Y0-BBD-859

INTRODUCTION TO SOCIAL PSYCHOLOGY

Russell A. Jones, University of Kentucky
Clyde Hendrick, University of Miami
Yakov M. Epstein, Rutgers University

Sinauer Associates Inc. • Publishers
Sunderland, Massachusetts

INTRODUCTION TO SOCIAL PSYCHOLOGY

Copyright © 1979 by Sinauer Associates Inc. All rights reserved. This book may not be reproduced in whole or in part, for any purpose whatever, without permission from the publisher. For information, address Sinauer Associates Inc., Sunderland, Mass. 01375.

Printed in U.S.A.

Library of Congress Cataloging In Publication Data

Jones, Russell A
   Introduction to social psychology.
   Bibliography: p.
   Includes indexes.
   1. Social psychology. I. Hendrick, Clyde, joint author. II. Epstein, Yakov M., 1941-   joint author. III. Title.
HM251.J513   301.1   78-20857
ISBN 0-87893-367-0

ABOUT THE BOOK

This book was set in V.I.P. Souvenir by David E. Seham Associates, Inc. Designed in the early 1900's by Morris Fuller Benton for the American Type-founders Company, the typeface was virtually ignored until redesigned in 1971 by Edward Benguiat of International Typeface Corporation. It is now experiencing a surge of popularity.

The book was designed by Wladislaw Finne of Yarmouth, Maine. Line art and cartoons created especially for this book were produced by Fredric J. Schoenborn and Steven DuQuette, respectively. Joseph Vesely coordinated production and the book was manufactured by The Murray Printing Company.

CONTENTS

Critical reviewers xiv

Preface xv

Part I
Foundations of social psychology

Chapter 1. Social psychology in perspective 2

The individual in a social world 4
Defining social psychology / Relating social psychology to psychology and sociology

Historical background 9
Recurring questions / Oversimplified answers

The dawn of the modern era 13
The theoretical foundation of social psychology / The research tradition

Summary 16

Chapter 2. Research methods 17

Research strategy: the basis for research methods 20

Participant observation 22
The method applied: life on the wards / Evaluation of participant observation

Survey research 27
The method applied: hawks, doves, and candidates / Evaluation of survey research

Content analysis 31
The method applied: cultural differences in delay of gratification / Evaluation of content analysis

Archival research 34

The method applied: threat and authoritarianism / Evaluation of archival research

Experimentation 38

The method applied: impression management / Evaluation of experimentation

Summary 45

Part II
Becoming a social creature

Chapter 3. The development of social behavior 48

Some basic issues of socialization 51

The Universal Parenting Machine / Are there universal issues of socialization?

Theories of becoming a social being 56

The psychoanalytic approach / Erikson: the psychosocial approach / The cognitive-developmental approach / The social-learning approach

Origins of early social development 68

Mother-infant interaction / Attachment / Maternal separation and deprivation / Child-rearing practices

The development of morality 74

The nature of morality / Psychoanalytic conceptions / The social-learning approach to moral development / The cognitive-developmental model

Sex-roles: "it" becomes "him" or "her" 84

The emergence of the person 88

Summary 89

Chapter 4. The development of self, language, and communication 90

Understanding the social world 92

Developing conceptions of other people / Developing conceptions of self / Role-taking: The basis for developing communication skills

Language 100

Communication 103

The social nature of communication / Speak that I may know thee: The many forms of communication / Context and embeddedness / Nonverbal communication

Summary 116

Part III
Cognition of the social world

Chapter 5. Person perception and attribution 120

Generalizing what we "know" about people 122

Forming impressions of others / Biases, illusions, and conceits in person perception / Individual differences in social perception

Acquiring new information about people 133

Observing behavior / Attribution processes / Attribution in action: explaining success and failure

Understanding ourselves: self-perceptions and attributions 141

Effects of self-perception on performance / Learning to identify and label our bodily states / Perceiving and explaining our own behavior

Summary 148

Chapter 6. Attraction and love 149

Determinants of attraction 151

Propinquity / Similarity / Complementarity / Reciprocity / Desirable characteristics / Physical attractiveness

Theories of attraction 162

A balance theory approach / Reinforcement theory

The nature of love 168

Romantic love / Liking versus loving / Passionate love / The colors of love

Summary 179

Chapter 7. Attitudes, beliefs, and behavior 180

The nature of attitudes 182

Attitude components: the classical view / A model of the relations among components

Origins and maintenance of attitudes 189
Prior experience / Reference groups and indoctrination / Functions of attitudes

Attitudes and behavior 197
Measurement pitfalls / Attitude-behavior consistency

Prejudice 204

Summary 208

Part IV
Forms of social influence

Chapter 8. Attitude change: the persuasive communication paradigm 210

The source: *who* says what to whom 212
Credibility / Similarity / Intent to persuade

The message: who *says what* to whom 222
One-sided versus two-sided communications / Conclusion drawing / Discrepancy / Fear-arousing messages

The audience: who says what *to whom* 236
Personality and persuasibility / Defense mobilization / Sleeper and Socratic effects

Summary 244

Chapter 9. Conformity and nonconformity 246

Recurring patterns of behavior 248

Conformity 249
The development of norms / The power of the group / Manipulating others

Compliance 255
Inequity and guilt / The foot-in-the-door technique / Obedience

The effects of conforming and compliance on private beliefs 259
Dissonance and forced compliance / Self-perception: my mouth was moving when I heard it

Nonconformity 265
Reacting to pressure / Rejection

Summary 270

Part V
Prosocial and antisocial behavior

Chapter 10. Altruism and helping behavior 274

The nature of altruism 277

What is altruistic behavior? / Conditions for altruistic and helping behavior / Theoretical approaches to altruism and other forms of helping behavior

Helping in emergency situations 284

Bystander intervention in emergencies / When will bystanders help?

Helping in nonemergency situations 293

To help or not to help / What makes a Good Samaritan? / Situational determinants of helping / Characteristics of the recipient of help / Sometimes it's hard to be grateful

Organized helping 296

Voluntarism / Are volunteers altruistic? / Altruism bought and paid for

Summary 300

Chapter 11. Aggression 302

What is aggression? 306

The components of aggression / A definition of aggression

Conceptions of aggression: instinct, drive, and social learning 310

Aggressions as instinctive behavior / Aggression as drive: does frustration cause aggression? / The revised frustration-aggression hypothesis / Aggression as a learned social behavior

Personality and individual differences in aggression 317

Are males more aggressive than females? / Genetic effects in aggression / Personality dispositions in aggression

Situational and environmental factors in aggression 319

Experimental methods for studying aggression / Environmental factors in aggression / Is television a cause of violence?

Forms of violence in society 327

Violence against individuals / Violence in the family / Violence as a social control mechanism: the Mafia / Large scale violence

Control and prevention of aggression 332

Punishment / Nonaggressive models / Cognitive factors / Social change as prevention

Summary 333

Part VI
The nature of groups

Chapter 12. The formation of groups: from "I" to "We" 336

Small groups 338

Sources of affiliation 340

Physical attractiveness / Similarity / Anxiety / Complementarity / Forming the family: an integration of similarity and complementarity / Which comes first, the membership or the motive?

Aberrations of affiliation 355

Groupthink / Risk and caution in groups / Commitment to the group

Summary 362

Chapter 13. Interaction in groups 364

Incidental consequences of interaction 366

Social facilitation: when others matter / Deindividuation: when others don't matter / Nonverbal communication and information management

Interaction processes 375

Attempts to analyze ongoing interaction / Stabilizing participation differences / Reacting to one's own behavior / Individual versus group performance

Retrospective misinterpretations: what really happened here: 386

Summary 388

Chapter 14. Leadership 390

The search for "leaders" 392

Dominance in nonhuman species / The Great Person theory of leadership

The situational approach to leadership 398

Presidential style and changing situations / All things to all people? / The contingency model of leader effectiveness

Leadership as a group process 406
Legitimacy and leadership / The influence of followers

Crises and change in leadership 409

Summary 412

Part VII
Social psychology and the environment

Chapter 15. Environmental psychology 416

The urban environment 418

The suburban environment / City life / Cognitive representation of cities / Neighborhoods / The cognitive mediation of stress / Environmental load / Effects of noise

The natural environment 433

Weather and behavior / Effects of heat / Suicides and mental hospital admissions / The value of wilderness / Energy conservation

Summary 440

Chapter 16. Environmental influences on social behavior 441

The use of space to regulate social behavior 443

Interaction distance / Spatial intrusion / The equilibrium model / Privacy / Territoriality / Cultural differences in human interaction

Crowding 455

The what and why of crowding / Crowded transportation settings / Sex differences in reaction to crowding / Residential crowding / Prisons / Architectural effects in reactions to crowding / "Tripling" students in two-person rooms

Effects of institutional environments 465

Total institutions / The physical environment of mental hospitals

Summary 470

Glossary 473
Bibliography 491
Credits 523
Author Index 525
Subject Index 533

Boxes

1. Social psychology in perspective
   A. A Group Is Not Just a Lot of People 6
   B. Courting, Conflict, and the Power-Oriented Male 13

2. Research methods
   A. Science and Psychotherapy 21
   B. Reason and Religion 24
   C. Internal and External Validity 39
   D. Expectations and the Experiment 42

3. The development of social behavior
   A. Discussion Questions Raised by the UPM Thought Experiment 54
   B. Kohlberg's Stages of Moral Development 81
   C. Examples of Responses to the Heinz Dilemma 82
   D. The Androgynous Person 87

4. The development of self, language, and communication
   A. Newspeak 104
   B. Communicating with a Chimpanzee 105
   C. "Punctuation" 111

5. Person perception and attribution
   A. My Friend is a Leftover Ham and Corn Casserole? 125
   B. Race and Belief Similarity in Social Choice 130
   C. Illusory Correlation, Availability, and Attribution 138
   D. The Illusion of Control 143

6. Attraction and love
   A. Examples of Some of the Great Loves of History 170

7. Attitudes, beliefs, and behavior
   A. Stereotyping Supporters of Women's Liberation 186
   B. Archie Bunker and the Eye of the Beholder 196
   C. The Window of the Mind 201
   D. The Scapegoat Theory of Prejudice 207

8. Attitude change: the persuasive communication paradigm
   A. Clean for Gene? 216
   B. Why are Laboratory and Field Results on Attitude Change Different? 229
   C. Making Political Speeches Easy to Swallow 233
   D. Censorship Changes Attitudes 239

9. Conformity and nonconformity
   A. Do Females Conform More Than Males? 253
   B. Legitimate and Illegitimate Requests 260
   C. The Rescuers 269

10. Altruism and helping behavior
    A. Application of the Concept of Distributive Justice to Helping Behavior 283
    B. The Murder of Kitty Genovese 286

12. The formation of groups: from "I" to "We"
    A. Self-Fulfilling Stereotypes about the Physically Attractive 343
    B. The American Ideal? 349
    C. Extremes of Commitment: The Cult That Killed Itself 354
    D. Brainstorming 358

13. Interaction in groups
    A. How're We Doing? Great! 373

    B. Are Men or Women More Sociable? Yes. 379
    C. Authoritarianism of Group Members and Social Change 382

14. Leadership
    A. Revolutionary Leaders and Long-Term Success 400
    B. The Peter Principle 403
    C. Relative Deprivation and Revolutionary Sentiment 408

15. Environmental psychology
    A. The Poet's Image of Suburbia 422
    B. A Superstar's Boyhood Neighborhood 429
    C. Madness and the Moon 437

16. Environmental influences on social behavior
    A. "Don't Break My Bubble" 449
    B. How Private Are You? 451
    C. Territorial Control and Crime 452

CRITICAL REVIEWERS

We deeply appreciate the help of the following people who critiqued parts of the book. Some served as specialty consultants and provided intensive examinations of individual chapters. Others served as section consultants by reading blocks of chapters for clarity and continuity. A few critiqued the entire manuscript. The final versions of the chapters benefited greatly from their combined expertise and wisdom.

Icek Ajzen
University of Massachusetts

Irwin Altman
University of Utah

Robert A. Baron
Purdue University

John H. Harvey
Vanderbilt University

Harvey A. Hornstein
Columbia University

Mark R. Lepper
Stanford University

George Levinger
University of Massachusetts

David R. Shaffer
University of Georgia

R. Lance Shotland
Pennsylvania State University

Mark Snyder
University of Minnesota

Sidney Rosen
University of Georgia

Mark P. Zanna
University of Waterloo

PREFACE

In a Utopian society, there might be little need for social psychology. In a perfectly harmonious social and political system, the study of social relationships would not be a pressing matter, because everyone would presumably be content, kind, and generous to a fault. A glance at any newspaper, however, should make it clear that we do not live in Utopia. Racial discrimination, crime, international and religious conflict, overpopulation, drug addiction, and individual depression are just a few of our problems. While all these problems appear quite diverse on the surface, they all have in common inharmonious social relationships.

People are all around us, and we need to know as much as we can about our relationships with them. How do we go about perceiving and understanding people? What kinds of mistakes are we likely to make in forming impressions of others? How do our attitudes originate, and how can they be changed? Under what conditions will interpersonal aggression occur? How are people likely to behave in groups? How does the environment influence our behavior? These are but a few of the questions we shall address in the chapters that follow.

PLAN OF THE BOOK

In Part I (Chapters 1 and 2), we begin by defining social psychology somewhat more rigorously than we have just done, and offer a brief history of the field. People have grappled with the issues involved in interpersonal relationships for eons, and some of the concerns of the ancient social philosophers can still be discerned in modern social psychology. But one of the major differences between modern social psychology and ancient speculation about social behavior is that modern social psychology is an active, empirical, data-gathering enterprise. Therefore, in Chapter 2 we describe and give examples of a number of research methods for answering our questions about the why and how of social behavior.

Social behavior involves individuals interacting with each other, and our understanding of social behavior is enhanced by knowing how those individuals got to be the way they are. Attitudes, stereotypes, and a willingness to help others, for example, do not just occur; often they emerge slowly, sometimes painfully, out of the process of socialization. Part II (Chapters 3 and 4) is concerned with socialization. Human infants are faced with the enormous task of learning to behave as people. To do this, they must master an array of social skills, not the least of which is communication via language, the topic of Chapter 4. Language provides a basis for taking various roles and looking at the world from someone else's perspective—an ability that is essential if social behavior is to proceed smoothly.

As we shall see, much of social behavior is a function of the internal cognitive and emotional processes of the individuals involved. We focus on such processes in Part III (Chapters 5, 6, and 7), beginning with the processes involved in perceiving and evaluating others. We attribute certain characteristics to others based on our observations of them, and these attributions often constrain and shape our interactions. To live a social life is to live affectively, liking and disliking, loving and hating. Such feelings are a pervasive part of our social world, and they are the topic of Chapter 6. It would be difficult to imagine a world in which people had no emotional involvement with each other, but our emotions extend to many things in addition to people. To have strong positive or negative feelings toward some object is part of what is involved in holding an attitude toward that object, so the nature and functions of attitudes are discussed in Chapter 7.

Our attitudes toward and beliefs about other people and objects are important—even crucial—to social behavior, because we act on them. We behave as though our perceptions, beliefs, and feelings about other people and objects reflect the way they really are. Of course, they often do. But often they do not. Fortunately for us all, attitudes, beliefs, and behavior can be changed. In Part IV (Chapters 8 and 9), we examine some of the circumstances under which social influence is successful. As we shall see in Chapter 9, social influence can sometimes be too successful, and people may be induced to behave in ways that they should not.

One of the enduring paradoxes of social behavior is the human capacity for both extreme love and tenderness and extreme hatred or barbarism. Much research has been devoted to the study of altruistic behavior (or helping behavior) and the conditions under which it occurs. The study of aggression is also proceeding apace, and these are the topics of Part V (Chapters 10 and 11). Research, theories, and thinking about altruistic behavior are discussed in Chapter 10, and the social psychological perspective on aggression is presented in Chapter 11.

Social psychology has sometimes been identified as the study of groups, and research on small, face-to-face groups continues to be a major focus of social-psychological endeavor. Humans seem to be group-oriented. We live out our lives in the context of groups, and there is a fascinating variety of group processes to be understood. The complex nature of groups is considered in Part VI (Chapters 12, 13, and 14). Chapter 12 introduces the study of groups by focusing on their formation. Chapter 13 discusses several aspects involved in ongoing group interaction, and Chapter 14 deals with the topic of leadership.

During the last few years, our society has become increasingly aware of pressing social problems, and social psychology as a discipline has begun to respond with research on the causes and consequences of a number of these problems. In Part VII (Chapters 15 and 16), we concentrate on the impact of the environment on social life. Chapter 15 deals with a variety of topics, such as the effects of noise, stress, and weather on the quality of life. Chapter 16 is concerned with how people use space and with the effects of institutional environments. A number of basic concepts are considered, including interaction distance, privacy, and crowding.

We shall discuss a variety of topics in the pages that follow, but despite the diversity there is a guiding theme. Each topic deals with how individuals affect and are affected by other people, and that, of course, is the subject matter of social psychology.

ACKNOWLEDGMENTS

In addition to the critical reviewers listed separately, many social psychologists contributed to the book by providing evaluative feedback on our initial plan. We are indebted to these many people who contributed generously of their time to provide comments:

Richard Baker, *Boise State University*
Jack W. Brehm, *University of Kansas*
Robert E. Brewer, *DePaul University*
Robert G. Bringle, *Indiana/Purdue University at Indianapolis*
Carol Burnett, *Rollins College*
Richard R. Burnette, *Florida Southern College*
Roland L. Calhoun, *Humboldt State University*
Ruth A. Cline, *Los Angeles Valley College*
Carl J. Cooper, *Curry College*
Stephen R. Deane, *Simmons College*
Caralyn C. Duncan, *Eastern Nazarene College*
Vernon P. Estes, Jr., *San Antonio College*
Ron Flint, *Winona State College*
John R. Forward, *University of Colorado*
Phillip S. Gallo, *San Diego State University*
Barbara Gentile, *Simmons College*
Carlos I. Goldberg, *Indiana/Purdue University at Indianapolis*
Anthony G. Greenwald, *Ohio State University*
Joseph E. Grush, *Northern Illinois University*
Sharon B. Gurwitz, *Northwestern University*
Raymond C. Harvey, *Samford University*
Joyce M. Hoffman, *Framingham State College*
Betsy Hornung, *Morraine Valley Community College*
Rosethel Howe, *Henry Ford Community College*
Homer Johnson, *Loyola University*
Patrick H. Keating, *Incarnate Word College*
Lindsey L. Keys, *Ferris State College*
Vladimir J. Konecni, *University of California at San Diego*
Edward Krupat, *Massachusetts College of Pharmacy*
Bibb Latané, *Ohio State University*
John M. Levine, *University of Pittsburgh*
Michael B. Lupfer, *Memphis State University*

Clara Mayo, *Boston University*
Lou Miller, *Texas A&I University*
Bob Newell, *Houston Baptist College*
Thomas Ostrom, *Ohio State University*
C. K. Patel, *Triton College*
Albert Pepitone, *University of Pennsylvania*
Hugh M. Petersen, *Pasadena City College*
Arthur R. Poskocil, *Hollins College*
Diana P. Rathjen, *Rice University*
Joan H. Rollins, *Rhode Island College*
Ralph L. Rosnow, *Temple University*
Fred Rowe, *Randolph Macon College*
John L. Roys, *Anderson College*
Lee Sechrest, *Florida State University*
Marvin E. Shaw, *University of Florida*
Mary T. Sheerin, *Regis College*
Vincent Shotko, *Humboldt State University*
Frank Sistrunk, *University of South Florida*
Phyllis W. Stevens, *Sweet Briar College*
Tom Tyndall, *Santa Rosa Junior College*
Harry Upshaw, *University of Illinois at Chicago Circle*
Daniel M. Wegner, *Trinity University*
A. Rodney Wellens, *University of Miami*
Eugene H. Welsand, *St. Joseph's College*
Robert Wyer, *University of Illinois*
Yoash Wiener, *Case Western Reserve University*
Edwin P. Willems, *University of Houston*
John P. Wilson, *Cleveland State University*
Robert S. Wyer, *University of Illinois*
Sheila G. Zipf, *San Francisco State University.*

We also wish to thank the many other people who gave us enormous assistance in preparing the manuscript. Irma Fox, Karen Jones, Martha Lancaster, Dorothy Manon, Sandi Racoobian, Joanne Ries, Ruth Stanton and Christine Kitschker contributed by the careful execution of many tasks, ranging from deciphering semilegible handwriting and converting it into neat typescript to tracking down abstruse references hidden away in dusty corners of libraries. Connie Day did a magnificent job of copyediting, for which we are all grateful. Finally, we offer special thanks to John Amacker of Sinauer Associates, who has shepherded the book through every phase of creation and production, from start to finish.

Russell A. Jones
Clyde Hendrick
Yakov M. Epstein

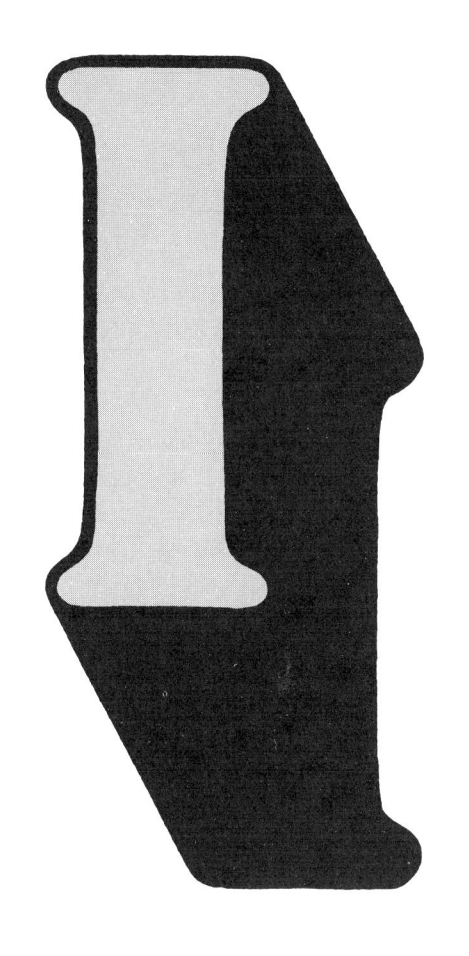

Foundations of social psychology

1

Social psychology in perspective

4 The individual in a social world

Defining social psychology
Relating social psychology to psychology and sociology

9 Historical background

Recurring questions
Oversimplified answers
   Pleasure seeking
   Power seeking

13 The dawn of the modern era

The theoretical foundation of social psychology
The research tradition

16 Summary

People have always been interested in social behavior. Since the dawn of history, our relations with other people have been the most important and, usually, the most intriguing part of a world filled with important and intriguing things. Other people and our relationships with them are of vital importance, so it is easy to understand why there has always been such keen interest in social behavior. But why should others be so important to us? Why do we spend so much of our time interacting with others, thinking about them, making efforts to please them, trying to anticipate how they are going to behave, and even dreaming about them?

As a partial answer, try to imagine what life would be like without other people around. If you are really honest with yourself, you should come up with a blank. Actually, *void* is the more appropriate and fashionable term for what life would be like without others. Think about it for a moment. First of all, of course, you would not even exist if your mother and father had not engaged in a certain type of social behavior some years ago. Second, you would not be able to speak, think, or understand the world around you if your parents, friends, teachers, and countless total strangers had not taken the trouble to teach you a language. And if you could not do any of these things, there is some question about whether you would be human.

We need others to exist. From the moment of conception until we draw our last breath, we are immersed in a social world. We are molded and shaped by others, but our experiences differ. Although similar in many ways to those around us, each of us becomes an individual and we begin quite early to exert a reciprocal influence on those who are shaping our lives. It's a two-way street. As individuals, we are both the products and producers of society.

The individual in a social world

In 1964, Lyndon Johnson was elected president of the United States by an incredible 16,000,000-vote landslide victory. Yet, barely 3 years later, he announced that he would not run for a second term. His popularity had reached such a low ebb that it was obvious to everyone that he would not win if he ran again. How could such a turn-around occur in so short a time? At first glance, the answer seems simple. He just did some unacceptable things, such as getting us more deeply involved in a very unpopular, tragic war. But why did he think he could do that with impunity? Why did he so overestimate his strength?

Clark and Sechrest (1976) suggest that Lyndon Johnson's case is an example of what they refer to as the MANDATE PHENOMENON. That is, the behavior of a leader is determined in large part by the support he or she perceives to be coming from the group. As the number of people voting for or favoring a particular leader increases, the less likely it is that the leader will anticipate criticism of his or her actions, and the more likely the leader is to feel able to do whatever he or she pleases. The idea is that Johnson perceived his 16,000,000-vote victory as a mandate from the people to do whatever he liked and was for too long unconcerned about criticism of his actions. Society gave the individual a particular view of himself as an invulnerable leader and he, in turn, imposed the consequences on society.

An interesting idea. If we left it at this level, however, it would be sheer speculation. We can never really know whether the mandate phenomenon played a role in Lyndon Johnson's fall from power. Even if he were alive, it is doubtful that he could accurately relate his thoughts and feelings of years ago. But we *can* find out whether the mandate phenomenon itself is real. We can test the idea that the larger the majority by which a leader is elected, the more likely the leader is to engage in risky behavior and to ignore criticism. More generally, we can take ideas about the relationships between individuals and groups, formulate those ideas into testable hypotheses and theories, and gather evidence on their validity. That, in fact, is the task of social psychology.

DEFINING SOCIAL PSYCHOLOGY

We feel a little uneasy about offering a concise, one-sentence definition of social psychology. This entire book, after all, is intended as a partial definition of

The mandate phenomenon. President Johnson's landslide victory in 1964 may have created overconfidence within his administration. The escalating war in Vietnam and inflation at home changed public opinion to the extent that in 1968 Johnson announced he would not seek reelection. Had his margin of victory not been so great in 1964, is it possible that he might have been more cautious afterwards, and recent history might have been quite different? (Wide World Photo)

A. A Group Is Not Just a Lot of People

One of the characteristics of a group is that the members have some awareness of each other as individuals and (usually) some degree of concern about what the other members may think of them. Thus we might expect that the behavior of an individual in a group would be somewhat inhibited compared to how the individual might behave if he or she were alone. On the othe hand, an aggregation of people, such as you might find on a crowded city sidewalk, usually consists of individuals who do not know each other and who are not concerned with the opinions of the others present. Thus we might expect that the behavior of an individual in such an aggregation would be somewhat less inhibited compared to how the individual might behave if he or she were alone. The surrounding mass of humanity provides a cloak of anonymity for the individual, and violations of social norms, such as littering, shoplifting, or spitting on the sidewalk, may become more likely.

To see whether aggregations and groups have these differing effects on individuals, Dale Jorgenson and Fred Dukes (1976) set up a simple observational study in the dining area of a university student union. There were a number of signs in the dining area requesting students to return their trays to certain locations near the exits when they had finished eating. Thus leaving the tray on the table was a minor violation of social norms. This was the behavior of interest. The return rate for students who were eating alone was compared with the rates for students eating with one, two, or three others. Observations were also made at times when the cafeteria was very crowded and at times when it was relatively empty.

Students eating alone when the cafeteria was very crowded had the lowest tray-return rate. Only about 50 percent of them returned their trays to the proper locations. Students eating together with others were much more likely to return their trays. However, even these small groups of diners were less likely to return their trays when the cafeteria was crowded than when it was not. It appears that being a member of a group may, under some conditions, increase the likelihood of adhering to socially approved patterns of behavior, while being surrounded by a larger aggregate of people may decrease conformity for both individuals and small groups.

---

the field. But we have to start somewhere. So let us begin by saying that social psychology is the study of social relationships and the cognitive and emotional processes accompanying such relationships. Note that we intend to emphasize social relationships and not just social interaction. INTERACTION occurs when two or more people engage in reciprocal, direct behaviors with each other. Interaction is usually face-to-face, but it can also take place by telephone or letter. RELATIONSHIP is a more general term. You can have a relationship with people and seldom interact with them. The presence of others may affect your behavior, even though you interact with none of them. (For an example, see Box A.) You may not see your grandmother or grandfather for years, but they can still have an impact on your day-to-day life. Lyndon Johnson never met most of the people who voted for him, but they certainly influenced his life, just as he influenced theirs.

The overt, visible aspects of relationships are important, but they are only one level of social life. Much of social life is unseen; it occurs in our heads. How many times in the course of a day do you think about other people? Keep track sometime and you'll be in for a surprise. We think about others literally hundreds of times a day. Whether it is just noticing a stranger walk by or trying to figure out why our best friend seemed a little peeved last night, we are constantly thinking about people. We are often emotionally involved with other people, we worry about those we love, and we plot ways to avoid those we dislike. The mental (or cognitive) and emotional aspects of social relationships are quite important, and they are an integral part of social psychology. If the mandate phenomenon really occurs, for example, it occurs because of what the elected leader *thinks* his or her overwhelming victory means.

Our definition of social psychology, then, implies that certain topics will be studied and others omitted. Some of the topics you might expect are the process of socialization, language, communication, how we form concepts of persons, liking, love, disliking, beliefs, attitudes, stereotypes, prejudice, conformity, persuasion, altruism, aggression, group interaction, leadership, and the impact of the environment on social life. All these topics involve interpersonal relationships, and they are the topics we shall cover.

There is one other aspect of our definition that we need to mention, and that is the word *study*. One can study something in many different ways. One can observe it, read about it, ask other people about it, or, in some instances, do something to it and *see* how it reacts. These approaches are actually different methods of conducting research, and, as we shall see in the next chapter, they all have properly dignified names. The point here is simply that social psychology must make use of a variety of methods.

For example, how would you study the mandate phenomenon? You might try a *case study* to begin with. That is, you could go back and identify those presidents, say, who had been elected by unusually large majorities and then find out what had happened to their programs and popularity during the terms following their elections. White (1975) took this approach in his analysis of Richard Nixon's slide from an 18,000,000-vote victory in 1972 to resignation less than 2 years later. Or you might try an *experiment* in which you set up some groups and have them elect leaders. By using secret ballots, you could induce the elected leaders to believe that they had received a unanimous vote of confidence or that they had received only a bare majority of the votes. You could then see if the ones who thought they had received a unanimous vote behaved any differently from those who thought they had only received the bare minimum of votes necessary for election. This was the approach chosen by Clark and Sechrest (1976). They found that the leaders who thought they had been elected by a unanimous vote did, in fact, commit their groups to riskier courses of action than leaders who thought they had just managed to slip into office by a vote or two.

Social relationships, then, can be studied in many different ways, and it is often a challenge for the investigator to pick the best approach for gathering evidence on a particular hypothesis or idea. In the next chapter, we offer some guidelines for picking the best method to investigate a particular question, but before we do, let us sharpen our definition of social psychology somewhat by distinguishing it from neighboring disciplines. To do this, we shall make use of a very curious phenomenon called the autokinetic effect. A dubious but fascinating story will explain what the autokinetic effect is as well as how it was supposedly discovered.

RELATING SOCIAL PSYCHOLOGY TO PSYCHOLOGY AND SOCIOLOGY

The story goes that, during the first World War, one of the problems confronting the Allied Forces in Europe was how to move convoys of supplies without being bombed by German aircraft. Both trucks and aircraft were just coming into widespread use at the time, and not many people had much experience with either. The solution seemed simple, however. Move the convoys of trucks at night, without lights. The enemy pilots would not be able to see them, and if they went slowly, they would be able to find their way along the roads without too much trouble. Even better, a small light could be mounted on the back of each truck so that the next truck could simply follow the one ahead. These small lights, of course, would be hooded so that they could not be seen from the air.

That seemed fine, but the strangest things started happening. Almost as soon as the convoys got under way, the trucks were running all over the roads. Some ended up stuck in ditches or plunging down ravines, others were scraping against the sides of bridges and buildings that lined narrow streets. The drivers were just as surprised as anyone. They always reported that they were just following the light on the truck ahead, but suddenly they would find themselves sitting alone in a ditch or wedged against the side of a building.

What was being discovered, at the cost of many stalled, stuck, and wrecked trucks, was the AUTOKINETIC PHENOMENON: a small, stationary light in an otherwise dark setting will appear to move. The light doesn't actually move, but it seems to go up, down, or off to one side. A truck driver who attempts to follow it off to the side will wind up in the ditch. Once the source of the difficulty had been identified, the solution was easy. Just put two lights on the back of each truck and the effect disappears. The autokinetic effect can be used to illustrate how the issues addressed by social psychology differ from those addressed by experimental psychology on the one hand and sociology on the other.

To study the autokinetic effect, we can use a darkened room with a small light source at one end. An experimental psychologist would typically ask questions about the conditions under which the autokinetic effect occurs. For example, does the room have to be totally dark before the light appears to move, or can there be some faint background light? Perhaps the amount of perceived movement depends on the amount of background light. Thus it might be important to ask how much the light appeared to move and not just whether or not it moved. Similarly, the size of the light might affect perceived movement. Must the light be only a pinpoint, or can it be quite a bit larger? Does it matter whether the person knows the light is stationary? Does alcohol, caffeine, or nicotine affect the amount of perceived movement? While the answers to these questions would help pin down the conditions under which the autokinetic effect occurs, they have nothing to do with interpersonal relations. They involve the nature of the visual system, and they are typical of the kinds of questions an experimental psychologist might ask in trying to understand perceptual processes.

A social psychologist might use the autokinetic effect as a vehicle for examining interpersonal influence. Sherif (1935), for example, accepted the basic fact of apparent movement as a given and asked whether the amount of perceived movement might be affected by the amount of movement perceived by another person. In one study (Sherif, 1936), two students were seated in a darkened room observing the pinpoint of light, and each gave an estimate of how far the light appeared to move on a series of trials. One of the students was actually an accomplice (or CONFEDERATE) of the experimenter and, unknown to the second student, gave a series of fabricated estimates that averaged about 5 inches. The question was whether these estimates would affect the responses of the other student. They did. Under a variety of conditions, the naive student's estimates followed those of the accomplice quite closely, and in most cases, the naive students were totally unaware of being influenced by the accomplice's estimates. Furthermore, the influence tended to persist over a long period of time. Obviously the social psychologist's interest in the autokinetic effect is quite different from that of the experimental psychologist. The social psychologist is interested in the effect only as a setting for the study of conformity. Other ambiguous settings might have served the purpose just as well.

How, then, might a sociologist employ the autokinetic effect? Like the social psychologist, a sociologist would probably use the setting to study susceptibility to the illusion of apparent movement. But sociology as a discipline is concerned with the nature, structure, and functions of society as a whole and not, usually, with interpersonal relations on an individual level. Thus a sociologist might select people from different sectors of society, such as Protestants versus Catholics or middle class versus working class, and examine their responses in the autokinetic setting. The sociologist would be interested in whether people from these different sectors of society varied in their susceptibility to the illusion, and if so, why.

Experimental psychology, social psychology, and sociology focus on somewhat different issues, but all three are concerned with how something relates to or affects something else. These "somethings" are usually called variables, and the specific task of research is to discover how variables relate to one another. In our examples we analyzed variables that affected the amount of perceived movement of the light. Perceived movement of the light was in each case the DEPENDENT VARIABLE, because we were concerned with the way it depends on, or is affected by, changes in certain other variables. The variables that we actively manipulate, or change, in order to study their effects are usually referred to as INDEPENDENT VARIABLES.

Although all three might focus on a similar dependent variable involving some aspect of perception, experimental psychologists, social psychologists, and sociologists differ in the independent variables that usually attract their interest. To reiterate, with the autokinetic effect as the dependent variable, an experimental psychologist might examine the effects of such variables as size and intensity of the light source. A social psychologist might look at such variables as the

	Experimental Psychologist		Social Psychologist		Sociologist	
	Size of the Light		Attempt to Influence		Socioeconomic Background of Subjects	
Independent Variable	Small Light	Large Light	Confederate Gives Fabricated Guesses of 5 Inches	Confederate Does Not Give Fabricated Guesses	Middle-Class Subjects	Working-Class Subjects
Dependent Variable (in all cases, the amount of perceived movement)	8 Inches	2 Inches	5 Inches	8 Inches	5 Inches	5 Inches

1. Three hypothetical sets of scores for the autokinetic experiment. Different independent variables are used by the experimental psychologist, social psychologist, and sociologist. The same dependent variable is used in all cases: the average amount of perceived movement. The scores in the bottom row are means for several subjects. The confederate is used as a constant source of influence by the sociologist with both middle-class and working-class subjects. These hypothetical data show that: (1) perceived movement is greater when a small light is used; (2) subjects conform closely to a confederate's guess; and (3) working-class and middle-class people do not differ in their susceptibility to influence by the confederate.

presence or absence of someone giving different estimates of the magnitude of movement. A sociologist might focus on variables of a societal nature, such as the socioeconomic class of the subjects. These different possibilities are summarized in Figure 1. In each case, there is a search for orderly relationships between independent and dependent variables. The focus is on different independent variables in each case, however, and different kinds of knowledge are obtained. One approach is not necessarily better or more interesting than another; they are simply different.

Later we shall examine the issues involved in the study of conformity, obedience, and nonconformity in some detail, but for now we should note one final feature of the autokinetic experiment. Sherif was not just concerned with conformity as a general concept or with conformity in the abstract. Rather, he was concerned with the conformity of individuals. One outstanding feature of social psychology as it has developed in the United States is that it focuses on individual behavior in a social or group context. SOCIAL PSYCHOLOGY, then, is concerned with interpersonal relationships and, in particular, with how the thoughts, emotions, and behaviors of the individual are influenced by others. As you might guess, many of the issues that intrigue social psychologists today have been with us for centuries. Let us take a brief look at the background from which modern social psychology emerged.

Historical background

Many of our ideas about social relationships had their origins in the works of ancient Greek philosophers such as Plato and Aristotle. At that time, conceptions of the social nature of humankind were an integral part of theories of government—an idea that was popular until about 100 years ago. In a sense, social psychology was an aspect of political philosophy for the first 2000 years of its history. Even so it is surprising how often the concerns of these ancient philosophers recur in modern social psychology.

RECURRING QUESTIONS

Plato lived at a time of upheaval and change in Athenian society. His teacher, Socrates, had been condemned to death after the overthrow of a group of elite rulers. Disgusted, Plato turned away from everyday affairs of state to formulate an ideal society, which he described in *The Republic* (Bogardus, 1960). Education was the most important social characteristic in his utopia, because ideas were supposedly the ruling force in life. Plato believed that a society came into existence because of the mutual needs of individuals who could not survive in isolation and that the ideal society would be stratified into three social classes: rulers, soldiers, and ordinary workers. The rulers were aristocrats, ruling by virtue of wisdom. One of the main tasks of education, then, was to teach people to be content with this division of social classes. Plato's advice was to teach children the rightness of this classification at an early age. They would then believe in it at maturity and, in turn, teach it to their children.

Thus a basic issue of social psychology was posed thousands of years ago, an issue that is as alive today as it was then. What is the proper function of education, or, more generally, what is the proper function of the socialization process? Is it to indoctrinate youth with the values, attitudes, and beliefs prevalent in society? Or should youth be trained to be independent and critical of society? The issue is not simple, because the individual needs society and its institutions in order to survive, just as society needs individuals in order to remain a society. This tension between the individual and society is clearly still with us. It may, in fact, be argued all over again at any school board meeting. One faction of parents may decry some textbook as subversive, un-Christian, and alien to democracy, while another group demands that children be exposed to a variety of ideas, even if the ideas are uncongenial to the status quo.

Compared to Plato, Aristotle had a more moderate view of the social order. Like Plato, he viewed humans as political animals who, by both nature and necessity, yearned for each other's company. But instead of an elite, he favored a large middle class in control of society. The extremes of great wealth and poverty, he thought, led to crime and social instability. In general, Aristotle was more trusting of democratic group processes than Plato and believed that, in the long run, the success of a government depends on the degree of virtue in the population. According to Allport (1968), the differences between Plato and Aristotle have come down to us as a basic option. Modern philosophers and social theorists tend to take either an elitist, Platonic stance or a democratic, Aristotelian stance in their theories of social behavior. But the major legacy of the Greeks is a diversity of views about the social nature of human beings—a diversity that still exists.

Many of the questions that concern social psychologists today have been with us for thousands of years. There seems to have always been a great deal of speculation about social relationships, groups, leaders and followers, friendship and altruism, the formation of attitudes, and so on. But up until about 100 years ago, those who were interested in such issues tended to propose single ideas or principles as *the* explanation of all human social behavior. These explanations were usually very simple. They were also usually sovereign, in the sense that they were supposed to explain everything about social behavior, not just one or two aspects. These twin characteristics prompted Allport (1968) to label this period the era of simple and sovereign theories. Let us look at some of these oversimplified answers to the recurring questions about social behavior.

OVERSIMPLIFIED ANSWERS

Why do people behave the way they do? When you pose the question this way, it almost seems that it *should* have a simple answer. Over the centuries, many simple answers have indeed been proposed. Everyday observation, for example, suggests that people usually seek out pleasant activities or states of being and avoid painful ones. Everyday observation apparently suggested this to the ancient Greeks as well, and many people since that time have proposed that humans are basically pleasure-seeking animals. The explanation of human behavior that sees humans as pleasure seekers is psychological HEDONISM: people do what they do to obtain the greatest possible pleasure.

Pleasure seeking. Apparently the first systematic philosophy of humans as pleasure seekers was advanced by Epicurus, whose name is the origin of the word *epicurean,* as in "epicurean delight." Epicurus was something of a Greek Hugh Hefner and James Beard rolled into one, who believed not only that pleasure seeking explained all human behavior, but that it was right that it should. Friends, for example, were of value only if they enhanced one's personal pleasure, and self-sacrifice and altruistic behavior were to be frowned on. One simply was not to do such things—unless, of course, they brought pleasure. You may have already spotted one of the fatal flaws in such simple theories of human behavior. They can account for everything (but usually after the fact) by assuming that whatever the person did must have brought him or her pleasure. They reason backwards.

During the eighteenth century, the English philosopher Jeremy Bentham formulated the principle of hedonism in a more systematic way. He agreed that an individual's every act is an attempt to maximize pleasure and also argued that people follow a sort of hedonistic calculus in adding up their potential pleasures. Pleasure and pain have several dimensions, such as duration, intensity, certainty, and purity, and these various dimensions can in principle be measured. If so, one could more precisely compare the amounts of pleasure that would derive from different courses of action and, hence, have a basis for deciding which would yield the greatest pleasure. Bentham also thought that people would attempt to maximize pleasure and that they should do so. The *would* is a psychological assumption, but the *should* is a moral evaluation, part of a social philosophy. One implication is that there should be as little governmental control as possible, because our natural inclination to pleasure will supposedly lead us to the proper form of government. Although Bentham's theory that individual pleasure seeking results in the greatest good for the greatest number has not been borne out, his philosophy is another example of how an assumption about the psychological nature of the individual is intimately related to ideas about the individual's place in society.

Herbert Spencer added a new twist to the doctrine of hedonism by connecting it to the Darwinian notion of survival of the fittest. Pleasurable actions are generally those that promote survival, and pain is symptomatic of danger and death. Thus pleasure seeking can be viewed as an evolutionary development. As a consequence of his ideas about hedonism, Spencer advocated *laissez-faire* government and advocated it with a vengeance. That government is best which governs least! The ideal state would be one that respected rugged individualism and interfered with people's lives as little as possible. This philosophy led Spencer, a highly civilized and moral man, to take a number of positions that most people today would find distasteful. For example, he opposed free public education and social welfare services of any kind.

Because psychological hedonism was so often connected with advocacy of *laissez-faire* governments, it fell into disrepute near the end of the nineteenth century. The abominable working and living conditions that grew out of the industrial revolution created enormous pressures for governmental protection of the ordinary person. It would be a mistake, however, to suppose that the principle of hedonism is no longer of any importance in social psychology. Under the guise of reinforcement, it has been kept alive and well by psychologists such as Thorndike (1898), Watson (1919), Freud (1922), and Skinner (1948). A reinforcement is simply anything that increases the probability that a particular behavior will occur. If you receive a good grade (the reinforcement) on a test after studying in a particular way (the behavior), you are likely to study in that same way for future tests.

There is no doubt that the principle of hedonism goes a long way toward explaining behavior, but it does not go far enough. There are simply too many kinds of behavior that apparently have nothing to do with pleasure seeking. For example, it has been found that the *less* a person is paid to advocate an attitudinal position he or she does not believe, the *more* likely the person is to subsequently adopt that position. We shall examine why this occurs in Chapter 9, but the point is that it is exactly the opposite of what a hedonistic, reinforcement theory would predict. Nevertheless, we shall use the notion of reinforcement many times in the chapters that follow. It helps us understand some (but not all) aspects of social behavior.

Power seeking. In contrast to the notion of hedonism, other writers have proposed that humans are driven primarily by a POWER-SEEKING MOTIVE and that all activities are devoted to seeking dominance and superiority over other people. The power motive is not completely independent of the principle of hedonism, but it has usually been viewed as more basic and as underlying the successful pursuit of pleasure. Thomas Hobbes, a seventeenth-century philosopher, believed that, in order to obtain pleasure, it was first necessary to have power over one's world. According to Hobbes, the craving for power is insatiable and life is nothing less than a state of war, all against all. Social constraints and government are necessary for common protection, because without them, we would soon destroy each other.

This bleak view of human nature has persisted over the centuries and was given an even more extreme twist by Le Dantec (1918). Le Dantec believed that each person is totally interested in self and that the individual ego is supreme. As Allport (1968) puts it, Le Dantec believed that

> All social varnish is superficial; at bottom the caveman remains. Even the most pious Christian is thrilled and excited by battle and by brute victory (p. 17).

Le Dantec's defense of egoism and self-interest as the basis of social life was totally uncompromising. He even reinterpreted the Ten Commandments. The injunctions not to steal, kill, or commit adultery, for example, really mean "Don't steal from me, kill me, or commit adultery with my sexual partner." In Le Dantec's view, civilization is a kind of hypocrisy in which the appearances of cooperative behavior barely mask total self-centeredness.

Modern treatments of the power motive tend to be somewhat more plausible and somewhat more limited in scope. Adler (1945), for example, was one of Freud's colleagues who felt that Freud had overemphasized the pleasure principle. Adler argued that striving for superiority and overcoming feelings of inferiority was a central motive in both individual and social life. To take another example, McClelland and his colleagues have developed a conception of ACHIEVEMENT MOTIVATION (McClelland, Atkinson, Clark, and Lowell, 1953) that is a somewhat tamer derivative of the power motive. The basic thrust of a strong achievement motive is to accomplish, to make one's mark in the world through useful work. People clearly differ in the extent to which they seek achievement, and recent research has turned up some interesting findings. You might expect that those who are very high in achievement motivation would be quite willing to take risks, to stick their necks out, and to take all sorts of chances to get ahead. But it turns out that people who are strongly oriented toward achievement are actually relatively cautious and tend to prefer moderate risks and ventures that have about a 50–50 chance of succeeding.

Another line of current research on interpersonal relations also stems from early speculation about the power motive. In 1513, Niccolò Machiavelli published a book called *The Prince* on how best to govern other people. According to Machiavelli, the ideal ruler should be both loved and feared, but fear is more important, because people are selfish, ungrateful, and totally concerned with their own welfare. Thus the ruler should take a detached, manipulative approach to social control. Christie and Geis (1970) have developed a test that measures how Machiavellian individuals are in their interactions with others. The MACH SCALE, as the test is called, basically measures the extent to which people are willing to use manipulative techniques to get what they want from others. As we shall see, people who score high on the Mach Scale are more likely to lie, if lying will serve their purposes, and they are more likely to look you straight in the eye while doing so. (For another example of recent research on the desire for power, see Box B.)

Simple principles, such as hedonism or the ruthless pursuit of power, have proved inadequate to explain the range and complexity of behaviors involved in social relationships. No one still views such single explanatory principles as exclusively important. Even so, threads of thought linking some areas of research in modern social psychology with the simple and sovereign theories of the past can still be discerned, as we have tried to illustrate. The hallmark of the modern era of social psychology is diversity of explanatory concepts. This modern era, as the saying goes, has a long past, but only a relatively short history.

B. Courting, Conflict, and the Power-Oriented Male

People seem to differ greatly in the extent to which they desire interpersonal power. Some seem to spend their lives pursuing the ever-elusive goal of total control. They want to influence others, persuade them, and hold their respect and attention. Other people seem to be quite content to go about their lives with little thought about their influence on the lives of those around them. The interpersonal influence they exert seems to make little difference to them; they find their satisfactions in other realms.

Abigail Stewart and Zick Rubin (1976) hypothesized that those people who have a strong desire for power over others are likely to be more dissatisfied with their interpersonal relationships than are those who have less of a need to dominate and influence others. Those with a strong desire for power over others, for example, should be less tolerant of differences in tastes, lifestyles, interests, and attitudes. Because of their great need to influence others, those high in desire for power would be less satisfied in relationships in which the other person maintained some degree of independent judgment. If they are unable to persuade the other to see things as they do, they have failed at something they value greatly, and nobody likes to be around reminders of past failure.

To see if those high in desire for power form less stable interpersonal relationships, Stewart and Rubin contacted a number of dating couples in the Boston area and secured their cooperation in taking a test, individually, that measured their desire for power over others. Two years later, at least one member of each couple was contacted again, this time via mail or telephone, to assess the status of the relationship.

Of those couples in which the male had been identified as having a high need for power over others, 50 percent had broken up in the 2-year period following the initial testing, and only 9 percent had gotten married. However, of those couples in which the male had been identified as having a low need for power over others, only 15 percent had broken up and over 50 percent had gotten married. It appears that the need for power in men is a source of stress and dissatisfaction in intimate relationships with members of the opposite sex. The pattern of results for women was less consistent. Approximately the same proportions of women high and low in desire for power were no longer with their companions by the end of the 2-year period. It may be that power-oriented women are better able to handle conflict than power-oriented men and so maintain their relationships better.

The dawn of the modern era

As we have seen, speculation about social relations has been going on for thousands of years, but two relatively clear turning points brought modern social psychology into being. The two essentials of any scientific endeavor are theory and research. As a systematic theoretical enterprise, social–psychological thinking seems to have been given focus by a Frenchman named Auguste Comte, who lived from 1798 to 1857. Social psychology as a research-oriented, data-gathering enterprise is even more recent, having begun around the turn of the century with some research by Triplett (1897) on whether bicycle racers did better when racing against the clock or when competing against other riders. (He found they did better when competing against other riders.)

THE THEORETICAL FOUNDATION OF SOCIAL PSYCHOLOGY

In the two centuries prior to Comte's life, the physical sciences had made tremendous progress and were already considered the epitome of what sciences should be like. There had already been several attempts to classify and systematize the various sciences, but Comte threw himself into the task, devoting most of his life to it. His argument was that knowledge evolves through three stages: theological, metaphysical, and positivistic. Initially, thinking about the world is theological or fictitious in nature, and myths abound on the origin and nature of things. As time passes, conceptions gradually shift from the supernatural but remain speculative and very abstract. This is the metaphysical stage. Finally, thinking becomes truly scientific or positivistic: ideas are tested, measurements are made, and speculation is no longer sufficient.

Comte believed that all areas of knowledge have evolved through these three stages (Coser, 1971; Ferre, 1970; Harris, 1968) and, further, that the various sciences emerged in a definite order. First there were mathematics and logic. Over the centuries, the physical sciences emerged and finally the realm of psychics, or what we would call the biological and social sciences (see Figure 2). Comte also envisioned the possibility of a true science of society, which he termed social physics but later referred to as sociology. Human nature was seen as both biological and social, and the sciences of biology and sociology were to deal with these twin aspects. But something was still missing. Humans are individual men and women, each unique and each with a highly developed moral sense. Comte thus proposed a new science, the highest of all, to study the unique and moral aspects of people. He gave the name *morale* to this new science, and it coincides roughly with what we would today call psychology.

Comte was quite proud of his invention. Morale as a science would be based on both biology and sociology. At times, biology would be more heavily emphasized, leading to the discipline of physiological psychology. At other times, the study of the individual in a social context would be emphasized, and this, of course, is the subject matter of social psychology. In this way, the conception emerged of social psychology as a hybrid science, containing elements of both psychology and sociology. However, Comte wanted to do more. He wanted to make his new conceptions into real sciences, but he lacked the necessary techniques, the research methods that we shall discuss in the following chapter.

THE RESEARCH TRADITION

It was not until around the beginning of the present century that active research into social-psychological phenomena began. We have mentioned Triplett's interest in comparing bicycle racers in competition and those racing against a clock. In modern terms, Triplett was interested in SOCIAL FACILITATION, the effects on one's performance of having other people around. This line of research is still active and has led to some interesting results. (There are only certain types of tasks on which you are likely to do better with others around. We shall return to this topic in Chapter 13.) Ten years after Triplett's research, in 1908, the first two social psychology textbooks were published. One was by E. A. Ross, a sociologist, and the other was by William McDougall, a psychologist. After that, things picked up rapidly. Research on social facilitation and on the issue of whether groups perform better or worse than individuals continued. Textbooks that still have a modern ring began to appear, such as one by Floyd Allport (1924), in which the value of experimentation was stressed.

During the 1930s, there was a veritable explosion of social-psychological research and writing. In addition, an event occurred that was to be of great significance for the development of social psychology as a modern, empirically oriented science: Kurt Lewin came to the United States. Lewin came to escape the Nazi regime in Germany, and, in the few years before his death in 1947, he gave tremendous impetus to the study of group processes. He and a group of gifted colleagues and students created a movement called GROUP DYNAMICS that continues to be influential.

It is very easy to talk about group processes and speculate about what goes on in groups. Everyone has some experience in groups and knows something about them. It is quite another matter, however, to find a way to study group processes in a rigorous, objective fashion. Lewin's creative genius lay in pointing the way toward orderly empirical inquiry into group processes and the effects that groups have on individuals. For example, suppose that you were interested in what leadership style is most effective in helping a group achieve its goals. Up until Lewin's time, it was felt that with an issue of this sort, the best one could do would be to observe existing groups. In a classic study, Lewin, Lippitt, and White (1939) were able to demonstrate that you could, in fact, *create* certain realistic group conditions in the laboratory. Adult leaders of boys' activity groups were trained to behave in different ways. Some leaders behaved in an authoritarian manner, giving orders, supervising activities closely, and making all decisions. In other groups, the leader behaved in a more democratic manner, allowing the entire group to share in decision making. In still other groups, the leader behaved in a *laissez-faire* manner, taking a generally passive role and letting the boys supervise their own activities.

Thus leadership style was the independent variable, and to manipulate this variable was to vary the group atmosphere or climate on a dimension ranging from strong dictatorial control (the authoritarian leader) to passive noncontrol (the *laissez-faire* leader). The issue was how these variations in group climate would affect group performance and member satisfaction. The results, unfortunately, were not very clear, though the authors seemed to prefer the democratic leadership style. As we shall see in Chapter 14, however, recent research has shown that what is best for a group depends on such things as whether the task facing the group is clear-cut or ambigious and whether the leader has good or poor relations with key group members. Sometimes a domineering, cold, authoritarian leader is best; sometimes a warm, friendly, democratic leader is more effective. Lewin and his colleagues were the first to demonstrate that something as subjective and nebulous as group atmosphere could be studied in a rigorous manner.

It has become increasingly clear that such seemingly nebulous, subjective notions about group processes and the behavior of individuals in groups can indeed be sharpened, clarified, and put to the test. What kind of speaker is more likely to persuade you to change your attitudes? Who are you likely to choose as your friends? How does prejudice originate, and how is it maintained? How do you go about forming impressions of other people? These are just a few of the many questions that we shall address in the following chapters, but we no longer have to rely on someone's opinion for answers. Instead we examine the evidence—evidence from experiments, surveys, systematic ob-

2. Comte's hierarchy of the sciences. Note that social psychology is a combination of sociology and "morale," which we would call psychology. (Adapted from Allport, 1968.)

Logics	Physics			Psychics		
Mathematics	Astronomy	Physics	Chemistry	Biology	Sociology	Morale

Social Psychology

Physiological Psychology

servation, and many of the other research methods that have become the tools of social psychology.

It is hard to overestimate Lewin's contribution to the development of modern social psychology. He was a strong advocate of experimentation and was able to translate his ideas about social processes into laboratory tests. Lewin also believed in the necessity of theoretical development and, in fact, coined the saying "There is nothing so practical as a good theory." Theories help us know where to look and what questions to ask. Lewin felt that systematically developing theories about social behavior and testing them by rigorous methods was the best way to acquire new knowledge and clarify what we might think we already know. Lewin also believed in applying the findings of social psychology to the solution of society's problems. He felt that social psychology ought to contribute to the solution of problems such as social discrimination, conflict, crime, and alienation. His ideal was a vigorous social psychology made up of ongoing theoretical developments, active research, and meaningful applications of knowledge to the solution of society's problems. In the chapters that follow, we hope to demonstrate that this ideal has been realized to a large extent, but that there is still much to be done.

Summary

We have defined social psychology as the study of interpersonal relationships and of the cognitive and emotional processes that accompany such relations. Although social psychology remains closely tied to its parent disciplines of psychology and sociology, there is a distinction among the three based on the types of independent variables that are studied. The variables of greatest interest to social psychology have to do with individual behavior in a social context. How is the individual influenced or changed by other people, and how, in turn, does the individual affect others?

Interest in social relations has been active for thousands of years, and social psychology was really a branch of political philosophy for a long time. Speculations about individual behavior in social contexts were tied to theories of the state and to ideas about the best forms of government. Characteristically, human behavior in these political systems was explained in terms of a single, all-inclusive principle, such as hedonism or desire for power. People were thought to behave the way they do in order to maximize pleasure or attain control over others. Vestiges of many of these earlier simple and sovereign theories of human behavior can still be found in modern social psychology, but it is now clear that human behavior is too complex for any single explanatory principle.

As a modern theoretical and empirical science, social psychology is still relatively young. Though it enjoyed a place in Comte's hierarchy of sciences at the interface of psychology and sociology, social psychology as a data-gathering, research-oriented enterprise did not really get under way until well into the present century. Thus there is still a sense of excitement about much of social psychology—an excitement that we hope to convey to you in the pages that follow.

2

Research methods

20 Research strategy: the basis for research methods

22 Participant observation

The method applied: life on the wards
Evaluation of participant observation

27 Survey research

Measurement
The method applied: hawks, doves, and candidates
Evaluation of survey research

31 Content analysis

The method applied: cultural differences in delay of gratification
Evaluation of content analysis

34 Archival research

The method applied: threat and authoritarianism
Evaluation of archival research

38 Experimentation

The method applied: impression management
Evaluation of experimentation

45 Summary

Abraham Maslow once observed that "if the only tool you have is a hammer, it is tempting to treat everything as if it were a nail" (1966). This chapter is about the tools available to anyone who is interested in studying social psychological phenomena—tools that help avoid the trap of treating everything as if it were a nail. There is, as we shall see, no one method or technique that can be used to study all aspects of social behavior. The particular method employed depends on the question being asked. We will define and give examples of five relatively distinct research methods. Our purpose is to make clear the peculiar advantages and disadvantages of each method.

Research strategy: the basis for research methods

Science, of course, involves asking questions, and scientific methods are techniques for obtaining answers to questions. The similarities between "scientific" and other human endeavors have been emphasized by many people. George Kelly, for example, has pointed out the basic similarity between science and "humanistic" psychotherapy (see Box A). The strategy implicit in most scientific research, and in Kelly's approach to psychotherapy, is that *in order to understand any phenomenon, one should devise as many plausible explanations for it as possible and systematically gather evidence on these explanations.* The question of interest may be as "scientific" as how diversification of species occurs in successive generations or as "unscientific" as why you do not have many friends. Is it bad breath? Are you a put-down artist? The key to gathering evidence is, first and foremost, accurate observation.

Observations, even scientific observations, are made by fallible human beings. Hence, it should come as no surprise that the desires and emotions and ambitions of people engaged in research can cloud their vision and bias their interpretations. Good researchers, however, devise ways of checking themselves. Darwin, for example, would make a special note when he came across data unfavorable to his ideas, because he knew he was more likely to forget such facts (Beveridge, 1957).

One of the most general techiques for checking on our observations and holding our biases at least partly in check is *triangulation of measurement* or *multiple operationism* (Webb, Campbell, Schwartz, and Sechrest, 1966). Although the names are forbidding, the technique itself is really a simple one, and we have already described it. If we observe a given phenomenon —that friends tend to be similar to each other, for instance—our confidence in the validity of this observation is increased if we obtain evidence for it under a number of different conditions, in a number of different situations, and using several different measures. More generally, when we become curious about some phenomenon, one of the most efficient ways to proceed is to generate as many plausible rival explanations of the phenomenon as we can and then devise ways for checking on the validity and/or explanatory value of these rival hypotheses. Perhaps an example will help illustrate the strategy.

In 1956, the state of Connecticut instituted a severe crackdown on speeders. At the end of the year, 40 fewer lives had been lost on the highways in Connecticut than were lost in 1955. Accordingly, the governor (Abraham Ribicoff) issued the following statement: "With the saving of 40 lives in 1956, a reduction of 12.3% from the 1955 motor vehicle death toll, we can say that the program is definitely worthwhile" (Campbell, 1969, p. 412).

Cracking down on speeders was followed by a clear decrease in traffic deaths. It is not clear, however, that cracking down on speeders *caused* the decrease in traffic deaths. What are some other possibilities? Campbell (1969) describes several other plausible hypotheses or possible explanations. Suppose 1956 had less rain and snow and consequently clearer and dryer roads than 1955. A possible consequence would be fewer accidents in 1956. This possibility can be checked out, of course, by looking at such readily available indices as total rainfall in Connecticut for the two years, total number of days on which *any* rain or snow fell, and so on. Another possible explantion is that 1956 had fewer days on which there was a conjunction of precipitation and temperatures below 32°F. Another possibility is that in cracking down on speeders, Connecticut instituted a "fasten-your-seat-belt"

A. Science and Psychotherapy

One of my tasks in the 1930's was to direct graduate studies leading to the Master's Degree. A typical afternoon might find me talking to a graduate student at one o'clock, doing all those familiar things that thesis directors have to do—encouraging the student to pinpoint the issues, to observe, to become intimate with the problem, to form hypotheses either inductively or deductively, to make some preliminary test runs, to relate his data to his predictions, to control his experiments so that he will know what led to what, to generalize cautiously and to revise his thinking in the light of experience.

At two o'clock I might have an appointment with a client (i.e., patient). During this interview I would not be taking the role of the scientist but rather helping the distressed person work out some solutions to his life's problems. So what would I do? Why, I would try to get him to pinpoint the issues, to observe, to become intimate with the problems, to form hypotheses, to make test runs, to relate outcomes to anticipations, to control his ventures so that he will know what led to what, to generalize cautiously . . .

At three o'clock I would see a student again. Likely as not he was either dragging his feet, hoping to design some world-shaking experiment before looking at his first subject to see what he was dealing with, or plunging into some massive ill-considered data-chasing expedition. So I would again try to get him to pinpoint the issues, to observe open-mindedly, to become intimate with the problem, to form hypotheses—all the things that I had to do at one o'clock.

At four o'clock another client! Guess what! He would be dragging his feet, hoping to design a completely new personality before venturing his first change in behavior, or plunging into some ill-considered acting-out escapade, etc., etc. But this, of course, was not my hour for science; it was my hour for psychotherapy. And what I had done with that student the hour before, that was obviously not psychotherapy. It was science!

I must say that this sort of thing went on for a long time before it ever occurred to me that I was really doing the same sort of thing all afternoon long. It seems incredible now that it took me so long to realize this, but at the time it seemed so perfectly obvious that science and psychotherapy were different, even contrasting kinds of experiences.

From G. Kelly. "The autobiography of a theory," in B. Maher (ed.), *Clinical psychology and personality,* New York: Wiley, 1969, pp. 60–61.

To test a hypothesis, we must ask specific, testable questions. When the answer to our question is positive, we have gained some information about the way things work. On the other hand, if the answer is negative we do not know what to conclude. Is the answer really "No," or did we make an error in the way we put the question to the test?

campaign. If so, the decreased death toll may have been due to the decreased likelihood of fatal injuries in accidents, not to decreased accidents. The plausibility of this explanation could also be easily checked by simply looking up total number of accidents for the two years and comparing numbers of accidents in which a fatality occurred. Another plausible hypothesis is that death rates had been steadily declining at about the same rate for several years. Campbell uses a simple time-series plot to rule out this alternative explanation (see Figure 1). It is apparent from the figure that traffic fatalities had not been steadily declining prior to the crackdown on speeders; one alternative explanation for the decrease in death tolls between 1955 and 1956 is ruled out.

One could generate a number of other possible hypotheses to explain why Governor Ribicoff's evaluation of the success of his crackdown on speeders may have been inaccurate. Enough have been mentioned, however, to exemplify the research strategy we are advocating. For any observed phenomenon that you wish to understand, generate as many plausible explanations as possible and use all the ingenuity you can muster to devise methods for gathering evidence on the validity of each of these various hypotheses, *one, all, some,* or *none* of which may turn out to be adequate.

Strategy is important, but strategy alone never won a war. We must also have the techniques, methods, and equipment for carrying out our strategy. Fortunately for those of us interested in understanding social behavior, there are a number of methods available to help us find explanations for why people behave the way they do. We shall define, describe, and illustrate five general categories of research methods often used by social psychologists. Each has certain advantages and disadvantages that we will try to illuminate. The specific examples selected for each of the various methods have been chosen, in part, to illustrate the range of questions that interest social psychologists.

Participant observation

There is a little more to *participant observation* than the name implies. Participation in and observation of an event are not alone sufficient. The participant observer is usually concerned with people's beliefs and behaviors in their natural setting. In order to understand the usually complex web of observed interrelationships, he or she gathers as much information about the people and their setting as possible. With the mass of data that quickly results from observations, inter-

22
Foundations of social psychology

views, and whatever records can be found, a particularly important aspect of participant observation is the systematic recording of data and observations.

Suppose, for example, one were interested in "doomsday cults," cults or groups of people who predict the end of the world on a certain day. In particular, suppose one were interested in what happens after their day-of-doom passes. Participant observation is an ideal technique for studying this issue. In October of a year in the early 1950s, a team of social psychologists (Festinger, Riecken, and Schachter, 1956) became participant observers in a group predicting that a cataclysmic flood would occur on December 21 of that year and inundate most of the western part of the United States. This prophecy had been revealed to the group's leader, Mrs. Marian Keech, through "automatic writing." Festinger and his colleagues hypothesized that when Mrs. Keech's prediction was disconfirmed (they were assuming, of course, that it would be), group members would find some way of rationalizing what had occurred and also begin to seek out new members for the group in an attempt to obtain social support for their shaken belief system. This is exactly what happened. When the long night of the prophesied flood came and went with everyone as dry as a bone, there was a new revelation. The world had been spared because of the group's devoutness, and the members were instructed to go forth and spread the word. Even so, and in spite of a flurry of publicity seeking in the days immediately following the disconfirmation, the group had dissolved within about a month.

The important point for our purposes is that the participant observers could not be content with simply observing and recording what went on in the group's meetings. Rather, they had to gather all the information available about the group: biographical informa-

the group's activities, information about group members who had drifted away and why they had left. Such data were obtained by conducting informal interviews, going through old newspapers, and using informants. These were necessary because the hypothesis that Festinger and his colleagues were investigating was anticipated to hold only under certain relatively specific conditions. The auxiliary information about the group helped establish that these conditions were met. More generally, however, the gathering of all pertinent information through diverse techniques helps the participant observer guard against bias, or seeing only what is expected.

Participant observation can be most useful when it is carried out to answer some specific question or test a specific hypothesis. Having a full-blown theory is not necessary, of course. Having a specific purpose in mind, a question to be answered, or a comparison to be made is, however, likely to enhance the value of participant observation. (See Box B for an illustration.) tion about each of the members, historical accounts of

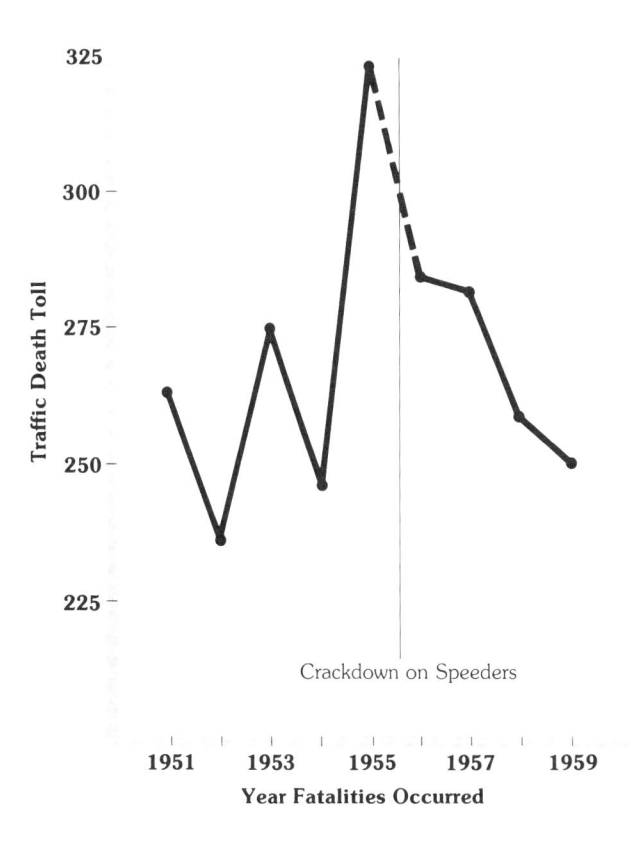

1. A time-series analysis of Connecticut traffic fatalities. The essence of a time-series design is taking some measurement periodically and introducing an experimental change at some point in the series. Here the change introduced is the crackdown on speeders. (From Campbell, 1969, Figure 2, p. 413.)

B. Reason and Religion

Does all human behavior make sense? Can differences in lifestyles be understood scientifically, or is there some irreducible residue of custom and tradition before which we must simply throw up our hands and say "that's just the way things are"? Marvin Harris, one of America's leading anthropologists, points out that if we begin our study of human behavior by assuming that there are some questions that cannot be answered, we shall indeed never find the answers.

Harris' own work (1974) has demonstrated that many peculiar, even bizarre aspects of human behavior have reasonable, plausible explanations. All it takes to uncover those explanations is an understanding of the historical and cultural context in which the behavior occurs. This, of course, is easier to state than to acquire.

Consider, as an example, the Hindu's refusal to eat beef. To an outsider, this seems extremely odd. How can it be that there are all those millions of cows wandering around the countryside in India and, at the same time, famine is endemic there? Why don't they just eat some of those cows? This would not only provide an immediate source of food, but it would also save for human consumption the food that the slaughtered cows would have eaten in the future.

It comes as something of a surprise to find that those sacred cows have to be kept alive, at all costs, or India's rather shaky economy would collapse. Harris found that India has 60 million farms and each needs at least one pair of oxen or water buffalo for traction animals. There are only 80 million traction animals available, however, a shortage of 40 million. This shortage of draft animals is a serious threat to the Indian peasant farmer, because should he lose an ox, say, he would be unable to plow and would lose his farm. Oxen, of course, come from those "sacred" zebu cows, and even a skinny, old cow can breed.

Further, Harris points out that India's cattle annually produce 700 million tons of recoverable manure, about half of which is used for fertilizer and the rest for cooking. The annual thermal equivalent of the cow dung used for cooking would be 27 million tons of kerosene, 35 million tons of coal, or 68 million tons of wood—resources that India simply does not have. Harris also points out that the cows are effective scavengers and that what they eat is usually not fit for human consumption.

There is more to the story, but the point is simply that many apparently nonfunctional aspects of human behavior have reasonable explanations. We have to be willing to look for those explanations, and we have to start with the assumption that most human behavior is understandable.

Given these various aspects of participant observation, let us commit ourselves to a definition. PARTICIPANT OBSERVATION is the method in which the researcher enters for some length of time into the routine of the people or situation under study, observing and systematically recording things that happen, informally or formally interviewing all who might have information pertinent to the events under study, and gathering auxiliary information relevant to his or her purpose. The researcher may adopt any degree of candor varying from complete openness about why he or she is there to complete secrecy and the assumption of a disguise.

Many social-psychological examples of participant observation could be used to illustrate our definition. The particular example that follows was chosen because it addresses an important issue relevant to our understanding of the relationship between the individual and the society of which the individual is a member: What happens when an individual is labeled "insane"? Also, it points out some of the advantages and disadvantages of the technique.

THE METHOD APPLIED: LIFE ON THE WARDS

In the past few years, a great deal of controversy has arisen over the question of whether "mental illness" really exists. Thomas Szasz (1961), one of the most outspoken critics of the concept, points out that "Psychiatrists have traditionally regarded mental illness as a problem apart from and independent of the social context in which it occurred" (p. 52). The reason for this neglect of social context was that the concept of mental illness developed by analogy with physical or bodily illness, which was usually treated without regard to the social environment of the victim. Szasz argues that the result of this pseudomedical analogy has been to locate mental illness in the victim when, in fact, what we are usually talking about when we say that someone is mentally ill is that the person in question has interpersonal problems—problems in his or her social relationships—problems, in short, in living. Concurrently with the line of reasoning advanced by Szasz and others (Scheff, 1966), there has developed a large and growing body of data questioning the reliability and usefulness of psychiatric diagnosis (Chapman and Chapman, 1967). As if this were not enough to give one pause, anthropological field reports have repeatedly made the point that behaviors defined as deviant or insane in one culture are frequently looked on with equanimity in another.

Thus many people have come to the conclusion that psychological and psychiatric categorization of those with emotional and interpersonal problems, the so-called mentally ill, is at best useless and may even be actively harmful. Critics of psychiatric/psychological diagnostic procedures (Szasz, 1961) even go so far as to say that such diagnoses are more a function of the mind of the diagnosticians than of the behaviors of the diagnosed. If this is true, normal or "sane" people who take up residence in a psychiatric ward and act normally would go undetected. On the other hand, if normality is distinct enough from abnormality, such pseudopatients would be detected and expelled. Participant observation seemed to be the ideal research method.

To check on which of these outcomes occurred, Rosenhan (1973) and seven co-workers became participant observers by gaining secret admission to the psychiatric wards of 12 different hospitals. Each pseudopatient gained admission by claiming to hear voices saying such things as "empty" or "hollow," a symptom chosen because of its similarity to the self-questioning that occurs when people wonder about the meaningfulness of their lives. The participant observers also employed pseudonyms and, in several cases, gave false occupations to protect their true identity. As soon as they were admitted, however, all pseudopatients began to behave normally. They stopped simulating *any* symptoms. Rosenhan cites evidence from nursing reports to confirm that the behavior of the pseudopatients was in no way disruptive. Nurses on the wards described the pseudopatients as uniformly friendly and cooperative.

On entering, each pseudopatient had been told that he or she would be discharged when the staff became convinced of his or her sanity. Yet even though they stayed an average of 19 days and at least one stayed as long as 52 days, not one of the pseudopatients was ever detected. Not one was ever deemed sane by the staff.

During the course of their stays, the pseudopatients took notes and systematically recorded what went on in the wards: the number and types of drugs given (although these were people with no bodily or mental problems, they were administered over 2000 pills), the amounts of time that staff spent on the ward, the behaviors of their fellow patients. One of the things that became clear from the notes is that once a person has been labeled schizophrenic, as most of the pseudopatients had been, interpretation of that person's subsequent behavior is strongly colored by the label. For example, Rosenhan notes that patients would often congregate outside the cafeteria entrance half an hour or so before mealtime, because life on the wards was so dull and meals were one of the few things patients could anticipate with pleasure. On observing their behavior, however, one of the ward psychiatrists commented that it was typical of the oral-acquisitive nature of the syndrome from which the patients suffered.

Aside from such reinterpretation of normal behaviors so that they would fit into what the staff "knew" about the pseudopatients, the pseudopatients quickly began to experience depersonalization. Physical exams were often conducted in semipublic rooms; staff would often discuss a patient within his or her hearing; staff avoided eye contact with patients and failed to acknowledge their questions; morning attendants often woke patients with "Come on, you m - - - f - - - - -, out of bed!"

There are other implications of the results, but the important point is that the pseudopatients were never detected by the staff in spite of their normal, appropriate, and sane behavior. By means of participant observation, the pseudopatients determined that the meanings read into their every behavior were largely a function of the environment and the manner in which they had been labeled. The study calls into question the notion that mental illness or mental health is contained in the individual.

One piece of research is never sufficient evidence. The Rosenhan study is suggestive, nothing more. It provides a point of departure for future studies and future thinking about the problem. The study itself can be attacked on several methodological grounds. For example, just as the pseudopatients' behaviors were misinterpreted in many instances, the pseudopatients themselves probably misinterpreted certain staff behaviors. The study does, however, illustrate an appropriate use of participant observation to obtain some evidence on a question that would have been difficult to attack by other methods.

EVALUATION OF PARTICIPANT OBSERVATION

The advantages of participant observation over other research methods all revolve around the completeness or "range" of information gathered. Becker and Geer (1970) even go so far as to say that participant observation is the yardstick by which we should gauge the completeness of other data-gathering techniques. That, however, is a slight overstatement. As Trow (1970) points out, it assumes that all events could be studied by participant observation, an assumption that is simply unjustified. For appropriately selected problems, however, participant observation can be beneficial in at least three ways.

First, there are many things that people are unwilling or unable to discuss with others. Participant observation provides a way of obtaining information about such topics. Becker (1963), himself a jazz musician, was able to learn about values, habits, and prestige hierarchies among dance musicians by intimately participating in that culture. Much of the information obtained by Becker would never have been revealed to outsiders or "squares." A second advantage of participant observation has to do with language. Many groups develop certain idiosyncratic terms and phrases to refer to aspects of their environment. The participant observer, as Becker and Geer (1970) note, can learn the meanings of such words ("crock," "alley apple") with great precision. A third advantage of participant observation is that the participant observer is likely to become aware of the existence of varying perspectives within the group or situation being studied. Hence, the participant observer is often able to avoid hasty generalizations and misunderstandings.

The disadvantages of participant observation stem primarily from the biases and limitations of the observer. As we pointed out in connection with the Rosenhan study, observers are human also. They have hopes, expectations, and prejudices, just like the observed. There will be some people in a group with whom the observer establishes rapport much more easily than with others; hence, the particular perspective of those people is likely to be given undue prominence. Further, the observer(s) cannot be everywhere at once. Data are likely to be missed, information lost, and a biased picture formed. Rosenthal (1966) has demonstrated repeatedly that observers make errors in line with their expectations—they see what they expect to see. Although it is not quite fair to call it a disadvantage of the method, there are certain types of research problems for which participant observation is just not appropriate. For example, suppose you were interested, as Durkheim (1951) was, in suicide rates in different groups? Suppose you were interested in the relationship between economic cycles and mob violence? Suppose you wanted to learn how Democrats feel about birth control? Participant observation is simply not an appropriate technique with which to seek answers to these questions. For each of these questions, however, one of the methods we will discuss in the following pages is appropriate. As you read on, see if you can match the questions with the appropriate methods.

Survey research

For the general public, survey research is one of the most visible forms of social–psychological research. Results of "the latest poll" appear in the news with ever-increasing frequency. Such polls are usually concerned with opinions about some issue or person: "Do you think the President is doing a good job?" "If the election were held tomorrow, for whom would you vote?" "What do you believe to be the most important issue facing the nation at this time?"

The descriptive and predictive information obtained from such polls is useful for a number of practical purposes, from predicting election outcomes to marketing attractive products. Survey research can also be used to gather information relevant to important social-psychological questions, and we will be concerned with this latter use. First we need to be a little more specific about what is involved in such research.

SURVEY RESEARCH usually involves interviewing a selected sample of people and asking each person in the sample the same questions. The answers given by such a sample of people are compiled and often reported in terms of the number or percentage of people who hold certain opinions. Thus, there are two aspects to a survey: (1) selection of the people to be interviewed and (2) interviewing. Both of these aspects are approached with the research objectives in mind. If we were interested in whether child-rearing practices are related to emotional adjustment, it would be absurd to select our sample of respondents (people to be interviewed) from a nunnery.

The key to respondent selection is the notion of sampling. SAMPLING is selecting part of a group about which we wish to make generalizations in such a way that the selected part fairly represents the whole group. The total group is generally referred to as the POPULATION. It is usually impossible to contact every member of the population—college students, mothers, motorcycle riders, firstborn children, whatever particular population is of interest. If reaching each member of the population is impractical, the ones who are contacted (the SAMPLE) must be chosen with great care. It is important to note that the answer is *not* simply a larger sample. A large biased sample is no better, and probably worse, than a small biased sample, because people are likely to place more faith in the biased results if the sample is large. The crucial point is that the sample must be as representative of the population as we know how to make it. If the population of interest were college students, for example, female sophomore out-of-state history majors enrolled at an exclusive New England college would not be a representative sample.

Once the research problem and an appropriate sample have been selected, the actual data-collection phase of a survey begins. The data-collection phase usually takes the form of an interview. It is important to remember that, while interviewing in one of its many forms is a necessary aspect of survey research, interviewing is often an integral part of other research methods also. We have already mentioned it in connection with participant observation, and we shall mention it again in connection with experimentation. We will discuss it in some detail here, because it is a crucial component of survey research.

Interviews can range from a few casual, open-ended questions to lengthy lists of questions with specific alternative answers, and, by stretching the definition only slightly, we can even include preprinted questionnaires that the respondent fills out on his or her own. Each of these procedures can be used as a RESEARCH INTERVIEW, defined by Cannell and Kahn (1968) as an interview intended to obtain information relevant to the interviewer's research objectives of description, prediction, or explanation. Thus the research interview is concerned with measurement.

Measurement. Since all of the research methods presented in this chapter are techniques for measuring, let us digress from our discussion of the interview for a moment and look at some general criteria for helping us decide when we are measuring well. There are three such criteria: reliability, validity, and precision. A measuring instrument exhibits RELIABILITY if, on repeated use under the same conditions, it gives the same results. The instrument is said to exhibit VALIDITY if it measures what it claims to measure—nothing more, nothing less. Measuring instruments also vary in their degree of PRECISION. That there are exactly 52 cards in a deck is a more precise piece of information than that there are fewer than 100 cards in the deck. Now let us see if we can illustrate each of these criteria in the context of a research interview.

Suppose we were interested in whether there was a relationship between how concerned people were about the threat of a nuclear war and whether or not they had taken any steps to protect themselves in case such a war occurred. (This is a specific example of an important social–psychological question that we will discuss in Chapter 7, the question of the nature of the relationship between attitudes and behavior.) Suppose we have already selected our sample of people to interview and made up our interview schedule—that is, the list of questions that we plan to ask each person. The data that we obtain from a given person would be perfectly *reliable* if different interviewers were to obtain exactly the same information from that person or if the person were to give exactly the same information if interviewed on Monday as if interviewed on Tuesday. Thus reliability has to do with repeatability.

The data obtained from our interviews would be *valid* if our questions were phrased so that they elicited accurate information about each person's concerns about nuclear war and accurate information about what they had done to prepare themselves. Thus an interview can produce reliable but invalid data. The questions may be such that they always evoke the same answers from the same people, but they may not measure the thing of interest. The question "Are you aware that India can produce H-bombs?" may always evoke a "Yes" or "No" answer from a particular person, but it is not clear that the question elicits any information about how concerned that person is over the threat of nuclear war.

The last criterion for evaluating a measuring instrument is its degree of *precision*; the more precise, the better. In our interview example this might be illustrated by the difference between the two questions "Are you concerned about the possibility of a nuclear war?" and "How concerned are you about the possibility of a nuclear war?" The latter question is likely to differentiate among people better in terms of their degree of concern.

One final point that may already be obvious is that, in evaluating a particular measuring technique, we often discern a trade-off among reliability, validity, and precision. We can make measures more reliable by sacrificing precision. When such trade-offs become necessary, it is well to keep in mind that *validity* is the most important criterion.

Numerous factors determine the extent to which a given research interview achieves the ideal of yielding valid, reliable, and precise information. Cannell and Kahn (1968) summarize these factors under the three concepts of accessibility, cognition, and motivation.

ACCESSIBILITY refers to the extent to which the respondent has the information sought by the interviewer in a form that can be easily and quickly communicated. Age is, for most people, a highly accessible item of information. The names of the subjects that they took in the tenth grade are probably somewhat less accessible, and information on their overall goals in life is probably even less accessible. Information sought by an interviewer may be inaccessible to the respondent for a variety or reasons. It has been forgotten, it was never known, it has been repressed, or the interviewer's question may be so poorly phrased that the person does not know what is being asked. The latter reason also involves the interviewee's COGNITION, or understanding of what is expected, his or her role vis-à-vis the interviewer, and what sort of information is required. The final requirement for a successful interview is that the person being interviewed be motivated and willing to provide complete and accurate information. Many things determine the MOTIVATION to provide such information. A few of the forces acting to increase or decrease this motivation are summarized in Figure 2. We will mention motivation again; lack of motivation can be a serious handicap to the survey researcher.

We are ready now to briefly describe an example of the use of survey research to address a theoretically important social–psychological topic.

THE METHOD APPLIED: HAWKS, DOVES, AND CANDIDATES

A topic of considerable interest to many social psychologists is the question of whether people (P's) maintain consistency or "balance" among various aspects of their world of other people (O's) and things

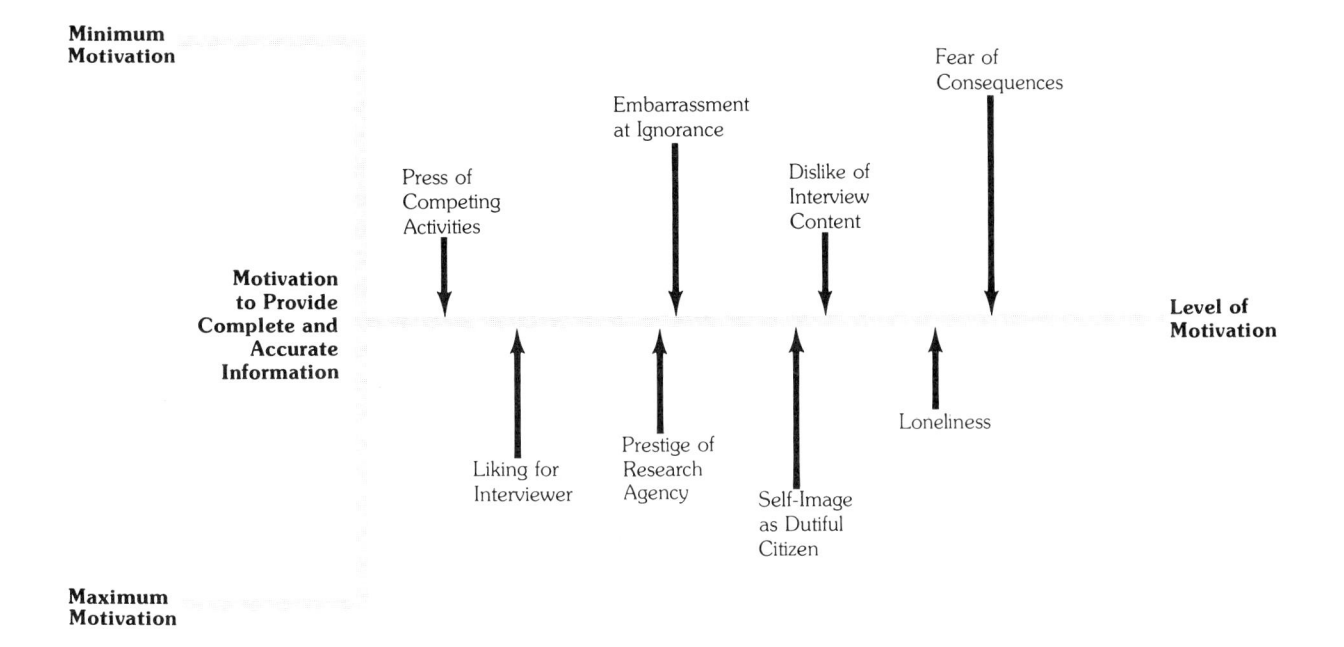

```
Minimum
Motivation

                    Press of              Embarrassment         Fear of
                    Competing             at Ignorance          Consequences
                    Activities                      Dislike of
                                                    Interview
                                                    Content
Motivation
to Provide                                                                          Level of
Complete and         ↓         ↓         ↓         ↓                                Motivation
Accurate
Information
                     ↑         ↑         ↑         ↑
                                                              Loneliness
                  Liking for   Prestige of
                  Interviewer  Research
                               Agency      Self-Image
                                           as Dutiful
                                           Citizen

Maximum
Motivation
```

2. Motivation to supply answers to an interviewer is a function of many things. If the respondent likes the interviewer or feels duty-bound as a good citizen to respond, the inclination to answer accurately increases. If the respondent is busy with other activities or embarrassed about not knowing how or what to answer, the motivation to answer accurately decreases. (From Cannell and Kahn, 1968, Figure 2, p. 539.)

(X's). For example, suppose a person (P) strongly favors abortion (X) and also very much likes another person (O) who abhors abortion (X) and equates it with murder. For P, this could be a very uncomfortable situation. Heider (1946), one of several researchers who have been concerned with this problem, postulated that it is psychologically unpleasant to disagree with someone you like and similarly unpleasant to agree with someone you dislike. Heider further assumed that people prefer psychologically pleasant or "balanced" states and tend to avoid the unpleasant, "imbalanced" states.

Putting this reasoning in the context of an election, Granberg and Brent (1974) noted that "As a consequence, one would expect that individuals would tend to minimize differences on policy issues with a preferred candidate and to minimize similarities on policy issues with a nonpreferred candidate" (p. 688). The most salient policy issue during the 1968 presidential election was United States involvement in Vietnam. The major candidates were Hubert Humphrey and Richard Nixon.

Before and after the election, the University of Michigan Survey Research Center interviewed 1673 adults, a nationwide sample. Among the questions asked were for whom subjects had voted, how they would place each of the candidates on a seven-point "Hawk" (7) to "Dove" (1) scale, and how they would place themselves on the same scale. Granberg and Brent report a number of results, and the most important ones for our purposes are summarized in Figure 3.

First, note the two solid lines in the figure. These lines plot the position on the Hawk–Dove dimension attributed to Nixon and Humphrey *by the people who voted for them*. As can be seen, the more hawkish the voter, the more hawkish his or her candidate is perceived to be. The other two lines in the figure, the

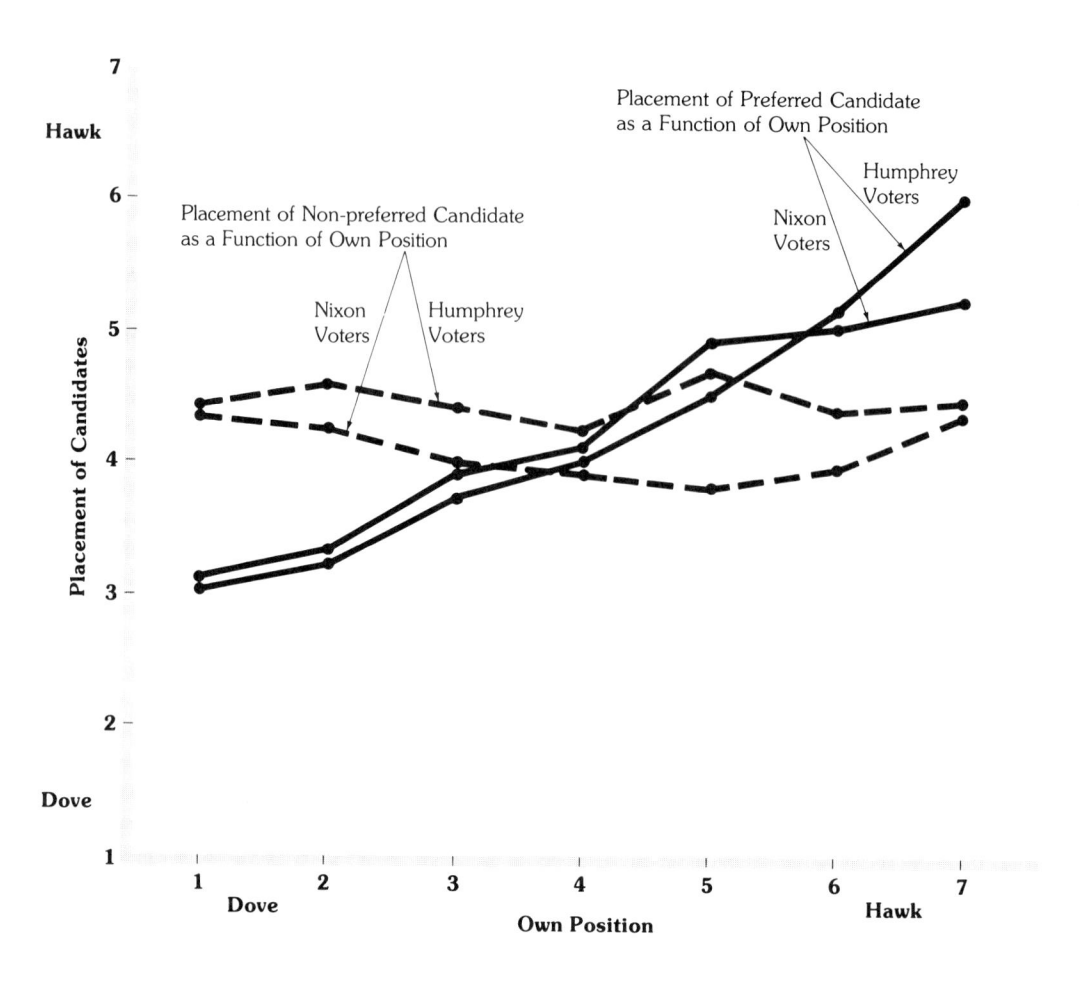

3. Voters tended to see the candidate they preferred as having a position very similar to their own. Hawkish voters who favored Humphrey, for example, believed him to be a hawk, while doves who favored Humphrey believed him to be a dove. Whether voters were hawks or doves made little difference in their perception of the candidate they did *not* favor. (From Granberg and Brent, 1974, Figures 1 and 2, pp. 690-691.)

roughly horizontal dashed lines, show that the voter's own hawkishness has little influence on his or her judgment of the hawkishness of the nonpreferred candidate. In summarizing these results, Granberg and Brent note that apparently Nixon and Humphrey "presented themselves in such a way as to be many things to different people; at least this held true of those who supported each of these two major candidates" (p. 693). Thus voters do appear to minimize differences on policy issues with a preferred candidate. Doves who voted for Nixon tended to see him as somewhat dovish. Hawks who voted for Nixon tended to see him as somewhat hawkish. As Granberg and Brent note, however, there is no evidence in this study for the other prediction from Heider's notions about balance: that voters will minimize similarities with a nonpreferred candidate. Thus we are left with a puzzle for future research and theory. Why was one prediction upheld and one not? Was it something about this particular study, or is there a need to revise the notions of balance and imbalance? Perhaps only certain kinds of imbalance are unpleasant.

EVALUATION OF SURVEY RESEARCH

In addition to the disadvantage all research methods share—that is, that there are certain problems for which they are simply inappropriate—the disadvantages of survey research fall into two main classes or

30
Foundations of social psychology

categories. These two categories correspond to the two major facets of survey research: sampling and interviewing.

Sampling is a complex problem, and perhaps we have passed over it too lightly by implying that the solution is to get a representative sample. The problem, of course, is that the researcher rarely knows what a representative sample really is. Suppose that we are interested in voting behavior during the 1984 presidential elections and want to interview a representative sample of voters both before and after the election. How can we ever define the population from which we want to sample before the election? There is no foolproof way to know ahead of time who is and who is not going to vote. There are techniques for minimizing sampling error, but sampling must still be done with care. An inappropriate or biased sample invalidates the results of a survey even before the survey is conducted.

The second major disadvantage of survey research concerns the interview. An interview is, after all, an interpersonal encounter. All of the nuances of gesture, voice inflection, body position, status symbols, prejudices, and even odors that both interviewer and respondent bring to that encounter can adversely affect the validity of the information obtained. Bias in the interview is a research problem that has been actively attacked. Scores of papers have reported the detrimental effects of variables ranging from the interviewer's own political views (Rice, 1929) and race (Williams, 1964) to the respondent's need to maintain a socially approved front (Lamale, 1959). Even when the respondent is motivated to be as accurate as possible, difficulties are often introduced by the wording of questions. For example, Mauldin and Marks (1950) found that a large number of respondents who answered the question "What is the highest grade of school you have completed?" would answer "No" when subsequently asked "Did you complete that grade?" We have already mentioned some other disadvantages of the interview under the concepts of accessibility (the respondent may have forgotten, repressed, or never had the information requested), cognition (the respondent may not understand what is being requested even if he or she has the information); and motivation. In spite of this host of potential sources of invalidity, the interview is an indispensable tool and can yield reliable, valid, and precise information when constructed and used with care.

It is clear that survey research is applicable to research questions for which participant observation is not appropriate. It should also be clear that there are numerous interesting questions for which neither participant observation nor survey research are appropriate methods of seeking answers. For example, suppose we were interested in the question of how expressions of certain values, like achievement, are related to stages in the development of a civilization (McClelland, 1961). Content analysis is a research technique that can be used to investigate such a question.

Content analysis

What does content analysis involve? As Holsti (1969) notes, many people are surprised to find that, since learning to read, they have been constantly performing informal versions of content analysis. The specific definition that we endorse comes from Stone, et al. (1966). CONTENT ANALYSIS is a research technique by which certain characteristics of printed or spoken material are systematically identified (p. 5).

The starting point for any content analysis is a question, a hunch, a theory—some anticipation of a relationship between things. As in any other method, the research question is crucial, because it guides the entire process. In content analysis, the first things determined by the question are the texts to be compared. If we are interested in the extent to which newspaper editorial support for a political candidate is reflected in biased news coverage, our texts are determined. We would look at editorials and news stories about candidates. We would not look at the candidates' campaign literature or televised political commercials or political billboards. Given that we would look at newspaper editorials and news stories, there would still be a sampling problem. We could not possibly look at all newspaper editorials and news items about all political candidates at all times in all places. So we would set up some rules for selecting a sample. We might decide to look only at presidential candidates in the 1960, 1964, 1968, and 1972 elections and use editorial and news items from 10 daily papers with circulation of 100,000 or more. That is, for each candidate in each election, we would find 10 such papers that supported the candidate editorially. We would then have to choose a time period within which to sample. Would we examine news items in each paper every day for three months preceding the election? Two months? Six months? Every third day for three months? Every fourth day for six months? The point is that, given even a relatively clear-cut research question, as in our example, we must make a series of important sampling decisions in the process of selecting the texts to be compared.

Once the texts have been selected, the key process of content analysis remains: "specification of the coding categories and rules for deriving indices." The object here is to come up with a set of categories into which the content of the text can be coded. Holsti (1969) notes the following general principles of category construction. Categories should (1) reflect the purposes of the research, (2) be exhaustive, (3) be mutually exclusive, (4) be independent, and (5) be derived from a single classification principle. It should be obvious that the categories into which the content is to be coded must reflect the purposes of the research. If we were interested in the relationship between the concepts of freedom and equality in the essays of fifth-graders, for example, we would not have a category for references to 10-speed bicycles. That the categories be exhaustive means there must be a category into which each relevant item can be placed. That the categories be mutually exclusive means that each item should be capable of being placed in only one category. That the categories be independent means that assignment of one item to a given category should not affect the assignment of other items. Use of a single classification principle means that the categories cannot mix conceptually different levels of analysis.

Specifying the set of categories into which our texts are to be coded is extremely important in content analysis, and it is also a good example of an important problem that occurs with all research methods—the problem of operationalizing the concept or question or variable we are interested in. When we want to measure a concept such as "conservatism" or "attitudes toward Mexicans" or "intelligence" we must be able to point to something and say "I am willing to take this as an example of X." Thus we OPERATIONALIZE a concept, or define a concept operationally, by specifying instances of that concept in the empirical world. There are several points to note in this admittedly oversimplified definition. First, it is possible to operationalize a concept in more than one way. We might take as an example of intelligent behavior the ability to solve a certain set of anagrams in less than 60 seconds. Or we might take a student's grade-point average (GPA) as an index of intelligence. Both of these are fallible indices: they are both determined by a number of factors other than intelligence. Because many of the concepts encountered in science are difficult to specify in ways acceptable to everyone, it is imperative that we be as clear and as precise as possible about how a particular concept is being operationalized. Second, people may argue about the particular index with which we choose to measure a concept. The evidence may indicate that the way we have chosen does not produce results similar to what is already known about the concept (that is, our index may be invalid), but until we specify what our index is, we cannot even enter the debate.

To return to content analysis, once we have selected the texts and defined our categories, we read the text and record the frequency of category appearance. This process must be checked for reliability. The usual technique is to have two or more coders independently code the same portions of the text. If their agreement about the relative frequency of occurrence of the various categories is high, we can be encouraged that our coding scheme and categories are well defined. What we conclude or what we infer from any given content analysis depends, of course, on the research question we started with, the texts we decided to sample, the category system we constructed, and how the text fits into the categories. An example of content analysis should help to focus these several considerations.

THE METHOD APPLIED: CULTURAL DIFFERENCES IN DELAY OF GRATIFICATION

One of the difficulties of doing cross-cultural research is that a given behavior may mean very different things in different cultures. Further, since most social psychologists are middle-class whites, there is a constant danger of their using middle-class, white norms as standards to determine the meanings of certain behaviors in other cultures. For example, in connection with a comparison of Hawaiian and Japanese-American orientations to the future, Gallimore, Weiss, and Finney (1974) make the point that from a Hawiian-American perspective, spending most of one's pay buying drinks for fellow workers is like buying insurance. In future crises, one's workmates will help out. To a non-Hawaiian, however, such behavior may be seen as simply another example of the Hawaiians' supposed inability to delay gratification and accumulate capital.

A number of observations suggested to Gallimore, et al. that, while Hawaiian youths might be more inclined to spend resources immediately than the Japanese-American youths living in the same physical location (rural Oahu), such immediate "squandering" does not necessarily indicate an inability to delay gratification or invest for the future. To the extent that resources were spent on friends and family (as opposed to self), such expenditure might be viewed as an investment for the future, given a general cultural emphasis on social relations and social reciprocity.

To check on their reasoning, Gallimore, et al. asked each of two groups of high school students—Hawaiians and Japanese-Americans—to write essays in response to the question "If someone gave you $1500 dollars, what would you do with it?" Each essay was indendently rated by two raters in terms of the extent to which the writer intended to defer use of the $1500 for some later purpose. In addition, each essay was coded in terms of the intended use of the money. Four code categories were used: (1) family and others, (2) save or invest, (3) personal, and (4) save for education.

There were a number of results, but only two are directly relevant to our purposes. First, as determined by independent ratings of their essays, the Hawaiian youths were much more inclined to indicate that they would use the money immediately. However,

> In terms of intended usage, there were two significant between-groups differences: Hawaiians more often elected expenditures to aid 'family/others'; the Japanese more frequently chose education. The absence of a reliable difference in percent electing to spend for personal use suggests that despite their reputation, Hawaiians are no more likely to seek immediate personal pleasure or 'impulse gratification' than are the Japanese (p. 76).

In terms of middle-class American values, "saving for an education" is an obvious example of ability to delay gratification, but within the cultural system of Hawaiian-Americans, expenditures that reinforce group ties may also be examples of the ability to defer gratification.

EVALUATION OF CONTENT ANALYSIS

As Stone, et al. (1966) point out, content analysis focuses on behavior once removed—that is, on recorded speech and writing. Such a focus has inherent difficulties. The really crucial documents one may need to test a certain idea may have been destroyed, altered, never written, or unattainable for a variety of reasons. Another serious difficulty is that content analysis is literally blind to whole aspects of human behavior, such as nonverbal communication.

As an example, read the minutes of the next meeting you go to and then compare their Spartan quality to your memory of what actually went on, who sat next to whom, the innuendo and sarcasm expressed, the angry glances, the flirtations, the audible sighs when the more long-winded started to speak. Further, as Holsti (1969) points out, even when the documents of interest are available, content analysis can usually tell us nothing about the truth of assertions in the text or about such nebulous qualities as the aesthetic appeal of the text.

On the other hand, there are decided advantages to the use of content analysis. Often the only information we have that is pertinent to a particular issue or research question is in documentary form. With such data, content analysis forces the investigators to make explicit the categories and coding rules on which their conclusions about such documents are based. Another advantage of content analysis is that it is usually an unobtrusive measure that is not confounded and biased by the research subject's knowledge that he or she is participating in research (Webb, Campbell, Schwartz and Sechrest, 1966). Having subjects generate text (as in Gallimore, et al., 1974) and then content analyzing the text is an increasingly accepted use of content analysis. Originally, content analysis was employed primarily with preexisting documents, reflecting its beginnings in journalism and political science.

As we have seen, content analysis is a tool for drawing inferences from "text," or verbal communications of one sort or another. There are, of course, numerous other sources of information relevant to social-psychological phenomena in addition to verbal communications. The next section describes the use of such additional sources of information.

Archival research

Nearly everyone is aware of vast amounts of information about human behavior that are not contained in verbal communications. Yet the overwhelming majority of social science research depends almost exclusively on interviews and questionnaires. This research is subject to three general classes of biases: bias due to the respondents themselves, bias due to the interviewer, and bias due to poor selection of respondents. Given these sources of error, should the interview, questionnaire, participant observation, and content analysis approaches be discarded? No one would advocate such a solution.

The solution advocated here is TRIANGULATION OF MEASUREMENT. If the same result is obtained using several different measuring instruments or several different research methods, then the likelihood that the result is erroneous, artifactual, or unrepresentative of the real state of affairs is greatly diminished. The solution, in short, is to take a multimethod approach to any research question. This section is about two nonreactive approaches, both of which are concerned with the use of what might be called by-product indices. Webb, et al. (1966) cite some examples of the use of such indices:

> The floor tile around the hatching chick exhibit at Chicago's Museum of Science and Industry must be replaced every six weeks. Tiles in other parts of the museum need not be replaced for years. The selective erosion of tiles indexed by the replacement rate is a measure of the relative popularity of exhibits.

> The accretion rate is another measure. One investigator wanted to learn the level of whiskey consumption in a town which was officially "dry." He did so by counting empty bottles in ash cans.

> The degree of fear induced by a ghost-story-telling session can be measured by noting the shrinking diameter of a circle of seated children.

> Library withdrawals were used to demonstrate the effect of the introduction of television into a community. Fiction titles dropped, nonfiction titles were unaffected.

> The child's interest in Christmas was demonstrated by distortions in the size of Santa Claus drawings.

> Racial attitudes in two colleges were compared by noting the degree of clustering of Negroes and Whites in lecture halls (p. 2).

These examples fall into three classes: use of archival records (library withdrawals and museum maintenance records), use of physical evidence (bottles in ash cans, Santa Claus drawings, and museum tile replacement), and simple observation (clustering of Negroes and Whites, fear during ghost-story telling). We will discuss only the first two of these classes. The issues involved in the third, simple observation, are the same as those we considered when we discussed participant observation.

The use of *physical evidence* has been largely ignored in social psychology. There are, however, two broad classes of physical evidence that can be employed. First are EROSION MEASURES, wherein the degree of wear gives the index. Suppose, for example, we were interested in the relative activity levels of boys and girls attending a day-care center. We might require their parents to purchase a special pair of gym shoes for the children to keep at school and wear during school hours. We could then periodically measure the extent of wear on the soles and heels. We would, of course, need to supplement our measure of activity level with another method—say, observers' ratings of how active each child was. If the two methods yielded comparable results, we would have greater faith in the finding than if our only evidence were the degree of shoe wear and tear. If we had to rely only on the physical evidence, we would be in a quandary even if the boys' shoes wore out more quickly than the girls' shoes. Maybe the boys just weigh more. Maybe they drag their feet when they walk.

The second type of physical evidence is *accretion,* wherein the deposit of some material gives the index. Detective novels and TV shows often hinge on a crucial accretion index—a particular type of blood on the suspect's coat sleeve, a certain kind of soil between the treads of the suspect's car tire, a particular size footprint. Numerous accretion measures might be employed for various social–psychological questions. The number of fingerprints on objects displayed in a store might be used as an index of the object's appeal. Household litter and garbage contain a wealth of information about families: information on eating habits, buying habits, alcohol consumption, aspirin consumption, and the like. Social psychologists seem to have been somewhat reluctant to get their hands on (or into) these kinds of data. Literally tons of valuable information are thrown out each day.

Accretion and erosion measures can be important sources of data, particularly when they are employed in conjunction with other research methods. We referred to these earlier as by-product indices, a term intended to imply that, while the situation may or may not be contrived by the researcher (requiring special gym shoes for our day-care students versus looking through garbage cans for empty whiskey bottles), the measure is produced *incidentally* in conjunction with normal activities. A third and vastly more important type of by-product research is the extraction of indices of interest from archives.

Webster defines ARCHIVES as public records and documents. We would define it a little more broadly to include both public and private records of any sort. All societies produce vast amounts of useful records—votes, births, deaths, budgets, divorces, crime rates, health statistics. Webb, et al. (1966) point out that research workers should occasionally give thanks to those literate record-keepers of yesteryear who have provided us with such a wealth of material that bears on many questions of current interest.

In the previous section on content analysis, we made the point that once the research question has been phrased, the key process is the construction of a set of categories into which the texts can be coded. Analogously, in the use of archives, once the research question has been phrased, the key process is the definition of an index to be extracted from the archives. The index must be chosen with care, because any records maintained continuously for long periods of time are subject to a number of factors that may threaten their accuracy. The record-keeping system or the persons in charge of making entries may have changed, for example, and some record-keepers make more errors than others. The problem of index construction is the problem of operationalizing our research question in such a way that the measure we extract from the archives reflects the concept of interest and as little else as possible.

Perhaps an example will help clarify this point. Suppose we are interested in the effect on crime rate of introducing a "home-cruiser" program allowing police officers to take their patrol cars home with them and use them when not on duty. The idea behind such a program is that it makes the police more visible in neighborhoods, at shopping centers, etc., and that this increased visibility serves as a deterrent to crime. The data we want to look at in order to check this hypothesis are contained in police archives—records of crimes reported, arrests made, convictions, and so forth. The point here is that whatever index we finally select, it could *not* be a simple before–after measure of number of crimes reported. At the very least, our index would have to take into account population changes. Suppose the population were increasing rapidly, the home-cruiser program were instituted, and the following year crime were up. Would we conclude that the home-cruiser program led to an increase in crime? Another thing we would need to incorporate into our index is some recognition of seasonal variations in crime. If the home-cruiser program were instituted on June 1, and we compared number of crimes reported in the previous three months with number reported in the following three months, we might again be tempted to draw an invalid conclusion about the effect of the program. In general, crime increases in the summer.

Index construction is usually highly idiosyncratic to the particular research problem. There are, however, two general principles to follow. First, one should have a *specific* research purpose, question, or hypothesis clearly in mind. Second, one should begin a sort of trial-and-revision process in which a possible index is proposed and then subjected to critical scrutiny. The scrutiny should be aimed at discovering what plausible interpretations (such as the population changes or seasonal variations we mentioned) will be allowed by this index in addition to the one intended by the hypothesis. The trial-and-revision process should be relaxed only when an index is discovered that is susceptible to no plausible interpretations other than that intended in the research question. To illustrate both the use of archival data and the concept of triangulation of measurement, we have chosen the following study by Sales (1973).

THE METHOD APPLIED: THREAT AND AUTHORITARIANISM

During the middle and late 1940s, a group of personality and social psychologists employing questionnaire data and intensive clinical interviews defined a new personality type—the authoritarian. Early investigators of this personality type found a bizarre pattern of ideas and beliefs. The authoritarian seemed to at once admire science and rationality and yet was filled with irrational and unscientific beliefs. He or she seemed to be both enlightened and superstitious, a fierce individualist and abjectly afraid of being different, strongly independent and inclined to genuflect to any authority. The authoritarian syndrome as detailed by Adorno, Frenkel-Brunswick, Levinson, and Sanford (1950) is a complex web of such contradictory impulses. There are, however, a number of specific markers of authoritarianism that Adorno and his colleagues singled out for study. In contrast to others, authoritarians seemed to greatly admire power and strength, to have a cynical contempt for humankind, to believe in mystical determinants of one's fate, to maintain submissive attitudes toward anyone in power, to reject those who violate in-group values, and to be particularly harsh toward those who violate sexual norms. One of the situational factors hypothesized to bring about increases in authoritarianism is environmental threat. Further, if a threatening or unsatisfying situation does tend to evoke increases in authoritarianism, it should be measurable in each aspect of authoritarianism—in increased belief in and popularity of mysticism, in increased admiration of power, in greater harshness toward sexual deviates, etc.

To test the hypothesis that increased environmental threat leads to increased authoritarianism, Sales (1973) chose to look at the two decades 1920-1929 and 1930-1939. The 1920s was a prosperous time for the United States and one of the few decades during which the United States was not involved in a war, while the 1930s was an economic disaster.

> Unemployment rose from a yearly average of 4.98% in the 1920s to an average of 18.23% during the 1930s, while per capita disposable income fell from a yearly average of $629 in the 1920s to an average of $485 during the 1930s. . . . Further, the threat of the Depression was exacerbated late in the 1930s by the portent of a new European war. If environmental threat were to have any impact upon authoritarian behavior, its effects would surely be seen during these two decades (p. 45).

Sales chose a number of different indices to test the hypothesis that increased threat leads to increased authoritarianism. We shall describe three of these indices.

First, if an aspect of the authoritarian personality is to demand submission to in-group values, then it should follow from the hypothesis that a time of increased threat (the 1930s) should lead to greater demands for toeing the party line than a time of low threat (the 1920s). Sales found that only 8 states passed statutes requiring loyalty oaths from school teachers in the 1920s. During the 1930s, however, 17 states passed such laws. Thus it appears that increased demands for submission to in-group norms occurred during the 1930s. This occurred in spite of the fact that, at the beginning of the 1930s, there was a smaller remaining pool of states without such laws than at the beginning of the 1920s.

A second index Sales chose was the amount of support for police forces during the 1920s and 1930s. It should follow that, if authoritarians condemn those who violate in-group values, they will support forces in society charged with apprehending and punishing the violators. Further, during times of increased threat, their support for such forces should increase. Looking at the proportion of New York City and Pittsburgh budgets devoted to police, Sales found that during the 1920s police were allocated 9.44 percent of the budget in these cities, while during the 1930s they received 10.14 percent. While this increase fits the hypothesis, it is ambiguous until at least two additional types of data are brought to bear. First, was crime on the increase? If so, such an increase might explain greater percentage allotments for the police. Sales found that the *Uniform Crime Reports for the United States* indicate that the increased funding for police forces occurred in the face of a decline in crime between the 1920s and the 1930s. The second type of data needed before interpreting the increase for police support is information on other aspects of the budgets. Maybe the cities were generally increasing expenditures for services—police, garbage collection, fire—and cutting back other aspects of the budgets. Sales selected the fire department allotments for comparison and found that these allotments declined from the 1920s to the 1930s. Thus it appears that, relative to other city services and in the face of a decline in crime (but in line with the hypothesis), New York City and Pittsburgh increased their support for police in the 1930s compared to the 1920s.

A third index that Sales selected was designed to see whether there was an increase in the harshness with which sexual offenders were treated during a period of increased threat (the 1930s). Going through court records of Allegheny County, Pennsylvania, he found that during the 1920s, rapists received sentences averaging 3.41 years in prison, but during the 1930s, the average sentence for rape was 4.65 years in prison. For a major nonsexual crime serving as a control, no such increase in sentence length occurred between the 1920s and the 1930s. Again the result is in line with the hypothesis.

Sales employed a series of additional indices taken from archival sources to test the hypothesis about the relationship between environmental threat and authoritarianism: sales of books dealing with mysticism, cynicism expressed in magazine articles, power of the heroes of comic strips originating in the 1930s versus the 1920s. Each of these indices has limitations; none is an infallible indicator. The result with each, however, was generally in line with the hypothesis. The relationship between threat and authoritarianism revealed itself with each of these imperfect indices. Thus our confidence in the hypothesized relationship has been greatly enhanced by the triangulation of measurement.

EVALUATION OF ARCHIVAL RESEARCH

A number of major advantages argue for the use of archives, records, and other by-products whenever possible. The first is a practical one: such research is generally very inexpensive. Literally millions of archives pertinent to social-psychological questions are available for research. Public records, information almanacs, old newspapers—the list is almost unlimited. The data are there waiting for researchers to think of a use for them.

The second advantage of using such data is that they can provide research results with a generality that cannot be attained with the more conventional methods of social psychology. They can provide EXTERNAL VALIDITY for our results (see Box C). The issue of external validity is the issue of generalizability: To what other populations and variables can we extend our results? As Webb, et al. (1966) put it,

> If a research hypothesis, particularly for social behavior, can survive the assaults of changing times and conditions, its plausibility is far greater than if it were tested by a method which strips away alien threats and evaluates the hypothesis in an assumptive, one-time test . . . if the events of time are vacillating, as they usually are, then only the valid hypothesis has the intellectual robustness to be sustained, while rival hypothesis expire (p. 84).

The third advantage of archival research is that it is generally the most nonreactive or unobtrusive set of techniques available. The interpersonal biases inherent in participant observation and survey research are largely absent. Selective perception on the part of the researcher may still operate to some extent (Rosenthal, 1966), but its range of detrimental influence is vastly reduced.

Finally, for some research purposes, there is simply no alternative to archival research. Webb, et al. give the example of suicide, for which one must simply wait until a group defines itself by committing the act. Then one can try to piece together a picture of the individuals from suicide notes, biographical details, and whatever else one can find. One cannot, of course, interview the subject, engage in participant observation with the subject, ask the subject to fill out a questionnaire, or ask the subject to take part in an experiment.

There are serious drawbacks to archival research, however. The most pervasive of these have to do with selective deposit and selective survival. With the use of both physical evidence and archives, SELECTIVE DEPOSIT can be a problem. The researcher who goes through people's trash cans should be aware that things like letters from secret lovers are likely to be burned and not thrown out with the trash. Some years ago, a group of industrial spies was exposed whose principal source of data had been the contents of a rival firm's trash bins. Since then, many companies have installed paper shredders. More mundane motives may also influence selective deposit. Even such "genuine" public documents as the *Congressional Record* are subject to this source of bias. Senators and representatives are allowed to edit and alter things entered in the *Record* and many take this opportunity to improve (or have their aides improve) their grammar.

The problem of SELECTIVE SURVIVAL is also a serious one. As several authors have noted, archeologists tend to be pottery and burial experts. Pottery is durable and tends to survive the onslaught of the elements, and primitive people often took great care to preserve the bones of their departed. And as Webb, et al. point out,

> For the student of the present, as well as of the past, the selective destruction of records is a question. Particularly in the political area, the holes that exist in data are suspect. Are records missing because knowledge of their contents would reflect in an untoward way on the administration? Have files been rifled? If records are destroyed casually, as they often are during an office move, was there some biasing principle for the research comparison which determined what would be retained and what destroyed (pp. 56–57)?

Other questions come to mind, particularly with the use of records. Has there been a change in the record-keeping system? Who was responsible for keeping the records? Do independent sources exist that can be used to check the accuracy of the records?

In spite of these potential difficulties, we are enthusiastic about the largely untapped potential for research represented by the use of physical and archival data. It is something of a paradox that, in a time when many are demanding "answers," pertinent, unused, interpretable data are lying about waiting for someone to ask questions. People differ in the way they like to phrase questions. Although we heartily endorse phrasing questions so that they can be answered with archival data, many prefer to ask and attempt to answer questions experimentally.

Experimentation

All research methods can be thought of as ways of attempting to insulate observations from error (Kaplan, 1964). From this perspective, the difference between experimentation and the other methods we have described is simply a matter of degree. In general, an experiment provides greater insulation from error. The crucial aspects of an experiment that help to achieve this are manipulation and control.

Most people already understand both of these concepts. MANIPULATION simply means changing something: trying a large picture instead of a small one over the mantle (if we are interested in the aesthetic effect produced by our living room wall); trying high-test gasoline instead of regular (if we want to stop the ping in our engine); using Brand Y mouthwash instead of Brand X (if we want people to stand closer when we talk). The parenthetical phrases indicate that we usually manipulate with a purpose in mind. We want to see "what happens if. . . ." Even when people claim they manipulated something "just for the hell of it," there usually is a purpose hidden away somewhere. Perhaps the purpose is as mundane as relief of monotony, but it is usually there.

The concept of control is closely tied to the notion of manipulation. If we change something, we want to know whether the change has any effect. Suppose we switch to high-test gas and get the car tuned up on the same day. The ping stops, but we don't know whether the different gasoline had an effect or not. Similarly, if we switch to Brand Y mouthwash, get a new wardrobe, and make it a point to be nicer to people all at the same time, we will not know whether switching to Brand Y had anything to do with the fact that others seem friendlier. Thus, when we are interested in whether a given manipulation of some aspect of the environment has any effect, we need to CONTROL, or hold constant, other aspects of the environment.

C. Internal and External Validity

Donald Campbell and Julian Stanley (1966) have made a distinction between two basic categories of variables that may jeopardize the validity of findings from various experimental and quasiexperimental designs. The first set of variables may threaten the *internal validity* of the design. That is, there are many things that may occur incidentally during the course of an experiment or because of the particular way in which an experiment is conducted, and these extraneous variables may cause changes in the dependent variable of the experiment. An experiment is said to be internally valid when the changes in the dependent variable are a function of changes in the independent variable and nothing else. Campbell and Stanley list eight variables that might jeopardize the internal validity of a design:

1. History: Specific events that occur during the course of an experiment other than changes in the independent variable.
2. Maturation: Changes in the experimental respondents or subjects that are purely a function of time passing.
3. Testing: Changes in responses of subjects that are a function of having been tested more than once.
4. Instrumentation: Changes in the measuring instruments or observers during the course of the experiment.
5. Statistical regression: When subjects have been selected because they are extreme on some variable, a later measurement may reveal them to be less extreme due to random variation in their responses.
6. Selection: Subjects assigned to the various comparison groups may not have been selected in the same manner.
7. Experimental mortality: Subjects may drop out of the various comparison groups at different rates.
8. Selection–maturation interaction: Because of the nature of what subjects in one group are asked to do, changes due only to passage of time may occur more rapidly for them than for subjects in other groups.

A second set of variables may jeopardize the external validity of the design. That is, even if an experimental design is internally valid, the findings may be of no use to us if we cannot generalize them to other settings and populations. Campbell and Stanley list four variables that may limit external validity:

1. Reactive effect of testing: If a pretest was used in the experiment, it may turn out that the independent variable produces changes in the dependent variable only among subjects who have been pretested.
2. Interaction of selection biases with the independent variable: Similarly, the independent variable may produce changes in the dependent variable only among subjects similar to those used in the experiment.
3. Reactive effects of experimental arrangements: Other aspects of the experimental setting may have effects similar to the reactive effect of testing.
4. Multiple-treatment inference: What is true for one variable in isolation may not hold when that variable is embedded in several others, and vice versa.

We cannot, of course, hold all other aspects of the environment constant. We cannot run time back and replay situations at will to introduce our manipulation. We can never know *exactly* what would have happened had we done A instead of B in a particular circumstance. We can only try doing A in the future in similar circumstances. Given that everything except our manipulation cannot be held constant, what things should we attempt to control? We need to hold constant or control those other aspects of the environment that might plausibly be expected to interfere with or obscure observation of the change produced by our manipulation. When we switch to high-test gas, it probably doesn't matter if we get the car washed on the same day, or buy a new battery, or have the windshield wiper fixed. None of these improvements can explain why the engine stopped pinging. On the other hand, we should not get the engine tuned up or have the valves adjusted. These changes might plausibly explain a quieter running car, and we would not know for sure whether the gasoline change had any effect.

The aspect of the environment that we choose to manipulate in an experiment is usually referred to as the INDEPENDENT VARIABLE. As Aronson and Carlsmith (1968) point out, in most social–psychological experiments the experimenter must decide whether the independent variable will be produced by instructions to the subject or will be some event that happens to the subject. As an example of the former, Byrne (1969) has conducted a large number of experiments testing the general hypothesis that similarity leads to attraction. In these experiments, similarity has usually been manipulated by giving subjects information about the attitudes of a "stranger." That is, either the stranger had attitudes and opinions very similar to those of the subject, or the stranger had very dissimilar attitudes and opinions. An example of the "event" type of manipulation is an experiment by Piliavin, Rodin, and Piliavin (1969) in which subway riders were confronted by a man who fell to the floor of the car and seemed to be in need of help. One aspect of this situation that was manipulated was the apparent source of the man's difficulty. On some occasions, the man smelled strongly of whiskey and appeared to be drunk. On other occasions he appeared to be ill.

While the jargon itself is not important, when we have an independent variable that is either present or absent—changing to high-test gasoline versus not changing, for instance—we usually say that the independent variable has two LEVELS. Thus an independent variable may have two (a minimum) or more than two levels. Bryne has manipulated attitudinal similarity by employing finer gradations than simply similar versus not similar. When we have a variable we want to manipulate, the different levels or degrees of the variable are referred to as TREATMENTS, and a common procedure is to expose some subjects to one treatment, some to another treatment, and some to no treatment at all. Data from the latter subjects serve as a baseline or control with which to compare the data from the experimental subjects. For example, suppose we were interested in the effect of varying degrees of food deprivation on the tendency of subjects to "see" food-related items in ambiguous shapes such as those formed by inkblots. We might deprive some subjects of food for 24 hours, some for 48 hours, and some not at all. We would need the data from the undeprived subjects as a control or comparison in order to interpret the data from the two experimental conditions (24 and 48 hours of deprivation).

The aspect of the environment that we look at or measure to see if our change in the independent variable has had any effect is usually referred to as the DEPENDENT VARIABLE. In our food-deprivation example, the dependent variable might be some measure of the total amount of food-related imagery in response to five different inkblots. In Byrne's studies manipulating the similarity of a stranger's attitudes to the subject's attitudes, the dependent variable is usually some measure of attraction: how much the subject thinks he or she will like the stranger. In the study by Piliavin et al. (1969), the major dependent variable was how many people came to the aid of the man on the floor.

The things to be held constant in a given experiment, as we have said, are those things (other than the independent variable) that might plausibly be expected to influence the dependent variable. Since many experiments involve comparisons of the responses given by subjects exposed to the independent variable with the responses of subjects not exposed to the independent variable, one thing that might plausibly be expected to influence those responses are any preexisting differences between the groups of subjects. To take an extreme example, no thinking experimenter interested in the effects of caffeine on weight-lifting ability would compare the amounts lifted by male college students who had had a cup of coffee with the amounts lifted by female college students who had not had a cup of coffee. The comparison would be worthless except, perhaps, as an example of how not to do research. There are several techniques for controlling the influence of preexisting group differences. The most general and widely used is that of RANDOM ASSIGNMENT of subjects to groups. In principle, such randomization is simple. We simply need to ensure that there are no systematic ways in which subjects in the experimental and control groups differ. In assigning subjects to groups, any given subject should be as likely to be assigned to one group as to another (see Figure 4).

In practice, achieving true random assignment can be very difficult, and all sorts of subtle biases may operate in determining which subjects get assigned to which group. To use volunteer subjects in one condition or treatment and paid or coerced subjects in another would be an obvious error, because the motivations of the two groups differ sharply. To use an eight o'clock section of students in the experimental group and a ten o'clock section of students enrolled in the same course in the control group is also nonrandom assignment. Students who schedule their classes at eight o'clock may be quite different from students who schedule their classes at ten o'clock.

Thus the key aspects of an experiment are manipulation and control. The independent variable is manipulated, and its effects on the dependent variable are measured. Those aspects of the situation other than the independent variable that might plausibly affect the dependent variable are held constant, or controlled. (For an example of something that must be controlled in most social-psychological experiments, see Box D.) Random assignment of subjects to treatments is one facet of control. It is a way of controlling for preexisting differences among subjects exposed to the various treatments. The purpose of control is to achieve what Campbell and Stanley (1966) refer to as internal validity. INTERNAL VALIDITY concerns whether the results are due to experimental treatment or can be explained by some artifact of the procedure. The difference between our weightlifters who drank coffee and those who did not may not have been due to caf-

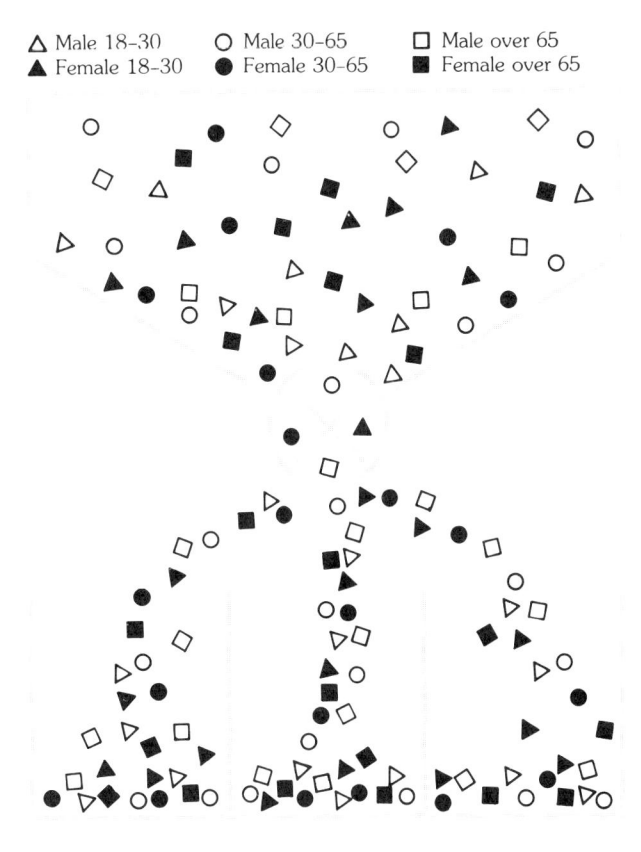

4. In a well-designed experiment, we would not put all males in one condition and all females in another, or all old people in one condition and all young people in another— unless, of course, we were interested in sex or age differences. Random assignment of subjects to the conditions of an experiment helps insure that differences in results are due only to the manipulated, independent variable. With random assignment, all subjects have the same likelihood of being assigned to any of the experimental conditions. It is then unlikely that any of the subjects' personal characteristics will systematically influence the results of the experiment, because the personal characteristics reflected in the various conditions should average out about the same.

D. Expectations and the Experiment

In a series of studies beginning in the late 1950s, Robert Rosenthal and his colleagues demonstrated the pervasive influence of expectations on research findings. Although people had long been aware of the influence of expectations in perception, one of the more important findings from Rosenthal's research was that, even in apparently well-controlled laboratory settings, experimenters who expected their subjects to respond in certain ways were more likely to obtain those responses than were experimenters who had no such prior expectations.

In a number of studies, for example, Rosenthal (1966) and his colleagues asked experimenters to administer a person-perception photo-rating task to subjects. Experimenters were to show a series of photos to each subject and ask the subject to rate each photo in terms of whether the person pictured "has been experiencing success or failure" (p. 144). The ratings were to be made on a scale running from -10 (extreme failure) to $+10$ (extreme success). The photos had previously been selected so as to actually be neutral on this scale. Some experimenters were led to believe that the subjects' ratings would average about $+5$, and other experimenters were led to believe the ratings would average about -5. It was found in many studies that experimenters with the former expectation obtained significantly more positive ratings from their subjects than experimenters with the latter expectation. Since the experimenters had all read the same instructions to subjects, their expectations were apparently communicated to subjects via some relatively subtle aspects of their behavior.

The search for what these subtle aspects of behavior might be began almost immediately and still continues. The experimenter's tone of voice, inflection, number of smiles, number of mutual glances exchanged with the subject, and several other behaviors have been implicated as channels by which the experimenter's expectations can be communicated to the subject and, thus, may determine how the subject responds.

Regardless of the exact means by which such expectations are communicated, ways must be found in any research endeavor to hold this source of bias in check. One general procedure that has been useful in a variety of settings is to keep the experimenter "blind" to the condition each subject is in. Presumably, if the experimenter does not know how the subject is expected to respond, he or she will not be able to unintentionally induce subjects to respond as expected.

---

feine (the experimental treatment). Rather, the difference may have been an artifact of our nonrandom assignment of males to one group and females to another.

Before discussing the advantages and disadvantages of experimentation relative to the other research methods we have described, we will give an example of experimentation.

THE METHOD APPLIED: IMPRESSION MANAGEMENT

In recent years, a number of investigators have suggested that under certain conditions our behavior is shaped by the expectations of others. For example, Zanna and Pack (1975) hypothesized that, if we are strongly attracted to someone and know that he or she admires a particular kind of person, we may try to present ourselves as if we were that kind of person in the hope of winning that certain someone's admiration. If, in doing this, we change the way we normally present ourselves, our behavior will have been molded by our knowledge of the other's expectations. However, if we do not care whether the other person likes us or not, we may pay no attention to what that person expects.

Specifically, Zanna and Pack suggest that if one were about to meet an attractive, eligible member of the opposite sex and one knew the characteristics that this person admired, one might well overemphasize the extent to which one possessed those characteristics. The basic proposition is very simple. As the desirability of the other person increases, so should one's motivation to make a good impression. If, for example, an extremely attractive, desirable male were known to admire dependent, conforming, "traditional" females, females first meeting this person might be inclined to present themselves as fulfilling these qualifications. If the same male were known to admire independent, nonconforming, "untraditional" females, then the *same* females might first be more inclined to present themselves as possessing the latter qualifications.

To see whether this sort of IMPRESSION MANAGEMENT does occur, Zanna and Pack recruited 80 female undergraduates of Princeton University to participate in a study dealing with personality traits and opinions. At an initial pretest session, subjects were asked to rate the extent to which certain statements were characteristic of themselves. The statements dealt with a number of sex-role stereotypes, such as the extent to which the subject was dependent, aggressive, career-oriented, sentimental, emotional, easily influenced, and interested in her appearance. Three weeks later these same subjects were individually brought back to the lab to take part in a "different" study, a study of impression formation.

This time, the subject's task was to form an impression of her "partner" based on some information the partner would provide, and *he*, in turn, would form an impression of the subject based on information that she provided. Subjects assigned to the High Desirability conditions were led to believe that their partner was a 6'1", 21-year-old Princeton senior with no girl friend and that he was most interested in meeting some female college students. He also happened to have a car and was interested in sports. On the other hand, subjects assigned to the Low Desirability conditions were led to believe that their partner was only 5'5", 18 years old, and a first-year student at another school. He also had a girl friend, owned no car, and was not particularly interested in meeting female college students.

Following receipt of this initial information about her partner, each subject was given information about her partner's view of the ideal woman. For half of the subjects in each of the desirability conditions, the partner's ideal woman was very traditional: dependent, conforming, home-oriented, and passive. For the remaining subjects, the partner's ideal woman was very un-

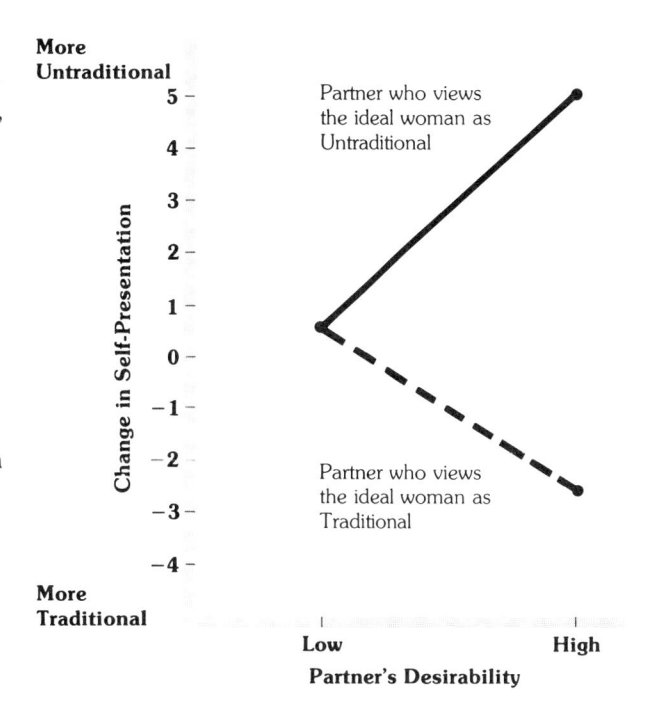

5. When the partner's desirability was high, female subjects who believed that the partner admired untraditional women were likely to present themselves as untraditional. When they believed the partner admired traditional women, they were inclined to present themselves as traditional. These changes did not occur when the partner's desirability was low. (From Zanna and Pack, 1975, Table 1, p. 588.)

traditional: competitive, ambitious, independent, and nonemotional. Finally, subjects were asked to furnish some information about themselves for their partner by rating themselves on a series of scales. These scales were the same as those they had filled out earlier in the "other" study, so changes in the extent to which subjects presented themselves as traditional or untraditional could be determined. These changes in self-presentation as a function of the partner's desirability and view of the ideal woman were, of course, the major interest of the study. They are presented in Figure 5.

As shown in Figure 5, when the partner is low in desirability, his image of the ideal woman makes little difference in the self-presentations of the female college students in the study. On the other hand, when the partner is high in desirability, the subjects present themselves as being closer to his image of the ideal woman, regardless of whether that image is traditional or untraditional.

EVALUATION OF EXPERIMENTATION

There are essentially three advantages of experimentation over the other research methods we have described. The first is the degree of control over extraneous and possibly contaminating variables. For example, in the Zanna and Pack study, random assignment of subjects to conditions made it relatively unlikely that any initial, or preexisting, differences among subjects in the various conditions could influence the results. There is no reason to believe that more traditional students were assigned to the High Desirability–Traditional Ideal condition than to the other conditions.

The second major advantage of experimentation is that it offers the opportunity to manipulate variables of interest. Being able to manipulate variables, as opposed to merely observing and recording changes, allows one to isolate and specify precisely what is making a difference. In the field, variables are often complex and many-faceted. The laboratory experiment is often the best way to tease out the important component of a complex variable.

The third major advantage is that the experiment can provide us with the least ambiguous evidence about the relationship between an antecedent (independent) variable and a consequent (dependent) variable. We have purposely limited our use of the term "causation." A judgment that X causes Y involves knowing a great deal more than a simple experiment can tell us. Further, most of the phenomena of interest to social psychologists have multiple antecedents. Our position is that investigators should be less concerned with isolating the cause and more interested in specifying the conditions under which antecedent A predominates in producing the effect in question and determining how those conditions differ from the conditions under which antecedent B predominates. Experimentation can provide us with the clearest definitions of those various sets of conditions.

The disadvantages of experimentation stem primarily from its artificiality. Many people (Aronson and Carlsmith, 1968) have commented on the elaborate stage-setting and deception that may be involved in an experiment. In the experiment by Zanna and Pack, for example, subjects had to be convinced that they were about to meet a partner who was either high or low in desirability when, in fact, there was no partner.

In their discussion of the problems of social–psychological experiments, Aronson and Carlsmith introduce the concepts of mundane realism and experimental realism. EXPERIMENTAL REALISM refers to the extent to which the situation confronting a subject in an experiment is involving and must be taken seriously. It concerns the extent to which the situation has impact and holds the subject's attention. MUNDANE REALISM, on the other hand, refers to the extent to which the laboratory situation is similar to things that occur in the "real world." These are not polar opposites. A given situation can be high on both mundane and experimental realism, low on both, or high on one and low on the other. (Note also that these concepts are *not* the same as external and internal validity.)

The disadvantages of experimentation in social psychology are often linked with the attempt to create situations that are high in experimental realism. In an attempt to create such situations, many experimenters create elaborate scenarios or cover stories that deceive the subject by keeping the true purpose of the experiment hidden but may arouse suspicion on the part of the subject about what is really going on. An example of a cover story appears in the Zanna and Pack experiment when subjects were led to believe that the purpose of the second session was to study the impresssion-formation process. It has often been pointed out that when individuals participate as subjects in such experiments, they are usually motivated to perform well. Further, most subjects have the idea that the experimenter is trying to prove something, and they very often view their task in terms of helping the experimenter find what he or she is looking for. Therefore, all the cues that convey an experimental hypothesis to subjects become significant determinants of their behavior. Orne (1962) has called the sum total of such cues the DEMAND CHARACTERISTICS OF THE EXPERIMENTAL SITUATION. The purpose of elaborate cover stories is often to keep demand characteristics to a minimum. The problem is that, in minimizing demand characteristics, the experimenter often introduces extraneous, confounding variables. A second problem is that the cover stories often involve deception and raise ethical considerations. A further disadvantage of the experiment is that it is simply not appropriate for many of the most important social–psychological questions.

We would like to make some final comments about methods. It will become obvious that the five methods we have described are rarely used in pure form. They blend together and are often intermixed in the actual conduct of research. A participant observer may conduct an informal experiment to check out a hunch. An experimenter may conduct extensive postexperimental interviews to determine whether subjects perceived the manipulations as intended. A survey researcher may seek out archival data to round out his or her information. Furthermore, there are other methods that can be employed to investigate social–psychological questions. Computer simulation is an example (Abelson, 1968). However, the methods we have described and their various combinations probably account for about 99 percent of all social–psychological research at present. In reading the following chapters, keep in mind the question of whether a particular researcher chose wisely among these methods. Could the question have been better addressed with a different method?

As Webb, et al. (1966) point out and as we have tried to make clear in this chapter, no research method is completely bias-free. The key to advancing our knowledge of social processes is the careful selection of those methods that are most appropriate for the question being asked. When we say "those methods" we refer, of course, to the multimethod approach. Social processes and human behavior are complex, and to attempt to capture that complexity with single, isolated methods and measures is naive.

Summary

We began this chapter with a general discussion of the nature of research, pointing out that there is nothing mysterious about scientific research that sets it apart from other human activities. Research always begins with a question, with something about which we are curious, and research methods are simply procedures for helping us answer our question. Because each method is fallible, however, and carries with it a number of sources of potential bias, one should obtain evidence by using several different procedures whenever possible. In other words, one should triangulate measurements. Further, because most social–psychological phenomena do not have single, simple causes, we recommended the following general research strategy. *When trying to understand some phenomenon, one should generate as many plausible explanations for the phenomenon as possible and then systematically set about gathering evidence on these multiple hypotheses.*

We then described and illustrated five general categories of research methods frequently employed in social–psychological research: participant observation, survey research, content analysis, archival research, and experimentation. Each of these methods has certain advantages and disadvantages, and each is only appropriate for some, not all, research endeavors. The primary advantage of participant observation, for example, is the completeness or range of information that the sensitive participant observer can gather about a particular setting or situation. The primary shortcomings of participant observation are the enormous possibilities for bias and information selectivity on the part of the participant observer who is, after all, only human. Similarly, each of the other methods has its own peculiar advantages and disadvantages. The experiment, for example, allows for a great deal of control over bias and contaminating influences, but it often appears artificial and takes the phenomenon of interest hopelessly out of context. No method is without its limitations. The researcher must pick that method or combination of methods most appropriate for his or her research question.

The research question, or hypothesis of interest, must guide the entire process. One of the worst and, unfortunately, one of the most common errors made in research is to assume that data will speak for themselves. Unless one asks a question and asks it well, the data won't say a word.

II

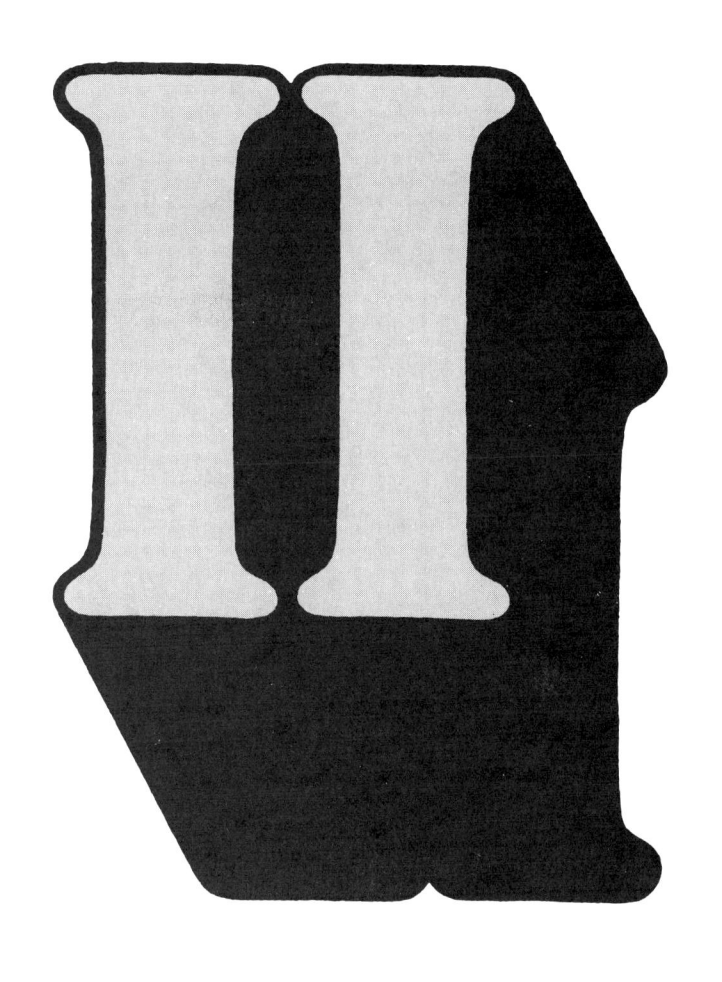

Becoming a social creature

3

The development of social behavior

51 Some basic issues of socialization

The Universal Parenting Machine
   The imaginary experiment
   Are there universal issues of socialization?

56 Theories of becoming a social being

The psychoanalytic approach
   The structure and dynamics of personality
   Identification
   The psychosexual stages of development
Erikson: the psychosocial approach
The cognitive-developmental approach
   Jean Piaget
   The nature of cognitive development
   Social development
The social-learning approach
   Neo-Hullian theory
   Elements of Bandura's approach

68 Origins of early social development

Mother-infant interaction
   Infant sensory and response capabilities
   The interaction system
Attachment
   How attachment begins
   Must attachments form for the infant to become human?
Maternal separation and deprivation
   Short-term effects of maternal separation
   Long-term effects of deprivation
   What is crucial—mother deprivation or stimulus deprivation?
Child-rearing practices

74 The development of morality

The nature of morality
   The three components of morality
   Consistency in moral conduct
Psychoanalytic conceptions
   Evidence for the psychoanalytic approach
The social-learning approach to moral development
   Moral prohibitions
   Self-control: the role of reinforcement
   Self-control: the role of punishment
   Self-control: the role of imitation
The cognitive-developmental model
   Piaget's approach to moral development
   Kohlberg's approach to moral development

84 Sex roles: "It" becomes "Him" or "Her"

88 The emergence of the person

89 Summary

The study of such topics in this book as conformity, leadership, and attitude change takes as its subject a socialized human being who has a distinctive conception of self, an ability to communicate and use language, and the capacity to see the world from the point of view of other people. In this chapter and the next, we explore some of the concepts, theories, and research related to SOCIALIZATION, the development of the infant into the sophisticated social being called an adult. We focus on six issues.

1. *What are the basic problems of socialization?* Many years ago, anthropologists and some psychologists believed in CULTURAL RELATIVISM, the idea that all the customs, values, and behaviors of a given society are unique to that society. If every society is unique, the problems and principles of socialization in one society have no bearing on socialization in another society. Today, social scientists question cultural relativism. Perhaps certain problems crop up in all societies. If so, they are universal problems that all societies must deal with in socializing their youth. We need to explore what some of these universal issues of socialization might be.

2. *What are the major theories of how the infant becomes a social being?* There is no single, uniform view of the socialization process. Rather there are several different approaches. We will briefly examine three theories: the psychoanalytic, social-learning, and cognitive-developmental approaches.

3. *How does the immature infant begin to be a human being?* At birth, the infant seems to be a small, noisy machine that sleeps, eats, eliminates, and thoroughly exhausts its parents in the process. By the end of the first year, however, it smiles, vocalizes, perhaps walks, and seems attached to its parents. How does this marvelous transformation occur?

4. *How does the amoral infant become a moral agent?* The infant has no conception of the values and moral codes of its society. During the course of socialization, the child internalizes rules, notions of right and wrong, and feelings of social responsibility and learns to engage in moral judgments and actions. We consider in some detail the various conceptions of moral development.

5. *How does the infant become male or female?* Sexual identity is only partly a matter of biology. Every society has a complex set of ideas about what it means to be a man or a woman. During the course of socialization, the child acquires a SEX-ROLE IDENTITY, or adopts the society's conception of his or her basic identity as male or female.

6. *How does the infant become a person?* At maturity, the individual is conceived by his or her society as a PERSON. The notion of personhood is a complex concept, and to be a person (as opposed to being merely a biological organism) is to be many things. Personhood includes several attributes: (a) self-determination, (b) decision-making capacity, (c) relative autonomy of self in the world, (d) competence to do certain things and not others, (e) desire and ability to achieve goals, and (f) organized and distinctive behavior patterns that make the person unique and recognizable compared to all other people.

Thus socialization may be viewed as a journey that begins at birth and involves transformation and change throughout life. The early years are oriented toward the establishment of identity as a person, which is roughly achieved at physical maturity, but which continues to evolve more slowly throughout life.

Some basic issues of socialization

It will be useful to raise some of the issues of socialization in terms of a fantasy experiment or, as it is sometimes called, a thought experiment.

THE UNIVERSAL PARENTING MACHINE

Every child is born into an ongoing culture that affects the child from the moment of birth until death.

Consequently, it is impossible to disentangle the effects of culture from the genetic endowment of the species. Ideally, an experiment would be conducted in which some children were raised without benefit of culture and compared at age 18 with children who were raised normally. Of course, such an experiment is impossible. But we can *pretend* that it is possible and think through the implications.

The imaginary experiment. Suppose that six infants are placed immediately after birth in a "universal parenting machine" (the UPM). To enliven the scenario, we may suppose that three infants are male and three female. The UPM is conceived as an enclosed building with advanced machinery capable of satisfying all of the infants' physical needs from immediately after birth to maturity. The most crucial feature of the UPM is that it is constructed so that the subjects will have no human contact (except with each other) during their first 18 years of life. In fact, they will not even know that other human beings exist. The question of interest is what kind of creatures the children would be at age 18.

For the sake of argument, we will assume that creation of the UPM is technically possible. However, numerous problems would arise in the design of the apparatus, because the instruments themselves might become an important part of the socialization process and influence the course of the children's development. For example, there must be some way to feed the infants, and at first a nipple device that mimics a mother's breast would be required. This device could be a mechanical arm that extended periodically into the cradle from a wall of a general instrumentation module, or it could be part of a mobile robot programmed to pick up the infant periodically and insert a nipple into its mouth. The perceptual difference between an anonymous extension from a wall and the more "personal" service of a robot might well affect the course of development.

Another technical problem with developmental implications concerns the nature of the sensory environment. Human infants, like other creatures, need a rich diet of sights and sounds, touches and tastes. There is abundant evidence that an impoverished sensory environment is detrimental to development (see Stone, Smith, and Murphy, 1973, for an extended review).

Clearly our UPM infants should experience many sights and sounds. But what kind of sights and sounds? Humans are group animals, so presumably they should have visual and auditory contact with each other from the beginning. Perhaps the UPM should be a garden of Eden with flowers and shrubs. Perhaps it should be encased in a huge transparent dome so that the subjects could experience the daily movement of sun, moon, and stars in the cycle of day and night (see Figure 1). Perhaps the sounds of birds and insects are important in sensory development.

We will assume that our UPM infants have been raised in a protected garden of Eden with a transparent dome—a physical environment similar to that in which children are normally raised. Their physical needs are met, and they have access to each other as they grow up. Now we must pose several interesting questions. The answer to each question is problematic, but we can speculate.

1. *Would the children develop a language?* We know that the capacity for speech is innate, but its full flowering depends on the existence of a linguistic community. Since the brain and vocal apparatus develop with increasing age, it is reasonable to assume that a rudimentary vocal system of communication might develop. It seems unlikely, however, that such a system could be very sophisticated. The point is made in Chapter 4 that language enables us to label and define reality and that without language there would really be nothing to communicate about. Thus we would expect our UPM children to have only a rudimentary conception of external reality. It also follows that the sense of self as a unique and distinct creature would be very ill-defined.

2. *Would the children become attached to mothering robots in the same way that infants become attached to their natural mothers?* The concept of IMPRINTING suggests that attachment to a mothering robot might occur. Imprinting is very rapid perceptual learning exhibited by some species during early life (Hess,

1. Sketch of the imaginary Universal Parenting Machine. In such an environment, all of the child's physical needs would be satisfied, but there would be no contact with humans except the other children being "raised" by the UPM.

**53
The development
of social behavior**

1964). For example, baby geese and chicks often follow any available moving object shortly after birth and thereafter show an apparent attachment to that object.

It is unclear whether humans and other primates go through such periods of rapid perceptual learning. We do know that infants show a preference for human faces compared to other shapes during the first few weeks of life (Schaffer, 1977). It might well be that our UPM infants would become attached to mothering robots in a way that would not occur for a mechanical feeding arm extended from a fixed wall.

3. *Would the UPM children become sexual creatures at maturity?* While it may seem that they would discover sexuality naturally, that outcome is by no means certain. In primitive species, sexual behavior is triggered largely by instinctive mechanisms. At higher levels of the phylogenetic scale, and particularly with humans, sexual behavior is largely learned. Whether or not copulation would be discovered by our little group seems quite chancy.

4. *Would the children come to love each other?* Love, like hatred, is a complex human emotion, and it is presumably modeled by the early experience of mother love. Strange as it may seem, love may not be a required ingredient of human social life. Schaffer (1977) offers the dramatic example of the Ik, a small tribe in northern Uganda. Due to their location, the Ik were constantly faced with the possibility of starvation. Their attitude toward life was one of total selfishness. There was no room for sentiments such as love. Children were only grudgingly fed and cared for and then only until the age of three. At that age, they were turned out of the parents' hut to fend for themselves, and the parents guarded their own food supply to make sure the children did not steal it. Love did not exist among the Ik. Given this range of variation in human society, we cannot predict what kind of emotional life and affective ties would develop among the UPM group.

Other questions pertaining to the thought experiment are listed in Box A.

ARE THERE UNIVERSAL ISSUES OF SOCIALIZATION?

The thought experiment was designed as a way to get at the root of the human condition when all the complications of culture have been stripped away. Trying to answer the questions posed by the experiment makes it clear that human biological nature is completely intertwined with the ongoing culture into which the human infant is born. Because social behavior is so diverse across different societies, many social scientists have assumed that nothing is universally true about socialization and that each society is unique and must be studied within its own framework. But as we have said, social scientists are increasingly questioning this doctrine of cultural relativism (Triandis, 1978).

It is now assumed that there are common (or universal) problems of socialization shared by all societies.

A. Discussion Questions Raised by the UPM Thought Experiment

1. All known societies have some conception of religion with one or more powerful forces or Gods. Would the UPM group develop a concept of God?
2. All human groups develop rules about excretion. Would some kind of "modesty" rules develop in the UPM group?
3. Would some of the group members become leaders? If so, how would they exert power over the others?
4. Would the group explore their environment and perhaps try to escape into the larger world?
5. Would members of the UPM group be basically peaceful toward each other, or would they be aggressive?
6. Would the males dominate the females at age 18? Male dominance is a fact of life in most cultures. Is it based ultimately on the fact that males are physically stronger, or is male dominance a cultural development?

The search for universals of social development was stimulated by the book *Child Training and Personality* (Whiting and Child, 1953). These authors assumed that there are five areas in which children, regardless of the culture they belong to, have to be socialized in one way or another. These areas or behavior systems (Zigler and Child, 1969) are eating and oral behavior, excretion, sexual behavior, dependence, and aggression. It is hypothesized that the way children are socialized in these behavior systems may affect their personality and social behavior as adults. Other social scientists have considered other behavior systems (Endleman, 1967), and about ten such systems have been identified so far.

1. *Eating and oral behavior.* The infant's world revolves around eating, which is both a biological act and a social interaction with the mother. Out of this interaction, which is repeated hundreds of times during the first year of life, the infant develops an awareness of its social world. These early feeding experiences may be crucial for the child's long-term personality development. For example, unless the infant has repeated close contact with adults via feeding, it may not learn that it is a human being! This possibility led to our speculation about the feeding experiences of the UPM infants. Perhaps the mothering robot would have to be "humanlike" for the infants to develop any human identity.

Beyond the basic question of human identification within the context of early feeding experience, there are a host of specific questions. Does it matter whether the infant is breast fed or bottle fed? Does the mother's attitude while feeding the infant affect the infant's development? At some age, the child is shifted from infant modes to adult modes of eating. Weaning may be either gradual or abrupt. Thus there are many possibilities for early frustrations. Do such frustrations have temporary or long-term effects on development? Because feeding the infant is necessary in all societies, it is clear that the problems associated with feeding are indeed a universal dilemma of socialization.

2. *Excretory behavior.* Toilet training is a problem area that all cultures must deal with. It may begin very early or be delayed until the child is several years old, and parents may be more or less severe in their training demands. Since every child is toilet trained in one way or another, the fact of toilet training is another universal issue.

3. *Sexuality.* Although middle-class American folklore tends to deny that the young child has sexual feelings, everyday observations of children indicate otherwise. Small children manipulate their genitals and show much interest in sexual anatomy. Parents and other adults may be indulgent of sexual curiosity, or they may reprimand and repress. The parents' handling of the child's early sexual expression may conceivably affect attitudes and behaviors in adulthood.

4. *Aggression.* Small children often interfere with each other's behavior and goal direction. Such interference often results in various kinds of aggressive behavior, and the expression of aggression must be socialized in one way or another. The severity of the parents' reaction to the child's aggressiveness may potentially influence the course of adult social development.

5. *Dependence and independence.* All infants are totally dependent physically and emotionally on the adult world. During the first several years of life, various modes of dependent behavior become habitual. With increasing maturity, independent modes of behavior must be substituted.

6. *Emotional development.* The capacity for emotional feeling appears to be innate, but the circumstances, settings, and intensity of emotions are highly conditioned by social training. The development of love (or attachment, as it is called) is nearly universal, and it is enormously important in the type of group life a culture develops.

7. *Achievement.* Humans can engage in an almost infinite variety of activities. Any group prizes some acts more than others and socializes its young in those favored directions. Transmission of the urge for culturally prescribed achievement must be accomplished with every new generation.

8. *Competition and cooperation.* The inborn desire to live for self and the necessity of yielding to the desires of others are the horns of a dilemma faced by every human being. Everyone must learn complex patterns of striving to benefit oneself in some areas of life and complex accommodations to other people in other areas. The child's socialization will be affected by the relative emphasis his or her culture places on competition or cooperation. This emphasis may vary enormously from culture to culture.

9. *Self and other role conceptions.* The sense of

self is not something that comes automatically, as does physical growth. Rather it develops out of social interaction and use of linguistic symbols. Other key roles in life, such as husband, mother, and worker, must also develop. Cultures vary widely in terms of how much a strong, individualistic self-concept is emphasized. The nature of the self-concept the culture promotes helps shape the nature of adult social relations.

10. *Universal existential problems.* There are certain problems that we must all face as basic facts of existence. These problems include: (1) continual renewal of the group by birth, (b) marriage and mating, (c) the grim reality of death, (d) sickness and pain, and (e) the various moral rules for right and wrong that a society establishes.

It seems reasonable to conclude that these ten behavior systems are aspects of human infancy and childhood that all human groups must deal with. In this sense, they are universal issues of socialization. The range of ways in which societies handle each system is very great. That is probably why people differ so much from society to society.

Despite the diversity of custom and behavior, there is a common "humanness" the world over. We recognize others as humans no matter how strange their mode of dress or behavior patterns. What are the limits beyond which creatures who are biologically human would have no conception of their own humanity? The thought experiment suggests some of those limits. Without exposure to language, without exposure to the tender touching, holding, smiling, and laughing of human contact, it is doubtful whether a human organism can truly become a person. The members of the UPM group would have the physical shape of human beings, but functionally they might as well be members of another species.

Thus SOCIALIZATION is the process by which the raw material of the biological infant is transformed into a person. We explore some aspects of this fascinating transformation in the following sections.

Theories of becoming a social being

Different theories often make very different assumptions about human nature.

1. Are humans by nature inherently good, inherently bad, or neither?
2. Are humans merely passive agents or active agents in their own socialization?
3. Is human development a continuous progression from infancy to adulthood? Or is it discontinuous, as the person passes through a series of very different stages?

Some early philosophers, particularly Thomas Hobbes, viewed human nature as basically evil. According to this view, each person is filled with insatiable egoism, and socialization of the young consists largely in taming evil impulses or at least keeping them in check. This view may be called the doctrine of ORIGINAL SIN, a philosophy that grew out of early Jewish and Christian religions. Psychoanalytic theory accepted this basic assumption, which substantially determined its underlying concepts.

Other philosophers, such as John Locke, believed that the child is neither good nor bad but rather a TABULA RASA, or "blank slate," that can be molded in any one of many directions. This philosophy is congenial with the notion that we are basically the products of our experience. This basic assumption underlies the various social-learning theories of development.

Another view, subscribed to by such philosophers as Rousseau and Kant, may be called the doctrine of INNATE PURITY. According to this view, the child is a "noble savage" who interacts actively with the environment. The process of active interaction with the environment will lead to a happy and fulfilled adult, unless severe deprivations or frustrations intrude during the course of development. Various cognitive-developmental theorists, especially Piaget, come closest to assuming innate purity. This approach focuses on the rational, cognitive aspect of human nature and downplays the irrational, impulse-ridden image. The cognitive approach also views development as proceeding through a series of stages.

THE PSYCHOANALYTIC APPROACH

Sigmund Freud is perhaps the most familiar name in social science. He was originally trained as a physician and specialized in the treatment of nervous disorders (Hall and Lindzey, 1957). He studied techniques of hypnotism with the French psychiatrist Charcot for a year, but he decided that hypnosis was of limited value. He then explored the "talking cure" that a Viennese physician, Breuer, was using with patients. Freud was impressed with the results of patients talking out their problems, and he soon elaborated the general technique into methods of eliciting free association, taking life histories, analyzing dreams, and interpreting verbal material.

In this way, psychoanalysis was born. In 1900 Freud published a major work, *The Interpretation of Dreams,* and for the next 40 years developed his theory and wrote prodigiously (there are some 24 volumes of his collected works). A number of eminent students, such as Jung, Adler, and Rank, came to study with him. Some developed their own theories; others elaborated and extended Freud's thinking. By mid-century, psychoanalytic theory had become a major cultural phenomenon, heavily influencing clinical practice and several scientific disciplines.

The structure and dynamics of personality. According to psychoanalytic theory, the personality consists of three systems, id, ego, and superego. The ID is the original and primitive instinctual system. It does not recognize time or the demands of reality, but only the needs of immediate reduction of tension. This principle of tension reduction is called the PLEASURE PRINCIPLE. Tension reduction is achieved by reflex actions (such as a sneeze or cough) and the PRIMARY PROCESS, which is the calling up of the image of a need-satisfying object. For example, a hungry person may have images of food. Such wish-fulfilling images are the only reality the id knows; it cannot distinguish desire from reality. Inevitably this causes frustrations, and the need to overcome such frustrations is the impetus for the formation of the ego.

The EGO is sometimes called "the executive of the personality." It comes into existence to channel the desires of the id into appropriate selection of time, circumstance, and object. Its main job is to coordinate the instinctual demands of the id, the demands of the external world, and (as the child matures) the demands of the superego. The ego is never really independent of the id, because it draws its energy from the id. But if development is successful, the ego increasingly becomes master of the personality.

The SUPEREGO consists of the conscience and ego ideal and is the last system of the personality to develop. It is the moral aspect of the person. The bad things for which a child is punished are internalized as the CONSCIENCE, so that ultimately the child punishes himself or herself for misbehavior. The standards and ideals of the parents are internalized by the child as his or her EGO IDEAL and become part of the individual's self-concept. The superego is the internalized representative of society. As such, it is the mechanism by which the child eventually becomes a moral agent.

Freud believed that the organism is a set of physical energy systems, some of which are diverted to the various psychological systems. He felt that the instincts of the id were the source of psychic energy and that all the instincts collectively constituted the total sum of energy available for the personality. In his later writing, Freud elaborated on two classes of instincts: the life instincts, comprised of hunger, thirst, and sex, and the death instincts (discussed briefly in Chapter 11). The work of the life instincts is performed by a general energy known as LIBIDO. The sex instincts were given prominence because a number of body parts, primarily mouth, anal, and genital areas, are quite sensitive to stimulation. Reduction of stimulation to these erogenous zones is experienced as pleasure. The fusing of these various zones at maturity led to Freud's emphasis on the PSYCHOSEXUAL nature of humanity. It should be emphasized, however, that the Freudian emphasis on sexuality was quite broad. It was not the narrow focus on genital activity that we usually mean when we talk about sexuality in everyday life.

Identification. During early life, the primitive id system has a monopoly on psychic energy. As we have noted, the primary process of the id invests energy in wish-fulfilling images in an attempt to satisfy an instinctual need. Such an investment of energy is called an OBJECT-CHOICE or OBJECT-CATHEXIS. Since the id does not distinguish between image and reality, it cathects (invests psychic energy in) an image as easily as it cathects the real object. But images do not satisfy needs, and the person is forced to discriminate between mental images and the outer world. Concurrently, the person has to learn to match the image in the mind with the physical object in the world. Learning to match the mental symbol with the actual reality is called IDENTIFICATION.

Identification is a most important concept. It accounts for the eventual energizing of both ego and superego systems. The infant very early develops a cathexis for the mother and later for other adults, because these adults satisfy important physical needs. Gradually the infant cathects both the prohibitions and the ideals of the parents. In time, he or she comes to match those cathected items with the external reality of the parents' wishes and, in so doing, makes an identification with the parents. The mechanism of identification is the main channeling device by which the infant is guided through the various psychosexual stages of development into adulthood.

The psychosexual stages of development. Freud felt that the various erogenous zones are differentially sensitive to stimulation at different times. The investment of libido in a bodily zone during a given period of time makes that source of sexuality particularly significant. Either overindulgence or underindulgence of the instinctual needs of that bodily zone may have a strong impact on the type of personality that emerges in adulthood.

The investment of libido in each bodily zone constitutes a stage of psychosexual development. These stages proceed in fixed order throughout the first six years of life.

1. ORAL STAGE. During the first year of life, eating is the most pleasurable activity. The mouth and lips are very sensitive to tactual stimulation. Sucking and swallowing form a prototype for generalized "taking in" behavior. As teething begins, biting becomes another source of oral pleasure. If the infant does not receive enough oral gratification, this need may persist into adulthood, and the person may become acquisitive for symbolic food substitutes such as money, fame, and the like. A mother who withholds her breast or weans abruptly may condition the child to cling to her, and if this behavior generalizes, the result may be an overdependent adult who lacks self-reliance.

2. ANAL STAGE. During the second year of life, the child develops some control over the anal sphincters. As we have noted previously, the emotional climate associated with toilet training may affect personality development. Strict, punitive parents may create a hostile child who reacts by defecating inappropriately out of spite. If this habit generalizes, the result can be an anal-expulsive adult with traits of cruelty, wastefulness, and disobedience to authority. Parents who strongly praise bowel movements may instill the notion that feces production is important. The concept may generalize, creating adult traits such as generosity and creativity. The reverse is possible. The child may get the idea that feces are extremely important, try to hoard them, and end up as an anal-retentive adult with traits of stubborness and stinginess.

3. PHALLIC STAGE. By the age of 3 to 5 years, the child matures to the point where libido flows into the genital area. The child develops a strong sexual cathexis for the parent of the opposite sex and a hostile cathexis for the same-sex parent. This attitude is called the OEDIPUS COMPLEX after the mythical king of Thebes who unwittingly killed his father and married his mother. Resolution of the Oedipus complex is considered enormously important for successful personality development. Basically, resolution of the Oedipus complex consists of repression of sexual and hostile impulses toward one's parents and identification with the same-sex parent. Success in identification is crucial for sex-role identity and full development of moral concepts.

4. LATENCY STAGE. Freud considered this a sexually quiescent stage, lasting from about age 6 to age 12. The period is devoted to ego development, and the formation of a wide range of interests and activities sets the stage for adulthood.

5. GENITAL STAGE. The onset of puberty leads to a spurt of growth and maturation of the sexual organs. Cathexes toward members of the opposite sex are formed. During this period, the aim of the sex instincts becomes reproduction. The emergence of the genital stage, which lasts throughout life, prepares the way for adult social relations, particularly marriage and family formation.

Freud's thinking, particularly about the psychosexual stages, constitutes a theory of social development. Clearly the emphasis is on the emotional, nonrational aspects of human nature. Human life is viewed largely as sexualized affective relationships. All our many complex activities and occupations are viewed as derivatives of the various psychosexual stages and the way in which they were experienced.

Freud attracted many followers, but some of them disagreed with him and developed their own versions of psychoanalytic theory. One of the more prominent variations on psychoanalytic theory was developed by Erik Erikson.

Table I Comparison of Freud's psychosexual stages with Erikson's psychosocial stages

Chronological age	Psychosexual stage	Significant persons	Psychosocial stage
Infancy (0-1 years)	Oral	Mother	Trust vs. mistrust
1-3 years	Anal	Parents	Autonomy vs. shame and doubt
3-5½ years	Phallic	Family	Initiative vs. guilt
5½-12 years	Latency	Neighborhood, teacher, school	Industry vs. inferiority
12-17 years	Adolescence (early genital stage)	Peer groups, outgroups	Identity vs. role confusion
17-22 years	Genital	Friends, opposite-sex partners	Intimacy vs. isolation
Adulthood		Wife, children	Generativity vs. stagnation
Maturity (old age)		Self, humankind	Ego integrity vs. despair

(From Shaffer, 1977, p. 160.)

ERIKSON: THE PSYCHOSOCIAL APPROACH

Erikson (1963; 1968) accepted many of Freud's ideas about personality structure. However, Erikson may be called an ego psychologist, because he focused on the ego and its transactions with reality, rather than on the chaotic id. Erikson also focused on social and cultural determinants of personality. Erikson's approach may therefore be characterized as a PSYCHOSOCIAL theory in contrast with Freud's psychosexual theory.

Erikson is also a stage theorist. He developed a schema of the "eight stages of man" (Erikson, 1963), in which each stage represents a basic conflict or dilemma that must be successfully resolved in order for development to continue in a healthy direction. A comparison of Erikson's and Freud's stages appears in Table I.

Stage 1: Basic trust versus mistrust. At birth, the infant is totally dependent on others. The first stage occurs during the first year, when the child's oral needs are strongest. The mother's relation to the child during this period is enormously important. Her tenderness, smiles, and expressions of affection in the context of feeding create a climate of warmth, an attitude within the infant that the world is okay and that people in it can be trusted. The development of a general attitude of basic trust underlies all future positive interactions with the world. Parental negligence, inconsistency, or rejection may shape the infant in the direction of basic mistrust instead. Such a child will view the world as a dangerous, unpredictable place, and if neurosis or psychosis are avoided, the child will probably emerge as a lonely, alienated adult, cut off from strong emotional ties with other people.

Stage 2: Autonomy versus shame and doubt. Between the ages of 1 and 3, the child gains physical autonomy of movement and action. The crisis of this stage comes from the necessary restrictions parents impose and their shaping of the child's various activities. If parents actively encourage the child's explorations while gently restricting prohibited acts, the child will be able to develop a strong sense of autonomy and self-reliance. Restrictive, punitive parents inhibit the growth of autonomy and create feelings of shame and doubt that can persist throughout life.

Stage 3: Initiative versus guilt. This stage emerges at about the time of Freud's phallic stage. A strong sense of self begins to emerge. Conflicts between self-centered desires and the needs of others occur. The sense of conscience also begins to emerge. The dilemma for the child is to feel an appropriate degree of guilt when he or she commits transgressions but to feel guiltless about his or her own need to take initiative in growth and social exploration. The Oedipus complex is viewed as an attempt to reach out and establish social relations. It is largely resolved when strong group relations are established with play and peer groups.

Stage 4: Industry versus inferiority. This stage corresponds roughly to the Freudian latency stage. The child is moving toward adultlike activities but clearly recognizes that adult competence is not yet available. Feelings of inferiority are common. It is important that the child become industrious in various academic, play, and work pursuits during this period. The development of a basic sense of competence—confidence that one can do things—is necessary for success at the next stage

Stage 5: Identity versus role confusion. The famous identity crisis described by Erikson occurs during this stage. Puberty is a time of many changes. Childhood is gone, but full adulthood is not yet achieved. "Who am I?" is an incessant question. Rebelliousness, trying on new identities, and conformity to what is in vogue are common. The search is for a stable identity that one can be comfortable with as one moves into the adult world. Developing a strong self-concept is not an easy task, but it is necessary for achieving a sense of purpose and meaning in life.

Stage 6: Intimacy versus isolation. Establishment of a sense of identity prepares the person for true interpersonal intimacy in early adulthood. True intimacy requires the ability to achieve a shared identity with another person. An intimacy crisis is common during this stage. Intimacy is risky, and many young adults do not yet feel secure enough to take the risk. Emotional isolation results. Erickson doubts that the final two stages can be negotiated successfully unless a truly intimate relationship with one other person can be established.

Stage 7: Generativity versus stagnation. Until recently, partly due to the influence of psychoanalytic theory, developmental mythology viewed adulthood as a smooth movement over the years. Recent writers (Sheehy, 1974) view adulthood as a series of "passages," each with its own crisis. Erikson felt that the mature adult must make a series of choices throughout adulthood. The choice that leads to generativity means willingness to develop new interests, concern for others and desire to help them, and a general desire to make the world a better place. Stagnation means a pattern of living that involves self-absorption and ultimately leads to a sense of purposelessness during middle age.

Stage 8: Ego integrity versus despair. Erikson believes that aging people choose one of these two contrasting perspectives. Ego integrity means the ability to look back over one's life with a sense of closure, with a feeling that what had to happen did happen, and with some sense of satisfaction with one's accomplishments. People who have not resolved previous developmental crises are likely to be dissatisfied with life, fearful of death, and in a general state of despair.

Erikson's approach to psychoanalytic theory has been well received. The notion of an identity crisis is a concept that many college students can relate to easily. The theory appeals to today's common-sense notions more readily than Freud's deterministic, more heavily sexualized language. Much work remains to be done on the theory. For example, it is unclear whether polar states, such as trust and mistrust, are the best descriptions of reality and whether they are amenable to rigorous scientific investigation. However, Erikson's model points out one fruitful direction for a good theory of social development.

THE COGNITIVE-DEVELOPMENTAL APPROACH

The cognitive-developmental approach is couched in very different language from psychoanalytic theory, and it is concerned with different aspects of development.

Jean Piaget. Cognitive-developmental theory was largely created by Piaget, who has studied children and published prodigiously (Piaget, 1929; 1930; 1950; 1952) for over 50 years. During the last two decades, his theory and research have been widely investigated by other scholars (Kohlberg, 1969).

Identity versus role confusion. The identity crisis of adolescence can take many forms. Violence may provide one mechanism for forging a stable identity. The young man, though clearly in trouble with the police, may by that very fact be creating a tough, "masculine" identity. (Eugene Richards/The Picture Cube)

61
The development
of social behavior

62
Becoming a
social creature

Piaget was a precocious Swiss youngster who published his first article at age 11 on the albino sparrow (Helms and Turner, 1976). He was interested in biology and epistemology, an area of philosophy that deals with the nature of knowledge. Piaget specialized in zoology and earned his Ph.D. in 1918. After a year of work in clinics and laboratories in Zurich, he traveled to Paris and took a position in which his work involved standardizing the famous Binet intelligence test. These tests are administered individually to children, and Piaget soon became curious about the incorrect answers that children gave. At any given age, a similar type of reasoning seemed to lead to incorrect answers. Further, it seemed that the reasoning process was quite different at different age levels. These observations fascinated Piaget. From that point on, his research was largely concerned with the course of cognitive development. Piaget's early theories originated from careful observation of his own children, as he spent hundreds of hours watching their behavior and posing simple intellectual problems for them to solve.

The nature of cognitive development. Intelligence is one of the basic life functions that helps an organism survive and adjust to its environment. Intelligence is not just an innate capacity, but rather a continuously evolving set of mental skills that emerges from the child's interaction with the environment. Intelligence has *content, structure,* and *function*. The content is the "what" of thought (I am a little boy; mommy is good). COGNITIVE STRUCTURES (Piaget called them SCHEMATA) are the organizational frameworks of the mind. Schemata emerge out of reflexes. For example, sucking is an innate reflex. But soon the infant learns to coordinate bodily movement so that the thumb can be placed in the mouth. Thus thumbsucking is an early schema, and such structures provide the basis for the eventual development of mental schemata. Piaget believes that mental structures evolve from these early behavioral structures.

All life activity, including intellectual activity, has two inherent functions, adaptation and organization. ORGANIZATION is the tendency of an organism to arrange its physical and mental structures into coherent whole systems. Structures start at a low level, such as the grasping–sucking schema, and are slowly integrated into ever-higher levels of complexity. The goal of organization of the various structures is to promote ADAPTATION, which occurs by the complementary processes of assimilation and accommodation. ASSIMILATION is a general process of shaping or changing environmental events so that they can be incorporated into existing structures. For example, an infant who sees a new ball may try to assimilate it into a grasping structure in the same way that he or she has previously assimilated rattles and small toys (Shaffer, 1977). Most efforts to assimilate also require ACCOMMODATION, which is an attempt by the organism to meet the demands of the environment rather than shaping the environment to familiar structures. Thus assimilation and accommodation are two sides of the same coin. Development occurs because the organism is constantly applying its present structures to a novel world. In trying to assimilate that world, the organism makes accommodations, and the organism changes. This change creates a new state of mental organization that will itself soon be transformed in turn into another state of organization.

These concepts are the basis of Piaget's theory of cognitive development. The theory is a stage theory. The main stages are as follows:

1. *Sensorimotor stage (0–2 years)*. The infant begins with reflexes and during the first two years gains knowledge of its world by acting on surrounding objects. In this way, various motor habits and action schemata develop. Near the end of this period, the infant becomes able to represent such action patterns in its head. This development permits the infant to begin to solve problems symbolically and to invent new mental combinations of perceptual images.

2. *Preoperational thought (2–7 years)*. During this period, children gain the power of language, which greatly increases their ability to develop mental schemata. Symbolic play is now possible. For example, the child can pretend a stick is an airplane. How-

Ego integrity versus despair. Erikson's last stage of life may encompass the despair and hopelessness exemplified by the "street lady" who has no home and nowhere to go with her few possessions. Or, the last stage may be one of ego integrity—contentment, and a sense of life well lived. (above, Wide World Photo; below, Bobbi Carrey/The Picture Cube)

ever, children are still EGOCENTRIC in the sense that they cannot take the point of view of another person. OBJECT PERMANENCE, the realization that objects continue to exist when out of sight, develops during this stage. Object permanence is a prerequisite for the formation of emotional attachments to other people.

3. *Concrete operations (7–11 years)*. During this stage, children develop rapidly in their ability to think logically about concrete objects and events. CONSERVATION develops: The child becomes able to recognize that certain properties of an object remain constant even though the object's appearance changes. Conservation of volume is an example. If two containers of the same size have the same amount of water in them, and an adult pours the water from one of them into a taller, narrower container, a nonconserving child will say that the taller container now has more water. The child is unable to distinguish the constancy of amount (a mental concept) from the perceived change of shape. During this stage, children also become able to think numerically, arrange objects into classes, and construct mental images of complex actions.

4. *Formal operations (age 12 and beyond)*. As this stage develops, the child can think logically about abstract objects, events far removed in time and space, and hypothetical propositions. Thinking becomes quasi-deductive, similar to scientific reasoning. Apparently not all adults are able to achieve the level of formal operations in their thought processes.

Quite clearly, Piaget focused on cognitive development more than social or emotional development. The libidinal and aggressive impulses of the Freudian id are omitted from the theory, and development is conveyed as a stage-by-stage movement toward rationality. However, Piaget's theory is general enough to encompass social development, and his theory has been applied by several scientists, especially Lawrence Kohlberg (1969).

Social development. The development of the child as a social creature depends on the successful development of cognitive structures (Shaffer, 1977). Kohlberg's (1969) extension of the theory rests on several assumptions.

1. Emotional development occurs in parallel with cognitive development. Love of mother, for example, cannot occur until the child develops a conception of object permanence. True interaction (particularly altruistic acts) requires the ability to take the perspective or role of another person. Thus egocentrism has to be relinquished before a truly social creature can emerge.

2. The concept of self may be thought of as an organized cognitive schema. Social and personality development are viewed as a restructuring of the self-concept over time. This change also requires restructuring of one's conceptions of other people.

3. Schemata for social cognitions develop. The child learns that he or she has thoughts, needs, and intentions. By learning to take the role of other people, the child learns that others also have similar thoughts and needs. Thus the child's growth in self-concept parallels the development of cognitive structures about other people.

4. Social and personality development occur in the direction of equilibrium or reciprocity between the child's behaviors and the behavior of other people toward the child. The main task is the development of a stable identity, or sense of self, across all the situations and people the child experiences. The establishment of a stable self-identity is in some respects analogous to the concept of conservation: the child learns that self-identity is conserved across transformations of the social world.

Kohlberg argues that social and personality development proceed through a set of fixed stages comparable to the stages of cognitive development. The behavior content of each stage depends on the level of cognitive development and the specifics of the social experiences the child has. Learning is important, because the child assimilates and accommodates to a social experience in the same way as to an intellectual experience. But what is learned and what can be learned from experience depends heavily on the stage of the child's cognitive development. The same argument holds for moral development, which we will consider later in this chapter.

THE SOCIAL-LEARNING APPROACH

There are three distinct schools of social-learning theory: the neo-Hullians, the Skinnerians, and the Bandurians (Shaffer, 1979). Followers of B. F. Skinner

Concrete operations. A child who has developed conservation of volume will say that the tall and short containers hold the same amount of water when the water from one short container is poured into a tall container. A non-conserving child confuses the height of the container with the quantity it holds, and will say that the two containers hold different amounts. (Eric Roth/The Picture Cube)

Observational learning or modeling. Children learn much of their social behavior by observing and imitating a model. Both prosocial and antisocial behavior may be acquired in this way. (Eugene Richards/The Picture Cube)

have applied his "radical behaviorism" to the study of social development with some success (Skinner, 1953). Clark Hull developed a deductive theory of learning in the 1930s, and, beginning in 1936, a diverse group at Yale began to apply his ideas to some of Freud's psychoanalytic notions. The result was a wide-ranging series of publications by several distinguished people (Miller and Dollard, 1941; Dollard and Miller, 1950; Sears, 1951).

Neo-Hullian theory. Briefly, the neo-Hullian approach replaced the notion of instinct with the concept of DRIVE. Personality was not viewed as a set of stages through which one develops, but rather as a set of habits that one acquires through learning. Learning occurs because the organism has drives that must be reduced. Any response that reduces a drive is acquired and becomes a part of the organism's habit set. Primary drives, such as hunger, thirst, pain avoidance, and the like, are innate. Secondary drives are the wide range of human motives that people acquire through association of stimuli with one or more primary drives. Therefore social learning is presumed to obey the same laws as other types of learning, and the principles are the same throughout the course of development.

The neo-Hullian approach was moderately successful in explaining some types of social behavior. However, it tended to downplay cognitive and symbolic activity. This lack led to an evolution in the form of social-learning theory. Perhaps the most distinguished representative of the more recent version of the theory is Albert Bandura (1969; 1977).

Elements of Bandura's approach. Like the other learning theories Bandura's theory assumes that personality and social behavior are determined by experience. Terms such as *cue, response, reinforcement, discrimination,* and *generalization* are freely used. However, the notion of drive is not used as a key concept. Like Skinner, Bandura views drive as a circular concept with little explanatory power. The major tenets of Bandura's theory are as follows:

1. Bandura believes that all learning based on direct experience can occur vicariously, simply by observing other people's behavior. Other learning theories assume that a response must first be performed and then reinforced before it is learned.

2. Bandura's approach may be called OBSERVATIONAL LEARNING, or MODELING. Children (and adults) observe a model and may later imitate the model's performance. (Observational learning is applied to the acquisition of aggressive responses in Chapter 11.)

3. Most of our behavior consists of responses we have learned by observing other people. Reward or reinforcement is irrelevant to learning per se.

4. Reinforcement has its greatest effect on performance. Bandura distinguishes between learning and performance. If a child sees a model punished for a behavior, the child is unlikely to perform the behavior. At a later time, the same child may eagerly perform the behavior if given the proper incentive. Quite clearly, the child learned the behavior by observing it but suppressed performance because of anticipated punishment.

5. Delayed imitation requires: (a) attention to the other's behavior, (b) retention of the behavior in memory, (c) motor reproduction of the act, and (d) a reason or motive to reproduce the act.

6. Retention can occur by recall of sensory images of another's performance or by application of an abstract verbal code. These two types of cognitive symbolism are then translated into motor acts similar to the model's acts.

7. There is strong emphasis on symbolic representation. Bandura's theory views cognitive processes as having causal powers. This means that humans have the power of self-control and self-regulation. We can set performance standards for self, evaluate self, and reward and punish self.

It is evident that the three major approaches to social development are very different in their areas of emphasis. Psychoanalysis focuses on the emotional, nonrational side of human nature. The conflicts and stresses, as well as the sensual joys of unfolding development, are the images portrayed. Cognitive-developmental theory focuses on the mechanisms of the mind and the ways in which they unfold. About equal emphasis is placed on the ways in which the infant is "prewired" genetically and the ways in which experience activates and matures the constitutional endowment of the mind. Social-learning theory focuses more heavily on experience. Social behavior is learned behavior; scant attention is paid to the way the infant is genetically or constitutionally disposed to behave. In the following sections, we draw on research studies generated by these contrasting theories as we attempt to reconstruct the course of human social development.

Origins of early social development

At birth, the human infant exhibits primitive responses to the social world. Years ago, many child experts thought that the infant was functionally blind and deaf for the first few weeks after its birth. We now know that this is untrue; the infant is responsive to a wide range of stimulation and matures in its perceptual capacities very rapidly. Nevertheless, it appears that the infant is stimulus-directed rather than person-directed (Schaffer, 1971). That is, the infant at first responds to patterns of stimulation such as fuzziness, softness, shape, tone, and visual configuration. Preference for some aspects of stimuli rather than others appears to be innate. It takes some time before these stimulus patterns blend into the perceptual pattern of "mother" or "father."

How does it happen? How does the tiny infant begin its journey into adulthood, a journey that will soon transform "it" into "him" or "her," with a unique identity and meaning to the significant people in the infant's world? We will discuss a few of the topics related to early social development. We first consider mother and infant as an interaction system that lays the foundation for the emergence of social behavior. We then consider the development of attachment in the infant, maternal separation and deprivation, and the effects of specific child-rearing practices.

MOTHER-INFANT INTERACTION

Earlier research viewed the infant as a passive recipient of stimulation from mother and other adults, its behavior shaped entirely by the acts of the caretakers. More recently, recognition has been accorded to what common sense suggested all along: the infant has a tremendous effect on its caregivers, socializing as well as being socialized by them. In fact, there are now entire books about such topics as the effect of the infant on its caregiver (Lewis and Rosenblum, 1974), maternal-infant bonding (Klaus and Kennell, 1976), and the nature of mothering (Schaffer, 1977). The literature now stresses parent-infant interaction (Hofer, 1975; Hartup and Lempers, 1973). Social behavior is largely interactional behavior, and although mother-infant interaction is qualitatively very different from the interaction of adults, it appears to be the primary basis of the infant's early social development.

To understand adult-infant interaction, we must have some notion of the infant's perceptual skills and ability to respond to others.

Infant sensory and response capabilities. Modern thinking views the development of sociability as rooted in the infant's perception of its environment (Schaffer, 1971). It seems likely that the infant is innately attuned to certain features of the environment—features that promote survival. Characteristics of the parents are probably the stimuli to which the infant is inherently sensitized. Parents in turn structure the sensory environment to make sure the infant pays as much attention to them as possible. Hence parents begin as the most interesting stimuli available, and they rapidly become overwhelmingly important in the infant's sensory world.

Until one month of age, infants cannot accommodate their visual response to moving targets but are locked in at a focal distance of about 8 inches. Interestingly, this is about the distance to the mother's face when the infant is feeding. Other studies show that infants prefer patterned complexity in visual stimuli and that the preferred level of complexity increases over the first several months. Infants are also differentially responsive to different sound patterns. And, they attend to moving targets more readily than to stationary ones. It appears that the small infant may be more attuned to certain features of the human face, especially the eyes, than to other types of geometric designs (Schaffer, 1971). Adults move about, emit varied stimulation, and are likely to stimulate a number of the infant's senses. Adults are thus consistent sources of complex stimuli that maximize sensory impact on the infant and are likely to become strong objects of attention.

The infant's response capabilities are also relevant to its growth into the social world. The small infant has two such primary response modes, crying and smiling. Wolff (1969) identified three types of cries: (1) a basic hunger cry that starts at low intensity and increases in volume, (2) an angry cry, and (3) a pain cry that has a sudden onset. Caregivers can distinguish among the three types of cries quite reliably.

The smiling response occurs near the end of the first month. At first it is apparently only a physiological response, but it quickly becomes a social response. During the very early months, the smile is elicited by a variety of stimuli. There is some evidence that facelike stimuli are the strongest elicitors of smiling. Spitz (1965) suggested that the eyes and surrounding area of the face may have an innate releasing effect in stimulating the smile.

The interaction system. The infant's cries, and slightly later smiles, are powerful stimuli in activating the mother and other adults. It has been suggested that these two responses appeal to instinctive caretaking needs in adults. Darwin felt that the smile definitely has survival value, because it draws the adult close to the infant, increasing the odds that the adult will take good care of the child.

During the first several months of life, parent and child engage in a wide variety of interactive behaviors. They gaze at each other, vocalize to and touch one another, smile at each other and so on. One interesting example is mimicry, a type of imitation. Mothers prompt imitation by first clapping their own hands and then the infant's hands, by playing peek-a-boo, and by mimicking the various sounds that babies make. The interaction is so intense that we can refer to mother and infant as a DYADIC SYSTEM, or small social system consisting of 2 people (Hartup and Lempers, 1973).

Schaffer (1971) notes that the basic characteristic of interpersonal behavior is reciprocity. Reciprocal behavior involves long chains of coordinated interaction sequences. Each partner serves as a stimulus for the other and responds in turn to the response of the other. Mother and infant are no exception. Their behavior is highly reciprocal, and it increases in complexity as the baby matures. The intensive study of adult and infant from the interaction perspective is just beginning. It is an important area of study because much of the joy, as well as the alienation, of adult life is traceable to the nature of child–adult interactions during the first years of life.

ATTACHMENT

The term ATTACHMENT signifies the baby's sense of affection and love for the people around him or her. At one time, *dependency* was the preferred term. Some authors distinguished between instrumental and expressive dependency, the former term meaning the literal physical dependency of child on adult and the latter term meaning affection or love.

Both psychoanalytic and learning theories view love as developing out of the basic physical dependency of the child. Parents meet many needs over and over, especially hunger. Drive reduction is pleasant, and since the mother is constantly associated with reduction of primary drives, she should through stimulus generalization become a secondary reinforcer in her own right. In Freudian language, the baby should come to cathect the mother. In Erikson's terms, the baby should develop a sense of basic trust in her because of the warm nurturing environment that she provides. In everyday language, we would say that the child learns to love the mother.

These traditional approaches view all of the many secondary attachments, preferences, and interests of childhood and adulthood as deriving from satisfaction of primary needs in infancy. It is a neat and simple theoretical approach. The problem is that it is not true.

How attachment begins. Most of us probably make the common-sense assumption that the infant learns to love mother and later father, because they take care of it. Bowlby(1958) coined the term ATTACHMENT to describe the situation in which mother and infant try to maintain physical closeness to each other. Bowlby (1969) also believes that attachment and dependency are distinct behaviors. Dependency means reliance on parents for the satisfaction of needs. During the first few months of life, the infant is completely dependent on others in this sense but is not yet emotionally attached to them. Bowlby's distinction between attachment and dependency has been widely adopted; indeed an entire book has been devoted to the topic (Gewirtz, 1972).

Attachment is a complex behavior (Ainsworth, 1973) that develops slowly during the first 18 months of life. It is based on affection, and it implies specific positive acts toward some people and not toward others. Since the infant cannot talk, its attachment has to be inferred from behavior. Infants who are attached to their mothers show a variety of positive behaviors. They smile at mother, cry when separated from her, try to stay physically close to her, and (once crawling begins) use mother as a secure base from which to explore the surrounding environment.

Attachment during the first year of life moves through four fairly distinct phases (Cohen, 1976):

1. First few months. The infant is indiscriminately responsive to everyone who approaches.

2. Approximately 3 to 6 months. The infant is differentially responsive to the mother to some extent but is still responsive to other people as well.

3. Approximately 6 to 9 months. The infant becomes strongly attached to the mother. Strong protests arise when she is absent. Also at this age, strangers elicit a strong fear response. The infant may now be frightened even by people it has previously seen irregularly.

4. Approximately 9 to 12 months. During this period, fear of strangers decreases somewhat, and the infant may become attached to several other familiar figures, most often the father.

The attachment process is striking. Infants vary in how quickly they go through the sequence. Some do not form attachments until well into the second year. Others give signs of strong attachment but do not exhibit severe fear of strangers. Many authors now believe that the development of the attachment bond is partially innate. That is, we are prewired as a species to become attached to others if we have the proper kinds of experiences during the first year of life.

What kinds of experiences should the infant have? It appears that a diet of rich sensory and social stimulation is the key to the growth of attachment. Quite clearly, the notion of drive reduction is inadequate to explain the process. The infant has had its drives reduced consistently for 7 or 8 months before it gets attracted to anyone, and then the attraction develops rather rapidly. The perverse little creature may also become strongly attached to father at the same time as to mother (Schaffer and Emerson, 1964), even though father may have done less work than mother in taking care of the infant.

Thus it appears that stimulation rather than care as such is crucial. Much of the stimulation may be visual in nature, although touch and hearing are probably also important. According to Piaget, the infant does not develop a sense of object permanence until the seventh or eighth month of life. Until object permanence occurs, it is "out of sight, out of mind," and attachment presumably could not occur. It is interesting that the strong onset of attachment occurs at about the same time that the sense of object permanence develops.

Must attachments form for the infant to become human? The question is a most interesting one. If the infant were handled by so many different adults that it could not become attached to a single one, how would emotional development be affected? The question cannot be answered at present, but some suspect that the result would be an emotionally sterile human at maturity. On the other hand, if we are prewired to become attached, an infant might become attached to any convenient object in the environment. The continuing legends of feral children over the centuries—children reportedly reared by animals—suggest that such attachments are conceivable.

The question is of great importance for the UPM infants described in the thought experiment. If attachment occurs innately, then each of the six infants would form a bond to some aspect of the physical caretaking environment. Whether such bonds would later prevent humanlike attachments to each other is an open question.

It is clear that attachment to other species does occur in animals. The reason for bringing home a puppy before it gets too old is so that it will become a member of the family, basically identifying itself as a human instead of a dog. Similar findings with rhesus monkeys have been reported. Harlow (1958) reared infant monkeys with mother SURROGATES, inanimate replicas of a mother monkey. The surrogates were constructed of either wire mesh or soft warm terry cloth (both versions supplied nourishment). The infant monkeys clearly preferred the terry cloth mother, clung to it, and returned to it regularly after forays into the wide world.

In conclusion, it appears that emotional attachment is a developmental behavior that occurs in a great many species. We are just now beginning to learn about it in detail. It will be most important to understand the attachment process and the ways in which it can go wrong.

MATERNAL SEPARATION AND DEPRIVATION

Until a decade or so ago, it was common to keep children without parents in orphan homes or other institutional settings. In 1945, Rene Spitz published an article that had a dramatic effect and, with additional research, eventually led to the abolition of such institutions. (Today such children live in foster homes.) Spitz reported that young children raised for the first years of life in such an environment were devastated by it. As time progressed, the infants Spitz observed became increasingly withdrawn, seldom cried, and were indifferent to the world around them. They also became increasingly retarded intellectually. They were more susceptible to disease, and, of a total of 88 children up to age 2½ years, 23 died.

Spitz referred to the infants' pattern of behavior as HOSPITALISM, and felt that it was due to inadequate stimulation. A nurse was in charge of a dozen or more infants, so each child received very little attention. Spitz felt that the lack of handling, touching, and movement caused the child to withdraw from the world.

Spitz' research and much more that soon followed raised several questions about the effect of early experience on social development. What are the short-term effects of separation from the mother? What are the long-term effects of separation and/or deprivation of normal adult care? Is stimulus deprivation or maternal deprivation the key variable in causing the effects of separation?

Short-term effects of maternal separation. It often happens that a young child must be separated from its mother for a period of time, ranging from a few days to the rest of its life. Such separation often results from an emergency, and the child may be cared for by strangers in a strange situation. The short-term effects are quite clear (Schaffer, 1977). The child seems to go through three phases of adjustment.

1. A period of acute distress occurs. The child cries for the mother and will not be comforted by anyone else.

2. The distress phase is followed by a period of despair. The child becomes quiet and apathetic.

3. After a time, a period of detachment occurs. The child apparently gives up his or her emotional tie to the mother and may fail to establish trust with anyone in the new environment. If the mother returns after the child reaches the point of detachment, the emotional bond can be reestablished only with great difficulty.

This is a generalized picture, but it is fairly typical for children separated from their mothers between the ages of 6 months and 5 years. As noted previously, strong attachment to the mother and a correlated fear of strangers develops at about 7 to 8 months of age. Separation from the mother should be particularly traumatic at this age. The stage of detachment is in some respects similar to the hospitalism syndrome noted by Spitz. Thus the withdrawal of the institutionalized infants may have been due to some extent to separation, rather than to an impoverished environment.

It is clear that separation from the mother has a traumatic short-term effect. What are the long-term effects of deprivation on social development?

Long-term effects of deprivation. Early reports by writers such as Spitz indicated that the effects of inadequate mothering in early life are irreversible. A socially deprived child becomes a socially crippled adult. Today the picture is not so clear. We briefly review several lines of evidence on the issue. Harry Harlow spent many years studying the social development of rhesus monkeys (Harlow and Harlow, 1966; 1970). One facet of this research concerned the effects of rearing the young monkeys under various degrees of social isolation. Monkeys were reared in isolation for either 3, 6, or 12 months. If removed after 3 months of isolation and placed with other monkeys, the young monkeys experienced a state of shock. They appeared terrified, clutched at themselves, tried to bury their head in their arms, and generally avoided social contacts. However, these monkeys eventually recovered and by adulthood had established effective social relations. Monkeys reared in isolation for 6 months or longer never recovered from the effects of isolation. They failed to develop normal social and sexual behavior as adults and often remained isolated all their lives.

This research implies that the first 6 months of life may be crucial for proper social development. If deprivation is too severe and lasts too long, the damage may be irreversible. However, more recent work by Suomi and Harlow (1972) challenges this notion. Monkeys raised in isolation for 6 months were then exposed to 26 weeks of "therapy." The therapy consisted of placing each isolate with a female rhesus who was only 3 months old at the time therapy began. The younger "therapist" provided a nonthreatening model who clung to the isolate monkey. In time, the isolate began to accept the younger monkey, and by the end of the 26-week period had overcome the devastating effects of spending the first 6 months of life in isolation. Thus Harlow's more recent work indicates that the effects of early deprivation can be overcome under special conditions.

Many of the early studies of institutionalization (such as Spitz, 1945, and Ribble, 1943) have been rightly criticized for poor methodology. However, more recent work has yielded similar results. For example, Provence and Lipton (1962) studied 75 physically healthy institutionalized infants, who were provided with excellent food and physical care but received little social stimulation. They behaved like a normal control group until 3 months of age but thereafter showed increasing signs of retardation. They seldom cried or babbled, lost interest in their surroundings, and were retarded in language development at 1 year of age. Such recent studies rule out physical or genetic abnormalities as the cause and indicate rather clearly that social deprivation has disasterous effects. Could such effects be overcome if a strong intervention program were established?

The mystery deepens when we consider a report by Kagan and Klein (1973), who studied Indian children raised in Guatemala. In that culture, infants are raised for the first 10 to 15 months of life in small, windowless, mud huts. They are rarely spoken to or played with and receive little stimulation. By American standards, these children are quite retarded. Speech does not appear until they are 2 years old. On tests of cognitive abilities, they lag about 5 months behind American infants. But by age of 10–12 years, these children have recovered completely and are quite comparable to American youngsters of the same age!

A few children are occasionally socially and emotionally deprived, even though reared in the home by parents. Such children exhibit apathy and a forlorn appearance similar to that of institutionalized children. Gardner (1972) has discovered that such children often experience glandular disturbances that slow growth. This syndrome is called DEPRIVATION DWARFISM (see Figure 2). These children received adequate physical care, and Gardner feels that the condition is caused directly by social and emotional deprivation. When placed in a hospital where they received much social attention, the infants typically began to grow rather rapidly.

What is crucial—mother deprivation or stimulus deprivation? There is abundant evidence that severe restriction of stimulation has harmful effects. If the restriction approaches true sensory deprivation (raising young animals in the dark for example), the negative effects may be irreversible. It seems clear that a monotonous, bland environment contributes to hospitalism in infants and to the lack of responsiveness in Harlow's monkeys. The dullness of the infants in Guatemala is probably due to the restriction of sensory stimulation.

Deprivation of stimulation (perhaps from the day of birth) probably retards development, but it can be distinguished from the impact of separation or rejection. If the infant has already made an attachment when separation occurs, the emotional trauma may yield symptoms like those of deprivation. If the child is placed in an impoverished sensory environment, the withdrawal into apathy may be quite complete. Within limits, on the other hand, pure stimulus deprivation can be overcome. The Guatemalan children are a case in point. The early restriction is cultural; the parents believe this is the way to raise children. Since the parents love their children, they begin to provide good interactions around 18 months of age. From that point on, these children have a good diet of both sensory and social stimulation, and they recover.

It is not so clear what will happen when infants are rejected emotionally. The case of the deprivation dwarfs indicates that rejection constitutes a total assault on the sense of self. Even though such children receive enough pure physical stimulation, they do not experience the complex patterns of social stimulation that we call love and caring. Dramatic developmental effects result, and it is not so clear that such effects can be overcome.

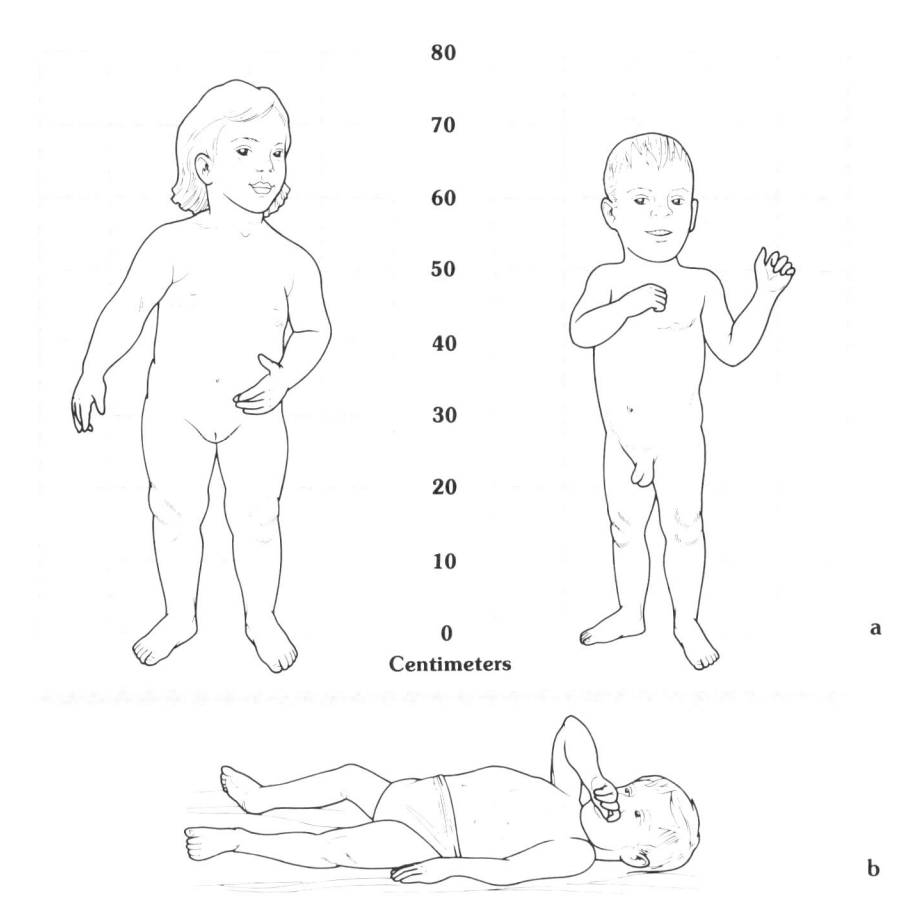

Is *maternal* stimulation necessary for proper social development? In the sense of one mother figure ministering to the infant's needs the answer appears to be no. For example, Israeli children raised on a communal kibbutz have many caregivers. The caregiving is rich and comprehensive, however, and these children mature into socially responsive adults.

Based on all the evidence to date, we can draw the following conclusions with some confidence:

1. Human infants need a rich diet of sensory stimulation to develop properly, as do other species. The effects of stimulus deprivation, if not too severe or prolonged, can be overcome.

2. Human infants also need stimulation through interaction with other humans in order to develop normally (Shaffer, 1979). The stimulation does not have to come from a specific person, though it may be important that an attachment to at least one person develop. Also, the stimulation does not necessarily have to be all love and attention. (Children of parents who

**2. Deprivation dwarfism. (a) These twins, normal and dwarfed, offer evidence of the effect of emotional deprivation on infants. This drawing is based on photographs made when the children were almost 13 months old. The girl was near normal in weight and stature, but her twin brother was the size of a 7-month-old. Some 4 months after the twins were born, a period of stress began between the parents; the father then lost his job and left home. It appears that the mother's hostility toward her husband was directed at the son but not the daughter.
(b) A three-year-old, treated for deprivation dwarfism 18 months earlier, actually lost weight on return to the care of a mother who appeared detached and unemotional in her relationship with the boy. His skeletal maturity on return to the hospital was at the level of a 15-month-old's; he was listless and lay on his back most of the time, his legs spraddled in a characteristic "frog" position. (From Gardner, 1972, pp. 77–78.)**

periodically beat them severely often become deeply attached to their parents.) What is apparently required is a lot of social interaction. Parents who reject and ignore produce emotional cripples. At this point, it is unclear whether the effects of prolonged deprivation of human interaction can be overcome.

These conclusions have some implications for our UPM infants. Even though these infants have visual access to each other, they necessarily have little or no physical contact during the first 6 months of life. Neither do they receive the rich stimulus of an adult figure, and they are therefore unable to begin learning to respond and participate in interaction. The most likely outcome is severe retardation; the UPM infants appear unlikely ever to become socialized human beings.

CHILD-REARING PRACTICES

The previous section was concerned with the gross effects of stimulation or lack of it. There is also massive literature on the specific effects of various socialization practices on social development. The nature of this research can be illustrated by a few typical questions. Is it better to breast feed or bottle feed an infant? Does it make any difference whether the child is weaned early or late? Should the infant be fed on a firm schedule or whenever it seems to want food? How early should toilet training begin, and how quickly should it be concluded?

These are practical questions that all parents want to know about. Furthermore, our previous discussion of psychoanalytic theory raised the possibility that the answers to such questions are very important. The presumed importance of Freudian stages of oral and anal eroticism, for example, implies that the way parents handle feeding, toilet training, and early sex play has a strong formative effect on personality and social development.

Literally hundreds of studies have been conducted on the effects of specific practices on the development of various personality traits. Several extensive reviews of this work (Caldwell, 1964) indicate almost no systematic effects. Variables related to feeding, sucking, and toilet training have not been shown to be related to adult personality styles or even to behavior in later childhood.

The most immediate implication is that parents can relax. Whether the infant is bottle fed or breast fed probably doesn't make much difference. What probably matters most is that parents genuinely want and love the child and interact with the child intensely. It is common sense, but many parents have problems in fulfilling the role adequately. The child who receives such loving care in childhood has a good chance of leading a happy, productive life. If insecurity and rejection fill childhood, the odds against a happy life increase somewhat, but a happy outcome is not impossible.

The road to full humanhood is securely anchored in the early social environment of the child. Mother and infant, or more generally adult and infant, are best viewed as an interaction system. Each member of the system has a socializing effect on the other member. In Schaffer's (1971) terms, mother and infant develop a reciprocity of interaction. By means of this rich interplay, the child gradually becomes a social creature. The child learns that he or she is loved and in turn learns how to love. The sense of self begins to form, the child's capabilities expand, and more complex patterns of stimulation are explored.

In addition to parents, the child experiences a wide range of other socializing agents. Peer groups have an enormous impact and are being studied intensively. School and the mass media are also potent socializing agents. The effects of television on children's aggressiveness will be discussed in Chapter 11.

From the early beginnings of socialization, the child goes on to become a moral agent, a person who has internalized the values and rules of the society. In the next section, we examine several conceptions of moral development.

The development of morality

The infant and young child are often described as amoral, which means that the child's behavior is without morality; it is neither moral nor immoral. An important part of socialization is the transformation of the child into a moral agent, a creature with concepts of right and wrong, good and bad, and shalls and shall nots. Human life is governed by an endless number of rules, prohibitions, codes of ethics, and behavioral injunctions. Acquiring these various rules and codes is what is meant by becoming a moral agent.

Morality is an interesting notion. The purpose of training the child in the rules and regulations of the culture is so that she or he will *internalize* them, making them part of self. When the moral rules are fully incorporated, the individual is considered responsible for his or her own behavior and held accountable for his or her actions. Thus a person as a moral agent is viewed as a self-determining system; the cause of moral behavior comes from within the person. By contrast, certain views of scientific determinism, such as B. F. Skinner's, conceive of the individual's behavior as caused by external stimuli. Behavior is a function of external controlling conditions.

A psychological account of moral development cannot pass judgment on the *content* of moral acts. It can describe how the transformation of the child from amoral to moral agent occurs without ruling on the validity of moral conceptions. The latter belongs to philosophy and religion. Likewise, psychology cannot say whether a moral agent is self-determining. Such speculation belongs to the philosophy of science. Psychology can only describe the various beliefs about self-control and responsibility that people subscribe to and investigate the ways in which such beliefs develop.

In this section, we first examine the nature of morality and then discuss notions of moral development within the framework of the three major theories of social development.

THE NATURE OF MORALITY

In some respects, it is misleading to speak of morality. There is no one entity or trait that is morality. Rather, morality refers to beliefs, attitudes, values, and behaviors considered relevant to moral conduct. The problem of conception is more manageable if we focus on two issues:
1. What are the basic components of morality?
2. Is there consistency across these components?

The three components of morality. The *affective* or emotional component of morality involves feelings of self-worth and pride when one behaves properly and feelings of guilt, shame, and unworthiness when one misbehaves. Freud and other psychoanalysts were concerned largely with the affective component of morality.

The *cognitive* component of morality consists of moral reasoning. Piaget and other cognitive-developmental theorists deal largely with this aspect of morality. They focus on the process of reasoning about moral acts and the ways in which reasoning changes during the course of development.

The *behavioral* component of morality involves the things people do. There are two types of moral acts (Shaffer, 1979). Acts of *commission* are positive deeds that one is supposed to do, such as sharing and helping. Acts of *omission* are negative deeds that one is not supposed to do, such as cheating or stealing. Proper moral conduct is a balance of performing positive acts and inhibiting negative acts. The behavioral component of morality has been studied most by social-learning theorists. They have focused on such things as how children resist temptation and inhibit behaviors that violate moral rules.

The three-component approach to morality draws attention to the issue of consistency among the components. A person may have a highly developed reasoning ability about moral matters and still behave overtly in immoral ways. Or one may behave morally in one situation but not in another.

Consistency in moral conduct. If a person were consistent across all three components of morality, knowledge of where the person stood on one component would allow us to predict his or her standing on the other two components. For example, if a person has developed a coherent set of moral principles to reason with, we would predict strong feelings of guilt when a transgression is committed, resistance to tempting situations, and positive acts directed toward others.

Many studies have dealt with the issue of consistency among the three moral components. Several investigators have ranked children in the maturity of their moral *reasoning* and then recorded their overt *behavior* in laboratory tests of cheating and ability to resist temptation. There is no relationship between reasoning and overt behavior for young children, but there is a modest relationship in adolescents. We can conclude that only a slight degree of consistency among the three components exists by adulthood.

Almost the same conclusion emerges when we look at consistency within moral behavior. A famous study by Hartshorne and May (1928) investigated the moral conduct of 10,000 children aged 8 to 16. Several situations were set up that gave the children opportunities to lie, steal, or cheat. The major finding was that the children's behavior was not consistent across situations. Willingness to lie, steal, or cheat in one situation did not mean that the child would perform such behaviors in another situation. Hartshorne and May concluded that moral behavior is situation-specific; there is no such thing as a stable trait of honesty. Later reanalysis of these data by Burton (1963) revealed somewhat more evidence for consistency than the original investigators found. However, specific situational factors were still most important.

In conclusion, there is little evidence for consistency of morality across the three moral components or within a single component. Indeed, it has been suggested (Shaffer, 1979) that moral affect, reasoning, and behavior may develop as three separate moralities. They may be more or less integrated in adulthood by some people, but for a great many people, unified integration may never occur.

PSYCHOANALYTIC CONCEPTIONS

Freud's account of moral development was based on the concept of the child's identification with the parents. During the phallic stage, incestuous desires for the parent of the opposite sex occur. These desires cause anxiety and even fear. For example, little boys reputedly develop fears of castration. Clearly, such a conflict cannot last long. It is resolved by the child trying to make himself or herself identical to the same-sex parent. This identification is a "swallowing whole" of the many attributes of the parent, including the parent's standards of morality. The former incestuous desire for the opposite-sex parent is transformed into a harmless affection and vicarious sense of possession.

This is the resolution of the famous Oedipus complex by which the formation of conscience is supposed to occur. Freud spelled out the process most clearly for boys. He was unsure about girls and in general felt that they developed weaker superegos than males. Needless to say, few women agree with this position.

Other psychoanalytic writers, particularly Erikson (1963), disagreed with Freud's sexual emphasis on the development of morality. Parents restrict and control children, subject them to toilet training, and punish them. Therefore children are necessarily frustrated by parents and come to resent them, perhaps even to the point of wishing that they could be rid of them. But children realize that they could lose their parents' love. They resolve the dilemma by repressing the hostility and becoming as much like the parents as possible. Thus identification is based on the need for love. Identification is a kind of insurance; children reason that if they make themselves just like the parents, then the parents will have to love them.

Neoanalytic writers tend to stress that the ego and the superego are both important in moral development. The ego comes into existence to channel the id and resist its impulses until proper objects of gratification can be found. Thus ability to delay gratification and not act impulsively is an ego function more than a superego function. In general, moral behavior relies on both the internalized rules of the superego and the restraining forces of the ego.

Evidence for the psychoanalytic approach. The evidence tends not to support Freud's views. One example will illustrate the tests of his ideas that have been conducted. If morality is based on identification, then children of harsh, moralistic parents should develop strong superegos. The evidence indicates the opposite. Children with parents who are cold and punitive tend to develop weak superegos (Hoffman, 1970).

The evidence for the neoanalytic position is somewhat better. In general, the neoanalytic position holds that identification occurs because of the child's anxiety over loss of love. One implication is that love-oriented discipline, such as scolding and withholding affection, should lead to stronger moral development than power-assertive techniques such as spanking and denial of privileges. Sears, Maccoby, and Levin (1957) conducted a large interview study of mothers with children about 5 years old. Children who were rated high on conscience development had mothers who used love-oriented discipline and were also high in emotional warmth and affection. Hoffman and Saltzstein (1967) obtained similar results, but they also found that love-oriented techniques work only if the parent explains why the child's acts were wrong. This amounts to giving cognitive justification for behavior change, and it, rather than anxiety over loss of love, may be the crucial variable in love-oriented discipline strategies. Thus the neoanalytic claims may perhaps be interpreted in terms of the other two theoretical approaches.

THE SOCIAL-LEARNING APPROACH TO MORAL DEVELOPMENT

Social-learning theorists (Aronfreed, 1976; Bandura, 1969; Mischel, 1974) tend to focus on moral behaviors, which are viewed as situation-specific. Moral behavior is seen as a wide variety of socially acceptable responses that are self-reinforcing by their commission. Failure to commit negative acts is reinforcing through avoidance of guilt, anxiety, or punishment. Moral responses are presumably learned in the same way as other responses, by direct teaching and observational learning. Most attention has been given to the learning of acts of omission, such as resistance to temptation, and reactions to transgressions.

Moral prohibitions. Suppose you do something you think is wrong—an act of transgression. You may experience two kinds of reactions, an internal emotional reaction such as guilt or shame, or an external reaction such as confession or self-criticism. From the standpoint of society, it is more important that people resist temptations to transgress than that they feel guilt after transgression. Without strong internal deterrents to commit antisocial acts, the social order could hardly continue to exist.

Both resistance to temptation and internal reactions to transgressions may be considered types of self-control behaviors. Resistance to temptation is maintenance of self-control. The various reactions after a transgression may be thought of as attempts to reestablish self-control, to bring oneself back to the degree of control that existed before the prohibition was broken. Social-learning researchers have studied three types of variables relevant to maintenance of self-control: the effects of reinforcement, punishment, and imitation.

Self-control: The role of reinforcement. In the lore of learning theory, positive reinforcement is presumed to be more important than punishment in shaping desired responses. For positive acts of commission such as helping others and sharing, this is undoubtedly true. However, for failure to perform bad acts (that is, acts of omission), the role of reinforcement is less clear. An actual transgression is usually visible, so the child often receives a reprimand or other punishment. On the other hand, since it is often difficult to know when a child has successfully resisted temptation, children are unlikely to receive regular rewards for resistance. Thus in training the inhibition of bad acts, punishment may play a larger role than positive reinforcement.

Self-control: The role of punishment. Almost every child is punished at one time or another. Even a psychologist who ardently believes in the value of positive reinforcement will occasionally punish his or her child. Most parents undoubtedly assume that some punishment is desirable in teaching children proper moral behavior.

Despite the common-sense belief that punishment is necessary for proper socialization, research on this complex topic is inconclusive. It would seem that the effectiveness of punishment cannot rest on fear of detection. People disposed to commit immoral acts would simply inhibit them until the odds of being detected were small. Thus the learning of self-control does not rest primarily on fear of detection. What is required is that fear be attached to the acts that are punished (Shaffer, 1979). Desire to avoid the prohibited act itself must be developed. But how does punishment instill an aversion toward the prohibited act?

The answer that social-learning theorists give conforms to their theories of other types of emotional learning. When a child behaves badly and is punished, the punishment causes anxiety. If the punishment is properly timed and administered, an association between the act and the punishment is formed. The anxiety aroused by the punishment is associated with, or conditioned to, the act. On future occasions when the child thinks of doing the immoral act, the aversive conditioned anxiety is aroused anew. Because anxiety is painful, the child decides not to engage in the act and will perhaps push it out of his or her mind altogether. Inhibiting the act and/or thoughts of it reduces the anxiety, so inhibition of the act is self-reinforcing.

In general, then, learning of self-control is possible

because of avoidance learning. One learns to avoid the anxiety associated with punishment by learning to avoid the act that was punished. Within this general framework, many specific issues about punishment still need to be addressed. A few of the more salient research results are summarized in the following paragraphs.

Most of us have heard a small child say "bad boy" or "bad girl" or something similar after they have done something for which they were previously punished. This self-criticism seems to be the forerunner of confession. An old proverb maintains that "confession is good for the soul." That may be, but the question is whether it plays some role in inhibiting immoral acts. The answer is that it probably does not. Children learn self-criticism because their parents criticize them. Often parents punish first and conclude the session with criticism. What the child may learn is that criticism is associated with the end of an anxiety-producing event. That child probably engages in self-criticism thereafter because it is anxiety-reducing. It is not clear that learning to make self-critical remarks helps the child inhibit the bad act in the first place.

Punishment does affect the way children resist temptation (Shaffer, 1979). Many experiments have been conducted on resistance to temptation. In a typical experiment, children are presented with toys and asked to do something with them. A very attractive toy is placed in the set, but whenever the child picks it up, he or she is punished with a "no", or the toy is taken away brusquely. Children usually learn to avoid the prohibited attractive toy after only a few training trials. Later the child is left alone in the room with the attractive toy. The measure of resistance to temptation is how long the child waits before beginning to play with the prohibited toy. Several interesting findings have emerged.

1. The longer the delay in punishing the prohibited act, the lower the child's resistance to temptation. The general rule is that punishment for committing a prohibited act should follow the act immediately and directly.
2. Intense punishment creates stronger resistance to temptation than mild punishment. This conclusion must be tempered by the fact that intense punishments were relatively mild in these experiments, probably milder than a spanking or severe scolding by the parent. Since there is evidence that children withdraw from and avoid punitive adults (Redd, Morris, and Martin, 1975), it would be unwise to conclude that harsh punishment is better than mild punishment in everyday life. Even if stronger inhibitions are instilled, the resulting hostility generated by harsh punishment may offset the moral gains.
3. Consistency of punishment for a deviant act is important. Inconsistent punishment may actually increase the strength of the act. Thus undesired acts should be punished on a regular basis from the time they first occur.
4. Punishment is most effective when administered by a person who has a warm, nurturant relationship with the child. Punishment by a warm, loving parent may by simple contrast have a stronger impact than punishment by parents who are somewhat cold and withdrawn from the child.

Punishment without "rhyme or reason" is often ineffective. The child may actually not know why he or she is being punished, even though it seems obvious to the parent. Punishment seems to work best when it is accompanied by a careful explanation to the child of why he or she is being punished and what should and should not be done in the future. A focus on the child's intentions may be particularly effective when the child approaches school age.

It seems clear that punishment does have an important role to play in children's learning to inhibit undesired acts, and it is therefore an important technique for teaching self-control. Much remains to be learned about the effects of punishment, and the generalizations we have made should be regarded as tentative rather than absolute.

Self-control: The role of imitation. It has generally been assumed that children imitate, or model, the moral acts of adults in the same way that they imitate other acts. It is clear that imitation of positive acts of commission, such as helping responses, does occur. However, it is not clear that the child is able to imitate an inhibited act. There is a logical problem involved, because the child would have to imitate an act that does not occur. Much of the parent's behavior is internal to the parent, and the child does not have access to it (Shaffer, 1977). The child must develop the ability to take different perspectives and to understand sophisticated verbal instructions before access to the parents' desires and intentions is possible. This is a gradual process, lasting throughout childhood. What the research does show is that models who yield to temptation have a disinhibiting effect on children who observe them, but models who do *not* yield do not exert an equally strong inhibitory effect. The conclusion seems to be that parents of small children must be consistently exemplary in their behavior.

The social-learning approach to moral development is strongly empirical in its orientation. Much of value has been learned. The focus on situation-specific behavior has not promoted a unified, coherent picture of how the child evolves step-by-step from an amoral little being into the moral adult. Indeed, this approach denies that there is any overall consistency in moral behavior. We turn now to the cognitive-developmental approach. This theory does try to develop a coherent structural scheme for the emergence of morality.

THE COGNITIVE-DEVELOPMENTAL MODEL

The basic assumption of the cognitive-developmental approach is that moral development depends on cognitive development. As a consequence, this approach has focused heavily on the nature of moral reasoning, rather than moral feelings or conduct. Jean Piaget (1932) founded the study of moral development within this tradition. His approach has been extended considerably by Lawrence Kohlberg (1969; 1976). We will summarize the research of each of these scholars.

Piaget's approach to moral development. Piaget believes that moral maturity implies respect for social rules and a sense of social justice. His task was to discover how the amoral infant eventually achieves moral maturity. His studies were done informally. Basically, he played various games, such as marbles, with children of different ages. He observed their concepts of rules, asked questions about the origins and legitimacy of rules, and inquired about what should happen when rules are violated. He eventually constructed stories containing various types of moral dilemmas, presented them to the children, and noted how they resolved the dilemmas. For example, he told children the story of a little boy who is called to dinner, opens the dining room door, and knocks over a tray of 15 cups that was on a chair near the door, breaking them all. The boy did not know that the tray was there. The same children then heard a second story about a little boy who tries to get some jam out of a cabinet while his mother is away and in the process breaks one cup. Piaget asks whether the two boys were equally guilty; if not, who was most guilty; and what punishments should be given. Note that the boy in the first story did a lot of damage unintentionally, and the boy in the second story did slight damage in the process of committing an intended moral transgression (raiding the jam). Younger children tended to assign guilt according to how much damage was done; older children tended to take the boy's intentions into consideration.

According to Piaget's findings in this and other experiments, the child's morality matures through a series of stages, each succeeding the other. The moral stages are correlated with the stages of cognitive development and depend on them. He describes the premoral period, the period of moral realism, and the period of moral relativism.

1. *The premoral period.* The child is largely unaware of rules prior to school age. In the earlier years, children do not play marbles to win a game, but for the sheer joy of handling the marbles. By age 4 or 5, children become aware of the rules by watching older children and imitating them, although they do not yet grasp the cognitive meaning of rules.

2. *The period of moral realism (or heteronomous morality).* Children between ages 6 and 10 look on rules as moral absolutes and believe that rules should be obeyed at all times. Children assume that rules are "God given" and do not grasp the arbitrary nature of game rules. Children are moral realists at this stage. They focus on the consequences of an act (such as how many cups were broken) rather than on the intention behind the act. Children at this stage often believe in IMMANENT JUSTICE, the notion that violations are invariably punished by God or natural forces. In addition, they favor EXPIATORY PUNISHMENT—punishment for its own sake because of the transgression—and have very little conception of "making the punishment fit the crime." In summary, children at this stage are literal and concrete about the nature of rules, about justice, and about punishment for transgressions.

3. *The period of moral relativism (or autonomous morality).* By age 10 or 11, children begin to develop a sense of autonomous morality. They realize that rules are arbitrary social inventions and can be changed if the people involved agree to change them. Children at this stage reject expiatory punishment and favor RECIPROCAL PUNISHMENT—punishment appropriate to the nature of the misdeed in such a way that the rule-breaker will understand the nature of the punishment and its relation to the transgression. They no longer believe in immanent justice. By now they have violated too many rules without getting caught and punished to buy the idea that "God always punishes wrongdoers."

The child moves from heteronomous to autonomous morality because of cognitive growth and social experience. Children are EGOCENTRIC during the heteronomous stage, which means that they are unable to take roles and view the world from differing perspectives. As a result of egocentrism, children are literal realists, confusing their own thoughts and feelings with objective reality. This confusion makes children susceptible to the influence of powerful authority figures such as parents. Neural growth and social experience help overcome egocentrism and realism. For example, as children age, they gain experience with peers and develop equal-status relationships. In the push and shove of peer life, children learn that sometimes they can exert power, that other children have different rule concepts, and that there are many points of view on the world. Slowly, concreteness gives way to the relativity of autonomous morality.

Research has provided some support for Piaget's theory, but not complete confirmation. The findings indicate that, more so than older children, younger children focus on consequences, favor expiatory punishment, believe in immanent justice, and consider rules absolute. However, it is not clear that the child progresses evenly through a series of stages. The level of maturity seems to vary somewhat across situations. Also, recent research indicates that children take intentions into account much earlier than Piaget had assumed. There is also some evidence (Schleifer and Douglas, 1973) that children can be trained to give moral reasons at a stage quite different from the stage they are presumably at, indicating that moral reasoning (or at least the expression of moral reasons) is sensitive to social influence. In short, there is considerable evidence that children do progress from heteronomous to autonomous morality, but there are many irregularities in this progression and it is susceptible to cultural and modeling effects.

Kohlberg's approach to moral development.
Kohlberg has worked for many years to refine and extend Piaget's theory, and in the process, he has basically constructed his own theory. His approach was to ask boys of age 7 to 16 years to resolve a series of moral dilemmas posed in the form of short stories. Each story required a character to choose between an authoritative rule or law and some other act that promoted some human value. One of these well-known dilemmas is as follows:

> In Europe, a woman was near death from a special kind of cancer. There was one drug that doctors thought might save her. It was a form of radium that a druggist in the same town had recently discovered. The drug was expensive to make, but the druggist was charging $2000, or 10 times the cost of the drug, for a small (possibly life-saving) dose. Heinz, the sick woman's husband, borrowed all the money that he could, about $1000, or half of what he needed. He told the druggist that his wife was dying, and asked him to sell the drug cheaper or to let him pay later. The druggist replied, "No. I discovered the drug and I'm going to make money from it." Heinz then became desperate and broke into the store to steal the drug for his wife. Should Heinz have done that (from Shaffer, 1979)?

Kohlberg was not so much interested in whether the child answered yes or no as in the reasons the child gave to support his or her answer.

Kohlberg found that his data were somewhat different from Piaget's. For example, the obedience to rules found in younger children seemed to be based on fear of punishment rather than respect for authority. Also, Kohlberg found that moral development is not complete at age 12 or so, as Piaget had thought, but continues to become more complex until early adulthood.

Analysis of the data suggested that moral development proceeds through an invariant sequence of three moral levels, each comprised of two distinct stages. The progression is invariant, because each succeeding stage is built on a reorganization of the previous stages. The higher the stage, the higher the level of moral development. Kohlberg's levels of moral development and stages of moral reasoning are given in Box B. Examples of possible responses to the Heinz dilemma at each stage appear in Box C.

B. Kohlberg's Stages of Moral Development

Level 1: Preconventional Morality. At this level, morality is truly external. The child conforms to rules imposed by authority figures in order to avoid punishment or to obtain personal rewards. The preconventional level consists of the following two stages:

Stage 1: Punishment and obedience orientation. At this stage, the child determines the goodness or badness of an act on the basis of its consequences. The child will defer to authority figures and obey their commands in order to avoid punishment. There is no true conception of rules however; if the child can "get away" with an act, it is not considered bad. The seriousness of a violation depends upon the magnitude of its consequences (the amount of punishment received and/or the amount of objective harm done).

Stage 2: Naive hedonism or instrumental orientation. A person at the second stage of moral development conforms to rules in order to gain rewards or to satisfy personal needs. Doing things for others is "right" if the actor will benefit in the long run. This low-level reciprocity is quite pragmatic: "you scratch my back and I'll scratch yours" is the guiding philosophy of the Stage 2 individual. The seriousness of a violation now depends, in part, on the intent of the actor.

Level 2: Conventional Morality. At this level, the individual strives to obey the rules and regulations set forth by others (parents, peers, social groups) in order to win praise and recognition for virtuous conduct, and/or to maintain social order. The following two stages are the components of conventional morality:

Stage 3: Good boy or good girl orientation. Moral behavior is that which pleases, helps, or is approved by others. Actions are evaluated on the basis of the actor's intent. "He or she means well" is a common expression of moral approval at this stage. A primary objective of a Stage 3 respondent is to be thought of as a "nice" person.

Stage 4: Law-and-order orientation. At this stage, the orientation is toward authority, established rules and regulations, and the maintenance of the social order. Laws are accepted without question and must be obeyed. Students often refer to this law-and-order orientation as redneck or Archie Bunker morality.

Level 3: Postconventional Morality or the Morality of Self-accepted Moral Principles. The individual who has attained this third level of moral reasoning is personally committed to a set of rules or standards that are shared with others and yet transcend specific authority figures. In other words, moral standards are internalized and become the person's own. Postconventional morality includes the following two stages:

Stage 5: Social contract or legalistic orientation. This stage has utilitarian overtones. Right actions are those that express the will of the majority or maximize social welfare. There is an awareness that laws may be unjust, but the feeling is that unjust rules must be obeyed until they can be changed by social consensus (such as through an orderly election). In contrast, the Stage 4 individual would not challenge an established law, and might be suspicious of those who do. This fifth stage of moral reasoning represents the "official" morality of the United States Constitution.

Stage 6: The universal ethical principles orientation. At this "highest" stage of moral reasoning, the individual defines right and wrong on the basis of the self-chosen ethical principles of his or her own conscience. These principles are not concrete rules like the Ten Commandments. They are abstract moral guidelines (such as the Golden Rule, the greatest good for the greatest number, and the categorical imperative) or principles of universal justice (and respect for individual rights) that are to be applied

Box B (*continued*)

in all situations. Deviations from these self-chosen moral standards produce feelings of guilt or self-condemnation (the Stage 6 conscientious objector may refuse to conform to a draft law that violates his pacifist beliefs. To comply would bring self-degradation, a punishment that may be much more aversive to the conscientious objector than a short prison sentence.)

(From Shaffer, 1979.)

C. Examples of Responses to the Heinz Dilemma

Stage 1: Punishment and obedience orientation

Pro-theft: It isn't really bad to take it. He did ask to pay for it first. He wouldn't do any other damage or take anything else, and the drug he'd take is only worth $200, not $2000.

Anti-theft: Heinz doesn't have permission to take the drug. He can't just go and break through a window. He'd be a bad criminal doing all that damage. That drug is worth a lot of money and stealing anything so expensive would be a big crime.

Note: Both of these answers disregard Heinz's intentions and judge the act in terms of its consequences. The pro-theft answer minimizes the consequences while the anti-theft answer maximizes them. The implication is that big crimes warrant severe punishment.

Stage 2: Naive hedonism or instrumental orientation

Pro-theft: Heinz isn't really doing any harm to the druggist, and he can always pay him back. If he doesn't want to lose his wife, he should take the drug.

Anti-theft: The druggist isn't wrong, he just wants to make a profit like everybody else. That's what you're in business for, to make money.

Note: Heinz's intentions are apparent in the pro-theft answer, while the intentions of the druggist come out in the anti-theft answer. Either Heinz or the druggist is "right" for satisfying his own needs or goals.

Stage 3: Good boy or good girl orientation

Pro-theft: Stealing is bad, but this is a bad situation. Heinz is only doing something that it is natural for a good husband to do. You can't blame him for doing something out of love for his wife. You'd blame him if he didn't save her.

Anti-theft: If Heinz's wife dies, he can't be blamed. You can't say he is heartless for failing to commit a crime. The druggist is the selfish and heartless one. Heinz tried to do everything he really could.

Note: Both answers seek to resolve the dilemma by advocating what others would approve of under the circumstances. In either case, Heinz is described as a well-intentioned person who is doing what is right.

Box C (*continued*)

Stage 4: Law-and-order orientation

Pro-theft: The druggist is leading the wrong kind of life if he just lets somebody die, so it is Heinz's duty to save her. But Heinz can't just go around breaking laws. He must pay the druggist back and take his punishment for stealing.

Anti-theft: It is natural for Heinz to want to save his wife, but it is always wrong to steal. You have to follow the rules regardless of your feelings or the special circumstances.

Note: The obligation to the law transcends special interests. Even the pro-theft answer recognizes that Heinz is morally wrong and must pay for his transgression.

Stage 5: Social contract or legalistic orientation

Pro-theft: Before you say stealing is wrong, you've got to consider this whole situation. Of course the laws are quite clear about breaking into a store. And even worse, Heinz would know that there were no legal grounds for his actions. Yet, it would be reasonable for anybody in this kind of situation to steal the drug.

Anti-theft: I can see the good that would come from illegally taking the drug, but the ends don't justify the means. You can't say that Heinz would be completely wrong to steal the drug, but even these circumstances don't make it right.

Note: The judgments are no longer black and white. The pro-theft answer recognizes that theft is legally wrong but that an emotional husband may be driven to steal the drug—and that is understandable (although not completely moral). The anti-theft answer recognizes exactly the same points. Heinz would commit an immoral act if he were to steal the drug, but he does so with good intentions.

Stage 6: Universal ethical principles orientation

Pro-theft: When one must choose between disobeying a law and saving a human life, the higher principle of preserving life makes it morally right to steal the drug.

Anti-theft: With many cases of cancer and the scarcity of the drug, there might not be enough for everybody who needs it. The correct course of action can only be the one that is "right" by all people concerned. Heinz ought to act not on emotion or the law, but according to what he thinks an ideally just person would do in this case.

Note: Both answers transcend law and self-interest and appeal to higher principles (individual rights and the sanctity of life) that all "reasonable" people should consider in this situation. The pro-theft answer is relatively straightforward. On the other hand, it is difficult to conceive of an anti-theft stage 6 response, unless the drug were scarce and Heinz would deprive other equally deserving people of life by stealing the drug to save his wife.

(From Shaffer, 1979.)

Kohlberg's theory has generated much research. A substantial amount is cross-cultural, and much of it supports the theory. In most societies, stages 3 and 4 (conventional morality) are dominant, and only a small percentage of the people reach stages 5 or 6. Not all research confirms the theory. Recent longitudinal studies indicate that the sequence of moral development may not be so invariant as Kohlberg thought. According to the theory, regression to a lower level of moral reasoning is not supposed to happen, but in fact it is rather common. There is also the interesting possibility (Kohlberg, 1969) that stages 4, 5, and 6 may be alternative pathways branching off from stage 3. That is, instead of 5 being higher than 4, and 6 higher than 5, stages 4, 5, and 6 might simply be "alternative moralities." Finally, Kohlberg (1973) has speculated that there may be a seventh stage of moral development, although the details remain to be specified.

Clearly, Kohlberg's theory has captured the imagination of many researchers. It is an interesting theory that continues to evolve. At present, it is the best and most comprehensive theory of moral development that we have.

The study of moral development is an important aspect of the study of socialization. Each of the three theoretical viewpoints offers valuable insight into the course of moral growth. However, the psychoanalytic approach has not fared well when subjected to empirical tests. The social-learning approach is probably the most viable from an empirical point of view. However, many people find the notion of morality as situation-specific displeasing. They feel morality somehow *ought* to be consistent and unified within the person and progress steadily to high and rarefied levels. This need for unity and progression has stimulated stage theorists such as Piaget and Kohlberg. Their theories are quite different from the social-learning approach. There is much value in both approaches, and the years ahead will see serious attempts to integrate them.

Sex-roles: "it" becomes "him" or "her"

An infant is often referred to as "it" instead of "him" or "her," even though biologically the baby is quite obviously male or female. Sexual identity begins with biological gender, but it is determined primarily by the expectatons, values, and behaviors of the society into which the infant is born. In almost every society, the social definition of maleness is quite different from the definition of femaleness.

There are no data on whether the attending physicians who administer the proverbial slap on the behind at birth actually slap female babies more gently, but beginning very soon thereafter, male and female babies are treated in systematically different ways by their parents, their peers, and society generally. In fact, Bem and Bem (1970) argue that this differential treatment of males and females is so pervasive that it results in the almost universal adoption of what they term a nonconscious ideology about the "natural" role of women. As they point out,

> Not only do most men and women in our society hold hidden prejudices about the woman's "natural" role, but these nonconscious beliefs motivate a host of subtle practices that are dramatically effective at keeping her "in her place." Even many liberal Americans, who insist that a black skin should not uniquely qualify its owner for janitorial and domestic service, continue to assume that the possession of a uterus uniquely qualifies its owner for precisely that (p. 89).

These subtle and not so subtle practices begin early. Block (1973), for example, reported data from parents who responded to a series of 91 items dealing with practices they did or did not employ with respect to their children. The parents of boys were significantly more likely than the parents of girls to respond affirmatively to such items as: "I encourage my child always to do his best"; "I teach my child to control his feelings"; "I feel it is good for a child to play competitive games"; and "I have strict rules for my child." On the other hand, the parents of girls were significantly more

As the stereotyped sexual image for females is reevaluated, new behaviors are possible. These include pursuing careers and working in positions that would have been considered impossible—or highly improbable—for women even a few years ago. (Steven M. Stone/The Picture Cube)

84
Becoming a
social creature

85
**The development
of social behavior**

likely than parents of boys to respond affirmatively to such items as: "I feel a child should be given comfort when upset"; "I find it difficult to punish my child"; "I encourage my child to talk about his troubles"; and "I don't go out if I have to leave my child with a stranger" (p. 516). As Block points out, the emphasis of the reported child-rearing practices for boys is on achievement, competition, control of feelings, and playing the game according to the rules. For girls, the emphasis is different. They are given comfort and reassurance more readily, they are not encouraged to play the game and "take their knocks," and there is much more importance attached to interpersonal relationships.

Observational studies of mothers and fathers interacting with nursery school children (Block, 1973) paint essentially the same picture. With boys, the parents are much more demanding of objectively correct solutions on a puzzle task; they tolerate poorer solutions and more non-task-oriented play from girls.

It should follow, then, that after years of this sort of differential treatment by parents on many, many tasks, boys and girls develop different images of themselves. They come to think of themselves in different terms, primarily because others have treated them in such different ways, have demanded different things from them, and will not usually let them be until these demands and expectations are met. Boys should come to think of themselves as more competitive, assertive, and practical than girls, because they have, in fact, been forced to be more competitive, assertive, and practical. The evidence indicates that such differential self-perceptions do exist, at least by middle and late adolescence (Wylie, 1961, p. 147; Block, 1973). It may well be that an "ideal" person should incorporate aspects of the usual self-conceptions of both sexes (see Box D).

It is not, of course, just parents who reinforce the appropriateness of these differential self-images. Very early in life, children learn their gender identification, and the message that impinges on them continually from television, advertising, the comics, and the behavior of others is that girls behave differently from boys and women behave differently from men. Consider the images of males and females that appear in picture books for preschool children. Weitzman, Eifler, Hokada, and Ross (1972), in an analysis of several groups of such books, found that girls and women are almost invisible. That is, they seldom appear in the titles or pictures and only rarely in the stories themselves. For example, in a sample of 18 books that had won recognition by the American Library Association, there were 261 pictures of males and only 23 pictures of females. In the stories themselves, females usually played secondary roles (if they appeared at all), and their roles were dull and stereotyped compared to those of males. Similarly, Hunter (1976) reports that a historical survey of attitudes toward women in Greece, Rome, Judeo-Christian religious writings, and down through the Middle Ages converges on three dominant images: woman as love object, woman as inferior, and woman as evil. Furthermore, since the late 1940s, an image of women very similar to that conveyed in the preschool picture books has found its way, via television, into the vast majority of American homes.

Do society and women in particular accept this image of females as generally inferior? The evidence indicates such acceptance. Pheterson, Kiesler, and Goldberg (1971) asked 120 female college students to evaluate a series of paintings. For each painting, half of the subjects thought it had been painted by a male artist and half thought it was the work of a female artist. For some subjects, the paintings were depicted as having won a prize; for other subjects, the paintings were described as entries in a show. When the paintings were believed to have won a prize, the artists were evaluated as equally competent and promising regardless of whether they were male or female. However, when the paintings were described as entries in a show, the artists were evaluated as being more competent and promising when they were believed to be male than when they were believed to be female. It is important to remember that the subjects in the Pheterson, et al. study were not men but women, and relatively well-educated women at that. Speculating on why women devalue the work of other women, Pheterson, et al. mention that many groups—women, blacks, Jews—who feel themselves to be the objects of prejudice and discrimination often adopt the attitudes of the dominant majority surrounding them. They appear to incorporate the misconceptions of others into their self-conception and define themselves as they are defined by others: a vicious circle indeed.

The key question, however, is whether the images

D. The Androgynous Person

Masculinity and femininity have usually been approached as an "either-or" affair. The more masculine a person, the less feminine; and the more feminine, the less masculine. Recently, a number of people have argued that masculinity and femininity might more appropriately be considered independent dimensions, thus allowing for the possibility that someone might have both masculine and feminine characteristics. As Berzins (1975) points out, even though the single masculine-feminine dimension is deeply rooted in "common sense,"

> it needlessly confounds components of psychological self-definition (I am an assertive person; I am a nurturant person) with biological sex differences, differences in bodily size or muscular strength, traditions regarding the division of labor in the family, choice of vocation, and even with preferences in sexual partners. While these jumbled strands no doubt are still treated "as one" and enshrined in the sex-role socialization practices in American society . . . members of the human liberation movement have increasingly called our attention to the stultifying effects of the prevalant "either-or" perspective on sex roles. For example, it is not at all clear why the "appropriately feminine" woman should not only internalize societal standards for feminine behavior but should simultaneously learn to repudiate standards for highly desirable "masculine" behaviors.

The best of both worlds may be possible. That is, there is no reason why one person could not incorporate desirable "feminine" qualities (concern for others, nurturance) and desirable "masculine" qualities (achievement motivation, curiosity). Such an ANDROGYNOUS person might be able to function better in a wider variety of situations than one who was bound by sex-role stereotypes and felt constrained to be masculine or feminine only. By definition, the androgynous person should show greater cross-situational adaptability.

Berzins (1975), Bem (1974), and others have devised scales for measuring psychological androgyny, and these scales appear to be promising research tools. Berzins, for example, administered his scale to a diverse sample of male and female psychotherapists and found proportionately more sex-typed male therapists while there were relatively more androgynous female therapists. He speculates that this may lend some credence to the feminist contention that "female patients have a higher probability of benefitting from female than from male therapists."

---

of "typical male behavior" and "typical female behavior" that are conveyed to young children influence their behavior. Is there any evidence that children consciously model themselves after the stereotypical characters depicted in picture books, on television, in magazine advertising, and almost everywhere else they look? Unfortunately, the answer is yes. Consider the following study by McArthur and Eisen (1976). Male and female nursery school children were individually read one of three illustrated storybooks. In one, the Stereotype Storybook, a little boy was described saving a little girl from a goat, buying a model ship-in-a-bottle kit, figuring out how to get the ship into the bottle, and, finally, succeeding in constructing the ship. In this same Stereotype Storybook, the little girl was described as being frightened by a goat, calling for help, watching the boy working on the ship model, and suggesting that they ask an adult to help with the ship. In the Reversal Storybook, the behaviors depicted were identical, but the roles were reversed; that is, the little boy was frightened by the goat and saved by the girl, and the little girl constructed the ship model while the little boy watched.

Following the storybook reading, each child was

given an opportunity to work on a terrarium in a bottle very similar to the bottle in the storybooks. The task involved using a pair of long wooden tongs to stand up some plastic flowers lying on their side in the narrow-necked bottle. The dependent variable was simply how long the children persisted on this task. The results showed that boys persist longer after having been read the Stereotype Storybook, whereas girls persist longer after having been read the Reversal Storybook. As McArthur and Eisen (1976) put it,

> One implication of the present findings is that if one wishes to promote more equal representation of men and women in "achieving" roles in our society, a change in the representation of females in children's books may be a useful step forward. Admittedly, the effects of storybooks on achievement behavior measured in the present investigation were only short-term, but so was the exposure to these stories . . . it does not seem unreasonable to expect that young girls' prolonged exposure to stereotypic children's books may contribute to their lower levels of adult "achievement" as compared with men (p. 473).

The models that are available to people of either sex convey society's expectations and how they should define themselves. As we have seen, these societal expectations and stereotypes are incorporated into the self-conceptions of developing girls and boys at an early age. People begin to measure their worth by the extent to which they meet the expectations of others. The tragedy is not that they may become a "typical" male or a "typical" female, because many such males and females lead happy, healthy, productive lives. The tragedy is that they may never be aware of alternatives, that they may never perceive that they have a choice.

The emergence of the person

We have traveled a long conceptual journey in this chapter. We began by pondering some of the basic issues of socialization and asking whether parents are really necessary ingredients in socialization. We found that conceptions of development vary widely, from the sexualized Freudian theory to the more mundane approach of social-learning theory. We saw the child emerge from its first beginnings in a mother–infant interaction system to become a creature who forms attachments of love—attachments that are susceptible to disturbance and disruption. Successful socialization does not occur automatically. It is won over the long haul by successfully surmounting the hurdles of life. Slowly the child advances, assimilating the rules and values of the culture, and eventually becoming a moral agent. With a set of moral norms fully instilled, the individual assumes the status of a person.

The notion of personhood is complex; it partakes of common-sense philosophy rather than scientific psychology. Development of an internalized moral sense is probably the prime requirement for personhood. But there are many other milestones before the mature person is fully realized. We can do no more here than list a few of them.

1. A firm, subjective sense of self must develop.

2. A definite sex-role identity must develop. This aspect of personhood is enormously important and complex.

3. A person must have a sense of competence in the world. One must feel effective in maneuvering in the world and mastering the tasks that the world poses. White (1959) has proposed that the motive to be competent is powerful, is perhaps intrinsic to the species, and must be considered in any adequate theory of human behavior.

4. A person must strike a balance between independence and interdependence with other people. Along with competence, a full sense of self-autonomy must be achieved. To some extent, every person is an island, and we must all learn to move and function as separate, independent entities. At the same time, we are caught up in a vast web of relationships with others; we are interdependent with them. Achieving a delicate balance between independence and interdependence is an important aspect of socialization.

5. Full personhood means a life of productive accomplishment at chosen tasks. Apparently various cultures instill different levels of the desire to achieve in their young. Much work has been done on the achievement motive and how it develops (McClelland, 1961; Shaffer, 1979). The internalization of some degree of achievement motivation seems to be an important facet of socialization.

There are many other tasks of socialization. Full treatment of the subject would require a book on social development (Shaffer, 1979), and the focus of books and courses on social development is somewhat different from the goals of a text and course on social psychology. Nevertheless, the many facets of socialization are relevant to the host of topics on social behavior discussed in this book. We hope we have conveyed the importance of socialization in the development of a comprehensive social psychology.

Summary

Socialization is an important aspect of social psychology, because study of such topics as conformity, leadership, and attitude change assumes a well-socialized human being as its subject. One important question is whether certain basic aspects of socialization are universal across all cultures. We explored this question via an imaginary thought experiment, in which a Universal Parenting Machine raised a group of children from birth without any direct human intervention or contact at all.

Jean Piaget created the cognitive-developmental approach to socialization. According to Piaget, the child proceeds through a set of cognitive stages: the sensorimotor stage (0–2 years), the preoperational stage (2–7 years), the concrete operations stage (7–11 years), and the formal operations stage (12 years and older). Cognitive development and its progress determines the child's rate of social and emotional development.

Social-learning theory explains social development by applying principles of learning. Certain theorists, such as Bandura, have stressed observational learning and imitation, and the effects of positive reinforcement. Sophisticated versions of the theory focus on how learning becomes internalized so that the individual's behavior is self-regulated.

Early social development is best viewed as beginning within an interaction system consisting of mother and new infant. Early development leads to emotional attachment to others, a necessary step for an individual to become a full-fledged human being. Attachments occur rather rapidly around 7–8 months of age. Separation from mother and deprivation of parental attention can have devastating effects. Short-term effects often include emotional outbursts, a period of despair, and withdrawal into apathy. Long-term deprivation can have a variety of effects, such as deprivation dwarfism, a pattern of stunted growth that appears to be due to extreme deprivation of emotional ties.

Moral development is an important aspect of social development. Morality can be examined in terms of an affective component, a cognitive component, and a behavioral component. Psychoanalytic theory deals primarily with the emotional component, social-learning theory with overt behaviors, and cognitive-developmental theory with the cognitive component, including moral reasoning.

Development of sex-role identity is another important aspect of socialization. What it means to be male or female depends more on the values and expectations of society than on the biological gender of the child.

The concept of personhood is a complex notion. Personhood has many requirements, such as moral responsibility, a subjective sense of self, feelings of competence, a balance between independence and interdependence, and a motive to achieve goals.

4

The development of self, language, and communication

92 Understanding the social world

Developing conceptions of other people
Developing conceptions of self
Role-taking: The basis of developing communication skills

100 Language

103 Communication

The social nature of communication
Speak that I may know thee: The many forms of
    communication
Context and embeddedness
Nonverbal communication
    Body language
    Visual interaction

116 Summary

William James once referred to the world confronting the newly born as "booming, buzzing confusion." Sounds, lights, shadows, smells—millions of stimuli that somehow, in the course of development, have to be sorted out and made sense of, if the infant is to survive. The necessity of understanding and interpreting our surroundings is not, of course, confined to infancy, but it continues and grows progressively more difficult and complex as we mature, our horizons broaden, and our knowledge increases. Fortunately humans are a culture-learning species, so each infant does not have to experience everything firsthand in order to learn about it. The infant can profit from the experience and knowedge of parents, older brothers and sisters, teachers, authors, and even television writers.

However, in order to profit from the experience of others, one must be able to communicate with them—to ask them questions and understand their answers, to read what others have written, and to listen to what others say. This is not quite so easy as it sounds. For effective communication to take place, one must not only have a clear conception of one's own view of the object or event being discussed, but one must also be able to understand that the other person's view of the same object or event may differ. Understanding that people see things differently is not by any means given at birth. The infant must achieve it through hard work, and until it is achieved, effective communication is impossible. The infant must learn that what sound like random noises to him or her mean something to others. And in order to communicate with those others, the infant must learn what the noises mean to them. Thus the first major cognitive task facing the developing infant is the differentiation of self from others. That accomplishment paves the way for the development of skill in taking the others' point of view (role-taking ability), the use of language, and communication. Let us see how these things fit together.

Understanding the social world

Every adult is familiar with at least one language. In modern civilizations, it is difficult to avoid being exposed to some spoken, written, or printed word for more than 5 or 10 minutes at a time. We are bombarded by words, words from radios, books, magazines, newspapers, and road signs. Even television, a "visual" medium, pours forth an almost uninterrupted stream of verbiage. Because of this constant immersion in language, many people fail to appreciate its importance in the development of the child's understanding of his or her world. Without language, neither individual thought nor human society as we know it would be possible.

Why is language so important? Why does what Bram (1955) defines as a "structured system of arbitrary vocal symbols" make such a difference? Surely, one might argue, humans could exist without language—animals do. That, of course, is the point. Language and the ability to communicate separate humans from the lower animals. It is the ability to communicate, to exchange symbols, and to symbolically refer to things not physically present that allows the transmission and inheritance of culture and raises humans above their biological imperatives. Language and the ability to communicate make us human. Without language, furthermore, we would not only not have the ability to communicate, but we would *have* nothing to communicate. That is, it is only through a process of communication with others via language that we learn to label both external and internal reality. The bond between language and thought is an intimate, inextricable one. Far from serving as a mere tool of expression, language structures our ideas. Some even say it makes thinking possible.

Most terms in the lexicon (vocabulary) of a language, such as *boy, mother,* and *book,* are composed of a bundle or cluster of meanings. Linguists

(Stockwell, 1969) refer to the individual units in such clusters as sememes or sememic components. A SEMEMIC COMPONENT can be thought of as a dimension consisting of two or more values, such as male–female. Thus, the term *father* and *son* share the same value on one sememic component (maleness) but differ from each other on a second (generation). A given word, then, is defined by its relationships to other words, and one of the major tasks facing a child is to develop some comprehension of the interrelations among words and among concepts. How is an orange like an apple? How is a truck like (and how different from) a car? How are mommies like aunts and daddies like uncles? This task is a major part of what Brown (1958) refers to as the "Original Word Game," the crucial game of linguistic reference that all children must play if they are to learn a language. For social psychology, of course, the most important domain in which the game is played concerns conceptions of other people and how these conceptions develop.

DEVELOPING CONCEPTIONS OF OTHER PEOPLE

The general theoretical orientation that has dominated this area of interest combines the ideas of Murphy (1947), Werner (1948), Piaget (1954), and Bruner (1951). While there are major differences among the positions of these four investigators (Anglin, 1973), they all believe that cognitive development proceeds through various stages characterized by increasing degrees of both differentiation and integration. DIFFERENTIATION here refers to the child's gradually increasing ability to perceive and label the various components of his or her environment. INTEGRATION refers to comprehension of the interrelationships among these various components.

An early study of the development of person concepts (Hartley, Rosenbaum, and Schwartz, 1948) offers some tentative evidence on this view of cognitive development. Eighty-six boys and girls between the ages of 3 and 10 years were interviewed and asked such questions as "What is Daddy?," "What is Mommy?," "What are you?," and "What does it take to be Jewish?" The responses were categorized in order to explore the ways in which the children identified themselves and others. Among the younger groups, almost *no* children spontaneously attributed personal characteristics such as "intelligent," "sweet," or "warm" to others. Rather, they responded in terms of global role categories: "Mommy takes care of me" or "Daddy drives a truck." In the older age groups, there was an increasing tendency to attribute distinguishing or differentiating personality characteristics to significant others.

Some evidence exists for increasing differentiation of person concepts with increasing age. Is there any evidence for greater integration of these increasingly differentiated perceptions of others? An important technique by which integration occurs, of course, is the abstraction of some common attribute from an apparently diverse set of objects or concepts. A dog and a whale are different, certainly, but they are both mammals. Gollin (1958) offers some evidence that with person concepts, as in other linguistic domains, increasing age means increasing ability to abstract commonalities from (and hence integrate) apparently diverse phenomena. He presented a five-scene silent motion picture about an 11-year-old boy to three groups of boys and girls who differed in age (group averages were 10.7 years, 13.6 years, and 16.6 years). In one of the movie scenes, the actor was simply shown; in two scenes he was shown engaging in socially approved behavior; and in two scenes he was shown engaging in socially disapproved behavior. As anticipated, with increasing age there was a dramatic increase in the percentage of subjects who were able to integrate both the "good" and the "bad" behavior into their descriptions of the boy.

One of the major problems in trying to examine how children organize their conceptions of others is how to avoid predetermining the outcome. Dubin and Dubin (1965) rather pessimistically note in their review of children's social perception that technologies measuring intrapersonal factors tend to confound the results: "When relations are measured the variables discovered are relations . . ., when the responses are limited to role categories the results are in terms of roles" (p. 817). Investigators have usually attempted to circumvent this problem by using an open-ended, unstructured interview ("Tell me about _____") coupled with some sort of content analysis of the responses.

An example of this approach is a study by Yarrow and Campbell (1963). In that study, 267 boys and girls were interviewed shortly after their arrival at a summer camp and again after 2 weeks at camp. At each interview, campers were asked to choose one child (from his or her cabinmates) about whom the child knew the most and to "tell all about him (her)." On the average, the children gave 11 units of descriptive material, though some gave as many as 27. The descriptions were coded according to personality characteristics, such as aggressive behavior or affiliative behavior. It was found that if a child used a particular characteristic in the first interview, he or she was significantly more likely to employ it in the second interview than were children who had not used it initially. This was true even if a different child was being described in the second interview. It appears that each child develops a perceptual framework for perceiving others and treats this framework as if it has general applicability to *all* others, even though it may not.

In an elaboration of this study, Dornbusch, Hastorf Richardson, Muzzy, and Vreeland (1965) addressed themselves to the relative contributions of perceiver and perceived in person perception. Again information was solicited from boys and girls in summer camps. Each child was interviewed twice and was asked in each interview to describe two other children who shared his or her tent. A set of 69 content-analysis categories was developed (see Table I), and the descriptions were reliably coded into these categories. Without exception, there was greater category overlap when one child was describing two other children than when two children were describing the same other child. This finding held up even when the two descriptions from a given child were elicited a week apart.

The preceding studies support the idea that people begin quite early in life to impose categories and place constructions on their perceptions of others. Apparent contradictions may be resolved by switching to a more abstract level, a level that allows integration of superficially unrelated behaviors in others. Furthermore, the linguistic categories into which the behaviors of others are coded often seem to be more a function of the perceiver than of the perceived.

The conceptions of things that we acquire from society are, of course, continually changing as society itself changes and as our position in society shifts. Such shifts and reorganizations do not cease at any particular point in life, even though the studies we have cited in this section dealt primarily with children. For example, Friendly and Glucksberg (1970) reasoned that novices in a particular culture often lack understanding of the way full-fledged members of the culture view things. Full-fledged members of a culture often seem to make discriminations and differentiations that are lost on newcomers. An example is the old standby about Eskimos being able to discriminate (and having different words for) a large number of kinds of snow. Friendly and Glucksberg were also interested in whether experience in a particular culture or subculture led to changed perceptions about the relationships among people and their characteristics.

With the aid of undergraduate informants, Friendly and Glucksberg selected 20 trait names peculiar to the undergraduate culture at Princeton University (Ivy Type, Meatball, Lunch, and so on) and asked one group of first-year students (novices in the culture) and one group of seniors (old hands) to sort these traits and 40 additional personality characteristics. The structures underlying the perceived relationships were then obtained separately for the two groups. For the first-year students, two dimensions of meaning were adequate to account for the variations they perceived among the 60 terms. Seniors perceived these same two variations, but they also perceived a third. The latter variation had to do with socially approved behavior for Princetonians—a discrimination that the first-year students did not yet make.

DEVELOPING CONCEPTIONS OF SELF

At some point relatively early in life, children begin to realize that other people have intentions and purposes that differ from their own and that one cannot focus only on overt behavior in order to understand

Table I   Dornbusch's content-analysis categories.

Demographic variables
  1. Spatial location
  2. Age
  3. Race
  4. Ethnicity
  5. Religion
Organic variables
  6. Handicap
  7. Health
  8. Physical description
  9. Physical attractiveness
Recreational variables
  10. Physical recreation
  11. Nonphysical recreation
Aggression
  12. Physical aggression
  13. Verbal aggression
  14. General aggression
Quality of interaction
  15. Described to describer
  16. Describer to described
  17. Others to described
  18. Described to others
  19. Described and describer to others
  20. Others to describer and described
  21. Reciprocal relationships
Frequency of interaction
  22. Described and describer
  23. Others and described
  24. Described, describer, and others
Interpersonal relations
  25. Relations with describer
  26. Relations with father
  27. Relations with mother
  28. Relations with siblings
  29. Relations with other family members
  30. Relations with nonfamily adults
  31. Relations with nonfamily children
Group status
  32. Membership in a specific collective
  33. Inclusion or exclusion by others in a group
  34. Executive—holding an office in a specific collective
  35. Socioeconomic status
Modes of interaction
  36. Generosity
  37. Giving aid
  38. Needing aid
  39. Cooperation
  40. Competition
  41. Trust
  42. Humor
  43. Dominance-submission
  44. Interpersonal skill
Moods of interaction
  45. Happiness
  46. Excitability
  47. Confidence
Total personality
  48. Adult terms
  49. Children's terms
  50. Undifferentiated positive comments
  51. Undifferentiated negative comments
Abilities
  52. Verbal communication
  53. Physical ability
  54. Mental ability
  55. School ability
Norms
  56. Grooming and manners
  57. Honest-dishonest
  58. Swearing, cursing, drinking, smoking
  59. Conformity to expectations of peers
  60. Conformity to expectations of family adults
  61. Conformity to expectations of nonfamily adults
Miscellaneous
  62. Possessions of the child
  63. Possessions of the family
  64. Magic and autism
  65. Occupation of child
  66. Occupation of adult
  67. Family
  68. Sexual
  69. Residual

Categories used to code children's descriptions of others. (From Dornbusch, et al., 1965, Table 1, p. 436.)

another person. One has to try to figure out what the behavior was intended to accomplish. This, of course, is a very useful strategy for simplifying the universe. Rather than trying to keep track of millions of behaviors that another might perform, one only need know what his or her intentions are and interpret all the behaviors in terms of a few underlying purposes. For example, Rappoport and Fritzler (1969) employed animated cartoon sequences to study the extent to which children focused on the overt behavior of depicted geometrical objects or on the underlying "intentions" of the objects. First-grade subjects responded primarily to movements, whereas sixth-graders responded by attributing intentions.

In a related but somewhat less artifical study, Peevers and Secord (1973) analyzed open-ended descriptions of both liked and disliked peers from five groups of subjects: preschoolers, third-graders, seventh-graders, eleventh-graders, and college students. The descriptions were coded in terms of their level of descriptiveness, the extent of personal involvement of the describer, the evaluative consistency of the description, and the "depth" of the description. Although fewer items overall were used to describe disliked peers, dispositional items (attribution of enduring personality traits) were much more common in the descriptions of disliked peers. It appears that attribution of a negative quality is more likely to be taken as a sufficient explanation of "all there is" to that person than is attribution of a positive quality. Of particular interest here, however, is that egocentrically phrased descriptions of others were much more common among younger subjects. Peevers and Secord use *egocentric* to refer to descriptive units that describe the other person in subjective, self-oriented terms—for example, what he or she *did to me*.

An earlier "programmed case" study by Rockway (1969) revealed a similar egocentricity. At a number of choice points, subjects had to decide which one of three behaviors seemed true or real for the person being described in the case. After each choice, the subject was asked to explain his or her choice and then was given immediate feedback about whether the choice was right (based on data from the actual case history). A response was called egocentric if the choice was justified in terms of what the subject would have done had he or she been confronted with the situation.

Among sixth-, ninth-, and twelfth-grade boys, egocentric responses decreased from early to middle adolescence but, surprisingly, showed a slight increase in late adolescence (twelfth-grade subjects). Rockway (1969) interprets the latter finding as a kind of enlightened egocentricity. That is, while the younger children may always assume that how they would have responded is the key to understanding how others respond, older adolescents may focus on their own past experiences to predict another's behavior only when it appears logical to assume that they and the other are in some way alike.

Signell (1966) reports a finding that seems congruent with this interpretation. She elicited descriptions of persons from children 9 to 16 years old and found

The way in which we dress and such seemingly unconscious things as the postures we assume often convey a great deal of information about how we view ourselves and how we want others to view us. This is Robert Welch, founder of the politically conservative John Birch Society. (Eric Roth/The Picture Cube)

that, as they increase in age, children seem to increase the complexity of the person concepts they employ. Hence, while younger subjects might base a prediction such as that requested by Rockway on whether the person in the case was "like me," older subjects might base the prediction on whether the person was "like me in terms of how he or she responded to X." As the self-concept becomes more differentiated, people apparently become aware that they behave differently and, to some extent, actually have different characteristics in different situations. When they are secure, they are likely to be kind to others; when insecure, they are likely to be tense and even cruel. As children become aware of such relationships in their own life, they probably come to expect them in others. As the study by Rockway suggests, adults apply these expectations selectively, only when it seems that self and others are in some way *alike*. This is one of the basic suppositions of social-comparison theory (Festinger, 1954), which we shall discuss more fully in Chapter 9.

The idea that perceptions of others are tied to one's own self-concept and/or life situation is underscored by Olshan (1970). Olshan used children in the third, sixth, and ninth grades as subjects and employed a sentence-completion task to determine the traits most frequently used in person perception at each of these levels. ("My mother is _____." "A firefighter is _____.") Once these traits had been obtained, subjects at each grade level were asked to sort a number of traits into piles, each pile corresponding to a different type of person. Using a rather sophisticated scaling procedure, Olshan was able to determine the organizational structure underlying the way in which subjects sorted the traits. An important observation is that the sortings were interpretable in psychologically meaningful ways in terms of the stage of life of the subjects. Adult–child, for example, is a highly significant dimension in third-graders' personality perceptions, but this dimension fades with the beginning of adolescence. On the other hand, preadolescents do not perceive sex as a dimension, whereas adolescents do. Such findings make sense in terms of the life of the subjects. They also emphasize that as one's life situation changes, salient interpersonal expectations also change, and one organizes those expectations in terms of current preoccupations and social interactions.

Not only do maturing children continually reconstrue their perceptions of others, but they also learn that what others expect from them continues to change. A 6-year-old is treated differently from a 10-year-old. The antics of an 8-year-old that are laughed at and approved by adults are frowned on when performed by teenagers. Through the application of such mundane rewards and punishments—and the often plaintive plea to "act your age"—children learn these shifting role expectations. As Sarbin and Allen (1968) put it, they learn that certain rights and duties are associated with certain stages in life and with certain positions in society. They learn to expect different things from different people and, conversely, that different people—their parents, their peers, their teachers—expect different things from them. They learn, in short, to play various roles.

The work of Erving Goffman (1959, 1961, 1963) is closely identified with the metaphor "all the world's a stage." Goffman conceives of individuals as staging performances in virtually all of their day-to-day activities, performances that are geared to specific audiences and intended to project particular definitions of both the situation and the performer's self. As performers, we all attempt to control or manage the available information about our self to which the "audience" has access in order to insure that the audience perceives us as we intend to be perceived. Complications arise, however, because every performer plays multiple roles and cannot be onstage for a particular audience at all times. Goffman's distinction between front and back regions takes this into account. The "front region" is simply the place or setting in which a particular performance is given. The "back region" is a place, relative to a particular performance, where self-definition fostered by the performance does not have to be maintained. Goffman (1959) illustrates the discrepancy between behavior in front and back regions with data from his study of the Shetland Islands and with auxiliary information culled from various sources. In the dining room of the Shetland Hotel, for example, British middle-class standards of decorum and cleanliness were maintained by the staff, whereas

> in the scullery wing of the kitchen regions, mold would sometimes form on soup yet to be used. Over the kitchen stove, wet socks would be dried on the steaming kettle. . . . Tea, when guests had asked for it newly infused, would be brewed in a

pot encrusted at the bottom with tea leaves that were weeks old. . . . Another interesting example of backstage . . . is found in radio and television. Thus an announcer may hold the sponsor's product up at arm's length in front of the camera while he holds his nose with his other hand, his face being out of the picture (pp. 117–119).

In most of Goffman's work, the key issue is the nature of the relationship between the individual and society. How does the individual maintain and project a particular identity in the face of the multiple roles that must be enacted and the varying expectations of others? If all the world's a stage, is the self merely a sequence of different costumes behind which there is little or no substance? Goffman is not so cynical as this question implies. Rather, he sees the self as the common elements that persist through the various roles we play. We recognize what is common in our apparently diverse actions and infer from that who we are and what we are capable of doing. An important implication of playing a particular role, whether it be that of good friend or loyal brother, is that one is the sort of person who can *be* a good friend or a loyal brother.

Such a view of the relationships between self and others descends directly from the thinking of James (1890), Cooley (1902), and Mead (1934), who see self-conception as reflecting the reactions of others to one's behavior. It is also closely related to Bem's (1965, 1967) line of argument, which we shall return to in Chapter 9. For now, let us simply note that as the reactions of others to our behavior changes, our self-conception changes. Thus, Epstein (1973) has argued that it makes sense to think of the self-concept as a "self-theory," a theory each of us has about what we are like, what we will or will not do under various circumstances, how we relate to other people, and what our strengths and weaknesses are. One of the advantages of Epstein's conception of the self is that it makes explicit the expectation of change. Unfolding events may demonstrate that one's view of oneself is inadequate, that one has over- or underestimated certain abilities, or that others do not treat one as the theory predicts. When such disconfirming events occur, we have a choice: we can change our behavior or we can change our theory of ourself.

We began this section by looking at several studies demonstrating the gradual differentiation of self and others. Early in life, children act as if they believe everyone shares their intentions, desires, and perspectives. They are egocentric, believing their view of the world to be *the* view of the world. Only later do they begin to realize that other people have different intentions and perspectives, as well as certain clear-cut expectations about how *they* should behave.

In the course of this shift from an egocentric to a POLYCENTRIC view of the interpersonal universe, the self-concept emerges. Children come to realize that they are "different," that they have certain qualities, features, desires, intentions, perspectives, and history that others do not share. An important question is how this shift from an egocentric to a polycentric view of the interpersonal universe is reflected in communication. At what point in life are children able to incorporate their sense of varying perspectives into the communications they address to others?

ROLE-TAKING: THE BASIS FOR DEVELOPING COMMUNICATION SKILLS

Werner and Kaplan (1963) make a distinction between INNER SPEECH, which they define as self-directed symbolic communication, and EXTERNAL SPEECH, or other-directed symbolic communication. To examine the different characteristics of these two types of communication, Werner and Kaplan asked subjects to write descriptions of unusual stimulus objects either so that they themselves would be able to recognize the objects from the descriptions at some future time or so that, given the descriptions, another person would be able to identify the objects. The two resulting types of communication differed in a number of ways. For example, inner speech tended to be much more concise, laconic, and less explicit than external speech. Fewer words were used overall. Further, Werner and Kaplan analyzed the descriptions in terms of the relative predominance of communal versus idiomatic referents. A COMMUNAL REFERENT was defined as a word or phrase making use of conventional, easily recognizable properties of the stimulus objects, such as height, color, shape, or quantity. An IDIOMATIC REFERENT, on the other hand, was defined as a word or phrase making use of similes, metaphors, evaluative expressions, or other subjective reactions to the stimulus objects. As anticipated, communal referents were much more common in speech intended for others.

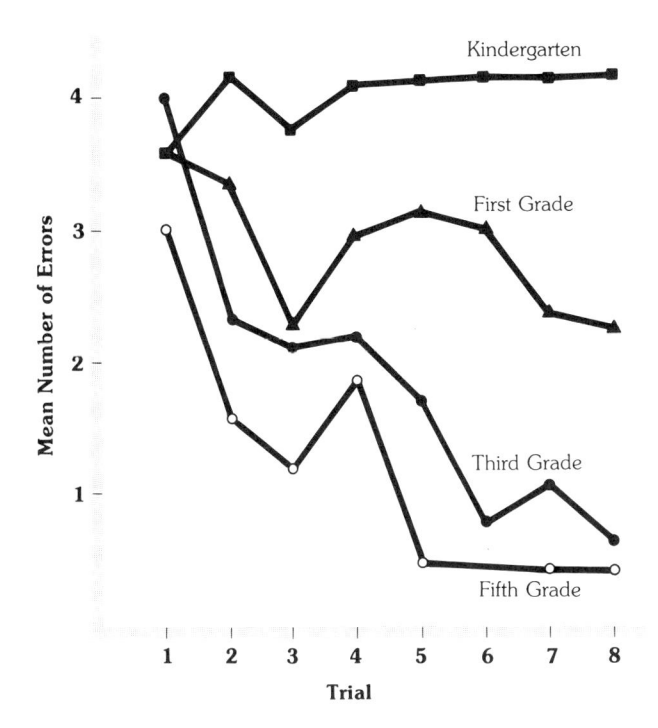

1. Performance of children at four grade levels on a simple communication task. The graph shows the mean number of errors over trials for matched age pairs in the four grades. (From Krauss and Glucksberg, 1969, Figure 3, p. 260.)

The major communication problem confronting the growing child, once he or she has mastered the essentials of grammar, is that of shifting from inner to external speech. The child has to learn that others do not share his or her understanding of idiomatic referents, so more conventional symbols must be employed. While it may be perfectly true that some strange object a child is trying to describe to another "looks like Mommy's hat," such a communication is inadequate because the other child has a different Mommy who has different hats. The child must develop an appreciation of what words mean to others.

A growing body of literature documents the development of this ability to adopt another's perspective and, hence, to communicate with words the other will understand. Krauss and Glucksberg (1969), for example, recruited pairs of subjects from kindergarten, first grade, third grade, and fifth grade and assigned them a simple communication task. The members of each pair were separated and seated on opposite sides of a screen so that they could hear but not see each other. On the table in front of each were six blocks, each block having a novel graphic design stamped on it. The two sets of blocks were identical. One subject of each pair was designated a "speaker" and the other a "listener." The task for the speaker was to stack the blocks on top of each other, describing each block in the process so that the listener on the opposite side of the screen could stack his or her blocks in the same order. When the blocks had been stacked, the two stacks were compared and the number of errors noted. The blocks were then unstacked and the task was repeated seven times for a total of eight trials. The results appear in Figure 1.

As the figure shows, kindergarten children do not do well at this task, and first-graders improve only slightly over trials. However, third- and fifth-graders were communicating quite accurately by the fifth or sixth trial. One question that might be raised about this study, however, is the extent to which the better performance by the older pairs was a function of the speaker's greater ability to describe the blocks so that the listener would understand, or the listener's greater ability to make sense of what the speaker was saying. To answer this question, Krauss and Glucksberg designed a second experiment in which the listeners were all adults and the speakers were either kindergarteners, first-graders, third-graders, or fifth-graders. Accuracy scores for this version paralleled those in the first experiment, indicating that third- and fifth-grade speakers are better able to convey understandable information to a listener than are kindergarteners and first-graders. Further, Glucksberg, Krauss, and Weisberg (1966) offer some evidence that children can understand descriptions and references that adults make long before they themselves are capable of putting such communications into words.

Appreciation of the need to phrase communications in words that will be understood by the listener is, of course, only one aspect of what is commonly thought of as role-taking ability. As Weinstein (1969) points out, the socialization process is concerned with equipping individuals to participate in a society composed of other individuals. In order to do this, they must develop the interpersonal skills that will enable them to project and maintain desired self-identities when interacting with others and to get others to think, feel, or do what they want them to. This competence is based on three things:

> First, the individual must be able to take the role of the other accurately; he must be able to correctly predict the impact that various lines of action will have on alter's [the other person's] definition of the situation. This is what is meant by empathy if we strip the concept of its affective overtones. Second, the individual must possess a large and varied repertoire of lines of action. Third, the individual must possess the intrapersonal resources to be capable of employing effective tactics in situations where they are appropriate (pp. 757–758).

Partly because there are several diverse skills involved in role-taking, Glucksberg, et al. (1975) conclude that the concept is too general to be used as a guide to research.

Several other lines of research bear on particular aspects of role-taking ability and interpersonal competence. For example, there have been a number of studies of empathy and of the accuracy of inferences that people make about others based on relatively external cues (Jones, 1977). There are situations, of course, in which adults are reasonably accurate in anticipating the responses of others, but under some circumstances they are quite inaccurate. The relevance of the cues from which predictions are to be made and the ego-involvement of the predictor are just two of many variables that have been shown to affect level of accuracy. But even in this relatively circumscribed field of study, there are many unanswered questions about why a person is or is not accurate in such interpersonal predictions (Cronbach, 1955, 1958). Similarly, Flavell (1968) and his associates have attempted to classify role-taking behaviors and determine how they relate to the inferences children make about others. But, as Weinstein (1969) points out, even though there has been a fair amount of research on the relation of role-taking ability to inferences, relatively little is known about its causes and course of development. Much remains to be learned.

Of particular interest here is the possibility that our attempts to anticipate the reactions of others have a constraining effect on those reactions. That is, by responding to others as if we expected them to do certain things, we may increase the likelihood that they will respond as expected. At least, we will have made it somewhat more difficult for them to respond otherwise. Further, consider the person whose responses are anticipated. If many others appear to hold similar expectations for that person's behavior, then sooner or later the person may be forced to incorporate these expectations into his or her self-conception. The process is circular, of course. When particular people or categories of people are expected to respond in certain ways, they often find that interpersonal encounters with others run more smoothly if they behave as expected. They do so, and they wind up thinking of themselves as people who do indeed respond in certain ways.

It appears that the ways in which we organize our conceptions of others and the ways in which we conceive of ourselves are susceptible to reconstruction and reorganization. This process does not stop at some point in late childhood, but continues throughout life. Reconstruction and shift in perspective are possible because of language and the fact that most words in the lexicon of a language are composed of bundles or clusters of meanings. That is, they share certain aspects of their definitions with other related words. Both a horse and a mule, for example, are four-legged mammals, but each has additional properties that the other does not share. Let us examine this aspect of language a little more closely, because it is crucial to effective communication.

Language

One of the things that never ceases to confuse and confound is that words often seem to mean different things to different people. This is true even when there is clear agreement about the referent of a particular word—the thing to which the word "points." Two people may easily and always agree about whether certain four-legged mammals are dogs, but the word *dog* may still mean quite different things to each. Each may associate a different set of additional attributes to the word, or each may call to mind unique past experiences with members of the class of things labeled "dogs." In short, the connotative meaning of any word may vary from individual to individual.

As an example, consider the word *work*. To the typical middle-class or upper-middle-class American, work is often considered an end in itself. One works because it is interesting, fulfilling, and challenging and gives one a feeling of accomplishment. Lawyers, doctors, business executives, teachers, craftspeople—all are identified by their work and find a sense of self-worth in working. Hence, it is difficult for such people to understand or sympathize with those who disdain work and evade it at every opportunity. But, as Weller (1966) points out, for the rural poor in Appalachia, the word *work* has an entirely different meaning.

> For the mountaineer, work has never been particularly enjoyable. It was a necessity. He did not plan to enter a particular kind of occupation because he liked it—he worked at whatever there was to do because he had to make a living. The concept of choosing a vocation, becoming trained in that field, and traveling wherever it called him was—and is—largely foreign. . . . One works to live and for no other reason. Work means hard physical labor . . . in timber, coal mines, and hillside fields . . . The Protestant ethic of "work hard, save, get ahead" or the idea of work as a vocation . . . are foreign to the mountaineer's understanding. His experience does not confirm them (pp. 102–105).

Thus there is more to the meaning of a word than the thing it signifies. One must examine what Whorf (1956) referred to as the "connected ideas."

The technique of FREE ASSOCIATION, which Freud (1924) instituted as part of psychoanalysis, was in fact based on the notion that in order to discover the real meaning of a particular object, event, or memory, one must explore the associated thoughts and ideas called to mind by the event, or word, or object in question. Hence, patients in psychoanalysis were often asked to name the first thing that came to mind in response to particular words or concepts. Freud believed that this technique of free association formed the first bridge between experimental psychology and psychoanalysis in that it provided a way of exploring the structure of an individual's cognitions, a topic of great interest to both fields. As a practicing psychoanalyst, however, Freud was not much interested in quantifying the network of associations, the "meanings," he might obtain from a given patient.

In the early 1950s, however, Osgood and his associates began a program of research specifically addressed to the question of whether such a nebulous thing as meaning could indeed be measured. The measuring device they devised is surprisingly simple and has proved useful in literally hundreds of studies. Subjects are simply asked to rate a concept of interest—such as *me, mother, father, the future, blacks, work*—on a series of bipolar scales like those shown in Figure 2. The connotative meaning of a concept is its profile of ratings on the scales. As Osgood, et al. (1957) point out:

> Given stability of learning experiences within a particular culture . . . meanings of most common verbal signs will be highly similar (e.g., the adjective *sweet* will be heard and used in much the same types of total situations regardless of the individual in our culture). On the other hand, the meanings of many signs will reflect the idiosyncrasies of individual experiences, as, for example, the meanings of *father, mother,* and *me* for individuals growing up in "healthy" versus "unhealthy" home environments (p. 9).

Using factor-analytic techniques to condense the ratings made by hundreds of subject samples for thousands of concepts on tens of thousands of rating scales, Osgood and his associates have repeatedly found that three properties account for a great deal of variation in connotative meaning: evaluation, potency, and activity. EVALUATION is defined by contrasts such as good–bad, clean–dirty, and valuable–worthless. POTENCY is defined by such contrasts as strong–weak, heavy–light, and large–small. ACTIVITY is defined by scales such as active–passive, fast–slow, and hot–cold. These three factors do not, of course, exhaust the connotative meaning of a particular concept for a given individual. Individuals can, and often do, structure their cognitions in idiosyncratic ways. But these three factors appear to be widely shared dimensions of connotative meaning, not only within our culture, but cross-culturally as well (Cole and Scribner, 1974).

By asking individuals or groups of individuals to rate concepts on a set of semantic differential scales, we can determine the extent to which the connotative

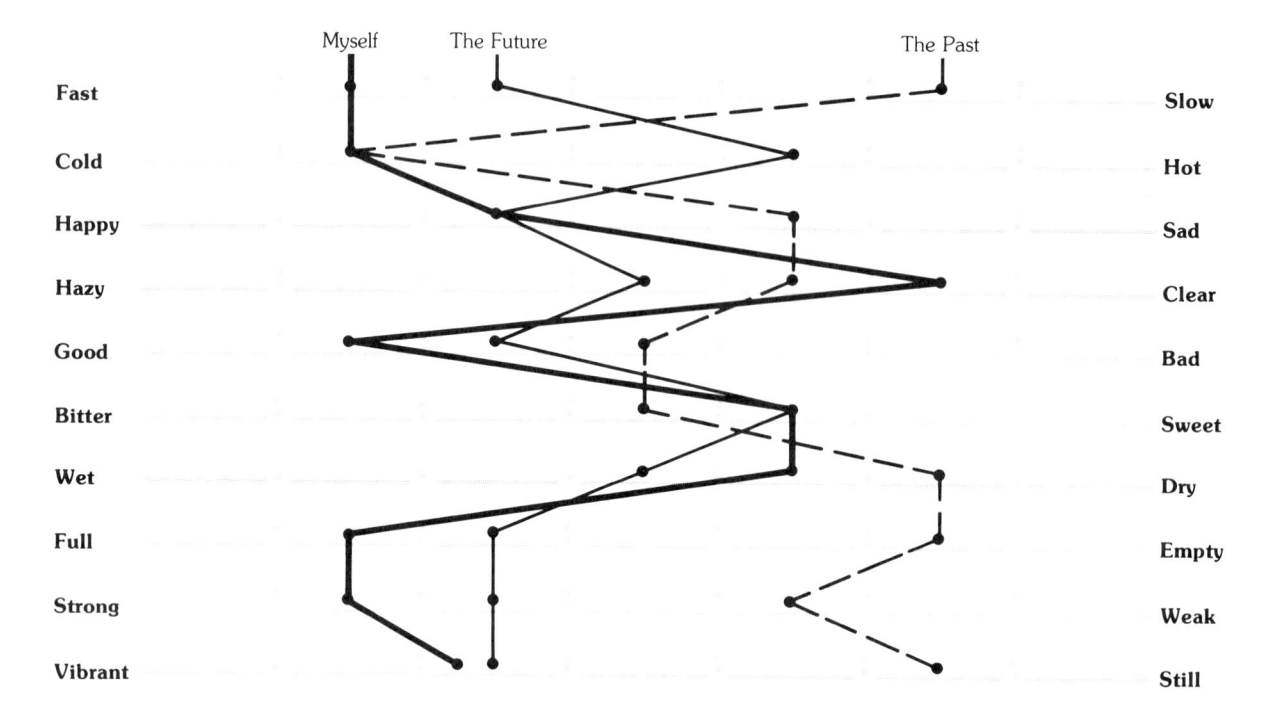

[Figure showing semantic differential profiles for Myself, The Future, and The Past on ten scales: Fast-Slow, Cold-Hot, Happy-Sad, Hazy-Clear, Good-Bad, Bitter-Sweet, Wet-Dry, Full-Empty, Strong-Weak, Vibrant-Still.]

2. Hypothetical ratings of three concepts on ten semantic differential scales. On separate questionnaires, ratings are made for *myself, the future,* and *the past* on all ten criteria. For comparison, the ratings for the three concepts are graphed on a single questionnaire. The graph for a concept is called its profile, and the profile is interpreted as the the meaning of the concept to the subject. Similarity of meaning between two concepts is defined as the degree of closeness and similarity in form of two profiles to each other. In this example, *myself* is more similar in form and closeness to *the future* than to *the past.* Therefore, *myself* and *the future* share a more common meaning than either concept shares with *the past.* (From Osgood, Suci, and Tannenbaum, 1957, p. 91.)

meanings of the concepts differ for the individuals or groups. For example, prior to the presidential elections in 1952, Osgood, et al. (1957) asked 30 Stevenson supporters and 36 Eisenhower supporters to rate a number of concepts on a 10-scale semantic differential defined by the adjective pairs wise-foolish, dirty-clean, fair-unfair, safe-dangerous, strong-weak, deep-shallow, active-passive, cool-warm, relaxed-tense, and idealistic-realistic. The concepts to be rated included *Stevenson, Eisenhower, Truman, MacArthur, socialism, McCarthy, atom bomb,* and the *United Nations.* The results are shown in Table II. Each group of voters saw its own candidate, but not his opponent, as being good, strong, and active. Further, although there are some similarities ("United Nations"), by and large the connotative meanings of the eight concepts were different for the two groups. The concept *Harry S. Truman,* for example, is clearly different for the two groups, even though they would no doubt have agreed unanimously on what Harry S. Truman looked like and could have pointed to him had there been occasion to do so. Agreement on the referent of a word does not guarantee agreement on its connotative meaning.

CONNOTATIVE MEANING, the semantic network of associations that we have to particular objects, events, and words, is very important in our day-to-day life (see Box A). As we shall see in Chapter 7, the belief system and stereotypes that we carry around in our heads can be conceptualized as extensions of the semantic associations that give rise to connotative meaning. For now, let us look at some of the ways in which the connotative meanings of words and some related concepts can enhance communication or make it more difficult.

Communication

We have all had the experience of failing to communicate, of saying something and being met with a blank, uncomprehending look from the person to whom we are talking. Our first impulse is usually to repeat what we just said, only a little louder—as if the problem were simply that our well-formulated and precise communication was obscured, somehow, by nearby noise. When an increased volume also fails to get our message through, we may resort to question-begging phrases ("You know!") and various gestures. If the intended receiver of our message still has knitted brows and a genuinely questioning look, we may try mentally searching through our linguistic repertoire for ways of paraphrasing what we said. Another version of such failures to communicate is miscommunication. That is, we may say something to someone and later find out that the listener completely misinterpreted what we were saying, although at the time he or she (and we) thought they understood us perfectly.

THE SOCIAL NATURE OF COMMUNICATION

Such mundane breakdowns in communication reveal that the conception of language as a code, in which the symbols bear a one-to-one relationship with the things they stand for (referents), is inadequate to explain communication. Of course, language is essential to human communication as we know it, but there is more. The use of language is usually embedded in a social context of some sort in which the reciprocal perceptions of speaker and listener, the physical and linguistic contexts, the individual goals of participants, and their linguistic repertoires are all important variables in determining what will be said and what will be communicated. Figure 3 depicts the interrelationships of some of the perceptual, intellectual, motivational, and interpersonal variables involved.

Vocalization is not essential for referential communication (see Box B), nor is referential meaning the same as denotative meaning. The DENOTATIVE MEANING of a word or phrase refers to a category of objects or events that are examples of the idea or concept expressed in the word. Pipe wrenches, crescent wrenches, box-end wrenches, and Allen wrenches are all denoted by the word *wrench*. However, asking someone to bring you a wrench from the toolbox when all these types are in the box would probably not get you the type of

Table II Mean semantic differential ratings made by Eisenhower and Stevenson supporters in 1952

	Ratings made by Eisenhower Supporters			Ratings Made by Stevenson Supporters		
Concept	Evaluation	Potency	Activity	Evaluation	Potency	Activity
Stevenson	.95	.68	1.22	2.27	2.22	2.24
Eisenhower	2.05	2.17	2.13	1.16	1.41	2.02
Truman	−1.14	−1.22	.80	.95	.75	1.93
MacArthur	1.23	1.40	1.53	.56	1.56	1.50
Socialism	−1.16	−.86	.62	−.40	−.39	.97
McCarthy	−.59	.42	1.70	−1.47	.07	2.04
Atom bomb	.34	.87	1.24	−.26	1.46	1.47
United Nations	1.35	.11	.69	1.43	.17	1.16

Ratings range from −3 to +3. (From Osgood, Suci, and Tannenbaum, 1957, Table 12, p. 109.)

A. Newspeak

In George Orwell's frightening portrait of a totalitarian society, *1984,* the task that the Party in power had set for itself was the complete control of consciousness. This was to be accomplished in part by a continual rewriting of history (so that no evidence of anything contrary to the Party's current doctrine would exist) and absolute power over all sources of information available to the public, such as newspapers, books, television, and radio. The primary method by which consciousness control was to be achieved, however, was the construction of a new language, Newspeak. As for the purpose of Newspeak,

> It was intended that when Newspeak had been adopted once and for all and Oldspeak forgotten, a heretical thought—that is, a thought diverging from the principles of Ingsoc—should be literally unthinkable, at least so far as thought is dependent on words. Its vocabulary was so constructed as to give exact and often very subtle expression to every meaning that a Party member could properly wish to express, while excluding all other meanings and also the possibility of arriving at them by indirect methods (p. 246).

Newspeak was designed, then, not to extend but to diminish the range of thought. For example, the names of all organizations, countries, institutions, and doctrines were cut down into a compound, easily pronounced, single word. Thus "English Socialism" became "Ingsoc." The idea was that abbreviating names in this way narrowed their meaning and excluded old associations. A similar technique was to simply do away with shades of meaning by throwing out many words that referred to variations on a theme and retaining only one word for the core meaning. Thus, *magnificent, excellent, splendid* and the like were cast out of the dictionary. The whole range of goodness and badness was covered by compounds of *good: doubleplusgood, plusgood, good, ungood, plusungood, doubleplusungood.* By these and other techniques for purging words of ambiguities and secondary meanings, the range of consciousness was to be gradually restricted and made more amenable to control.

> A person growing up with Newspeak as his sole language would no more know that *equal* had once had the secondary meaning of "politically equal," or that *free* had once meant "intellectually free," than, for instance, a person who had never heard of chess would be aware of the secondary meanings attached to *queen* and *rook.* There would be many crimes and errors which it would be beyond his power to commit, simply because they were nameless and therefore unimaginable (p. 246).

---

wrench you want. As Glucksberg, Krauss, and Higgins (1975) point out, the REFERENTIAL MEANING of a word or phrase is always in relation to a particular context, which includes nonreferents—objects, events, or relationships that the speaker wishes to distinguish from the referent. In referential communication, a speaker formulates a message and conveys it to a listener in the hope that the message contains sufficient information for the listener to distinguish the intended referent from the other objects, events, and/or relationships (nonreferents) with which it might be confused. Thus, to get the wrench you want, it might be better to request "the big wrench with the red handle that has a number 6 on it."

Of course, if the particular wrench that we wanted were the only one in the toolbox, nestled among screwdrivers, nuts, bolts, wires, pliers, and hammers, then "bring me the wrench" would suffice to differentiate the item to which we referred. The key to referential communication, then, is effectively differentiating

B. Communicating with a Chimpanzee

Although there have been several systematic attempts, efforts to teach chimpanzees to imitate human speech sounds have generally not been very successful. This is apparently because the vocal apparatus of the chimpanzee is quite different from that of humans and because chimpanzees engage in relatively little spontaneous vocalization, except when aroused. On the other hand, chimpanzees are quite dexterous. This, coupled with the fact that chimps are generally recognized as an intelligent species capable of learning a wide variety of behaviors, prompted psychologists Allen and Beatrice Gardner at the University of Nevada at Reno to "adopt" an infant female chimpanzee and attempt to teach her sign language.

Washoe was obtained quite young and put in an environment of human companions, all of whom had mastered American Sign Language (ASL) and used it *exclusively* in Washoe's presence. ASL is similar to pictograph writing in that some symbols are representational and others quite arbitrary. A variety of techniques were employed in teaching ASL to Washoe, from using procedures analogous to classical conditioning to holding the chimp's hands and forming the appropriate signs in a given context. In addition, Washoe showed both spontaneous immediate imitation and delayed imitation of things she had seen or experienced. As Gardner and Gardner (1969, 1978) point out:

> At the outset we were quite sure that Washoe could learn to make various signs in order to obtain food, drink, and other things. For the project to be a success, we felt that something more must be developed. We wanted Washoe not only to ask for objects but to answer questions about them and also to ask us questions. We worked to develop behavior that could be described as conversation (pp. 664–672).

Within 22 months of the beginning of the project, it was clear that it was a success. Washoe had acquired a variety of signs that were used reliably and in the appropriate context. A few of these are listed here.

Sign	Description	Context
Hear–listen	Index finger touches ear.	For loud or strange sounds: bells, car horns. Also for asking someone to hold a watch to her ear.
Open	Flat hands are placed side by side palms down, then drawn apart while rotating to palms up.	At door of house, room, refrigerator; on containers such as jars.
Clothes	Fingertips brush down the chest.	For Washoe's jacket, nightgown, and shirts.
Hat	Palm pats top of head.	For hats and caps.

At the time of the Gardners' report in 1969, Washoe's acquisition of signs was continuing to accelerate. It does indeed appear that sign language is "an appropriate medium of two-way communication for the chimpanzee."

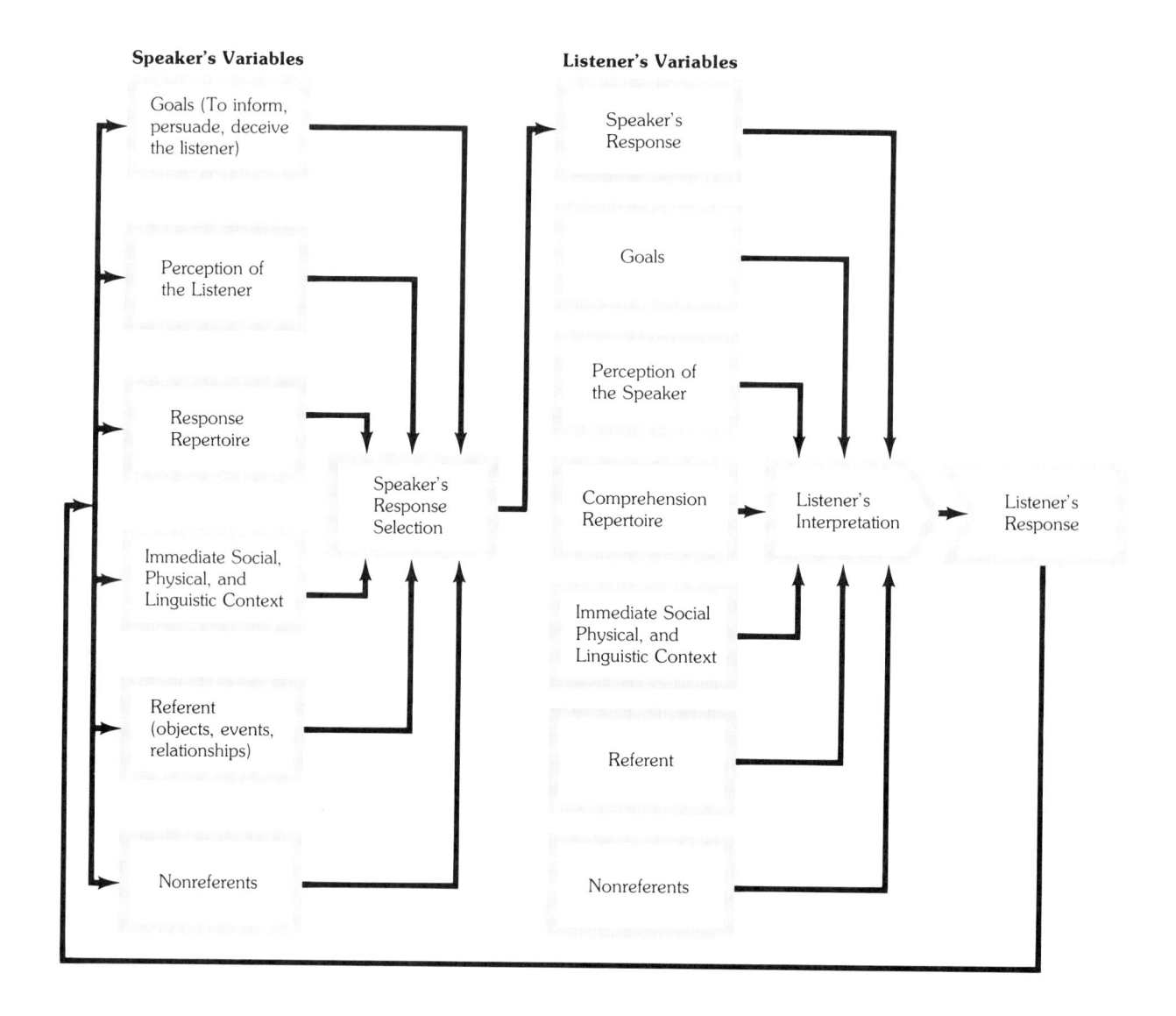

3. Many things determine whether or not what a speaker intends to communicate to a listener actually is communicated. The diagram illustrates some of the variables that may make a difference in the clarity with which the message is conveyed. (From Rosenberg and Cohen, 1967, Figure 1, p. 57.)

the referent from nonreferents. If our wrench were the only one in the toolbox, "the big red wrench with a number 6 on the handle" would still distinguish it from the other assorted tools, but such a phrase would be unnecessary and inefficient. "The wrench" would do.

Questions such as "Is that clear?" and even pauses during which the speaker raises his or her eyebrows and gazes toward the listener are requests for feedback, and feedback that the message is getting through can have dramatic effects on a speaker. To examine the effects of feedback on message length, Krauss and Weinheimer (1966) devised a task consisting of a number of trials. On each trial, a speaker was to encode messages about novel geometric figures, and a listener had to determine which of several figures was being described. Krauss and Weinheimer hypothesized that CONFIRMATION (feedback in the form of information that the listener's subsequent behavior was in line with the speaker's intention) would result in a decrease in the length of subsequent messages addressed to the listener.

They also reasoned that CONCURRENT FEEDBACK (free discussion between speaker and listener while the figure was being described) would result in a greater decrease in subsequent message length than a situation in which such discussion was not allowed. Over a series of 15 trials, message length decreased more when concurrent feedback was allowed and when speakers received confirmation that their message had had the intended affect. Furthermore, 100-percent confirmation led to a greater decrease in message length than 50-percent confirmation, or confirmation on only half the trials (see Figure 4). As Krauss and Weinheimer point out, ". . . these results support the notion that concurrent feedback and confirmation serve as two separate sources of information which affect a speaker's encoding in communication" (p. 346).

Another interesting thing about referential communication is that the particular words a speaker chooses to distinguish the referent from the nonreferents can tell us a great deal more than which object or event is the referent and which the nonreferent. Since language is not a code in which the symbols bear a one-to-one correspondence with the real world, there is a great deal of latitude within which a speaker may pick and choose how he or she wishes to describe a particular referent. Listeners know that this latitude exists, so a speaker's choice of words may itself convey information in addition to that required to distinguish referents from nonreferents.

SPEAK THAT I MAY KNOW THEE: THE MANY FORMS OF COMMUNICATION

One kind of information to which listeners are quite

4. Knowing that a communication has been understood (confirmation) and being able to carry on a free discussion with one's listener (concurrent feedback) result in messages becoming more concise over trials. (From Krauss and Weinheimer, 1966, Figure 2, p. 345.)

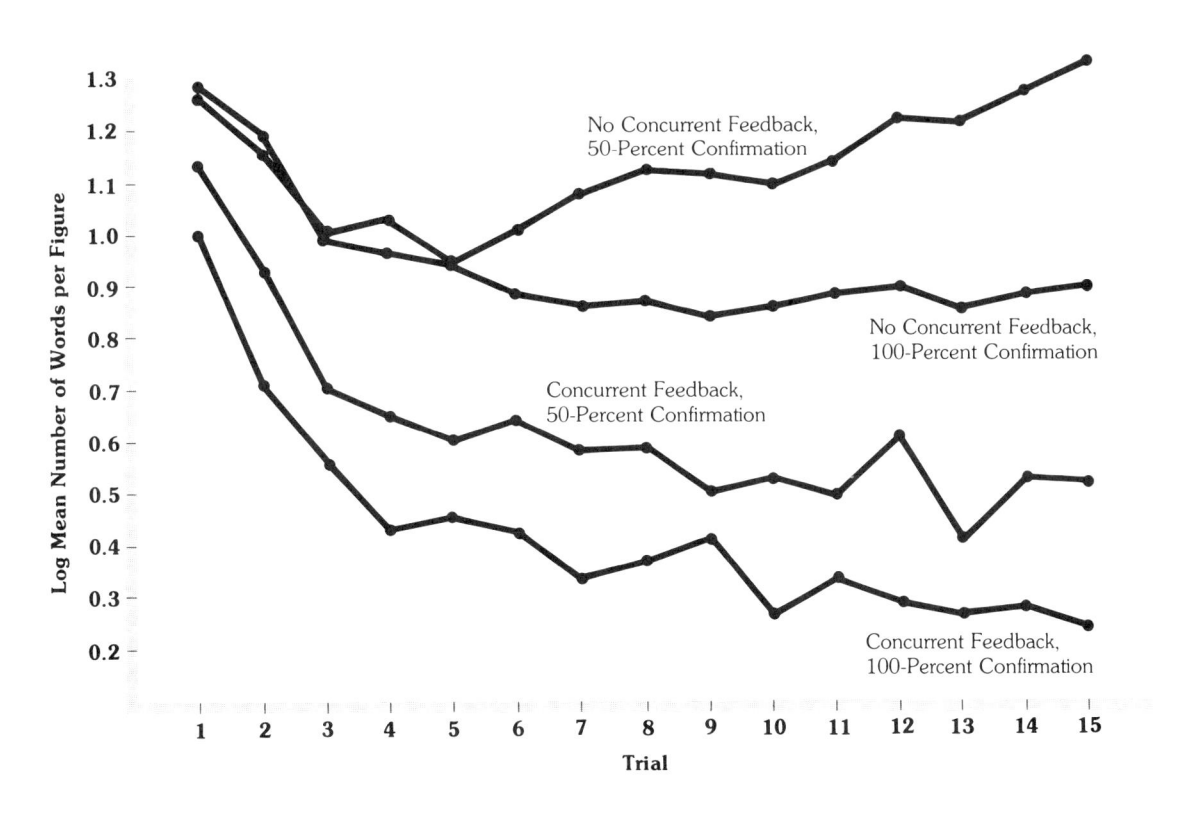

sensitive is information about the affective state of the speaker. Weiner and Mehrabian (1968) have introduced a concept they call "immediacy" and argue that immediacy is an aspect or channel of verbal communication that carries important information about the speaker's affective state. Non-immediacy is defined as "any variations in word usage which indicate differences in the degrees of separation or non-identity among the communicator, the addressee, the object of communication or the communication itself" (p. 31). Consider the following examples, which are arranged roughly on a continuum of immediacy–non-immediacy:

> We
> He and I
> John and I
> Mr. Smith and I
> Mr. John Smith and I
> That person with whom I

Given the appropriate circumstances, each of these expressions would clearly differentiate referents from nonreferents. However, the stilted "That person with whom I" suggests a psychological distance between the speaker and "that person," while the intimate "We" does not. Non-immediacy, or separation of the speaker from the person or object referred to, can be indicated by other linguistic components, such as verb tense, the order in which objects are introduced in a communication, the frequency with which reference is made to certain persons or objects, and various other linguistic devices.

Weiner and Mehrabian (1968) review several studies in which subjects were asked to write descriptions of others whom they either liked or disliked. Using a content-analysis scheme based on their conception of immediacy, Weiner and Mehrabian were able to demonstrate that when subjects dislike the person being described, they use more non-immediate verbalization. This is different from referring to the person being described in negative terms, attributing more negative characteristics, or even saying such things as "I dislike him." One can convey negative attitudes toward another while *saying* positive things! Weiner and Mehrabian review several additional studies indicating that not only do speakers use different vocal patterns when discussing liked and disliked others, but listeners can reliably (though not perfectly) interpret these vocal behaviors.

In addition to verbalizations expressing the affective state of the speaker, listeners are particularly sensitive to word choices by the speaker that express the nature of the relationship between speaker and listener. Several languages, such as French, German and Spanish, often give the speaker an explicit choice of singular pronouns of address with which to refer to his or her listener. The primary difference between these pairs is that one pronoun signifies an intimate, close, familiar relationship and the other a formal, distant, and respectful relationship. Brown and Gilman (1960) suggest that usage of familiar versus polite pronouns may have begun in the Roman empire during the fourth century when the Latin plural *vos* began being used to address the emperor. At that time, there were actually two emperors—one of the Eastern and one of the Western Empire—and speech to one was, by implication, addressed to both. By a process of generalization, the plural pronoun came to be used to address other (singular) power figures; it expressed respect for and deference to the individual addressed. The emperor, of course, and other personages of power continued to address their inferiors with the singular Latin *tu*.* Brown and Gilman term this differential usage the POWER SEMANTIC and note that

> Power is a relationship between at least two persons, and it is nonreciprocal in the sense that both cannot have power in the same area of behavior. The power semantic is similarly nonreciprocal; the superior says T and receives V (p. 255).

Everyone is familiar with nonreciprocal forms of address, even though in English few people use the singular familiar *thou* anymore, and *you* serves as both singular and plural. Even so, we address those who have power over us with, for example, titles or titles plus last names, and we allow them to address us by our first names. On the other hand, we address those we perceive to be our social equals in the same manner in which they address us. But what will it be? Do we use reciprocally familiar forms of address or reciprocally polite, formal modes? As with most interesting

---

*Following Brown and Gilman, we shall use T and V (from the Latin *tu* and *vos*) to stand for familiar (T) and polite (V) pronouns.

questions, the answer is "it depends," and Brown and Gilman argue that what it depends on is the perception of solidarity—that is, similarities between the people in question that make for "like-mindedness or similar behavior dispositions." The more solidary two people are, the more likely they will address each other with the familiar (T) forms of address, while less solidary people are more likely to use polite (V) forms. We might refer to this principle as the SOLIDARITY SEMANTIC.

Brown and Gilman (1960) note that the power semantic has prevailed and nonreciprocal forms of address have been the norm throughout much of history, not only between emperors and slaves and officers and soldiers, but even between parents and children. In the last few hundred years, however, there has been a shift. Static feudal societies and monarchies have given way to democracy, socialism, and communism, all of which are based on an ethic of equality. Nonreciprocal forms of address have consequently become less common. Employers and employees address each other as "Mr. _____" or "Ms. _____"; officers and soldiers use a reciprocal "Rank plus last name"; parents and children use reciprocal familiar modes of address. But the power semantic is still around. We all recognize differences in ability, prestige, and importance. We defer to those we respect and address them in a polite, formal manner. Employers are still more likely to receive "Title plus last name" than are employees. Officers are still more likely to use only a soldier's last name without prefixing rank than vice versa.

There is a conflict between the power semantic and the solidarity semantic. Brown and Gilman felt that the extent to which one refused to employ the power semantic (the extent to which one insisted on addressing everyone in the familiar mode) might reflect more than just a peculiarity of speech. It might reflect a general ideological orientation toward "*liberté, égalité, fraternité.*" That is, a person who in French used the familiar *tu* with everyone, an American who called everyone by his or her first name, and a Russian who addressed everyone as *Comrade* might be expected to be somewhat more liberal politically than their counterparts whose speech reflected the power semantic and who used the polite, formal mode of address to employers, teachers, and other power figures.

To check on this possibility, Brown and Gilman administered two questionnaires to a group of French students. On one, the students were asked about the pronouns they used to address various categories of people: parents, teachers, peers, government officials, waiters, and so on. The second questionnaire was an inventory of attitudes about religion, sex, economics, politics, and associated matters (Eysenck, 1957). From answers to the first questionnaire, an index was derived that reflected the degree to which the students used the familiar mode of address. In general, the more diverse the situations in which the student said he would use familiar modes of address, the greater the expression of liberal ideology on the second questionnaire. Brown and Gilman (1960) note that

> There is enough consistency of address to justify speaking of a personal-pronoun style which involves a more or less wide use of the solidary T. Even among students of the same socioeconomic level there are differences of style, and these are potentially expressive of radicalism and conservatism in ideology. A Frenchman could, with some confidence, infer that a male university student who regularly said T to female fellow students would favor the nationalization of industry, free love, trial marriage, the abolition of capital punishment, and the weakening of nationalistic and religious loyalties (p. 272).

These consistent personal differences in mode of address do not, of course, give the listener a complete picture of the speaker's unique personality. They do, however, convey a great deal of information about the speaker's probable attitudes and opinions.

Labov (1970) defines a sociolinguistic variable as a variation in speech that is correlated with some nonlinguistic aspect of the social context. The use of familiar versus polite modes of address is thus a sociolinguistic variable, but there are literally hundreds of others. Some of the most common are differences in pronunciation of words and letter combinations as a function of the social class and/or geographic origin of the speaker. In addition to these regional and social-class dialects, there are variations in pronunciation within social classes as a function of the situation: some things are pronounced differently in informal conversation from the way they are pronounced in reading aloud.

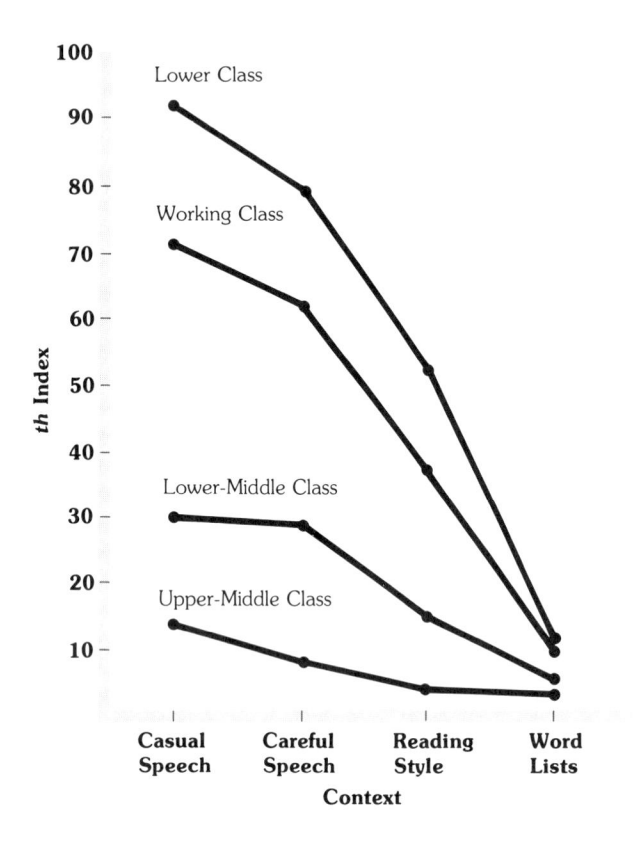

5. Both social class and the situation in which speech is called for affect pronunciation among these New York City residents. The *th* index reflects "correctness" of the pronunciation of *th*: the higher the *th* index, the "poorer," "less correct" the pronunciation. (From Labov, 1970, Figure 2, p. 67.)

Consider the letters *th* as they appear in words like *thing, three,* and *third.* Labov (1970) points out that there are at least three systematic variations in the pronunciation of this combination: (1) the fricative, in which the breath is quickly forced through a narrow opening between the teeth and the lips, (2) the affricative, in which the breath is more slowly released, and (3) the stop, in which the outgoing breath is completely stopped. The fricative is usually considered the "correct," or at least the most prestigious, pronunciation and the stop the least prestigious. Labov recorded speech samples in four different situations from lower-class, working-class, lower-middle-class, and upper-middle-class respondents in New York City and scored the samples on the pronunciation of *th*. A score of 0 was given for each fricative, a 1 for each affricative, and a 2 for each stop. Thus the higher the score, the "poorer" the pronunciation. The results appear in Figure 5. As the figure shows, there are both social-class and situational variations in pronunciation. The pronunciation of the upper-middle-class subjects was relatively consistent and "correct," regardless of whether they were engaging in casual conversation, reading, or pronouncing words from a list. The casual conversation of lower-class subjects was very poor on this index. When asked to pronounce words from a list, however, these subjects pronounced the words very much like the upper-middle-class subjects.

Not just what we say, but also how we say it conveys information to a listener. We communicate more than we intend to, and since language is subject to normative expectations just like other facets of a culture pronunciation that differs from the "approved" often serves as the basis for a negative evaluation of the speaker (Lambert, Hodgson, Gardner, and Fillenbaum, 1960). Labov's study also highlights the notion of context. It is clear that, for some groups, dramatic shifts in pronunciation occurred as a function of context. There is another, more important, way in which context makes a difference in communication. We use the context of a communication (often without being aware of doing so) to help us make sense of and interpret the communication.

CONTEXT AND EMBEDDEDNESS

The behavior of an individual engaged in social interaction cannot be interpreted except as part of a system, which is in part composed of the behavior of the other person or persons with whom the individual is interacting (see Box C). Communication is an active achievement by the listener as well as by the speaker. As Giglioli (1972) puts it, "Social reality is not a 'fact,' but an ongoing accomplishment, the often precarious result of the routine activities and tacit understandings of social actors" (p. 13). For example, consider the process by which we recognize another person. Berne (1961) argues that almost everything we do when we enter the presence of another person is of communicative significance, and he points out in particular that what we usually communicate is how we see the other person vis-á-vis ourselves.

Similarly, Ervin-Tripp (1969) notes that there are certain widely understood rules in our culture for how we should address people in different circumstances. When one of the parties to an interaction wants to define the other and the situation in a certain way, he or she can do it, in part, by the form of address. Consider a young, well-dressed, professional woman carrying an attaché case along a street in a business district. The accepted manner for a stranger to address her might be something like "Excuse me, Ms., I . . ." Other forms of address, particularly those beginning with exclamations or a reference to her physical attractiveness, would probably be viewed as attempts to redefine her from a professional woman into a sexual object. By

C. "Punctuation"

Watzlawick, Beavin, and Jackson (1967) use of term *punctuation* to refer to the manner in which an individual organizes his or her perceptions of the sequence of events in an interaction. They point out that disagreement about how to punctuate a given sequence of events is the source of many problems of communication. Consider the following example.

> Suppose a couple have a marital problem to which he contributes passive withdrawal, while her 50 per cent is nagging criticism. In explaining their frustrations, the husband will state that withdrawal is his only defense *against* her nagging, while she will label this explanation a gross and willful distortion of what "really" happens in their marriage: namely, that she is critical of him because of his passivity. . . . Represented graphically, with an arbitrary beginning point, their interaction looks somewhat like this:

> It can be seen that the husband only perceives triads 2-3-4, 4-5-6, 6-7-8 . . . where his behavior (heavy arrows) is "merely" a response to her behavior (thinner arrows). With her it is exactly the other way around; she punctuates the sequence of events into the triads 1-2-3, 3-4-5, 5-6-7 . . . and sees herself as only reacting to, but not determining, her husband's behavior (pp. 56–57).

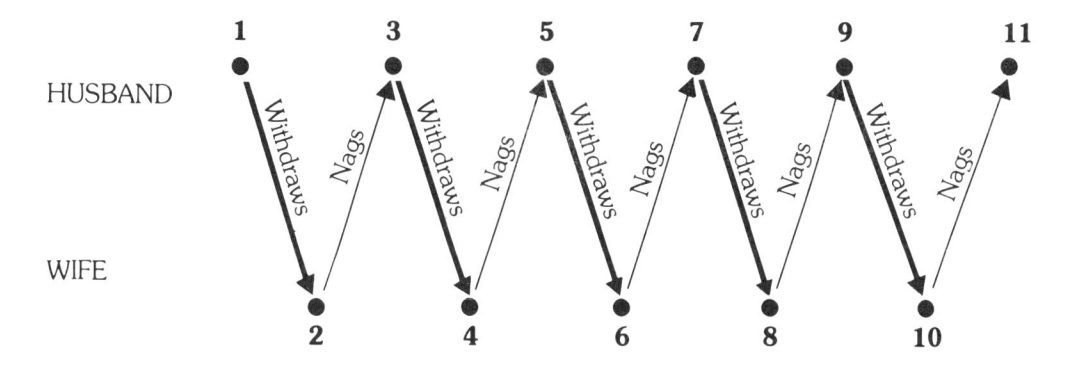

Such punctuation of a sequence of communicative acts serves to help the individual make sense out of what is going on and helps organize the ongoing interaction. However, the different participants in an interaction may punctuate the sequence differently and end up with totally different views of what has occurred in the interaction—even though they both observe precisely the same behaviors.

her style of dress and her attaché case, she projects a certain image of herself and a certain definition of the situation. By addressing her appropriately, the stranger signifies understanding of that image and situation.

As Watzlawick, et al. (1967) point out, a person may offer others a definition of self in many possible ways, but regardless of how it is done, what he or she is trying to communicate is "This is how I see myself." Others, of course, may or may not accept the projected image, as this passage from the memoirs of a black physician illustrates (Poussaint, 1967, p. 53. Quoted in Ervin-Tripp, 1969, pp. 97-98):

> "What's your name, boy?" the policeman asked.
> "Dr. Poussaint, I'm a physician."
> "What's your first name, boy?"

There was no problem of communication in this interchange. Both parties were acutely aware of what was going on. "Both were familiar with an address system which contained a selector for race available to both Black and White for insult, condescension, or deference, as needed. Only because they shared these norms could the policeman's act have its unequivocal impact" (Ervin-Tripp, 1969, p. 98).

For the most part, however, the self-images and situational definitions that people project are accepted, even if only temporarily and even if they are not believed in by others. The hesitancy that people apparently experience about calling what may appear to them to be a bluff—that is, a projected image of self or situation on the part of another that is unwarranted—stems from at least two sources. First, it seems safe to assume that most people prefer to avoid unnecessary interpersonal conflict and to make interaction with others run its course smoothly. Hence, we usually say nothing when someone presents a slightly exaggerated view of their own virtues, pretends to unattained accomplishments, or drops a few well-chosen names. Second, and perhaps more important in everyday interaction, it is often quite difficult to tell whether the situational and self-definitions projected by others are appropriate. We frequently have no clear contradictory evidence. Under such circumstances, the most reasonable course of action is to accept others at face value. We assume that they are what they appear to be and treat them accordingly.

The important point for our purposes is that people who communicate a given situational and/or self-definition have, in effect, delineated both what can be expected from them in the situation and what they expect from those with whom they are interacting. Thus impressions and situations are "managed" for a purpose, and the techniques people employ in their attempts at impression management are simply techniques for communicating expectations about how they are to be treated and how they intend to treat others. The extent to which attempts at impression management are conscious can vary from those features of personal style and habit so routine that we are no longer aware of them to overt, active attempts to present oneself in a particular light.

Gibbins (1969), for example, presents evidence that the messages conveyed by particular types of women's clothing are clearly perceived and that, within a given social group, consensus exists about the characteristics of women who wear particular items of apparel. Presumably the clothes that a person wears become a part of his or her daily routine, and the messages conveyed by one's manner of dress may indeed have slipped from awareness. On the other hand, there is the possibility that failure to attempt to convey anything by one's manner of dress in itself conveys something. Watzlawick, et al. (1967) argue that all behavior has communicational significance, and, since behavior has no opposite, it is impossible not to communicate. It is possible, of course, to attempt to miscommunicate. Such miscommunication may take several forms, including the sort of overt, conscious manipulation attempted by Sylvia Plath (1971) during an encounter with one of her psychiatrists:

> I began to feel pleased at my cleverness. I thought I only need to tell him what I wanted to and that I could control the picture he had of me by hiding this and revealing that (pp. 106-107).

Whether conscious or unconscious, impression management can be tricky. As Goffman (1959) notes, one is constantly in danger of letting cues slip that will destroy the projected image.

Another aspect of communication context involves the assumptions that each participant makes about the knowledge, experience, and personal situation of the other participant. Schegloff (1971) notes that in selecting terms to refer to physical locations, for example, a speaker must be sensitive not only to his or her and the listener's present location, but to the listener's knowledge of the place referred to. Giving directions to someone who is familiar with the local terrain is much easier than giving directions to someone who is not. Often, however, we assume that the person to whom we are speaking shares our geographical perspective and/or knowledge, and we may discover that this assumption was unwarranted. Schegloff (1972) gives the following example from a collection of calls to the police department of a midwestern city.

C: Uh, this is Mrs. Lodge calling from 121 Sierra Drive.
D: 121 Sierra.
C: Yes.
D: Ma'am, where's Sierra located?
C: It's on the corner of Sierra and uh-hh Smith Drive.
D: Sierra and Smith.
C: Yes...
D2: Uh, where is this Sierra and Smith located? We gotta know about this.
C: 121 Sierra Drive. It's right on the corner.
D2: Right on the corner of Si-uh of what? Sierra and Smith. Where is Smith?
C: Sierra Drive. Sierra and Smith.
D2: I wanna know where Smith is located.
C: Well, it's uh right off Flint Ridge.
D2: Off Flint Ridge.
C: Yeah.
D2: Where're you at ma'am, are you in the County? You're—you're in [nearby community] (pp. 83–84).

Both the caller and the police assumed a shared geographical perspective, and they were both wrong. The result was a lot of fumbling and repetition before communication begins to take place, in the last line of the quote.

The study of the interpretive procedures and techniques by which we attempt to make sense of the often incomplete and ambiguous messages we receive from others is part of ETHNOMETHODOLOGY (Garfinkel, 1967), the study of the "ethnomethods" by which we interpret our social worlds. We too often take it for granted that others see the world as we do, have similar past experiences, or have similar goals. This is frequently not the case.

To communicate accurately and efficiently, we need to understand what is really a part of us and how we differ from those with whom we wish to communicate. Often, however, we communicate in ways that we do not intend and without even speaking. One of the most interesting areas of social–psychological research in recent years is the investigation of such nonverbal behaviors.

NONVERBAL COMMUNICATION

The term *body language* was popularized by Julius Fast (1970) in a book by that title as an informal way of designating a vast area of research known as nonverbal communication. Body language is similar to verbal language in that it is structured and has communication value. Strictly speaking, NONVERBAL COMMUNICATION includes all aspects of behavior other than the use of words. It is convenient, however, to divide nonverbal communication into two general classes. One class is concerned directly with the body and the messages the body mediates. The other class is concerned with the physical possessions belonging to a person, such as clothing, jewelry, briefcases, handbags, and so on. Physical possessions help designate a person's wealth and status and in this way define permissible relationships with other people. One's possessions are often a potent nonverbal communication device.

Body language. With respect to the body as a medium of communication, it is convenient to arbitrarily distinguish between the head region and the rest of the body. The meanings of facial expressions and the issue of whether some facial expressions have universal cross-cultural meanings have received much attention (Ekman, 1973). What has been called "the language of the eyes" has also been studied in considerable detail (Exline, 1972). Other research has concentrated on the voice, particularly nonverbal messages communicated by the tone and intensity of the voice.

Visual interaction will be discussed in the next section. Our concern at the moment is with the rest of the body. The general posture, position, and orientation of the body may provide an observer with rich cues. The body in action also communicates messages. Hand gestures and their many meanings come readily to mind. The movement of the arms and legs when seated and the movement of the body when walking can also be scrutinized for unspoken meanings.

Birdwhistell, an anthropologist, made early and important contributions to the study of bodily movement. His work is summarized in *Kinesics and Context* (1970). The term KINESICS denotes the science of bodily movement that he is trying to develop. Birdwhistell's methodology is comparable to that of a linguist. Much work in linguistics has been devoted to the basic vocal building blocks of speech, called PHONEMES. Approximately 43 phonemes have been isolated so far, and from these basic sounds all the millions of words of spoken languages are constructed. Similarly, Birdwhistell takes a short motion picture of some simple behavior and subjects it to exhaustive analysis.

The purpose is to search for basic movement structures, called KINEMES (analogous to phonemes), from which the rich complexity of ongoing behavior can be constructed. Kinemes have been isolated for the head, face, and body. Birdwhistell believes that a total of between 50 and 60 kinemes will ultimately account for most movement. So far, 32 kinemes have been isolated in the face and head area. For example, there are 4 distinct kinemes for the eyebrow: lifted brows, lowered brows, knit brows, and single brow movement. As another example, there are 4 degrees of eyelid closure: over open, slit, closed, and squeezed. These elementary units have little meaning in isolation. Rather they combine in context with other kinemes to form larger units, kinemorphs, which are combined in turn into still larger units called kinemorphemic classes, and so on until the complex behavior of everyday life is reached.

Isolating kinemes and fitting them into context with other kinemes is demanding work. Most of us are more concerned with interpreting behavior or movement at the level of everyday life, and it may be difficult to see the usefulness of the elementary movement units isolated by Birdwhistell. The value of the general approach can be illustrated by the work of Scheflen (1965) on what he calls "quasi-courtship behavior" in psychotherapy and other interaction situations.

After extended observations, Scheflen was somewhat surprised to find courtship-like elements in most types of interactions: not only between lovers, but also in psychotherapy sessions, business meetings, parties, and so on. Since few of these interactions ended in actual sexual behavior, it seemed reasonable that there also existed qualifying signals that modified the function of the courtship-like behaviors.

According to Scheflen, there are three basic elements of kinesic behavior in the courtship situation: courtship readiness, positioning for courtship, and actions of appeal or invitation. Courtship readiness is indicated by high muscle tonus, erect posture, bright eyes, and variable skin color. Preening behavior, such as stroking the hair, rubbing the body discreetly, or adjusting clothing slightly, may also occur. Positioning for courtship involves a strong attentional orientation between two people. Usually they will face each other directly, lean toward each other, and screen other people out of the field of attention. In this position, the two people may adopt an intimate mode of conversation. Actions of appeal or invitation follow positioning for courtship. Language may become soft and hushed. Other behaviors may include flirtatious glances, extended gazing, cocking the head, and rubbing the hip or thigh. Women may cross the legs to slightly expose the thigh and turn the wrist or palm outward as an invitational gesture. Men may spread their legs apart slightly or hook their thumbs in the belt with fingers pointed toward the crotch region.

In an actual courtship situation, this sequence (along with the proper words at the proper time) often leads to sexual encounters. However, it is surprising that these same courtship elements exist in a great variety of noncourtship situations. Scheflen argues persuasively that we interject behavioral qualifiers that serve to define the situation as quasi-courtship and not the real thing. For example, some verbal or nonverbal reference may be made to the inappropriateness of the present context for courtship. A head movement or glance at a third person (or even a pretended third person) may effectively signal inappropriateness of the courtship elements. Other signals may include incongruent postures. For example, two people may sit facing each other directly but turn their bodies slightly away from each other. Another type of incongruence may involve saying soft, courtship-like words, but lean-

Nonverbal communication helps to define permissible relationships. What nonverbal communications are evident in this interaction? (Antonio Mendoza/The Picture Cube)

ing back away from the other person instead of toward him or her. The list of possibilities seems endless; the key point is that discrepant elements intrude, block the progression toward courtship, and define the situation as merely one of quasi-courtship.

Scheflen (1965) noted that such quasi-courtship behaviors occur quite extensively in psychotherapy and are often consciously used by the therapist as an effective interaction tool. Properly modulated, quasi-courtship is a stimulant to social interaction. It is based on sexuality, but its effect is to increase attractiveness, attentiveness, sociability, and readiness to relate to others. Essentially, the sexual drive is harnessed or sublimated to some optimal state between immediate sexual preoccupation and total sexual inhibition. Freud saw such diffusion of sexuality as the basis for civilization—for cooperativeness, creativity, and social interest. Thus it is perhaps not unexpected that the study of body language, starting basically from a nonsexual perspective, should find sexual overtones in most of our movements and actions. When you think about it, would you really rather have it any other way?

Visual interaction. The glance, the stare, mutual eye contact, and other forms of visual interaction are most important in everyday life. Two distinct themes about eye contact exist in literature. One approach views eye contact as a mechanism of dominance and evil acts. The other approach views eye contact as a means of conveying preference and affection.

There is an ancient myth of the "evil eye." Elworthy (1895) traced the history of the myth, concluding that "the eye was and is certainly considered the chief medium of communicating evil." Eye contact as a means of dominating others also appears frequently. The philosopher Sartre emphasized the threat to freedom in the glance: "Either the other looks at me and alienates my liberty, or I assimilate the liberty of the other" (cited in Exline, 1972, p. 166).

There is some evidence that eye contact can be aversive and act as a stimulus to either flight or fight. Ellsworth, Carlsmith, and Henson (1972) found that automobile drivers and pedestrians who were stared at crossed an intersection faster than control subjects who were not stared at.

The aversiveness of the steady stare may be general across primates, particularly between males. Exline (1972) reported one study in which a male experimenter stood directly in front of the cage of male rhesus monkeys and either stared directly at the eyes of a monkey or first established eye contact and then dropped the gaze deferentially. The monkeys reacted to the fixed stare with threat displays and sometimes charged to the front of the cage as if to attack. No such behavior occurred when the experimenter dropped his gaze. It appears that it really is impolite to stare, and the reason why may be part of our evolutionary heritage.

In humans, prolonged eye contact can also indicate positive regard for another person. Simmel (1924) emphasized the role of mutual glances in establishing meaningful interpersonal relations. Indeed, the prolonged eye contact of young lovers is so commonplace as to require little comment. There is, however, considerable experimental literature demonstrating the importance of eye contact in behaviors as diverse as liking for an interviewer, affiliation, and expectancies for social approval, and as a cue for sending and receiving information (Giesen, 1973). Eye contact is clearly an important component in social interaction.

Summary

We began this chapter by focusing on some of the relationships between language and cognition. Because the words we use to label and categorize reality are composed of interrelated bundles or clusters of meanings, it is possible to classify objects or events in more than one way. We can shift our perspective and categorize and recategorize reality as long as we continue to learn. This process was illustrated with children's developing conceptions of others. Following a gradual differentiation of the qualities of others, each child develops a perceptual framework that is to some extent unique and that he or she imposes on perceptions of others. This does not mean that the child's perceptual framework remains static. Some of the data we cited indicated a shift in the perceptual frameworks of college students as they became integrated into a new subcultural setting.

The phenomenon of connotative meaning is also

linked to the fact that labels for reality are composed of bundles of meaning. Even when people can agree on the referent for a given word, they may disagree on the word's meaning, because each associates different past experiences with the word or referent in question. Osgood and his associates derived a measuring device, the semantic differential, to try to measure connotative meanings. They found that the three properties of evaluation, potency, and activity account for a great deal of the variation in connotative meanings.

Following our discussion of connotative meaning, we turned our attention to communication, taking the view that context is crucial. The speaker must not only take into account the relationships between the referent and nonreferents, but he or she must also make judgments about the listener, the person for whom the communication is intended. Feedback from the listener is very helpful to a speaker, because it affords information about whether the assumptions the speaker made about the listener were warranted. We also discussed several lines of research indicating that the speaker's choice of words, pronunciation, and manner of addressing the listener convey a great deal of information about his or her own affective state, opinion of the listener, social class, and even political ideology. Furthermore, the listener is not a passive recipient of communication. The listener uses the context of a communication in a variety of ways to try to make sense of what the speaker is saying. When the speaker fails to take the listener's perspective into account, the listener must try to assume the speaker's perspective in order to understand what is being said.

III

Cognition of the social world

5

Person perception and attribution

122 Generalizing what we "know" about people

Forming impressions of others
Biases, illusions, and conceits in person perception
Individual differences in social perception

133 Acquiring new information about people

Observing behavior
Attribution processes
Attribution in action: explaining success and failure

141 Understanding ourselves: self-perceptions and attributions

Effects of self-perception on performance
Learning to identify and label our bodily states
Perceiving and explaining our own behavior

148 Summary

In Chapter 4, we examined some of the basic processes involved in our attempts to make sense of the world around us. We saw how we select and categorize what we perceive and how we place constructions on reality to order our experiences and make them meaningful. In this chapter, we continue our exploration of how we go about trying to understand the world we live in, but we focus on one particular aspect of that world—the people who inhabit it.

It will hardly come as a surprise to anyone that people are the most important perceptual "objects" around. They help us, they hurt us, they like us, they hate us. But whatever they do, it is clear that if we want to survive for long, we have to learn how to anticipate their actions and predict what they will do in the future. We do learn; not perfectly, of course, but we learn. In the process of learning how to anticipate what to expect from others, we weigh evidence carefully part of the time and let our prejudices and preconceptions sway us part of the time—just like scientists. The interesting question, of course, has to do with the circumstances under which we let our preconceptions lead (or mislead) us and the circumstances under which we seek out new information on which to base our judgments of others. When we do seek out new information about others, how do we go about it? And once we have a new item of information, how do the circumstances under which it was obtained influence what we infer from it? These are some of the questions we shall explore in this chapter. Let us begin by looking at how we use what we already know, or think we know, when we try to understand another.

Generalizing what we "know" about people

As we saw in our discussion of connotative meaning (see Chapter 4), people develop in the course of their experiences a semantic network of associations to objects, events, and words of all sorts. That is, they develop a set of expectations about what events or objects are likely to be associated or to occur together. It follows that everyone has a set of beliefs about what other people are like. One way to sensitize people to the existence of such beliefs is to pose such a question as "What do you think of a wise, cruel man?" This is a jarring inconsistency for most people, for whom wise men are generally kind, old, and sometimes jaded, but never cruel.

Rosenberg and Jones (1972) point out that there are really two components involved in these expectations about people: (1) the categories that one uses in his or her perceptions of the characteristics of others, and (2) one's beliefs about which of these perceived characteristics tend to go together and which do not. One may, for example, categorize others as intelligent or dumb, pompous or sincere, and arrogant or helpful. One may further believe that intelligent people are also likely to be sincere and that dumb people are likely to be arrogant. In any event, this system of categories and beliefs constitutes the rudiments of an implicit theory of personality (Bruner and Tagiuri, 1954) that each of us carries around in his or her head.

The idea that people have implicit theories that may differ from person to person has been around a long time, although it has appeared under several different aliases. For example, Newcomb (1931) and Guilford (1936, 1954) have described people's tendency to "package" information. They took this as an indication that people do have conceptions about which human characteristics go together. They viewed these conceptions as sources of error in making judgments about people and termed the bias the LOGICAL ERROR in judgments. For instance, if one knows that another is intelligent, it would be logical to assume that he or she reads a lot. Such an assumption or inference could lead to error, however, because there are many intelligent people who do not read much at all. The important point, of course, is that this sort of inference—a generalization based on our past experience with intelligent people—may get us into trouble when we are trying to form an impression of a new acquaintance about whom we know nothing except that he or she is intelligent. Let us look at this more closely.

FORMING IMPRESSIONS OF OTHERS

In 1946, Solomon Asch published a paper on impression formation that has since become a classic. In that paper, Asch took the point of view that, when we form an impression of another person, we do not see that person as simply a bundle of different characteristics. Rather, we interpret each of the person's characteristics in the light of all that we know about him or her; we see the whole and not each part.

To demonstrate this point, Asch prepared two lists of characteristics that were supposedly descriptive of a person and read these lists to two different groups of subjects. The two lists are as follows:

intelligent	intelligent
skillful	skillful
industrious	industrious
warm	cold
determined	determined
practical	practical
cautious	cautious

As can be seen, the two lists differ in only one respect: whether the fourth word in the list is *warm* or *cold*. After hearing the respective lists, both groups of subjects were asked to check, on a form provided, those additional qualities or characteristics that the person described would be likely to have. The resulting differences were dramatic. Subjects for whom *warm* had been included in the list were much more likely to describe the stimulus person as generous, wise, happy, good-natured, humorous, sociable, popular, humane, altruistic, and imaginative. It appears that subjects had clear expectations about what additional characteristics a "warm" person would have. When given no more information about that person than a simple list of traits, they were quite willing to generalize their expectations to this particular person.

Asch's basic result has held up quite well through a series of replications using different subjects and/or less artificial stimulus materials (Mensh and Wishner, 1947; Kelley, 1950). Kelley, for example, told students in classrooms that he was interested in the question of how they perceive and react to various instructors. He then gave students a brief biographical description of a visiting instructor. The information given to all students was the same except that for half of them the visiting instructor was described as *warm,* and for half he was described as *cold.* The instructor then actually appeared and led the class in a 20-minute discussion. After the discussion, the students rated him on a series of scales. Consistent with Asch's result, those subjects given the *warm* preinformation rated the instructor more favorably than those given the *cold* preinformation.

In one of the additional studies reported in the same paper, Asch (1946) demonstrated that manipulation of *polite-blunt,* instead of *warm-cold,* in the stimulus lists read to subjects, made little difference in the impressions formed by subjects. He interpreted this, in conjunction with the large differences obtained by changing *warm-cold* in the lists, as evidence that *polite-blunt* was a peripheral characteristic, whereas the warmth or coldness of a peson was a central characteristic. Presumably, a central characteristic is one the absence of which makes a difference. Hair color would probably not be central for most people, whereas intelligence would be. Asch seemed to be saying that people have no clear conceptions or expectations about characteristics that go with PERIPHERAL TRAITS, whereas they do have definite expectations about characteristics that accompany CENTRAL TRAITS.

One of the interesting things about Asch's initial study was that whether subjects heard the list describing the stimulus person as warm or cold made a difference in most, *but not all,* of their responses. For example, subjects were about equally likely to describe the stimulus person as reliable, important, persistent, serious, strong, and honest regardless of whether he had been described as warm or cold. Asch did not really interpret this lack of difference on some items, but a more recent study by Rosenberg, Nelson, and Vivekananthan (1968) does. In doing so, it clarifies the notion of a central trait.

Rosenberg, et al. (1968) used multidimensional scaling to obtain geometrical representations of the relationships among a set of 64 trait terms, a set that included the words used by Asch to describe the stimulus persons in his experiment. By asking subjects to sort the 64 terms into categories and to let each category be descriptive of a person, Rosenberg and his colleagues were able to obtain indices of perceived psychological distance among the various terms. The assumption is that the more often any two traits were put in the same category, the more closely related they were perceived to be. *Helpful,* for example, was often put in the same category as *sincere,* but rarely was *helpful* put in the same category as *vain.* Thus *helpful* and *sincere* are psychologically closer together than *helpful* and *vain.* Based on such a measure of psychological distance, Rosenberg, et al. were able to represent the interrelationships among the traits geometrically (see Figure 1). They were also able to show that the variations among the traits could be

1. Two dimensional representation of 60 traits showing the best fitting properties of social and intellectual desirability. To interpret the figure, select a trait such as *foolish*, which is near the bad-intellectual extreme. The placement of the trait in the figure means that *foolish* was seen as an intellectually undesirable characteristic. An intelligent person should not be foolish. On the other hand, *foolish* is relatively neutral (only slightly undesirable) as a social characteristic. It is close to the center of the good-social–bad-social axis. (From Rosenberg, et al., 1968, p. 290.)

124
Cognition of the social world

A. My Friend is a Leftover Ham and Corn Casserole?

One of the reasons for using trait adjectives in much of the research on impression formation is that a trait is assumed to summarize a great deal of information about another person. It is, in a sense, an abstraction of the essence of a number of diverse behaviors that the person might exhibit. Instead of describing the person as someone who catches on quickly, works crossword puzzles in ink, always wins at Scrabble, reads constantly, has a 3.9 grade-point average, and is handy around the house, we can simply say that she is an intelligent person. Some research by Miriam Rodin (1972), a clinical-social psychologist at San Diego State University, however, suggests that this assumption about the informativeness of traits may be unwarranted.

Rodin used 21 faculty members in the Department of Psychology in her research. The seven "most highly visible" of these were selected as targets to be described. Seven others were designated as encoders; they were to describe the seven targets. The final seven were designated as decoders; based on the encoders' descriptions, they were to try to match the descriptions with the targets. The encoders were to describe the targets in the following ways:

1. In terms of a typical behavior
2. Using an adjective or two
3. By answering the question, "What kind of animal is he?"
4. By answering the question, "What kind of entrée (main dish) is he?"

Rodin then computed how accurately a particular type of description described a target when it was used by several encoders or only one encoder. The results are depicted below:

	Typical Behavior	Trait Adjective	Animal	Entrée
Several Encoders	3.86*	2.86*	2.00	1.00
One Encoder	3.57*	2.00	2.14	2.00

*Significantly better than chance accuracy ($p < .01$)

As the table shows, the decoders are consistently more accurate than they might be by chance only when the targets are described in terms of a typical behavior, such as "catching you in the hall to start a conversation that could only be brought to a conclusion in a matter of hours." Thus trait descriptions may not be as informative as they are commonly assumed to be. Rodin suggests that laboratory studies of impression formation that use trait lists to describe hypothetical persons are poor simulations of how we really form impressions and that they are poor in at least two ways: the nature of the stimulus information and the use that judges make of that information.

> The trait information is clearly artificial in the sense that one does not form impressions of other people from bare traits lists outside the laboratory . . . [and] trait information is relatively uninformative as well (p. 344).

---

adequately interpreted in terms of each trait's positions on the two properties or dimensions plotted in the figure, *good-social–bad-social* and *good-intellectual–bad-intellectual*.

Comparing their results to Asch's *warm–cold* study, Rosenberg, et al. (1968) point out that the context traits presented to subjects—intelligent, practical, determined, skillful, industrious, cautious (that is, those common to both lists)—are all from the "good" end of the *good-intellectual–bad-intellectual* dimension. Further, the traits for which Asch did not obtain much of a difference as a function of whether subjects had heard the *cold* or the *warm* list are also pretty much on the *good-intellectual* side. On the other hand, *warm* and *cold* are about neutral on the intellectual dimension and at opposite ends of the social dimension.

What does all this mean? It means that the concept of centrality as Asch conceived it has been changed to the idea that a characteristic is important as an organizer of one's impression of another to the extent that the characteristic stands out as unique among all the other's characteristics. If this is true, then taking a pair of antonyms (such as *industrious–lazy*) from the poles of the intellectual dimension of Figure 1 and presenting them in a context of good traits on the social dimension (such as warm, sociable, good-natured, humorous) should make *industrious–lazy* the central characteristic. This was done by Zanna and Hamilton (1972), who also repeated the original Asch experiment in the same study. As anticipated, *industrious-lazy* was central when presented in the context of social good traits, just as *warm–cold* was central when presented in a context of intellectual good traits. As Zanna and Hamilton note, "Centrality is not a property of certain traits, but . . . a function of the inferential relationships among a set of traits" (p. 354).

One could argue that we really don't form impressions of others by reading lists of traits (see Box A), but another way of looking at this issue of centrality is to use the notion of cues. That is, some characteristics, qualities, or behaviors of others serve as cues to additional characteristics that these others might possess. For example, Dion, Berscheid, and Walster (1972) suggested that an important cue for many people is the physical attractiveness of another. They hypothesized that not only do people attribute desirable personality characteristics to physically attractive others, but that people also expect physically attractive others to lead better lives than unattractive individuals. To check on this, Dion, et al. (1972) asked male and female subjects to rate people depicted in photographs on 27 different personality traits. The photos had previously been selected to represent three different levels of attractiveness, and each subject judged one average, one attractive, and one unattractive other. Subjects were also asked to speculate about which of the depicted people would be most likely to have a number of different life experiences, such as divorce, professional success, or a happy marriage, and which would be most likely to engage in each of 30 different occupations. As anticipated, many more socially desirable personality traits were attributed to attractive individuals, and the latter were expected to attain more prestigious occupations, to be more competent spouses, and to have happier marriages. Subjects apparently believed that what is beautiful is good.

There have been a number of studies examining the various inferences that people make from such cues as physical attractiveness, sex, race, or height of forehead. Pheterson, Kiesler, and Goldberg (1971) found that women students at Connecticut College used the sex of the artist as a cue to the artist's "technical competence" and "artistic future." That is, when judging paintings entered in a contest, these women downgraded the artist more when told the artist was female than when told the artist was male. The paintings were the same in both cases. When we start talking about inferences based on such cues as sex or race or religion, we are getting very close to what most people think of as stereotypes. We shall discuss stereotypes more fully in Chapter 7 in connection with the cognitive component of attitudes. For now, let us look a little more closely at some of the cognitive processes that may interfere with our forming an accurate impression of another person.

BIASES, ILLUSIONS, AND CONCEITS IN PERSON PERCEPTION

One of the ways in which our implicit theories of personality may get us into trouble is that we may assume we know more about another person than we really do. From one or two cues or bits of behavior, we may infer a whole range of things, and these unfounded inferences may interfere with appropriate utilization of new information about the person. In a series of experiments, Dailey (1952) asked subjects to read autobiographical sketches written by stimulus persons and to predict how the stimulus persons would respond to specific items on a personality inventory. The criterion in each case was how the stimulus person had actually responded. Some subjects made

Actor-observer differences in attribution. Observers tend to attribute causes of behavior to characteristics of the person, whereas actors tend to attribute causes of behavior to the environment.

predictions after reading half of the autobiography and again after reading all of it. Other subjects made predictions only after reading all the information. The latter group did significantly better. Daily interprets this to mean that premature conclusions based on a small amount of data can apparently prevent the observer from learning as much from additional data as he or she would without having made a premature decision.

In later experiments, Dailey attempted to manipulate the importance of the information on which the premature conclusion was based, and, as expected, premature decisions were most detrimental when based on unimportant information. Further, simply allowing subjects to pause after reading some information had a biasing effect similar to asking for personality predictions on the basis of only a small amount of information! We mistake the inferences we have made about another for facts, and these "facts" keep us from being as open as we should be to new information about the other.

There is another way in which our perceptions of others may be biased. In the Dion, et al. study, we saw that we often use invalid cues, like physical attractiveness, to infer a host of additional characteristics. Nisbett and Wilson (1977) caution that the overall impression we have of a person—our "global evaluation"—may alter our perceptions of the person's specific attributes, such as his or her physical attractiveness. If we like someone, for example, we may perceive that person as more attractive than if we dislike him or her. This phenomenon is called the HALO EFFECT. It was defined by Thorndike (1920) over 50 years ago, though there was not much clear experimental evidence of its existence until recently.

To demonstrate the halo effect, Nisbett and Wilson (1977) asked male and female college students to watch short videotape segments of an interview with a college instructor who spoke English with a fairly heavy accent. Some subjects saw an interview in which the instructor appeared warm and friendly, seemed to like his students, and gave the impression of being quite enthusiastic about teaching. Other subjects saw an interview in which the instructor appeared cool and aloof, seemed not to trust his students, and gave the impression of being quite rigid in his approach to teaching. After viewing one of the two videotapes, subjects were asked to rate their liking of the teacher and the extent to which they found his physical appearance, his mannerisms, and his accent either irritating or appealing. As anticipated, subjects liked the teacher significantly more when he answered the interview questions in a warm and friendly manner than when he answered in a cool and aloof manner. Of particular interest here, however, are the subjects' ratings of the instructor's individual attributes as a function of their liking of him. These data are presented in Figure 2. The instructor's physical appearance, mannerisms, and accent were found irritating by the vast majority of subjects who viewed the *cold* tape, and these same characteristics were considered appealing by students who viewed the *warm* tape.* Nisbett and Wilson also present some evidence that subjects were apparently unaware of how their liking or disliking of the instructor had influenced their ratings of his specific attributes.

Some research by Ross, Amabile, and Steinmetz (1977) indicates another powerful bias on our perceptions of others—a bias of which we are often unaware. Ross, et al. point out that the social roles we play in our day-to-day life may make us appear to have qualities and characteristics that we really do not possess. As they put it, interpersonal encounters are typically constrained by roles such as teacher–student, police officer–traffic offender, and lecturer–audience, and

> roles confer unequal control over the style, content, and duration of an encounter; such social control, in turn, generally facilitates displays of knowledge, skill, insight, wit, or sensitivity, while permitting the concealment of deficiencies. Accurate social judgment, accordingly, depends upon the perceiver's ability to make adequate allowance for such role-conferred advantages and disadvantages in self-presentation (p. 485).

The point is simply that, in forming an impression of another, we may not give sufficient weight to the situation in which we observe the other's behavior. It might be that anyone put in that situation would behave similarly.

To see whether subjects really do fail to consider the situation in which they observe another's behavior, Ross, et al. recruited male and female undergraduates at Stanford to participate in a "quiz game" experiment. Subjects were recruited in pairs, and one subject was assigned the role of contestant and one the role of questioner. The questioner for each pair of subjects assigned to the experimental condition was instructed to compose a set of difficult, but potentially answerable, questions. The questions could be on any topic that the questioner desired. The contestant was to try to answer the questions. For the pairs of subjects assigned to the control condition, both questioner and contestant were informed that the questioners would simply ask questions prepared beforehand by someone else. During the actual quiz, the questioners gave the contestants 30 seconds to answer, then indicated whether the given answer was correct, and supplied the correct answer if it was not. Immediately following the quiz, the subjects rated themselves and their partners on their general knowledge. The results are shown in Table I.

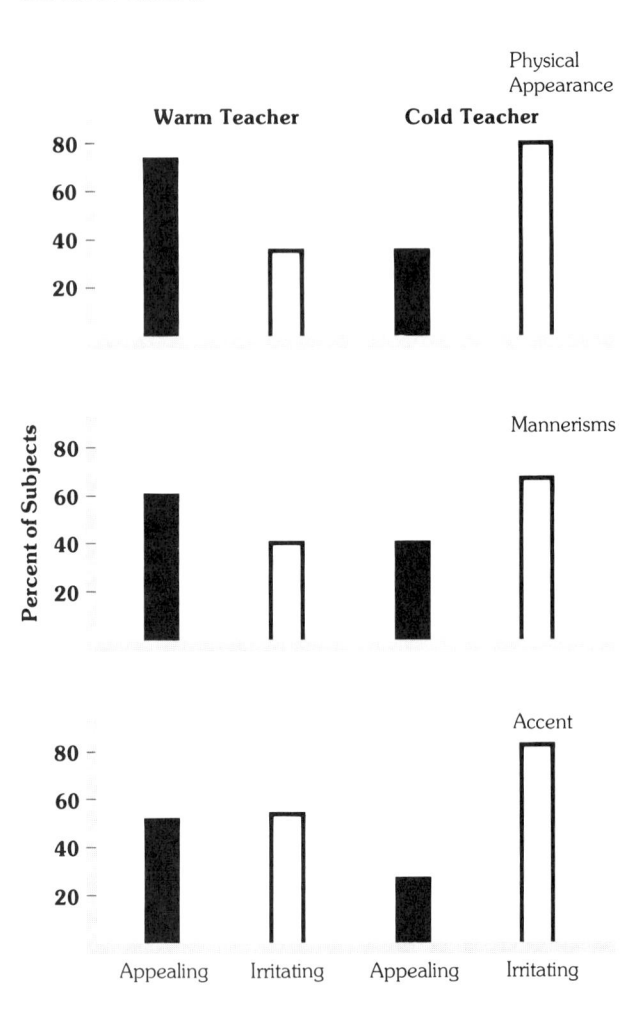

2. **Ratings of teacher's physical appearance, mannerisms, and accent in a demonstration of the halo effect. The same characteristics were rated differently depending on whether the teacher appeared warm or cold in the videotaped interview. (From Nisbett and Wilson, 1977, Figure 1, p. 253.)**

---

*An independent group of subjects who viewed the videotapes without the soundtrack revealed no significant differences in their ratings of physical appearance and mannerisms of the instructor.

Table I Mean ratings of general knowledge of questioners and contestants immediately following quiz

	Experimental		Control	
	Rating of self	Rating of partner	Rating of self	Rating of partner
Questioner	53.5	50.6	54.1	52.5
Contestant	41.3	66.8	47.0	50.3

The higher the number, the more general knowledge the person is believed to have acquired. (From Ross, et al., 1977, Table 1, p. 489.)

Contestants in the experimental condition, but not in the control condition, rated themselves as significantly less knowledgeable than their partners. This is in spite of the fact that the contestants knew the questioners had been given the task of selecting questions about isolated bits of knowledge that they happened to possess. Had the roles of questioner and contestant been switched, the new questioners could easily have dreamed up questions that could not be answered by most people. Nevertheless, contestants apparently failed to consider the self-presentation advantage enjoyed by their questioners. In a subsequent experiment, Ross, et al. were able to demonstrate that observers who watched the quiz game and who also heard the instructions given the questioner made the same error as the contestants in the original experiment. That is, they estimated that the questioner had significantly more general knowledge than the contestant. It appears that if you are allowed to define the game, not only will you win, but others will perceive you as a winner.

We have looked at several ways in which what we infer about another—what we think we know—can get us into trouble. We may jump to conclusions based on insufficient evidence, we may succumb to the influence of a halo effect, and we may pay insufficient attention to the situation in which we observe another when we are trying to form an impression. In the context of personality assessment and prediction, Dawes (1976) has recently noted that we seem to suffer from COGNITIVE CONCEIT. We overvalue our own cognitive capacity and fail to rely on evidence that contains much valid information about a person's general motivation and abilities. These are all general pitfalls of the impression formation process, general in the sense that we are all susceptible to them. But surely we do not all form impressions in exactly the same way or look at the same cues when we form an impression. What evidence is there for individual variations in person perception?

INDIVIDUAL DIFFERENCES IN SOCIAL PERCEPTION

In the late 1940s and early 1950s, Bruner, Postman, McClelland, and their colleagues carried out a number of studies demonstrating that the human perceiver is anything but passive. Subjects in the experiments appeared to approach ambiguous stimuli, such as blurred images briefly exposed on a screen, with sets of hypotheses about what they were seeing. Furthermore, the hypotheses of individual subjects seemed to be related to their current motive states, their moods, their values, and other aspects of their personality. Subjects who had been without food for 24 or 48 hours, for example, tended to see many more food-related objects among the blurred images than did well-fed peers. Are there similar individual differences in the hypotheses that people form regarding which human characteristics can co-occur in others? If so, are such individual differences related to other aspects of personality?

If the human organism is an integrated system, definite relationships among the various subsystems should exist. Perception, for example, aids us in adjusting to the external world. Hence, we would expect some relationship between an individual's characteristic personality traits and his or her perception of others. Let's take the authoritarian personality syndrome as an example. As we saw in Chapter 2, a person exhibiting an authoritarian personality is supposedly characterized by submissiveness to authority figures, rigidity, belief in things mystical and supernatural, opposition to subjectivity, exaggerated condemnation of sexual deviance, and a host of other undesirable traits (Adorno, et al., 1950). Is there any reason to believe that authoritarians will perceive others differently from nonauthoritarians?

Scodel and Mussen (1953) reasoned that a person high in authoritarianism would not be likely to be particularly sensitive to the characteristics of others. In fact, descriptions of the authoritarian syndrome seemed to emphasize that the authoritarian divides people into "those like me" and "others." Others include anybody of different color, religion, nationality, sexual preference—anybody, in short, who might have a different set of values. If authoritarians are given no basis for suspecting the "others" category,

B. Race and Belief Similarity in Social Choice

Rokeach (1968) has argued that one of the most important factors in our perception of others is whether we perceive them to have beliefs and values similar to our own. He suggests that not only do we tend to reject others when we perceive them as having different beliefs, but that in areas where racial prejudice is not socially institutionalized, perception of belief dissimilarity may be a more powerful determinant of prejudice than race.

To test this idea, Rokeach designed an ingenious field experiment. The study was conducted in the employment offices of two mental institutions in Michigan, and the subjects were actual black and white job applicants for positions as janitors, laundry workers, and ward attendants. When each applicant had completed some initial forms, he was taken to a waiting room where four other applicants were seated. The other applicants were actually experimental accomplices, two white and two black. When all five—including the real applicant—were present, each was handed a mimeographed sheet listing five problems that arise in working with mental patients. While the experimenter was temporarily out of the room, the four confederates started a "spontaneous" discussion about the topics. The topics were questions such as "What would you do if a patient took off all his clothes?" On each topic, one confederate of each race took a hard-line, adhere-to-the-rule-book approach, and the other two took a more lenient and permissive attitude.

In each instance, the subject was gradually drawn into the discussion, his opinion on the issue being explicitly solicited if he did not volunteer it. When the experimenter returned to the room, he passed out cards, had each applicant introduce himself, and then had everyone write down the names of the two people with whom he would most like to work. The choice patterns are shown in the following table. Subjects overwhelmingly chose others who believed as they did, regardless of race.

Characteristics of The Two Partners Chosen

Subjects	S+O+*	S−O−	S+S−	O+O−	S+O−	S−O+
Black	15**	3	1	2	3	2
White	15	0	1	1	1	6

*S = Same race as subject; O = Other race; + = Agreed, − = Disagreed
**Frequency of choice of various combinations of two partners

Thus, in this setting, perceived similarity of belief was indeed more potent than race in determining social choice. Rokeach is careful to add that these results might not hold in other contexts or cultural settings, although a growing body of evidence suggests that these results may be quite robust, even in contexts where racial prejudice is more powerfully entrenched.

they will assume that someone whom they are forming an impression of is pretty much like themselves.

To check on this, Scodel and Mussen paired high- and low-authoritarian subjects of the same sex and instructed each pair to discuss radio, television, and music for 20 minutes. Following the discussion, each subject was instructed to fill out some personality measures of authoritarianism as he or she felt the other subject would respond. As anticipated, the high-authoritarian subjects estimated their partners to be about as authoritarian as they themselves were. On the other hand, low-authoritarian subjects estimated their partners to be considerably more authoritarian than themselves. While this result is intriguing and makes sense in terms of the personality dynamics associated with authoritarianism, it is ambiguous. It may not mean that nonauthoritarians are more sensitive to the characteristics of others at all; it may simply mean they are more cautious. The estimates of the nonauthoritarians very closely correspond to the overall mean of the group from which the highs and lows had been selected. The nonauthoritarians could have simply been guessing that their partner was about average, since they really did not know much about the partner. However, data indicate that perceived belief similarity may be quite important in social perception, and not just for authoritarians (see Box B).

A number of later studies have taken variables correlated with authoritarianism and essentially replicated the format of the Scodel and Mussen study. Burke (1966), for example, found that subjects high in dogmatism—subjects who tend to see the world and others in either–or terms as good or bad, for me or against me—estimate others to be about as dogmatic as themselves, whereas subjects low in dogmatism estimate others to be considerably more dogmatic than themselves. Unfortunately, such studies don't tell us very much about what specific characteristics dogmatic versus nondogmatic or authoritarian versus nonauthoritarian subjects infer about others, but there have been a few studies relating the perceiver's personality to his or her specific inferences about others.

Benedetti and Hill (1960), for example, administered the Gordon Personal Profile to a large group of students at the University of New Mexico and divided the students into high, middle, and low subgroups on the basis of their sociability scores. Each subject was

Table II Mean number attributing preferred traits

Stimulus person	Subject's own sociability		
	High	Middle	Low
Sociable	32.35	30.75	30.25
Unsociable	12.30	17.00	21.60

When the stimulus person had been described as sociable, all subjects tended to attribute socially desirable traits to the stimulus person, regardless of the extent to which they were sociable themselves. However, when the stimulus person had been described as unsociable, subjects who were themselves highly sociable tended to attribute very few socially desirable traits to the stimulus person. Subjects who were themselves low in sociability attributed comparatively more favorable traits to a stimulus person who had been described as unsociable. (From Benedetti and Hill, 1960, p. 279.)

then read a list of traits that were supposedly descriptive of another person. Half of the subjects in each of the sociability groups were read list A and half within each group were read list B:

A: intelligent, skillful, industrious, sociable, determined, practical, cautious.
B. intelligent, skillful, industrious, unsociable, determined, practical, cautious.

Each subject was then asked to select one trait from each of 20 pairs of traits. The traits in each pair differed in social desirability, and the selected traits were supposed to be those that best fitted the subject's impression of the stimulus person. The mean numbers of subjects in each condition who selected the more socially desirable trait of each pair are given in Table II.

As Table II shows, when another is described as unsociable, subjects attribute different characteristics to the other as a function of their own level of sociability. The failure to find a similar result (though in the opposite direction) when another is described as sociable is puzzling, and could be due to a number of factors. For example, subjects who are themselves examples of a particular characteristic (high in sociability) may be more discriminating among others with respect to that particular characteristic than subjects who are not examples of the characteristic (those middle and low in sociability). This is another way of saying that personality variables may not be symmetrical. Those high in authoritarianism, sociability, security, or whatever may not be mirror images of those low in authoritarianism, sociability, or security.

Because of these and a number of other problems in examining individual differences in impression formation, many researchers have turned the approach around. That is, instead of selecting subjects on the basis of some personality variable that *should* make a difference in how they perceive people and seeing if those differences can be identified, they have identified stable individual differences in the perception of others and then figured out additional personality characteristics of different perceivers. Hamilton and Gifford (1970), for example, constructed 52 personality profiles such that each profile gave 9 items of information about a young man. Of these pieces of information, 4 were biographical or demographic, while the other 5 items were personality-related (the man's standing on each of 5 bipolar personality scales). Subjects were asked to study each profile and make a judgment about how liberal or conservative the man was. Based on a factor analysis of the correlations of each subject's liberal–conservative ratings with those of each other subject, 6 subgroups of subjects (or judges) were identified in terms of the cues they placed the most emphasis on. These 6 subgroups relied, respectively, on:

1. The stimulus person's race—using "black" as a cue to liberalism
2. The degree of cultural refinement and home region of the country
3. Biographical cues and ignored personality
4. Conscientiousness and responsibility of the stimulus person
5. Race in conjunction with emotional stability
6. Extroversion of the stimulus person in inferring liberalism

It appears that different people use different cues on which to base the same inference—in this case, how liberal the stimulus persons were.

A similar study is one by Wiggins, Hoffman, and Taber (1969). These authors went further in that they not only identified subgroups of judges, but also differentiated the subgroups on the basis of other characteristics. The judgment or inference of interest in this case was intelligence, and the stimuli were profiles of college students, each of which involved nine cues coded on scales from 0 to 100: high school grade rating, ambitiousness, degree of self-support, correctness of written expression, responsibility, mother's education, study habits, emotional anxiety, and credit hours per semester. Eight subgroups of subjects were identified in terms of the cues they placed most emphasis on in making judgments of intelligence. For example, the first two groups relied most heavily on either high school grade rating or correctness of written expression. These subjects tended to be intelligent, to be conventional with respect to religion, to be low in ethnocentrism, and to have good mechanical comprehension. Another group of subjects placed emphasis on responsibility and study habits in making their judgments of intelligence. These subjects were themselves not particularly intelligent, but rather authoritarian and conventional in religion.

There have been a number of similar studies within this realm. Sherman and Ross (1972) asked subjects to rate the similarity of 20 American politicians who had been selected to cover a large portion of the political spectrum (from Wallace to McGovern). Seven types of variations were perceived among the politicians, and these variations were systematically related to the liberalism of the subjects making the judgments. For example, the more conservative a subject was, the less likely he or she was to use a hawk–dove dimension in differentiating the politicians. Liberal subjects were likely to place great emphasis on the power of the politician within his own party as a basis for differentiation.

Thus data are accumulating that indicate clear and definite relationships between the personality of the perceiver and how he or she organizes beliefs about others. Our discussion, of course, has only scratched the surface. Both domains (cues and aspects of personality) are probably infinite. But experimental results leave no doubt that definite relationships exist between the personality of the perceiver and how the perceiver organizes beliefs about others.

We have been discussing how we utilize information that we already have, or think we have, to help us form an impression of another person. Based on associations that we believe exist among characteristics generally, we infer that a person who possesses certain characteristics also possesses the qualities we believe to be associated with those characteristics. We generalize our knowledge to new circumstances and, as we have seen, our generalizations are often inappropriate. We cannot simply rely on old knowledge. We must, and we do, seek new information on which to base our understandings of others and ourselves.

Acquiring new information about people

We have used the phrase *person perception* several times, but you may have noticed that we really have not discussed person *perception* at all. Rather, we have been discussing PERSON COGNITION, inferences we make about others or how we think about others. However, in order to talk about the processes involved in seeking new information about others, we must talk about the perception of persons. If we want to find out something about another person, one of the best approaches is to begin by observing that person—watching, listening, smelling, comparing what he or she does with what others do, and comparing what he or she does with what we would have done in the same situation.

OBSERVING BEHAVIOR

In recent years, a number of social psychologists have warned that we may have spent too little time simply observing behavior. Deaux (1978), for example, reports an informal quiz of graduate students in psychology in which they were asked such questions as "What is the frequency of aggressive behavior?" and "How often do people make attributions?" The students could discourse at length on the causes of aggressive behavior and theories of attribution, which we shall cover in the next section, but they were at a loss with these oversimplified questions about how often people behave in various ways.

Barker (1968) points out that basic normative information about its subject matter is crucial to any science, so normative information about the distribution of behaviors is crucial to psychology. Part of the reason for the lack of such vital information, according to Barker, is that psychology seems to have skipped its "natural history" phase. That is, it jumped from philosophy to the experimental laboratory without taking time to marvel at behavior in the world around us. As we shall see in Chapter 15, there is evidence that this situation is changing. Many social psychologists are becoming interested in the developing field of environmental psychology and in observing and understanding behavior as it occurs in natural settings.

An intriguing line of research by Newtson (1973, 1976, 1977) and his colleagues has recently focused attention on the perceptual processes involved when we try to make sense of what another person is doing. The basic assumption behind Newtson's research is that the perceiver does not passively take in information about the behavior he or she is observing. Rather, the perceiver actively participates in the perceptual process by organizing the ongoing observed behavior into meaningful segments or actions. Thus, to a large extent, the perceiver controls the amount and kind of information obtained when observing another's behavior and may literally generate more or less information from a given behavioral sequence, depending on such factors as his or her expectations and attentiveness.

In one of his first experiments, Newtson (1973) hypothesized that perceivers who break down an observed ongoing behavior sequence into small units are subsequently more confident of the validity of their impressions of the observed person and have more differentiated impressions of that person than perceivers who break down the observed behavioral sequence into larger segments. The assumption is that by breaking the behavior down into small segments, we obtain more information. The more information we have, the more confident we are about our impression and the more differentiated the impression is likely to be. To check on this, Newtson asked first-year male students at the University of Wisconsin to observe a 5-minute videotaped behavioral sequence. The subjects were furnished with a continuous event recorder, synchronized with the videotape, on which they were to mark off the behavior of the person on the videotape into meaningful segments. However, half the subjects were told to mark off the behavior into the *largest* units that seemed natural and meaningful, and half the subjects were told to mark off the behavior into the *smallest* units that seemed natural and meaningful.

After watching the tape, subjects were asked to rate the observed person on a number of social qualities and a number of intellectual qualities and to indicate how confident they were of their ratings.

Newton found that subjects instructed to use the smallest meaningful units did, in fact, divide the videotape into significantly more segments than those instructed to use the largest meaningful units (52.1 versus 21.3). As anticipated, the former subjects were more confident of their impressions. Further, the correlation between the ratings of social and intellectual qualities was high and positive for subjects using large units and virtually nonexistent for subjects using small units. That is, small-unit subjects had more differentiated impressions.

In subsequent research, Newtson, Engquist, and Bois (1977) have shown that observers segment the behaviors they are watching at BREAK POINTS, points in the ongoing stream of behavior where a noticeable change occurs in one or more of the features that the observer is monitoring. Thus, Newtson's point is that the information we obtain from observing another's behavior is defined by *changes* in the relative positions of the actor's features. The observer has a great deal of choice in how he or she segments the observed behavior. The observer's purpose, of course, is to gain enough information from the observed sequence to understand what the observed person is doing. As a sequence of behavior becomes predictable, Newtson has found that observers gradually begin to segment the behavior into larger and larger units. It is as if they feel they don't have to pay so much attention, because they know what is going on. However, Newtson has also found that if an unexpected or unusual behavior occurs in the sequence being observed, perceivers quickly shift back to fine units, apparently in order to gain sufficient information to reestablish predictability.

Consider the following sequence of behavior, which one might observe on any spring or summer day on hundreds of campuses. Someone is seen jumping high into the air, extending the left arm overhead, mouth open, opening and closing the left hand, landing on the ground, feet wide apart, left foot slightly forward, twisting the head and torso to the right, mouth closed, left arm curling around the right hip, twisting back to the left, eyes forward, head level, quickly swinging the left arm forward with a flick of the wrist, opening and closing the left hand, frowning, and then smiling. What are we watching? Modern dance? Open-air mime? Of course not. It's a left-handed frisbee player. Once we have organized the behavioral sequence by attributing the purpose of "playing frisbee" to the actor, not only does the whole sequence make more sense, but we no longer find it necessary to pay as much attention to everything the actor is doing. We simply see someone catching and throwing a frisbee.

Zadny and Gerard (1974) hypothesize that attributing a purpose or intent to an actor allows us to organize a behavioral sequence into larger units *and* that, after having done so, we tend to pay attention only to those aspects of the other's behavior that are relevant to the attributed purpose. These attributed intentions can either enhance the accuracy of our perception of another's behavior or make it extremely difficult to understand what's going on. As Zadny and Gerard put it, when we attribute an intent we pay attention primarily to "intent-related" behavior, which, from the observer's point of view, is the crux of the action sequence.

To test their ideas, Zadny and Gerard recruited subjects for "a study of rumor transmission" and had them observe a farcical skit in which a college student attempted to enroll for classes. The student at one point dropped an armload of assorted items, gathered them up, made his way to a registration table, and inquired about registering in a number of required courses, all of which were closed out. Prior to this skit, observer-subjects had been led to believe that the student was either a chemistry major, a music major, or a psychology major. The items that the student dropped and the courses he inquired about were related to chemistry, music, and psychology—some of each. After the skit, subjects were asked to list all the objects the student dropped and all the courses he mentioned in trying to register. As anticipated, subjects who had been led to believe the student was a chemistry major recalled a higher percentage of the chemistry-related items and courses than those who believed the student was a psychology or music major. Similarly, those who believed the student was a psychology major recalled more psychology-related items and courses, and those who believed the student was a music major recalled more music-related items and courses. In a subsequent experiment, Zadny and Gerard were able to demonstrate that this effect is due to differential selective perception and not simply to differential recall. The effect does not occur if observers are informed of the actor's intent *after* observing his or her behavior.

In perceiving another's behavior, we tend to simplify as time goes on. We start out observing discrete actions marked off by noticeable changes in the features we happen to be monitoring and gradually organize these discrete actions into larger units (such as catching and throwing in our frisbee example). It helps us in this transition to larger behavioral units if we can assume that the observed person has some purpose, some intention, and that his or her behavior is not simply movement for movement's sake. Once we have attributed an intention to the person, we may become selectively attuned to behaviors relevant to that intention. However, we are rarely satisfied to stop at this point. We usually want to know *why* the person has a particular intention, *why* he or she is doing whatever we have observed. A number of social-psychological theories are pertinent to the issue of how we use information about others in our search for the causes of their behavior.

ATTRIBUTION PROCESSES

One of the things that scares people off when someone starts discussing theory is the vision of some elaborate superstructure made up of hot air and gas, which—as one might expect with such a composition—rarely touches ground. Such a preconception is unfortunate, because theories are necessary to achieve any sort of integration of knowledge. Also, such a preconception is usually just plain wrong. As we shall see, most of the theories relevant to attribution processes are not in the least difficult to understand. Some are even elegant in their simplicity.

Theories, of course, vary in scope. Some theories of attribution seek to explain only a small portion of how cues are utilized in attributing causes to behavior, while others are much broader in terms of what they seek to explain. Cohen (1961), for example, was concerned with a single aspect of the attribution process, one's reason for trying to understand another. Making use of Zajonc's (1960) concepts of reception tuning and transmission tuning, Cohen suggested that these two orientations should make a difference in how one handles information about another person. In TRANSMISSION TUNING, the individual expects to have to communicate his or her impression to others. Hence, he or she needs to be able to articulate that impression clearly and concisely. Such an orientation would tend to lead one to ignore or minimize inconsistencies and form a definite impression. In RECEPTION TUNING, on the other hand, the individual expects to continue to receive information about the other. Hence, he or she is more likely to suspend judgment, resulting in a less clear-cut impression.

Cohen gave subjects a list of traits that were supposedly descriptive of another person. Half of the subjects were told that, after reading the traits, their job would be to communicate to others all they could about the described person. The remaining subjects were told that, after reading the traits, they would find out how others perceived the person described by the traits. Further, there were a number of inconsistent traits in the lists that the subjects read. As expected, subjects set to transmit their impressions were more likely to form clear, consistent impressions and to ignore any contradictory material. Subjects set to receive more information had greater desire for more information and for more information on both sides. It appears that the purpose for which an impression is being formed does make a difference.

Others have concerned themselves with similarly specific questions about the process of cue utilization. Blanchard (1966) addressed the question of relevance of the information available to the type of attribution being made. It stands to reason that we need pertinent cues in order to make accurate predictions about another. It comes as no surprise, then, that Blanchard found that accuracy of prediction about another's subsequent behavior was higher when the cues given subjects were relevant to the predictions being requested.

The theorists who have been most influential, however, have formulated somewhat broader conceptions about the process involved in making attributions about others. Notable among these are Bruner (1948), Heider (1958), Sherif and Hovland (1961), Jones and Davis (1965), and Kelley (1967). We have already mentioned Bruner's work in Chapter 4, and we shall discuss Sherif and Hovland's in Chapters 8 and 12. Here we shall focus on Heider, Jones and Davis, and Kelley.

Heider (1958) took as his basic premise the principle that

> man grasps reality and can predict and control it by referring transient and variable behavior and events to relatively unchanging underlying conditions, the so-called dispositional properties of his world (p. 79).

If you observe someone kicking a cat, it helps you understand what is going on if you can assume that the person in question is just plain mean, an *internal* attribution. However, if you know that the person is genuinely kind and loving, you cannot understand the action unless it can be attributed to something *external* to the person, something about the environment or situation. Perhaps the person was just bitten or scratched by the cat and kicked it in anger. Maybe the cat has rabies and the person was trying to keep from being bitten. According to Heider, any given outcome or action depends on a combination of such personal (internal) and environmental (external) forces. If we are trying to decide why a particular outcome occurred (why someone is behaving strangely, say), we may first seek an environmental or situational cause. If the person who is behaving strangely fell off her bicycle yesterday and suffered a mild concussion, our search for a cause may end. The blow on the head would probably be a sufficient explanation of strange behavior. On the other hand, if we cannot find an environmental or situational cause, we are likely to infer that there is something about the person that makes him or her behave this way. In order to make such an attribution, however, we have to be able to convince ourselves that the person both has the *ability* to do whatever it is (say, succeeding on a difficult task) and was *trying* to succeed (it wasn't just luck). Thus, according to Heider, an outcome is determined by some combination of environmental and personal factors, the latter being a combination of ability and motivation. Heider diagrams these relations as follows:

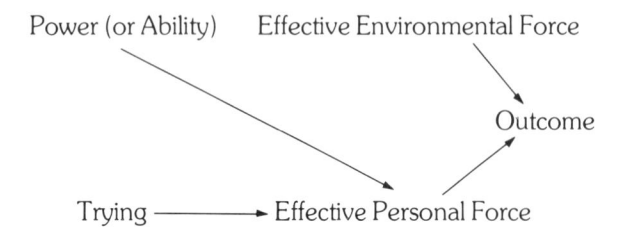

```
Power (or Ability)      Effective Environmental Force
             \                      \
              \                      → Outcome
               ↘                    ↗
Trying ────→ Effective Personal Force
```

As an example, consider the task facing a faculty promotion committee whose members are trying to decide whether a young assistant professor should be promoted. They know that our young academician has published ten articles in the last three years (outcome) and they want to know something about the quality of this outcome. Their first step might well be to look at the journals in which he or she has published. If the publications are in prestigious journals with notoriously high rejection rates, it would be difficult to attribute the productivity to a weak restraining environmental force. Hence, they are likely to infer high quality (or that the person has ability). The sheer volume of production has already assured them that the person is trying. On the other hand, if the publications are in journals that take anything from anybody, they are likely to infer that the quality is not so good. The restraining environmental force here is weak; almost anyone could have done the same if he or she had simply tried.

Building on Heider's basic premise, Jones and Davis (1965) developed a theory to explain some of the processes going on between the observation of a particular act of another person and the attribution of a particular disposition to that person. The key to their conception is the idea that a given act represents a choice among several possible acts. Each act has one or more possible effects. Any effects of the act which are common or belong to all the possible choices are called COMMON EFFECTS, and cannot explain why the given act was chosen. The effects unique to a given act may provide evidence as to why that act was chosen. Effects belonging only to a given act are called NONCOMMON EFFECTS. A given act may have only one or several noncommon effects. In the case of several noncommon effects it would still be quite difficult to know the underlying disposition which caused the act, since any or all of the noncommon effects may have contributed to causing the act.

Jones and Davis assume, as does Heider, that the more an act appears to be caused by the environment, the less informative that act is about the person who performs it. Specifically, acts that are high in general social desirability, such as being polite, saying "hello" on meeting someone, or inquiring about their health, do not tell us much about a specific person because nearly everyone does these things. On the other hand, acts low in social desirability, such as getting into street brawls or spitting on the classroom floor are likely to tell us more about a person because these actions are not done by most people.

Jones and Davis use the term CORRESPONDENCE to refer to the extent to which an observed act and the disposition which we attribute to an actor on the basis of that act are similarly described by the inference (e.g., if you see a person display an act of aggressive behavior, you might infer that person has an underlying disposition of aggressiveness). An inference is correspondent if the act performed has a small number of noncommon effects (preferably only one), and if the noncommon effects are socially undesirable.

The concept of correspondence is illustrated in Table III. The rows of the table indicate that the number of noncommon effects may be high or low, and the columns indicate that the desirability of the act is high or low. As noted above, there is high correspondence of inference when the noncommon effects are few in number and the desirability of the act is low. Jones and Davis refer to the other three possible combinations as trivial clarity, trivial ambiguity, and intriguing ambiguity. In each of these situations the perceiver is unable to make an underlying inference with any certainty; in terms of the theory, there is a lack of correspondent inference.

Table III Effect desirability and effect commonality as determinants of correspondence

Number of noncommon effects	Assumed desirability of observed act	
	High	Low
High	Trivial Ambiguity	Intriguing Ambiguity
Low	Trivial Clarity	High Correspondence

Only when there are few noncommon effects and the social desirability of an action is low are we likely to learn much about the person performing the action. (From Jones and Davis, 1965, p. 229.)

Jones and Davis incorporate two further concepts into their theory, hedonic relevance and personalism. HEDONIC RELEVANCE refers to the idea that an actor's actions or their effects may be relevant to the life or situation of the perceiver. With hedonically relevant acts, the perceiver may be more certain about inferences from the acts because he or she can calculate the internal rewards or costs more easily. Thus, hedonic relevance increases the perceiver's correspondence of inference. PERSONALISM is said to characterize acts that the perceiver believes are *directed* toward himself or herself. Thus, perception is likely to involve the ego of the perceiver in various ways and may lead to stronger and more active inferences by the perceiver in ways that would not occur if there were no vested self-interests. Because the inference process is more active, personalism may also enhance correspondence of the inference process. (For a discussion of another perceiver bias see Box C.)

The most direct descendent of Heider's and Jones and Davis's formulation of how we go about making inferences is the work of Kelley (1967, 1973). In analyzing the problem of how a perceiver goes about deciding whether an event (particularly a human response) is caused by the external evironment or the inner disposition of the person, Kelley says we need to consider four criteria: (1) distinctiveness, (2) consistency over time, (3) consistency over modality, and (4) consensus.

For example, we may feel confident in our attribution that George is an anti-Semite if he responds with hostility to any mention of Jews, but not blacks (distinctiveness), if he has responded in this manner as long as we have known him (consistency over time), if he responds with both verbal and nonverbal indices of hatred (consistency over modality), and if known anti-Semites have behaved as he has (consensus). It is important to note that Kelley, Jones and Davis, and Heider are all dealing with the subjective validity of one's inferences and are not concerned with objective accuracy. That is, they are not concerned with whether George is really an anti-Semite, but with how one convinces oneself about George.

One of the basic tenets of Kelley's approach to attribution is the idea that, in trying to understand why someone behaved as they did, we look for things that covary with the behavior that occurred—things that are present when the behavior is present and absent when the behavior is absent. One of the reasons why Kelley's ideas about attribution have generated more research than all the other attribution theories put together is that Kelley claimed that we apply this covariation principle to ourselves as well as others. That is, in trying to explain our own behavior, we engage in similar sorts of analyses as when we try

C. Illusory Correlation, Availability, and Attribution

In making causal attributions, people often have to make relative judgments about the frequencies with which various classes of events have occurred. The basis for many such judgments appears to be a simple law of repetition: the more frequently an event has occurred, the stronger the associative links to that event. Strength of association to the event is later used as an aid or clue in making judgments of the event's frequency. The ease with which instances of a particular class of events can be brought to mind has been termed AVAILABILITY by Tversky and Kahneman (1973), who point out that availability is a valid clue for judging frequency, because frequent events are usually easier to recall or imagine than infrequent ones.

There are things other than repetition, however, that affect the availability of a particular class of events. Anything that makes a particular class more salient or distinctive than related classes will make that class more available. Since frequent events are generally more available in memory than infrequent ones, bias occurs when the frequencies of related classes do not correspond to the ease with which those classes can be retrieved from memory.

The notion of availability has been used by Tversky and Kahneman to account for ILLUSORY CORRELATION—that is, the belief in a relationship between two variables when the relationship is weaker than believed, the opposite of what is believed, or nonexistent. The definition of illusory correlation comes from a study by Chapman (1967) in which subjects were shown pairs of words projected on a screen and were later asked to recall how many times particular pairs had been shown. For example, one series consisted of 12 word pairs, each shown 10 times for a total of 120 presentations. The 12 word pairs were constructed by pairing each of the four words on the left with each of the words on the right:

boat	tiger
lion	eggs
bacon	notebook
blossoms	

Chapman found that on the recall task, subjects erred by overestimating pairs, such as lion–tiger, for which there was a preexisting association and by overestimating the frequency of pairs composed of atypically long words, such as blossoms–notebook.

Rather than implicating two *different* bases of illusory correlations, however, Tversky and Kahneman point out that these data may be viewed as indicating that

> illusory correlation is due to the differential strength of associative bonds. The strength of these bonds may reflect prior association between items or other factors, such as pair distinctiveness, which facilitate the formation of an association during learning. Thus, the various sources of illusory correlation can all be explained by the operation of a single mechanism—the assessment of availability or associative strength (p. 224).

to explain someone else's behavior. This extension of attribution theories to the self has led to some interesting results and some intriguing hypotheses about actor and observer differences in explaining behavior. Let us look at some of the issues involved by examining research on how we account for the fortunes and misfortunes that befall people—ourselves as well as others.

ATTRIBUTION IN ACTION: EXPLAINING SUCCESS AND FAILURE

Basing their analysis on some of Heider's comments, Weiner, Heckhausen, Meyer, and Cook (1972) conclude that one may distribute the causes of success and failure on a task to four elements: ability, effort, task difficulty, and luck. Further, they argue that these four elements vary along two attributional dimensions, which they term stability and locus of control, in the manner depicted in Table IV. Thus a perceiver is assumed to attribute the causes of success or failure on a task to either fixed or variable factors that may be internal or external to the person being observed. Furthermore, how one distributes or allocates responsibility for success or failure among these four factors is hypothesized to be an important determinant of expectations about subsequent performance. If, for example, you see someone fail at a task and decide that the failure was due to lack of ability, your expectation for the person's future success at the task is likely to be lower than if you decide the person was simply unlucky at the time.

Do we attribute the causes of success or failure differently if we ourselves have succeeded or failed than we do if we have observed someone else—in the same circumstances—succeed or fail? Jones and Nisbett (1971) claim that we do. In fact, they claim that people usually attribute their own actions to situational requirements and attribute the same actions in others to stable personal dispositions.* In terms of Table IV, we would use internal attributions to explain the successes and failures of others: they tried hard or not hard enough, they are smart or not smart enough. On the other hand, we would use external attributions to ex-

---

*Jones and Nisbett acknowledge that there are many exceptions to this proposition and that, at best, they are talking about differences in predominant tendencies.

Table IV Stability and locus of control

Attribution of stability	Attribution of locus of control	
	Internal	External
Fixed	Ability	Task Difficulty
Variable	Effort	Luck

The four elements that Weiner et al. used to explain success or failure on a task vary along two attributional dimensions: stability and locus of control. (From Weiner, et al., 1972.)

plain our own successes and failures: the task was easy or hard, we were just lucky or unlucky. First, let us see why this difference in self/other attributions should occur. Then we shall see if there is any evidence that it does exist.

The major reason behind the Jones and Nisbett hypothesis is that, with respect to any given ongoing behavioral segment, different information is salient for an actor engaged in the behavior than for an observer witnessing the actor's behavior. The observer is likely to pay little attention to the environment. For the observer, the most salient feature of the situation is likely to be the actor's behavior—what the actor does. On the other hand, the actor's eyes are not well situated to observe his or her own behavior. The actor pays primary attention to the environment, to the cues that elicit his or her behavior or to those aspects of the environment to which his or her behavior is a response. Focusing on the actor's behavior, the observer is likely to infer that the actor did whatever he or she did because that is the type of person he or she is. Focusing on those aspects of the environment that shaped their behavior, actors are likely to infer that they did whatever they did because of the situation they were in.

To see if this sort of difference in explanations really occurred, Nisbett, Caputo, Legant, and Marecek (1973) recruited pairs of female college students to participate in an experiment. Before the experiment actually began, however, one of each pair was designated as an actor and one as an observer. The actor was approached with a request to spend some time on an upcoming weekend showing the wives of some

Implicit theories of personality. Often individuals make inferences about another's personality based on just a few cues.

potential financial backers of the university around the campus. For this she was offered either $1.50 an hour or $.50 an hour. The observer watched this entire interchange. After the actor had either volunteered or refused, the actor and observer were separated and asked some questions about the actor's behavior. Of interest here is a question asked of both actor and observer about how likely they thought the actor would be to say "yes" if requested to volunteer to canvass for the United Fund. The results appear in Table V.

As the table shows, there is a distinct difference in the actors' and observers' answers. Actors see themselves as no more likely to volunteer for a future task simply because they had just volunteered for something else. Observers, on the other hand, seem to attribute a disposition to volunteer to those who had agreed to show the women around campus and a disposition to refuse to those who refused. Similarly, actors were apparently responsive to the payment being offered. Only 24 percent of those offered $.50 volunteered, whereas 68 percent of those offered $1.50 volunteered. Observers, however, took the volunteering of the high-payment group as evidence for a disposition to volunteer, whereas actors who received the high payment did not see themselves as more likely to respond favorably to the future request. As Nisbett, et al. point out, "observers are inclined to make dispositional inferences from behavior under circumstances in which actors infer nothing about their general inclinations" (p. 157).

There is, however, another factor involved in this tendency to explain others' behavior by attributing dispositions to them. As Wortman (1976) and others have noted, people make causal attributions as a way of enhancing their feelings of control. If some disaster befalls our best friend and we attribute it to chance, we are in grave danger. It could just as easily have happened to us. If, on the other hand, we can find some flaw in our friend's character that might possibly explain why fate sought him or her out, then we can proceed about life with relative calm and assurance. All we have to do to avoid a similar disaster is to keep our own character untarnished. We need to believe in a

Table V Estimates of the probability of volunteering for a similar task

	Actor's behavior		Amount offered	
	Volunteered	Did not volunteer	$1.50/hr	$.50/hr
Actor's Ratings	3.31	3.92	3.73	3.38
Observer's Ratings	4.27	2.78	4.25	2.71

The higher the number, the more probable the actor would volunteer for a similar task. (From Nisbett, et al., 1973, Table 1, p. 157.)

just world, a world in which people get what they deserve.

As Lerner (1970) puts it, we want to believe that we live in a world where good things happen to good people and bad things happen *only* to bad people. If we seriously believed otherwise, it would be more difficult to continue to work and struggle to make our way in the world. At any moment, it might all be made meaningless—a bolt of lightning, a flood, cancer, or any of another thousand disasters could strike. Because our need to believe in a just world is so strong, we develop hedges (he shouldn't have been on the golf course or they should have built their house on higher ground or she should have stopped smoking) and explanations that place the blame on the victims. In an intriguing series of studies, Lerner and his colleagues (Lerner and Simmons, 1966) demonstrated that we do, in fact, derogate people whom we see suffering, and we derogate them for no reason other than the fact that they are suffering. Our belief in a just world is maintained by assuming that if they are suffering, they must deserve it.

Nevertheless, we do not always seek the causes of others' behavior in their internal characteristics and place the cause of our own success or failure in the environment. Other motivational factors influence our attributions. If, for example, we have failed on a task that is important to us, we may well explain that failure by our lack of effort, an internal attribution. Conversely, if someone we dislike succeeds, we may well explain it away as luck, an external attribution. We add these disclaimers simply as reminders that the processes involved in explaining our own behavior and the behaviors of others are complex and likely to be influenced by many situational, cognitive, and motivational variables. Even so, there is some evidence for the tendencies identified by Jones and Nisbett.

With the exception of portions of this last section, most of the present chapter has focused on how we perceive and understand the behavior of others. We have said little about self-perception: how we make sense of the things we feel and do. Surely, one might argue, that is as it should be. A chapter on person perception and attribution should be devoted to the perception of others, because, after all, we know what *we* are like. We all know what we are experiencing and what we believe and what we can and cannot do. Why belabor the obvious? But let's see. It may be that our knowledge of ourselves and our abilities is not always so clear and precise.

Understanding ourselves: self-perceptions and attributions

Epstein (1973) has suggested that our self-concepts are really theories that each of us has constructed about what we are really like. Thus, like the implicit theories that we have about others, we presumably build up out of our experiences a theory about ourselves: how we are likely to respond in certain situations, what we are and are not capable of doing, the sorts of people we like, and the sorts of people we dislike. The fundamental purpose of the self-theories we carry around in our heads is to optimize our control over the environment and ensure ourselves the greatest pleasure at the least possible cost. For example, it is very useful for us to have at least a rough conception of our physical abilities so that we will know which mountains we can climb and which we should simply admire from a distance.

As Epstein points out, no theory is ever completely valid. Whether it be a widely accepted theory of the origin of the solar system or the self-theory of your next-door neighbor, there are bound to be flaws and incorrect hypotheses and inconsistencies and poorly defined concepts. Part of the problem with self-theories appears to be that we often make mistakes in explaining our own experiences. If it stopped at that, it might not be so bad; there would simply be a lot of people walking around with misconceptions about themselves. However, explanations for past behavior that are incorporated into our conceptions of ourselves have consequences for our performance on various tasks, for our understanding of our feelings and emotions, and for what we think we believe.

EFFECTS OF SELF-PERCEPTION ON PERFORMANCE

Let us return to our discussion of the attributions involved in accounting for success and failure. How one distributes or allocates responsibility for one's success or failure may be an important determinant of future performance. Thus, if you learn that you have failed at some task and you decide your failure was due primarily to lack of ability or to task difficulty (fixed factors), your expectation of future success on similar tasks may be lower than if you decide your failure was due to lack of effort or to bad luck (variable factors). Convinced that you don't have the necessary ability or that the task is too difficult, you may not try so hard the next time, because you already "know" you can't do it.

Some evidence of this comes from a study reported in Weiner, et al. (1972), in which 39 male high school students were given 5 trials of a digit–symbol substitution task. On each trial, subjects were interrupted after they had completed various portions of the task but before they were able to finish. Hence, failure was induced on each trial. Following each trial, subjects were asked the extent to which they believed their failure was due to lack of effort, lack of ability, luck, or the difficulty of the task. They were also asked to indicate how likely they thought they would be to succeed on the next trial. As anticipated, the more subjects attribute their failure to lack of ability and task difficulty, the less they expect to succeed on the next trial. Further, the more they attribute failure to lack of ability and task difficulty, the more slowly they actually *perform* on subsequent trials. Subjects who attribute their failure predominantly to lack of effort, on the other hand, feel more likely to succeed and perform more quickly on later trials. Weiner, et al. conclude that perhaps any causal attribution for failure which maintains "hope" will have a facilitating effect, or at least not result in performance decrements. As Epstein would put it, if you incorporate into your self-theory the idea that you can do something, you are more likely to do it than if you convince yourself that you cannot do it. (Box D illustrates how we sometimes err about what we think we can do.)

Several studies have yielded similar results. Steiner (1957) found that subjects with positive self-appraisals tended to avoid internal attributions to explain their poor performance on a word-formation task. In a somewhat better-controlled study, Zajonc and Brickman (1969) employed a reaction-time task in which subjects were to throw a switch as quickly as possible following the onset of a stimulus light. After several blocks of trials on this task, feedback was introduced independently of performance. One-third of the subjects were led to believe they were achieving the reaction time required for success on only 20 percent of the trials, one-third were told they were achieving 80 percent success, and one-third continued with no feedback. In general, subjects tended to raise their expectations for subsequent performance after success and to lower them after failure. However, those subjects who received failure feedback and who did not lower their expectancies, or lowered them relatively less, improved on subsequent trials, while those who lowered their expectancies more did not improve. Again, it appears that if we explain our failures in ways that allow us to maintain a favorable conception of our ability to perform, we do indeed perform better.

On the other hand, suppose we have no explanation for our failures except our own lack of ability. If we use this explanation often enough, we approach what Seligman (1975) has termed LEARNED HELPLESSNESS. According to Seligman, the perception that one is helpless decreases the likelihood of initiating and sustaining task-relevant behaviors and thereby decreases the likelihood of success. In fact, it almost always ensures failure. The initial finding that seems to have stimulated Seligman's work on helplessness was a study of conditioning in dogs. It is reported by Overmier and Seligman (1967). Using a box with two compartments, Overmier and Seligman found that dogs placed in one side of the box behaved very differently if they had previously been subjected to certain classical-conditioning procedures than if they had not. If the floor in their compartment was electrified, naive dogs quickly learned to jump the barrier between the two compartments and escape the shock. However, if the dogs had previously learned to associate a tone with an inescapable electric shock while restrained in a harness, they failed to escape shock when later placed in the two-compartment box. The key words here are *inescapable* and *while restrained*. Apparently the latter dogs had learned during the prior experience with inescapable shock that their responses were to no avail, so their motivation to initiate responses that might lead to escape was now absent.

Another way of saying this is that the dogs were inappropriately generalizing their failure to escape in one situation to a new situation in which they could have escaped easily. Extending his research to humans, Seligman (1975) argues persuasively that such inappropriate generalization of helplessness is at the core of

D. The Illusion of Control

Most attribution theories and attribution theorists emphasize the rationality of the ways in which we go about explaining why something occurred or why someone behaved as he or she did. Some research by Ellen Langer suggests that the neat analyses of attribution theorists may have left something out. Consider the distinction between an outcome that is determined by skill and one that is determined by chance. In principle, this distinction can be made easily. In skill situations, one can presumably influence the outcome; in chance situations, one cannot. Langer hypothesizes, however, that in reality this distinction is often blurred if not totally ignored. People often act as if things that can only influence skill-related outcomes could also influence chance outcomes.

For example, in skill-related competitive situations, it is true that the more competent one's opponent, the more likely one is to lose. The less competent one's opponent, the more likely one is to win. But, what if the outcome is determined by chance, by the toss of a coin or the luck of the draw? Then, of course, the competence of one's opponent is completely irrelevant. One has the same chance of winning against Walter Mitty as against Bruce Jenner. Langer, however, reasoned that if people confuse skill and luck situations, they may let the characteristics of their opponent influence their behavior even in the latter. To check on this, she recruited male undergraduates at Yale to play a simple card game in which they and another "subject" each drew for high cards after placing bets between 0 and 25¢. For some subjects the opponent was neatly dressed, clean, and apparently competent, while for others the opponent was awkward, shy, and apparently incompetent. The major dependent measure was the average amount bet. As anticipated, subjects bet significantly less when their opponent was neat, clean, and confident than when their opponent appeared to be a schnook.

In subsequent research, Langer (1975) has found that subjects allowed to select their own ticket from a box of lottery tickets are significantly more reluctant to part with the chosen ticket than those who are simply handed a ticket from the box. All tickets, of course, had precisely the same chance of winning, but apparently the act of selecting the ticket gave subjects a feeling of greater control over the outcome.

---

those diverse psychological states that are loosely referred to as depression. Seligman, an experimental and clinical psychologist, reports that he has been repeatedly struck by the fact that many students he has come in contact with (college students who, objectively, are extremely fortunate) seem depressed, listless, and uninterested in the world around them. Seligman hypothesizes that this is partly because many of these students have never made a connection between their actions and the good and bad things that come their way. They have received much of the best that life has to offer, but not so much by virtue of their own efforts as by living in an affluent society or having rich parents. Seligman suggests that:

> what produces self-esteem and a sense of competence, and protects against depression, is not only the absolute quality of experience, but *the perception that one's own actions controlled the experience.* To the degree that uncontrollable events occur, either traumatic or positive, depression will be predisposed and ego strength undermined. To the degree that controllable events occur, a sense of mastery and resistance to depression will result (p. 99).

Seligman reports some success in treatment of hospitalized depressives with the use of simple tasks that demonstrate to the patients that they can exert control over aspects of the environment. The extent to which mastery of such simple tasks will generalize to the patients' life outside the hospital is a major question facing research on learned helplessness.

There is another way in which attributions may sustain or disrupt performance. When one has embarked on a long and arduous task, accurate perception of the amount of fatigue one is experiencing might be very unpleasant and could interfere with performance. It seems plausible that underestimating the amount of fatigue that one is experiencing might contribute to one's ability to keep trying for long periods of time. Consider the following example:

> Suppose a person embarked on a 10-mile hike. Near the end of the hike we would expect him to be perfectly aware that he was extremely fatigued. The very thought of hiking for an additional 10 miles might appear noxious or even impossible. If, however, the same person had embarked on a 20-mile hike, walking at the same pace and in the same manner as the 10-mile hike, at the end of 10 miles he might feel less fatigued; the experience of great fatigue would be incompatible with his knowledge that he must hike an additional 10 miles. Thus, we would expect him to suppress such a feeling or underestimate its intensity (Walster and Aronson, 1967, p. 42).

In other words, if two people who have each performed at the same level on the same task for the same amount of time have different perceptions of how far away the goal is, the one who perceives the goal to be closer should be more fatigued.

To test this idea, Walster and Aronson (1967) designed a very simple two-condition experiment in which, for repeated trials, subjects in both conditions were asked to perform highly fatiguing tasks. One task was marking X's in squares of graph paper at the rate of one X per second for 10 minutes, the pace being set by a metronome. The second fatiguing task involved measurement of the subject's visual threshold. In addition, prior to beginning either of these tasks, subjects had been required to dark-adapt for 45 minutes and to answer a lengthy questionnaire. After dark-adaptation, subjects in the long-expectancy condition were told that they would be given five trials at the X-marking and visual-threshold task, whereas subjects assigned to the short-expectancy condition were told there would be only three trials. On each trial, subjects were asked to indicate how fatigued they were on a scale ranging from 0 ("as fresh as I have ever been") to 13.5 ("as tired as I have ever been"). The results on this measure showed essentially no differences between the long- and short-expectancy groups on trials 1 and 2. On trial 3, however, the short-expectancy group indicated a sizable increase in fatigue, whereas the long-expectancy group did not. It appears that expecting to continue a fatiguing activity mitigates one's perception of one's own fatigue. "Individuals tend to underestimate the extent of their fatigue until they feel that they have virtually completed their task" (p. 45).

Such misattribution may indeed play a part in sustaining performance over long periods of time. Unfortunately, there has not yet been much research on whether this kind of self-deception may be involved in the pursuit of long-term, real-life goals. It does seem clear, however, that the ways in which we explain our successes and failures influence our future performance. The work on learned helplessness also indicates that believing one's actions have no effect on the outcome is a depressing, motivational disaster. On the other hand, when we believe that we can do something, we may even go so far as to trick ourselves into ignoring our own fatigue, a ploy that helps us do what we think we can. Let us look a little more closely at some of the things involved in this sort of misperception of one's own bodily states.

LEARNING TO IDENTIFY AND LABEL OUR BODILY STATES

In a series of important studies, Schachter and his colleagues (1964, 1971) explored the general proposition that the experience of internal physiological changes (such as a vague discomfort or arousal of some kind), in the absence of an understanding of the source of that experience, is likely to lead one to attribute the cause of the experience to the situation in which one finds oneself.

To test this idea, Schachter and Singer (1962) recruited subjects for an experiment that was supposedly designed to examine the effects of a new vitamin compound, Suproxin, on vision. Subjects received an injection of this "vitamin" and were told there would be a short waiting period for the vitamin to take effect before the vision tests began. Actually, the injection was either a placebo or epinephrine, a stimulant that causes several detectable physiological changes, such as hand tremor, flushed face, a feeling of warmth, and an increased heart rate. Some subjects were correctly informed about the physiological effects the injection would produce; other subjects were either told nothing about these side effects or misinformed about the effects they would experience. The subjects correctly informed about the nature of the effects they would experience have a completely adequate explanation for their flushed face and pounding heart. They should not be inclined to look around in their environment for an explanation. On the other hand, subjects who were left ignorant or misinformed about the effects of the injection do not have an explanation for their trembling hands and racing pulse. They, according to Schachter and Singer, should be more likely to try to explain what they are experiencing by the situation in which they find themselves. Subjects given a placebo, of course, have nothing to explain; they were not given a stimulant that induces physiological changes.

To manipulate the labels available for subjects to explain their physiological arousal, Schachter and Singer arranged for each subject to spend the brief waiting period in the company of another "subject" who behaved in either an extremely euphoric or an angry manner. During this period, the subject and the euphoric or angry accomplice were observed through one-way mirrors. At the conclusion of the waiting period, the subjects filled out several self-report mood scales. Although somewhat weak, the results were generally as anticipated. Subjects given the injection and correctly informed about its effects were less likely to label what they were experiencing as either euphoria or anger (depending on the stooge's behavior) than were subjects given the same injection with either no explanation or an incorrect explanation of its effects.

In subsequent research, Schachter and his colleagues extended their research into such areas as perception of pain, hunger, thirst, and various emotional states. For example, Nisbett and Schachter (1966) hypothesized that one may be able to tolerate more or less pain depending on how one interprets the physiological arousal and other effects accompanying the pain. If one believed that the pain-produced symptoms were in fact due to, say, a drug that one had taken, one should be able to tolerate more pain than if one believed the symptoms to be a direct result of the pain-producing agent. To check on this, Nisbett and Schachter recruited subjects for an experiment on skin sensitivity in which the test of sensitivity was to be their responsiveness to electric shock. Subjects were told that the experimenter was interested in the effects of a particular drug on skin sensitivity. All subjects were given the "drug," which was actually a placebo. However, in one condition (Pill Attribution) the description that subjects were given of the side effects of the drug was really a description of the effects produced by electric shock. In a second condition (Shock Attribution), the description of the side effects was not at all similar to the effects produced by shock. The idea, of course, was that subjects in the former condition would attribute their symptoms to the pill and think the shock was not so bad, whereas the latter subjects would blame everything on the shock. Subjects were administered a graded series of gradually increasing levels of shock and were asked to tell the experimenter when they could first feel the shock (Sensitivity Threshold), when the shock became painful (Pain Threshold), and when it became too painful to go on (Tolerance Threshold). The results appear in Table VI. Subjects who attributed their arousal to the pill had higher pain thresholds and higher tolerance thresholds. Nisbett and Schachter point out that Schachter and Singer had shown that the label attached to artificially induced bodily states could be manipulated and that the present study demonstrated that the labeling of bodily states that occur naturally is similarly manipulable.

One intriguing extension of Schachter's ideas about labeling bodily states involves eating behavior and

Table VI Mean shock thresholds from a series of 37 increasingly intense shocks

	Sensitivity threshold	Pain threshold	Tolerance threshold
Pill Attribution	4.58	11.58	25.75
Shock Attribution	4.58	8.00	15.75

Labeling of pain is manipulable in terms of whether the subject believes the sensation is a direct result of a pain-producing agent (shock) or a side effect of another condition (pill). (From Nisbett and Schachter, 1966, Table 4, p. 235.)

how we decide when we are hungry. Schachter (1971) notes that one possible explanation for the overeating of the chronically obese is that they never learn to discriminate the internal physiological cues by which people of normal weight tell when they are hungry. That is, they either do not have the same internal cues as normal-weight subjects or, if they do have these cues, they don't label them as hunger. In any event, it seemed to Schachter that part of the problem is that obese subjects rely too much on *external* cues, such as time of day, amount of food available, and quality of the food itself, to define for them when they are hungry and how much they should eat. Normal-weight subjects attend to these cues also, of course, but they seem to place a great deal more reliance on internal cues than do the obese.

In one of a series of experiments designed to test these ideas, Schachter and Gross (1968) hypothesized that the obese would pay more attention than normal-weight subjects to time of day in regulating their eating behavior. Thus, if an obese person were induced to believe that it was past dinner time, he or she would eat considerably more than if he or she believed it was still earlier in the day. Normal-weight subjects, on the other hand, should be less responsive to time of day and should eat about the same amount—depending on how hungry they were—regardless of what time they thought it was. To check on this, both obese and normal-weight subjects were recruited for an experiment on physiological reactions. On arrival at the laboratory (always at 5 P.M.), each subject was attached to a few electrodes, had his watch and rings removed if he had any, and left alone in a room that was bare except for a table, chairs, and a wall clock. The subject was told that there would be an initial base-line recording of his physiological reactions at rest, so all he had to do was sit there. The electrodes were actually dummies, but they apparently led through a conduit in the wall to some electronic gadgetry in the next room.

The only manipulation in the experiment had to do with the clock on the wall. For all subjects, the experiment had begun at 5 P.M. For some subjects, however, the clock ran much slower than normal, and for other subjects, the clock ran much faster than normal. For example, when subjects had actually been in the room for 40 minutes, those with the slow clock thought it was only 5:25 P.M., whereas those with the fast clock believed it was 6:10 P.M. At about 5:40 P.M. (real time), the experimenter returned to the room, fiddled with the electrodes and gave the subject a brief questionnaire to fill out. He also brought a box of crackers with him, left them in the room, and told the subject to help himself if he wanted any. He then left the subject alone for another 10 minutes. The measure of interest was how much the subject ate during this last 10 minutes, and the results are shown in Figure 3. The experimenter, of course, knew how much was in the box when he brought it in. Obese subjects ate almost twice as much in the fast-clock condition as in the slow-clock condition. For normal-weight subjects, this finding is reversed. In fact, postexperimental questioning re-

3. Amount eaten by subjects in the four conditions. Obese subjects responded to an external cue (a manipulated clock) in deciding how much to eat. Internal cues seemed to be ignored or nonexistent. (From Schachter, 1971, Table 28, p. 93.)

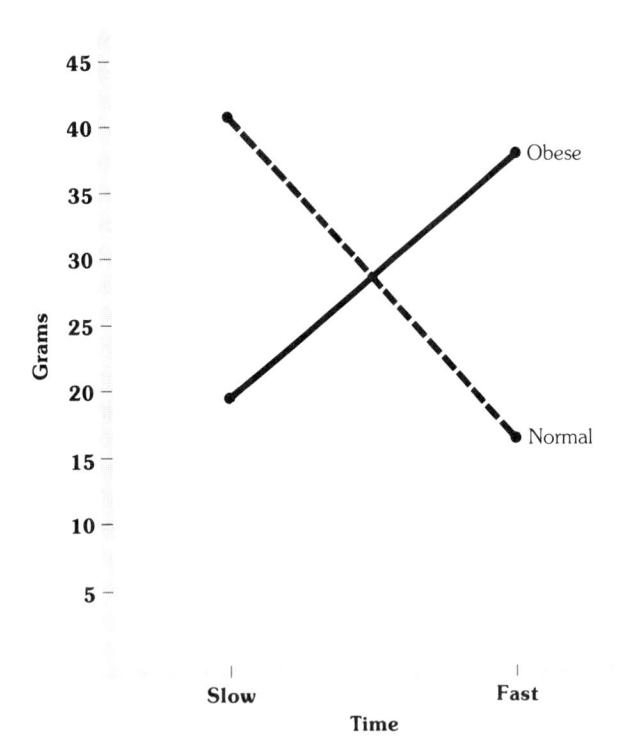

vealed that normal-weight subjects had specifically inhibited their eating in the fast-clock condition because they did not want to spoil their appetite for dinner. For obese subjects, the approaching dinner hour apparently made little difference as an inhibitor. The later it is, by the clock on the wall, the more they eat.

Thus, in Schachter's approach to the labeling of bodily states, both internal and external cues are important, though in some instances, such as the eating behavior of obese people, internal cues may be minimal or even nonexistent. Of course, Schachter would say that this demonstrates his point. Without those cues, the obese are not very accurate about labeling their experiences. They are overresponsive to external cues. There is another line of research on self-labeling, however, that dispenses entirely with internal cues and argues that, in many instances, we can very appropriately rely on simply observing our own behavior in order to understand what we feel or believe or intend.

PERCEIVING AND EXPLAINING OUR OWN BEHAVIOR

According to Bem (1965), we often make sense of our own behaviors and explain them by relying on precisely the same data that an observer would use. That is, we observe our own behavior and the circumstances in which it occurs. The crucial distinction that Bem makes about behavior is whether or not it is seen as occurring freely or as having been coerced by some environmental contingency, "an offer you can't refuse." If we see our behavior as having been coerced, we infer that it does not reflect our true beliefs, attitudes, or feelings. On the other hand, if the behavior does not appear coerced (such as going to a Chinese restaurant repeatedly when there are all sorts of other restaurants around), we infer that the behavior tells us something about ourselves (we must really like Chinese food). Thus, somewhat paradoxically, Bem suggests that one's response to a particular stimulus situation may partially determine how one perceives that situation. The usual view, of course, is that how one perceives a stimulus situation determines one's response.

To clarify this idea, consider the following experiment by Bandler, Madaras, and Bem (1968). Bandler, et al. recruited male college students to participate in what was billed as a pretest to help determine appropriate shock levels for a later experiment. Each student received a series of shocks under each of three conditions: Escape, No Escape, and Reaction Time. In the Escape condition, subjects were told that they *should* press a certain button to turn off each shock as it occurred but that they did not have to. In the No Escape condition, they were told they *should not* press the turn-off button, but they could if they really had to. In the Reaction Time condition, subjects were simply told to press the button as soon as the signal light came on (it came on ½ second after the shock began in all conditions). Following each shock in all conditions, subjects rated the discomfort it produced. Actually, the shock intensity was always the same for a given subject, regardless of condition. The idea behind the experiment was that the perceived discomfort of the shocks should be greater when subjects saw themselves as escaping from the shock than when they saw themselves enduring it. The Reaction Time condition was essentially a control condition in which subjects do turn off the shock, as in the Escape condition, but do not perceive themselves as doing so in order to escape. As anticipated, the mean ratings of discomfort in the Escape condition were significantly higher than those in the No Escape and Reaction Time conditions. It appears that one may look back at one's behavior in response to an aversive stimulus to help one decide how uncomfortable or painful the stimulus really was.

In the foregoing experiment, it was crystal clear that one's escape behaviors were relevant to the shock and that one could therefore use those behaviors as evidence about how one felt about the shock. Many behaviors we perform, however, have no clear relevance to any particular belief, feeling, or attitude we hold. Kiesler, Nisbett, and Zanna (1969) point out that we will use such neutral behaviors to make inferences about, say, what we believe, only when someone or something cues us that the behavior is relevant to the belief. Thus, if you try to conserve energy during a coal strike simply because that seems like the thing to do, it may never occur to you that someone could say you must be anti-union. You must not care anything about the coal miners' plight. The point, of course, is that energy conservation helps the large utilities and mine operators withstand the strike. Until the relationship between conservation behavior and attitude toward the U.M.W. was made explicit, however, you would not have used such behavior as an indicator of your feelings toward the union. Once the relationship has been pointed out to you, you might.

Some evidence on this possibility is reported by Kiesler, et al. (1969), who asked male college students to help them determine the optimal number of arguments to use in a persuasive communication. The students were to do this by stopping passers-by in the street, pointing out the importance of combatting air pollution, and urging them to sign a clean-air petition. A confederate was to try out similar sets of arguments about promoting auto safety. While the experimenter was explaining this to the subject and the confederate, the latter either said he would be glad to do this because he believed in auto safety (this was defined as the Belief-Relevant condition) or said he would participate because the experiment might have some value (this was termed the Belief-Irrelevant condition). The idea, of course, was that only in the former (Belief-Relevant) condition would the real subject be likely to infer that his agreeing to do what the experimenter asked could be taken as evidence that he was really in favor of a clean-air movement. This is precisely what occurred. On a postexperiment questionnaire, subjects in the Belief-Relevant condition were significantly more opposed to air pollution that were subjects in the Belief-Irrelevant condition.

It appears, then, that under some conditions people do indeed look at their behavior in order to decide what they believe. They may make a mistake or an incorrect inference about their belief, but the evidence they use is often the same evidence that an external observer would use. Bem's theory of self-perception is indeed an intriguing one. We shall discuss it in more detail in Chapter 9.

Summary

We began this chapter by examining the implicit theories of personality that we carry around with us. The evidence seems to indicate that we use our implicit theories to fill out our impressions of another. Given one or two items of information about another, we are all too ready to infer additional qualities, qualities that the person may or may not have. It appears that any characteristic of a person that stands as unique may have a disproportionate effect on what we infer about the person. From our consideration of implicit theories, we turned to a set of interrelated phenomena having to do with the effects of premature conclusions about another, halo effects, and the extent to which a person's social role may bias our impressions of that person. We also pointed out that, although there are large areas of overlap in the implicit theories of different people, there are also strong individual differences in their perceptions of others. Further, a growing body of evidence seems to indicate that these individual differences are not just random variations, but that clear and definite relationships exist between the personality of the perceiver and how he or she organizes beliefs about others.

We then turned to a closer examination of the actual processes involved in perceiving others' behavior and in how we go about deciding whether the behavior tells us anything about the person. The point was made that the perceiver actively participates in organizing another's ongoing behavior into meaningful units. Once a perceiver has succeeded in discovering what he or she believes to be the intention of an actor, perception is likely to become increasingly selective, and behaviors pertinent to the intention are likely to stand out. The work of attribution theorists such as Heider, Jones and Davis, and Kelley, however, demonstrated that we are rarely content with an intention. We want to understand the causes of behavior. In order to do so, we evaluate evidence in a relatively rational manner, looking for causes that covary with the observed behavior. As an example of attribution processes, we looked at some of the variables involved in explaining success and failure. We came across a systematic variable of some importance: whether the success or failure to be explained was our own or someone else's. We seem more inclined to blame (or praise) others and to see ourselves as simply doing what the circumstances dictate or as being lucky or unlucky.

To the extent that we do attribute our own triumphs and disasters to something about ourselves, such attribution affects our self-conception and our future performance. There is a plasticity about our feelings, abilities, and beliefs, and we often seem to rely on external cues to tell us what we are or are not capable of, what we believe or do not believe, and what we do or do not feel. Like any good theory, our conceptions of ourselves are continuously evolving.

6

Attraction and love

151
Determinants of attraction

Propinquity
Similarity
Complementarity
Reciprocity
   Reciprocity of liking
   Attraction and self-disclosure
Desirable characteristics
Physical attractiveness
   The matching hypothesis
   What is beautiful is good—or is it?

162
Theories of attraction

A balance theory approach
Reinforcement theory
   Reinforcement-affect theory of attraction
   Gain-loss theory of attraction

168
The nature of love

Romantic love
Love as exchange
Liking versus loving
Passionate love
The colors of love

179
Summary

Our daily lives are filled with other people. On a college campus, we may see literally hundreds of people each day. Most of them we do not know and may never see again. Many are slight acquaintances, some we know well, and a few are placed in a special category called "good friend."

We are not neutral in our feelings toward other people, particularly people with whom we are acquainted. Some people we like very much, some we like a little, and there are usually a few we detest. Liking and disliking others, or interpersonal attraction, is a pervasive aspect of social life. It makes life meaningful, gives it zest, and ensures our intense participation in the social world. Attraction is such a common, everyday occurrence that social psychologists were late in recognizing it as a phenomenon worthy of study. During the past two decades, however, attraction has received more attention. There are a great many interesting questions: Why do I like some people, but not others? How can I get other people to like me? Do opposites really attract? Or do birds of a feather flock together? Is liking different from loving, and if so how? Can you love and hate someone at the same time? The list is endless, and the answers are immediately useful, because we are always involved in the ongoing processes of liking and disliking.

ATTRACTION (which includes both liking and disliking) can be thought of as a type of affective or emotional force that propels us toward or away from another person. This definition conceives of attraction as a special type of attitude. (Attitudes are discussed in Chapter 7.) To like or dislike someone is to hold a positive or a negative attitude toward that person. An attitude can be thought of as pertaining to an abstract entity, such as mathematics, the United States, ethnic groups, etc. Some of the same basic dynamics seem to be involved in the development of attitudes toward people that are involved in the development of attitudes toward abstract concepts.

Attraction as it occurs in everyday life is one facet of our affiliation with groups. Our likes and dislikes occur in the context of the groups in which we are socialized, mature, and spend our lives. The affiliative (or behavioral) aspect of attraction is discussed in Chapter 12, and in the present chapter we are concerned with attraction as an attitude.

Determinants of attraction

In everyday life, attraction between people can take many forms. We may have mild positive feelings about people we see occasionally, intense affection for certain friends, respect for others with admired attributes, and an intense feeling called love for a few very special people. Social psychologists have not generally tried to sort out the qualitative differences in the types of attraction that we experience toward others. Most of the research has used a relatively undifferentiated concept of attraction that is measured on a numerical rating scale. Attraction has nearly always been treated as a dependent variable, and most of the research has sought the causes of attraction.

The effects of a great many independent variables on attraction have been examined Some of the major ones are *propinquity, similarity, complementarity, reciprocity, socially desirable attributes,* and *physical attractiveness.*

PROPINQUITY

PROPINQUITY is proximity or nearness. In attraction research, it refers to spatial proximity. There is an old saying that "somewhere in this world there is one true love just for you, and the chances are that he or she lives only a few blocks away." The adage summarizes the results of a great deal of research on friendships and mate selection, to the effect that other things being equal, the closer together two people are geographically, the more likely that they will be attracted to one another. There is extensive evidence that propinquity within residential areas or housing units is associated with friendship choices and mate selection.

A study by Segal (1974) tested the propinquity-attraction hypothesis. A questionnaire was mailed to

52 students (all male) in the Training Academy of the Maryland State Police. The students, who had known each other for six weeks at the time, were asked to name their three closest friends on the force. Students were assigned to rooms and to seats in classes by the alphabetical order of their last names. Thus, propinquity was based on the accident of one's birth name and so came close to serving as a true independent variable. The results showed that alphabetical ordering did have a strong effect on friendship choices. A total of 65 friendship choices were made, and of these 29 (45%) were given to trainees adjacent to the chooser's name in alphabetical order. Segal concluded that propinquity contributes to attraction but noted that the trainees were very similar to each other on a large number of variables. It may well be that propinquity is a powerful variable only when people in a geographical area are all relatively alike.

We can conclude that propinquity is related to attraction but does not cause attraction directly. Propinquity sets up the conditions for interaction to occur, and the quality of that interaction determines whether and how much people will like or dislike each other.

SIMILARITY

There is an old adage that "birds of a feather flock together." When translated into more scientific language, the proverb becomes the hypothesis that the more similar two people are on any of a wide variety of attributes, the more attracted to each other they will be.

Extensive correlational and observational evidence going back many years supports this hypothesis (Byrne, 1971). It has been found that spouses are more similar in opinions and preferences than unrelated couples. Friends have also shown substantial correlations between various beliefs and values. One problem with much of this research is that it is unclear what causes what. Similarity may have been a causal variable in the formation of friendships and marriages, but the hypothesis that people become more similar as a result of association is equally plausible.

Donn Byrne has conducted a vigorous research program over the past 15 years concerned with the relationship between similarity and attraction. Most of Byrne's experiments have followed a standard experimental procedure. Subjects first complete a questionnaire that may measure their attitudes or personality dispositions. One frequently used measure is a 56-item "Survey of Attitudes." Two items from the questionnaire are shown in Figure 1. Based on the subject's responses, a fabricated questionnaire is constructed to be either very similar or very dissimilar to the subject's questionnaire. The bogus questionnaire, which is attributed to another person, is presented to the subject for evaluation. The task is to form an impression of the person and rate the person on several items on the "Interpersonal Judgment Scale." The two critical items are shown in Figure 1. The seven response alternatives for each item are scored from 1 to 7, and the scores for the two items are added together. The sum is considered a measure of the subject's attraction to the hypothetical stranger.

This procedure allows precise variation in the degree of similarity of the subject to the hypothetical stimulus person. One variable that proved to be of major importance was the proportion of attitudes that the subject and stranger shared. Byrne and Nelson (1965) found that as the proportion of similar attitudes increased, attraction as measured by the Interpersonal Judgment Scale increased in almost perfect step.

The strong relation between similarity and attraction was found for many other types of similarity as well. A few of these include similarity on economic grounds (Byrne, Clore, and Worchel, 1966), personality characteristics (Byrne, Griffitt, and Stefaniak, 1967),

1. **Byrne's Method of Studying Similarity and Attraction. Subjects first complete a 57-item questionnaire composed of statements like item 5 (Belief in God) and item 19 (Premarital Sex Relations). Later they examine the same questionnaire, purportedly completed by another student, that includes responses which are either very similar or very different from their own. Subjects then rate on the Interpersonal Judgment Scale how much they feel they would like this other student. The two critical items are "Personal Feelings" and "Working Together in an Experiment." Responses to these two items are given numerical values and added together to obtain an overall attraction score. (Adapted from Byrne, 1971, pp. 416–427.)**

and self-esteem (Hendrick and Page, 1970). Variation in similarity on almost any dimension seems to work.

COMPLEMENTARITY

The notion that "opposites attract" has existed in our society for a long time. The basic concept is that people who differ on some attribute or on two different attributes are able to provide satisfactions to each other in ways that would not be possible if the difference did not exist. Such attributes may range from basic personality dispositions or psychological needs to relatively simple behaviors. One common example is the pair of personality needs of NURTURANCE and SUCCORANCE. A person with a strong nurturance need desires to take care of, nurture, or otherwise fuss over another person. A person with a strong succorance need desires to be taken care of and nurtured by another person. Two people, one high in nurturance and the other high in succorance, would be complementary on this pair of needs.

Most of the research on COMPLEMENTARITY has focused on personality needs, such as nurturance-succorance, and has been concerned specifically with

Two Items from Byrne's "Survey of Attitudes"

5. Belief in God (check one)
   ___ I strongly believe that there is a God.
   ___ I believe that there is a God.
   ___ I feel that perhaps there is a God.
   ___ I feel that perhaps there is no God.
   ___ I believe that there is no God.
   ___ I strongly believe that there is no God.

19. Premarital Sex Relations (check one)
    ___ In general, I am very much opposed to premarital sex relations.
    ___ In general, I am opposed to premarital sex relations.
    ___ In general, I am mildly opposed to premarital sex relations.
    ___ In general, I am mildly in favor of premarital sex relations.
    ___ In general, I am in favor of premarital sex relations.
    ___ In general, I am very much in favor of premarital sex relations.

The Two Major Items from "Byrne's Interpersonal Judgment Scale"

5. Personal Feelings (check one)
   ___ I feel that I would probably like this person very much.
   ___ I feel that I would probably like this person.
   ___ I feel that I would probably like this person to a slight degree.
   ___ I feel that I would probably neither particularly like nor particularly dislike this person.
   ___ I feel that I would probably dislike this person to a slight degree.
   ___ I feel that I would probably dislike this person.
   ___ I feel that I would probably dislike this person very much.

6. Working Together in an Experiment (check one)
   ___ I believe that I would very much dislike working with this person in an experiment.
   ___ I believe that I would dislike working with this person in an experiment.
   ___ I believe that I would dislike working with this person in an experiment to a slight degree.
   ___ I believe that I would neither particularly dislike nor particularly enjoy working with this person in an experiment.
   ___ I believe that I would enjoy working with this person in an experiment to a slight degree.
   ___ I believe that I would enjoy working with this person in an experiment.
   ___ I believe that I would very much enjoy working with this person in an experiment.

friendship formation and marital choice. Interest in the latter undoubtedly stems from our occasional observation of two married people who seem most unsuited for each other ("as different as night and day") but also seem quite happy with each other. What proportion of successful friendships or marriages are actually based on such an interaction of opposites? Given that similarity is generally important, in what situations or under what conditions would complementarity be expected to also enhance attraction? We cannot answer the first question at present, but in the following discussion we will present one tentative answer to the second question.

Robert Winch (1958) has been the major advocate of a theory of complementary needs. Winch believes that one person's gratification of another's needs automatically leads to attraction. Winch does not deny the importance of similarity on such variables as age, socioeconomic status, race, educational level, etc. during the initial phases of the mate-selection process. However, such variables only create mate-selection possibilities; they do not determine actual marital choices. Actual choice is made on the basis of personality needs that require fulfillment. There are two types of needs.

> Type I. The *same* need is gratified in both Person A and Person B because the need exists at different levels of intensity. An example of Type I needs might be one person with a high need for dominance, and a second person with a low need for dominance (Seyfried, 1977).
>
> Type II. The needs are different in type, but are of about the same intensity. Nurturance-succorance is an example of a Type II need.

As a major test of this theory, Winch studied 25 young married couples. At least one member of each couple was a student at Northwestern University at the time of the study. Each person was interviewed to assess his or her various needs and to obtain case-history material about the person's background. The subjects also took various personality tests. This mass of data was quantified in several ways, and correlations were computed between the various measures. The pattern of correlations was such that Winch claimed the data supported the need-complementarity hypothesis.

Although Winch's studies have been criticized (Murstein, 1971), the complementarity notion is appealing, and other researchers have investigated variations on the basic hypothesis. One of the more interesting attempts is the filter hypothesis of Kerckhoff and Davis (1962). This hypothesis states that initial attraction and pairing are based on similarity of values and interests. However, similarity alone is not enough to move the relationship to permanent status. Such movement requires complementary gratification of important needs. Kerckhoff and Davis interviewed and tested couples of college students who were contemplating marriage and then retested them several months later to ascertain the status of the relationship. The results indicated that couples whose relationship had lasted 18 months or less, and who were similar in values, felt there had been greater movement toward permanence than did couples who were complementary in needs. However, for couples whose relationship had endured 18 months or longer, those couples who were complementary in needs had progressed toward a more permanent relationship. For the long-duration couples, similarity of values and attitudes did not seem very important.

Presumably, couples who had only initial similarity going for them eventually broke up. However, for couples who were also able to complement each other's needs, there was a higher probability that the relationship would endure, and the importance of similarity diminished over time. Unfortunately, the results of this research were not replicated in a study by Levinger, Senn, and Jorgensen (1970), who suggested that there may have been major shifts in the nature of the college population over the several years between their study and the Kerckhoff and Davis study.

Despite difficulties in replicating the results of much of the research concerned with complementarity, the important notion was introduced that different variables may be important at different times during the course of the development of a relationship. A relationship is somewhat analogous to the growth of a living organism. Different needs arise and different experiences are required at different stages of life. Growth means change, and the principle seems to apply to the growth of a relationship as well as to the growth of a person.

RECIPROCITY

RECIPROCITY means give and take or mutual exchange: "You scratch my back and I'll scratch yours."

People engage in reciprocal behaviors endlessly, ranging from the exchange of physical commodities to subtle sentiments, expressions of approval, and love. It seems reasonable that reciprocity of at least some behaviors is related to the development of attraction. In fact, Lickona (1974) believes that "reciprocity is at the heart of human attraction" and is "a central dynamic in human attraction, with meaning for everything from making conversation to making love."

Many scholars view reciprocity in human behavior as highly significant for social life. Gouldner (1960), a sociologist, hypothesized a universal positive NORM OF RECIPROCITY which has two components: (1) people should help others who have helped them, and (2) people should not hurt others who have helped them (see Chapter 10 for a more extensive discussion). There is also a negative form of the norm, though perhaps not as universal, that people should repay harm and injury in kind.

We will discuss two aspects of reciprocity and attraction: reciprocity of liking and reciprocity of self-disclosure and its relationship to attraction.

Reciprocity of liking. A friend is someone who likes us, and it is almost a truism that we tend to like someone who likes us. Most of us have at one time or another been informed by an acquaintance that so-and-so likes us. It is almost impossible not to have an immediate feeling of warm regard in return for so-and-so. We have reciprocated perceived liking for us with liking for the other.

Reciprocity of liking stems from the fact that having someone like us is a potent source of reward. Only in a society in which people have a strong need for the approval and esteem of others would perception of their liking have such a strong effect. Berscheid and Walster (1969) concluded that we do indeed live in such a society. Advertising presents the message in a massive way; if you will buy and use brand X, other people will approve of you and like you better.

If liking from another is a reward, then when people receive information that others like them, they should reciprocate that liking. Backman and Secord (1959) tested this hypothesis by forming small discussion groups of subject strangers who, prior to the initial meeting, were each informed that (bogus) personality test information indicated that certain other members of the group would be highly attracted to the subject. An informal group discussion was held at the first meeting. Afterwards the experimenter told the group that they might eventually be divided into two-person groups. Each member was asked to indicate the three other members of the group whom he or she would most prefer as a discussion partner. The entire group continued to meet for six sessions, and the same ranking of preferred discussion partners was obtained after the third and sixth sessions. The results showed that at the end of the first session, subjects clearly preferred as potential discussion partners the other group members who the experimenter had indicated (falsely) would like them. However, this preference had disappeared by the third group meeting. Subjects were no more likely to choose expected likers than other members of the group as a discussion partner.

Backman and Secord's (1959) experiment is important because it demonstrates that people do tend to reciprocate anticipated liking initially. If the feelings are genuine, very often the interaction should be rewarding enough so that strong mutual attraction will develop over time. An exception is when the liking of the other is directed toward us for ulterior reasons. The other person is feigning liking in an attempt to ingratiate himself or herself with us. If we suspect such ulterior motives, the other person will not be liked and may instead be strongly disliked.

Attraction and self-disclosure. People differ enormously in how much they disclose about themselves. Topics vary in degree of intimacy, and what is considered intimate or nonintimate is to an extent culturally determined. Most of us will talk with a variety of other people on nonintimate topics. However, the degree to which we will disclose intimate facts or feelings depends on our personality dispositions, the situation, and our sex. Jourard (1964) constructed a self-disclosure scale and found that subjects differ widely in how much information they will divulge about themselves. There are also sex differences: females in our society tend to disclose more than males. Situational constraints on disclosure are also apparent. Some situations are defined as appropriate for high disclosure, while others are not. It is appropriate to reveal the most intimate details of your life to your psychiatrist; the same intimate detail related to your classmate will get you in trouble.

Jourard (1964) believed that there is an optimum

level of self-disclosure. To fully know one's own self, it is necessary to allow a few significant other people to know the core of one's being. To be nonintimate with all other human beings is to be alienated from one's self, to not know one's self. On the other hand, an individual who discloses self to anyone and everyone is likely to be viewed as egocentric and maladjusted and will be avoided. The modern movement of the weekend encounter group, sensitivity training, and the like may have increased the number of "instant disclosers." It is uncomfortable (and boring) to be trapped for two hours at a party by a person who insists on revealing all the details of his or her life with great gusto and even pride. For most of us, such an instant pace seems inappropriately fast; we prefer a much more guarded and leisurely rate of self-disclosure.

The objection is to the timing, not necessarily to the process. There is general consensus that exchange of intimate disclosures is necessary for the development of close friendships (Levinger, 1974; Derlega, Wilson, and Chaikin, 1976). Some mutuality of disclosure is necessary for strong and enduring attraction to develop between two people. The reciprocity effect may depend on modeling (one person serves as a model for the other) and trust (Rubin, 1973). The creation of trust seems most important. When a person reveals intimate information to you, that person signals that you are trusted with his or her welfare; and since you are trusted, you are probably liked. You are also given power over the person, since by implication you are viewed as the type of individual who would not abuse privileged information. Such a conferral of trust almost seems to demand reciprocity, at least in the typical unstructured situations that lead to friendship. Altman and Taylor (1973) have proposed a theory of social penetration which assumes that mutuality of disclosure, progressing gradually to more intimate levels, is crucial. Trust builds mutually, and the reciprocity of disclosure continues until the level of intimacy is reached that seems appropriate for that particular relationship. The conclusion from both theory and research is that self-disclosure, reciprocally given, is necessary for a high level of attraction.

Numerous experiments demonstrate that fairly high levels of self-disclosure between two strangers can be achieved in experimental periods of an hour or less. Nearly all of this research used an experimental confederate as one of the strangers. Derlega, Wilson, and Chaikin (1976) questioned whether such a reciprocity effect would occur between already well-established friends. Female subjects were recruited for the experiment and asked to bring a female friend who "knows your deepest thoughts." At the lab the pair were separated, and the subject engaged in an information exchange with either the best friend or a stranger who was in reality an experimental confederate. The friend was taken into the confidence of the experimenter and induced to write a note of either low or high intimacy to the subject. When the other was a stranger (the confederate), the note sent by the confederate was the note that had been sent by the actual friend of the pre-

Self-disclosure increases at an appropriate rate as a relationship develops. Too much or too little disclosure at the wrong time may harm a relationship or prevent its development.

vious pair of subjects. This procedure is called YOKING, because two different subjects were yoked together by the same initial note received from the other person, either a good friend or a stranger.

The variable of interest was the amount of disclosure the subject revealed in response to the low- or high-intimacy note received from the other person. The results showed that when the other was a stranger confederate, subjects gave intimate self-disclosures if the stranger gave an initial intimate self-disclosure, but low self-disclosures were given if the stranger gave low self-disclosures. When the other was a friend, however, subjects gave low self-disclosures regardless of the level of intimacy that the friend disclosed.

Thus, the precise reciprocity of self-disclosure that has been observed many times between strangers seems not to occur between good friends. By the time two people have become close friends, they have probably outgrown the need for "tit for tat" matching of disclosure. They have long since disclosed fully, up to the level of that particular friendship. If one of the pair feels a strong need to disclose at a given time, the other feels no need to reciprocate. And indeed, the discloser may instead need sympathy, comfort, advice or some other behavior than reciprocal disclosure.

This disclosure process appears to be more complicated than first imagined. Some degree of mutual disclosure that allows deep knowledge of the other person seems necessary for strong attraction to develop. Once a friendship is formed, however, routine reciprocation of disclosure is no longer needed or expected. During the acquaintance phase, disclosure is not a rote process that runs off automatically. Rather, it is a process of delicate negotiation, with one person assuming the lead, which is in turn reciprocated, which in turn stimulates another initiative by the leader. The content of the disclosures is presumably important. The content must indicate some basis of value, belief, or personality similarity, or a basis of complementary need satisfaction (Daher and Banikiotes, 1976). If such bases do not exist, mutual disclosure will cease, and the interaction will probably be broken off.

DESIRABLE CHARACTERISTICS

It is probably true that we like people with pleasant characteristics better than people with unpleasant characteristics (Aronson, 1969). One example is a study by Hendrick and Brown (1971), who found that both introverted and extroverted subjects preferred and were more attracted to an extroverted stranger than to an introverted stranger. In our society, outgoingness seems to be a highly valued trait. Introverts preferred this ideal on some (but not all) of the measures instead of opting for similarity to self.

The propensity to be attracted to others with highly valued traits poses an interesting dilemma with regard to similarity. Giving ourselves the benefit of the doubt, most of us have moderately positive amounts of desirable traits. Suppose we meet someone who has these traits in superabundance. Will we like that person more or less than someone else who has the same amounts of the traits that we do? An interesting ambivalence is created.

John Kennedy was an immensely popular president. He was youthful, handsome, very intelligent, rich, and had a beautiful wife. The Bay of Pigs fiasco in Cuba early in his presidency was characterized by Aronson (1969) as "one of history's truly great blunders." Yet Kennedy's personal popularity increased immediately after the debacle. Why?

Aronson reasoned that if someone else has too many good qualities or too much ability, that person may indeed be threatening to us. If someone of outstanding ability commits a blunder, however, the person is reduced to our own stature, merely human, therefore similar, and our attraction for the person may increase. To test this reasoning, Aronson, Willerman, and Floyd (1966) performed an experiment in which subjects listened to a tape recording of a student ostensibly trying out for a College Quiz Bowl. The questions posed by the interviewer were very difficult. The candidate answered either brilliantly, demonstrating superior ability, or rather ineptly, demonstrating only average ability. For half of the subjects, the tape ended at the end of the interview. However, the other half of the subjects heard the student commit the clumsy blunder of spilling a cup of coffee all over himself near the end of the interview. In this way, four experimental conditions were created. A student of superior ability or a student of average ability either committed a clumsy blunder or did not commit such a blunder. After the interview tape was finished, subjects indicated on several scales how much they would like the candidate.

The results are shown in Table I. The higher the

Table I Mean attraction ratings of candidates

	Clumsy blunder	No blunder
Superior Ability Candidate	30.2	20.8
Average Ability Candidate	−2.5	17.8

The higher the number, the more attractive the candidate. (Adapted from Aronson, et al., 1966, p. 228.)

mean, the more attracted the subjects were to the candidate. The results were as predicted. When the superior candidate spilled coffee on himself, he was liked more than in any of the other conditions. However, when the average candidate made the same blunder, he was relatively disliked. In the no-blunder condition, the candidate of superior ability was liked somewhat more than the candidate of average ability, as might be expected.

Demonstration of clumsiness apparently made the candidate similar to the subjects, because everybody goofs once in a while. The positive effect of similarity apparently added to the positive effect of superior ability to create a highly liked candidate. Based on the results for the average candidate, however, the moral seems clear for the rest of us. If we spill coffee on ourselves, we should expect to be perceived as clumsy oafs—unless we can quickly convince people around us that we are really brilliant by muttering our disgusted oaths in Greek or launching other such face-saving behavior.

PHYSICAL ATTRACTIVENESS

Physical attractiveness, particularly in members of the opposite sex, is of considerable interest in everyday life, and probably always has been. It is curious that the research interest of social psychologists in physical attractiveness developed late, in the mid-1960s. Perhaps the neglect was due to the bias of general psychology toward environmental determinants of behavior; physical beauty is a constitutional variable not very receptive to stimulus manipulations (Aronson, 1969; Berscheid and Walster, 1974b). In any event, the situation has changed dramatically. There has been an explosion of research in physical attractiveness and its effects. Most of the work has been concerned with heterosexual attraction.

We will consider two questions. (1) Will people of similar physical attractiveness be attracted to each other? (2) Do beautiful people prosper more than ugly people? An answer of "yes" to the first question would confirm what is called the MATCHING HYPOTHESIS—people at about the same level of social desirability, including physical attractiveness, tend to pair off, ugly with ugly, average with average, and beautiful with beautiful. Sociologist Erving Goffman (1952) eloquently stated one version of the hypothesis: "A proposal of marriage in our society tends to be a way in which a man sums up his social attributes and suggests to a woman that hers are not so much better as to preclude a merger or a partnership in these matters" (p. 456).

The second question is concerned with whether there is a general physical attractiveness stereotype in our society. An answer of "yes" to this question would tend to confirm the hypothesis that "what is beautiful is good" (Berscheid and Walster, 1974b).

The matching hypothesis. An experiment by Walster, Aronson, Abrahams, and Rottmann (1966) was conducted to test the matching hypothesis. The researchers ostensibly conducted a "computer dance" in which 376 males were paired with 376 females, presumably on the basis of personality test information collected at an initial session to which subjects reported to sign up for the dance. In fact, males were randomly paired with females for the upcoming dance. The subjects had been surreptitiously rated on physical attractiveness at the first session. The researchers hypothesized that pairs who by chance were of the same social desirability level would be more satisfied and attracted to each other than pairs of unequal social desirability. On the night of the dance, the couples danced and talked for a couple of hours. Then males and females were separated during intermission and completed a questionnaire assessing their date. Results showed that the only variable determining how much a subject liked his or her date, how much the subject wanted to see the date again, and how often the man did ask the woman for future dates was the physical attractiveness of the date. The more physically attractive the date, the more he or she was liked. Thus Walster, et al. did not find support for the matching hypothesis.

Some experiments have yielded evidence supporting the matching hypothesis. For example, Murstein (1972) took photographs of 99 couples who were either engaged or going steady and had judges rate the attractiveness of each member of each couple. A control set of photographs was formed by randomly pairing the male with the female photographs. The results showed that the difference in attractiveness between male and female for couples engaged or dating was significantly less than the difference in attractiveness of randomly formed couples. The inference is that actual couples tend to match each other more closely in attractiveness than would occur if, instead, couples were formed on a random basis. More recent work by Murstein and Christy (1976) showed that middle-aged, middle-class couples tend to be matched on physical attractiveness. The authors also hypothesized that equality in physical attractiveness between spouses would be related to marital adjustment, but this was not the case.

Although there are some discrepancies in the data, there does appear to be a tendency for people of similar physical appearance to select each other as romantic partners. However, the literature also indicates a very strong tendency to prefer highly attractive partners, regardless of one's own physical attractiveness. People want to be associated with beautiful people. Presumably we operate on the everyday theory that what is beautiful is good.

What is beautiful is good—or is it? Perhaps it seems only common sense that more physically attractive people will be preferred as dating and mating choices. However, there is another research tradition that goes back half a century (Berscheid and Walster, 1974b) in which people consistently rank looks much lower in importance than other qualities such as sincerity, personality, and character when asked to list the prized qualities of a prospective date or mate. Such studies contradict the strong preference for physical attractiveness found in the research we have just reviewed.

At one level, there seems to be a cultural dictum that we should not be dazzled by good looks, that we should not "judge a book by its cover." This dictum may be especially salient when people are simply asked to list the desirable personal attributes of another person. However, the opposing cultural dictum that "what is beautiful is good" may be especially salient when one is actually exposed to attractive stimulus persons or to their photographs.

If there is a tendency to believe that what is beautiful is good, then there exists a physical attractiveness stereotype in which beautiful people are assumed to be more intelligent, interesting, successful, and so on. Dion, Berscheid, and Walster (1972) conducted an experiment to determine whether such a physical attractiveness stereotype exists. They had male and female college students study the photographs of three people (one physically unattractive, one average, and one attractive) and rate each person on a large number of characteristics. Half of the students of each sex rated same-sex photographs, while the other half rated opposite-sex photographs. The researchers expected that when subjects rated same-sex photographs, there might be a jealousy effect for the very attractive photograph resulting in some decrease in the ratings.

The results showed that the more physically attractive people were judged to have more socially desirable personalities, greater occupational success and more marital happiness, general social and professional happiness, and total happiness in life than the less attractive stimulus persons. There was no evidence of a jealousy effect. Dion, et al. concluded that a physical attractiveness stereotype exists and that it is compatible with the thesis that what is beautiful is good.

Sigall and Landy (1973) provided further evidence for the stereotype in male subjects. The researchers had groups of three subjects report to the laboratory. In actual fact, two of the subjects in each group were confederates of the experimenter. There was one male and one female confederate. Half of the time the female confederate was very attractive, and half of the time she was made up to appear unattractive. In addition, half of the time the two confederates represented themselves as being together, and the other half of the time they appeared to be two strangers reporting for the experiment. After a brief period, the experimenter led the male confederate and the actual subject to

Commercial messages are one of the prime sources of the "what is beautiful is good" stereotype, the idea that physical attractiveness leads to success and happiness. The contrast with the world most people face is quite distinct. (Antonio Mendoza/The Picture Cube)

separate cubicles. The subject was asked to rate the male confederate on several scales. The results showed that when the male confederate was associated with an attractive female, he made a much more favorable overall impression and was better liked than when he was associated with an unattractive female or when the female was present but the male confederate was unassociated with her. These results were obtained from both male and female subjects. Sigall and Landy concluded that a beautiful woman has a radiating effect on a man who is associated with her. The desirable qualities of the beautiful woman transfer to the male in terms of other people's perceptions of him.

More recent studies have provided further evidence for the physical attractiveness stereotype. Landy and Sigall (1974) had subjects rate the quality of an essay and the writer's ability when a photograph of the writer (which varied in attractiveness) was attached to the essay. The results showed that more attractive stimulus persons received more favorable ratings of their essay, and these ratings were independent of the actual quality of the essay, which had been experimentally varied. It appears that beauty can bias assessment of the quality of the beautiful person's work in a positive direction.

The research discussed so far used contrived laboratory situations. Krebs and Adinolfi (1975) collected data about 60 male and 60 female students in the naturalistic situation of a college dormitory. The subjects completed several personality tests. More important for present purposes was the fact that, for each subject, sociometric data were collected from dormmates who knew the subject fairly well. The sociometric test asked dorm residents to list such things as a person you "would want as a roommate," and "a person you try to avoid." Based on the sociometric measures, the subjects were divided into four groups: Accepted (many favorable responses received), Control (average number of favorable responses received), Isolated (neither favorable nor unfavorable responses), and Rejected (unfavorable responses). A photograph of most subjects was available, and the photographs were rated by judges on physical attractiveness.

The data were surprising. The most physically attractive subjects, for both males and females, were in the Rejected group. The attractiveness levels of the other groups were, in order, Accepted, Control, and Isolated. It should be stressed that the degree of social acceptance by the sociometric test was based on choices by *same-sex* dormmates. It is possible that the results represent a jealousy effect. The most physically attractive subjects may have been threatening to their less attractive dormmates, who reacted by rejecting them. The personality test data for the subjects showed that the more attractive subjects tended to be ambitious, independent, and achievement-oriented. Although these characteristics are considered generally desirable, they are also self-centered characteristics and might become aversive to other people in a dorm-living situation. Whatever the reasons, the study demonstrates that in a real-life situation, the most beautiful people are not necessarily the most preferred by their same-sexed peers. They may, in fact, actually be rejected.

The many studies indicate that people do tend to respond positively to others who are physically attractive. Such people are assigned a host of favorable qualities based solely on their physical attractiveness. This phenomenon is qualified, however, by the mixed reactions of others of the same sex to the attractive person. Because very attractive people are attributed good qualities, they probably receive many rewards during the course of their socialization. Such individuals may sometimes tend to behave in ways which are perceived as overly self-confident and vain. In addition, the behavior of an attractive person toward another may have a much more potent effect than the same behavior received from a person of average appearance. Sigall and Aronson (1969) found that male subjects liked an attractive female confederate who evaluated them positively but disliked her when she evaluated them negatively. When the confederate was made to appear unattractive, her evaluations of the subjects, either positive or negative, had little effect on subjects' degree of liking for the confederate.

It appears that because beauty is prized, the behaviors received from a beautiful person have a more potent reward or punishment value than the same behaviors received from average people. Beautiful people may often hurt others' feelings, perhaps unintentionally, with slight nuances of behavior that are overlooked in average persons. It is a fair conclusion that highly attractive people should perhaps monitor their behavior more closely than others. In return for the favorable accolades that go with the designation "beautiful person," they must live in such a way as to confirm the positive stereotype or risk rejection if their behavior deviates from it. In a sense, beautiful people are relatively restricted behaviorally, compared to average people. It is doubtful, however, that this mild lack of behavioral freedom is very confining. Few beautiful people would choose to become ugly in order to gain it.

Attraction has many causes. Propinquity, or nearness in space, is important because it provides the basic physical setting for interaction out of which attraction can emerge. One of the more important psychological antecedents of attraction is similarity. A mass of research has shown that the more similar people are on a variety of attributes, the more they will like each other. Complementarity, or attraction of opposites does sometimes occur, but the effect of complementarity seems to occur much less frequently than the effect of similarity. The development of attraction within a relationship also depends on reciprocity of behavior between two people. Reciprocity in liking and reciprocity in self-disclosure are two of the more important areas in which reciprocity promotes liking. Other antecedents of attraction are the desirability of the other person's characteristics, and the physical attractiveness of the other. Within limits, more desirable and more attractive people are better liked in our society.

When we look at the variables one by one, we lose something of the big picture. We need a comprehensive scheme or overview that will allow full conceptual understanding of the phenomenon of attraction. We turn now to the major theories of attraction to see whether such a conceptual understanding is available.

Theories of attraction

There are two major theoretical approaches to the study of attraction. One approach follows *consistency* or *balance* principles. The other approach is based on *reinforcement* notions. Both approaches have been implicit in our discussion of some of the antecedents of attraction. These theories will be discussed briefly here; they will receive further consideration in the chapters dealing with attitudes. It is not surprising that the same theories apply to both attraction and attitudes, since attraction toward another person is one specific type of attitude.

A BALANCE THEORY APPROACH

Balance means harmony or equilibrium among elements in a set. There are several different balance theories, but all are based on a version proposed by Heider (1958). For our purposes, we will study a version proposed by Newcomb (1961), because it pertains most directly to attraction. Newcomb's theory, called the A-B-X model, consists of three conceptual elements: the actor A whose perspective is being taken; another person B perceived by A and related to A in some way; and object X, which may be another person. Actor A also perceives the relationship between B and X. For simplicity, only two perceived relationships are allowed—liking and disliking. The possible combinations of liking and disliking among A, B, and X are shown in Figure 2. The solid lines represent a liking relationship; the broken lines represent disliking.

All possible combinations of liking and disliking that are balanced are shown in the top row of Figure 2; the possible combinations for disliking are shown in the second row. Some examples may be helpful. In case 1, A likes B, and A likes X. It ought to follow that B also likes X. Since B does like X, the triad of three elements is in balance with respect to their liking relationships, as perceived by A. Consider case 6 as an instance of imbalance. A likes B; perhaps they are friends. A also likes X, who for the example may be considered as another person who is a friend of A. But A perceives that B dislikes X. This perception causes imbalance for person A. It is unpleasant to have two good friends one of whom dislikes the other.

Content can be given to each of the other cases in the same way. There is a simple rule that can be used to determine whether a triad is balanced or imbalanced. If the product of the three signs of the three relationships is positive, the triad is balanced. If the product of the three signs is negative, the triad is imbalanced. The products of the three signs of all four cases in the top row of the figure are positive, and all four cases are balanced. The product of the signs of the

```
   1           2           3           4
   A           A           A           A
 +   +       +   -       -   +       -   -

B  +  X   B  -  X   B  -  X   B  +  X

   5           6           7           8
   A           A           A           A
 -   -       +   +       +   -       -   +

B  -  X   B  -  X   B  +  X   B  +  X
```

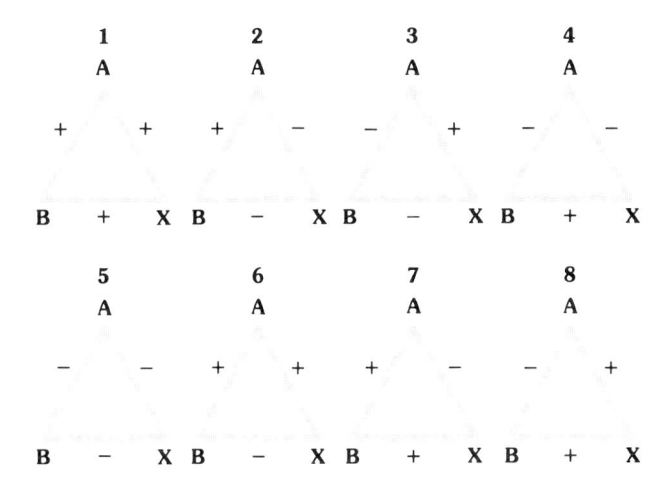

2. Examples of Balance and Imbalance. Solid lines represent liking; broken lines represent disliking. A triad of three elements is balanced if the product of the three signs is positive when all three are multiplied together. Thus all four triads in the upper panel are balanced and all four in the lower panel are imbalanced.

four cases in the bottom row are negative, and all four cases are imbalanced.

Balance theories assume that balance is a natural, intrinsically pleasant state of affairs and that imbalance is intrinsically unpleasant. When a situation is imbalanced in the perception of A, there is a motive to restore balance, or a "strain toward symmetry" (Newcomb, 1961). Of course, the situation can also be schematized from person B's point of view, and B may or may not perceive the situation in the same way that A perceives it. If both people perceive imbalance, however, there should be strong pressures to restore the balance. Persons A and B will communicate with each other about the unpleasant state of affairs. In case 6, for example, person A might try to persuade person B to like X. If the persuasion is successful, all three signs become positive and the triad is balanced. Balance would also be restored if person B persuaded person A to dislike X. The triad would then have two negative signs and one positive sign.

There is some evidence supporting a balance approach to attraction (Miller and Norman, 1976), although it is not as strong as one would like. Most of the relevant studies have used paper-and-pencil ratings of abstract situations. One intruding variable is that subjects tend to be very concerned about agreement and attraction between persons A and B and will often sacrifice overall balance to ensure that relations between A and B are positive.

Balance theory can be applied fairly directly to several of the antecedents of attraction. For example, let X represent person A's attitudes. Person A approves of his or her attitudes, so the A-X line is +. Suppose that person B has attitudes dissimilar to X. Person A will infer that B will dislike or disapprove of A's own attitudes. Therefore, A would probably dislike B. A balanced triad is preserved in this way. Suppose, instead, that B's attitudes are similar to A's attitudes, X. Person A will infer that B will approve of X and therefore will like B. Balance is maintained because all of the relationship signs are positive.

Aronson and Cope (1968) conducted an interesting experiment that tested case 3 in Figure 2. This situation can be described by the hypothesis that "my enemy's enemy is my friend," the title of Aronson and Cope's article. In the experiment, subjects wrote essays that were purportedly measures of creativity. The experimenter informed each subject that his or her essay was uncreative, but the evaluation was delivered very harshly to half the subjects and very pleasantly to the other half. Just after the appraisal of each essay, the experimenter's supervisor called the experimenter outside the room and delivered either a blistering condemnation or lavish praise for a report the experimenter had written. The experimenter returned to the room and sent the subject to the psychology office to get his or her credit points. The departmental secretary administered a questionnaire and also asked the subject if he or she would be willing to make phone calls to recruit local residents as subjects for a research project the supervisor was conducting. The number of phone calls the subject was willing to make was the dependent variable.

The results are shown in Table II. They indicate that subjects were willing to work more for a supervisor who treated a harsh experimenter harshly (my enemy's enemy is my friend) than for a supervisor who treated a pleasant experimenter harshly (my friend's enemy is my enemy), or for a supervisor who treated a harsh experimenter pleasantly (my enemy's friend is my enemy). And a relatively large number of calls were made for a supervisor who treated a pleas-

Table II Mean number of phone calls volunteered on behalf of supervisor

Experimenter's behavior	Supervisor's behavior to experimenter	
	Harsh	Pleasant
Harsh	12.1	6.2
Pleasant	6.3	13.5

The higher the number, the more phone calls volunteered. (Adapted from Aronson and Cope, 1968, p. 11.)

ant experimenter pleasantly (my friend's friend is my friend). Since the supervisor's treatment of the experimenter was unrelated to the experimenter's treatment of the subject, the results offered relatively pure and striking support for balance theory.

REINFORCEMENT THEORY

Reinforcement theories are most closely associated with learning theories. Two general types of learning theories were developed: theories of classical conditioning and theories of instrumental conditioning. In CLASSICAL CONDITIONING, any stimulus (the conditioned stimulus) associated spatially or temporally with an unconditioned stimulus (any stimulus that "naturally" elicits some type of unconditioned response) will, on repeated pairings, come to elicit a conditioned response similar in form to the unconditioned response. For example, when a hungry dog is presented with food (unconditioned stimulus), it will start to salivate (unconditioned response). When the dog is presented with food and the sound of a bell simultaneously, it will, after several pairings of food and bell, start to salivate when the bell is presented alone. The bell is the CONDITIONED STIMULUS, and the salivation that comes to be elicited by the bell is the CONDITIONED RESPONSE. Thus the dog is trained, or conditioned, to salivate to a stimulus that would not naturally elicit salivation.

INSTRUMENTAL CONDITIONING is exhibited when any response that is closely followed by a REINFORCER becomes more frequent over time. A rat in a Skinner box given a food pellet (the reinforcer) for pushing a bar will push the bar more and more frequently in order to obtain additional food pellets. The reinforcer of food for a hungry rat is said to control the behavior of bar pressing.

We will consider two specific reinforcement theories of attraction: a reinforcement-affect theory (Byrne, 1969; Clore and Byrne, 1974; Lott and Lott, 1974) and the gain-loss theory proposed by Aronson (1969).

Reinforcement-affect theory of attraction. As Aronson (1969) noted, all of the major antecedents of attraction—similarity, complementarity, and so on—can be summarized under a general reward-cost or reinforcement theory of attraction.

In its purest form, reinforcement theory assumes that attraction toward a person can be conditioned in the same way in which a dog can be trained to salivate. For example, if you give a hungry person food, the person will experience pleasure (an unconditioned response) from receiving the food. The pleasure from the food will then be attached to you. This pleasure or attraction to you is a classically conditioned attraction response. Dislike for another person can be conditioned in the same way if the unconditioned stimulus is unpleasant, such as shock.

Attraction can also be instrumentally conditioned. For example, a mother who praises a child is administering a reinforcement. In time, the child will learn to work hard for such reinforcement. By the time people are adults, expressions of social approval have become potent sources of reward, and we become attracted to individuals who express approval of us.

Byrne (1969) has perhaps developed the reinforcement model of attraction most completely. The general assumption is that "attraction toward X is a function of the relative number of rewards and punishments associated with X" (p. 67). The formulation is general because X can be almost anything, a nonliving object or another human being. Rewards and punishments vary widely. What is punishment for one person may be reward for another. It is assumed, however, that the variety of rewards and punishments to which adults respond can be traced back to association with the direct physical experience of pleasure and pain in infancy and childhood. The rewards and punishments associated with X can be associated in many different ways. The association may be arbitrary, as is sometimes the case in classical conditioning. Or the association may be the direct administration of rewards or punishments by X, when X is another person.

Byrne has tentatively proposed a law of attraction stating that attraction toward X is a positive linear function of the proportion of positive reinforcements received from X. This statement means that as reinforcements from X increase, liking for X increases directly.

The law of attraction was first formulated to account for the effects of similarity and dissimilarity on attraction. As we have indicated, attraction to a stranger can be predicted accurately if we know how many attitudes we share with the stranger. An interesting question is why similarity is positively reinforcing and dissimilarity punishing or negatively reinforcing. One possible answer is that exposure to similar and dissimilar attitudes creates within the person a specific motivational state called EFFECTANCE (White, 1959; Byrne and Clore, 1967). White proposed that people have a very general need (the effectance motive) to be competent in dealing with their environment—a need to understand, cope with, be effective in, and master the world around them.

In terms of social relations, to be competent means to be able to understand other people, to predict their actions, to have a sense of certainty about them and one's own actions. Much of the reality that we experience is *social* reality (Festinger, 1950), which is the socially defined and arbitrary conventions of life, by contrast with the reality of the physical world. Should you eat fried chicken with your fingers or your fork? Nature does not tell you which course of action is correct; social convention dictates the correct choice. Therefore social reality resides in people's opinions, attitudes and values.

If another person holds the same attitudes and values that you hold, that person gives validity to your sense of competence in dealing with the social world. In short, the person satisfies your effectance motive. Dissimilarity is threatening to one's social definition of the world and calls into question one's competence in dealing with the world. Such negative arousal of effectance is very unpleasant. One way of reducing the unpleasantness is by rejection of the person. Thus similarity or dissimilarity of attitudes serves as a powerful source of reinforcement, which results in various degrees of liking or disliking.

One interesting issue is the question of which is most rewarding, a constant series of positive evaluations received from another person, or an initial negative series of evaluations followed by a positive series of evaluations. A similar question may be posed for punishment. Is a constant series of negative evaluations more punishing than a series that begins positive but turns negative over time? The effects of the sequencing of evaluations on attraction was studied by Aronson (1969) and his students in a series of experiments designed to test what is called the gain-loss model of attraction.

Gain–loss theory of attraction. In an initial experiment, Aronson and Linder (1965) proposed that gain or loss of esteem from another person is a more potent source of reward and punishment than is constant praise or criticism. The prediction was that a person who provided a gain in esteem would be better liked than a constant rewarder and that a person who provided a loss in esteem would be more disliked than a constant punisher.

The experiment was very cleverly designed and rather complex. Subjects were female college students who reported individually for the experiment. They were seated in an observation room with a one-way window to a main experimental room. However, the experimenter told the subject that two women were needed, a "helper" and a "learner," and that since she had arrived first, she would be the helper. A few minutes later, another woman (the learner) arrived. This second woman was in fact a confederate of the experimenter, but from the point of view of the helper in the observation room, the second woman was a naive subject unfamiliar with the experiment. The experimenter seated the confederate learner so that she could be observed by the helper and then went into the observation room to instruct the helper. The experimenter told the helper that he was going to engage the learner in a conversation and reinforce her by saying "mmm hmmm" every time she said a plural noun. This was described as "verbal conditioning" of the learner. The helper's task was to listen in and record the plural nouns used by the learner and later to have a series of conversations with the learner while the experimenter listened to see if the learner continued to use plural nouns. The experimenter and helper would alternate talking with the learner until seven brief conversational sessions were completed.

The experimenter at this point told the helper that she was going to help him with a deception. The helper was told that the learner must not know that the experiment involved verbal conditioning; that he would therefore tell the learner that the experiment was about attraction; that the learner would think that the experiment was about attraction; that the learner would think that the conversations were for the purpose of forming impressions; and that between each of the seven conversations, the learner would be questioned about her impression of the helper at that point.

Thus the scenario allowed the confederate learner to give evaluations of the helper on seven different occasions, which the helper of course overheard. After the "verbal conditioning" phase of the experiment was over, the unsuspecting naive subject (the helper) was interviewed by an assistant. During the interview, the dependent variable, a measure of the real subject's attraction toward the confederate, was obtained.

The sequence of evaluations of the helper by the confederate was the manipulated independent variable. In one condition, the confederate was always positive in her statements about the helper. In a second condition, the confederate was always negative. In a third condition, the confederate started off negative but gradually became quite positive over the seven sessions (the gain condition). In the fourth condition, the confederate started off positive but gradually became negative (the loss condition).

The helper's attraction toward the confederate in each of the four experimental conditions is shown in Table III. The higher the mean, the greater the attraction. The confederate was liked more in the gain condition than in the condition of all positive evaluations and was disliked more in the loss condition than in the condition of all negative evaluations. As predicted, change (or gain and loss) in evaluations received from another had a more potent effect on attraction than constancy of evaluations. The gain–loss theory was neatly supported.

One may reasonably ask why gain and loss exert a strong effect on attraction responses. Aronson (1969) gave several possible explanations.

1. Anxiety reduction. Negative evaluations from others cause anxiety. The gain condition is one of strong anxiety reduction, with consequent high positive affect toward the evaluator. Likewise, a positive evaluation that changes to negative stimulates a great deal of anxiety, more so than continuous negative evaluation.
2. Competence. If an evaluator changes his or her opinion over time, it may be due to the efforts of the person being evaluated. In the gain condition, a positive sense of competence would be created; in the loss condition, a strong loss of competence may be experienced.
3. Discernment. The change in opinion of the evaluator over time may imply that he or she is a discerning individual. In the gain condition, the discernment works in the "right way" to prove that one is indeed a worthy individual. Unfortunately, in the loss condition, the discerning evaluator proves that one is perhaps a dolt after all. The evaluation in the loss condition hurts very much and may cause intense rejection of the evaluator.
4. Contrast. Positive things that follow negative things may seem even more positive by way of contrast. The same reasoning applies to negative things that follow positive things.

All of these explanations may be involved to some extent in accounting for gain–loss effects. A large number of relevant experiments have been conducted during the past decade (many are reviewed in Mettee and Aronson, 1974). Generally, the gain effect is easier to obtain than the loss effect (Clore, Wiggins, and Itkin,

Table III Mean liking of the confederate

Experimental conditions	Liking
(A) Constant evaluations	
1. All Positive	6.42
2. All Negative	2.52
(B) Changing evaluations	
1. Negative, then Positive (gain)	7.67
2. Positive, then Negative (loss)	.87

The higher the number, the more the confederate was liked. (Adapted from Aronson and Linder, 1965, p. 163.)

1975). The latter authors conducted an interesting replication of the gain–loss experiment from an attributional viewpoint. Subjects viewed a 5-minute segment of film showing an actress interacting with a partially visible male. The actress was trained to behave in a "warm" or "cold" manner by exhibiting such nonverbal behaviors as smiling, head nodding, frowning, looking around the room, and the like. Four tapes were created, based on the behavior of the actress during the first 2½-minute segment (warm or cold) and during the second 2½-minute segment (warm or cold). Accordingly, subjects viewed one of four different types of behavior: warm–warm, cold–cold, cold–warm (gain), or warm–cold (loss). After viewing the film, subjects rated the probable attraction of the male to the female, the probable attraction of the female to the male, and the subjects' own attraction to the female.

Generally, there were no differences among the four conditions on ratings of the female's liking for the male or the subjects' liking for the female. On ratings of the male's probable liking for the female, however, exactly the same pattern of results was obtained as in the original Aronson and Linder (1965) experiment shown in Table III.

One interesting implication of gain–loss theory may be called the "law of marital infidelity" (Aronson, 1969, p. 167), which says in effect that you always hurt the one you love. A spouse or other loved one provides many rewards. In fact, the loved one may be operating at near ceiling level with positive reinforcements and may therefore be unable to provide a gain. However, by *withdrawing* his or her affection, the loved one provides powerful punishment that hurts much more than the same nasty words said by a stranger. Thus an anomalous prediction occurs. In a long-term stable relationship, one has long since adapted and come to expect praise from the partner. The next round of praise provides only a luke-warm "ho-hum" experience. However, if an attractive stranger says exactly the same thing, one is likely to feel very, very good. The stranger provides a distinct gain of much reward against a background of no previous reward (by definition, since the other is a stranger). The result is that you cannot reward a loved one as well as a stranger can, but you can hurt a loved one much worse.

Bersheid, Brothen, and Graziano (1976) pointed out that the "infidelity extension" of gain–loss theory really involves two sets of evaluations occurring at different times, one from an admiring stranger and the other from a loved one. Bersheid, et al. questioned whether gain effects would occur when one set of positive evaluations was pitted simultaneously against a set of gain (negative, then positive) evaluations.

The essential logical features of the original Aronson and Linder experiment were replicated by Berscheid, et al., except that subjects watched the evaluator on a television monitor instead of through a one-way window. In *single-evaluator* conditions, subjects heard either a consistently positive evaluator or a gain evaluator. Replicating the original experiment, subjects liked the gain evaluator better than the consistently positive evaluator.

In *double-evaluator* conditions, subjects could watch one of two evaluators who were simultaneously presenting their evaluations. Subjects could switch the monitor back and forth between the two evaluators. One evaluator gave consistently positive evaluations, while the second evaluator gave a series of gain evaluations. The results are quite different in the double-evaluator situation. The positive evaluator was better liked than the gain evaluator—just the reverse of the result usually obtained. However, at least during the second half of the evaluations, the gain evaluator was watched significantly more than the consistently positive evaluator. The moral for the law of infidelity seems to be that you may pay more attention to an admiring stranger than to a loved one, but in the competitive triangle you will like the consistently positive loved one more. Berscheid, et al. pointed out that their results do not invalidate gain–loss theory, but only the particular extrapolation of it dubbed the law of infidelity.

What the Berscheid study does, and quite forcefully, is to show the importance of the actual context in studying attraction. In the traditional single-evaluator conditions, different groups of subjects are in the gain and the constant positive conditions. In the double-evaluator conditions introduced by Berscheid, et al. the same subjects are exposed to both stimulus patterns, gain as well as constant positive. In this situation, the results for attraction were exactly reversed from the results in the single-evaluator situation. Such dramatic changes suggest that future experiments on attraction must be very sensitive to the effects of background context on liking and disliking responses.

Both balance theories and reinforcement theories provide fairly adequate general explanations of attraction, although reinforcement theories seem to work somewhat better. The reinforcement approach takes a frankly hedonistic view of liking and disliking other people. Though they vary in their specifics, all reinforcement theories predict that we will like other people to the extent that they reward us and dislike them to the extent that they punish us. It is a crass view of human nature, but it may be correct. However, there is a tendency in us to rebel at such crassness. Surely a reward–punishment philosophy cannot explain a beautiful sentiment such as love? But perhaps love is very different from attraction. Or is it? We turn now to a consideration of the nature of love.

The nature of love

"I like you" and "I love you" signify to most people quite different sentiments. The difference seems obvious until you try to say exactly what it is. Most of us like many people whom we would not claim to love. It does, however, seem to be a common belief that if you love someone, you should also like that person, although the behavior of some spouses bears witness that no matter how much they love each other, they surely do not like one another. Despite such exceptions, it seems most natural to consider love as a profound kind of liking that involves a deep and intense emotional commitment. The continuity may be far from perfect, however, and anyone who has been in love may deny that it is merely intense liking.

There are many different kinds of love, perhaps as many as there are different kinds of people. There is the love of parent for child, of child for grandparents, of brothers and sisters for each other, and so on. Each relationship is different; each has its own rules of behavior and sentiments exchanged. One type of love that preoccupies most people a substantial part of their lives is love for one (or more) members of the opposite sex. Romantic love has a profound impact on nearly everyone's life at one time or another. It is enormously important from a social–psychological point of view, because it instigates and guides heterosexual relationships, often resulting in the semipermanent, contractual relationship known as marriage.

We will discuss this concept of romantic love, its effect on heterosexual relationships, and the relation between romantic love and marriage. In another section, we will consider research that attempts to distinguish liking from loving. An interesting conception of passion and its relationship to love will also be described. Finally, we will present a typology of love and lovers that has recently been proposed.

ROMANTIC LOVE

The conception of romantic love as a valued ideal apparently arose during the twelfth century among European nobility as a kind of grand game. Its major features were "beliefs that love is fated and uncontrollable, that it strikes at first sight, transcends all social boundaries, and manifests itself in turbulent mixtures of agony and ecstasy" (Rubin, 1973, p. 185).

Rubin provides an example of the early romantic ideal and the way it worked:

Courtly love in its traditional, extramarital form was epitomized by the *Frauendienst* (or "service of woman") of Ulrich von Lichtenstein, an Austrian knight of the thirteenth century. When he was a boy of five, Ulrich later reported in his autobiography, he first heard older boys saying that true honor and happiness could come only from serving a noble woman, and when he was twelve, he first saw and fell in love with the princess, already married, to whom he was to devote the next fifteen years of his life. After years of silent devotion as a page in her court, he finally dared to send her news of the many tourneys he had won for her sake. She sent back news that he was presumptuous and ugly. Undaunted, Ulrich had his harelip fixed, and the princess graciously responded by accepting his service. When the princess once pouted that Ulrich had falsely spoken of losing a finger in battle for her, he pulled out his knife, hacked off a finger, and sent it to her in a green velvet case with a gold clasp, together with an appropriate song. This must have made an impression, for it was only a few months later that Ulrich, after an unprecedented jousting expedition from Venice to Bohemia during which

168
**Cognition of
the social world**

he was dressed up as the goddess Venus, was allowed to visit the princess and, ultimately, granted her love. What this entailed was probably the right to embrace and kiss her, to fondle her naked body, and possibly—here the authorities are in some doubt—to engage in sexual relations. Regardless of what the prize may have been, as Morton Hunt notes, "sexual outlet was not really the point of all of this. Ulrich had not been laboring nearly fifteen years for so ordinary a commodity; his real reward had always been in his suffering, striving, and yearning." After two years, in fact, he tired of court life and moved on to new conquests (p. 186).

Slavish attention to and yearning for the princess are clearly recognizable as emotions that nearly any youngster might experience today. However, an important transformation has occurred. During most of the history of romantic love, it was considered appropriate only for extramarital relationships. (Ulrich had a wife and children back at his home castle.) Today romantic love between man and woman is considered a desirable and perhaps necessary condition for entry into marriage. Romantic love as a condition for marriage is, in fact, relatively rare (see Box A). Throughout most of history, marriages were arranged, usually by parents, and although it was considered desirable for spouses to show affection for each other, romantic love was not expected and indeed might even be detrimental to a good marriage.

There have been many disputes about whether love is the proper basis for marriage. The initial intensity of romantic love always seems to subside. Marriage based on such a flimsy edifice must surely be unstable. The anthropologist Ralph Linton (1936) observed that all societies have recognized that violent emotional attachments occasionally occur between the sexes, but American society is practically the only one to make such attachments the foundation for marriage.

To a considerable extent, marriage has always been a family affair. It matters to your relatives whom you marry, for several reasons. Parents quite naturally want their children to have happy and fulfilling lives. Beyond such altruistic considerations, there is the "pride of the family name" to maintain, which is enhanced if children form "desirable" liasons with other families. The right kind of person usually means someone rather similar to the family in socioeconomic, religious, racial, ethnic, and class background.

The danger of romantic love, from the societal viewpoint, is that it threatens established social structure. A harmonious, smoothly working society requires that most people remain in their allotted niches. Unpredictable marriages across racial, social class, and other backgrounds can be very disruptive to the social order.

One possible solution is to maintain the ideal of romantic love as the proper basis for marriage, but to arrange the social order in such a way that the probability of meeting and mating the right type of person is considerably higher than the probability of meeting and mating the wrong type of person. That is exactly what tends to happen. It is trite but true that you will not marry someone you have not met. And whom do you meet? You meet the people who live close to you in your neighborhood, people you attend classes with day after day, people at your job, people in your church, and so on. People living in the same neighborhood tend to be more similar in social class and ethnic background than people from different neighborhoods. Because of background similarity and the greater interaction resulting from propinquity, people in a neighborhood usually share common values and attitudes on a wide variety of topics. The result is that the odds of meeting, falling in love with, and marrying a person similar to oneself on a variety of attributes are high.

Several studies have found that residential propinquity is highly related to who marries whom. Generally, the largest number of marriage licenses are issued to couples who live within a few blocks of each other, and the number progressively decreases as distance increases. Other studies have shown that people tend to marry others of similar religious and racial background. Over 90 percent of U.S. marriages are within the same major religious category, and 99 percent or better are within the same racial background (Rubin, 1973).

Since similarity is such a strong determinant of attraction, it is reasonable that it is also an important factor in the development of romantic love. The social structure is in fact organized so that, on a day-to-day basis, individuals have more contact with similar others than with dissimilar others. The field of actual eligibles for marriage partners therefore tends to be a field of

A. Examples of Some of the Great Loves of History

Antony and Cleopatra, who defied convention and Julius Caesar in order to be together.

As Antony lay dying, his last words were to Cleopatra:

> I am dying, Egypt, dying; only
> I here importune death awhile, until
> Of many thousand kisses the poor last
> I lay upon thy lips.
> *Antony and Cleopatra,* Act IV: scene xiv

Romeo and Juliet, the young star-crossed lovers, probably the ultimate romantics:

> But, soft! What light through
> yonder window breaks?
> It is the east, and Juliet is the sun. . .
> See, how she leans her cheek upon her hand!
> O, that I were a glove upon that hand,
> That I might touch that cheek!
> *Romeo and Juliet,* Act II: Scene ii

David and Bathsheba:

> And it came to pass in an eveningtide, that David arose from off his bed, and walked upon the roof of the king's house: and from the roof he saw a woman washing herself; and the woman was very beautiful to look upon. . . And David sent messengers, and took her; and she came in unto him, and he lay with her."
> *The Bible,* II Samuel 11:2,4

> King David wanted Bathsheba for himself, so he sent her husband, Uriah, to the front lines of battle in the Israelite war. Uriah was killed, and David and Bathsheba were married.

Elizabeth Barrett, spinster and semi-invalid, left her family home to marry poet Robert Browning. She became a famous poet herself and wrote one of the best-known love sonnets of all time.

> How do I love thee? Let me count the ways.
> I love thee to the depth and breadth and height
> My soul can reach, when feeling out of sight
> For the ends of Being and ideal Grace.
> I love thee to the level of everyday's
> Most quiet need, by sun and candlelight.
> I love thee freely, as men strive for Right;
> I love thee purely, as they turn from Praise.
> I love thee with the passion put to use
> In my old griefs, and with my childhood's faith.
> I love thee with a love I seemed to lose
> With my lost saints,—I love thee with the breath,
> Smiles, tears, of all my life!—and, if God choose,
> I shall but love thee better after death.
> *Sonnets From the Portuguese,* XLIII, p. 102.

similar others. Hence it is generally safe to let romantic love run its course and determine marriage, since the outcome would not be much different if practical-minded parents selected marriage partners for their children without regard for their children's affections.

It seems clear that, although love is a powerful emotion that can verge on the irrational, the object of love is not randomly selected. We generally manage to hold the fevers of love in check until the right person, more or less, comes along. Thus romantic love appears to have an element of social deception built into its fabric. It is uncontrollable, yet controlled just enough so that the right type of person is the recipient of its uncontrolled passion. Though it can transcend all social boundaries, it almost never does.

The development of a love relationship is a complex and sophisticated ritual of interaction that may be analyzed in many different ways. We present one analysis based on exchange theory (Homans, 1961; Thibaut and Kelley, 1959), which is a type of reinforcement theory that draws on the example of the market place. In a trading situation, people exchange goods and services and incur rewards and costs during the process. The interaction between the two parties engaged in trade is instrumental. The relationship can be said to be *extrinsically* motivated by the goods and services each can deliver to the other. In contrast, many interaction relationships are primarily *intrinsically* motivated. In an intrinsic situation, the reward itself is the mutual exchange of behaviors and positive sentiments; there is no expectation of material gain as an outcome of the relationship. Mutual liking would be an example of an intrinsic relationship. Exchange theory assumes that intrinsic relationships can be analyzed as a type of exchange in the same way as extrinsic relationships.

Love as exchange. Blau (1964) has provided a description of love from an exchange viewpoint. He defines love as the polar or extreme case of intrinsic attraction, which has associated with it the gamut of emotional experiences generally recognized as components of romantic love.

The very early stage of love can be quite painful. The other person intrudes into one's thoughts and causes emotional stirrings. There is great uncertainty about how the other person feels. If the growing attraction is openly expressed, one reveals his or her growing dependence on the partner—and in doing so risks rejection. Therefore, during the early stage of love, each person has a vested interest in not revealing the depth of his or her feelings. The social ritual known as flirting provides a mechanism to get beyond this early stage of uncertainty, while minimizing the costs if failure should occur.

> Flirting involves largely the expression of attraction in a semi-serious or stereotyped fashion that is designed to elicit some commitment from the other in advance of making a serious commitment oneself. The joking and ambiguous commitments implied by flirting can be laughed off if they fail to evoke a responsive chord or made firm if they do so (Blau, 1964, p. 77).

As the relationship moves beyond the initial stage, lover's quarrels occur frequently. These serve the function of testing the relationship. One or both parties engage in a temporary withdrawal from the relationship. If the threat of termination is sufficiently painful, the partners make up and in this way express a renewal and deepening of commitment to the relationship.

During the growth of the relationship, the lovers exchange many rewards, which may range from gift giving that is effective mostly because of its symbolic value to shared expressions of each other's intrinsic values ("I love you because you are you"). The perception of increasing attachment by the partner is itself a powerful reward that may stimulate a reciprocal increase in attachment. Giving favors, giving presents, and exerting efforts for the loved one are all signs of love. The self-perception of doing these many things may work to promote self-attributions of love for the other ("I keep saying I love you; therefore I must really love you").

The proper progression of the love relationship requires a nicely balanced degree of mutuality. The more in love one is, the more one wants to please the other. Therefore the partner less deeply involved in the relationship has a power advantage over the other, which may lead to exploitation in various ways. Some slight imbalance of power may actually solidify a relationship, since the committed person will make extra efforts to please the less committed partner, which will in turn really please the less committed partner so that a further surge in his or her commitment may be stimulated. Too much of a power difference, or exploitation of it, will eventually cause frustration that exceeds the level of reward the less powerful member obtains from the relationship, and the resulting quarrels may well terminate the relationship.

Love between two people never occurs in a social vacuum. Rather, its value to each member is socially defined. The value of the relationship is in part defined by how valuable the loved person might be to other prospective love partners. If the partner could have many other potential relationships, his or her value is enhanced for the one in progress. If the relationship in progress is the only one potentially available for the partner, his or her value depreciates proportionately. The value of the relationship also depends on the cues that the partner gives. If the partner is too eager, expresses much commitment, and does so rather quickly, the other is likely to assume that the partner's value is rather low on the love market and depreciate it accordingly.

Closely related to perception of value is the importance of timing, or sequence, in the growth of the relationship. If one person's love grows much faster than the other's love, the other may be "scared off" if he or she does not feel ready for that degree of commitment. Alternatively, great unevenness in commitment often leads to exploitation. Thus there are pressures on both partners not to get in too deep, or at least not much deeper than the other. But there are also counterpressures to express one's love—both for the direct rewards to be experienced and to satisfy the expectancies created in the earlier stages of the relationship. The social network around the couple also defines for them an acceptable sequence of steps toward a permanent relationship. This sequence and its speed varies considerably across social classes, age groups, and geographical areas. There are general norms of timing, however; a man proposing marriage the first time he sees a woman is likely to be considered a little peculiar. A man proposing that the couple get married in 15 years is also not likely to be taken very seriously. Whatever the particular social norms governing timing, it seems crucial that the deepening commitment progress at roughly a mutual pace. If not, as in any other exchange relation, one member of the trading pair will get an inequitable deal, and the transaction will cease.

The exchange approach to love should not be considered as simply true or false. It is useful as a theoretical approach, because it conceptualizes the strange social behavior called love in the same terms and mechanisms as any other everyday behavior. Other theoretical approaches are also valid, and, because love is treated in popular culture as something almost holy, no doubt some other theory of love would be preferable to most people.

LIKING VERSUS LOVING

The discussion to this point implies that loving is something different from liking, although no proof has yet been offered. Rubin (1970; 1973; 1974) developed two questionnaires, one to measure liking, the other to measure romantic loving. Love was defined as an attitude held by a person toward a particular other person. This definition is very similar to a definition of liking, and Rubin intended that love be viewed as one type of interpersonal attraction. The results from the two scales would have to be used to decide whether liking was something actually different from loving, or whether the two scales really seemed to measure the same thing.

It will be useful to specify the criteria that Rubin followed in the development of his love scale and the rationale by which liking would be distinguished from love.

1. The items should be based on current popular and theoretical conceptions of love.
2. Answers to the items should measure a single underlying attitude of love. Operationally, all of the items should be highly intercorrelated.
3. The love scale should be complemented by a parallel scale of liking. All of the items on this scale should also be highly intercorrelated. However, if love and liking are separate or independent concepts, then the correlation between the love scale and the liking scale should be fairly low, although some degree of positive association might be expected.

A large number of items were initially obtained and sorted by judges into love and liking categories. From this procedure, 70 items were obtained, rated by students in an introductory psychology course, and evaluated by correlational methods. From this analysis, 13 items each for a love scale and a liking scale were obtained. Sample items from these two

Sample Love-Scale Items
   A. If I could never be with _____, I would feel miserable.
   B. If I were lonely, my first thought would be to seek _____ out.
   C. I would forgive _____ for practically anything.

Sample Liking-Scale Items
   A. I think that _____ is unusually well-adjusted.
   B. _____ is one of the most likable people I know.
   C. _____ is the sort of person whom I myself would like to be.

3. Sample items from Rubin's Love-Scale and Liking-Scale. Each scale contains 13 items. High correlations exist between items within each scale, and only a modest correlation exists between the two scales. For example, neither scale includes an item on attractiveness, since this item could pertain equally to love or liking. Therefore, love and liking, as measured by the two scales, should be relatively independent of each other. (Adapted from Rubin, 1970, p. 267.)

questionnaire scales are shown in Figure 3. The love items seem to tap affiliation and dependence needs, desire to care for the other, and exclusiveness, possessiveness, and intimacy toward the other. The liking items tap favorability of evaluation, respect, perceived similarity, and so on.

The two questionnaires were tested and validated by recruiting 158 couples to complete them. Subjects also completed the questionnaires again by rating a close, same-sex friend. Each item on the questionnaires was rated on a 9-point scale.

The results provided some support for Rubin's distinction between love and liking. The love scale (for females) had an average interitem correlation of +0.84; the liking scale had an average interitem correlation of +0.81. However, the correlation between the liking and loving scales was only +0.39 for women. The results for males showed average interitem correlations of +0.86 for loving and +0.83 for liking. However, the correlation between liking and loving was also quite high, +0.60. Rubin suggested that women may distinguish more sharply between liking and loving than men do.

Some interesting differences in average ratings emerged between males and females. These means are shown in Table IV. The means shown are total scores, computed by adding each subject's responses to all 13 questions on a scale.* Both men and women showed the same overall level of love for each other. The women liked their partners as much as they loved them. However, men liked their partners less than they loved them, and they liked the partners less than the partners liked them in return. (This difference may have been because men tend to get higher ratings on items such as intelligence, good judgment, and leadership potential than women do.) Both sexes loved their best friend of the same sex considerably less than they loved their partner of the opposite sex. They liked their best friend of the same sex considerably more than they loved him or her, but still somewhat less than they liked their romantic partner.

Rubin's data do not completely convince us that love is different from liking because of the high correlation between the two scales for men. However, it is a valiant first attempt to operationalize and scientifically distinguish between the two sentiments. Emotions are very difficult to distinguish in concrete terms. We all know that liking is different from loving, but proving it is something else again.

One possible difficulty is that differences in emotions may not be due to different kinds of physiological arousal, but may be due merely to how a person de-

---

*The most recent version of the scale contains only 10 items.

Table IV Means for loving and liking in Rubin's study

	Women	Men
Love for partner	89	89
Liking for partner	88	85
Love for friend	65	55
Liking for friend	80	79

The higher the number, the more the other is liked or loved. (Adapted from Rubin, 1970, p. 268.)

fines a state of arousal (recall Schachter's theory of emotional attribution discussed in Chapter 5). This possibility implies that whether a given state is liking or loving may depend pretty much on how the individual interprets the situation. One extension of this reasoning is that if a person is in a state of intense arousal, he or she may decide that it is sexual arousal, or fear, depending on the cognitions the individual has of the situation. We examine this interesting interpretation of passionate love in the next section.

PASSIONATE LOVE

Passionate love is basically the same as romantic love, except that the focus is more specifically on passion and emotional intensity. A theory of passionate love has been developed by Berscheid and Walster (1974a; Walster, 1971) based in part on Schachter's (1964) theory of emotional response. They argued that passionate love is not just intense liking and that reinforcement theory does not account for passionate love as well as it does for attraction. Liking relationships seem to depend on actual rewards; in passionate love, fantasy and imagined gratifications may occur out of all proportion to actual rewards received. Another difference is that friendship and liking seem to grow over time, but romantic love and especially passionate love seem always to become diluted with the passage of time. Liking seems to be associated rather consistently with positive reinforcements. Passionate love seems to be associated with conflicting emotions, as witnessed by teenagers' frequent question about whether it is possible to love and hate someone at the same time.

Because of these differences, Berscheid and Walster believed that some theory other than reinforcement theory could best account for passionate love. They selected Schachter's two-component theory of emotion as the best current candidate. Berscheid and Walster suggested that an individual will experience passionate love when two conditions occur.

1. The individual is intensely aroused physiologically.
2. The cues in the situation dictate to the individual that passionate love is the appropriate label for his or her feelings.

Both conditions are necessary. One will not experience passionate love unless physiologically aroused; and given arousal, it is still not love unless the individual labels it as love. The labeling is quite important in the theory. If the situation is such that it is reasonable to attribute the aroused state to passionate love, the individual will experience love. However, "as soon as he ceases to attribute his arousal to passionate love, or the arousal itself ceases, love should die" (Berscheid and Walster, 1974a, p. 363).

There are several negative experiences that can generate a state of arousal. Fear-provoking stimuli, social rejection, and sexual frustration provoke physiological arousal. There is some evidence that such negative states can be interpreted as passionate love. The rejected suitor sometimes redoubles the intensity of his passion. The arousal from the fear and anger created by being a combat soldier in war also seems to stimulate passionate love. In his fascinating account of life as a soldier in wartime, Gray (1959) devoted a chapter to love in war. In 1944, he wrote in a letter to a friend that "the Greeks were wise men when they matched the god of war with the goddess Aphrodite. The soldier must not only kill, he must give birth to new warriors" (p. 70). The increased intensity of eroticism for both men and women during war is also vividly described:

> If we are honest, most of us who were civilian soldiers in recent wars will confess that we spent incomparably more time in the service of Eros during our military careers than ever before or again in our lives. When we were in uniform al-

most any girl who was faintly attractive had an erotic appeal for us. For their part, millions of women find a strong sexual attraction in the military uniform, particularly in time of war. This fact is as inexplicable as it is notorious. Many a girl who had hitherto led a casual and superficial existence within a protective family circle had been suddenly overwhelmed by intense passion for a soldier met by chance on the street or at a dance for servicemen. It seems that the very atmosphere of large cities in wartime breathes the enticements of physical love. Not only are inhibitions on sexual expression lowered, but there exists a much more passionate interest of the sexes in each other than is the case in peacetime. Men and women normally absorbed by other concerns find themselves caught up in the whirlpool of erotic love, which is the preoccupation of the day. In wartime marriages multiply and the birth rate increases. We can safely assume that the number of love affairs, if they could be reduced to statistics, would show an even greater rate of expansion (Gray, 1959, p. 73).

Berscheid and Walster's theorizing would predict just such an effect. The rigors of soldiering in wartime would tend to keep one in a state of physiological arousal much of the time. The context and situation are very different from the peacetime situation. The mere sight of a member of the opposite sex may be a sufficient stimulus to define the situation as one appropriate for passionate arousal.

Naturally positive experiences as well as negative experiences may generate the necessary physiological arousal. Berscheid and Walster note that sexual arousal during the excitement phase is physiologically very similar to the physiological responses of fear and anger. Any activity that generates a sense of danger and excitement may serve as an arousal stimulus. In fact, many people value passionate love just because it is a source of excitement, which is positively valued.

It seems reasonable to conclude that a wide variety of experiences, both positive and negative, can generate the state of physiological arousal that serves as one of the conditions necessary for passionate love to exist. The labeling process seems to be culturally learned and relatively stereotyped. We are taught as children to label our feelings in a wide variety of situations, and by the time we are adults, we have an idea of the appropriate emotion to experience in most situations. The turmoil experienced at the funeral of a relative is unlikely to be experienced as sexual arousal instead of grief; such feelings are inappropriate at a funeral. The physiological excitement experienced after half an hour of vigorous kissing is unlikely to be interpreted as grief; social learning dictates that you label the excitement as sexual arousal. The state of physiological arousal may be quite similar in both situations; the difference in labeling dictates what emotion is experienced.

THE COLORS OF LOVE

We noted earlier that romantic love has been an ideal in Western society for several hundred years, although the concept has caused considerable ambivalence. The literature on love, its nature, and its types, is vast, jumbled, and often contradictory. Two general conceptions of love have recurred most frequently over the centuries. One conception was defined by the ancient Greeks, who called it *eros*. The other conception is associated most closely with the Christian tradition. It has been called *agape* (pronounced "ah-gah-pay").

Rubin (1973) noted that the two types can be conceived as polar extremes of a dimension. Eros is a needing or taking extreme at one end of the dimension, while agape is a giving or caring extreme at the other end of the dimension. Eros is described by strong desires to be with and have contact with the loved one and to have the loved one's approval, care, and intense attention. Agape stems from the religious notion that God is love and that the most perfect embodiment of this love at the human level is unconditional caring for other persons, without expecting or demanding reciprocity. Agape is completely altruistic. Erich Fromm (1956) discussed the tender care of a young infant by its mother as a relatively pure example of agape. He generalized that "Love is the active concern for the life and the growth of that which we love. Where this active concern is lacking, there is no love" (p. 22).

Clearly these two conceptions are quite different from each other. They are based on conceptual

21. After X and I started going out together, the other person I was going out with:
   a. Remained deeply involved with me, so that I was going out with two people and falling in love with both of them.
   b. Remained a good friend, but we both knew it wasn't "love."
   c. Was very upset. We went on seeing each other for a time, then broke off.
   d. Broke off with me right away.
   e. Was dropped by me.
   f. Other
   g. Remained unaware of the fact that I was dating X.

43. The night after I met X:
   a. I could hardly get to sleep. For a long time I lay there thinking.
   b. I dreamed about X.
   c. I woke up earlier than usual the next morning and started to think about X.
   d. I slept quite normally.
   e. I wrote a letter to X (or telephoned).

4. Two sample questions from the 170 items in Lee's Love-Story Card-Sort. (From Lee, 1973.)

reasoning and analytic distinctions. The question arises of whether there may not perhaps be other types of love as well that are different from eros and agape. The answer is yes. There are other types of love, and they have been described from empirical study. This conclusion is based on the monumental studies of love between the sexes that sociologist John Alan Lee reported in his book *Colours of Love* (1973).* Lee tried several different research methods and eventually evolved a combination interview–questionnnaire format called the *Love-Story Card-Sort*.

The Card-Sort consists of 170 basic statements or questions about a love relationship, each on a separate card. A series of answer cards is provided for each statement card, and the subject selects the answer (sometimes more than one) most appropriate for him or her. Two sample items appear in Figure 4.

The subject is asked to focus on one major love relationship that may either be in progress or have oc-

*Lee's research was initially reported in a doctoral dissertation completed at the University of Sussex, England, which was over 900 pages long. The research took over 10 years to complete.

curred in the past. The Card-Sort essentially allows the subject to tell the story of the love relationship, how it started, what the problems and satisfactions were, whether other people were involved, the intensity of each partner's feelings, the various behaviors, the development of the relationship, and how it terminated (if it did). The Card-Sort is applicable to homosexual as well as heterosexual love, although the initial sample of 112 people all described heterosexual relationships.

The initial sample was composed of male and female Canadians and English subjects under age 35. The subjects were recruited on the streets to participate in the study. If they agreed, they later reported individually to the researcher's office. The Card-Sort and related instruments took approximately half a day to complete. Apparently subjects found the task highly absorbing. The Card-Sort often served as a memory stimulus and helped individuals reconstruct their relationships in considerable detail. The data were analyzed by a series of complex and elaborate methods.

A major purpose of the data analysis was to discover how many distinctly different types of love relationships the sample of subjects had experienced and to identify the salient characteristics of each type of love. During the analyses, Lee realized that the various mixes and blends of behavior and emotions the subjects had experienced could be described well by analogy to a modified version of the color wheel. There were three primary types of love relationships, *eros, ludus,* and *storge.* Some subjects seemed to represent rather pure cases of one or another of the three primaries. However, other subjects were best described as a combination of two of the primaries. These were secondary types. Actually there were two distinct classes of secondaries. One class seemed to be a true *compound,* in which the essential nature of the two primaries was completely transformed to create a new type. The other class of secondaries was a *mixture* of the two primaries. A distinctly new type was created, but various elements of the two primaries were still clearly recognizable in the mixture. The compound secondaries were named *mania, pragma,* and *agape.* The mixture secondaries were named *ludic eros, storgic ludus,* and *storgic eros.* No pure cases of agape were found in the subject sample, although the response patterns suggested that agape should remain as a theoretical possibility. With this reservation, however, it should be stressed that the types emerged from the data; they represented different and distinctive types of love relationships that these people had experienced. A brief description of the major characteristics of the three primary and the three compound secondaries follows.

Eros. The erotic lover considers love as life's most important activity but will not harm or destroy himself or herself for love. There is a definite physical stereotype of the type of person the erotic lover prefers. Strong approval and attraction toward the other person are usually evoked on the first meeting. This attraction has a strong physical component, which is expressed verbally and by touching. Considerable contact is desired, daily if possible. There is strong pleasant anticipation about the other and very little anxiety about the relationship. The erotic lover attempts to quickly develop a rapport with the loved one, which includes openness, honesty, and sincerity in the relationship. The erotic lover wants the relation to develop mutually but tends not to demand mutuality from the partner. Finally, the erotic lover enjoys intense emotions, seeks early sexual relations with the partner, and enjoys variety in sexual activities. An erotic lover tends to focus exclusively on the partner but is not possessive or afraid of rivals.

Ludus. Ludic love is love practiced as a game or pleasant pastime. It was developed into something of a skilled art form in the courts of European aristocrats in preceding centuries, but it still survives as a value orientation toward love held by many people. Ludic love is best played with several partners in ongoing relationships.

The ludic lover does not make deep emotional commitments, likes a variety of physical types of the opposite sex, and can easily switch from one type to another. A ludic lover does not become overly excited after meeting the partner, and life goes on as usual, because there are no plans to include the partner in a long-term future life. Too frequent contact with the partner is avoided in order that intense feelings may be avoided. Ludus is very wary of a partner who begins to get too intense and tries to help the partner retain the same sense of self-control and detachment. The game is played for mutual enjoyment, and this requires just the right level of intensity; too little or too much by either partner may unbalance the relationship. Lies and insincere behavior are justified as part of the rules of the game. A ludic lover would never be jealous or possessive and indeed may encourage the partner to have other relationships to help keep their own relationship at the required distance. The ludic lover enjoys sex and variety in sexual activity but tends to consider sex as good fun, not a means to deep emotional rapport.

Storge. "Storge is love without fever or folly, a feeling of natural affection such as you might have for a favorite brother or sister. An unexciting and often uneventful kind of loving, storge is rarely the stuff of dramatic works or romantic novels" (Lee, 1973, p. 77). According to Lee, this type of love develops most often in semirural areas where people know each other over long periods of time, often grow up together, and perhaps go to school together. The storgic lover tends to come from a stable background and considers love as the basis of society and the family. Storge does not expect love to be exciting, but an extension of friendship instead. There is no preferred physical type. One should get to know the partner gradually and incorporate the partner into more and more of life's activities. The relationship is generally relaxed because there are no strong emotions to control. There is a tendency to share interests and activities but to avoid expression of direct feelings about the relationship. Storge also tends to be shy about intense contact and sexual behavior, assuming that after commitment (probably via marriage) any sexual difficulties will be worked out. Love is not exciting to the storgic lover, but it is solid, incorporated into the ongoing flow of the person's life.

Mania. The components of mania discovered by Lee overlap considerably with the traditional conception of romantic love discussed earlier. In fact, literature over the centuries has linked elements of both manic and erotic love under the general rubric of romantic love. However, Lee's data indicated that mania is something quite different from eros in the pure form. The contradictions inherent in manic love suggested that it is best conceived as a full compounding of eros and ludus, and as such, presents itself as a distinctly different type.

The typical manic lover feels that childhood was unhappy and tends to feel lonely and have few friends as an adult. The manic type yearns for love yet expects it to be painful. There is no set preference for physical types, and the search is often for a contradictory set of qualities in the partner. Ambivalence toward the partner and even actual dislike may be felt on the first meeting. However, the manic lover soon becomes preoccupied and even obsessed with thoughts of the partner. There is much imaginative construction of a future with the partner, but it is fraught with anxiety. The desire to see the partner frequently is intense, and frustration of this desire causes much unhappiness. If no particular problems exist, the manic lover will create them in order to intensify feelings but then periodically struggle to get his or her feelings under control. There is a sense of loss of control over one's feelings. The manic lover is very possessive and tries to force the partner into greater expressions of love and affection. The mutual frustrations created often prevent enjoyment of intimacy. The manic lover can convince himself or herself that life without the partner's love is not worth living (though suicide seldom occurs) and will abuse himself or herself in order to win the partner's love.

Pragma. "Pragma is the love that goes shopping for a suitable mate, and all it asks is that the relationship work well, that the two partners be compatible, and satisfy each other's basic or practical needs" (p. 124). The pragmatic lover is looking for contentment and a mate to whom he or she is well suited. This usually means similarity of characteristics and perhaps some complementarity of satisfaction of emotional needs. The pragmatic type is predisposed to select a partner with whom he or she is already familiar, such as a worker at the office. The calculation involved in the selection process is similar to the calculating intent of ludus, but the purpose of long-term, compatible companionship is more like storge. The pragmatic type wants to avoid emotional extremes; gets to know the partner well over time; expects a measure of reciprocated affection but will not force it; believes that sexual compatibility is important but that any problems can be worked out mutually; and feels that, although a satisfactory mate is an important part of life, no particular person is worth too much sacrifice to achieve one's love objectives. Pragmatic love is well described by its name—it is pragmatic first and foremost.

Agape. As noted earlier, agape comes from the Christian tradition.

> When Saint Paul wrote to the Corinthian members of the early Christian church telling them that love is patient and kind, not jealous or boastful, not arrogant or rude, does not insist on its own way, but believes all things and endures all things, the Greek translation for love was *agape*. This concept of love implies a duty or obligation to care about the other person, whether you want to care or not, and whether the love is deserved or not. Agape is "gift love," without ulterior motives and with no strings attached. It is completely altruistic and deeply compassionate (p. 139).

Given the lofty requirements for agapic love, it is no wonder that Lee found no pure types in his research. Agapic love is cognitive more than emotional. Thus it has difficulty knowing what to do with sexuality. Since the body is the "temple of the spirit," sex would have to be a lofty, sacramental act. But given the biological nature of the act, it is difficult to keep the emotions uninvolved. The ultimate consequence is that advocacy of agapic love tends to go with the view that one should not seek sexual gratification. The early Christian church attempted an experiment in which both sexes lived together and slept together without sexual contact. The point was to shun pleasures of the flesh but to enjoy the spiritual ecstasy of closeness to another human. As Lee noted, sufficient pregnancies resulted from this experiment for it to be discontinued. The church continued to downplay sexuality over the centuries, however. Thus intercourse for pleasure alone was forbidden. Sex was permissible only as an act of procreation. The struggle between the reality of biology and the equally real ideal of agapic love has continued unabated for some 2000 years.

No claim is made that Lee's typology is perfect. It is a helpful device to represent empirical reality, but it should not be confused with that reality. The typology is, however, a considerable advance over previous conceptualizations of love, and it has the great advantage of being based on empirical research. The typology lends itself well to future research. One fascinating issue is whether entirely new types will be discovered in other cultures or whether the current types exhaust what exists around the world. Future work should also relate the various styles of love to personality and dispositional variables. Manic love appears to be pursued by people of low self-esteem, while erotic love obviously requires a strong ego. Many fascinating relationships are likely to be discovered.

The types of love relationships might best be seen as lovestyles. Although an individual may have a strong preference for one style over another, the styles are not fixed by the genes. A person's preferred lovestyle may change over a lifetime, or even during the course of a given love relationship. Indeed, an individual may be involved in an erotic relationship with one person and a ludic or other type of relationship with a second person. The types are conceptual ideals that map empirical reality. Like all maps, they are representations and not mirror images of reality itself.

Summary

Attraction toward another individual is conceived as a type of attitude. Liking and disliking others has been studied primarily in terms of classes of independent variables that result in liking or disliking. The most important of these variables are propinquity; similarity on various attributes; complementarity of needs and role behaviors; reciprocity of liking, self-disclosure, and other behaviors; desirable characteristics such as ability; and physical attractiveness.

The two major theoretical approaches to attraction are balance theories and reinforcement theories. The A-B-X model proposed by Newcomb (1961) is discussed as one example of a balance theory. Two approaches to reinforcement theory are a reinforcement–affect theory developed primarily by Byrne (1969) and the gain–loss model developed by Aronson (1969). Both balance and reinforcement theories can account for much of the data on attraction, although reinforcement theories are more popular.

In the past, love has been treated by social psychologists as an intense form of liking, though this tendency is changing. We discussed the social–cultural complex of attitudes called romantic love and presented one specific interpretation of love from the viewpoint of exchange theory. The more recent work of Rubin (1970) on a distinction between loving and liking is described in detail. A recent theory of passionate love is also presented. Finally, Lee's (1973) typology of the different kinds of love relationships is discussed in some detail.

7

Attitudes, beliefs, and behavior

182 The nature of attitudes

Attitude components: the classical view
A model of the relations among components

189 Origins and maintenance of attitudes

Prior experience
Reference groups and indoctrination
Functions of attitudes

197 Attitudes and behavior

Measurement pitfalls
Attitude-behavior consistency
    "Pseudoinconsistency" of attitude and behavior
    Conditions promoting consistency
    General attitudes

204 Prejudice

208 Summary

What could something as ugly and disastrous as the religious conflict in Northern Ireland have in common with fund-raising activities or peaceful election results? What could the racial confrontations that occurred across the United States in the 1960s have in common with the innocent display of a bumper sticker or a campaign button supporting your favorite candidate? As diverse as these various events and activities are, each has in common the expression of attitudes. Each gives evidence of feelings of like or dislike toward some situation, object, or group, evidence of beliefs about that situation, object, or group, and evidence of an intention to behave in relevant ways—whether the behavior involves dropping a vote into the ballot box or a bomb into a crowd.

Hardly a day goes by when attitudes and the behaviors that follow from them are not front-page news. On a more mundane level, we have already seen in Chapter 6 that our attitudes toward other people play a major role in our day-to-day affairs. We like some people and dislike others, we believe certain things about our friends and other things about our enemies, and we behave quite differently toward friends and enemies. Individual people, however, constitute only one class of the many objects, situations, and groups that may be the focus of an attitude. In this chapter, we shall examine the concept of attitude more closely.

We begin by presenting what might be referred to as the classical view of attitudinal structure in which attitudes are seen as having three components: affect (likes and dislikes), cognition (beliefs), and behavioral tendencies. We shall discuss each of these in turn and shall present a recent model which, with some alteration in terminology, makes the interrelations among the components explicit. For example, do our beliefs about some object determine whether we feel positively or negatively about the object, or vice versa? We shall see. We shall also pay particular attention to the formation of attitudes and to some of the social-psychological phenomena that stabilize and maintain our attitudes. Although attitudes are of interest in their own right, the major reason for studying attitudes is to see whether they help us in trying to understand and predict behavior. In the final section, we shall examine some of the literature on the relationships between attitudes and behavior. As we shall see, the apparent inconsistencies between attitudes and behaviors are more apparent than real.

The nature of attitudes

Eagly and Himmelfarb (1978) point out that attitude was the single most important concept in social psychology for many years and, after a brief absence from the limelight, it is once again regaining center stage. Although social psychology might like to claim attitudes as its own, there has been widespread interest in the concept in other disciplines as well. Philosophers, political scientists, and historians, to name only a few, have all concerned themselves with attitudes and their effects.

But what, exactly, is an attitude? Has anybody ever seen one? And if so, what did it look like? No one, of course, has ever seen an attitude, and no one ever will. An attitude is something we attribute to a person to help us understand why certain situations, stimuli, or events evoke similar responses from that person. For example, suppose that over the last few years you have observed one of your friends denounce Betty Friedan as a communist agitator, claim that "woman's place is in the home," and refuse to hire any female employees for his business in other than secretarial jobs. You might very well infer that he has a negative attitude toward the women's liberation movement. Your attribution of such an attitude to him would help

Looking at this photograph, you probably "feel" something—most likely negative—about the person you see. In this chapter we explore the elements of what you feel and how you might act as a result. (Wide World Photo)

183
Attitudes, beliefs,
and behavior

you anticipate his future behavior. For example, you could probably guess how he might feel about his daughter wanting to go to West Point.

There are literally scores of definitions of the word *attitude* (Allport, 1935; McGuire, 1969). The essence of these various definitions seems to incorporate the following points. First, an ATTITUDE is something we infer that a person has. In our example, we infer that your friend has a negative attitude toward women's liberation. Second, the attitude has a focal object. The object of your friend's attitude is, of course, the women's liberation movement. Third, we base our inference about attitudes on apparent consistencies in behavior. Your friend not only denounced Betty Friedan, but he did other things that seemed consistent with such behavior. By subsuming his various behaviors under a blanket "negative attitude toward women's liberation," we make it easier for ourselves to keep track of and account for his future behavior. Finally, we usually assume that one's attitudes proceed from one's experiences with the objects of the attitudes.

ATTITUDE COMPONENTS: THE CLASSICAL VIEW

From the time of Plato to the present, many philosophers, psychologists, and others have distinguished three components of attitudes: the affective, cognitive, and behavioral components. The cognitive component consists of beliefs and ideas that the attitude holder has about the attitude object. The affective component consists of feelings of like and/or dislike toward the object, and the behavioral component consists of tendencies to respond in particular ways toward the object. These three components are part and parcel of every attitude.

As an example, consider the following comments of an urban public school teacher, which display and contrast her attitudes toward two groups:

> I loved the Polish people. They were hardworking. If they didn't have money, they helped out by doing housework, baby-sitting for ten cents an hour. No work was beneath them. But here, these people—the parents—come to school in the morning. This is a social outpost for them. They watch their kids eat free breakfasts and lunches. There isn't any shame, there isn't any pride. These Polish people I knew, there was pride. You didn't dare do anything like that. You wouldn't think of it.
>
> I see these parents here all the time. A father brings his kids to school and he hangs around in the hall. I think it's dangerous to have all these adults in the school. You get all these characters. I'm afraid to stay in my room unless I lock the door (Terkel, 1975, p. 631).

The affective components are clearly present. She "loved" the Polish, but now she is "afraid." The beliefs about the Polish contrast starkly with the beliefs about the new group. The Poles were "hardworking," and "no work was beneath them." Now, the parents apparently don't do anything but "hang around the hall" and they are such "characters." The behavioral tendencies toward the groups are also clear; she feels she must "lock the door" when she is in her room.

The affective components of attitudes toward various racial, national, and ethnic groups, then, are represented by statements such as "I dislike French people. They make me feel ill at ease" or "I really enjoy being around people from Sweden. They make me feel so comfortable."

When dealing with attitudes toward such groups, we often refer to beliefs about the attributes of the groups (the cognitive components of the attitudes) as STEREOTYPES. For example, in an early study of stereotypes, Katz and Braly (1933) asked 100 Princeton undergraduates to select from a list of 84 adjectives those they believed to characterize each of 10 groups (Germans, Italians, Irish, English, Negroes, Jews, Americans, Chinese, Japanese, Turks). At intervals of 18 years, the Katz and Braly study was repeated at Princeton, employing the same 84 trait objectives and asking for attributions to the same 10 groups (Gilbert, 1951; Karlins, Coffman, and Walters, 1969). A sampling of some of the beliefs about the 10 groups, which seem to be changing over time, is presented in Table I. One thing that emerges clearly from results such as those shown in Table I is that people do have different beliefs about the characteristics of various groups—beliefs that, according to the classical view, are a part of their attitudes toward the groups. (For another illustration of beliefs about an attribute of a group, see Box A.) To complete our example, attitudes toward various groups would also be expected to have behavioral

Table I Comparison of stereotypes attributed in three studies.

Group	Trait	Katz and Braly 1933	Gilbert 1951	Karlins, et al. 1969
Germans	Scientific	78	62	47
	Intelligent	65	50	59
	Progressive	16	3	13
Negroes	Superstitious	84	41	13
	Lazy	75	31	26
	Ignorant	38	24	11
Jews	Shrewd	79	47	30
	Ambitious	21	28	48
	Mercenary	49	28	15
Americans	Materialistic	33	37	67
	Alert	23	7	7
	Intelligent	47	32	20

People apparently have beliefs about group characteristics, though these beliefs seem to be changing over time. (From Karlins et al., 1969, Table 1, pp. 4 and 5.)

components, tendencies to behave toward the groups in particular ways: to discriminate against them and to avoid them or to seek out their company and promote their best interests.

Some people have argued that it is pointless to distinguish among components of an attitude. McGuire (1969), for example, claims that even though the three components can be conceptually distinguished, they usually turn out to be highly interrelated. Why, then, should we bother distinguishing them? The reasons for distinguishing them are simple. They are measured in different ways, serve different functions, and, even though they often are interrelated, they often are not.

In order for the components to be interrelated, one must be able to recognize that a particular course of action, say, has a bearing on some attitude object about which one feels positively or negatively. If you do not know that a certain charity supports goals that you feel are worthwhile, not contributing to that charity can hardly be considered a case of inconsistency between affect and behavior. It is a truism, of course, that different people like, or have positive attitudes toward, different things. Even in well-controlled laboratory experiments, different subjects may be there for different reasons. Some may do what the experimenter requests because they are intellectually curious about research, some may only want the money, some may want approval from the (usually) higher-status experimenter, and some may simply want to master whatever task is set for them. Thus, we should be able to increase the correlation between the subjects' affect and behavioral tendencies by leading them to believe that their current behavior is an appropriate way to obtain the things they feel positively about.

In line with this reasoning, French (1958) hypothesized that people who are achievement-oriented (that is, those who feel positively about success and its trappings) would improve in performance of a group task when given positive feedback about their apparent efficiency and mastery of the task. Conversely, she hypothesized that people who are less achievement-oriented but more concerned with affiliation and social relations would improve more in performance of the *same task* when given positive feedback about their apparent ability to work well together. To test these hypotheses, 256 Air Force trainees were selected from a larger group of potential subjects who had been tested for the strength of their achievement and affiliation motives. Half of the subjects were high in achievement motivation and low in affiliation motivation, and half were high in affiliation motivation and low in achievement motivation. Subjects were divided into motivationally homogeneous 4-person groups and assigned a story-construction problem. For three 10-minute work periods, they were to attempt to construct a story out of 20 phrases or short sentences that had been written on cards and distributed among the group members, 5 to each member. Group members were not allowed to show their cards to others, so the entire task had to be done by conversation.

The variable of interest here was termed task versus feeling feedback and was manipulated during a break between work periods. For half of the groups, the experimenter said, "This group is working very effi-

A. Stereotyping Supporters of Women's Liberation

Goldberg, Gottesdiener, and Abramson (1975) obtained photographs of 30 female undergraduates at Connecticut College and asked these same 30 students to respond to a questionnaire assessing their attitudes toward women's liberation. Half of the group indicated that they strongly supported the movement, and half indicated that they either supported the movement with serious reservations or did not support it. The former group was designated strong supporters and the latter, mild supporters. A control group of 40 male and 29 female introductory psychology students were then asked to rate each of the 30 photographs in terms of attractiveness. For these 69 students, no mention was made of women's liberation. There were no significant differences in the rated attractiveness of the photos of strong versus mild supporters of the women's liberation movement.

Next a new group of subjects, including both males and females, were asked to inspect the photographs and divide the women into (1) those they believed were strong supporters of women's liberation and (2) those they believed were not supporters of women's liberation. Based on ratings already obtained, the experimenters calculated the average attractiveness of the photos assigned to the two groups. For both male and female subjects, the average attractiveness of the women believed to be strong supporters of women's liberation was significantly lower than the average attractiveness of the women assigned to the other group. As Goldberg, Gottesdiener, and Abramson point out,

> The general results seem clear: Women who support the feminist movement are believed to be less attractive physically than their sisters who do not support the movement, though the evidence is that there is no true difference in attractiveness between the two groups (p. 115).

It is interesting to note that female as well as male students subscribed to this particular stereotype of the supporters of women's liberation.

---

ciently'' and mentioned 5 specific task-related behaviors that had been observed (task feedback). For the remaining groups, the experimenter said, "This group works very well together" and mentioned 5 specific behaviors of a social nature (feeling feedback). The argument here is that for achievement-oriented groups, the task feedback is more likely to enhance the expectation of attaining the goal of interest to them and thus facilitate performance, whereas for the affiliation-oriented groups, the feeling feedback is more likely to have this effect. This is precisely what occurred. In terms of the number of points obtained on problem solution, task feedback was more effective with the achievement-oriented groups, and feeling feedback resulted in better performance by the affiliation-oriented groups.

Thus the affect toward a particular object is more likely to be translated into overt behavior when one is aware, or is made aware, that the behavior in question is indeed a means of approaching the attitudinal object. There are meaningful differences, then, among the components of attitudes. Behavioral tendencies are related to affect only under certain conditions, and those who would ignore the distinctions among the components are now in a distinct minority (Oskamp, 1977). In fact, ignoring the distinctions would, by definition, make it impossible to understand the circumstances under which we might expect the components to be related and how those circumstances differ from the ones in which we would expect the components to be unrelated.

One of the problems with this view of differing components of attitudes, however, is that researchers have too often left unspecified exactly how and when the components are related. Early investigators seemed to think that affect toward an object, beliefs about the object, and one's behavioral tendencies toward the object *should* be related under *some* conditions, but that those conditions would just have to be found by research. That could turn out to be like looking for a needle in a haystack. What is needed, of course, is something to give a little direction to the search.

A MODEL OF THE RELATIONS AMONG COMPONENTS

Fishbein and Ajzen (1975) use the term *attitude* to refer only to what we have been calling the affective component of attitudes. For Fishbein and Ajzen, statements such as "I really dislike those new triangular-shaped cars" or "I thought the party was very pleasant" represent attitudes. Another way of saying this is to say that attitudes can be measured only by a procedure that allows one to place the attitude object on a bipolar evaluative scale, such as good–bad, or like–dislike. In this view, then, an attitude is synonymous with one's evaluation of the attitude object.

Beliefs, on the other hand, relate a particular attribute, characteristic, or property to the object. We have already seen several examples of beliefs in Table I. But the objects do not have to be ethnic groups, and the attributes do not have to be personality characteristics. An example of a belief is "Smoking" (the object) "causes cancer" (the attribute). Another is "Jogging" (the object) "prevents heart attacks" (the attribute). In contrast to attitudes, which are measured on an evaluative scale, beliefs differ in strength, or the perceived probability that the object really does have the attribute in question. You may believe it is almost certain that smoking increases the likelihood of cancer, but members of the tobacco industry are not so sure.

In addition to attitudes (affect) and beliefs (cognition) about an object, Fishbein and Ajzen define a third class of variables, one's INTENTIONS (behavioral tendencies) toward the object. Intentions are also measured in terms of subjective probabilities, such as how likely you are to donate blood or to give to charity.

If this were all there were to the model, it would hardly be worth presenting, but there is more. Fishbein and Ajzen propose that one's attitude toward an object *is based on* one's beliefs about the object. Specifically, each belief associates a particular attribute with the object, say X (X is——; X has——; X does——), and these attributes are themselves either favorably or unfavorably evaluated. If one's beliefs about the object associate it with predominantly favorable attributes, one's attitude toward the object will be favorable. If one's beliefs associate the object with predominantly negative attributes, one's attitude will be unfavorable. Further, it is the attitude (affect) toward the object that determines one's intentions with respect to the object. Webster, in fact, defines the verb *affect* as "to have an effect on; influence; produce a change in." Thus when we feel positive about, like, or love some object, our behavioral intentions toward that object are different from when we feel negatively about the object or dislike it. The relations among beliefs, attitude and intentions are diagrammed in Figure 1.

Even the best (or worst) of intentions sometimes go astray. We shall devote the final section of this chapter to a discussion of whether we can really predict someone's behavior toward an object from knowledge of their beliefs, attitude, and intentions pertinent to the object. For now, let us look at some research on how we combine information taken from our beliefs about an object to determine what our attitude (affect) is toward the object—that is, how we feel about it.

Suppose that you wanted to decide how you felt about a proposal made by the Army Corps of Engineers to dam a scenic river a few miles from your home. The only items of information you have about this proposal are the following beliefs:

1. The dam will form a lake over what is now one of the most beautiful canyons in the state.
2. The dam will cost 4 million dollars to construct.
3. The dam will allow better flood control downstream.
4. The lake created by the dam will dispossess more people than are likely ever to be inconvenienced by flooding.

Each of these beliefs relates an attribute to the dam (and the lake it will create), and each of these attributes is something that you can evaluate. If you put the attributes down on a common scale running from good to bad, they might look something like this:

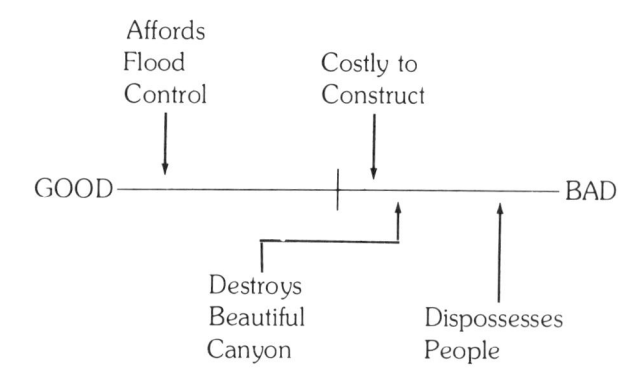

```
                Affords
                Flood        Costly to
                Control      Construct
                   |            |
                   ↓            ↓
    GOOD ──────────────┼──────────────── BAD
                         ↑        ↑
                  Destroys        |
                  Beautiful       |
                  Canyon    Dispossesses
                             People
```

The question is, "What is your overall attitude (affect) toward the dam construction under these circumstances, and how is it arrived at?"

There is now a fairly large body of research (Anderson, 1974) indicating that, under the circumstances described, you would probably feel quite negative toward the dam. You would arrive at this feeling by averaging your evaluations of all the characteristics you had attributed to the dam. There is a little more to the story, however, in that your feeling toward the dam would actually be a WEIGHTED AVERAGE. That is, some of our beliefs about an object are more salient or important to us than others, and we give these beliefs more weight in determining our feeling toward the attitude object.

Once you have decided the extent to which you like or dislike an attitude object, do your intentions follow directly? Fishbein (1967) suggests that one's intentions toward a given action which is related to an attitudinal object depend upon (a) affect toward the object and the specific action, and (b) a particular kind of general belief called a subjective norm. A SUBJECTIVE NORM is an individual's belief about other people's attitudes toward a given behavior or object. Thus a person's intentions are influenced by both liking (or disliking) for the object and a subjective norm, the perception that relevant other people think the behavior in question should or should not be performed. Of course, one must be motivated to comply with what these relevant others think before their perceived beliefs make a difference. You might, for example, really want to do something physical to that taxi driver who just pulled out in front of you, but you also believe your insurance agent and that police officer standing on the corner might not approve. Hence, the negative affect you feel will probably be channeled into certain less-than-polite verbal behavior rather than the intention to ram the back of the cab.

To see if these sorts of variables do influence one's intentions, Davidson and Jaccard (1975) interviewed a large sample of married women about their beliefs, intentions, attitudes, and perceived normative beliefs (subjective norms) with respect to family planning. The women were first contacted by phone, and an appointment was made for a female interviewer to go to the homes of the interviewees. After obtaining some preliminary information, the interviewer gave each woman a questionnaire containing a number of

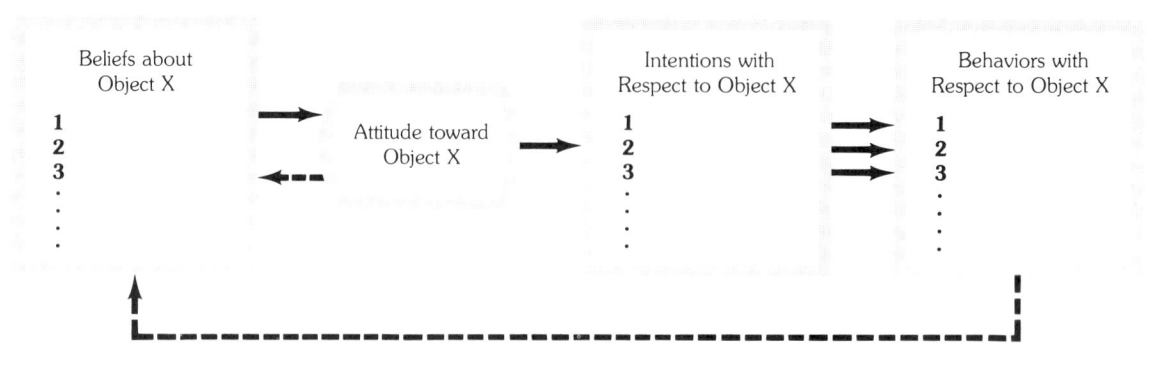

1. An attitude toward an object is partly obtained by beliefs that are held about the object. The attitude, in turn, determines the intentions to behave in certain ways toward the object. The diagram shows a conceptual framework relating beliefs, attitude, intentions, and behaviors. (From Fishbein and Ajzen, 1975, Figure 1, p. 15.)

```
  Beliefs about              Intentions with          Behaviors with
    Object X                 Respect to Object X     Respect to Object X
       1         →                    1                      1
       2     Attitude toward →        2          ⇒            2
       3      Object X                3          ⇒            3
       .     ←---                     .          ⇒            .
       .                              .                       .
       .                              .                       .
       ↑                                                      |
       └──────────────────────────────────────────────────────┘
```

semantic differential scales (see Chapter 4). The following are examples of the items used in the questionnaire:

I intend to have one and only one child in my completed family.
unlikely __: __: __: __: __: __: __: likely

Having one and only one child in my completed family would be
good __: __: __: __: __: __: __: bad

My parents think I should have a one-child family.
unlikely __: __: __: __: __: __: __: likely

General speaking, I
want to do	do *not* want
what my	to do what
parents	my parents
think I	think I
should __: __: __: __: __: __: __: should

The first item is a measure of behavioral intentions, the second is a measure of attitude (affect), the third is a measure of perceived normative beliefs, and the last is a measure of motivation to comply with the perceived normative beliefs. Davidson and Jaccard found that the women's behavioral intentions with respect to family planning could be predicted quite well from knowledge of their attitude toward specific aspects of family planning and their perceptions of the normative beliefs of others about those aspects of family planning.

It is important to remember that studies such as this deal with intentions to behave and not with actual behavior. We shall make the extension to behavior later. Before we do, however, let us look a little more closely at some of the ways in which attitudes are formed and maintained.

Origins and maintenance of attitudes

One of the nice things about attitudes is that they often furnish us with ready-made responses to objects and situations that recur. That is, we do not have to respond to each occurrence of some event in all its uniqueness if we can categorize it as a member of a class of objects about which we already have a full-blown attitude, including positive or negative affect, a set of relevant beliefs, and behavioral intentions. As Jones and Gerard (1967) put it,

> Because these dispositions grow out of the triumphs and embarrassments of the past they are not to be lightly discarded. Reliance on them is part of a fundamental economic or "least-effort" principle: whenever possible, apply past solutions to present problems. The person imposes as much system on the environment as he can get away with in order to free his attention and energy for coping with surprises (pp. 227-228).

Thus we have a vested interest in stabilizing and maintaining our attitudes and continuing to use our prior experiences. But how does our prior experience result in an attitude?

PRIOR EXPERIENCE

Staats and Staats (1958) have proposed that the affective components of many attitudes may be established by a process of classical conditioning. That is, the attitude object or its symbolic representation is presented repeatedly, and each time it occurs, some other stimulus that the subject already feels positively (or negatively) about is also presented. Presumably, the positive or negative affect attached to the second stimulus will thus be conditioned to the first. A child, for example, who hears references to blacks or Jews or southerners or New Yorkers made in sneering, condescending tones will develop negative affect toward these groups long before he or she can justify the experienced affect.

To demonstrate that such affective conditioning can indeed occur, Staats and Staats presented subjects with six national names (*German, Swedish, Italian, French, Dutch,* and *Greek*) repeatedly flashed on a screen one at a time in random order. As each name appeared, the experimenter read aloud one word from a list of 108 words that had previously been rated on an evaluative scale. For some subjects, each time the name *Swedish* appeared, the experimenter read a word that had positive evaluative meaning, and each time the name *Dutch* appeared, the experimenter read a word that had negative evaluative meaning. For other subjects this was reversed. For all subjects, the remaining 4 names were always paired with words that were approximately neutral on the evaluative scale. As anticipated, when asked to rate the 6 names on a pleasant–unpleasant continuum at the end of the experiment, those subjects for whom *Swedish* had always been paired with a positive word rated *Swedish* as more pleasant than *Dutch*. Conversely, those subjects for whom *Dutch* had always been paired with a positive word rated *Dutch* more pleasant than *Swedish*. Zanna, Kiesler, and Pilkonis (1970) obtained a similar result in a somewhat less transparent experimental setting. Thus the effect seems to be a real one and not an artifact produced because the subjects guessed the purpose of the Staats and Staats experiment.

The repeated co-occurrence of an attitudinal object and extraneous positive or negative affect is a relatively subtle technique by which the extraneous affect may be attached to the attitude object. However, Zajonc (1968) has suggested that an even more subtle set of circumstances may induce us to feel positively or negatively about particular objects. According to Zajonc, contrary to the old sayings that "familiarity breeds contempt" and "absence makes the heart grow fonder," the mere repeated exposure to some object may induce us to feel increasingly positive toward that object. To test this idea, Zajonc constructed a set of Chineselike characters—symbols that were meaningless in themselves but which resembled the symbols of Chinese caligraphy. He then exposed these characters repeatedly to subjects, who were simply asked to look at each one closely as it was presented. The presentation of the various characters was arranged so that some were never presented, some were presented only once, some twice, some 5 times, some 10 times, and some 25 times. Following this procedure, the subjects were told that the characters they had just seen actually stood for adjectives and that they were to try to guess their meaning on a good–bad scale. The results appear in Figure 2. As the graph shows, the more frequently a subject had seen a given symbol, the more positively that symbol was rated.

Why repeated exposure to an attitude object should lead us to evaluate that object more positively is not as yet clear. Matlin (1970) offers some evidence that a novel stimulus produces conflict, or RESPONSE COMPETITION. That is, we do not know quite how to respond to a novel stimulus or even what parts of it to look at or how to make sense of it. This conflict is reduced with repeated exposure, and with the reduction in conflict we begin to feel increasingly positive (or at least less negative) about the stimulus.

There is at times a very fine line between processes that result in the development of an attitude and those that serve to maintain or stabilize an already-existing attitude. Consider, for example, what happens in the various groups to which we belong or to which we aspire.

REFERENCE GROUPS AND INDOCTRINATION

The information to which people are exposed is never random. To underscore this point, take an extreme example: a religious sect such as the Amish. Hostetler (1963) points out that to the Amish, the biblical injunctions "Be not conformed to this world" and "Be ye not unequally yoked together with unbelievers" are taken quite literally and serve as the bases

2. Average rated "goodness" of Chinese-like characters. The more often a subject has seen a given symbol, the more positively the symbol is rated. (From Zajonc, 1968, Figure 2, p. 14.)

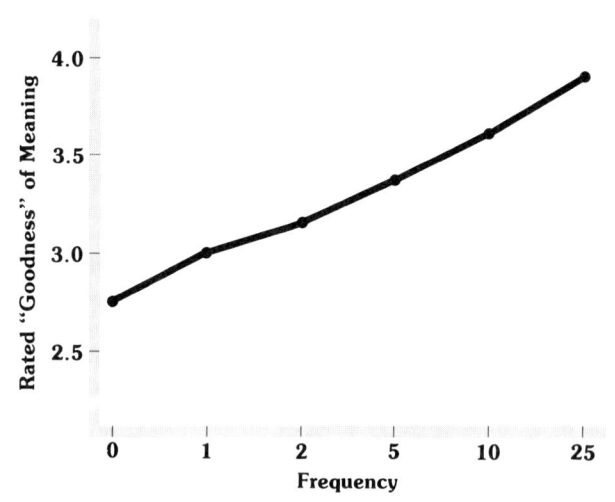

A major device used by politicians to get elected is the campaign poster. These offer the voter no substantive information that will help cast an intelligent ballot, but according to Zajonc's theory, repeated exposure to a candidate's name makes us feel more positively toward him or her than toward a candidate whose name is unfamiliar to us.

for much of Amish life. The Amish do not conform to the lifestyles typical of modern industrial society, and they have as little interchange as possible with non-Amish "nonbelievers." As Hostetler notes,

> The rules of the Amish church cover the whole range of human experience. In a society where the goal is directed toward keeping the world out, there are many taboos, and customs become symbolic. The most universal of all Amish norms across the United States and Canada are the following: no electricity, telephones, central-heating system, automobiles, or tractors with pneumatic tires; required beards but not moustaches for all married men, long hair. . . , hooks-and-eyes on dress coats, and the use of horses for farming and travel. No formal education beyond the elementary grades is a rule of life (p. 61).

Thus the Amish perforce tend to live in isolated farming communities with no radios, televisions, or telephones, and the typical young adult is actively discouraged from continuing his or her education beyond the elementary grades and from learning more about the world beyond the Amish community. The result, of course, is an incredible homogeneity of beliefs and attitudes. Everyone is likely to end up believing exactly the same things and holding precisely the same attitudes. Such a tendency is reinforced by the practices of *Bann und Meidung,* excommunication and shunning. Those who violate the church norms are cast out of the church and systematically excluded from the social and economic life of the community. They cannot even eat at the same table with church members, which would normally include their own family.

One way of conceptualizing the Amish situation is to say that the typical member of an Amish community has only one REFERENCE GROUP, the Amish community. On the other hand, an average person in middle-class society may have many reference groups in which he or she aspires to attain or maintain membership. A university professor, for example, may be a Roman Catholic, a psychologist, a member of N.O.W., a Democrat, and a member of an outdoors club. Each of these parent bodies (the Catholic Church, the Democratic Party, etc.) would serve as a reference group for the professor to evaluate his or her attitudes, beliefs, and values. The important point, for purposes of contrast with the Amish, is that these various groups may take different stands on certain issues and that it is up to the individual to integrate their divergent stances. The result of millions of such individual decisions, on the level of society, is a heterogeneity of beliefs and attitudes unknown in communities like that of the Amish. As we shall see in Chapter 9, the result is really not quite so benign, because reference groups have both comparative and normative functions—that is, they not only set standards, but they often try to enforce them. For now, let us look at a study demonstrating the importance of confluence of reference group (a group we *aspire* to belong to) and membership group (a group we actually belong to) for attitude stability.

Siegel and Siegel (1957) employed a naturally occurring sequence of events at a university to set up a field experiment that has since become a classic study of the influence of reference and membership groups. In the spring of each year, all first-year women students at the university participated in a drawing for

**192
Cognition of
the social world**

Table II Summary of experimental design used by Siegal and Siegal.

Subjects	End of first year		End of second year	
	Membership group	Reference group	Membership group	Reference group
A	Non-Row	Row	Row	Row
B	Non-Row	Row	Non-Row	Row
C	Non-Row	Row	Non-Row	Non-Row

(From Siegal and Siegal, 1957.)

housing for the following year. Sophomore students could participate if they wanted to change their housing, but sophomores did not have to participate. The options in the drawing were either dormitories of various sizes ("non-Row houses") or several small houses ("Row houses") located along what had once been Fraternity Row. Row houses had considerably more status than the dormitories. Earlier research at the same university had revealed that residents of Row houses and those women who indicated a preference for Row housing tended to have more authoritarian attitudes than non-Row residents and women who indicated a preference for non-Row housing.

By following three groups of students, all of whom had indicated a preference for Row housing at the end of their first year, Siegel and Siegel were able to implement the experimental design shown in Table II. In the table, Membership Group refers to where the students were actually living, and Reference Group refers to where they wanted to live, as indicated by their participation in the housing drawing. Thus group A consisted of students who were actually assigned Row housing for their sophomore year. The reference and membership groups of these students corresponded during their sophomore year. Group B consisted of students who had expressed a desire for Row housing

For some individuals, an organized religion is an extremely powerful reference group. The Hare Krishna movement, for example, becomes the only reference group for its devotees, who forsake the more usual reference groups of their peers. (Bobbi Carrey/The Picture Cube)

at the end of their first year, but who did not get it. However, they maintained Row houses as their reference group, because they again expressed a desire for such housing at the end of their sophomore year. During their sophomore year, then, their membership and reference groups were different. Group C also consisted of students who had expressed a desire for Row housing at the end of their first year and who did not get it, but for group C, the reference group changed from Row to non-Row during their sophomore year. At the end of the second year, this group no longer expressed a preference for Row housing.

To assess the stability of authoritarian attitudes under these three conditions, Siegel and Siegel obtained measures of authoritarianism from all subjects at the end of their first year and again at the end of their second year. Remember that it had already been established that residents of Row houses were generally more authoritarian than residents of non-Row houses. Hence, those students moving into Row houses found an atmosphere that supported their initial authoritarian attitudes, whereas those moving to a non-Row house found a nonauthoritarian atmosphere at variance with their initial attitudes. The results indicate that at the end of the second year, members of group A had indeed retained their authoritarian attitudes. Members of group B were less authoritarian at the end of the second year, and members of group C were least authoritarian. As Siegel and Siegel (1957) note, these results show the importance of both membership and reference groups on attitude stability. Compared to groups A and B, who had not changed reference groups, the attitudes of group C were least stable. Compared to groups B and C, who had nonsupportive membership groups, the attitudes of group A were most stable.

De facto selective exposure is not the same thing as the sort of motivated selective exposure usually found in political campaigns, wherein it often turns out that most of the people who hear a particular candidate's speech already intended to vote for him or her anyway. Rather, *de facto* selective exposure has to do with the related, accompanying attitudes and values to which one is exposed because of some particular choice. In the Siegel and Siegel study, for example, those girls who expressed a preference to live in Row houses did so because of the higher social status associated with such living quarters. They did not seek out Row houses so that their authoritarian attitudes would be supported and maintained. The latter was, from their point of view, entirely gratuitous.

De facto selective exposure, then, is partly a function of the fact that we seldom have isolated attitudes. Any given attitude is usually embedded in a cluster of associated attitudes. Katz and Stotland (1959) take the position that individual attitudes are often organized into larger structures, which they term VALUE SYSTEMS. These value systems are said to be integrated around some abstractions concerning general classes of objects. Thus one might build a value system around the concept of *freedom*. Woven into this value system might be a host of specific attitudes ranging from one toward the American Civil Liberties Union, with accompanying beliefs and behavioral tendencies, to one toward fresh air, open spaces, and sunshine.

The exact manner in which attitudes are interrelated is very difficult to specify. In fact, there is probably not any *one* way in which attitudes combine into larger systems or clusters. Some attitudes may be tied together because of common elements in the cognitive components of each. Others may be associated because the attitude objects were both present during some traumatic situation. Jones and Gerard (1967) propose that an attitude can be approached as the conclusion of a syllogism (a form of deductive reasoning) in which the major premise is an evaluative (affective) statement and the minor premise is a belief (cognitive) statement. As an example, consider the following syllogism:

(Belief, minor premise) Building a dam on the Red River will destroy a scenic area.

(Evaluation, major premise) Destroying scenic areas is bad.

(Attitude, conclusion) Therefore, building the dam is bad.

An implication of this approach is that attitudes have both a horizontal and a vertical structure. HORIZONTAL STRUCTURE refers to the fact that the same attitude may be the conclusion of several different syllogisms. VERTICAL STRUCTURE refers to the fact that the components of any given syllogism may themselves be the conclusion of other syllogisms. The major premise above, "Destroying scenic areas is bad," is an example of a component that is itself the attitudinal conclusion of another syllogism.

An important consequence of the interrelatedness of attitudes is that apparently simple attitudes may be very resistant to change, because they are woven into a tapestry of beliefs and other attitudes. A change in one aspect of the interconnected system might have far-reaching implications. We are assuming, of course, that there is some pressure toward consistency among the components of an individual's value and belief systems. Katz and Stotland point out, however, that such mechanisms as rationalization and wishful thinking are too prevalent for consistency to be a useful predictive tool unless we can specify the conditions under which it operates. Fortunately, as we shall see in the next two chapters, considerable progress has been made in detailing the conditions under which consistency is a factor in attitude and behavior change.

The fact that attitudes seldom exist in isolation, but are interwoven with other aspects of personality, raises some interesting questions about what functions attitudes serve in the individual's total personality. What, for example, do attitudes *do* for the person?

FUNCTIONS OF ATTITUDES

In the period immediately following World War II, there was a great deal of interest in what came to be known as the "new look" in perception. The basic argument of the new look was that our perceptions are often erroneous, but that the perceptual errors we make are not random. Rather, our errors are systematic and are a function of our attitudes, values, expectations, and current mood states.

It often happens that a particular approach or theory

fits in so well with what common sense and everyday experience dictate that it is difficult to believe that anyone could ever have believed otherwise. How could anyone have really believed that attitudes, moods, and other personality factors did not influence perception? Yet the very title "new look" clearly implies that someone, somewhere did not believe that attitudes, for example, were relevant to perception. For decades, in fact, most experimental psychologists tried to study humans as if they were passive receivers and processors of information. However, in the late 1940s and early 1950s, Bruner, Postman, McClelland, and their colleagues carried out a number of studies demonstrating that the human perceiver is anything but passive. Subjects in these early experiments appeared to approach the perception of ambiguous stimuli, such as blurred images briefly exposed on a screen, with certain ready-made interpretations. Conversely, other stimuli—stimuli that there was reason to believe the subjects felt negative about—seemed to be somewhat difficult for the subjects to perceive. It was as if their attitudes toward these objects were serving a protective function and making it more difficult for the subjects to perceive them.

There was a great deal of controversy about these early studies, and a number of telling methodological critiques have been advanced. Even so, the concepts emerging from the research have proven very fruitful. Two of these concepts are the notions of perceptual defense and perceptual vigilance. PERCEPTUAL DEFENSE is simply the idea that one will be slow to perceive or identify negatively valued stimulus objects. PERCEPTUAL VIGILANCE refers to an enhanced readiness to perceive or identify positively valued stimulus objects. Let us look at an example of how perceptual defense might be a factor in certain prejudicial racial attitudes.

Technically prejudice can refer to positive or negative orientations, but in the realm of intergroup relations, it has come almost exclusively to mean a negative orientation. Ashmore (1970) points out that there are two types of negative orientation, *moving against* (aggression) and *moving away from* (avoidance), and that both are apparent in intergroup relations. In black–white relations in the United States, moving against (in the sense of overt physical aggression) seems to have decreased in recent years, while moving away from or avoidance continues to be a frequent mode of response in whites' reactions to blacks, and vice versa.

If a person has strong negative affect toward any ethnic group, it seems reasonable to suppose that exposure to that group might be avoided whenever possible. Such avoidance fits in rather nicely with the idea of perceptual defense, which might also explain why "All those (whites, blacks, Chinese) look alike" to the prejudiced person. He or she simply does not pay sufficient attention to them and avoids them at every opportunity. Using black and white male subjects, Malpass and Kravitz (1969) have obtained evidence that there is indeed better recognition and memory of faces belonging to one's own race than there is for faces of another race. Whites, for example, recognize and remember white faces better than black faces.

Taking this one step further, Sensenig, Jones, and Varney (1973) attempted to relate subjects' level of prejudice (their attitude toward blacks) to their avoidance of black faces in a photo-inspection task. Prejudiced and nonprejudiced white subjects, who had been selected from a larger group on the basis of their responses to two measures of prejudice, were contacted individually and asked to participate in a yearbook evaluation. As part of the study, they were to inspect a series of 50 pictures taken from various yearbooks and rate each picture. Some of the pictures were of whites, and some were of blacks, and the main dependent measure was the amount of time spent inspecting white versus black pictures. As anticipated, nonprejudiced subjects spent approximately the same amount of time inspecting white and black pictures. By contrast, prejudiced subjects spent significantly less time looking at black pictures than at white pictures.

While this study may be taken as suggestive evidence for the operation of perceptual defense among prejudiced subjects, it is possible that prejudiced subjects simply found pictures of blacks easier to rate than pictures of whites. That is, prejudiced subjects may not have been avoiding black pictures relative to white pictures, but may simply believe that less variation exists among black faces and, hence, that black faces can be rated more quickly. Such a process becomes a self-fulfilling prophecy (Jones, 1977); belief in less variation leads to less inspection time and, consequently, actual perception of less variation.

Thus one of the things that attitudes do for us is

smooth our progress through the world by keeping us alert and sensitized to perceive those objects we feel positively about (perceptual vigilance). Conversely, attitudes help us ignore those things we dislike and want to avoid thinking about by blocking or at least retarding our perception of those objects. (For another example of how attitudes affect our perceptions, see Box B.)

Attitudes serve us in other ways as well. In addition to helping us make sense of what is going on around us, attitudes may help protect our sense of well-being. Katz (1960) terms this latter function the ego-defensive function of attitudes, and its operation can be seen quite clearly in the authoritarian personality. As we saw in Chapter 2, the authoritarian personality is made up of a complex web of contradictory and irrational beliefs and impulses. The authoritarian, for example, seems to be a great admirer of science and technology but is filled with superstitions and unscientific beliefs. Authoritarians seem to greatly value strength and power in leaders, but they feel everyone should be an individualist and stand on his or her own two feet.

In the early research on this personality type, Adorno, et al. constructed a number of scales to measure various aspects of personality and attitude thought to be associated with authoritarianism. Some of these, such as the anti-Semitism (AS) and ethnocentrism (E) scales, were intended as direct measures of negative attitudes and beliefs toward Jews and other groups, including blacks. The political–economic conservatism (PEC) scale was intended to obtain some index of the extent to which people preferred to main-

B. Archie Bunker and the Eye of the Beholder

One of the most popular television series in recent years has been CBS's *All in the Family*. Since January 1971, Archie Bunker has loudly voiced his ultraconservative, superpatriotic views on almost everything and, in the process, has derogated, insulted, and made fun of almost every ethnic group imaginable. Blacks, Jews, Puerto Ricans, gays, southerners, Californians, Mexicans, "women's libbers," and many more have been the object of Archie's often awkwardly worded, but always negative, pronouncements.

Archie's main antagonist on the show is his liberal son-in-law Mike, who lived with the Bunkers for a while and then moved next door. Most of Mike's views are directly contrary to Archie's, and much of the show revolves around this conflict. Mike repeatedly points out the glaring inconsistencies and irrational elements in Archie's convoluted logic. Archie, the bigot, is made to look ridiculous. But does he? And if so, to whom?

Neil Vidmar and Milton Rokeach, two social psychologists, selected a large number of adolescent and adult subjects in both the United States and Canada and asked them a number of questions about their perceptions of *All in the Family*. The subjects were also asked to fill out measures of prejudice, indicating how they themselves felt about certain groups such as blacks, Canadian Indians, or French-Canadians. The results were surprising.

The perceptions of what occurred on the show were quite different for prejudiced versus nonprejudiced subjects. Prejudiced subjects, for example, were significantly more likely than unprejudiced subjects to think Archie usually won his arguments with Mike. Prejudiced subjects were also more likely to admire Archie and to feel that it was okay for him to use the ethnic slurs and derogatory statements that have become his trademark.

It appears that many people, especially the prejudiced, do not see *All in the Family* as the satire on bigotry that its producers claim it is. Rather, all too many identify with Archie and think he tells it like it is. Vidmar and Rokeach (1974) suggest that the program may reinforce prejudice; at least, it may reinforce prejudice among the prejudiced.

tain the status quo (or even go back to "the good ole days"). The implicit antidemocratic trends (or F, for fascist) scale was intended as a measure of basic personality tendencies that support prejudice. Some examples of items from these scales appear in the following list. For these and other items on the scales, subjects were simply asked to indicate the extent to which they agreed or disagreed with the items by assigning a number from +3 (strong agreement) to −3 (strong disagreement).

Obedience and respect for authority are the most important virtues children should learn. (F scale item)
We are spending too much money for the pampering of criminals and the insane, and for the education of inherently incapable people. (E scale item)
The best way to eliminate the Communist menace in this country is to control the Jewish element which guides it. (AS scale item)
The best political candidate to vote for is the one whose greatest interest is in fighting vice and graft. (PEC scale item)

In addition to having subjects complete these scales, Adorno, et al. conducted intensive interviews and clinical assessments of the highly prejudiced subjects and compared the results to those obtained from subjects who had scored low in prejudice. Of interest here is the finding that the highly prejudiced were much more likely to externalize their personal problems, conflicts, and concerns. That is, they were more likely to blame others, particularly identifiable groups such as Jews and blacks, for the things that bothered or frightened them. By doing so, of course, they could protect their own self-esteem: it (whatever it is) isn't their fault. Suffering from vague and formless fears or simply suffering from things that one cannot do much about also seemed to be made more tolerable by giving such problems a focus and blaming someone, and the highly prejudiced were more likely to pursue this route to psychological comfort.

The highly prejudiced were more likely, then, to seek a scapegoat, and this observation led to what is called the SCAPEGOAT THEORY OF PREJUDICE. If you can blame your problems on someone else, then not only do you not have to shoulder any responsibility, but you can also justify your negative feelings about them and your discrimination against them. We shall return to the scapegoat theory of prejudice later (Box D), but first let us look at some of the issues concerning the relationship between attitudes and behavior. Some of the major criticisms (Kirscht and Dillehay, 1967) leveled against studies such as *The Authoritarian Personality* have made much of the paper-and-pencil, interview nature of the data, while the real issue is whether authoritarians behave differently from nonauthoritarians. More generally, the issue is whether we can predict people's behavior from knowledge of their attitudes.

Attitudes and behavior

There is a sizable literature purporting to show that affect toward an attitude object and behavior toward that object are often, even *usually*, inconsistent. LaPiere (1934), for example, traveled around parts of the United States with a Chinese couple, stopping at over 250 restaurants, cafes, hotels, and motels. Only once were they refused service because of the race of the Chinese couple. However, LaPiere later mailed a questionnaire to each of the places in which they had been served asking if they would serve Chinese patrons, and over 90 percent of those responding said no! Is this evidence that attitudinal affect and behavior are inconsistent?

As Dillehay (1973) has pointed out, it is not. The LaPiere study and similar studies often cited as evidence for inconsistency between affect and behavior are essentially irrelevant to the inconsistency question, because they probably did not have a measure of affect and behavior for the same people. No one has ever claimed that you should be able to predict Sam's behavior from knowledge of Dolores's affect toward the object in question. How likely is it, for example, that the host or hostess who seated LaPiere and his friends at a restaurant also handled the correspondence for the restaurant? Not very likely, but even if he or she did, LaPiere never asked for a verbal expression of attitudinal affect toward Chinese. His letter asked for a statement of institutional policy. Thus we need to be careful about this question of predicting behavior from attitudes. There are many traps for the unsuspecting to fall into. To help us avoid a few of them, let's look at some of the more common.

MEASUREMENT PITFALLS

One of the first things that should concern anyone who wants to relate attitudes to behavior is what, exactly, we want to relate. We have argued that attitudes have several components, so it seems unreasonable to suppose that we can arrive at *a number* to represent an attitude in the same sense that we can arrive at a number to represent the length of a board. While we might be able to represent the affective component on a simple scale running from positive to negative, how would we represent the multiplicity of beliefs that make up the cognitive component on such a scale? Further, the evidence (Sherif, Sherif, and Nebergall, 1965) seems to indicate that even the affective component cannot be adequately represented on such a scale.

Scott (1968) points out that a number of properties of attitudes can be conceptualized, measured, and presumably related to behavior. He lists the following examples, but he claims there are more:

1. Direction: the positive versus negative aspect of the affective component
2. Magnitude: the degree to which the affect toward the object is positive or negative
3. Intensity: the degree of commitment or strength of feeling with which one holds a particular positive or negative position
4. Salience: the importance or prominence of the attitude to the person
5. Relative salience of components: the degree to which the affective as opposed to, say, the cognitive component is the focus of the attitude
6. Ambivalence: the extent to which the person has both positive and negative feelings toward the attitude object
7. Cognitive complexity: the "richness" of the cognitive component, the number of beliefs and/or amount of information the person has about the attitude object
8. Overtness: the likelihood that the attitude will be translated into behavior
9. Embeddedness: the extent to which the attitude is related to other attitudes
10. Flexibility: the susceptibility of the attitude to change or modification
11. Consciousness: the extent to which the attitude is verbalizable by the person

As Scott (1968) points out, however, most of these properties have not been operationalized very well in the attitude literature. In fact, most of them have received very little attention. Almost all the research on attitude measurement has been focused on the affective component and, in particular, on the magnitude of the affective component. Even with such a limited focus, progress has been difficult.

For example, look back at Table I and note in particular the apparently decreasing favorableness of beliefs about Americans and the apparently increasing favorableness of beliefs about blacks. Sigall and Page (1971) have pointed out that these changes in beliefs about blacks and Americans may be more apparent than real. That is, college students in the late 1960s may simply have been more concerned about giving socially desirable responses than were their counterparts in 1951 and 1933. As Sigall and Page (1971) put it, favorable descriptions of blacks and self-criticism of Americans may have been "fashionable" at the time. In an attempt to reduce such socially desirable responses and more accurately assess beliefs about blacks and Americans, Sigall and Page employed a technique referred to as the "bogus pipeline," which involves convincing a subject that the experimenter can measure his or her attitudes precisely via a direct physiological index similar to a lie detector.

Subjects were seated at a fancy electrical console called the EMG. Recording electrodes from the EMG were strapped to their arms, and they were asked to grip a large wheel that presumably picked up unconscious muscle movements. A meter on the EMG with a 7-point scale (-3 to $+3$) was ostensibly controlled by hand pressure on the wheel. The wheel was locked in place so that the meter was set at zero. The experimenter said that although the wheel was locked, their implicit muscle tendencies would deflect the needle in a -3 or $+3$ direction in response to attitude statements that would be read to them. The subjects were told the purpose of the experiment was to assess perceptions of various ethnic groups. The labels "Characteristic"

(+3) and "Uncharacteristic" (−3) were then inserted on the EMG meter, and subjects were told that they would be read a list of traits. For each trait, they were to try to predict what the EMG would show about how characteristic they believed that trait to be of blacks or Americans. The idea, of course, is that the subject, believing the EMG is going to record true feelings from implicit muscle responses, will be more accurate and *not* give socially desirable responses as predictions of the EMG readings. The subject does not want the experimenter to think he or she is lying. For comparison purposes, another group of subjects were simply asked to rate how characteristic they believed each of the traits were of Americans and blacks. Some of the results appear in Table III.

As the table shows, Sigall and Page were apparently correct about the extent to which social desirability may determine responses to questions about characteristics of ethnic groups. For example, subjects seem to believe that Americans are more, and blacks less, intelligent than the subjects say when simply asked to rate how characteristic intelligence is of the two groups. Similarly, they apparently believe that laziness is less characteristic of Americans, but more characteristic of blacks, than they say in a simple rating task. In short, we need to beware of taking verbal reports of beliefs about attitude objects at face value.

Suppose, however, that two people were to make precisely the same verbal report of their beliefs about some object. Could you then assume that they felt equally positive or negative toward the object? Unfortunately, no. In a demonstration of this point, Hovland and Sherif (1952) took a large number of statements about blacks and asked subjects to sort them into categories in terms of how favorable or unfavorable the statements were perceived to be. Categories 0, 1, and 2 represented the unfavorable extreme, and the categories ranged through neutral up to 9, 10, and 11, the most favorable extreme. One group of subjects who were asked to sort the items were recruited among white students at the University of Oklahoma who had participated in a number of problack activities. A group of antiblack subjects was recruited from among various housing units at the same university. The placement of the statements into categories was quite different for the two groups. The average placements for a sample of items by the two groups are shown in Figure 3. The problack subjects displace most of the items toward the unfavorable end of the scale. For the antiblack subjects, on the other hand, 7 of the same 11 items are seen as favorable statements about blacks.

A number of other potential biasing factors may enter into one's response to an attitude questionnaire or rating scale. For example, if several items in an attitude questionnaire are all worded so that agreement with the items indicates, say, favorability toward the attitude object, then the responses may be contaminated by what has been termed an ACQUIESCENT RESPONSE STYLE (Cronbach, 1960). That is, some people seem more inclined to agree with anything than others and to agree more readily than they disagree. This potential bias can usually be handled by reversing some of the items in the questionnaire, making it so that the subject *has* to disagree with some statements and agree with others in order to display a favorable (or unfavorable) attitude toward the object. Other biases, such as the giving of socially desirable responses and related attempts to ingratiate oneself with the person administering the questionnaire (Jones, 1964), are not quite so easily corrected.

On a general level, the problems are those of obtain-

Table III Mean assignment of traits to Americans and blacks

	Condition			
	Americans		Blacks	
Trait	EMG	Rating	EMG	Rating
Happy-go-lucky	.53	.53	.93	−.13
Honest	.60	−.27	−.33	.67
Ostentatious	1.70	1.27	1.13	.33
Intelligent	1.73	1.00	.00	.47
Stupid	−1.07	−.20	.13	−1.00
Physically dirty	−1.67	−1.53	.20	−1.33
Sensitive	1.47	.07	.87	1.60
Lazy	−.80	−.40	.60	.73

Assignment by subjects who believed their "true" responses could be determined (EMG) and subjects who simply rated the two groups. On a scale of +3 to −3, the more positive the number, the more the trait was seen as being characteristic of the group. The more negative the number, the less the trait was seen as being characteristic. (From Sigall and Page, 1971, Table 1, p. 250.)

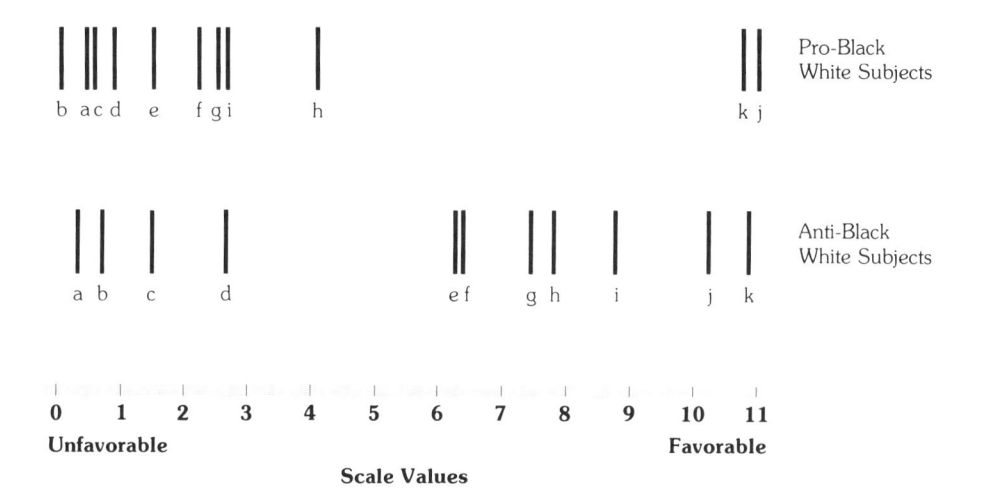

3. Scale values of 11 selected items for two groups of white subjects who differed in attitude toward blacks. Whether certain statements about groups are interpreted as favorable or unfavorable varies with the subject's general attitude toward the group. (From Hovland and Sherif, 1952, Figure 2, p. 829.)

ing reliable and valid indices, which we discussed in Chapter 2. In the realm of attitude assessment, the pursuit of reliable and valid indicators has led a number of investigators to abandon such direct techniques as rating scales and questionnaires. Seeking to escape the confoundings introduced by selective perception, social desirability, acquiescence, and other sources of bias, they have turned to indirect and unobtrusive methods of assessment. These methods often have problems of their own (see Box C), but they do get around some of the ambiguities introduced by overreliance on paper-and-pencil measures of attitudes.

Thus one of the reasons why attitudes have seemed inconsistent with behavior is that early research in this area was plagued by measurement problems. With the increasing sophistication of researchers and their alertness to these problems, things are beginning to look better for the attitude–behavior relation. Let us see.

ATTITUDE-BEHAVIOR CONSISTENCY

"Pseudoinconsistency" of attitude and behavior.
Nearly everyone has had the experience of wanting to do something, even wanting to do something badly, and yet voluntarily not doing it. Why not? Probably within the last week or two, you yourself have foregone something you really wanted to do. Why? If you asked a large number of people this question, you would no doubt get hundreds of different answers, but many of the answers could probably be grouped into one of two categories: (1) the people had something else that they wanted to do even more, and the foregone behavior would have interfered; or (2) they perceived that someone whose favorable opinion was important to them would have disapproved. As an example of the former, try to remember the last time you went to a nice restaurant with a big, diverse selection on the menu. Did you have a hard time deciding what to order? If you are like most people, you probably made up your mind two or three different times and then changed one final time just as the waiter or waitress came to take your order. Or you let your companions order first so that you would have a couple of extra minutes to decide. Everything looked so good! But in order to choose one, you had to forego the others. As an example of the second category of answers, consider the plight of the teenager with a part-time job. It would be great to go out and spend each paycheck on movies and records and snacks, but mom and dad get upset if at least some of it is not safely stored away. So it's off to the bank.

These are but two of many reasons why we sometimes do not behave in ways that are consistent with

C. The Window of the Mind

Eckhard Hess, a psychologist at the University of Chicago, has conducted a series of investigations into the relationship between pupil dilation and one's interest in or attitude toward the object at which one is looking. The typical procedure employed involves having a subject peer into a large box-like apparatus. At the opposite end of the box is a screen on which pictures of various objects or scenes can be projected. Through a series of mirrors, a movie camera simultaneously takes pictures of the subject's eyes while he or she is looking at the projected images.

In one study (Hess, 1965), male and female subjects were shown five slides: one of a baby, one of a mother and child, one of a male pinup, one of a female pinup, and one of a landscape. From the films of the subjects' eyes taken while they were observing these slides, the percent change in pupil size was calculated. The results are depicted below:

As can be seen, female subjects show the greatest enlargement in pupil size to the slides depicting a baby, a mother and child, and a male pinup. On the other hand, males show the greatest pupil dilation when observing the slide of a female pinup.

Unfortunately, the initial promise of pupil dilation as an indicator of attitude has not been fulfilled. Subsequent research controlling for brightness of the slides indicates that the percent change in pupil size is actually quite a lot smaller than it was thought to be at first, often on the order of 4 or 5 percent. It is also not clear exactly what pupil dilation means. Is it a measure of positive affect toward the object or of interest in the object? Perhaps these two are the same, but they may not be. There is also the problem introduced by the finding that very unusual, shocking stimuli such as scenes of dead soldiers on a battlefield—stimuli that would theoretically be expected to produce pupil constriction—initially produce large pupil dilation. A final problem is simply the cumbersome apparatus involved in using pupil dilation as a measure of anything. For the time being, Hess's index of pupil dilation as a measure of attitude will remain itself the object of investigation. Its practical usefulness as a measure of attitude is yet to be demonstrated.

our attitudes: we have many different and sometimes competing attitudes, and we sometimes perceive norms and expectations of others that are contrary to our attitudes. Oskamp (1977) and Fishbein and Ajzen (1975) list a number of other factors that may make attitudes appear inconsistent with behavior. For example, attitudes may change over time. If someone asks us in September which political candidate we favor, there is no guarantee that we will feel the same way in November when the election rolls around. Between September and November, we might find out that our favorite candidate has been on the take for years. Another reason why attitudes may appear inconsistent with behavior is that irrelevant, extraneous events and circumstances may prevent us from behaving as we intended. You may have been planning for weeks to go see that Peter Sellers movie. But on the last night it was in town, a storm came up, there was a power blackout, and the theater closed early.

There are other reasons for what we might term the pseudoinconsistency (Oskamp, 1977) of attitudes and behavior, but it should be clear that behavior in any given situation has many determinants, only one of which *may be* the affective component of a relevant attitude. There are situational pressures to do or not to do particular things, social norms, conflicting attitudes, and other factors (Kiesler, 1971) that may intervene to make one's behavior different from what it would have been if it had been determined only by the single focal attitude. Even with all of these interacting forces, however, there are some identifiable conditions under which we may anticipate a fairly consistent relation between attitudes and behavior.

Conditions promoting consistency. Heberlein and Black (1976) suggest that the more specific the attitude, the more likely that the attitude is related to a specific behavior. Many people say and genuinely feel that we need to be more careful about preserving and protecting our environment; that is, they have a positive attitude toward taking ecology seriously. But what does that mean in terms of specific behaviors? Are they likely to save papers and cans for recycling? Do they eat only organically grown foods? Do they write letters to their representatives and senators urging them to support environmental-protection bills? And if they don't do those things, are they being inconsistent? Heberlein and Black argue that in order to know which, if any, of these various behaviors will be performed, we need to be more precise when measuring attitudes. Instead of asking a general question such as "To what extent are you in favor of a cleaner environment?" we need to ask questions such as "Do you feel that saving paper and cans for recycling is a good idea?"

To see whether increasing the specificity of the attitude being measured increased the extent to which one could predict a specific behavior from knowledge of the attitude, Heberlein and Black designed an interesting field study. Service station operators were asked to note the license number and general appearance (age, sex) of purchasers of lead-free gasoline and, for comparison, the license number and general appearance of regular gasoline purchasers. The names and addresses of the car owners were then obtained from the open records of the state Motor Vehicle Bureau, and the owners were sent a questionnaire. The study was done at a time when the purchase of lead-free gasoline was not required by law or most car manufacturers' specifications, and lead-free gas cost about 2 cents more per gallon than regular. The assumption was that purchasing lead-free gas under these conditions would serve as a behavioral index of a positive attitude toward cleaning up the environment.

The questionnaire that the identified subjects received contained questions at four different levels of generality, ranging from global questions about being concerned with environmental issues down to very specific questions about purchasing lead-free gasoline as a step toward helping clean up the atmosphere. A sample question from the most specific level is "How much personal obligation do you feel to purchase lead-free gasoline?" Possible responses to this particular question ranged from "some obligation not to buy lead-free" to "strong obligation to buy lead-free." (Remember that the people who filled out the questionnaire had already been observed actually buying or not buying lead-free gas.) As anticipated, as the questions on the questionnaire became more specific, they became better predictors of behavior. The answers to the general questions about environmentalism were not at all predictive of who had or had not purchased lead-free gas. However, the more specific questions about attitudes toward purchasing lead-free gas were predictive. A person who indicated that he or she felt an obligation to buy lead-free gas was much more likely to actually do so than someone who did not feel so strongly about this particular action.

In addition to being more specific about the attitude we want to relate to behavior, there is another factor that we can take into account to increase the extent to which we are able to predict behavior. Attitudes are translated into behavior in certain situations, and we can have an attitude toward the situation just as we can have an attitude toward some object present in the situation. For example, suppose you really like a particular kind of cheese, but the only place you have been able to find it is a little specialty store about three miles away. Furthermore, every time you go in there, the jerk behind the counter manages to make you wish you had stayed home. Clearly you've developed an attitude toward the situation in which the cheese (the object of the initial attitude) must be purchased. Rokeach and Kliejunas (1972) point out that if we take both the attitude toward the object and the attitude toward the situation into account, we are likely to be more accurate in our predictions of behavior. We could improve our accuracy even more if we got some measure of the relative importance of the object and the situation. How important is it to you to have that particular kind of cheese, and how important is it to you to avoid interacting with the snide clerk who sells it?

To demonstrate that prediction of behavior from a knowledge of attitudes is greatly improved by taking the attitude toward the situation into account, Rokeach and Kliejunas attempted to predict how often college students would cut class by measuring their attitudes toward attending class generally and their attitudes toward the particular professor teaching the class. Subjects were also asked about the relative importance of these two attitudes to them. When these three things were taken into account—the attitude toward the general idea of attending class, the attitude toward the particular professor, and the relative importance of these two attitudes to the student—the behavior of cutting class could be predicted quite well.

General attitudes. We have been looking at this issue of attitude–behavior consistency mostly from the attitude side, and we have seen that specific attitudes are better predictors of specific behaviors than are more general attitudes. But what about those more general attitudes? After all, the major reason for studying attitudes is to predict behavior. If we have to ignore all our more general attitudes, we may be admitting defeat in our attempts to predict behavior. Surely the fact that a person is strongly in favor of socialism should mean that the person's behavior is different in many ways from the behavior of someone strongly opposed to socialism. We would expect two such people to take different newspapers or, if they took the same newspaper, to read different columns. We might expect them to buy different books, to support different political candidates, and to have different friends. While we might not be able to foretell precisely which behaviors of the two people would differ, we would certainly expect many differences.

In line with this reasoning, Fishbein and Ajzen (1974) suggest that studies of attitude–behavior consistency should include measures of multiple as opposed to single behaviors. In the study by Heberlein and Black, for example, a single behavior was to be predicted: buying lead-free gasoline. For that single behavior, the subjects' general attitude toward environmental issues was not a good predictor. However, had Heberlein and Black included many different behaviors related to environmental concerns, such as buying lead-free gas, collecting paper to be recycled, and belonging to the Sierra Club, it might have turned out that the subjects' general attitudes toward environmental issues *would* have been predictive. That is, the more favorably the subjects look upon environmental protection, the greater the *proportion* of these different behaviors they would have performed, even though they might not perform any *specific* one, such as buying lead-free gasoline.

To demonstrate that general attitudes are predictive of multiple behaviors, Fishbein and Ajzen constructed a list of 100 specific behaviors dealing with matters of religion—behaviors such as praying before meals, taking a religious course, donating money to a religious institution, and dating someone of a different religion. For a group of 62 subjects, they then determined which of these behaviors each subject had actually performed and asked each subject to fill out several attitude scales indicating how favorable or unfavorable they were toward religion generally. The 100 behaviors differed, of course, in the extent to which each could be considered a proreligious behavior, and an independent group of judges rated each on the extent that it was pro- or antireligious. Thus Fishbein and Ajzen had a measure of each subject's general religious attitude, a measure of which of 100 different behaviors each subject had performed, and knowledge of the extent to which each of these behaviors was considered pro- or antireligious. As anticipated, the more favorable the subject's attitude, the greater the number of proreligious behaviors the subject had actually performed. On the other hand, there was no consistent relationship between a subject's attitude and the likelihood of having performed any particular proreligious behavior.

What, then, are we to make of the relationship between attitudes and behavior? We have seen that the influence of a particular attitude on behavior may sometimes be obscured by conflicting attitudes and situational pressures, such as social norms and the anticipated disapproval of others. Even so, it is clear that attitudes are predictive of behavior. If we want to predict a specific behavior, however, we need to measure a relatively specific, pertinent attitude. We can further improve our predictive accuracy by taking into account attitudes toward the situation as well as the object of interest. Finally, the more general attitudes that are so important to all of us are indeed predictive of multiple behaviors, even though they may not tell us anything about the likelihood of someone's engaging in any particular, specific behavior. As an area of research in which attitudes, attitude formation, and attitude–behavior consistency have been central concerns, let us look at some of the issues involved in the study of racial prejudice.

Prejudice

PREJUDICE is an attitude toward some group or toward anyone perceived to be a member of that group (Ashmore, 1970). Technically one can be favorably as well as unfavorably prejudiced, but in social psychology the word *prejudice* has come to mean an overall negative attitude toward some group and/or its representatives. As an attitude, then, prejudice toward a particular group would be accompanied by beliefs about the characteristics of the group (stereotypes) and predispositions to behave toward the group in particular ways. It is also safe to say that the behavioral predispositions accompanying any overall negative attitude will be tendencies to behave in predominantly negative ways, such as avoidance, aggression, and discrimination.

There are some curious things about prejudice. How, for instance, does it originate? Why is it that historically there has always been greater prejudice against blacks in the south than in the north? Perhaps southerners are generally more authoritarian than northerners, and, as we have seen, a general tendency to distrust and dislike those who are different is part of the authoritarian personality. The evidence seems to indicate that this explanation will not suffice, however. Generally speaking, southerners are no more or less authoritarian than northerners (Pettigrew, 1959). Besides, if antiblack prejudice were due to greater authoritarianism of southerners or to greater "mental illness" among Southerners (a possibility that was seriously entertained some years ago), how would we explain the fact that anti-Semitism is stronger in the north than in the south? And how would we explain the waves of prejudice against particular groups that have occurred at various times and places in history, such as the strong anti-Catholic sentiments that swept Massachusetts in the mid-nineteenth century and the anti-Japanese furor in California around 1900?

Though almost anything one says about prejudice is bound to be something of an oversimplification, the best explanation seems to be that prejudice originates in realistic group conflicts. Groups are often forced into competition for scarce resources, and in that sense the competition or conflict is both rational and realistic (Campbell, 1965). In the impoverished agrarian economy of the post–Civil War south, blacks and whites were in direct competition for land and jobs. In the middle 1800s, large numbers of Irish–Catholics migrated from Ireland to Massachusetts, providing masses of laborers eager for jobs at almost any wages. Similarly, in California in the late 1800s, as immigration from Japan increased and the Japanese became more numerous, they became a source of cheap labor, willing to take jobs at wages below those demanded by whites. The result was an escalation of prejudice against them (Daniels, 1968).

Once a group comes to be thought of as "less worthy," discriminatory practices against members of the group are seen by some as being justified. A vicious circle is set up: having poorer and fewer facilities at their disposal, the members of the group are less able to behave in ways similar to the other members of society. (Ebony Magazine)

In one of the few experimental tests of the idea that realistic group conflict can produce intergroup prejudice, Sherif, Harvey, White, Hood, and Sherif (1961) randomly assigned 11- and 12-year-old boys to one of two groups. The two groups occupied separate sites in a large camping area near Robbers' Cave, Oklahoma, and for a number of days, they were not even aware of each other's existence. During this period, each group developed some traditions of its own and generated considerable *esprit de corps,* even adopting names for themselves: the Rattlers and the Eagles. After a few days of this blissful wilderness experience, the two groups were allowed to discover each other's presence. Almost immediately they challenged each other to competitive sports such as baseball. In addition, the experimenters arranged a series of tournaments complete with prizes that could only be won by one of the groups.

The games and contests began in a spirit of good sportsmanship, but it quickly evaporated. The Eagles were defeated in a tug of war, for example, and after the Rattlers had gone away victorious, the Eagles removed and burned the Rattler flag from a stand where it had been left. A scuffle broke out the following day, and soon group contacts had degenerated into reciprocal name-calling, assaults, and raids on each other's camps. The intergroup hostility became so intense that the experimenters had to intervene several times to calm things down. The point, of course, is that while cultural, language, and other differences between groups may increase the likelihood of intergroup prejudice, they are not necessary. Competition for scarce resources among groups artificially formed with members from equivalent backgrounds was sufficient to arouse intergroup prejudice. Sherif, et al. (1961) also found, however, that when the two groups subsequently had to cooperate in order to achieve goals they both valued but could not achieve alone, there was a sharp reduction in hostility. (For another theory about the origins of prejudice, see Box D.)

Of course, other factors come into play if the group conflict results in one group conquering or dominating the other. The members of the dominated group are likely to be forced into subordinate roles, and, as incredible as it sounds, with the passage of time they may come to think of these roles as the only ones appropriate for them. Frederick Douglass, the fiery nineteenth-century black leader, once commented that in his fight against slavery he had to contend not only with whites, but with many of his own people who seemed to think it was natural for the white race to dominate the black. Many young black and white civil rights activists in the south in the early 1960s reported similar attitudes among older blacks toward maintaining the status quo. It is possible, of course, that some of this was prompted by a realistic fear of violent retaliation from whites, but it appears that a more subtle and insidious effect of the decades of segregation was also responsible: the lowered self-esteem and self-hatred that have often been found to characterize blacks (Proshansky and Newton, 1968).

If society defines the members of any group as second-class citizens and limits their access to educational resources and other opportunities, a vicious circle is set in motion. Not only are the individual members of the group likely to become genuinely disadvantaged because they do not have access to the means to improve themselves, but they soon come to think of themselves as unworthy of anything better. Members of the more privileged groups in society are likely to inadvertently help keep this deadly circle spinning once certain beliefs about "second-class citizens" become widespread.

For example, it has been well documented that many white middle-class teachers believe lower-class black students will perform poorly in school. What effect is this belief likely to have in the classroom? To find out, Rubovits and Maehr (1973) asked each of 66 white female undergraduates enrolled in a teacher-training course to teach a brief lesson about television to groups of four seventh- and eighth-graders. In each group of four, there were two white and two black students. The interactions between teachers and students were observed, and each teacher's behavior was coded into a set of categories. White students received significantly more attention than black students. Further, fewer statements were requested of black students, more statements by black students were ignored, and black students were praised less and criticized more. It is likely that the greater participation demanded of the white students gives them the opportunity to clarify their thoughts more through dialogue with the teacher. By having to articulate their ideas more precisely, they come to understand those ideas better. And, of course, both black and white students sense that the teacher has different expectations of

D. The Scapegoat Theory of Prejudice

Originally, a scapegoat was a live goat used in religious ceremonies. The idea was that the sins of the people could be symbolically transferred to the goat and the goat then allowed to escape into the wilderness, thus cleansing the community of its sins. In a fairly straightforward extension of this, the term SCAPEGOAT has come to mean someone or some group who takes the blame for others.

The scapegoat theory of prejudice is based on the frustration–aggression hypothesis, which we shall discuss in more detail in Chapter 11. The basic idea is that when our access to something we want is blocked (frustration), we tend to lash out at (aggress against) the object or person that we perceive to have produced our frustration. Often, however, we cannot aggress against those who produce our frustrations. Children, for example, usually learn fairly quickly that they had better inhibit whatever tendencies to counteraggression they feel when they are being disciplined by parents. The parents are too powerful and would very probably retaliate with even more severe discipline. What is likely to happen, according to the scapegoat theory, is that a less powerful target is selected (a target unlikely to retaliate) and the pent-up aggression is loosed against this target. The aggression is displaced onto the cat, say, by a swift kick.

In an intriguing use of archival data to examine the scapegoat theory, Carl Hovland and Robert Sears found a negative relationship between the price of cotton in the south for the years between 1882 and 1930 and the number of lynchings of blacks each year. That is, the lower the price of cotton, which they took as an index of economic frustration, the greater the number of lynchings, the index of aggression. The economic system that produced the frustration and poverty was presumably too nebulous and vague to be a target for aggression. Hence, the aggression was displaced onto blacks.

Subsequent experimental research on the scapegoat theory of prejudice has yielded mixed results. Scapegoating does seem more likely to occur against targets that are already disliked. Ashmore (1970) points out that the perceived norms of one's own group are also important. That is, if you believe that most of your friends are not prejudiced against Jews, you are not likely to select Jews as targets for scapegoating.

---

them. A few years, or even a few months, of this and the white students are likely to be much further along in educational development, confirming (and also resulting from) the teacher's initial beliefs.

The effects of prejudice can be quite subtle and long-term. The grade-school child who falls behind today because the teacher doesn't think he or she is capable is more likely to be a high school dropout 10 years from now and chronically unemployed 30 years hence. Prejudice has a tendency to perpetuate itself. Beliefs about a particular group foster particular kinds of behavior toward members of the group, and this behavior tends to justify the belief. Also, prejudice is often (Pettigrew, 1959) perpetuated by sheer conformity to social norms. That is, even though realistic group conflicts, scapegoating, authoritarian personality patterns, and self-justification may all play a part in the origin and perpetuation of prejudice, most prejudice seems to be maintained by simple unthinking adherence to existing social norms.

As unfortunate as this is, it is actually an encouraging sign that prejudice can be reduced. In this chapter, we have been taking the point of view that attitudes determine behavior, and we have seen that, to a large extent, they do. However, as we shall see in Chapter 9, under certain conditions the opposite effect seems to occur, and behavior determines attitudes. If we can induce someone to behave in an unprejudiced manner toward a particular group, the chances are that the person will begin to feel more positive about the group. It is as if the person justifies having behaved in an unprejudiced manner by saying, "They must not be so bad after all." But we are getting ahead of ourselves. We shall devote the next two chapters to examining the conditions under which attitudes, including prejudices, can be changed.

Summary

An attitude is something we infer a person has—an inference that helps us account for consistencies in the person's behavior. Each attitude has a focal object, and the object of an attitude can be something as concrete as a particularly comfortable chair or as abstract as the idea of freedom. The classical view of attitudes is that each has three components: affect (likes and dislikes toward the object), cognition (beliefs about the object), and behavioral tendencies (predispositions to behave toward the object in certain ways). Although this view of attitudes is still predominant, one of its major shortcomings is that the nature of the relationships among the components of an attitude has usually been left unspecified.

Because of this ambiguity, we next turned to a recent model of the relations among the components, in which the term *attitude* was reserved for the affect toward an object. In spite of the change in terminology, it was clear that the Fishbein and Ajzen model was dealing with the same three components as the classical view: beliefs (cognitive component), attitude (affective component), and intention (behavioral predisposition). The advantage of the Fishbein and Ajzen model was that it helped us specify how the components are related. As we saw, affect toward an object seems to be a function of beliefs about the object. Each belief associates a particular attribute with the object, and these attributes are themselves evaluated either favorably or unfavorably. Although there is still some controversy about exactly how these evaluations combine to determine the overall affect we feel toward the object, it seems that we usually combine them by taking a weighted average of the individual evaluations. Another advantage of the Fishbein and Ajzen model was that it made explicit the notion that intentions to behave in particular ways are a function not only of the affect we feel toward a particular object, but also of our perception that others will approve or disapprove of our behavior.

Next we turned to an examination of some of the ways in which attitudes are formed and maintained. Affect toward an object may be established by relatively subtle conditioning techniques. The repeated co-occurrence of an initially neutral object with one we feel positively about may condition the positive affect to the initially neutral object. Further, the mere repeated exposure to an object may lead us to feel more positive toward it. Attitudes are very useful in that they free us from having to respond to each situation in all its uniqueness. Because of the economy of thought and action it provides, an established attitude is usually not given up easily. Also, the *de facto* selective exposure that results from surrounding ourselves with similar others tends to stabilize preexisting attitudes by reducing the likelihood that we will come in contact with attitudes and beliefs that differ from our own.

In examining the question of whether attitudes are predictive of behavior, we pointed out that we must be very careful in measuring attitudes to ensure that we get a valid and reliable index of the attitude of interest. We saw that a number of factors, such as the tendency of many people to give socially desirable responses, may make it difficult to predict behavior from verbally reported attitudes. We pointed out that there are many reasons for the appearance of inconsistency between attitudes and behavior, but we were also able to identify a number of conditions under which there is a fairly consistent relationship between attitudes and behavior. When we want to predict a specific behavior, we need to measure a relatively specific pertinent attitude. It helps improve our predictive accuracy if we can get not only a measure of the attitude toward the object of interest, but also a measure of the situation in which the object would be approached (or avoided). Finally, we saw that more general attitudes are also predictive of behavior, though they may not tell us anything about the likelihood that a particular behavior will be performed.

Finally, we took a brief look at prejudices—negative attitudes toward groups or anyone perceived to be a member of those groups. Prejudice has many sources, including realistic group conflicts, scapegoating, personality syndromes that predispose one to reject all who are different, and slavish conformity to existing norms. One of the most troublesome aspects of prejudice is that it tends to be self-perpetuating, setting in motion self-fulfilling prophecies that give the appearance of justifying the prejudice.

IV

Forms of social influence

8

Attitude change: the persuasive communication paradigm

212 The source: <u>who</u> says what to whom

Credibility
Similarity
Intent to persuade

222 The message: who <u>says what</u> to whom

One-sided versus two-sided communications
Conclusion drawing
Discrepancy
   Dissonance theory
   Social-judgment theory
Fear-arousing messages

236 The audience: who says what <u>to whom</u>

Personality and persuasability
Defense mobilization
Sleeper and Socratic effects

244 Summary

As we have seen, attitudes can be formed in many ways and, as you might expect, they can be changed in many ways. In this chapter, we shall examine one of the two most common settings for attitude change, the persuasive communication paradigm (see Figure 1). In spite of its fancy name, the PERSUASIVE COMMUNICATION PARADIGM is nothing more than a situation in which someone (a source or communicator) formulates a message to try to persuade others (the audience) to change their attitude toward some object. We begin by looking at several variables that enhance the effectiveness of particular sources: their prestige, credibility, similarity to the audience, and their announced or apparent intent to persuade. These are complex variables, and they interact with each other and with additional aspects of the communication setting. We shall also take a look at the nature of the message. The way it is organized can make quite a difference in its effectiveness. Under some circumstances, a message that mentions and refutes opposing arguments may be more effective than one that ignores the opposition. A tightly reasoned logical appeal may have no effect in some instances and produce massive long-term changes in others. A communication that advocates a great deal of change may actually produce less change than one that advocates only a little. We will try to make sense of these and other pertinent bits and pieces of evidence about what kinds of messages will be most effective in producing attitude changes. Finally, we shall examine some of the characteristics of the AUDIENCE, the people to whom a persuasive communication is addressed, that may be expected to enhance or reduce the effectiveness of particular messages and source–message combinations.

The source: who says what to whom

In the 1930s and 1940s, there were a number of studies of what was referred to as PRESTIGE SUGGESTION. The idea was that the more prestigious a particular figure, the more likely others would accept, or positively evaluate, his or her pronouncements. A particular statement would presumably have a greater chance of acceptance if it were attributed to Abraham Lincoln than if it were attributed to Al Capone. A study by Lorge (1936) illustrates this line of research.

Lorge asked a large group of adults to rate their respect for each of 70 well-known world figures. Three days later, these same subjects were asked to respond to 100 quotations by rating their agreement with the quotations and by guessing which of two names listed below each was the true author. One item from this part of Lorge's experiment was as follows:

> "Labor is prior to, and independent of, Capital. Capital is only the fruit of labor, and could never have existed if labor had not first existed."

☐ Abraham Lincoln: Civil War President of the United States.
☐ V. I. Lenin: Leader of the Russian Communist Revolution

After another lapse of time, the respondents were asked to rate all the quotations again, but only the true source of each quotation was listed below it this time. Lorge found that when the true source was more highly regarded than the guessed but incorrect source, subjects indicated greater agreement with the quotations. The prestige of the more highly regarded sources apparently rewarded subjects for agreeing. (As we have seen, balance theory predicts that it is more pleasant to agree with those we like and respect.)

In a sweeping critique of such studies, Asch (1948) offered a somewhat different interpretation of the results. The basic proposition of the prestige-suggestion studies was that an unchanged object of judgment undergoes a change in evaluation by being associated with a prestigious source. This, according to Asch, was just not so. Rather, a statement attributed to, say, Abraham Lincoln may be taken to mean something entirely different from what the same statement is taken to mean when it is attributed to Richard Nixon. The change, then, is in the object of judgment—the statement itself—rather than in the judgment of the statement. As an example, consider the statement "I hold that a little rebellion now and then is a good thing." The meaning and implications of "a little rebellion" are quite different if one believes that statement was made by Lenin than if one believes it was made by Thomas Jefferson. The former attribution may evoke images of anarchy and bloodshed, while the connotations of the latter are more likely to involve liberty and human dignity. In a reanalysis of data from the earlier prestige-suggestion studies, Asch (1948) found that there was, in fact, little evidence for simple prestige effects. Subjects' evaluation of and agreement with quotations seemed to be a function of what they understood the quotations to be saying, and this, of course, was partly a function of the source of the quotation.

Note that even though Asch's critique of the prestige-suggestion studies was generally correct, it still remained possible that simply having a positive, as opposed to a neutral or negative, evaluation of a source might increase our tendency to agree with the source of a persuasive communication. On the other hand, it seems much too simplistic to deal with an overall evaluative judgment of a source. A more fruitful approach might be to ask why particular communicators are effective in certain situations but not in others. Are there identifiable factors that will enhance one's effectiveness in producing attitude change?

CREDIBILITY

One of the attributes of a communicator that has been demonstrated to influence effectiveness in producing attitude change is the communicator's credibility. CREDIBILITY seems to have two components: expertise and trustworthiness. A highly credible communicator, then, is one who is very knowledgeable about the topic at hand and who has no ulterior motive for trying to persuade you. Obviously a person who is a credible communicator on one topic in one situation, or to one audience, might totally lack credibility if speaking on another topic, in another situation, or to a different audience.

In an early study of communicator credibility, Hovland and Weiss (1951) demonstrated that communicators high in expertise and trustworthiness were significantly more effective in producing attitude change on their respective topics than were com-

1. The persuasive communication paradigm. This chapter is concerned with "who says what to whom with what effect." The communicator (or source), the message, and the audience are complex independent variables, each of which has numerous components that may effect persuasion (attitude change) which is the dependent variable. It may prove useful to refer back to this figure while studying this chapter.

Source characteristics (Who)	Message characteristics (Says What)	Audience characteristics (To Whom)

A. Prestige suggestion
B. Credibility
   1. expertise
   2. trustworthiness
C. Similarity
D. Intent to persuade
	A. Message structure
	   1. one- versus two-sided communications
	   2. conclusion clearly drawn, or not drawn
	   3. discrepancy between audience's position and the position being advocated by the message
	B. Message Style
	   1. Type of appeal
	      a. pleasant messages
	      b. fear-arousing messages
		A. Personality variables
		   1. attention
		   2. comprehension
		   3. disposition to yield
		B. Defense mechanisms
		   1. counterargument
		   2. agreement (favorable thoughts)
		   3. inoculation against opposing beliefs
		C. Time factors
		   1. sleeper effects
		   2. Socratic effects

municators lacking these attributes, even when the latter delivered precisely the same messages. The basic finding has held up quite well in subsequent research and is firmly established: high-credibility communicators, when speaking on topics pertinent to their expertise, are more effective than low-credibility communicators.

In an extension of this finding, Bergin (1962) reasoned that when people hear a highly credible source advocate a position that differs from their own position on some issue, then the greater the discrepancy, the greater the pressure on them to change their attitudes. Since they cannot discredit the source, greater discrepancy should result in greater attitude change. On the other hand, a low-credibility source offers a second option: one can simply derogate the source. By assuming that the source does not know what he or she is talking about, one reduces the pressure to change.

To see whether these different responses actually did result after exposure to high- and low-credibility communicators, Bergin recruited male and female undergraduates at Stanford for two personality-assessment sessions. In the first session, subjects rated themselves on femininity–masculinity, and in the second session they received information on their masculinity–femininity from either a high- or low-credibility source, whose evaluation was either moderately, highly, or extremely discrepant from their own self-ratings. In the high-credibility conditions, the sessions took place in the Psychiatry Department of the Stanford Medical Center, and the experimenter was presumably the director of a personality-assessment project. In the low-credibility conditions, the sessions took place in a decrepit room in the basement of another building on campus, and the discrepant ratings were simply the "impressions" of another student (an experimental accomplice). Following exposure to the discrepant ratings, subjects were asked to rate themselves again. The changes in self-ratings in response to these conditions are shown in Figure 2. The more discrepant the communication from a highly credible communicator, the greater the change produced. The more discrepant the communication from a low-credibility communicator, the less the change produced. Ratings of the communicators revealed that the low-credibility communicator was perceived as significantly less of an expert and that this perceived degree of expertise

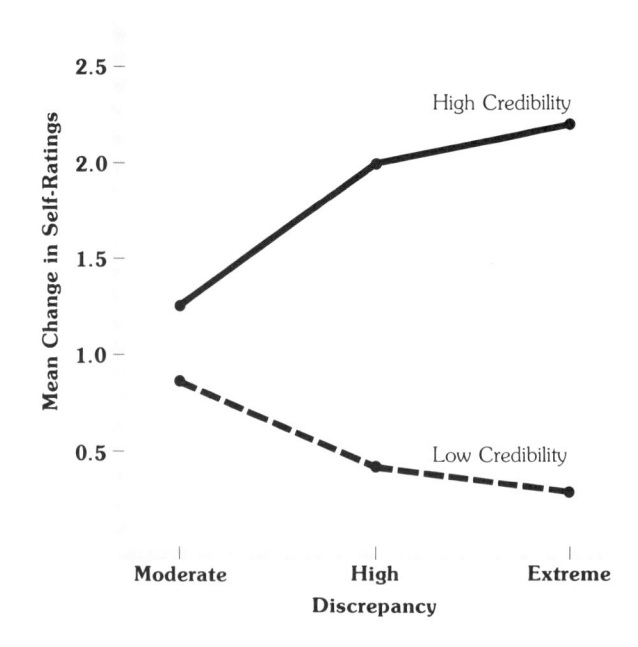

2. Mean change in self-ratings based on communicator's credibility and amount of communication discrepancy. The more discrepant the communication from a highly credible source, the greater the change produced. The more discrepant the communication from a less credible source, the less change produced. (From Bergin, 1962, Figure 1, p. 433.)

declined as the descrepancy of the communicator's message increased. Thus a low-credibility communicator is more likely to be derogated than he or she is to produce attitude change.

A number of investigators have addressed themselves to the conditions under which a low-credibility communicator's effectiveness in producing attitude change might be enhanced. In the Hovland and Weiss study mentioned earlier, subjects read the communications and the name of the author appeared at the end of the article. Husek (1965) reasoned that the effectiveness of a low-credibility source might actually be improved by not mentioning the source until after the communication has been delivered. To check on this, he played to 498 high school students a 20-minute talk attempting to promote more favorable attitudes toward mental illness. For about a third of the presentations, the speaker mentioned at the outset that she was a former mental patient; for another third, this was mentioned at the end of the presentation; and for the remaining students, it was never mentioned. As anticipated, mention at the outset of the fact that the speaker was a former mental patient resulted in significantly less positive attitude change than in the other two conditions. It is possible that withholding negative information about the source until after the talk allows the quality and reasonableness of the talk itself to influence the subjects' attitudes, whereas mentioning this information at the outset may promote inattention and/or a tendency to greater critical analysis of the argument. As McGuire (1969) points out, the keys to attitude change via persuasive communication are attention, comprehension, and yielding. A message must be attended and understood before it can have the desired effect.

In Husek's experiment, it appears that subjects were, in effect, discounting anything that a low-credibility source might have to say when they knew the source before hearing the communication. Sigall and Helmreich(1969) hypothesized that under some conditions, however, people will believe anybody. Specifically, they reasoned that when people are in a state of high stress, they may be so in need of support that they ignore the credibility of communicators who address them. People not experiencing stress may be more critical of a communicator's credentials and somewhat more selective about whom they believe. In support of this, Sigall and Helmreich found that subjects not experiencing stress (anticipation of a painful experience), were influenced significantly more by a highly credible communicator whose credentials were relevant to the topic than by either a low-credibility communicator or a communicator of high credibility whose credentials were irrelevant to the topic. (Actually, by our definition, the communicator whose credentials were irrelevant to the topic was *not* credible—expert and trustworthy—on this topic.) On the other hand, subjects experiencing stress were about equally influenced by all three communicators.

Thus a low-credibility communicator is relatively more effective in producing attitude change when the audience is under stress. Walster, Aronson, and Abrahams (1966) have found that a low-credibility communicator is also more effective when perceived to be arguing against his or her own best interests. In this case, the perceived trustworthiness and sincerity of the communicator would apparently be enhanced. But surprisingly, Walster, et al. (1966) found that if a communicator mentions arguments opposed to his or her own best interests, the audience also thinks of the communicator as more of an expert. It is less clear why this should be so. People may believe that someone who is able to set self-interest aside and look at the big picture is knowledgeable and intelligent. One of the most important turning points in intellectual growth, as we saw in Chapter 4, comes when a child learns that his or her view of the world is not the only one possible and probably not the most important one. It may be that subjects perceive the ability to shift perspectives as a cue to intelligence.

The credibility of a source, then, is an important determinant of his or her effectiveness in producing attitude change. But even when a particular source is lacking in expertise and trustworthiness, there are several ways in which his or her effectiveness may be enhanced. One example is given in Box A. Another interesting ploy, frequently used in political campaigns, is the communicator's attempt to shift the basis of evaluation from expertise to similarity. The appeal of the familiar "man of the people" is that "I'm just one of the folks." In any election year, scores of satiric political cartoons take their inspiration from it. Such an appeal has sound theoretical basis, however, and research indicates that it often works quite well.

SIMILARITY

There are several theoretical reasons for expecting that similarity between the source of a communication and the audience might, under certain conditions, enhance the effectiveness of the source in producing attitude change. As we saw in Chapter 6, for example, there is considerable evidence that similarity leads to liking. It follows from balance theory that liking for a communicator who advocates a given position on some issue should increase the probability of adopting that position, provided, of course, that we have not created dissonance for ourselves by voluntarily choosing to hear a communicator we dislike. With a similar result from a different perspective, social comparison theory, which we shall discuss in Chapter 9, predicts that we turn to others similar to ourselves on pertinent attributes to evaluate our attitudes and allow ourselves to be influenced by them.

A. Clean for Gene?

When Eugene McCarthy was running for president of the United States, there was a movement among his supporters to "Get Clean for Gene." The idea was that many of McCarthy's supporters would be more effective campaigners if they presented themselves to middle-class America with jacket and tie, short hair, and a generally wholesome, clean-cut appearance. Cooper, Darley, and Henderson (1974) suggest that this reasoning may have been wrong, or at least incomplete:

> if an anti-hippie voter, for instance, is induced to agree to listen to the political arguments of some army-jacketed, long-haired, bearded "freak," he cannot rationalize his listening by his liking for the hippie. On the other hand, listening to similar arguments from a conventionally dressed person can be justified on the basis of liking and tolerance for that person. From the basis of dissonance theory, then, it can be predicted that deviant-appearing campaigners will produce more voter agreement with their message than will more conventionally dressed campaigners (p. 753).

Dissonance theory suggests that when a person voluntarily exposes him or herself to a discrepant persuasive communication, dissonance is produced. The knowledge that one has a certain attitude is dissonant with the act of having chosen to listen to someone advocate the opposing view. The tendency is then to reduce that dissonance by one means or another. If one can find extrinsic reasons for having chosen to listen, such as the attractiveness of the communicator, there will be less dissonance and less pressure to change one's attitude. If such extrinsic justification cannot be found, one is more likely to reduce the dissonance by convincing oneself that the message indeed has merit and, hence, changing one's attitude.

To test this idea in a field setting, Cooper, et al. contacted voters by telephone and obtained a measure of their attitude toward a proposal to introduce a state income tax. This was an active political issue in the area, and most voters were opposed to the tax. Prior to obtaining this initial measure of subjects' attitudes, however, the telephone solicitor had explained that the "Henderson Economic Institute," which was conducting the survey, would like one of its workers to call at the subject's home for 5 or 10 minutes later that day and explain what the Institute was trying to do.

Subjects who agreed to let the worker drop by were greeted sometime later by either a conventional-looking worker (clean-shaven, short hair, jacket, and tie) or a deviant-looking worker (excessively long hair, bearded, blue-jeans). After gaining admittance to a subject's home, all the workers delivered a 3 to 4-minute, rational, persuasive communication explaining why the Institute was for the introduction of the state income tax. As soon as the communication had been delivered, the communicator claimed that he was running short of time and had to leave. (This was to keep the communication situation as standard as possible and to keep the subjects from asking questions.) Two to four days later, those subjects who had seen either the deviant or the conventional communicator and matched subjects assigned to a Control condition were contacted by an apparently independent survey organization and asked a number of questions, one of which was how they felt about the introduction of a state income tax.

The results indicated that subjects who had voluntarily exposed themselves to an unattractive, deviant communicator were more influenced by the communicator's message than were subjects who had been given the same message by an attractive, clean-cut communicator. The latter subjects and those assigned to the Control conditions were more steadfastly antitax.

Similarity on relevant dimensions—body style, clothing, and age—suggests similarity in general value orientation which under many conditions increases a communicator's persuasive effectiveness. (Jonathan Goell/The Picture Cube)

There are many ways in which people can be similar, and, as Simons, Moyer, and Berkowitz (1970) point out, there are both relevant and irrelevant similarities. Both the door-to-door salesperson and the customer may be fans of the Green Bay Packers, but this is largely irrelevant to the customer's need for an encyclopedia. However, if the customer has three children who are not doing well in school and the salesperson has three children who were not doing well until they got a set of the encyclopedias, this similarity may be relevant indeed. A relevant similarity between communicator and audience, then, is one logically related to the message the communicator is advocating. Simons, et al. (1970) go on to suggest that, from the point of view of the recipient of a persuasive communication, these relevant similarities with the communicator are effective in producing attitude change if they are perceived as informative and useful by the audience.

In a field study conducted in the paint department of a large retail department store, Brock (1965) was able to manipulate a relevant similarity between source and audience and to do it in such a way that the similarity did have implications for the audience. Two part-time paint salesmen were trained to deliver a persuasive communication to customers who had already decided to buy paint and who had actually proceeded to the cash register with the paint. For half of the customers, the salesman waiting on them said that he had purchased a similar amount of paint several weeks ago for a job he was helping his dad with. They had used "type X," however, a paint that was either higher or lower in price than the one the customer was about to buy, and it turned out beautifully. The salesman went on to note that he had also tried the paint the customer had and that it did not turn out well at all. The spiel ended with a strong recommendation to try the other type of paint. For the other half of the customers, the spiel was essentially the same except that the salesman began by stating that he had recently had occasion to buy and use 20 times the amount of paint that the customer was buying. That is, he was dissimilar to the customer and perhaps more of an expert on paint. Thus the design of the study was such that a similar or a dissimilar communicator advocated that the customers purchase a higher- or a lower-priced paint than the one they had already decided to buy. The results appear in Table I. As the table shows, the similar communicator was significantly more effective in producing change than the dissimilar communicator.

Prior to conducting his study, Brock had the part-time paint salesmen deliver their spiels to classes of college students who rated them on a number of scales. The dissimilar communicator turned out to be rated higher in expertness than the similar communicator. In this situation at least, people are more willing to allow themselves to be influenced by someone similar to them than by an expert. We would not, of course, expect that finding to hold for all times and places. The question of the circumstances under which experts are more effective than similar others in producing attitude change has been around a long time. Moore (1921), for example, asked subjects to judge the offensiveness of certain linguistic expressions and personality traits, and also to determine the most pleasant-sounding musical chords. He later asked subjects to make these judgments again after being informed how a "majority" or an "expert in the field" had judged each. The hypothetical expert and majority did not differ in inducing subjects to change their judgments of the musical chords or the personality traits, but the majority was more effective in inducing judgment reversals on the offensiveness of linguistic expressions. The important question, of course, is how these types of judgments differ. What are the differences between those situations in which similar others are more influential and those in which an expert is influential?

A partial answer to this question has been provided by Goethals and Nelson (1973). Following Kelley's (1967) analysis of the attribution process, Goethals and Nelson reasoned that when the issue is one of a belief about *objective reality* (a belief that is potentially verifiable by appeal to physical evidence), people would be made more confident about their position by discovering that others very dissimilar to themselves believe as they do. If dissimilar others agree with us, our belief is confirmed and does not stem from our own peculiar perspective. On the other hand, if the issue is one of *value* (of the goodness or badness of some aspect of reality), people should become more confident about their position when they find that similar others agree with them.

Under the guise of an evaluation of college admissions procedures, Goethals and Nelson asked male

Table I Percent of paint purchasers who changed their decision

Direction of influence	Similar	Dissimilar
To a lower price	73 percent	45 percent
To a higher price	55 percent	32 percent

(From Brock, 1965, Table 2, p. 652.)

and female students to view videotaped segments of interviews with two supposed applicants. One applicant appeared to be interested in a broad range of things but was somewhat diffuse and nonspecific about educational objectives. The other appeared to have considerably narrower interests but also appeared more intelligent and articulate. Subjects were told that both applicants had been accepted and that both were doing well academically and socially. However, two sets of conditions were created. Subjects in the Belief conditions were told that one of the applicants had a somewhat better academic record and that, after viewing the tapes, they would be asked to guess which one. Subjects in the Value conditions were told that the experimenter was interested in their personal feelings and impressions and that, after viewing the tapes, they would be asked to indicate which of the two applicants they would prefer as a close friend and fellow student. The tapes were shown, and the subjects made their choice and rated their confidence in the choice. The experimenter then explained that each subject would get to look at an evaluation of the two applicants written by someone who had already participated in the study. In all cases, these evaluations agreed with the subject's own, but approximately half the subjects were led to believe that the evaluation they saw was written by someone very Similar to themselves, while the remaining subjects were led to believe that it had been written by someone very Dissimilar. Finally, subjects were again asked to rate their confidence in the choice they had made. The results appear in Table II. As the table shows, when the issue is one of value, agreement with a similar other bolsters confidence in one's position more. When the issue is one of belief, agreement with dissimilar others is more reassuring.

Note that Goethals and Nelson did not actually measure *attitude change*. It should follow from the theoretical reasoning behind their hypothesis, however, that the same pattern of results would hold for attitude change as for their measure of increase in confidence. Dissimilar others should be relatively more effective in changing our *beliefs* (the cognitive components of our attitudes), and similar others should be relatively more effective in changing our *feelings* (the affective components of our attitudes). If we assume that prejudiced white subjects see themselves as more similar to white than to black communicators, then there is some evidence in a study by Aronson and Golden (1962) that dissimilar communicators are indeed less effective when the position taken is essentially unverifiable by appeal to physical reality. In the Aronson and Golden study, a black or a white communicator, who was portrayed as either an engineer or a dishwasher, presented a communication extolling the value of arithmetic to groups of white sixth-graders. When the communicator was presented as an engineer, with presumably relevant expertise, he was more effective than when presented as a dishwasher. Also, compared to unprejudiced subjects, prejudiced subjects were influenced less by a black communicator, whether he was an engineer or a dishwasher.

The similar-dissimilar communicator issue has evolved as a refinement of the earlier global interest in expertise. The original assumption was that the expertise of a communicator was crucial in producing attitude changes, but, as we have seen, this is not always so. Communicators who are less expert but more similar to the audience are more effective under some cir-

Table II Changes in subjects' confidence

	Characteristics of other evaluator	
Condition	Similar	Dissimilar
Belief	6.38	17.38
Value	21.11	10.63

The higher the number, the greater the increase in confidence.
(From Goethals and Nelson, 1973, Table 2, p. 121.)

cumstances. A parallel development has emerged in research on the second component of credibility postulated by Hovland and Weiss (1951), a communicator's trustworthiness or objectivity.

INTENT TO PERSUADE

As McGuire (1969) points out, the hypothesis that has guided investigations studying the objectivity of a communicator may be a prime example of "bubbapsychology"—the psychological principles that grandmother knew but which aren't so:

> It was expected that the less objective the source was felt to be (that is, the more the receiver suspected that the source was really out to persuade him), the less opinion change he would produce (p. 183).

Surprisingly, research has uncovered a number of conditions under which the perception that the communicator intends to persuade *enhances* his or her effectiveness in producing attitude change.

Mills (1966), for example, asked male and female college students to read, under one of four conditions, an interview extolling general education. The interviewee was described as either liking or disliking college students very much, and he either expressed the hope that he would be able to persuade them to adopt his position or said that he did not care whether he influenced them or not. After they read the interview, subjects indicated the extent of their agreement with the communicator's position by responding to a number of attitude items concerning general education. As anticipated, when subjects believed the communicator liked them, they were more influenced by his message when he overtly stated his desire to influence. On the other hand, when subjects believed the communicator disliked them, they were more influenced when he said he did not care about influencing them.

In Mills' study, the information about the communicator's intent to persuade was, in a sense, a part of the communication itself. The subjects had been given a booklet containing a few introductory remarks describing the interviewee's liking or disliking for college students, and at the beginning of the interview itself, the communicator expressed his desire, or lack of desire, to influence college students. But suppose the warning about the communicator's intention to try to make the audience change its attitude were separated in time from the message itself and delivered somewhat earlier. Suppose subjects were given sufficient time for it to register that someone was going to try to make them change their attitude. What might occur in the postwarning–preattack interval?

McGuire and Millman (1965) suggest that, under these conditions, subjects may very well change their attitude in the direction of greater agreement with the anticipated communication before they ever receive the communication itself. The reason behind this prediction is that many people tend to be somewhat anxious about their ability to withstand attempts to influence them. They are afraid that they will be unable to defend their beliefs and, when they do succumb to persuasion, will appear gullible both to themselves and to others. One way they can avoid this, and thus maintain their self-esteem, is to adjust their attitude before they are exposed to the persuasive communication.

Table III "Emotional" and "technical" issues used by McGuire and Millman

Emotional	Technical
1. Likelihood of Communist takeovers in Latin America	1. Shortage of lab animals
2. Difficulties of finding a cure for cancer	2. Failure of earth sciences to find oil deposits
3. Probability of a serious depression	3. Continuing need for propeller planes
4. Likelihood of World War III	4. Likely abolition of sales tax

McGuire and Millman also suggest that the need to use this type of face-saving ploy should be partly a function of the nature of the topic of the persuasive communication. That is, if the issue is a straightforward, technical one and not an emotional or otherwise unverifiable one, the person might *not* be so likely to change beforehand, because he or she could always attribute a change after the fact to an open-minded receptivity to new information rather than an inability to resist persuasion. Thus McGuire and Millman (1965) hypothesized that a shift in attitude should occur after one is warned that one is going to be exposed to a persuasive communication advocating a position that differs from one's own on some issue. And this shift toward greater agreement with the anticipated communication should be more pronounced for emotional, unverifiable issues than for technical, matter-of-fact issues.

The results McGuire and Millman obtained appear to bear out their hypothesis. Postwarning–preattack shifts in the direction of greater agreement with the anticipated communication did occur, and such shifts were significantly more pronounced for emotional than for technical issues. Consider for a moment, however, the emotional–technical issues that McGuire and Millman used (see Table III). The only definition offered of this variable is that a technical issue is a matter-of-fact one and an emotional issue is an unverifiable one. It is certainly a matter of fact that it has been difficult to find promising leads for a cancer cure, yet this was used as an emotional issue. Likewise, the probability of a serious economic depression is no less verifiable than the likely abolition of the sales tax, but the latter was classed as a technical issue and the former as an emotional issue. It appears that whatever the issue variable was, it was not emotionality-technicality. It could have been involvement, interest, or importance. We just don't know.

On the other hand, the issues McGuire and Millman used do not seem likely to be of great day-to-day interest for the college students taking part in the study. As Apsler and Sears (1968) point out, people usually get really involved only with those issues that they expect to be important for their own lives. With such issues, warning about an impending attack on their attitude should increase their resistance to the attack, because they are likely to believe that agreement with the discrepant communication would have unpleasant consequences for them. Hence, they are likely to mobilize their resistances and, perhaps, not even attend to the communcation very closely. On the other hand, when the issue is not important to the subject, warning of an impending attack on his or her position may actually increase the effectiveness of the discrepant communication. The warning may call attention to the communication and thus make the subject more attentive and receptive than would otherwise be the case.

To manipulate involvement, Apsler and Sears convinced half of their subjects that a set of proposals they would read were to be instituted at their school the following year. The proposals, that is, would be tried out on them while they were sophomores. These, of course, were High involvement subjects. Low Involvement subjects were told that the proposal would not be instituted for another ten years or so. Half of the subjects in each involvement condition were then given a specific warning of the position to be taken in the proposals they would read. They were told that the proposals suggested replacing undergraduate professors with supervised teaching assistants. All subjects then read the same persuasive communication ("Proposals Made by the Faculty Commission on Undergraduate Instruction") and filled out a questionnaire concerning their agreement with the proposals. The results are shown in Table IV. Warning of the position to be taken in a forthcoming persuasive attempt enhanced agreement with the communication among uninvolved subjects, but it reduced agreement among involved subjects.

Table IV   Mean attitude as a function of involvement and warning

	Involvement	
	High	Low
Warning	1.5	2.4
No Warning	1.8	0.7

The higher the number, the greater the agreement with the communication. (From Apsler and Sears, 1968, Table 1, p. 164.)

In going from the McGuire and Millman study to the Apsler and Sears study, we have maintained our interest in the effects of a warning about persuasive intent and issue involvement, but we have shifted from a discussion of change that occurs *in anticipation of* a persuasive communication to change that occurs *as a result of* the communication. Cialdini, Levy, Herman, Kozlowski, and Petty (1976) suggest that the types of changes that occur in these two situations are, in fact, quite different. They hypothesize that shifts that occur in anticipation of being exposed to a persuasive communication that disagrees with one's own initial attitude are strategic self-presentation maneuvers designed to put one in the most favorable light in the current situation. Such shifts are seen as quite different from genuine attitude change and as occurring as a kind of adjustment to a particular situation. The idea is that one's positions on certain issues are rather elastic. They may be stretched somewhat or temporarily distorted to suit the occasion, only to snap back like a rubber band to the original position when the situation changes. In support of this reasoning, Cialdini, et al. (1976) were able to demonstrate that subjects who anticipated having a discussion with a classmate whose position was discrepant from their own modified their stand on the issue toward greater agreement with the classmate. However, this occurred only when the issue was one of little personal relevance to the subjects and when the anticipated discussion was to take place immediately. And when subjects found that the discussion had been canceled, their stand on the issue "snapped back" to its original position.

The conditions under which knowledge of a source's intent to persuade will enhance, or reduce, the source's effectiveness in producing attitude change are not yet clear (McGuire, 1969). It does appear that the importance of the issue to the audience is a crucial variable. The more involved, interested, or committed the audience, the more likely a warning of persuasive intent is to reduce the source's effectiveness. It also seems that much of the research on forewarning and intent to persuade has dealt with the sorts of elastic, self-presentational shifts identified by Cialdini, et al. (1976) and not with true attitude change. As we shall see, research on the nature of the source's message also bears on the issue of intent to persuade.

The message: who says what to whom

It has often been pointed out, sometimes in jest but usually in earnest, that the way in which something is said is as important as what is said. While we may be evolving into completely rational beings, we haven't made it yet. Indeed, if we want to convince someone of something, it is usually not sufficient just to lay out the evidence and assume that the other's rational evaluation of that evidence will coincide with our own. We must present evidence, to be sure, but the manner in which we present this evidence is of utmost importance.

Many have claimed to know the best way to organize and present one's message. Benjamin Franklin, for example, believed that:

> The way to convince another is to state your case moderately and accurately, then scratch your head, or shake it a little and say that is the way it seems to you, but of course you may be mistaken about it.

In its unqualified form, the question of the best way in which to organize a persuasive communication is unanswerable. We can refine the question, however, ask specifically about those aspects of a persuasive communication that are important, and try to specify conditions under which certain kinds of communications are more or less effective. Let us begin with the issue of one-sided versus two-sided communications. When trying to change someone's attitude, is it best to present only those arguments that support your position (a one-sided message)? Or should you also mention a few of the opposing arguments as well (the combination being a two-sided message)?

ONE-SIDED VERSUS TWO-SIDED COMMUNICATIONS

Early research on the effectiveness of communications that presented only arguments in support of the position advocated (one-sided) versus those that also mentioned opposing arguments (two-sided) was relatively atheoretical. That is, investigators usually just wanted to find out which type of communication would be most effective in a particular situation. Hovland, Lumsdaine, and Sheffield (1949) conducted such a study during World War II. The communications were presented to large numbers of soldiers as radio transcriptions of a news commentator's analysis of the Pacific War. The impetus for the study was the War Department's interest in finding the most effective means of convincing Armed Forces personnel that the war in the Pacific might continue for some time after the war in Europe had ended. Accordingly, the one-sided presentation offered only arguments that the war with Japan would be long and arduous. The two-sided presentation gave these same arguments, but it also included 4 minutes of arguments that stressed U.S. advantages and Japanese weaknesses.

In overall effectiveness, as measured by increases in the average estimation of the length of the war, there was no advantage for either communication. Since both approaches resulted in about 40 percent of the audience increasing their estimate of the war's length, there was no apparent difference in their effectiveness. Such overall findings of no difference were typical of the early research. However, Hovland, et al. (1949) carried out further analyses of their data, which have led to development of a theory about the conditions under which one-sided communications are more or less effective than two-sided communications. These subsequent analyses revealed that a two-sided communication was more effective for the better-educated members of the audience and for those who opposed the position being advocated. These findings led investigators to speculate that the perception of bias in the communication could account for the obtained results. Presumably a one-sided communication is more likely to be seen as biased by those who are aware of opposing arguments, those who initally oppose the position advocated, and those who are relatively well educated. These people would generally be more aware of arguments on both sides of the issue.

Evidence in support of this reasoning has been reported by Chu (1967). He exposed some of his subjects to pro and con arguments on an issue two weeks prior to presenting all subjects with either one-sided or two-sided communications. Subjects initially favorable to the advocated position showed no difference in postexperimental attitude as a function of either prior familiarity with pro and con arguments or one- versus two-sided communications. However, among subjects who were initially unfavorable, the two-sided communication produced more agreement with the advocated position among those familiar with the pros and cons than did the one-sided communication. Based on this and on some additional analyses, Chu concluded that differential responses to one- and two-sided communications were probably due to perceived bias in the communications. That is not the whole story, however. The one-sided communication tended to be perceived as relatively biased in all conditions, but it resulted in reduced acceptance of the communicator's position only for the initially unfavorable subjects who had been exposed to pro and con arguments. At best, then, perceived bias accounts for only part of the obtained effects.

Jones and Brehm (1970) suggest that reactance theory may account for many of the findings on one- versus two-sided communications. As applied to this issue, REACTANCE THEORY asserts that when a person feels free to adopt or reject any of several positions on an attitude issue, pressure to adopt a particular position threatens his or her freedom and arouses reactance. The greater the pressure, the greater the amount of reactance aroused, and the greater will be the tendency to restore or safeguard the threatened freedom. Two ways to restore the freedom are by resisting the pressure to adopt a particular position, or by adopting a position clearly at variance with the one recommended. A one-sided communication will normally be seen as exerting greater pressure to adopt a particular position than a two-sided communication. Hence when an individual is aware that there are two sides to an issue, a one-sided communication will be seen as more threatening. On the other hand, when the individual is quite ignorant about the issue and does not know whether there are really two sides, a one-sided communication is relatively effective because it does not require the individual to weigh alternatives.

To check out this reasoning, Jones and Brehm (1970) asked subjects to read through a booklet containing either a one-sided or a two-sided communication—different versions of the prosecution's summary to the jury in a bigamy trial. Prior to reading one of the communications, subjects in the

WE ARE THE FEW, THE PROUD, THE MARINES.

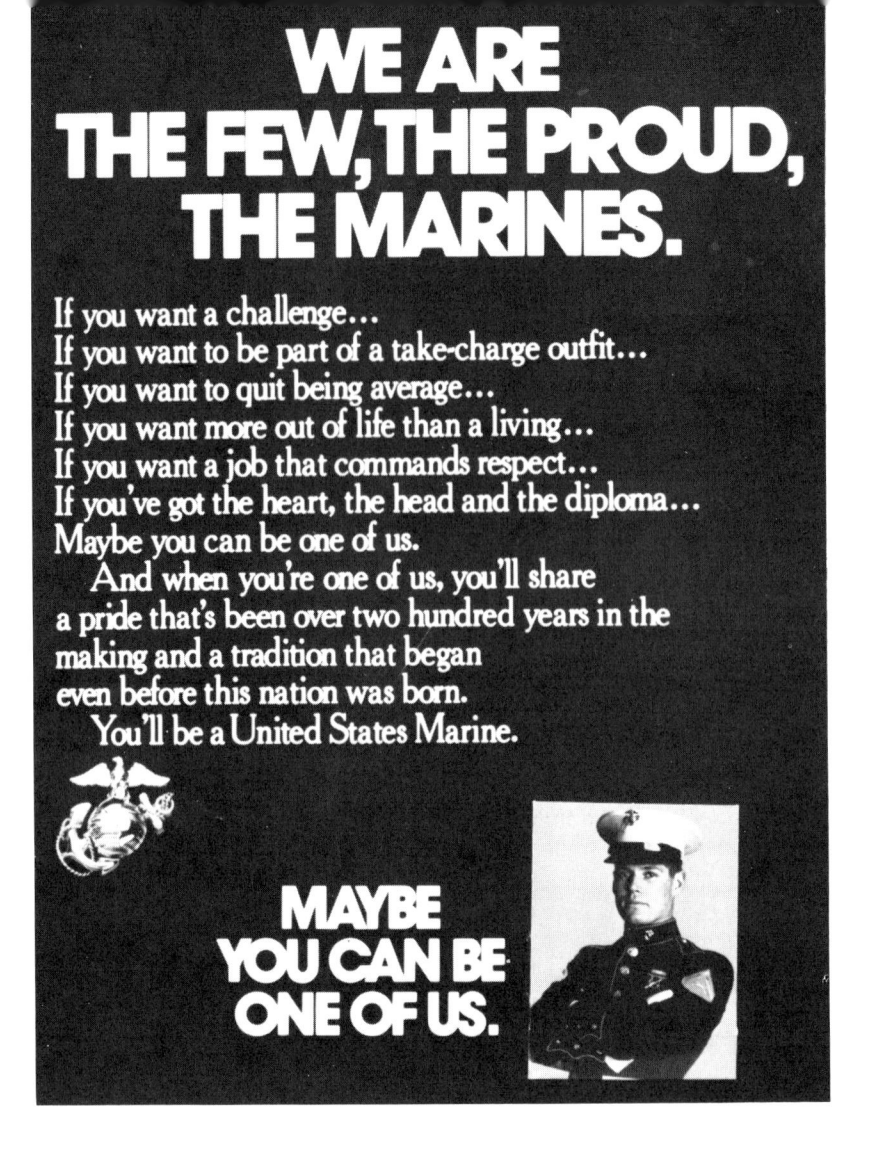

If you want a challenge...
If you want to be part of a take-charge outfit...
If you want to quit being average...
If you want more out of life than a living...
If you want a job that commands respect...
If you've got the heart, the head and the diploma...
Maybe you can be one of us.

And when you're one of us, you'll share a pride that's been over two hundred years in the making and a tradition that began even before this nation was born.
You'll be a United States Marine.

MAYBE YOU CAN BE ONE OF US.

Aware condition were informed that the case was definitely not of the open-and-shut variety and that there had been a number of seemingly competent witnesses for the prosecution *and* for the defense. Subjects in the Unaware condition simply read one of the communications. After reading either the one- or the two-sided communication, all subjects were asked to indicate the extent of their agreement with the prosecution's summary by responding to a 9-point scale on which 1.0 indicated certainty of the defendant's innocence and 9.0 indicated certainty of guilt. The results of this measure are shown in Figure 3. Even when the audience has no initial opposition to the position of a communication, a one-sided communication is reduced in effectiveness, relative to a two-sided communication, when the audience is aware there are two plausible sides to the issue.

In a theoretical development complementary to the reactance analysis of one- and two-sided communications Hass and Linder (1972) also devised an experiment using materials from a bigamy trial. They demonstrated that the *ordering* of the arguments in support of the communicator's position is a factor contributing to the effectiveness of two-sided communications. When the audience is aware of counterarguments, acknowledging and implicitly refuting those counterarguments early in the message produces greater attitude change than not mentioning the counterarguments at all or mentioning them at the end of the two-sided message. When the counterarguments are mentioned and implicitly refuted at the outset, the audience's defenses are defused before the communicator's own supportive arguments are stated.

224
Forms of
social influence

Although the need for an armed force has remained constant, the appeal to potential recruits (the message) has varied depending on circumstances. Before the repeal of the draft, the Army's message to potential recruits was duty to your country. After the elimination of the draft, friendly faces implied warmth and companionship. The Marines, however, primarily a volunteer force for some time, have always appealed to pride and esprit de corps.

I WANT YOU FOR U.S. ARMY
NEAREST RECRUITING STATION

Join the people who've joined the Army.

Attitude change:
the persuasive
communication paradigm

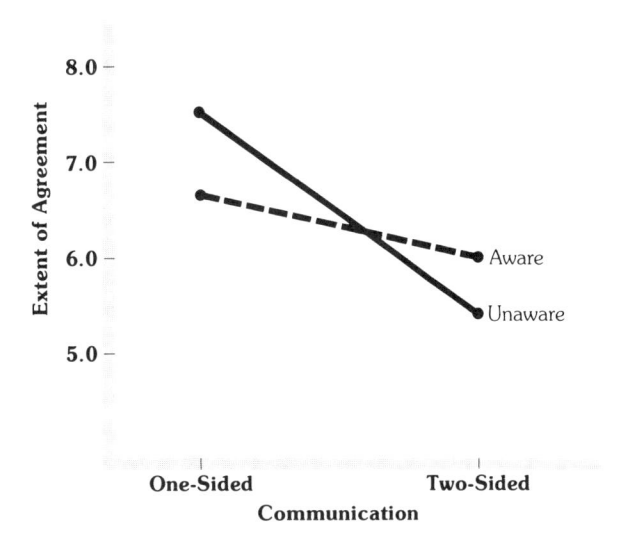

3. **Agreement with the advocated position depends on the awareness of a two-sided issue and whether or not the communication is one-sided or two-sided. The higher the mean, the greater the agreement with the advocated position. (From Jones and Brehm, 1970, Table 2, p. 53.)**

CONCLUSION DRAWING

In a discussion of factors contributing to the failure of many information campaigns, Hyman and Sheatsley (1947) point out that it is naive to assume that simple exposure to information will result in uniform retention and interpretation of the material. This, of course, presents problems for a communicator who is interested in getting an audience to agree with or appropriately interpret the material being presented. The question, then, is how one might go about ensuring that the audience does interpret the material appropriately. The most straightforward answer would seem to be that one should make the desired interpretation explicit—that is, one should draw the appropriate conclusion for the audience.

A reactance analysis of the conclusion-drawing situation suggests that it is actually somewhat more complex than this. Remember that the one necessary and sufficient condition for the arousal of reactance is that one perceive a threat to a free behavior. When the communication explicitly draws a conclusion, the free behavior that is threatened is the freedom of the message recipient to draw his or her own conclusion. But the amount of reactance aroused by a threat to a given free behavior is a direct function of the importance of the free behavior to the person. Thus, if the issue were one on which the message recipient did not feel competent, he or she would presumably not value the freedom to draw a conclusion. Hence, conclusion drawing by the communicator would be likely to produce both greater understanding of and agreement with the message. On the other hand, if the issue were one on which the audience did feel competent, conclusion drawing by the communicator would arouse reactance and attempts to safeguard the threatened freedom to draw one's own conclusion. Disagreeing with the communicator's conclusion is the clearest way to safeguard that freedom. Reactance theory predicts, then, that conclusion drawing will produce less agreement with the advocated position, the more competent the audience feels it is on the issue of the communication.

The classic study of conclusion drawing is that of Hovland and Mandell (1952), and their overall results seem fairly clear. Conclusion drawing by the communicator produced greater agreement with his message than leaving the conclusion implicit. To see if this result can be accounted for by the reactance hypothesis, we need to consider the message itself. The topic was the desirability of currency devaluation in the United States, and the communication was developed in such a way that the general principles of the topic were presented in addition to a statement of the conditions existing in the United States at that time. Also, two examples were given of foreign countries that had devalued their currency—one in which the devaluation had been successful and one in which it had not. Furthermore, the prevailing conditions in each of these two foreign countries were described. Imagine the task facing subjects for whom the conclusion was not drawn! They had to keep in mind the basic premises of the topic, the description of the conditions existing in the United States, the two examples of foreign countries that had devalued their currency, the two descriptions of the conditions that had caused one of these countries to be successful in its devaluation program and the other to be unsuccessful, and which set of conditions had gone with which country. In short, the complexity of both the issue and the communication make it fairly safe to assume that this was a topic on which the subjects (college students at N.Y.U.) would neither feel particularly competent nor value their freedom to draw their own conclusions. Conclusion drawing under such circumstances produces greater agreement with the message.

There is a question about whether Hovland and Mandell really measured *agreement with* or *comprehension of* their communication. The items from which they derived their scores for each subject were of the multiple-choice type, and because of their wording, they could very easily have been construed as simply questions about what the speaker said. Thistlethwaite, de Haan, and Kamenetsky (1955) designed an experiment on conclusion drawing in which they tried to separate the effects of comprehension and acceptance and, in addition, to test the hypothesis that among subjects who comprehend the intended point of a persuasive communication, conclusion drawing would be less effective in changing attitudes than no conclusion drawing. Using an issue somewhat less technical than that used by Hovland and Mandell—that the United States was right in fighting a limited war in Korea—Thistlethwaite, et al. varied both the conclusions drawn and the clarity of the message's organization. They found that the audience's comprehension of the message was positively affected by both of these variables. However, there was no sig-

Reactance and non-reactance situations in a one-versus two-sided communication.

nificant difference in attitude change when the conclusion was drawn or when it was not drawn for the audience. This, of course, is in apparent contrast to the Hovland and Mandell results. However, the subjects for the Thistlethwaite et al. study were Air Force recruits. Since the Air Force is made up almost exclusively of volunteers, it is fairly safe to assume that the commmunication was arguing for a position already held by the majority of the subjects—that, indeed, the United States was right in fighting a limited war in Korea—and, therefore, the freedom to draw a different conclusion was unimportant.

The more information one has that would lead one to agree with a conclusion drawn by a communicator, the less important is the freedom to disagree with that conclusion. This idea has received additional support from an experiment by Ferris and Wicklund (1974). It appears that one's felt competence to deal with an issue and/or the extent of one's knowledge about the issue are important determinants of whether conclusion drawing by the source of a persuasive communication enhances or reduces the tendency to agree with the position advocated. The more competent one feels and the more knowledge one has on the issue, the less likely conclusion drawing is to be effective. In a related but more general vein, McGuire (1969) hypothesized that we should expect conclusion drawing by a communicator to be less effective as the intelligence of the audience increases. The evidence from studies using this more global index of felt competence and knowledge is not, however, very clear. As we saw, there is also some evidence that the initial position of the audience, when the issue is one on which the audience has an initial position, may be important. The more discrepant that initial position from the one advocated by the communicator, the less effective is conclusion drawing compared to leaving the conclusion implicit.

The finding of Thistlethwaite, et al. that drawing the conclusion increases comprehension of the communication without necessarily increasing agreement has received support from other sources. In a review of the literature on the effects of mass communications, Klapper (1960) notes that a communication is more likely to be effective if an explicit conclusion is drawn, but he also points out that only the explicit material ("the facts") is likely to be successfully communicated, whereas the real goal of the communication (changing attitudes) is not likely to be attained. Some possible reasons for the failure of many information campaigns to change attitudes are discussed in Box B.

DISCREPANCY

At first glance, the literature on the effects of varying amounts of discrepancy between an audience's initial position on some issue and the position taken in a persuasive communication seems inconsistent and confused. Sometimes increasing discrepancy results in increased attitude change toward the position advocated; sometimes it results in less. Sometimes a greater discrepancy may cause a boomerang effect, or change away from the position taken by the communicator. Fortunately, at least two theoretical frameworks can be applied to the discrepancy research and findings to help us make sense of the apparent inconsistencies. These two theories make very similar predictions with respect to discrepancy but, as we shall see, for quite different reasons.

Dissonance theory. The first of the two theories is DISSONANCE THEORY, which we have already discussed in other contexts. According to Festinger and Aronson (1960), when one discovers that a credible communicator is advocating a position discrepant from one's position, one should experience dissonance, a psychologically uncomfortable state, and the greater the discrepancy, the greater the dissonance. There are a number of ways in which this dissonance can be reduced, but the most likely ways are (1) changing one's attitude toward agreement with the communicator and (2) derogating the communicator.

Aronson, Turner, and Carlsmith (1963) hypothesize that the relative emphasis given to, or the relative reliance on, these two ways to reduce dissonance depends on both the credibility of the communicator and the discrepancy of the position being advocated by the communicator. To take the two extremes, when the communicator is perfectly credible, he or she cannot (by definition) be derogated, no matter what. Hence, the greater the discrepancy, the greater the attitude change. When the communicator completely lacks credibility, he or she will be derogated completely and will produce no attitude change, no matter how small the discrepancy. Between these two extremes, however, both attitude change and derogation occur. For communicators with some (but not perfect) credibility, attitude change occurs when the position being advocated is only slightly discrepant, but with greater discrepancies, derogation of the communicator supersedes attitude change as the preferred mode of dissonance reduction. The more credible the communicator, the more discrepant the position he or she can advocate without running the risk of being derogated instead of producing attitude change.

To test this hypothesis that there is not *a relation* between discrepancy and attitude change, but a *family of*

B. Why are Laboratory and Field Results on Attitude Change Different?

One of the things that has puzzled many people about research on attitude change is the apparent discrepancy between results obtained in experimental studies of attitude change and results obtained in survey research on the effects of the mass media in changing attitudes. Examination of the experimental literature leaves the clear impression that attitudes are easily changeable. Subjects exposed to brief persuasive communications often show massive changes in attitude, frequently shifting completely from one side of an issue to the other. On the other hand, examination of the survey-research literature on the effectiveness of mass media leaves one with the impression that attitude change is genuinely rare. Millions of dollars have been spent in prolonged election campaigns, for example, but polls reveal that the attitudes of only a vanishingly small percentage of the electorate are ever changed.

In an analysis of the differences between the two types of research, Hovland (1959) suggested a number of factors that may account for the discrepancy. First, there is a difference in *discrepancy*. In an experiment on attitude change, subjects are usually exposed to a communication arguing for a position quite different from their own. In the naturalistic settings sampled by survey researchers, however, a great deal of self-selection takes place. That is, those people who show up at a political rally to hear candidate X are likely to agree already with most of what candidate X has to say. Hence, not much change is possible. A second difference is in the *nature of the issues*. Experimental research on attitude change often makes use of relatively uninvolving issues—issues not anchored in the subject's value systems and reference groups. On the other hand, survey researchers are typically concerned with socially and politically significant issues—issues deeply rooted in the respondents' world views, lifestyles, and reference groups. Another difference has to do with the *nature of communicators* and apparent sponsorship of the persuasive communications. As Hovland notes:

> in experimental studies, communications are frequently presented in a classroom situation [where] there may be some implicit sponsorship of the communication by the teacher and the school administration. In the survey studies, the communicators may often be remote individuals either unfamiliar to the recipients or [others] clearly known to espouse a point of view opposed to that held by many members of the audience. Thus, there may be real differences in communicator credibility in laboratory and survey researches (p. 9).

This difference in credibility again favors greater changes in experimental studies. A fourth difference between the two settings has to do with the *timing of attitude measurement*. Measurement usually occurs immediately after exposure to a persuasive communication in experimental studies, but considerable time may elapse between exposure and measurement in survey research. These and other differences between the two types of research lead Hovland to conclude that results obtained from the two are not, in fact, contradictory, but are understandable in terms of variables known to influence attitude change.

relations, Aronson, et al. (1963) asked subjects to rank order nine poems on an ambiguous criterion (the use of alliteration in poetry). Next, each subject was asked to read a two-page essay discussing the criterion. Each subject was then given an essay that used as an example of alliteration the poem that he or she had ranked 8 out of 9. For a third of the subjects, the essay claimed this particular selection was average (Slight Discrepancy), for another third, the essay claimed the selection was better than average (Moderate Discrepancy), and for the final third, the essay claimed the selection was one of the best (Large Discrepancy). Within each of these conditions, some subjects were led to believe that the author of the essay was T. S. Eliot (Highly Credible), whereas others were led to believe the communicator was a college student (Mildly Credible). The subjects were later asked to rank the selections a second time. The results, in terms of the changes in their evaluations of the poetry selections, appear in Table V. As the table shows, the mildly credible communicator produces greatest change at the moderate discrepancy level. Overall, the highly credible communicator produces more change, but there is a tendency for even the highly credible communicator's influence to level off when the position advocated is very discrepant from the subject's initial position. Apparently, the more credible the communicator, the more discrepant the position he or she can advocate before his or her effectiveness begins to level off and start to wane.

Social-judgment theory. Social-judgment theory (Sherif and Hovland, 1961), which we discussed in Chapter 7, offers a second set of reasons for expecting more than one relation between discrepancy and attitude change. SOCIAL-JUDGMENT THEORY postulates that an individual usually has a preferred position on any given attitudinal issue, but that there is also a set of positions that the individual perceives to be acceptable (the LATITUDE OF ACCEPTANCE), a set perceived to be objectionable (the LATITUDE OF REJECTION), and a set about which the individual is relatively neutral (the LATITUDE OF NONCOMMITMENT). Further, the relative sizes of these three regions are determined by how important the issue is to the person. The more ego-involved the individual is with an issue, the smaller the latitudes of acceptance and noncommitment and the larger the latitude of rejection. Sherif and Sherif (1969) make a further point with respect to the discrepancy of a communication from one's initial position. Social-judgment theory predicts that if a communication advocates a position in one's latitudes of acceptance or noncommitment, it will produce the greatest change. However, if the communication advocates a position in one's latitude of rejection, it will either produce no change or, if the communication is very discrepant from one's own position, it will produce a boomerang effect. A BOOMERANG EFFECT occurs when a communication produces change away from the position advocated.

Thus both (a) the extent to which one is ego-involved with a particular issue and (b) the corresponding sizes of one's latitude of acceptance, noncommitment, and rejection should determine the point at which increased communication discrepancy produces the most attitude change. The less ego-involved and/or important the issue is to the audience, the larger the discrepancy that can be expected to produce attitude change in the direction of the position advocated. The social-judgment predictions of attitude change for three individuals (A, B, and C) who differ in ego-involvement and latitudes of acceptance, noncommitment, and rejection are diagrammed in Figure 4.

Nemeth and Endicott (1976) have recently pointed out that one of the problems with both dissonance and social-judgment studies of discrepancy is that an important psychological characteristic of the issues used has generally been ignored. That is, some studies have employed an issue or scale on which there is a clear psychological midpoint at which the nature of the

Table V   Changes in evaluation of poetry selections

Communicator	Discrepancy		
	Slight	Moderate	Large
High Credibility	2.50	4.06	4.14
Mild Credibility	1.19	2.56	1.41

The higher the number, the greater the change toward agreement with the communicator. (From Aronson, et al., 1963, Table 1, p. 34.)

Figure caption (right column):

4. Expected attitude change toward (+) or away from (−) communications advocating positions of varying discrepancies from the positions accepted by persons with varying latitudes of acceptance, noncommitment, and rejection (cases A, B, and C). The social-judgment theory predicts attitude change as a curvilinear function of communication discrepancy from the latitude of acceptance. Increased change occurs as the communication departs from the acceptable range into the noncommitment range (NC). Communications falling in the latitude of rejection have progressively smaller effects, eventually crossing the zero line and resulting in change *away from* the position advocated (boomerang effect). (From Sherif and Sherif, 1969, Figure 21.5, p. 487.)

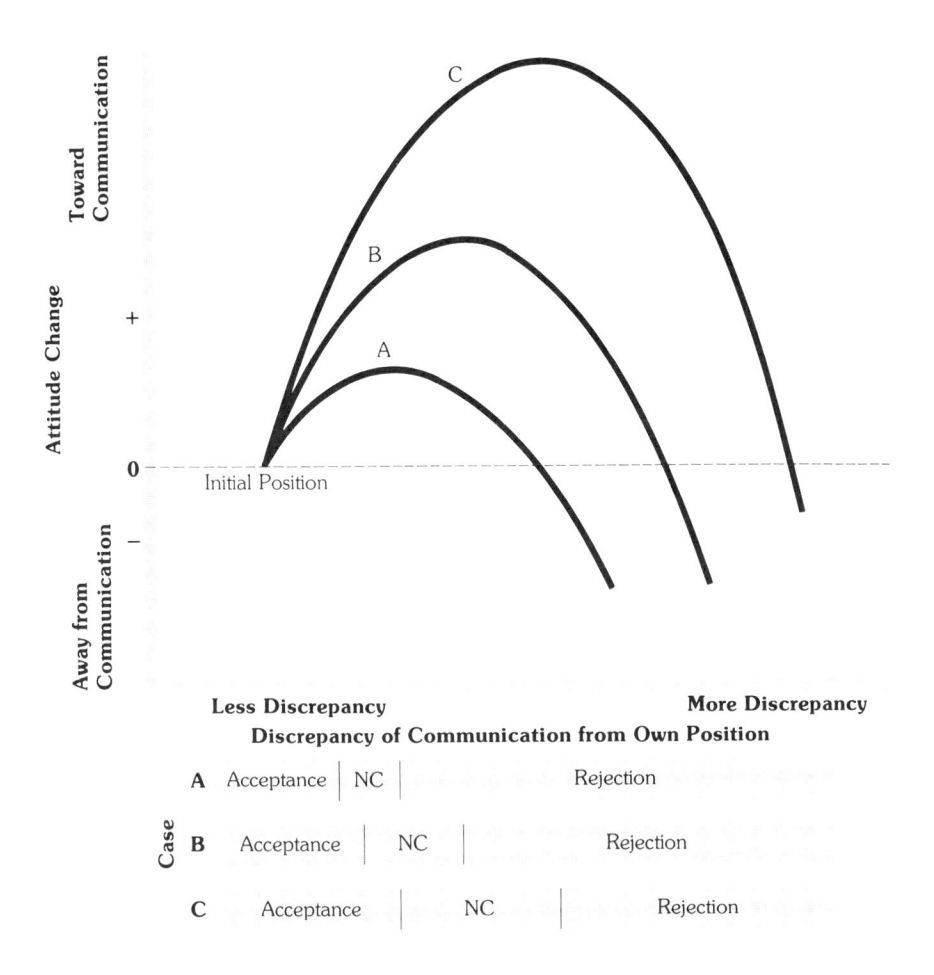

orientation to the attitudinal object changes—from positive to negative, say, or from agree to disagree. Other studies have emphasized scales or issues on which there was no discernible midpoint. The Aronson, et al. study we discussed is an example. Subjects in that study simply ranked nine poetry selections. For all we know, they could have liked or disliked all of them. Nemeth and Endicott note that this distinction between scales with and without midpoints is important for discrepancy research, because

> a midpoint that separates a scale of judgments into those which are on the same side of the issue as the subject and those which are on the opposite side of the issue will cause subjects to be more inclined to assimilate the positions on the same side and to contrast those on the opposite side, *even with discrepancy held constant* (p. 13). [emphasis added]

231
Attitude change:
the persuasive
communication paradigm

To check on this hypothesis, Nemeth and Endicott designed an experiment in which male and female eighth-graders heard a taped interview with a 14-year-old confederate who was posing as a fellow student. During the interview, the confederate argued for a position on a hypothetical problem that was either on the same side as or on the opposite side from the subject's own position on the problem and that was either small or large in terms of discrepancy from the subject's own position. The results appear in Figure 5. As the figure shows, greatest change in the direction of the advocated position was produced by a large discrepancy on the same side of the issue as the subject. Least change was produced when the advocated position was highly discrepant and on the opposite side of the issue.

5. **Mean change in the direction advocated by the communicator, relative to control group. Change is shown as a function of (1) whether discrepancy of communication from the subject's own position was small or large, and (2) whether the communicator took the same side of the issue as the subject or the opposite side. (From Nemeth and Endicott, 1976, Figure 1, p. 16.)**

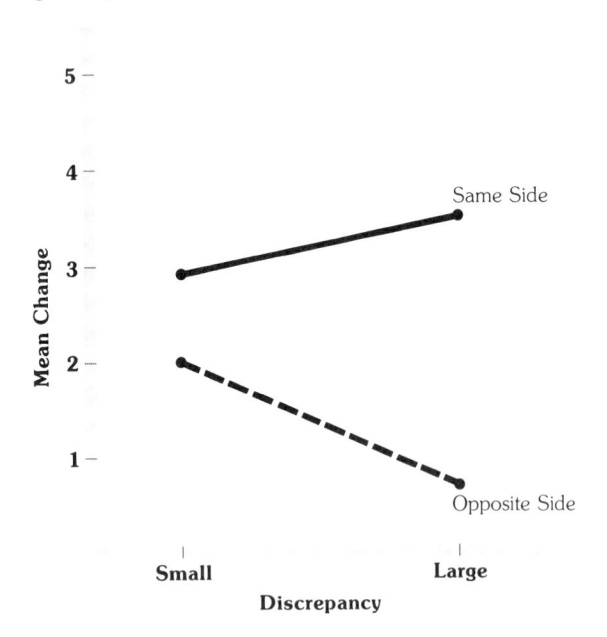

Thus it is much too simplistic to ask whether a large or a small discrepancy between the position advocated in a persuasive communication and the recipient's initial attitude produces greater change. As we have seen, the amount of change produced by a given discrepant communication may depend on the credibility of the communicator, the extent to which the issue is important to the recipient, and whether the position advocated is on the same side or the opposite side of the issue from the recipient's initial attitude. It may also depend on what other activity the recipient is engaged in (see Box C).

Questions about one- versus two-sided communications, effects of conclusion-drawing and the like are concerned with the *structure* of the communication. Other aspects of the communication may also be important in persuading an audience. One such variable is the emotional tone or style of the message. Some speeches or articles arouse pleasant emotions because they use soothing words and address mild or pleasant topics. Other communications arouse negative emotions. Most of the research has dealt with the effects of negative emotional arousal on persuasion. The bulk of this research has tried to determine whether fear-arousing messages lead to more or less persuasion.

FEAR-AROUSING MESSAGES

In the early 1950s, Janis and Feshbach (1953) published an experimental report that was assumed for a long time to have determined *the* relationship between fear arousal and attitude change. The subjects in the experiment consisted of the entire first-year class of a large Connecticut high school. The class was randomly divided into four groups. Three groups were exposed to communications urging the adoption of certain dental hygiene practices, and the fourth group served as a control. The talks given the three experimental groups were illustrated with a series of slides, and the three talks differed with respect to the amount of fear-arousing material presented. Subjects assigned to the Strong Fear group heard a talk emphasizing the painful aspects of tooth decay, diseased gums, and other assorted horrors that can result from improper dental hygiene. The slides these subjects saw were extremely vivid photographs of decayed teeth and diseased gums. Subjects assigned to the Moderate Fear group

C. Making Political Speeches Easy to Swallow

One of the ideas behind political picnics, barbecues, and banquets is that by offering good food and drink (extraneous reinforcement) along with political speeches (persuasive communications) the positions advocated in the speeches will go down easy and be readily accepted. Learning theory suggests, however, that an extraneous reinforcement—such as good food—will increase agreement only if the reinforcement is contiguous with or immediately follows the persuasive attempt. Dabbs and Janis (1965) point out that, while the extraneous reinforcement itself may increase persuasion, if the audience also thinks that the person who provides the extraneous reinforcement also positively endorses the persuasive communication, acceptance of it may be increased still further. On the other hand, if the provider of the reinforcement is perceived as disagreeing with the persuasive communication, almost no persuasion may occur.

To test these ideas, Dabbs and Janis exposed subjects to persuasive communications either while they were eating (soft drinks, mixed salted nuts, potato chips, corn chips) or immediately after they had eaten. Further, some subjects in each of these two conditions were led to believe that the experimenter personally agreed with the positions advocated in the communications and other subjects were led to believe that the experimenter personally disagreed with the communications. The results, in terms of attitude change based on measures taken prior to and immediately after the communications, are shown in the following table:

	Food Prior to Reading	**Eating While Reading**
Experimenter Endorses	1.64	4.57
Experimenter Disagrees	1.60	−0.36

The higher the number, the greater the agreement with the communication.

Greatest agreement with the positions advocated results when the experimenter endorses the communication *and* subjects are eating while reading. Least agreement (a negative value, in fact) results when subjects eat while reading a persuasive communication that they know the supplier of the food does not agree with.

Notice that if the subjects ate prior to reading, there was little persuasive effect, and it didn't matter whether the experimenter endorsed or disagreed with the communication. Dabbs and Janis concluded from this that eating and drinking while reading a persuasive message creates a momentary mood of compliance that decreases rapidly after eating. Thus, if you intend to persuade someone through their tastebuds, you had better catch them in the act of imbibing.

---

heard the dangers of improper dental hygiene described in a milder, more objective manner and saw slides depicting less extreme examples of oral pathology. Subjects assigned to the Minimal Fear group heard a relatively neutral talk about the growth and functions of the teeth and saw slides of healthy teeth and gums. All of the communications contained the same series of recommendations about oral hygiene practices. The main measure of interest was the extent to which subjects in each of the four groups indicated, on a questionnaire given one week after the communication, the degree of their conformity with the recommended practices. The same questionnaire had been administered to all students one week prior to the

Table VI Percent of subjects conforming to the various appeals

	Type of fear appeal			
Type of Change	Strong	Moderate	Minimal	Control
Increased Conformity	28%	44%	50%	22%
Decreased Conformity	20%	22%	14%	22%
No Change	52%	34%	36%	56%
Net Change	8%	22%	36%	0%

(From Janis and Feshbach, 1953, Table 6, p. 84.)

communication, so Janis and Feshbach were able to calculate changes as a result of the communications. The results (see Table VI) show that in terms of net change, the Minimal Fear appeal was most effective and the Strong Fear appeal least effective in producing conformity with the recommendations. Janis and Feshbach argue that a strong fear appeal, in the absence of sufficient reassuring recommendations, motivates an audience to ignore or minimize the importance of the threat and thus results in less conformity with the advocated practices. As Leventhal (1970) points out, however, Janis and Feshbach had no independent evidence for such a DENIAL HYPOTHESIS, even though it does seem quite plausible.

Whatever the real explanation for the negative relationship between fear arousal and acceptance of a persuasive communication, Leventhal (1970) goes on to reveal that such a finding has been the exception rather than the rule in subsequent research on fear-arousing communications. The more usual finding is that increased fear generally increases persuasion. There are, of course, circumstances under which this is not the case. Dabbs and Leventhal (1966), for example, hypothesized that the recommendations contained in a fear-arousing appeal may be crucial in determining whether one finds a positive or a negative relationship between fear arousal and acceptance of the communication. An audience may ignore recommendations that appear ineffective in forestalling danger. They may also ignore recommendations that seem too difficult or painful to carry out.

To check on this, Dabbs and Leventhal asked subjects to read a 10-page pamphlet discussing the dangers of tetanus and the effectiveness and painfulness of tetanus inoculations. For all subjects, the communications recommended getting a tetanus inoculation and gave specific instructions about where and how to do so, even providing a map showing the location of the University Health Department where the shots could be obtained. The communications differed, however, in their descriptions of the effectiveness and painfulness of inoculations and in the amount of fear-arousing material included about tetanus. Surprisingly, compliance with the recommended course of action was unaffected by the described effectiveness or painfulness of the inoculations. However, the high-fear communication was significantly more effective than the low-fear communication in getting subjects both to say they intended to get an inoculation and to actually do so, as determined by whether they turned up at the University Health Department within a month and requested the inoculations.

Dabbs and Leventhal (1966) also found an interesting interaction between self-esteem and fear arousal. This interaction reveals that subjects low in self-esteem were about equally responsive to the low- and high-fear communications in terms of their expressed intentions, whereas subjects high in self-esteem were more influenced by the high-fear communication than by the low-fear communication. It is possible that subjects high in self-esteem are more active in dealing with their environments and more able to tell when certain protective actions are appropriate. Inoculation for them is called for only when the danger of tetanus is great (the high-fear communication). Subjects low in self-esteem, on the other hand, may accept a communication's recommendation that inoculation is appropriate regardless of the probability of danger. Thus, as Leventhal (1970) argues, the perception of one's ability to cope with the threat posed by a fear-arousing communication is an important determinant of reactions to such communication. Further, the perception of being able to cope is influenced by many variables—for example, one's chronic level of self-esteem—in addition to the recommendations and/or threats contained in the communication itself.

Rogers and Mewborn (1976) postulate that the perceived effectiveness of a coping response is one of the three most crucial factors determining reactions to a fear-arousing communication. The other two are the degree of noxiousness the subject feels that he or she might experience as a result of the event, and the probability that the event will occur if no preventative measures are taken. One possible reason why the perceived effectiveness of the preventative measures manipulated in the Dabbs and Leventhal study failed to have any effect is that, regardless of whether the recommended inoculation was or was not effective against tetanus, subjects perceived tetanus as a very rare disease that they were unlikely to contract even if they did not get the inoculation. In a study using as subjects students who smoked an average of at least ten cigarettes a day, Rogers and Mewborn showed a film to manipulate noxiousness of the threatening event. The film depicted the case history of a man who discovers he has lung cancer. In the Low Fear (or low noxiousness) condition, the man is portrayed being interviewed by the physician and being prepared for the removal of his lung. In the High Fear condition, this same sequence was shown along with a 5-minute presentation of the actual surgery.

In addition, subjects in both conditions were asked to read and underline key phrases in a written communication about smoking and lung cancer. In the written communication, the probability of smokers getting lung cancer was described as being very high or relatively low; and in each case, the position was supported by a number of descriptive statistics and logical arguments. The effectiveness of the recommended preventive measures was also manipulated in the written communications. The High Efficacy message argued that the measures were quite effective in prevention of lung cancer, and the Low Efficacy message left the impression that the effectiveness of the preventive messages was somewhat uncertain. Of particular interest here is the interaction, shown in Figure 6, between the efficacy of preventive measures and the probability of the noxious event occurring. As the figure shows, in terms of expressed intentions to adopt the recommended practices, the efficacy of the preventive measures makes little difference when the probability of the noxious event is low. When the probability is high, however, the belief that the preventive measures will be effective enhances the intention to adopt them, while the belief that they are unlikely to be effective appears to decrease the strength of intention to adopt them.

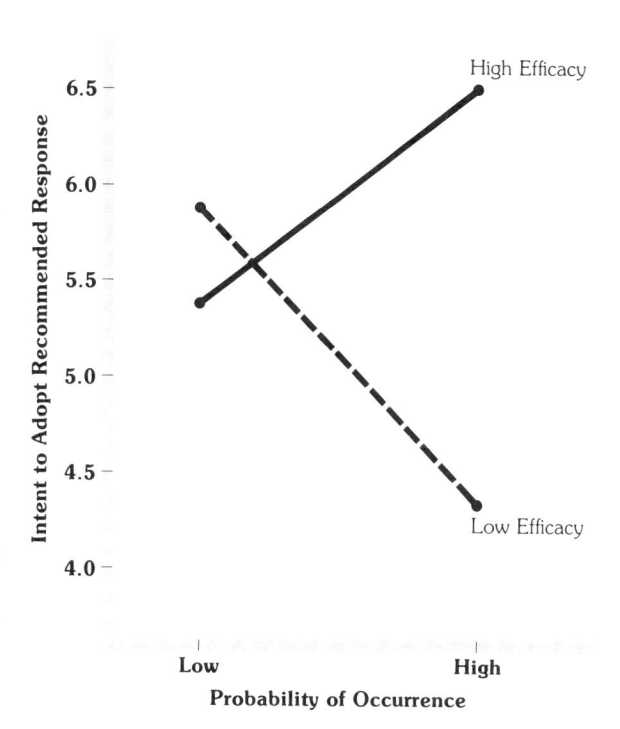

6. Interaction effect of (1) probability that a harmful event (lung cancer) will occur in the absence of preventive measures, and (2) efficacy of recommended preventive measures, on intent to adopt the recommended measures. (From Rogers and Mewborn, 1976, Figure 1, p. 58.)

Some correlational evidence in the Rogers and Newborn study suggests that severity of the threat and belief in the efficacy of coping responses were the most important predictors of intentions to adopt the recommended preventive measures. The more severe the perceived threat and the more effective the preventive measures were believed to be, the greater the strength of the expressed intentions to adopt those measures. Rogers and Mewborn believe that the interaction between the efficacy and probability variables (Figure 6) may explain why Janis and Feshbach (1953) found decreased acceptance of recommendations with increasing fear arousal. They suggest that the denial hypothesis promoted by Janis and

Feshbach "need not be limited to an interaction involving fear or noxiousness. The key variable seems to be the inability to ward off a danger" (p. 60).

Thus the effects of a fear-arousing communication are complex and multidetermined. Although the usual finding is a positive relationship between fear arousal and acceptance of the recommendations contained in the communication, this finding is apparently contingent on a number of variables, including the perceived effectiveness of the recommendations and the probability that the threatened event will occur if the preventive or avoidance measures are not followed. In the Dabbs and Leventhal experiment, we also saw an example of something that has frequently been found in studies of fear-arousing communication: differences in some personality characteristic among recipients may modify the effectiveness of fear-arousing communications. Rather than consider audience factors solely in the context of fear-arousing communications, however, let us look at the question more generally. The influence of audience factors is not, of course, peculiar to fear-arousing messages.

The audience: who says what to whom

The importance of audience characteristics in determining responses to persuasive communications has received a great deal of publicity in recent years as a result of the participation of social scientists and political activists in the jury selection process of several celebrated trials. One of these was the Harrisburg Conspiracy trial, in which Father Philip Berrigan, Sister Elizabeth McAlister, and five others were accused of conspiring to raid draft boards, kidnap Henry Kissinger, and blow up heating tunnels in Washington, D.C. The trial began on January 24, 1972. During much of the previous fall, Schulman, Shaver, Colman, Emrich, and Christie (1973) had interviewed prospective jurors in and around Harrisburg in an effort to determine whether the panel of prospective jurors was representative of the adult population living in the area. It turned out that the panel was not representative (members of a random sample taken in the judicial district were younger than people in the available panel). As a result of this survey, the presiding judge allowed a new panel to be selected before the jury was chosen. Schulman, et al. (1973) had volunteered their services to the defense in the hope of being able to help ensure a fair trial for the antiwar defendants. It seemed reasonable to anticipate that the personal qualities of the jurors themselves would influence the trial's outcome. The charges were rather vague and complex, leaving considerable leeway for each juror's own ideology, beliefs, and personal morality to influence the verdict.

Although Schulman, et al. actually helped select jurors for the trial and the trial itself resulted in a mistrial on the principal conspiracy charges, it is impossible to tell whether the jury selection procedures used by the defense were responsible for that outcome in this particular instance. There was no "control trial" in which a different jury, selected in the normal manner for that district, heard the same evidence presented in the same circumstances. There is some experimental evidence, however, that jury selection does affect the outcome of simulated court trials (Gerbasi, Zuckerman, and Reis, 1977). The nature of the audience makes a difference.

7. The relationship between intelligence and influenceability is irregular and difficult to predict, because intelligence has opposite effects on the two mediators of persuasion: reception and yielding (From McGuire, 1968, Figure 1, p. 1145.)

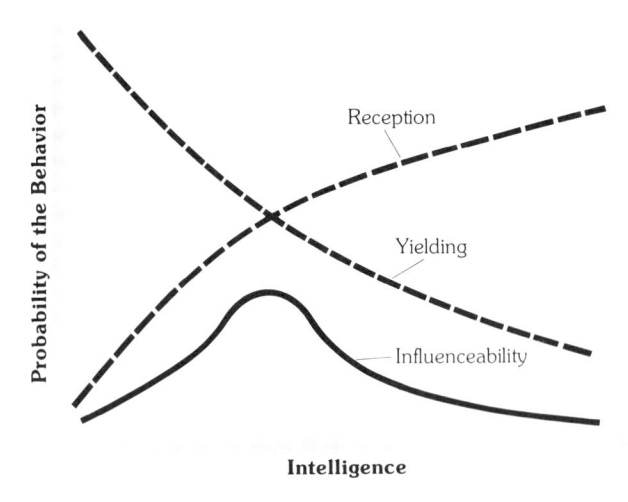

One could argue that all the variables pertinent to the persuasive communication paradigm are a function of the audience. It is not credibility that is important, for example, but *perceived* credibility. Similarly, discrepancy of a communication is defined by the audience's initial position. As McGuire (1969) points out, there is a sense in which all the factors that determine attitude change are receiver factors. In order to have an effect, each of them must operate on or via the recipient of the communication. In the three sections that follow, however, we shall take a somewhat more circumscribed view of audience factors. We shall first examine some general relationships between personality and persuasibility. Then we shall turn to some phenomena that may influence the actual reception of a persuasive communication—in particular, the extent to which the audience is prepared and/or motivated to defend against being persuaded. Finally, we shall examine two psychological processes that occur after a communication has been received and may influence long-term agreement with the position advocated.

PERSONALITY AND PERSUASIBILITY

McGuire (1968) suggests that the behavioral processes mediating persuasion can be reduced to two: reception of the message content and yielding to what is comprehended. The reception process includes attention to and comprehension of the message, and yielding is simply the tendency to accept and/or agree with the message. Of interest here is the idea that any given personality characteristic, whether it be intelligence, chronic anxiety level, self-esteem, or whatever, may have differential effects on the reception and yielding factors.

Take intelligence as an example. The more intelligent a person is, the more likely that he or she will be able to attend to and comprehend a persuasive communication. If the reception factor alone determined the response to a persuasive communication, we would expect a positive relationship between intelligence and attitude change as a result of being exposed to a persuasive communication. However, when we consider the yielding factor, we are led to anticipate a negative relationship between intelligence and attitude change. Intelligent people would have more confidence in their own opinion, would be better able to recognize flaws in the argument, and would exhibit more skill in forming counterarguments—would, in short, be less yielding to what they comprehended of the persuasive communication. The result of these twin, but mirror-image, relationships of the reception and yielding factors with intelligence is that intelligence should be related to influenceability in a NONMONOTONIC fashion. When there is a nonmonotonic relationship between two variables, as one increases, the other may increase and then decrease, or decrease and then increase. The nonmonotonic relationship is apparent in Figure 7, where we can see that the influenceability curve has been obtained by subtracting the yielding curve from the reception curve at each point along the intelligence axis.

Such a theoretical expectation about the influenceability–intelligence relationship may help us make sense of the existing literature. Some studies have found a positive relationship between the two variables, some have found a negative relationship, and some have found no relationship. As McGuire points out, inspection of the existing literature might tempt one to accept the proposition that intelligence is not systematically related to influenceability, but that simply seems unlikely. The hypothesized nonmonotonic relationship may help to systematize research findings by clarifying some of the conditions under which one might expect a positive, a negative, or no relationship between intelligence and influenceability. A similar analysis may help clarify the relationships between other personality variables and influenceability. Each such personality characteristic needs to be examined in terms of what effects it will have on the two factors that mediate attitude change: reception and yielding.

McGuire (1968) also points out that we must consider the situation when we try to analyze the relationships among reception, yielding, and influenceability. If the communication situation is distracting or the message confusing or complex, no one will be able to attend to or comprehend the message. On the other hand, if the message is very simple and clear, everyone in the audience will be able to attend to and comprehend it. For either extreme, personality variables cannot affect *reception* of the message; either everyone comprehends or no one does. In both cases, personality variables can only affect the audience's tendency to *yield* to the message. However, if the situation is intermediate in distraction or difficulty, personality variables, such as intelligence, may affect *attention* and *comprehension*. Highly intelligent members of the audience will be able to attend to and comprehend the message; less intelligent members will not be able to do so. In these cases a personality variable (intelligence) will affect persuasibility by its relationship to both receptivity (attention and comprehension) and yielding to the message.

Thus there is not likely to be any simple relationship between personality and persuasibility. Not only are the functions relating influenceability to single characteristics (such as intelligence or anxiety or self-esteem) likely to be multidetermined, but the characteristics themselves are likely to interact in affecting persuasibility. An intelligent person who is low in self-esteem, for example, responds differently from an intelligent person who is high in self-esteem.

In spite of this complexity, there are a few reasonably well-established results. Perhaps most important, there does seem to be a general trait of persuasibility. That is, people who are highly persuasible in one situation or in response to one persuasive communication are more likely to be persuaded by other communications and/or in other situations. Nevertheless, the magnitudes of the correlations that support this assertion are not overwhelming (Linton and Graham, 1959).

On the other hand, a few findings relating certain personality characteristics to persuasibility were once thought to be well established but now appear rather dubious, if not downright invalid. For many years, the evidence seemed rather consistently to indicate that females were more persuasible than males. Janis and Field (1959) present evidence that, in response to a series of persuasive communications on a variety of issues, female high school students were significantly more persuasible than male high school students. This apparent relationship between sex and influenceability was found so often that Gergen and Marlowe (1970) report that it became a part of the social–psychological folklore that females make the best subjects in experiments designed to demonstrate attitude change and/or conformity. It is reasonably easy to come up with a plausible psychological explanation of why intelligence, anxiety, and self-esteem should make a difference in persuasibility. With sex, however, a psychological explanation is very difficult. Even Janis and Field use a cultural explanation to account for the differences they found. They suggest that sex-role expectations in our society at that time were such that conformity, dependence, and passivity were believed to be appropriate behavior for females. Hence, females were more likely than males to accept and/or agree with persuasive communications addressed to them. If this explanation is correct, it follows that as sex roles change so that dependence is no more appropriate for females than for males, the relationship between sex and persuasibility should vanish.

Partly because of the complexity involved in dealing with personality variables in research on persuasibility, most investigators have taken a different approach to audience factors. Most have chosen to manipulate variables hypothesized to affect reception of and yielding to communications (see Box D) and have essentially ignored personality variables by randomly assigning subjects to conditions. This experimental approach has been somewhat more rewarding, as we shall see.

DEFENSE MOBILIZATION

Perhaps the most important question about the audience is: What is going on inside their heads while they are listening to a persuasive communication? Do they just sit there, take it all in, and decide when it's over whether or not they agree? Or are they more active? Do they engage in an implicit debate with the communicator even while they are listening to the message? To anyone who has been part of a group watching a TV address by an unpopular politician, the latter possibility is sure to seem more likely. The intermittent catcalls and jeers and cries of "What about _____?" testify that something is going on internally.

Petty, Wells, and Brock (1976) argue that a persuasive communication produces basically two kinds of implicit cognitive activity: counterargument or agreement with the position being advocated. If these ongoing cognitive processes are interrupted or made more difficult, then, depending on whether the predominant response to a communication was counterargument or agreement, the persuasive effectiveness of the message is enhanced or reduced, respectively. As Petty, et al. (1976) put it, if the dominant cognitive response to a communication was counterarguing, then distraction would lead to enhanced persuasion by interfering with the counterarguing process; but if the dominant cognitive response to a communication was agreeing or favorable cognitive responses rather than counterarguments, distraction would inhibit these favorable thoughts and lead to lowered acceptance (p. 874).

D. Censorship Changes Attitudes

According to reactance theory, when a person's freedom to perform a particular behavior is threatened or denied, the person becomes motivated to safeguard or restore the freedom in question. Censorship of a speech advocating position X on an attitudinal issue is, of course, a threat to one's freedom to adopt that position. It should follow, then, that such censorship would arouse reactance and that the individual's subsequent behavior would be directed toward assertion of freedom to adopt the censored position. If the person had initially *disagreed* with position X, the clearest way he or she can reestablish freedom is to actually adopt, or at least move closer to, that position. If the person had initially *agreed* with position X, the clearest way to reestablish freedom is to become *more* extreme on the same side of the issue as position X.

Ashmore, Ramchandra, and Jones (1971) designed an experiment to see whether censorship really does result in such changes in attitude. Subjects recruited for the experiment had initially indicated either moderate agreement or moderate disagreement with the statement "Police should never be allowed on college campuses." On arrival at the laboratory setting, subjects were assigned to a No Censor, a Censor Other Position, or a Censor Own Position condition. Subjects assigned to the No Censor condition were simply asked to again indicate their attitude regarding the "police on campus" issue. The remaining subjects were informed that the experimenter had intended that they should listen to and take a recall test on a tape-recorded speech advocating either that police should be allowed on college campuses whenever necessary or that police should never be allowed on college campuses. However, the experimenter said that she was not going to be able to play the tape because she had just received a note from the college dean forbidding her to play it to undergraduates. She then reiterated the position advocated on the tape and asked if the subjects would mind filling out a brief attitude questionnaire since they would not be able to go on with the experiment. The questionnaire, of course, contained an item asking their attitude on the issue of police on campus. A score for pre- to post-test change was computed for each subject in such a way that a positive score indicated movement toward the end of the scale initially endorsed, and a negative value indicated movement toward the opposite position. The means of these change scores were as follows:

Censor Other Position	No Censor	Censor Own Position
−2.00	−0.17	+1.75

Thus subjects who were told they were not going to be allowed to hear a speech that they already agreed with became even more favorably disposed to the position advocated in the speech. Subjects who were told they were not going to be allowed to hear a speech that they initially disagreed with changed their attitude in the direction of greater agreement with the speech. Subsequent research by Worchel and Arnold (1973) indicates that these effects seem to be due to reactance and not simply disliking for the censor. Dislike for the censor might, according to balance theory, induce subjects to adopt the censored position.

To test these ideas, Petty, et al. constructed two messages, both of which argued for a 20-percent increase in tuition at Ohio State University. One message was difficult to counterargue, because it contained logically sound and compelling points. The other was relatively easy to counterargue. The subjects in the experiment were students at Ohio State, and each subject listened to one of the messages under one of four distraction conditions. The distraction was provided by having subjects watch a screen while listening to the message and record the position of symbols flashed on the screen at varying intervals. For the No Distraction condition, no symbols were flashed; for the Low, Medium, and High Distraction conditions, symbols were flashed at the rate of 4, 12, and 20 per minute, respectively. Following presentation of the persuasive communications, subjects were asked to list their thoughts on the topic of increasing tuition and to indicate the extent to which they agreed that tuition should be increased.

The resulting attitude changes are shown in Figure 8. Increasing distraction decreased agreement with the difficult-to-counterargue message and increased agreement with the easy-to-counterargue message. The thoughts listed by subjects were scored in terms of whether they were supportive or nonsupportive of tuition being increased, and the results of this measure support the thought-disruption hypothesis. That is, distraction decreased counterargument production for the easy-to-counterargue message and decreased favorable thoughts for the difficult-to-counterargue message. It appears that audiences are not passive while listening to persuasive messages. They may be actively counterarguing, if that is possible, or entertaining a series of favorable thoughts linking points in the message to their own cognitive structure. Distraction, then, may enhance or reduce acceptance of the communicator's message, depending on which of these processes it disrupts.

McGuire (1964) postulates that when an individual has never heard a particular attitude or belief attacked, and hence has no practice counterarguing attacks on that attitude or belief, the individual will be particularly susceptible to persuasive attack against the attitude or belief. By analogy with the biological phenomenon of inoculation (an injection of a weakened form of some virus stimulates the body's defenses so that the inoculated person can later resist a more massive viral attack), McGuire suggests that an individual can learn to resist attacks on such previously undefended beliefs by being exposed to a mild form of attack on the beliefs. Such an attack would presumably motivate the individual to defend the beliefs and give him or her some practice in doing so.

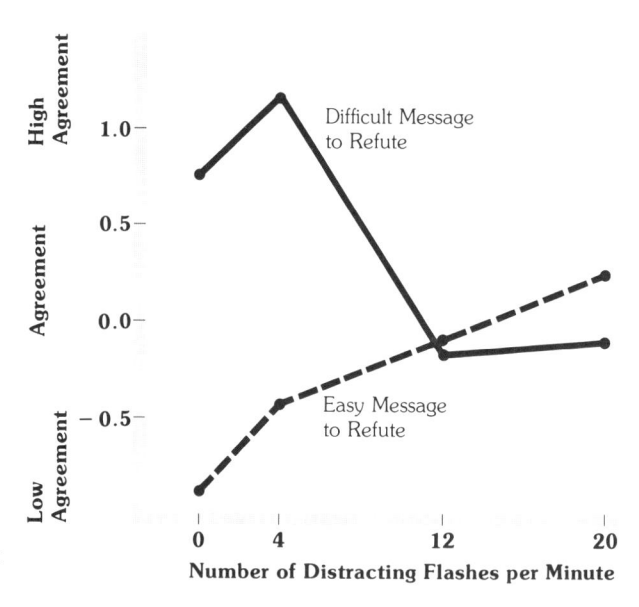

8. Mean attitude change in relation to how difficult the message is to refute and level of distraction. Increasing distraction decreased agreement with the message that was difficult to refute and increased agreement with the message that was easy to refute. (From Petty, Wells, and Brock, 1976, Figure 1, p. 879.)

To test his reasoning, McGuire first had to find some beliefs that people would indeed have had no experience defending because they had never heard them attacked. He had to find some CULTURAL TRUISMS: that is, beliefs so widely shared, so taken for granted by everyone, that one would be unlikely to have ever heard them attacked. Pretesting revealed that certain health beliefs, such as the following, qualified as cultural truisms:

It's a good idea to brush your teeth after every meal if at all possible.
Mental illness is not contagious.

The effects of penicillin have been, almost without exception, of great benefit to mankind.

Everyone should get a yearly chest x-ray to detect any signs of TB at an early stage.

Having found some beliefs that most people would be (1) unmotivated to defend because they had never heard them attacked, and (2) unpracticed in defending for the same reason, McGuire designed an experiment in which each subject participated in two sessions. In the first session (the defensive session), the subject was told that the study was concerned with reading and writing skills. Then, under varying conditions, the subject was exposed to either mild attacks (refutations) on the presumably unattackable truisms or to arguments supporting the truisims. In a Passive Reading condition, subjects simply read paragraphs either attacking or supporting the truisms. In a Reading and Underlining condition, subjects were asked to underline the crucial clause in each paragraph. In a Writing from Outline condition, subjects were exposed to statements of support or attack and given an outline from which to write paragraphs substantiating or refuting arguments, respectively. Finally, in a Writing without Guidance condition, subjects were exposed to statements of support or attack and simply asked to write paragraphs substantiating or refuting the arguments. Thus subjects were exposed in the first session to either supportive or refutational arguments about the truisms and were asked, under varying kinds of participation, to substantiate the supportive or refute the attacking arguments. In the second session (the attack session) some time later, the subjects were asked to read 1000-word essays, each mentioning four arguments *against* one of the health beliefs and presenting a paragraph substantiating each argument.

Following the attack sessions, subjects were asked to fill out assessment scales indicating the extent to which they believed the truisms. With 15.00 indicating complete adherence to the truism and 1.00 indicating complete disagreement, the results are shown in Table VII. As the table shows, the prior supportive defenses leave the beliefs very susceptible to attack. Adherence to the truisms is much reduced following attacks preceded by such reassuring supportive defenses. On the other hand, when the attacks have been preceded by weakened versions of the attacks themselves (the refutational defenses), the beliefs are much less vulnerable. The refutational defenses apparently motivate subjects to defend their beliefs and, by doing so, confer resistance to subsequent attacks on these beliefs.

In subsequent research, McGuire and his colleagues (Papageorgis and McGuire, 1961) demonstrated that the resistance-conferring powers of the prior refutational defense are not a function of the similarity between the attacks used in the initial refutational defense and the subsequent massive attacks. Prior refutational defense confers resistance even when the arguments used against the beliefs are completely different from those presented in the subsequent attack. Apparently the refutational defense works by stimulating the motivation to defend one's beliefs, not simply by causing the subject to develop the specific arguments used in countering the first, mild attack.

The audience, then, is not a passive recipient of persuasive communications and does not just sit there quietly gathering data for a later, rational decision about whether to accept or reject the communicator's message. Rather, the audience engages in both active, implicit counterargument and the production of thoughts favorable to the position being advocated. It is not yet clear what variables determine the relative predominance of these cognitive processes, but one can easily come up with a few testable hypotheses. For example, in our discussion of one-sided and two-sided communications, we argued that, to the extent that an audience is aware of opposing arguments, a one-sided communication is reduced in effectiveness, because audience members perceive it as a threat to their freedom to adopt a position different from the one being

Table VII Mean belief levels after attack

	Type of prior defense	
	Refutational	Supportive
Passive Reading	11.51	7.47
Reading and Underlining	11.13	7.63
Writing from Outline	9.19	7.94
Writing without Guidance	9.46	6.33

The higher the number, the greater the continued belief in the truism following attack. (From McGuire, 1964, Table 1, p. 207.)

advocated. But perhaps this reactance interpretation is not appropriate. Awareness of opposing arguments may simply make it more likely that the audience will engage in implicit counterargument, and, hence, be less persuaded by a one-sided communication. In any event, the cognitive activities of the audience do not cease abruptly when a persuasive communication ends. Instead, they continue over time to influence the individual's response to persuasive communications. Let us look at two ways in which this occurs.

SLEEPER AND SOCRATIC EFFECTS

In a study that we discussed earlier, Hovland and Weiss (1951) found that the amount of attitude change produced by highly credible communicators was significantly greater than that produced by low-credibility communicators when change was measured immediately after the communication. However (and this we did not mention in our earlier discussion of that study), these differences tended to disappear with the passage of time. That is, on measurements of attitudes obtained one month after exposure to the communications, the differences were less pronounced. During the month, there was apparently an increase in agreement with low-credibility communicators and a decrease in agreement with the high-credibility communicators.

To account for these effects, Kelman and Hovland (1953) suggested that the communication situation is something of a "package," including not only the content of the persuasive message but many additional factors, such as the characteristics of the source. Depending on their nature, these additional factors may stimulate acceptance or rejection of the message. However, when attitudes are measured some time after receipt of the communication, these extraneous factors are much less salient, and the content of the communication should be a more important determinant of long-term attitudes toward the object in question.

> If the communication situation contains factors which stimulate acceptance of the communication, and these factors disappear with time, we would expect a decrease in agreement at the time of delayed measurement. If, on the other hand, the communication situation contains factors which stimulate rejection, an increase in agreement at the time of the delayed measurement would be predicted (p. 327).

Further, Kelman and Hovland suggest that if, at the time of delayed measurement, those aspects of the communication situation that led to the initial inflated acceptance or exaggerated rejection of the message content are reintroduced, then the hypothesized effects should disappear.

To test this line of reasoning, Kelman and Hovland (1953) exposed high school students to a communication arguing for more lenient treatment of juvenile delinquents. The communication was disguised as a transcript of an educational radio program. For some subjects (Positive Communicator conditions), the speaker was introduced as a judge, the author of several books on delinquency, and a sincere, interested, and compassionate authority on the subject. For other subjects (Negative Communicator conditions), the speaker was described as a member of the studio audience chosen at random. However, this member of the studio audience turned out to be a borderline criminal who had had many scrapes with the law and was currently out on bail on a dope-peddling charge. All subjects then heard the same communication and immediately afterward filled out questionnaires assessing their attitudes toward lenient treatment of juvenile offenders.

Three weeks later, the delayed measurements of attitude change were obtained. For some subjects (Communicator Not Reinstated), their classroom teacher simply passed out the questionnaires and made no mention of the earlier session in which they had heard a communication. For the remaining subjects (Communicator Reinstated), the original experimenter reappeared and, before passing out the attitude questionnaires, reminded them of the earlier session and played the introduction to the radio program, in which the speaker was described. Thus, immediate postcommunication and delayed-attitude measures were obtained for subjects who heard either a positive or a negative communicator deliver a communication arguing for more lenient treatment of juvenile offenders. Immediately prior to the delayed assessment, some subjects were reminded of the

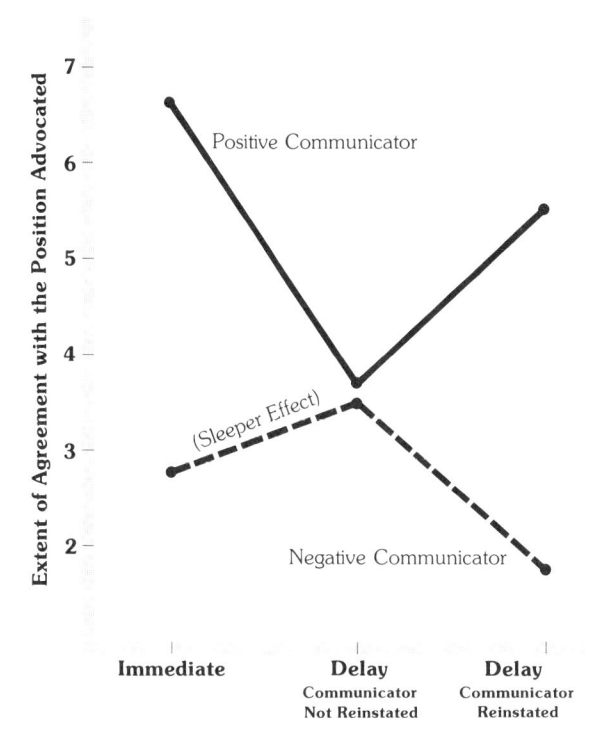

9. Agreement with the position advocated as a function of when the measurement was taken and whether the negative or positive communicator was or was not described (reinstated) when the delayed measurements were taken. (From Kelman and Hovland, 1953, Tables 3 and 5, pp. 331–332.)

character of the communicator and others were not.

The attitude-change data are presented in Figure 9. The figure shows that agreement with the positive communicator was significantly greater immediately following the communication. Three weeks later, however, when the subjects were not reminded of the communicators, agreement with the positive communicator had declined and agreement with the negative communicator had actually increased. It is the latter phenomenon that Kelman and Hovland term the SLEEPER EFFECT: agreement with the content espoused by a negative communicator increasing over time. On the other hand, when subjects are reminded of the communication sources prior to the delayed measurement, the difference in agreement with the positive and negative communicators is almost as large as the difference obtained on the immediate postcommunication measure. It should be noted that subsequent research by Gillig and Greenwald (1974) has found the sleeper effect to be an elusive phenomenon to demonstrate in the laboratory.

McGuire (1969) argues that the term *sleeper effect* should be used for any type of delayed action of a persuasive communication in which agreement with the communication is less immediately after the communication than it is at some later time. That is, there are presumably other types of delayed-action effects in addition to that produced by forgetting the negative source of some persuasive arguments. For example, he points out that the use of numerous complex and subtle arguments delays the impact of a persuasive communication. His point is that

> there is considerable inertia in the cognitive system; thus, material which is absorbed from a persuasive message makes itself felt for some time in all its subtle cognitive ramifications. Hence, if we measure the opinion-change impact of a rather complex and subtle message immediately after presentation, its ramifications on the more remote issues will not yet have occurred. Only after time has allowed for information processing does the communication's impact filter down to the more remote implications (p. 256).

There is, in fact, some evidence for such a Socratic effect, although Henninger and Wyer (1976) suggest that what appears to be a Socratic effect may actually be a function of repeated measurement rather than elapsed time. That is, when subjects are repeatedly asked their attitudes on a number of issues related to a persuasive communication, they may make their answers more consistent as they report them. A SOCRATIC EFFECT is the internal cognitive filtering down of the implications of a communication to remote issues. If Henninger and Wyer are right, such filtering may have little to do with what is usually taken to be a Socratic effect.

On the other hand, Cook and Insko (1968) have

found that a persuasive communication linking an attitudinal object with a large number of other values held by the audience produces an attitude toward that object that is more resistant to decay than the attitude produced by a communication linking the object with fewer other values of the audience. They also found that when the effects of the two communications were measured immediately after they had been received, there were no differences in the attitude toward the object as a function of the communication. Thus there is some evidence that a Socraticlike cognitive "working through" of the implications of a communication occurs; and the more far-reaching these implications in terms of the audience's value system, the more stable the initial agreement produced by the communication.

Summary

In this chapter, we examined the three major components of the persuasive communication paradigm: source, message, and audience.

Beginning with some old studies of prestige suggestion, we found that what a communication is understood to say is partly a function of who is believed to have said it, even when the actual content remains the same. We then analyzed some variables affecting credibility. The credibility of a communicator has generally been defined in terms of the communicator's expertise and trustworthiness. The usual finding is that high-credibility communicators are more effective in producing attitude change than low-credibility communicators. Subsequent research has shown that a number of additional variables enhance the effectiveness of a communicator who is low in credibility in terms of expertise and trustworthiness. If the low-credibility communicator's credentials are not revealed until after the audience has been exposed to his or her message, if the audience is under stress, or if the low-credibility communicator is perceived to be arguing against his or her own best interests, effectiveness is improved. We also found that communicators similar to their audiences are often more effective than dissimilar communicators, especially when the issue is one of value and not verifiable by appeal to external reality. Further, in contrast to early reasoning about the effects of a source's objectivity, we found a number of conditions under which a source's announced intent to persuade may actually produce greater attitude change. This seems to be the case, for example, when the audience believes the source likes him or her and when the issue is one with which the audience is not strongly involved. On the other hand, the more involved, interested, or committed the audience, the more likely a warning of persuasive intent is to reduce the source's effectiveness. It also seems that much of the research on forewarning and intent to persuade has induced temporary, elastic, self-presentational shifts and not true attitude changes at all.

In our discussion of the internal organization of persuasive communications themselves, we began with the issue of one-sided versus two-sided communications. Early research on this issue usually suggested no overall differences in effectiveness, but two-sided communications seemed to be more effective for the better-educated members of the audience. More recent research seems to indicate that the crucial variable is not educational level, but the extent to which the audience is aware of the existence of arguments on both sides of the issue. To the extent that they are aware, the effectiveness of a one-sided communication is reduced. Research on the effects of conclusion drawing by the communicator reveals a similar tendency. That is, one's felt competence to deal with an issue and the extent of one's knowledge about the issue are important determinants of whether conclusion drawing by the source of a persuasive communication will enhance or reduce one's tendency to agree with the position advocated. The more competent one feels and the more knowledge one has about the issue, the less likely conclusion drawing is to be effective in changing one's attitude though it may be effective in increasing comprehension of the message itself. Next we turned to research on discrepancy and found that the amount of change produced by a given discrepant communication may depend on the credibility of the communicator, the extent to which the issue is important to the recipient, and whether the position advocated is on the opposite side of the issue or the same side as the recipient's initial attitude. The final topic discussed in connection with the message was the extent of fear-arousing material contained in the communication. In general, the more fear aroused by a persuasive communication, the more likely the communication's recommendations are to be accepted.

However, this result is apparently contingent on the perceived effectiveness of the recommendations and the probability that the threatened event will occur if the recommended preventive measures are not taken.

Finally, we discussed the audience itself. We began our discussion of audience factors by looking at the issue of personality and persuasibility. Personality characteristics affect both reception of and yielding to a persuasive communication. As we saw with intelligence, however, a given personality characteristic may be positively related to the reception factor and negatively related to the yielding factor, or vice versa. There is no simple relationship between personality and persuasibility. Furthermore, the relationship of any given characteristic to influenceability is also a function of the situation and of other related characteristics. Most investigators interested in audience variables have avoided the complexity and ambiguity of personality research and have chosen an experimental approach. Much of the experimental research on audience factors has addressed the ongoing cognitive activities the audience engages in. It appears that, while the message is being received, the audience engages in active implicit production of counterarguments and/or production of thoughts favorable to the position being advocated. If these activities are disrupted, the effectiveness of the communication is changed. Similarly, if audience members are unmotivated to counterargue or unpracticed in counterarguing on a given issue, they are extremely susceptible to persuasion. Finally, we examined some delayed effects of communication, effects that are due in part to forgetting extraneous aspects of the communication situation and in part to a cognitive working through of the implications of the communication itself.

9

Conformity and nonconformity

248 Recurring patterns of behavior

249 Conformity

The development of norms
The power of the group
Manipulating others

255 Compliance

Inequity and guilt
The foot-in-the-door technique
Obedience

259 The effects of conforming and compliance on private beliefs

Dissonance and forced compliance
Self-perception: my mouth was moving when I heard it

265 Nonconformity

Reacting to pressure
Rejection

270 Summary

The basic issue in social psychology is the relationship of the individual to society. Human existence totally divorced from other humans is inconceivable. Try to imagine what it would be like. There would be no language, no thought, no cultural heritage. If we were willing to grant our hermit the ability to think and talk (provided he did not think about or talk to other humans), what would he think about and why would he need to talk? For better *and* for worse, individuals are immersed in society. They are both molded by and molders of their interpersonal worlds. The questions we shall discuss in the present chapter concern this reciprocal relationship between individuals and society. How does society attempt to mold the individual? Why do most people behave as expected most of the time and some people all of the time? What happens when someone resists pressures to be like everyone else and seeks a new and better way or simply does things differently?

Recurring patterns of behavior

In Chapter 3 we saw how, during the process of socialization, people are taught that certain behaviors are expected of them and that certain things are not to be done. Norms governing a great deal of day-to-day behavior are communicated to and impressed on the developing child with varying degrees of subtlety and varying degrees of success. The simplest and most general explanation for why children learn to adhere to such norms is that they are usually rewarded when they do what others want and punished when they do not (Bandura and Walters, 1963).

Parents seldom see this process as pressuring the child to conform, even though many changes in behaviors and beliefs are brought about (teaching the child to use the bathroom instead of soiling its pants, teaching the child to use a fork instead of its fingers, taking the child to church, and so on). Kiesler and Kiesler (1969) define CONFORMITY as simply a change in one's attitude or behavior or belief brought about by real or imagined pressure from others. If we accept such a definition, we must consider ourselves conformists in many of the things we do: driving on the right side of the road, eating with a fork, wearing clothes on hot summer days. Many such behaviors become so commonplace that we begin to think of them as right or natural. It is, of course, no more natural for women to wear skirts than for them not to smoke cigars. And it is less natural for men to have short hair than long hair.

If we behave like others in so many ways, why is it such a derogatory remark to call someone a conformist, an organization man or a yes-man? What we usually imply when we say people conformed in a particular situation is that they did something they did not believe in to gain approval, be accepted, or in some way deceive another. In common usage, the term carries the connotation of being manipulative, of not being honest and straightforward, of seeking to ingratiate oneself with another, of not doing what one would really like to do.

Thus we must be careful not to confuse conformity with simple group habits, customs, or established social conventions. If we drive on the right side of the road because everyone else does and we really don't care which side we drive on as long as we get there safely, we are simply following an established convention that frees us from the thousands of decisions we would have to make if there were no rules about which side to drive on. In fact, we usually describe groups by statements about their customs, the patterns that recur in their behaviors.

Conformity, on the other hand, involves a conflict between the desires or beliefs of an individual and the desires or beliefs of another individual or group of individuals. An individual can resolve such a conflict in a number of ways, not all of which demonstrate conformity. If the individual resolves the conflict by doing something he or she does not believe in and would not have done otherwise, we have an example of conformity. Many social psychologists argue that there are two types of conformity: PUBLIC COMPLIANCE and PRIVATE ACCEPTANCE. There are sound theoretical reasons for expecting private acceptance to *follow* conformity (new customs may even be established in this way), but true private acceptance is not conformity.

Conformity

We have already mentioned one of the classic studies of conformity, in which Sherif (1936) made use of the autokinetic effect. Recall that the situation was ambiguous to a naive subject. It was very difficult to tell precisely how far the light appeared to move. When subjects observed the pinpoint of light appear to move in the presence of a confederate of the experimenter who made all judgments within a certain range, the subjects' own judgments began to approximate those of the confederate.

In other conditions, Sherif put groups of naive subjects together, and no confederate was present. Here subjects tended to converge on a common norm of perceived movement. That is, two subjects who had in individual sessions been making judgments from 2-5 inches and 9-15 inches, respectively, might, when put together, wind up both making judgments of 6-8 inches. Sherif used these results to draw some very broad conclusions about the individual and society. He suggested that, in those many ambiguous situations in which groups have no customs to fall back on to tell them how they should behave, a common NORM or shared belief is likely to emerge. Members of the group then use this shared belief to structure the situation at hand and similar situations that occur in the future. Norms, then, develop in ambiguous situations. Once the norm has developed and people accept it, we are no longer dealing with conformity. Only the period between the perception of ambiguity (conflict) and the establishment of an accepted norm involves conformity. The key question, of course, is why people conform. Why do norms develop?

THE DEVELOPMENT OF NORMS

Evidence from many areas of psychology seems to indicate that people abhor uncertainty. Janis (1951), for example, notes that during World War II, residents of London actually seemed relieved when bombs began falling. Waiting each night for the bombing to begin was the hard part. Uncertainty seems to arouse anxiety, and anxiety is not pleasant. Unfortunately, in a rapidly changing society such as ours, there is an element of truth in the old saying that nothing is certain but death and taxes. Our society is caught up in the rapid social change said to result in rampant uncertainty and future shock (Toffler, 1970). Even apart from this, it is the very essence of human existence to be concerned with intangibles: love, affection, emotions, values, attitudes, beliefs. There is little objective physical reality in such concerns, so a great deal of uncertainty must be reduced if we are not to be paralyzed by anxiety. Who really knows what is right? Who really knows whether there is or is not a God? There is no unequivocal physical evidence to tell us what is the best form of government.

Given that most of our opinions, beliefs, attitudes, and values cannot be validated by physical reality, they must have something on which to rest so that the anxiety produced by uncertainty will not constantly distract and disturb us. Festinger (1950) was interested in this question and argued that people substitute social reality for physical reality when the latter cannot be used to validate a belief. SOCIAL REALITY is, in a sense, validation by consensus. Suppose, for example, that you believe things might have been less turbulent in the late 1960s if John F. Kennedy had not been assassinated. Obviously, you cannot appeal to physical reality to validate such a belief. Kennedy was assassinated, so there are no statistics or recorded history that you can use to support your belief. How would you decide whether your belief is correct? How would you validate your belief? You would probably rely to a large extent on the opinions of other people. If a number of your friends believe as you do, the belief is valid for you. Festinger goes on to point out that it is not necessary for you to feel that everyone you know agrees with you. Instead, we refer our opinions to specific groups to validate them. (Betty Friedan might check with Gloria Steinem or Shirley Chisholm, but not with Hugh Hefner.)

250
**Forms of
social influence**

The groups to which we turn to reduce our uncertainty about values, beliefs, and attitudes are called REFERENCE GROUPS (Kelley, 1952). Reference groups can serve at least two functions, normative and comparative. The NORMATIVE FUNCTION of reference groups is to set and enforce standards. The COMPARATIVE FUNCTION is to give individuals a basis of comparison against which they can validate their attitudes, beliefs, and values. Groups set and enforce standards for much the same reason that individuals seek to validate their own opinions by comparison with others: enforcing such standards keeps uncertainty and anxiety to a minimum. Consider the faculty committees that must decide whether a graduate student has satisfied the requirements for a Ph.D. In nearly all such committees, there is a strong feeling that students must thoroughly learn a great deal of the previous work in the field. Presumably, one of the functions served by continuing to require students to learn the material is to minimize the committee's own uncertainty about the value of the material.

The comparative function of reference groups poses something of a puzzle in real life. The problem is to decide which groups are appropriate reference groups for a given individual. Which group shall the individual use to validate a particular belief? The process is somewhat circular, because individuals tend to seek out others who agree with them and to avoid those who disagree. We can always find several people who will agree with us about almost anything, but are they the ones with whom we should be comparing our beliefs? One of the advantages of experimental research on conformity is that the appropriate reference group can be clearly defined. In the Sherif experiment, for example, the appropriate reference group for a given subject obviously consisted of those other people in the room who were also observing the point of light and its apparent movement.

One might argue, however, that the autokinetic phenomenon is so novel for subjects, and the apparent movement so ambiguous, that the subjects were not really conforming in the sense that we have defined conformity. That is, they were not aware of a conflict between their own beliefs and those of others. They did not really have any clear beliefs at all. The study of social influence is primarily concerned with the pressures on people to act in ways that are contrary to their beliefs and values. In what has since become one of the classic series of experiments in social psychology, Asch (1952) set out to observe directly what happens when an individual is confronted with such pressures from a group.

THE POWER OF THE GROUP

Asch arranged a situation in which naive subjects were confronted with a clear discrepancy between what they saw in front of them and what a group of apparently similar others said was there. The stimulus materials that Asch used were simple lines. Subjects were shown successive sets of two cards on one of which were three lines (the comparison lines) and on the other of which was one line (the standard line). For every set of cards, each member of a group of subjects was to indicate, in turn, which of the comparison lines matched the standard line in length. In each case there was a clear and obviously correct answer, as shown in Figure 1. Simple?

No. The plot is somewhat thicker. In each group of seven to nine people, only one (the subject) was responding authentically to the lines. Each of the others was an accomplice of the experimenter, and this group of confederates had been instructed to cooperate by sometimes giving unanimously incorrect judgments. On certain trials of the procedure, in other words, they would indicate that two clearly unequal lines seemed equal. Their estimates on these trials were obviously in error, such as saying that line 2 in Figure 1 was equal to the standard line in length. The naive subject was also seated in such a position as to give his or her judgment after most members of the group had already announced theirs.

The results were dramatic. Compared to control subjects who were not confronted with the discrepancy between what they saw and what the group appeared to see, subjects confronted with the conflict made almost five times as many errors in matching the standard and comparison lines! The erroneous an-

Often what appears to be conformity is simple imitation or social ritual. Conformity involves conflict between the individual's desire and what he or she is pressured to do. (Top: Eric Roth/The Picture Cube; Bottom: Michael Serino/The Picture Cube)

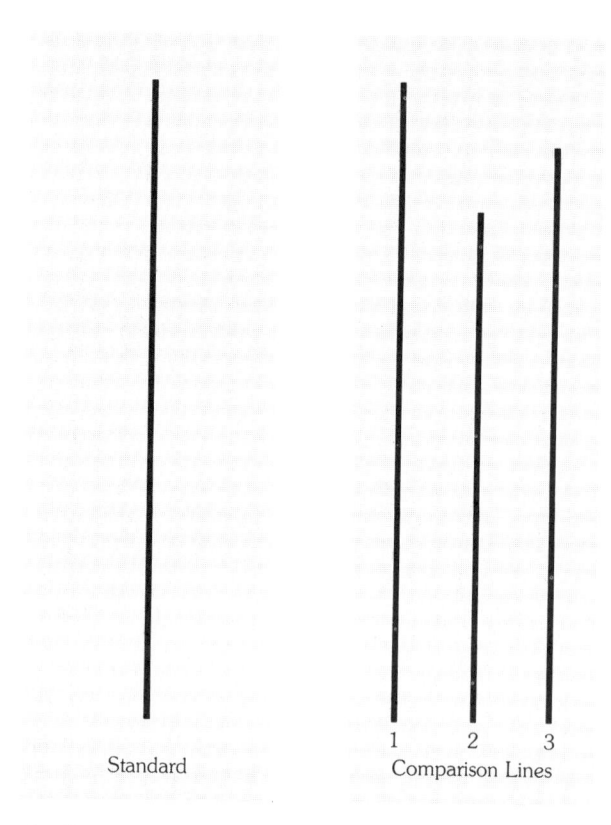

1. Experimental subjects confronted with unanimous false judgments by confederates made five times as many errors as control subjects in matching the standard and comparison lines. The cards on which the lines appeared were 17½ in. x 6 in. Standard lines appeared in the center of the card, while comparison lines were separated by a distance of 1¾ in. (From Asch, 1952, Figure 9, p. 452.)

nouncements of the majority contaminated one-third of the estimates of the naive subjects. Although two-thirds of the estimates by the experimental subjects were correct, the amount of conformity to the erroneous judgments of the group is still surprising.

There appear to be several reasons why people conform. The major reason is probably the desire for social approval: people want to be accepted by the group. In Asch's study, some subjects reported a fear of being thought inferior in some way. Others later said they had felt disturbed, puzzled, or like an outcast. Nearly all seemed to feel that if they continued to make judgments different from the group, the others would think they were peculiar. The desire for social acceptance and approval—and its underside, the fear of rejection and ridicule—are potent forces inducing conformity. The Asch experiment was a relatively benign demonstration of such forces. Many subjects were worried about the discrepancy between their judgments and those of the others, but they knew the group was not going to turn on them and harm them in any way. In contrast, individuals who want to live their lives in ways not generally approved by society must often fear physical injury. Consider the dilemma of homosexuals who would like to show their affection for each other openly but are genuinely afraid of what will happen if they do. They may become the object of leers, catcalls, or at least repugnant glances. In some places, they may even be subjected to physical abuse.

It is worth noting that self-doubt arose even among the subjects who did not conform in Asch's study. Some of those who initially appeared most confident of their judgments and who remained independent throughout the procedure later reported that they had become quite shaken. Although it had at first seemed clear to them that they were right and the others wrong, after a while they began to ask themselves how so many others could be wrong. They seriously began to mistrust their own vision. If subjects begin to doubt their own eyes on the basis of a few minutes of disagreement with a group of strangers, it is frightening to consider what they might be induced to believe through systematic, long-term indoctrination.

The Asch study apparently revealed an important social phenomenon. Numerous follow-up studies have investigated various aspects of the situation. For example, subsequent research by Asch himself showed that conformity is much reduced if even one member of the group appears to support the naive subject and agrees with his or her perception. Further, there seems to be little conformity when the group is composed of only one or two apparently similar others. Conformity increases dramatically when the group is composed of three others, but further increases in group size have little effect. Some researchers have investigated the effects of varying the relative ability of the naive subject and the group (Gerard, 1961). Not surprisingly, subjects yield less when they have been led to believe that they are really better at the task than the other members of the group. Surprisingly, the greater the subject's ability relative to the group, the more stress the subject experienced, as indicated by physiological measures. Jones and Gerard (1967) interpret this latter finding as indicating that a greater conflict is produced when the individual's own ability is high. The individual is then confronted with two very credible sources (himself or herself and the group consensus), so resolution of the conflict is more stressful. Subsequent research on conformity has also shown that the myth about females conforming more than males is incorrect (see Box A).

We have been discussing conformity from the point of view of the power of the group over the individual, a power that can make subjects doubt the evidence of their own senses, and the literature on this aspect of conformity continues to grow. There is another perspective on conformity, however. Conformity can be viewed as a conscious strategy by which an individual manipulates a group or another individual. Nobody has ever said that conformists were dumb. In fact, the prevailing view is that they know very well

A. Do Females Conform More Than Males?

Although it used to be widely believed that females conform more to social pressures than do males, actual research findings on this issue have been quite unclear for a number of years. Sometimes females were found to be more persuasible and/or conforming, sometimes males were, and sometimes there appeared to be no differences in conformity. In any event, the mixed results seemed to make one thing clear. Any explanation of sex differences in conformity that was based on the idea that females are generally socialized into dependent, passive, yielding roles was simply not adequate.

Frank Sistrunk and John McDavid suggested that many of the apparently discrepant results might be understandable in terms of the content or nature of the situations used in the research. That is, there are some topics and issues in our society with which males are generally more familiar than females. Similarly, there are other topics and issues on which females are generally better informed than males. Thus we might expect that males would yield less than females to social pressure on the former and that females would yield less than males on the latter. Earlier research gave inconsistent results, because no attempt was usually made to distinguish issues on which males and females had differing amounts of expertise.

To check on this idea, Sistrunk and McDavid (1971) designed a questionnaire containing a number of items, some of which had previously been judged to be of greater interest and familiarity to females than to males and some of which had previously been judged to be of greater interest and familiarity to males than to females. The questionnaire was then administered to several groups of males and females. In the margin beside each item there appeared an indication of how the "majority" of their peers had answered the item. The subjects were told that the information about the majority response might or might not be of interest to them in answering each item and that they were free to look at it or ignore it, as they wished.

Males yielded less to, or were less influenced by, the majority response on those items judged of greater interest and familiarity to males. However, females were less influenced than males by the majority response on those items previously judged to be of greater interest and familiarity to females. Females do not generally conform more than males. Both males and females may yield to pressure when the item or situation is of little interest to them or one with which they are not familiar.

what they are up to. They are out to gain something for themselves: a raise, approval, a promotion, or maybe just a pat on the head.

MANIPULATING OTHERS

Jones (1964) views opinion conformity as a type of ingratiation tactic. INGRATIATION is simply social behavior designed specifically to increase one's attractiveness to another person. For example, by frequently agreeing with the department chairperson, a rather mediocre assistant professor can become a valued commodity around the department. From the chairperson's point of view, the young ingratiator is obviously intelligent and discerning. After all, the two of them hold all the same opinions.

Christie and Geis (1970) consider the use of conformity as an ingratiation strategy to be one outcropping of a general orientation to interpersonal relations that they term MACHIAVELLIANISM. Author of *The Prince* and *The Discourses,* Niccolò Machiavelli lived in sixteenth-century Italy and wrote about the use and abuse of power in interpersonal relations. Machiavelli took a rather cynical view of human nature. He believed that people are basically selfish, ungrateful, and totally concerned with their own welfare. He felt that the key to success in handling others was to take a cool, detached, and manipulative approach. Christie extracted a number of relatively specific statements from Machiavelli's writings about how to implement this advice. "The best way to handle people," Machiavelli claimed, "is to tell them what they want to hear." "It is wise to flatter important people." And, "The biggest difference between most criminals and other people is that criminals are stupid enough to get caught."

Christie administered 20 such items to a large group of people. Based on the extent to which they agreed with the items, the people could be ranked in terms of the degree to which they adhered to Machiavelli's philosophy of interpersonal relations. This list of items has come to be called the MACH SCALE, and it has been used in scores of experimental studies investigating behavioral and attitudinal differences between those who score high and those who score low on the scale. Those who score high on the scale (that is, those who agree with statements such as the three we quoted) are much less likely to become emotionally involved with other people than are those who score low on the scale. The high Machs, as they are called, seem much more cool and deliberate. They are also more likely to concentrate on getting the best end of the stick in their interpersonal encounters.

Under certain circumstances, winning might require misrepresentation of one's score. It might be necessary to lie. Lying, of course, fits in rather nicely with our definition of conformity. It is clearly not a good thing, it involves a conflict between private beliefs or knowledge and behavior, and it is usually brought about by real or imagined pressure from others. There is, in fact, evidence (Geis and Christie, 1970) that high Machs lie and cheat more than low Machs when given rational justification—in other words, when they have something to gain. Not only are high Machs more likely to lie if the situation requires it, but they are more likely to do it while looking you straight in the eye (Exline, Thibaut, Hickey, and Gumpert, 1970).

Exline and his colleagues set up a study in which pairs of subjects worked on a series of ten tasks of increasing difficulty. At the end of the sixth task, the experimenter was called out of the room on some pretext. While he was away, one of the subjects (who was actually a confederate of the experimenter) looked up the answers to the remaining tasks. On his return, the experimenter finished administering the tasks, each of which required the two subjects to agree on both the number of dots on a large card and the shape of a figure represented by the dots. Following completion of all ten trials, the experimenter began asking about how the pair had decided on their answers in each case. In this interview, the experimenter became increasingly suspicious and finally accused the pair of cheating. The naive subject in each pair was implicated, because he or she had seen the confederate look up the answers and had not reported it when the experimenter returned. After the accusation, the experimenter turned to the naive subjects and interrogated them for several minutes. The experimenter was seated back to a one-way mirror behind which, unknown to the subjects, were observers, cameras, and other equipment to record the amount of eye contact between the naive subject and the experimenter. Several days prior to the subjects' participation in this study, they had been administered the Mach scale. As expected, the results of the study indicate that those scoring high on the Mach scale were more likely than those scoring low to look the experimenter in the eye while denying cheating, and they were also less likely to confess.

Lying about the extent of one's adherence to group norms can be interpreted as conformity and can result in some peculiar situations. Krech, Crutchfield, and Ballachey (1962) define PLURALISTIC IGNORANCE as a state existing in a group in which everyone pays lip service to norms that no one adheres to, but in which everyone thinks that everyone except themselves does adhere to the norms. If the norms are a minor part of some institutional structure whose goals people generally accept, each individual may come to believe that he or she alone is a deviate, a nonconformist. Individual violation of such norms may never be discussed with others, because to do so might imply overall rejection of the institution. The classic example of pluralistic ignorance is a study by Schank (1932) of a small rural community called Elm Hollow. In Elm Hollow, the Methodist Church was the focus of both religious and social life, and the church took a hard line on cigarettes, whiskey, and card playing. Data gathered through various interviews with the residents seemed to indicate that they accepted the church's position. Before Schank left, however, he had played cards and imbibed freely with many of the church members— but always behind locked doors and drawn blinds.

The card players and whiskey drinkers appeared to have the best of both worlds. On Sunday morning they were upstanding pillars of the community, as far as the community could tell. On Saturday night they could enjoy themselves, provided they took a few precautions. It is important to note that from the community's point of view (or more specifically, from the church's point of view), this was an unsatisfactory state of affairs. The goal of any such institution as a church is for the individual to accept the institution's doctrines and values. The mere public appearance of acceptance is not sufficient. In certain subcategories of conformity, however, the focus is entirely on public appearance.

Compliance

Many texts cite the Asch study that we discussed in the preceding section as an example of COMPLIANCE. We disagree for the following reasons. First, suppose the situation were real. It is unlikely that the majority would be satisfied for the minority of one to simply say the right thing. The majority would have a vested interest in getting the minority to accept the way they see things, because, if the minority of one really continued to see things differently, the majority members might have to question the evidence of *their* eyes. The Asch situation involves the minority and majority in mutual INFORMATION INTERDEPENDENCE (Jones and Gerard, 1967; Kelley and Thibaut, 1969). That is, both minority and majority group members are partially dependent on the information provided by others to validate the information obtained visually.

Second, in compliance and obedience, an individual yields to a direct request or command, respectively. The two parties involved, whether they be two individuals or an individual and a group, are caught up in mutual effect interdependence. Jones and Gerard (1967) define EFFECT INTERDEPENDENCE as existing when one person directly satisfies some need of another person. The latter is said to be dependent on the former for some effect. The person making a request or giving a command wants something. The person yielding to a request or obeying a command also wants something. Whether it is the simple social reinforcement of a "Thank you" or the freedom to go on living depends on the situation.

INEQUITY AND GUILT

There are many reasons why one might comply with another's request. Some of the reasons are rather obvious, and others are not so obvious. A particularly common source of compliance is the desire to maintain equity in our interpersonal relations. Social behavior involves us in continuous give and take, and several theorists believe that the process of exchange, of matching rewards and costs, is the very essence of life in society (Homans, 1961; Thibaut and Kelley, 1959). As Adams (1965) points out, however, there is always the possibility that someone will feel slighted, believing that the other person is taking more than he or she is giving or not pulling his or her share of the load. When someone feels this way, INEQUITY is said to exist. Give and take in a relationship can, of course, involve almost anything: money, effort, attractiveness, sex, time, emotional support. For example, if a husband works full time and a wife works part time, then the wife might be expected to do more around the house for equity to exist. On the other hand, if the husband were to get fired and the wife had to assume a full-time job, the husband would have to take over more household duties in order to reestablish an equitable relationship.

From the point of view of the person who is "ahead," one of the consequences of inequity is often a vague feeling of guilt, provided that the person is interested in maintaining his or her self-image as a fair and responsible person. Many parents appear to be experts in the strategic use of guilt to induce compliance in their children. The strategy is to simply make explicit the parent's large inputs ("all those years I worked for you") and small outcomes ("not a letter the whole semester") in the parent–child relationship. Once guilt has been induced, chances are that the guilty party is more likely to comply with requests in order to reestablish equity.

A study by Freedman, Wallington, and Bless (1967) provides some evidence for this reasoning. High school students who signed up for an experiment found themselves waiting in the same room with someone who had just taken part in the same experiment. The person with whom they were waiting was actually a confederate of the experimenter. The confederate initiated a conversation with the naive subject. For half of the naive subjects, the confederate interjected into the conversation a description of the test the naive subject was about to take and volunteered ideas about how the subject might do well on the test. For the remaining naive subjects, the confederate gave no details about the test.

After a few moments, the experimenter appeared and ushered the subject into another room where she described the test and said that she had to make sure the subject had neither taken nor heard about the test. She then paused for an answer. All subjects except one indicated that they had *not* heard about it. Thus half of the subjects were induced to tell a direct lie to the experimenter and presumably were experiencing some guilt. Later, after subjects had completed the test and were about to leave, the experimenter asked whether they would be willing to take part in another experiment run by someone with no funds to pay subjects. The measure of compliance was simply whether or not subjects agreed to take part in the additional experiment for no pay. The results, which appear in

Table I   Number of subjects complying in each condition

	Experimental (Lie)	Control (Nonlie)
Comply	20	11
Not Comply	11	20

Subjects who are experiencing guilt exhibit more compliance than those who are not. (From Freedman, et al., 1967, Table 1, p.119.)

Table I, show that there was greater compliance when the subjects were experiencing guilt than when they were not.

Suppose, however, that the experimenter in this study had not made a request of subjects as they were about to leave, but had simply paid them and sent them on their way. Is there any reason to believe that the subjects who had told a lie would have behaved any differently after leaving the lab from the subjects who had not lied? Specifically, if the subjects who had lied had been prevented from alleviating their guilt or reestablishing equity by doing something for the experimenter, would they have done something for someone else as a substitute? One occasionally hears tales of people who spend their lives doing good to expiate real or imagined guilt for something they did in the distant past.

In an attempt to obtain some evidence on this point, Darlington and Macker (1966) hypothesized that, if an individual who is experiencing guilt in one of his or her interpersonal relationships is prevented from doing something for the injured party, then he or she is likely to do something for someone else. Subjects recruited from a psychology class engaged in three tasks with a partner in another room. In order for the partner to obtain credit for participation (in the form of extra points added to his final exam grade), the subject had to successfully complete the three tasks. The tasks given the subject were actually impossible, so the partner received no extra credit.

Guilt was manipulated by the extent to which the extra credit was supposedly important to the partner. In the control condition, the partner was participating in the experiment merely out of interest and was totally indifferent to the extra points—he was only auditing the psychology course anyway. On the other hand, subjects assigned to the experimental condition found that the partner was almost overcome with troubles. He was working 20 hours a week, his wife was pregnant, his grade in the psychology course was borderline, and his graduation might depend on the few extra points he could receive by participating in psychology experiments. The subject's failure to complete his or her tasks, of course, ensured that the subject would not get those extra points. While the subject was seated alone in a room after the experiment, an accomplice came in, explained that she was soliciting donations for the University Blood Bank, asked for the experimenter, and, after a brief conversation with the subject, asked whether the subject would donate blood to the Blood Bank. Of 14 subjects in the control group, only 6 volunteered, but every subject in the experimental group volunteered. There does appear to be some evidence for the displacement of guilt. From society's point of view, maybe a little guilt is a good thing.

There are other reasons why people comply with requests, of course. Many people comply in the hope of gaining approval and securing some positive social reinforcement. McDavid (1965) found, for example, that subjects who volunteered for a psychological study for which they would receive no payment scored significantly higher than their classmates on a scale designed to measure strength of approval-seeking motivation. Often people comply because it seems to be the thing to do, particularly in ambiguous situations wherein they have no clear preference or the behavior requested is not very troublesome. Helson's (1948) ADAPTATION-LEVEL THEORY applied to studies of compliance postulates that responses to a request are a function of three factors: (1) the request itself, (2) the background against which the request is presented, and (3) residual factors deriving from such things as genetic predispositions and prior experiences.

In an early study of compliance, Rosenbaum and Blake (1955) found that subjects were significantly more likely to volunteer to take part in an experiment when they had just observed someone else (a model) volunteer than were control subjects who had not observed another's response to the request. Further, subjects who had just observed another refuse to participate were significantly less likely to volunteer than control subjects. The other's response presumably served as a model for the subject's own response to the request. Rosenbaum (1956) replicated these findings and also found that the willingness to volunteer was positively related to the intensity of the request. Other studies (Blake, Mouton, and Hain, 1956; Helson, Mouton, and Blake, 1958; Blake, Rosenbaum, and Duryea, 1955) have demonstrated similar effects on petition signing and donating money. The physical presence of an acquiescing or rejecting model was apparently not necessary in the latter studies. Merely seeing a list of names on a petition or a list giving the amounts that others had donated was enough to influence the petition-signing and donating behavior of subjects.

THE FOOT-IN-THE-DOOR TECHNIQUE

Freedman and Fraser (1966) have demonstrated that one's own previous behavior may function in a manner similar to the model's behavior in the earlier studies. That is, they were concerned with what door-to-door salespeople used to call the foot-in-the-door technique. The idea behind the FOOT-IN-THE-DOOR TECHNIQUE is that people who have been induced to comply with a small request, such as letting the poor salesperson have a glass of water, are more likely to comply with a larger request, such as buying his or her wares. Freedman and Fraser first asked some housewives if they would mind answering a few questions about soaps used in the home. Then, a few days later, they requested that the research team be allowed to inventory the entire household. Other housewives were simply presented the second of these requests with no prior inquiries about what soaps they used. The results offer evidence that the foot-in-the-door technique may indeed be valid. Over half of the housewives who had complied with the initial small request also complied with the subsequent larger request. On the other hand, less than one-fourth of the housewives who were only presented the large request complied. It is not clear just how the foot-in-the-door technique operates. Freedman and Fraser argue that what may occur is a change in the person's self-definition. That is, those who comply with the initial request are more likely to view themselves as people who help others and hence are more likely to comply with a later, larger request.

Thus compliance can occur for a number of reasons. It is a type of conformity that involves the person or group making the request and the person of whom the request is made in mutual effect interdependence. They both get something out of compliance—whether it is material benefit, social approval, alleviation of one's guilt, or validation of one's self-definition. Compliance is a type of conformity in which the requestor does not really care about the other's private beliefs as long as he or she does as requested.

OBEDIENCE

OBEDIENCE is a form of compliance in which the relationship is nonreciprocal between the person or group making the request and the person of whom the request is made. Because obedience involves a superior-subordinate relationship, it is more appropriate to speak of demands or commands than requests. Also, the question of equity does not arise in matters of obedience. As in compliance, however, the private beliefs of the person to whom the command is directed are of little importance to the person giving the orders. Reports of prisoners returning from the Korean War indicate that some 10 to 15 percent of the prisoners had chronically collaborated with the Chinese. They gave false confessions about war crimes they and their colleagues had committed, informed on fellow prisoners, signed anti-American petitions, and taped radio broadcasts of anti-American propaganda. However, none of these activities required a personal change of belief. The prisoners simply did as their captors demanded, and the reason was simple. As Schein (1965) points out, the captors were successful in inducing conformity to their demands because they had such total control over the prisoners. The Chinese, in short, had the power to command obedience. Refusal to obey was met with swift and forceful retribution.

The situation of prisoners of war is rather unique. More generally, one might wonder how people respond to orders from legitimate authority figures. Authority, after all, is an essential part of any society. Even in a pure and absolute democracy, the will of the majority usually assumes the force of authority. The average person submits to legitimate authority countless times during the course of a day: stopping at red lights, driving within the speed limit, paying for purchases, and so on. In addition, the early years of almost total dependence on parents mold and reinforce the tendency to obey authority figures. One begins to suspect that the very nature of life in society makes it difficult for the average person to resist authority, even when the authority is wrong or immoral or oversteps its bounds.

In a series of experiments that attracted international attention, criticism, and comment, Milgram (1963, 1964, 1974) created a surprisingly simple situation to observe what occurs when one person orders another to perform an act that harms a third person. The situation was designed to throw into conflict the apparently legitimate authority of the experimenter and the moral principle presumably held by the subjects that we should not harm anyone who is neither harming us nor threatening to do so.

Milgram's experiments involved two subjects, one of whom was a confederate of the experimenter, in a task in which the naive subject was to teach a list of word pairs to the other subject (the confederate) by administering an electric shock each time the learner made an error. The learner was put in a separate room and, while the real subject watched, had his arms strapped to a chair (supposedly to prevent excessive movement) and an electrode attached to his wrist. The teacher was then taken into an adjoining room and seated in front of an electrical apparatus, a shock generator with a row of switches ranging from 15 to 450 volts. In order to convince the subject that he would really be administering shocks to the learner, the subject was given a sample shock "just to show how the generator worked." The subject was told to shock the learner after each incorrect response and to move up 15 volts each time. The electrode attached to the learner was actually a dummy, and the learner never really received any shocks at all.

The experiment began with the subject reading word pairs, via an intercom, to the learner. After reading a list of pairs, the subject would then read the first word of a pair and four alternatives for the second word. The learner was to select the correct alternative and indicate his response by pressing one of four switches. The learner, of course, made a number of incorrect responses, and Milgram (1974) reports the shock levels quickly escalated:

> Conflict arises when the man receiving the shock begins to indicate that he is experiencing discomfort. At 75 volts the "learner" grunts. At 120 volts, he complains verbally; at 150 he demands to be released from the experiment. His protests continue as the shocks escalate, growing increasingly vehement and emotional. At 225 volts his response can only be described as an agonized scream (p. 4).

If, at any point, the subject turned to the experimenter and questioned whether he should continue shocking the "learner," the experimenter calmly directed him to continue.

The results of Milgram's study are both surprising and distressing. Over 60 percent of the subjects continued to shock the learner until the maximum shock had been delivered (450 volts!) and the experimenter terminated the study. This was in spite of the fact that many of the subjects were extremely concerned about the victim and repeatedly called out to him in an attempt to find out if he were okay. The victim fell silent after 330 volts and, for all the subjects knew, was either dead or unconscious. Some subjects made repeated efforts to get the experimenter to go see about the victim, yet they continued to administer the shocks. Transcripts of the verbal interchange with the obedient subjects indicate that many became extremely nervous, confused, and agitated by what was happening:

> I can't stand it. I'm not going to kill that man in there . . . Aach, but, unh, I'm not going to get that man sick . . . You better check in on him, sir . . . I'm shaking here . . . I'm worried about him . . . I'm shaking. I'm shaking. . . .

In variations of the experiment, Milgram found that obedience was reduced somewhat by bringing the victim into the same room as the subject, by having other subjects present who defied the experimenter, and by running the experiment in a seedy downtown office building away from the presumed prestige and authority of a university.

The basic finding is still disturbing, particularly in view of the fact that the only power the experimenter had over the subject was that which the subject allowed him to have (see Box B). Milgram (1974) concludes rather ominously that many people will simply do what they are told to do as long as they perceive the order to come from some kind of legitimate authority. People seem to be willing to obey such commands even when ordered to perform immoral acts that their consciences tell them are wrong. A particularly important question, which Milgram does not pursue, is what happens to conscience when we behave in ways that are contrary to its dictates. More generally, what happens to people's private beliefs when they behave in a way that is inconsistent with how they really feel?

The effects of conforming and compliance on private beliefs

We have all had the experience of having to be polite to people we genuinely dislike. Students are sometimes courteous and respectful to teachers for whom they really have no respect; conversely, teachers sometimes strive to appear interested in the questions of students who obviously have not done the very assignments that would have answered their questions. There are sound theoretical reasons for expecting that beliefs and attitudes that are initially discrepant with behavior may sometimes be brought into line with the behavior. Teachers who feign interest often enough may actually become interested. A piece of advice commonly given to those who are depressed and lonely is to perk up and to act happy. The idea, of course, is that when you act as if you were happy, you convince yourself that you are. Happiness does not always follow, but under certain circumstances it does. Dissonance theory helps clarify what some of those circumstances are.

DISSONANCE AND FORCED COMPLIANCE

Dissonance, according to Festinger (1957), is one of several types of relationships that can exist between cognitive elements. A COGNITIVE ELEMENT is simply an item of knowledge, such as "It is raining," "I like coffee," or "I do not believe in ESP." In DISSONANCE, two

B. Legitimate and Illegitimate Requests

Suppose a man were to walk up to you and say bluntly, "Would you please do 50 pushups?" You might give him a strange look and go on with your business. If, however, he prefaced his remark by explaining, "I'm conducting an experiment," and then added, "Please do 50 pushups," you might be more likely to comply (or try to do so). Subjects in experiments do all sorts of things they would not normally do. Would you, for example, sit at a table for an hour turning little pegs a quarter of a turn just because someone asked you to? (Subjects in a Festinger and Carlsmith experiment did just that.) What prompts subjects to do these things? Yakov Epstein, Peter Suedfeld, and Stanley Silverstein (1973) suggest that subjects hold an implicit contract about what they are obligated to do and what obligations the experimenter has. They surveyed over 300 students at Rutgers University and found the students believed that a subject in an experiment has an obligation to be cooperative, honest, punctual, serious, and not to inform other subjects about what transpired during the experiment. On the other hand, the experimenter's obligations are to be a decent human being and a competent professional.

Subjects in a second study were given a list of experimenter behaviors and asked to rate how appropriate and desirable they considered them. Of particular interest is the finding that, although subjects would consider experimental deception undesirable, they nevertheless feel that, given the nature of experiments, it is appropriate for experimenters to deceive them. Similarly, while the possibility of receiving an electric shock was seen as highly undesirable, subjects considered it an appropriate part of experimental procedure. Apparently, then, subjects in the Milgram experiment saw nothing inappropriate in the initial instruction that a learner be shocked for incorrect responses. The problem arose when the experimenter asked them to deliver *excessive* shocks. Here they were faced with the need to decide whether the experimenter was behaving professionally. We might hypothesize that subjects who refrained from obeying orders decided that the experimenter had stepped out of line. Since the experimenter was no longer living up to his end of the contract, they did not need to live up to their part of the contract, which called for them to cooperate with the experimenter's instructions.

---

such elements somehow do not fit together or follow from each other. For example, the two elements represented by the knowledge that your shoes are too small and the knowledge that you just paid $45 for them are dissonant. Dissonant relations between cognitive elements produce psychological tension, which people generally tend to avoid or reduce. To reduce the dissonance in our example, you might return the shoes, try to ignore the pain, or convince yourself that the shoes just need to be broken in. The relationship between two cognitive elements may also be consonant (liking sunshine and living in Florida) or irrelevant (liking sunshine and owning a watch). The latter two types of relations produce no psychological tension.

From even this brief description of dissonance theory, it should be clear how conformity can create dissonance. In a typical conformity situation, there are two dissonant cognitive elements. The cognitions that conformists have about their *behavior* do not fit with their cognitions about their private *beliefs*. This dissonance produces a tension that the conformist must somehow reduce. As Brehm and Cohen (1962) point out, when a person experiences dissonance, there is a tendency to change those dissonant cognitive elements that are easiest to change. If one of the elements involves a behavioral commitment that is difficult to undo, the dissonance is likely to be reduced by changing something other than the element involved in the commitment. A commitment, in Brehm and Cohen's terms, is active engagement in some overt behavior. It would be very difficult for the conformist to reduce dissonance by denying the act of conformity, because there are usually witnesses. It is somewhat easier to convince oneself that maybe the others were right after all.

As we have noted, however, only under certain circumstances is the act of conformity followed by private acceptance or belief change. The POWs mentioned by Schein did not become converts, even though they made speeches supporting communism. The reason for the failure of beliefs to follow behavior in that instance appears to lie in the conditions under which the behavior was performed. As Schein pointed out, the POWs were in an environment that was totally controlled. It was made clear to them that failure to do as their captors desired would result in extreme physical deprivation and possibly death. Thus there were not simply two cognitive elements ("I read a speech supporting communism" versus "I do not believe in communism"), but other elements as well ("If I had not read that speech, they would have killed me" and "I do not want to die"). If most of the relevant cognitive elements are consistent with a behavior, then the dissonance produced by engaging in that behavior is very small. When there is little dissonance, there is little pressure to reduce dissonance. The POWs in our example presumably experienced little dissonance, because the desire to live and knowledge of the consequences of not reading their "confessions" were consistent with their behavior. In short, they had such reasonable explanations for their behavior that they did not have to change their beliefs.

In an experiment designed to test this reasoning, Festinger and Carlsmith (1959) hypothesized that when a person is induced to say something that he or she does not actually believe, the dissonance produced by this act should decrease as the pressures on the person to perform the act—to lie—are increased. When subjects arrived to take part in the Festinger and Carlsmith study, they were put to work on extremely boring and repetitive tasks for a solid hour. At the end of an hour, the experimenter stopped the subject and, in a relaxed and casual manner, began to explain what the study was all about. The subject learned that the point of the study was to compare the way in which two groups of subjects perceived the tasks on which the subject had just been working. One group, which the subject was obviously in, was to perform the tasks with no initial explanation or introduction. A second group was to perform precisely the same dull tasks after having been led to believe that they would be exciting and interesting.

Up to the end of this explanation, all subjects who signed up for the experiment were treated exactly the same. Once this explanation ended, however, subjects were treated differently, depending on which of the following treatments they were assigned. Control subjects were simply asked some questions about how enjoyable they had found the tasks, whether they had learned anything, and whether they would like to participate in other such experiments in the future. The remaining subjects were told, after some apparent confusion and uncertainty on the part of the experimenter, that the confederate who was usually employed in "the other condition" to tell subjects that the tasks would be exciting and interesting had just called in and said that he couldn't make it. The experimenter was upset, because there was already another subject waiting outside who was supposed to be in the other condition. The upshot of this little scenario was that the experimenter asked the subject whether he or she would be willing to go out and, in effect, lie about the tasks by describing them to the waiting subject (who was actually a confederate of the experimenter) as enjoyable and interesting. The experimenter offered some subjects $1 and other subjects $20 to perform this little deceit. Following a brief conversation with the waiting subject, these subjects were asked the same questions as those in the control condition.

The idea is that $20 constitutes a great deal of pressure (external justification) for telling a fib about how interesting the tasks were, so there should be little tendency for $20 subjects to bring their opinion about the tasks into line with their behavior. On the other hand, $1 is not much justification for lying, so subjects in this condition were expected to experience more dissonance and to reduce it by convincing themselves that the tasks were not really so bad after all. In fact, it was kind of fun twisting those little pegs. The results, which are shown in Figure 2, strongly supported these predictions. Subjects paid only $1 to lie about the enjoyableness of the tasks wound up believing that the tasks were, indeed, more enjoyable than either control subjects or subjects paid $20 for lying found them.

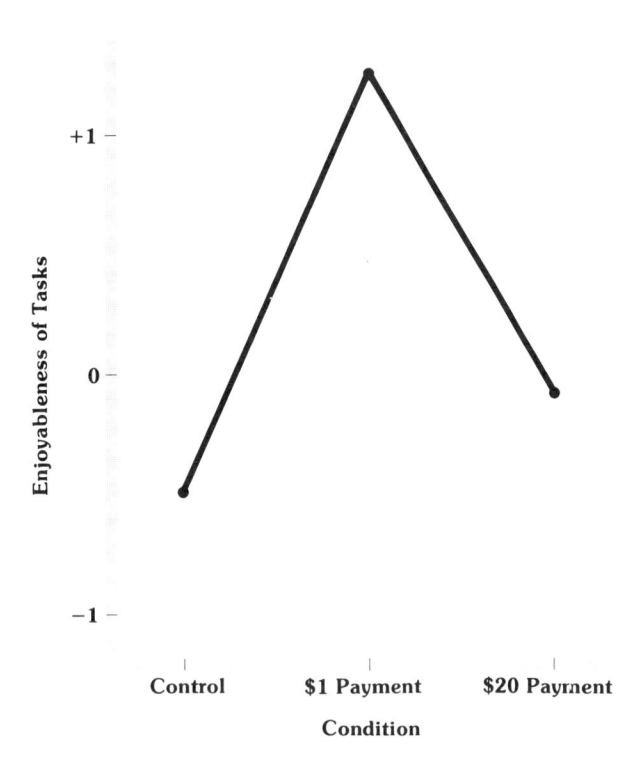

2. The greater the pressure to perform an act, the less dissonance the act produces and the less the tendency to bring one's belief into line with one's behavior. Subjects who were well paid for lying about the enjoyableness of tasks were less likely to come to believe the tasks actually were enjoyable. (Adapted from Festinger and Carlsmith, 1959, Table 1, p. 207.)

SELF-PERCEPTION: MY MOUTH WAS MOVING WHEN I HEARD IT

The results of the Festinger and Carlsmith study have spawned a continuing controversy (Insko and Schopler, 1972). One of the more interesting products of that controversy is a theory of self-perception (Bem, 1965, 1967) that makes essentially the same prediction as dissonance theory: an inverse relationship between the magnitude of pressures to conform and the effect of conformity on private acceptance. Bem, however, finds it unnecessary to postulate internal psychological tension (like dissonance) that must be avoided or reduced.

The basic point in Bem's analysis is that the statements we make about our attitudes and beliefs and the attitudes and beliefs that someone else would attribute to us are often functionally equivalent. He claims that we often infer our attitudes from observing our own behavior and the conditions under which it occurs in much the same way in which others infer our attitudes by observing how we behave. Some examples might help clarify this point. Bem points out that it is not unusual to see people consult their watch before responding to the question "Are you hungry?" Similarly, people asked whether they like television may reply, "I guess I do. I watch it all the time." The point is that there are many attitudes and beliefs on which people have never clearly articulated a position for themselves. When asked about their position, they look back at their relevant behavior and reason, "I did such and such; therefore, I must believe thus and so."

To test his ideas, Bem (1965) recruited 8 college students and had them come into the lab for two 40-minute sessions. In the first session, each subject was asked to rate the funniness of 200 cartoons. In the second session, subjects were led to believe that they would be making a tape-recording for use in a voice-judgment experiment. The alleged purpose of the voice-judgment study was to see whether listeners could tell when the voice on the tape was lying and when it was not. Thus preparation of the tape would require that subjects lie some and tell the truth some. At the beginning of the second session, each of the 8 subjects filled out a questionnaire that contained 49 questions and asked for such information as their first name, whether they were favorable or unfavorable toward fraternities and sororities, whether they believed in a Supreme Being, and so on. After completion of the questionnaire, the experimenter took it into another room and conducted the remainder of the experiment via an intercom. After repeating the fictitious purpose of making the tape, the experimenter continued:

> The procedure will be as follows: I will ask you questions, one at a time, from the list of information you just filled out. After I ask you a question, I will start the tape recorder, and you should answer the question into the microphone in front of you. Whenever I turn on the tape recorder, one of two colored light bulbs in the ceiling fix-

ture will also go on automatically. If the amber light goes on (amber light turned on) you are to answer the question truthfully; if, however, the green light goes on (green light turned on; amber light turned off), you should make up an untrue answer and speak it into the microphone as convincingly and as naturally as possible (p. 212).

The experimenter then proceeded through a lengthy list of questions. For half of the questions, the truth light came on, requiring the subject to be truthful. For the remaining questions, the lie light came on, requiring the subject to lie. The purpose of this procedure was to firmly associate certain conditions (amber versus green lights) with being truthful and with lying.

The experimenter then explained that, as part of the latter voice-judgment study, participants would be asked to look at 20 of the same cartoons that the subject had rated the day before. It was further explained to the subjects that, before making their own judgments, participants in the later study would listen to the subject's comments indicating that the subject had found the cartoons either very funny or very unfunny. The later study was purportedly to examine whether people were influenced by the comments of others in making their own judgments.

A notebook containing 20 cartoons that the subject had previously rated as neither funny nor unfunny had been placed on the table in front of the subject. The experimenter continued the instructions by telling the subject that he or she was to glance at each cartoon and decide whether it was funny or unfunny. Then, for each cartoon, he or she was to record the statement "I think cartoon such-and-such is very funny" or "I think cartoon such-and-such is very unfunny." So that the subject would know when the tape recorder was turned on and off, the experimenter said he would keep the amber and green lights hooked up and that the two colored lights would continue to flash on and off with the recorder in random sequence. This was the crucial part of the experiment. For half of the cartoons, the amber light came on while the subject recorded an evaluation, and for the other half, the green light came on.

The hypothesis was that recording a statement (behavior) to the effect that "I think cartoon No. 11 is *very funny*" in the presence of a light that had previously been associated with telling the truth would have more

Bem's truth and lie lights. Subjects were first trained to tell the truth when a truth light was on and lie when a lie light was on. Later, subjects made statements that neutral cartoons were funny when either the truth light or lie light was "inadvertently" left on. The subject depicted in the left panel then actually rated the cartoons as funnier when the truth light was on. Apparently the truth light served as an external cue that helped the subject infer his or her own behavior, in this case a belief. When the lie light was on (right panel), the cue light stimulated lying, and subjects maintained their original belief in the neutrality of the cartoons.

effect on the subject's actual beliefs about the cartoon than the same statement made in the presence of a light previously associated with lying. Ratings of the cartoon made immediately after the recording of the statements about the cartoons strongly supported the hypothesis. Seven of the eight subjects were persuaded by their own comments to a greater extent when those comments were made in the presence of the truth light than when they were made in the presence of the lie light.

The basic finding of Bem's study has held up relatively well in subsequent research. The situation surrounding behavior that is discrepant with one's beliefs determines in part the extent to which performing the behavior affects one's beliefs. For example, if your alternatives are to steal or to let your child die of starvation, stealing a loaf of bread will not have much effect on your opinion of yourself. There is really no choice, and everyone would have done the same thing. However, engaging in petty theft when you are relatively well off or stealing for a lark may lead to a negative opinion of your own honesty or morality. The key is the amount of pressure to which you are subjected. Hence Bem's self-perception theory reinforces dissonance theory. If the pressure is great to engage in behavior that is discrepant from your beliefs (to conform), then it is unlikely that your beliefs will change much. On the other hand, if the pressure is slight and you still conform, your beliefs are likely to change toward greater consistency with your behavior. It is as if people say to themselves, "I did it and I didn't really have to, so I guess I must have wanted to a little."

A study by Linder and Jones (1969), which was patterned after Bem's truth–light/lie–light study, confirms this reasoning. Subjects were told that they would record a series of statements, some of which would be true and others false. After completing a personal-information questionnaire similar to Bem's, subjects were asked to write two brief essays, one supporting socialism as the best economic system for the United States and the other supporting a free enterprise, capitalistic system. It had previously been determined that all the subjects believed in capitalism. Using questions from the 50-item questionnaire they had filled out, each subject was trained to answer truthfully in the presence of a distinctly colored truth light and to answer falsely in the presence of a differently colored lie light. Later, subjects were either induced to volunteer to tape record the essay supporting socialism, or they were given no choice but to record the essay.

The purported reason for recording the essay was to see if subjects in a later voice-judgment experiment could tell whether those reading the material agreed or disagreed with what they were reading. For some subjects, the experimenter said he would leave the lights used in the previous part of the experiment hooked up so that the subject could tell when the recorder was on. For other subjects, the experimenter used a different light to signal that the recorder was on. Thus each subject recorded his or her prosocialism essay in the presence of either the truth light, the lie light, or a light that had not been lit before. Finally, the subject was asked to complete a questionnaire designed to assess attitudes on socialism versus capitalism.

The results, which are shown in Figure 3, both repli-

3. Private acceptance of a counterattitudinal behavior (support of socialism) increased only when subjects volunteered to read a prosocialism essay and then actually read it under conditions previously associated with telling the truth (truth light on). When subjects were assigned to read the essay, or when they volunteered but read it in the presence of the lie light, their attitudes were not affected. (From Linder and Jones, 1969, Table 1, p. 477.)

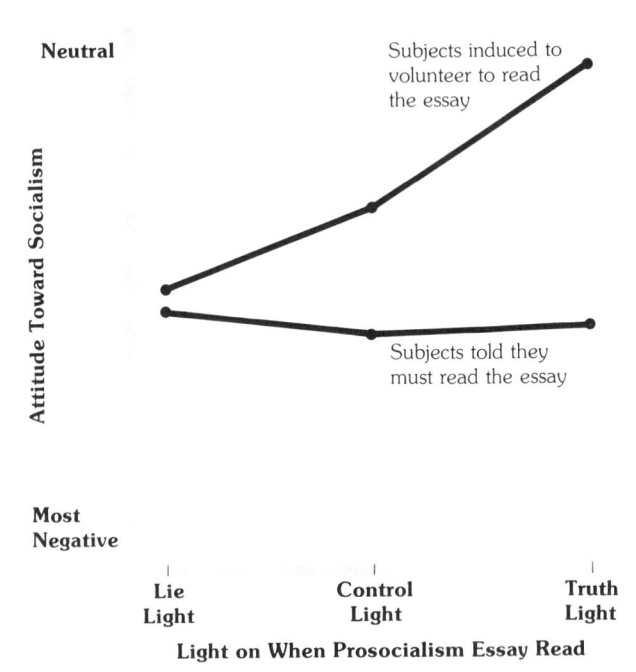

cate and clarify Bem's earlier results. When subjects were told that they had to read the essay, the conditions under which they followed orders had no effect on their private acceptance of the counterattitudinal behavior (supporting socialism). Only when subjects were induced to volunteer to read the counterattitudinal essay and when the situation surrounding such behavior had previously been associated with telling the truth was there a significant reduction in their private antipathy to socialism.

Under certain conditions, then, the consequences of conformity are changes in privately held beliefs toward greater agreement with the conforming behavior. The most general way of stating what those certain conditions are is to say that they involve *minimal justification*. When there is minimal pressure to conform and the person conforms anyway, there is likely to be a shift in beliefs to justify that conformity. When there is a great deal of pressure to conform (say, a gun to one's head), there is likely to be little or no shift in private beliefs. The implications are enormous. Consider the problem of how to teach children to refrain from particular kinds of behavior. How should we go about teaching a child not to steal? As Freedman (1965) points out, if our goal is to get the child to accept certain values or patterns of behavior, then we should not give too many reasons for the desired behaviors, nor should we promise tremendous rewards for behaving appropriately or threaten overwhelming punishments for behaving inappropriately. Rather, we should give the child the bare minimum justification necessary to get him or her to behave as desired. Learning under these conditions, the child is more likely to behave as desired in the future when the justification is absent.

We have been discussing conformity, the conditions under which it occurs, and its consequences. What about the other side of the coin? When and under what conditions can we expect nonconformity?

Nonconformity

Social psychologists have paid less attention to nonconformity than to conformity. This is not surprising, because the basic issue of social psychology is the nature of the reciprocal relationship between the individual and society, a relationship in which conformity is clearly implicated more than nonconformity. Nonconformists have appeared to be statistically infrequent, and quite often, when nonconformity is mentioned people think immediately of either villains or heroes.

If we take a somewhat less absolute view of nonconformity, we begin to see examples all around us. We all know people who appear to go along with the crowd 99 percent of the time but every now and then surprise us. Occasionally they do not go along but instead take a stand over what appears to be a petty or unimportant point. The husband may precipitate a scene by refusing to go to the concert for which his wife bought tickets without telling him. The friend who is usually willing and even eager to help is occasionally miffed when we take that help for granted. In the social-psychological literature, boomerang effects of attempted social influences are occasionally reported. A BOOMERANG EFFECT is said to occur when pressure on someone to do something has the paradoxical effect of making him or her even *less* likely to do it than if there had been no pressure.

REACTING TO PRESSURE

As a partial explanation of such effects Brehm (1966) has postulated the existence, under certain conditions, of a motivational state termed PSYCHOLOGICAL REACTANCE. Brehm's position assumes that people have a set of free behaviors, any one of which they might engage in at any given time. One's set of free behaviors is very broadly defined and includes overt physical activities as well as covert mental phenomena, such as thinking certain thoughts or believing what one wants to believe. A person may be free to go to the store for a bottle of soda in the same sense that he or she is free to believe that monogamy is unnatural. When an attempt is made by some external force, either personal or impersonal, to restrict someone's freedom of behavior, that person experiences psychological reactance. The goal of this motivational state is the reestablishment or safeguarding of the person's free behavior.

For example, suppose a controversial speaker has been invited to a nearby college to speak on abortion. Although you do not particularly agree with what this speaker usually has to say, you plan to attend. Arriving at the scheduled time and place, you find that the dean of the college has canceled the speech because he did not feel people should be exposed to the speaker's position. The dean's action has effectively eliminated your freedom to hear the speaker. As a result, according to reactance theory, you would become even more desirous of hearing what the speaker had to say and might even write and ask for a copy of the speech that was to have been delivered. The latter, of course, is one way of reestablishing your freedom to hear the speech.

According to reactance theory, the more important the free behavior that is threatened, the greater the magnitude of the reactance aroused, and consequently, the more persistently the person will attempt to safeguard the threatened free behavior. For a college professor, the freedom to discuss in class a controversial issue that is pertinent to his or her course is presumably more important than, say, the freedom to park in a particular parking lot. Another determinant of the amount of reactance aroused by a threat to a given free behavior is the magnitude of the threat itself. A weak threat arouses little or no reactance; a powerful threat arouses a great deal.

Although we mentioned that any external force (personal or impersonal) may threaten one's freedom, the vast majority of threats that one experiences in day-to-day activities are social in origin. They originate with other people. The driver in front of you pokes along at 20 miles an hour when you would like to be doing 50, someone zips into the parking space you were heading for, your office mates begin an animated conversation while you are trying to work, others try to pressure you to do certain things, and so on.

Brehm and Sensenig (1966) designed an experiment to test the hypothesis that if pressure to conform threatens people's freedom to decide how to behave there is in a tendency to reject the influence attempt. Pressure that threatens an important free behavior may result in nonconformity. High school students were recruited for a study that supposedly dealt with how people form impressions of one another. Each subject was told that he or she would look at pairs of pictures of people. From each pair, the subject was to choose the picture that he or she could work better with. For the chosen picture, the subject's task was to decide which of several descriptive statements about the picture was most accurate. The subject was led to anticipate a series of such choices, and the importance of being free to choose as he or she saw fit was emphasized by the experimenter, who said

> We are particularly interested in which pictures people choose to work on. We feel that we can tell quite a bit about a person by which pictures he chooses. It seems that different people choose different sorts of pictures, and how well a person does on matching the stories (description) to the picture depends on a person's choosing a picture which he understands (p. 704).

The subject was then led to believe that there was another student in a room down the hall who would be going through the same procedure as the subject. There was, in fact, no other student. In order to form an impression of the other subject, the naive subject first read a self-descriptive statement supposedly written by the other. In addition, as the task progressed, the subject was to receive a note from the other stating which picture of each pair the other preferred to work on. As we noted, the experimenter had said that one could tell quite a bit about another by the pictures he or she chose.

After some additional instructions and after subjects saw a pair of practice pictures, the experiment began. Immediately before looking at the first pair of pictures, subjects in the control condition received a note from the other subject that simply said, "I prefer 1-A." Subjects in the experimental condition received a note that said, "I think we should both do 1-A." Thus, in the experimental condition, the note stated the other's *preference and* threatened the subject's freedom of choice. In the experimental condition, then, the note constituted real pressure to conform. The major dependent variable was simply whether the subject chose A or B—whether or not the subject went along with the note. It is important to realize that in the control condition, there is some informational value in knowing the other subject's preference. The task itself was very ambiguous, and the pictures in each pair had been preselected so that there would be little or no preference for either one. Table II shows that, as expected, there was some positive social influence in the control condition. When the other subject simply stated a preference, 22 out of 30 subjects chose to

The world is full of signs that restrict our freedom and arouse reactance. How would most people respond to the signs in this public restroom? Would you say the threat is weak or powerful? (Melissa Shook/The Picture Cube)

Table II Incidence of acceptance or rejection of another's preference

	Accept	Reject
Control	22	8
Experimental	12	18

Subjects are more likely to select a picture which is suggested by another if no pressure to conform is involved. (Condensed from Brehm and Sensenig, 1966, Table 1, p. 705.)

work on the same picture. On the other hand, the data for the experimental condition show that, when the other attempted to usurp the naive subject's freedom of choice by stating that they both should work on a certain picture, 18 out of 30 subjects rejected the attempted influence.

If real or imagined pressure from a group threatens an important free behavior, we might expect the pressure to produce nonconformity rather than conformity. There are, in fact, many dramatic instances of nonconformity (see Box C). The overt expression of reactance-induced nonconformity might, of course, be masked or inhibited by other characteristics of the situation. If the rejection of pressure to conform is likely to bring down the wrath of the group on the nonconformist, he or she may not give vent to the aroused reactance. But suppose conformists do let it out. Suppose they overtly safeguard their freedom of behavior by not conforming. What are the consequences of nonconformity?

REJECTION

Earlier we defined conformity as behavior that is discrepant from an individual's private desires or beliefs and that results from real or imagined group pressure. NONCONFORMITY, then, is behavior that violates or deviates from the group's expectations. For behavior to qualify as nonconformity, the group must know about it. The closet homosexual may never be considered a nonconformist by unknowing officemates. The thief, from society's point of view, is not a thief until caught. According to Schur (1971), behavior is considered deviant to the extent that it departs from a group's normative expectations, involves acts that are considered personally discrediting to the person, and prompts reactions by the other group members that involve various attempts to punish, correct, or treat the person performing the deviant behaviors. The key to this perspective on nonconformity is the reaction of the group, not simply the action of the deviating individual.

That the action of a deviating individual is not all there is to nonconformity can be illustrated in a number of ways. Hollander (1958) introduced the concept of IDIOSYNCRASY CREDIT to account for the fact that a double standard seems to operate in many groups. That is, newcomers or initiates into the group are often expected to toe the line and conform rigidly to the group's expectations, while old-timers appear much more approximate in their adherence to group norms. Hollander argues that old-timers have built up credit by their proven support of the group and are allowed minor deviations. It is important to note that the notion of idiosyncracy credit implies that groups have a sliding definition of nonconformity that is, in part, a function of other characteristics of the deviating individual. For example, teenagers who get caught engaging in petty vandalism are more likely to be formally arrested if they happen to be lower-class blacks than if they are middle-class whites (Turk, 1969). An individual who has once been arrested, of course, becomes someone with a record, and any future violations are apt to be more harshly punished.

Once society has defined someone as a deviate, society's reaction frequently compounds, elaborates, and reinforces whatever impulses led the individual to commit the initial deviant or nonconforming action (Goffman, 1961). Consider those deviations that have been termed "mental illness." As we pointed out in Chapter 2, a growing body of informed opinion (Szasz, 1961) questions the very concept of mental illness. Nevertheless, society continues to label people as mentally ill, and the result is often tragic. Recently (1974), CBS aired a documentary about a man who had spent years in a mental hospital as a retardate when in fact he was of normal intelligence. The hour-long telecast concluded with the sentence, "A mistake in diagnosis in Larry Herman's case was made when he was a child many years ago. It is very unlikely that this could occur today." Unfortunately, it is very likely

C. The Rescuers

Milgram's study of obedience was stimulated, at least in part, by his concern over the high level of obedience to Nazi authority among many German citizens during the 1930s and 1940s. Many observers began to think of Germany as a nation of obedient, unthinking individuals. Yet even under the tremendous pressures exerted by the Nazis and in the face of dire threats, there were still individuals who risked their lives to save Jews.

Under the auspices of an organization in Oakland, California, known as the Institute for Righteous Acts, psychologist Perry London (1970) and several other researchers contacted and interviewed a group of such rescuers. These individuals were non-Jewish Germans who risked their lives to save Jews from the Nazi persecutions. On the basis of interviews with the rescuers, London was able to suggest some traits and life experiences that might help explain why some people resist the pressure to conform and why they can disobey the orders of authorities.

One trait that seemed to characterize the rescuers was adventuresomeness. They were a group of high-risk-takers, people who seemed to enjoy taking chances. For example, London found that one of his interviewees had rescued a jailed Jewish leader by simply walking into the jail and telling the guards that he had secret verbal orders to take the man. The orders, he explained, were too secret to be written down and from a source too high to be questioned. The implication was that the orders were from Hitler himself. The guards were taken in and released the Jewish leader into the rescuer's custody.

Another characteristic usually found among the rescuers was a very strong identification with one of their parents, who tended to be a highly moralistic, though not necessarily religious, individual. Thus part of the motivation for their courageous acts may have been due to the way in which they were socialized. A final characteristic of the sample was marginal social status. That is, many of these individuals were not strongly identified with mainstream German society.

Once again, we see how social behavior must be understood as a combination of personality traits and situational factors. These rescuers had personality traits, such as adventuresomeness, that enabled them to take risks involving resistance to authority and violation of societal norms. But it was also easier for them to violate the norms, because they did not identify with German society but identified instead with another reference group—their parents.

---

that this could occur today. In a critique of psychiatric classification and diagnosis, Draguns and Phillips (1971) note that, even among psychiatrists, there is widespread recognition that evidence of mental illness exists more in the mind of the diagnostician than in the behavior of the diagnosed.

Safeguards are supposedly built into the institutional structure of society to prevent individuals from being railroaded into mental institutions simply because they are old, behave differently, or in some other way violate expectations. Many states require sanity hearings prior to commitment at which, presumably, a board of experts can dispassionately decide whether a person is sane or insane. Such hearings have a hidden "Catch 22," however, because many of the experts appear to assume that appearance before a sanity hearing is *prima facie* evidence of insanity. In a study of 571 incompetency hearings in the state of Florida in 1965, Haney and Michielutte (1968) found evidence that many things other than the actual mental states of the alleged incompetents entered into the decisions. Similarly, Scheff (1964, 1974) points out that, legally, there are two criteria on which the judgment to commit a person to a mental institution may be based: (1) the dangerousness of the person to himself or herself and/or others, and (2) the degree of mental impairment. However, in 63 percent of the actual commitment procedures that he observed, Scheff found that the patients were neither dangerous nor impaired.

Most nonconforming behavior, of course, would not get one arrested or committed. Most nonconformity consists of minor differences of opinions, variations in dress, and peculiarities of one sort or another. The reaction to such behavior is surprisingly similar to reactions to criminals and the insane, though on a reduced scale. A male patron who appears without a tie at an exclusive restaurant may be offered one by the *maitre d'hotel*. If the patron declines, he is likely to be summarily ejected. The two elements here appear to be rather general in the treatment of nonconformists: an initial attempt to get the deviate to mend his or her ways followed by rejection if the attempt does not succeed.

A great deal of social–psychological research in the 1950s focused on the ways in which groups achieve consensus. Schachter (1951), for example, hypothesized that the pressure brought to bear on a group member to conform would vary directly with the cohesiveness of the group and the relevance of the deviant's opinion to the purpose of the group. Unfortunately, Schachter's results were rather weak. Although there appeared to be an increase in communication to a deviant group member in highly cohesive groups, followed by rejection when he or she continued to deviate, the results were not statistically significant. Later research, however, has established that not only with respect to opinions, but with abilities (Latané, 1966) and emotions as well (Schachter, 1959), individuals are likely to cease communicating with or forego opportunities to communicate with those who differ from themselves.

A cherished American ideal is that people have a right to dissent and a right to step to the music they hear. It is beginning to appear that this right extends only to those who agree with us. Or, if we are magnanimous enough to tolerate dissent, we apparently don't want to talk to the dissenters after it becomes obvious that they refuse to see the light. Farina, Chapnick, Chapnick, and Misiti (1972) point out that if people really tolerate dissent, there should be no relation between another's political views and, say, the intensity of shocks administered to them in a laboratory learning task. To check on this, they recruited 30 radicals and 30 conservatives to participate as teachers in a

Table III Intensity of shocks to learner as a function of differing political views

Teacher	Learner	
	Conservative	Radical
Conservative	4.5	5.0
Radical	7.0	4.5

The higher the number the more intense the shocks. (From Farina, et al., 1972, Table 1, p. 276.)

learner–teacher task. The task involved a series of trials on each of which the learner was to try guessing a pattern of 5 button presses. In each case, the learner was a confederate of the experimenter. During a preliminary part of the experiment, the confederate responded to some questions in the presence of the naive subject in a manner that clearly indicated either a radical or a conservative bent. Later, the naive subject's job was to inform the learner-confederate when his or her guesses on the button-pressing task were incorrect by administering an electric shock. The teacher-subject was free to vary the intensity of shock so as to best facilitate learning. As indicated in Table III, and contrary to the ideal of freedom to dissent, more intense shocks were given when the confederate's political views differed from those of the subject.

The consequences of persistent nonconformity are isolation and rejection. People do not like to be around deviants, and if they are around them, they appear not to want to talk. The nonconformists in our midst are constant reminders that we might be wrong about something; their very presence questions our values, our opinions, or our lifestyles. The staunchly middle-class couple may experience a little pang of uncertainty about the career–marriage–home–accumulation syndrome when they see Ken Kesey and The Merry Pranksters ride by laughing, singing, and stoned. As we mentioned earlier, one consequence of uncertainty is anxiety, and people don't like people who make them anxious.

Summary

We began this chapter by distinguishing between conformity and adherence to customs. To label someone a conformist implies that the person is being manipulative and/or dishonest. Conformity involves a conflict between one's beliefs and one's behavior. There are at least two perspectives on conforming behavior: it can be seen as a result of real or imagined group pressure, or it can be viewed as a conscious manipulative strategy on the part of an individual.

Many of the things we are concerned about have no concrete physical reality for us to use to check our interpretations and perceptions. Consequently, we substitute social reality as evidence on which to base our beliefs. The groups to which we turn to reduce our uncertainty about values, beliefs, and attitudes are our reference groups. Research by Sherif and by Asch was cited to illustrate conformity in the context of experimentally defined reference groups.

The notions of ingratiation and Machiavellianism were introduced in our discussion of conformity as an interpersonal manipulative strategy, and it was pointed out that lying and cheating fit our definition of conformity. Research by Exline and his colleagues illustrated one way in which a Machiavellian orientation to others can influence interpersonal behavior. Those who scored high on the Mach Scale were more likely to look another in the eye while lying and were also less likely to confess. We also introduced the notion of pluralistic ignorance in our discussion of conformity. Pluralistic ignorance occurs when no one believes, but everyone believes that everyone else believes—so everyone outwardly conforms.

In discussing compliance and obedience, we pointed out that they both involve a type of conformity in which the group or individual exerting pressure cares little or nothing about the private beliefs of the others, as long as they behave as requested or commanded. The notion of effect interdependence applies to these two types of conformity: each party relies on the other for direct gratification of needs. This was in contrast to the information interdependence involved in the Asch and Sherif situations, wherein both minority and majority members are partially dependent on the information provided by others to validate the information obtained visually.

Compliance was discussed in terms of some of the results of inequity in interpersonal relations, including guilt and displaced guilt. In general, experiencing guilt increases the likelihood that one will comply with another's request. People also differ in their need for approval. The stronger this need, the more likely they will comply. Adaptation-level theory was briefly cited to account for some of the effects of models on compliance. The foot-in-the door technique was also mentioned as a way to increase compliance. Obedience was discussed, with specific reference to Milgram's research and the extent to which life in society makes it difficult for people to resist authority even when the authority is immoral or illegitimate.

Dissonance theory and Bem's theory of self-perception were used to account for the consequences of conformity. Both of these theories predict that the circumstances surrounding conforming behavior will determine whether that behavior has an effect on the individual's private beliefs. If the pressure is great to engage in behavior that is discrepant from one's beliefs, it is unlikely that one's beliefs will change much. On the other hand, if the pressure is slight and one still conforms, beliefs are likely to move toward greater consistency with the behavior.

Nonconformity was discussed in terms of reactance theory. When an attempt is made to restrict people's freedom of behavior, they are likely to experience psychological reactance directed toward the safeguarding of their threatened free behavior. If the real or imagined pressure from a group threatens an important free behavior, we might expect that pressure to produce nonconformity rather than conformity.

Finally, discussing the consequences of nonconformity, we made the point that the reaction of the group is as important as the actual behavior of the nonconformist. The notion of idiosyncracy credits was introduced in connection with the idea that groups have various amounts of tolerance for nonconformity, depending on other characteristics of the deviant. Whatever lip service we may pay to the right to dissent, on both a societal and an individual level, the consequences of nonconformity appear to be isolation and rejection.

V

Prosocial and antisocial behavior

10

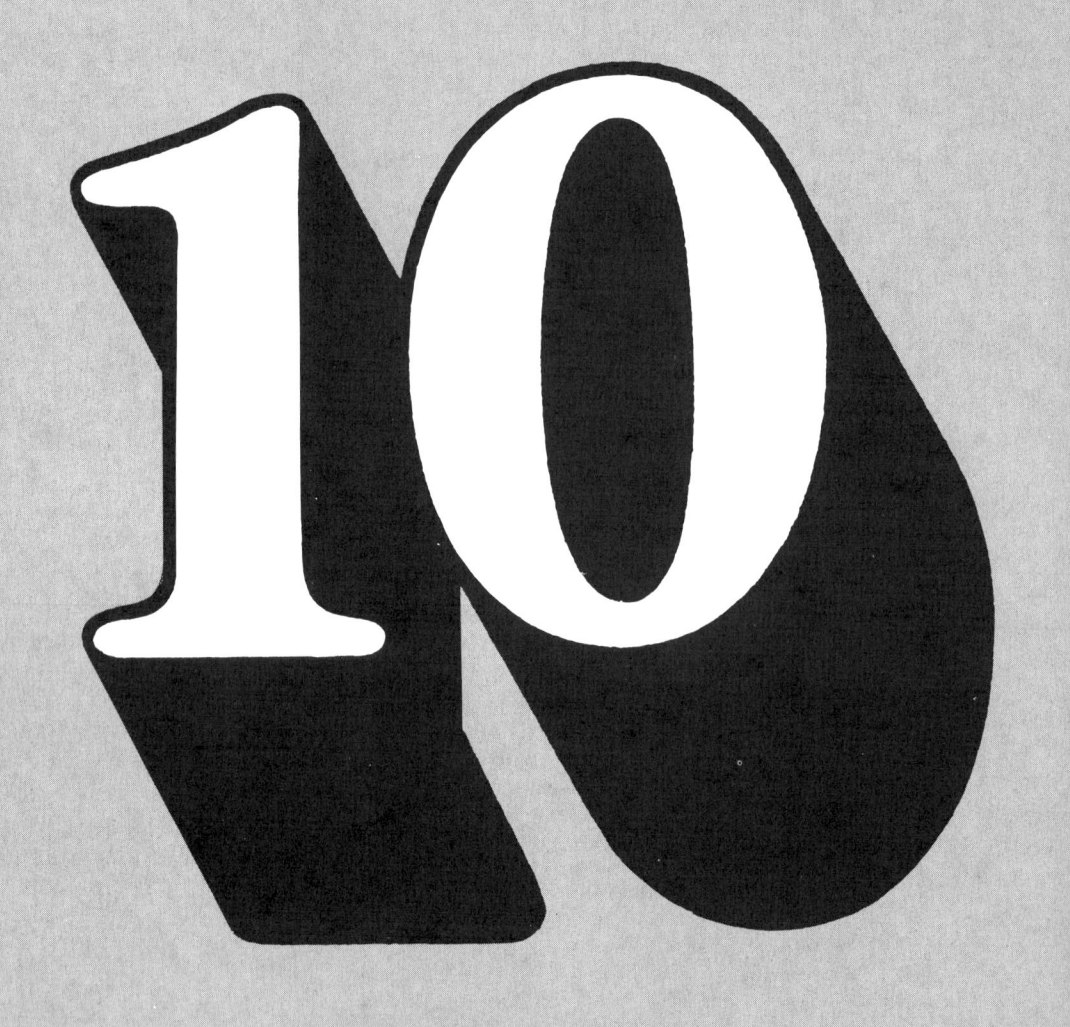

Altruism and helping behavior

277
The nature of altruism

What is altruistic behavior?
   Prosocial behavior and altruism
   A definition of altruism
Conditions for altruistic and helping behavior
   What is helping?
   Is helping instinctive?
   Social development and altruism
Theoretical approaches to altruism and
     other forms of helping behavior
   Theories of reciprocity behavior
   Social-norm theories

284
Helping in emergency situations

Bystander intervention in emergencies
   The nature of an emergency
   A decision-making model
   Research testing the model
   An arousal-reduction approach
When will bystanders help?

293
Helping in nonemergency situations

To help or not to help
   Awareness
   Assigning responsibility
   Costs and benefits
What makes a Good Samaritan?
   Sex, race, and personality variables
   Moods and feelings
Situational determinants of helping
   Social norms
   Modeling

Characteristics of the recipient of help
  Demographic characteristics
  Attractiveness
Sometimes it's hard to be grateful
  The recipient's view of the helping process
  Recipient characteristics
  Context characteristics

296
Organized helping

Voluntarism
  The history of voluntarism
  How widespread is voluntarism?
  The volunteer
Are volunteers altruists?
Altruism bought and paid for
  Historical development in the United States
  The community mental health center

300
Summary

A lawyer said to Jesus "And who is my neighbor?" And Jesus answering said,

A certain man went down from Jerusalem to Jericho, and fell among thieves, which stripped him of his raiment, and wounded him, and departed, leaving him half dead. And by chance there came down a certain priest that way: and when he saw him, he passed by on the other side. And likewise a Levite, when he was at the place, came and looked on him, and passed by on the other side. But a certain Samaritan, as he journeyed, came where he was: and when he saw him, he had compassion on him, and went to him, and bound up his wounds, pouring in oil and wine, and set him on his own beast, and brought him to an inn, and took care of him. And on the morrow when he departed, he took out two pence, and gave them to the host, and said unto him, 'Take care of him; and whatsoever thou spendest more, when I come again, I will repay thee.' Which now of these three, thinkest thou, was neighbour unto him that fell among the thieves? (Luke 10:30–36)

The nature of altruism

The parable of the Good Samaritan is universal in its appeal to the altruistic side of human nature. It may be considered an ethical mandate of several religions, specifying how people ought to behave when someone needs help. Let us make a few observations about the parable.

1. The Good Samaritan and the wounded man were strangers; there were no previous ties of kinship or past obligation between them.
2. Helping the wounded man cost the Good Samaritan something: effort, time, and money.
3. The help was given voluntarily.
4. The Good Samaritan did not expect repayment. Apparently he never expected to see the wounded man again.
5. The focus of the parable is very much on behavior, the act of helping. There is little reference to the Samaritan's inner states, such as sympathy or empathy. The statement that "when he saw him, he had compassion on him" indicates that the Samaritan probably had a general attitudinal set of kindliness and an intention to help. Beyond that, everything else is inference. We do not know whether the Samaritan was pleased with himself for helping, smugly felt that God would reward him for his good act, really disliked doing it but felt obligated, or perhaps hardly reflected on the act at all.

The parable of the Good Samaritan describes very well an act of altruism. In fact, it is a pure case. The ethical imperative of the story is that each of us should conduct our lives in a similar fashion. But quite frequently humans hurt each other more often than they help. (In contrast to altruism, we shall examine the components of aggression in Chapter 11.)

WHAT IS ALTRUISTIC BEHAVIOR?

The context of our discussion indicates that altruism is some kind of positive behavior. But what kind? Are all positive acts toward others altruistic? It will be useful to consider some examples that occur daily in social life in order to clarify the meaning of altruisic behavior.

1. A neighbor called soliciting money for the Heart Fund. Susan gave $20.
2. Joan moved to a new house. Mary offered to spend Saturday with her, cleaning and scrubbing the house.
3. A man in a shopping center lost a contact lens. Bill spent 15 minutes searching for the lens.
4. Joe had just begun to eat a delicious meal that he had prepared. His hungry wife wandered in

**277
Altruism and helping behavior**

at that moment, and Joe gladly gave her half of it.

5. Tanya and Barbara made an agreement that Tanya would assist Barbara at the PTA bake sale on Saturday morning, and Barbara would help Tanya collect for the March of Dimes the following Saturday.
6. Fred accidentally broke an expensive piece of china while visiting the Davidsons. The following day he came over and spent several hours cleaning their garage.
7. Tom saw an old couple struggling to get a large sack out of the trunk of their car. He felt a wave of sympathy as he walked by on his evening stroll.
8. Luke saw a disabled car on the freeway. He stopped and found a man with two small crying children. Their car would not start. Luke drove them to the next town and waited until a tow truck arrived to pick them up. He then drove on and was subsequently late for an important meeting.

Prosocial behavior and altruism. All these examples involve what is called PROSOCIAL BEHAVIOR (Bar-Tal, 1976): positive acts or sentiments directed toward other people. The behaviors are diverse, and a brief analysis of them will be useful.

Example 1 is an instance of DONATING, a common social activity.

Example 2 is an instance of HELPING. Joan and Mary are no doubt well acquainted; perhaps they are good friends. Mary may or may not have expected Joan to repay her at a later date. Helping of this type is quite common between friends. It is much less common for a person to offer this type of help to a stranger, though if Joan had just moved next door to Mary, most people would agree that Mary was beginning to establish a special relationship with Joan—that of a neighbor.

Example 3 is an instance of ASSISTING, another type of helping. It is a common occurrence and involves minimal cost. At the same time, Bill incurred this cost for a stranger, probably without expectation of repayment. We probably should call this an everyday instance of altruistic behavior.

Example 4 is a homey instance of SHARING. Good social relations in a society depend on millions of such acts every day. We would probably consider Joe a real grouch if he had refused his wife any of the food, but somehow it is difficult to wax eloquent about his altruism just because he shared it.

Example 5 is also a common prosocial behavior. It is an instance of COOPERATION, one of several types of RECIPROCITY BEHAVIORS (Bar-Tal, 1976). A trade-off seems to be involved: you help me and I'll help you. Both Tanya and Barbara incurred costs of time and effort in helping each other, but each did so in expectation of repayment. Their behavior is prosocial, but probably not altruistic.

Example 6 involves RESTITUTION. Fred tried to compensate for a harm done to the Davidsons by volunteering to engage in menial work for them. Restitution involves doing something costly (in time, money, or the like) for someone to compensate for a cost one has inflicted on the other party. Fred's clumsy behavior was costly to the Davidsons. He tried to create parity by offering to do work so that the Davidsons would not have to do it. A society probably could not endure without such acts of compensatory behavior. Restitution is prosocial behavior, but the motive seems to come from guilt or fear of disapproval, rather than from a positive desire to help.

Example 7 involves an emotional state. Sympathy or EMPATHY, the ability to put oneself in the victim's shoes, may often underlie acts of prosocial behavior. Tom experienced the emotional state but did not exhibit any helpful behavior. This example illustrates one point of the parable of the Good Samaritan: the important thing is the actual helpful act. The corresponding emotional state is secondary. In fact, some people might view Tom as something of a hypocrite. He indulged in a sentiment that felt good, but he was unwilling to incur any costs by actually helping. To continue our religious metaphor, "the road to hell is paved with good intentions."

Example 8 is similar to the parable of the Good Samaritan. Luke's effort was sustained and costly to him, and the help was given without any apparent thought of repayment. We would call his behavior altruistic.

A definition of altruism. Pondering the foregoing examples allows us to arrive at a tentative definition of altruism. ALTRUISTIC BEHAVIOR is a more or less costly act that is performed voluntarily, is intended to benefit another person, is performed without expectation of reward (Bar-Tal, 1976; Berkowitz, 1972; Krebs, 1970), and is performed with some degree of empathy for the other person (Aronfreed, 1970; Cohen, 1972).

Some authors would argue that feelings of empathy ought not to be included in the definition, because empathy cannot be observed and measured directly. However, empathy, sympathy, understanding, or some similar feeling state seems to be necessary to altruism. It is possible to satisfy the other three conditions and hate every minute of it. For example, a person may help a sick neighbor extensively, but really detest doing it. The act is helpful, but we would not call the person altruistic.

The definition of altruism presents a pure case of altruistic behavior. It describes a social ideal, a norm to which members of a society may aspire but will reach fully only on special occasions. The definition in pure form seems to imply that human nature is intrinsically good and that people help each other for no reason at all, beyond that intrinsic goodness. Our everyday experience suggests that pure altruism rarely occurs; people seldom act totally without expectation of reward. Why, then, do people behave altruistically on occasion even if there are no external rewards? One answer is that people give themselves *self-rewards* for altruistic behavior. That is, people have feelings of satisfaction and pleasure, and their self-esteem is elevated when they help others.

There is controversy about whether self-rewards should be allowed before an act can be called altruistic. Some authors (Rosenhan, 1972; Walster and Piliavin, 1972) believe that self-rewards are difficult to demonstrate and not useful as a research concept. There is also the possibility of circular reasoning: one can always appeal to self-rewards after the fact as an explanatory device. Self-rewards probably cannot be ruled out in acts of altruistic behavior. Pride and satisfaction in helping others clearly do occur, and such feelings may be an important motive force in much prosocial behavior. Therefore we should allow them as the reward for altruistic behavior, even though external rewards are ruled out.

We have seen that a given type of prosocial behavior can be very difficult to define precisely. It is even more difficult to study comprehensively in various research settings. In this chapter we will discuss many different types of helping behavior, and we will use the terms *altruistic behavior* and *helping behavior* interchangeably.

CONDITIONS FOR ALTRUISTIC AND HELPING BEHAVIOR

Most of the research has looked at the causes of helping and altruism. Before examining this research, we need to examine some of the factors underlying helping. Since prosocial behavior in one form or another seems to be universal across cultures, we also need to consider the possibility of a genetic basis for altruism and the extent to which it is a learned social behavior.

What is helping? All helping responses are conditioned to some extent by the situations in which they occur. In fact, current research strongly emphasizes the situational determinants of helping. Of course, we cannot simply say "the situation determines helping," because a situation is a complex of perceptions, need states of persons, relationships among persons, and the structure of the physical environment. We will consider the perception of need, the types of acts involved in helping, the personal cost of helping, the extent to which helping occurs in a crisis situation, and the relationship between helping and social roles.

1. *How perception of a need for help occurs.* Social life can be structured in many different ways, and it occurs in a multitude of settings. For any given setting at any moment, there is a shared understanding that all is well or normal. People are going about their business as beings in control of their own fate. This perception of normalcy can exist even when conditions of social disarray are extreme. For example, a street in a city may be a hangout for winos. The people look dirty, sick, hungry, and hopeless. If you walk past an old man sitting on the street dozing with his back against the wall, the sun reflecting brightly from his wine-soaked beard, you are unlikely to stop or perceive a need to stop. The old man is functioning normally in his world; he does not need your help. In fact, he needs massive changes in his life, changes we would call rehabilitation. But at that time and place, there is nothing he wants from you and nothing you can do for him.

Helping begins with a perceived need. Something has to change to cause the situation to deviate from normal. If the old wino started gasping for breath or calling for help, an immediate state of need would become part of the situation. You might or might not respond to the old man, but you would at least perceive a need.

Perception of need varies widely, of course, from seeing someone drop a pencil to witnessing someone's fall from a tall building. Occasionally one person perceives that another has a need when the other does not actually feel such a need. It can be embarrassing to offer help that is not needed or wanted, and people are sometimes reluctant to offer help because they are afraid of being embarrassed. It is also aggravating (as well as a source of social comedy) to have some insensitive clod insist on helping you when you don't want help and only want to be left alone.

2. *Types of helping acts.* Helpful acts are as diverse as behavior itself. Helping acts may be divided into two general classes. We perform *direct acts* to address a specific person's need after a problem has occurred. The behavior may be physical, such as lifting, moving, or holding; emotional, such as comforting or offering reassurance; or verbal, such as giving instructions or directions. We perform *preventive acts* to prevent an unfortunate situation from occurring (for example, grabbing a child from in front of an onrushing car) or to correct an unjust situation (for example, reporting or preventing a crime).

3. *The costs of helping.* Any behavior can be thought of as resulting in some reward and cost to the person who performs it. The general theoretical approach that views behavior as determined by rewards and costs is exchange theory. Such theorists as Blau (1964), Homans (1961), and Thibaut and Kelley (1959) have developed this conception, and their ideas are discussed in detail in other chapters. The general idea is that any act, such as helping an old person across the street, will carry some reward, perhaps a "thank you" or a feeling of pride in doing a good deed. Costs are also involved, such as the sheer physical effort of the helping response and time lost from other activities. The net profit (reward minus cost) presumably determines whether a given act will be performed.

4. *Crisis nature of helping.* In a sense, all helping is a response to a crisis. Our discussion of perception of need indicated that there must be some deviation from the normal state of affairs before helping is activated. Nevertheless, most deviations are not very serious; they do not cause much adrenalin to flow. Other situations are more serious. An auto accident, someone screaming for help, a robber with a pointed gun—all are real crisis situations. People in such situations are likely to be emotionally aroused and uncertain of what to do. It makes sense to consider helping in emergency and nonemergency situations separately, because different variables may be at work.

5. *Helping and social roles.* Much of social life is organized so that an individual's behavior follows well-defined patterns. An individual who behaves as expected is behaving in his or her role. For example, suppose someone has a heart attack and calls a hospital. The ambulance responds, picks up the victim, and delivers him or her to an efficient emergency room where a team of doctors and nurses saves the victim's life. We do not call the behavior of the ambulance driver, nurses, or doctors altruistic; they were just doing their job.

This example illustrates that a great deal of helping behavior is institutionalized, which means that behavior patterns are organized routinely so that helping can be performed as part of an occupational role. This type of organized helping is an important part of any society. The behaviors of individuals within the system are not altruistic, but the system as a whole works to perform a variety of helpful acts. We will discuss organized helping more fully in the last section of this chapter.

The example also helps clarify the nature of altruism at the individual level. We have defined altruism as behavior free of one's occupational or social role. In fact, one might say that altruism exists in a "role vacuum" (Leeds, 1963). Altruism occurs in situations in which behaviors are not prescribed. The person must be free to make a voluntary choice to help or not to help. This does not mean that a doctor or nurse, for example, could not behave altruistically toward a patient. But such behavior would have to be "above and beyond the call of duty." Otherwise it is behavior that is simply duty, and paid duty at that.

Let's consider another issue—the extent to which altruism is genetically determined or learned.

Is helping instinctive? Since helping others is such a common social response, it is reasonable to ask whether it might be genetically determined, at least in part. One distinguished social psychologist at first answered "yes" (Campbell, 1965) but later qualified his answer to the point of saying "no" (Campbell, 1972).

Campbell's initial argument was based on the premise that humans evolved as animals who live in small groups. Early human groups experienced many dangers, especially from other human groups. Survival depended on solidarity within the group. Solidarity was maintained by loyalty, cooperation, helping, and altruistic behavior, even to the point of self-sacrifice. The greater the altruistic behavior exhibited toward the group by its members, the more likely that group was to survive. In the long course of evolution, groups with altruistic members were more likely to pass their genes on to succeeding generations than groups with less altruistic members. In this way, altruism would gradually be selected as an individual trait of the species.

The problem with this argument, as Campbell (1972) later saw it, is that loyalty to the group involves not only helpful deeds to group members, but active defense of the group. A lot of people probably got killed in the process. In fact, one could argue that the more altruistic the individual, the more likely that he or she would be killed in defense of the group. If so, this would leave a pool of more "selfish" genes, not more altruistic ones. At best, the selection process probably balanced out genes promoting self-sacrifice versus self-preservation. Campbell's conclusion was that altruism is a product of sociocultural evolution, which is conducted through cultural indoctrination. Altruism is learned, in other words, and we should look for its origins in the social development of the child.

Social development and altruism. In Chapter 3, we examined social development, and particularly moral development, in detail. We were largely concerned with learning moral prohibitions. But learning positive acts of prosocial behavior may also be considered part of moral training. In fact, there has now been considerable research on the development of positive acts of prosocial behavior in children. Some of this work has been summarized by Staub (1975) and Bar-Tal (1976). The more important findings about the acquisition of prosocial behavior are as follows:

1. *Helping is learned.* Several studies have shown that various types of prosocial behavior increase steadily during the first several years of life. For example, Green and Schneider (1974) tested 100 boys ranging in ages from 5 to 14 on 3 tasks: helping to pick up pencils, sharing candy bars, and volunteering to make booklets for poor children. On the first 2 tasks, helping increased with increasing age, but age was unrelated to helping on the volunteering task. A number of other studies have yielded similar results.

2. *Helping is related to level of cognitive development.* In Chapter 3, we saw that moral reasoning is related to level of cognitive development, as predicted by Piaget's theory. There is some evidence that children's altruistic behavior is related to their level of moral judgment. Rubin and Schneider (1973) found that children's willingness to donate candy to poor children and to help a younger child stack tickets was positively correlated with the children's stage of moral development. Other studies (Rushton, 1975) have yielded similar results.

3. *Reinforcement promotes the learning of prosocial behavior.* Researchers within the social-learning tradition have demonstrated this result. Several studies (Midlarsky, Bryan, and Brickman, 1973) have shown that social reinforcements such as praise increase sharing and assisting behavior in children. Type of reward and relation to the reinforcing adult are also important, apparently in the same way as for other types of social learning.

4. *Prosocial behavior may become self-reinforcing.* Social-learning theory is concerned with the self-regulation of behavior and with how people learn to reinforce themselves. We noted earlier some of the objections to the concept of self-reward for altruistic behavior. However, some social-learning theorists (Aronfreed, 1968; Rosenhan, 1972) believe that a history of reinforcement and subsequent development of a self-reward mechanism is necessary before altruistic behavior can be fully acquired. Aronfreed believes that altruism is acquired by a type of emotional conditioning procedure. If Susan helps Mary, Mary's positive response may become a conditioned stimulus attached to the act of helping. This reinforces Susan's inner empathic response, which will be aroused by situations of need on subsequent occasions. With practice, the act of helping comes to serve as its own reward, because it is connected with the emotional response of empathy. It is unclear whether complete self-reinforcement is possible. Every once in a while, some positive feedback or approval from the person helped may be necessary to keep the self-reinforcement mechanism from extinguishing.

5. *Prosocial behavior is learned by modeling.* We saw in Chapter 3 that modeling and observational learning are important vehicles for the acquisition of social behavior. This statement holds true for the learning of prosocial behavior as well. A number of studies have shown that children imitate a variety of prosocial acts performed by models (see Bar-Tal, 1976).

6. *Model behavior is more effective than verbal statements.* The old proverb that actions speak louder than words certainly applies to children. In an interesting study, Bryan and Walbek (1970) had a model first verbalize (preach) either charity or greed and later practice either charity or greed. This procedure created four experimental conditions: preach charity/practice charity, preach greed/practice charity, preach charity/practice greed, and preach greed/practice greed. Results indicated that only a model's practice influenced a child's behavior. The preaching had no effect on behavior. Later studies have shown that verbalization about helping is sometimes effective, but not so effective as the actual behavior of the model.

7. *Role playing can increase children's altruistic behavior.* Staub (1971) trained children to enact roles of helper or helpee in five situations (a child falling off a chair, a child trying to carry too heavy a chair, and so on). After the training sessions in helping, the children were tested in different ways on two different occasions. Although there were some sex differences, the role playing of helping did enhance helping in the test situations. It may be that role playing stimulates children's abilities to take the role or perspective of others, creates empathy, and consequently leads to internalization of helping as a response style.

8. *Making children responsible for helping makes them more helpful.* In an experiment by Staub (1970), children given responsibility for helping helped more than children not given responsibility. Children were told, "If anything happens, you take care of it." The response measure was whether they went to help when sounds of distress from a hurt girl were heard next door. Staub's experiment on responsibility offers one possible explanation of how a norm of responsibility might originate. Adults at first impose responsibilities on the child from without. Through external reinforcement and self-reward, this sense of responsibility gradually becomes internalized. By adulthood it has become a norm, a part of one's value structure.

THEORETICAL APPROACHES TO ALTRUISM AND OTHER FORMS OF HELPING BEHAVIOR

Social life tends to proceed in the direction of stable forms of reciprocal behavior. In its crudest form, reciprocal behavior is a variant on "you scratch my back and I'll scratch yours." A great many theories postulate some reciprocity principle as a foundation for social life. Based on social life as we know it, this makes a lot of sense. This type of approach makes an explanation of altruism quite difficult, however, because altruism in its purest form is a nonreciprocal behavior. Unless one assumes that human nature is intrinsically good (and the discussion of aggression in the next chapter denies that possibility), one is left with the puzzle of explaining why altruism occurs.

There are two general theoretical approaches to the problem. One approach views altruism as somehow derivative of reciprocity behavior. The second approach views altruism as deriving from a social norm: people are altruistic because a social norm that somehow got established in the distant past is internalized by each successive generation. We shall examine both of these theoretical approaches.

Theories of reciprocity behavior. Most theories of reciprocity behavior assume that an individual has an internalized obligation to reciprocate favors or help. The sense of obligation does not necessarily stem from selfless motives, however, and may in fact derive from very egocentric motives. Following are brief discussions of several reciprocity theories.

EXCHANGE THEORY is a general approach to human interaction, as we saw in the chapter on conformity. Humans are viewed as engaging in an exchange relation when they interact. In the process they exchange goods, services, and social approval, which have various rewards and costs associated with them. An individual also brings to the interaction certain investments, such as age, social status, knowledge, wealth, and the like. Homans (1961) argued that people interact on the basis of DISTRIBUTIVE JUSTICE as the norm for proper exchange. Basically, the principle of distributive justice states that when two people interact, one person's profit (rewards minus costs) relative to investments should equal the other person's profit relative to investments:

$$\frac{\text{PERSON A}}{\text{(Rewards − Costs)}}{\text{Investments}} = \frac{\text{PERSON B}}{\text{(Rewards − Costs)}}{\text{Investments}}$$

Thus interaction is equitable when the *ratios* for persons A and B are equal. Note that *profits* do not have to be equal; one person may invest considerably more in the interaction than the second person, but as long as he or she also profits more, the interaction is equitable. The theory is applied to a superficially nonreciprocal act of helping in Box A.

As stated by Adams (1965), EQUITY THEORY is similar to the principle of distributive justice, though more general. The profit/investment ratios for two people must be close to equal in order for satisfactory interaction to take place. Inequality of the ratios results in inequity, which is aversive and motivates the people involved to restore equity. An entire volume on equity theory was recently edited by Berkowitz and Walster (1976).

Gouldner (1960) presented the idea that there exists a universal NORM OF RECIPROCITY stating that (1) people should help those who have helped them and (2) people should not hurt those who have helped them.

A. Application of the Concept of Distributive Justice to Helping Behavior.

Suppose that John, a brawny athlete, helps his friend Joe chop trees and saw them into firewood. The job is exhausting and takes all day Saturday. John enjoys working outdoors and likes strenuous exercise. Joe is frail and really needs the help. It would have cost Joe $100 to hire the help elsewhere.

Although John seems to be giving a lot and receiving little in return, the interaction may be equitable and both individuals may be satisfied. We must look at possible rewards and costs for each.

John		Joe	
Rewards	**Costs**	**Rewards**	**Costs**
Outdoor air	Fatigue	$100 saving	Hard work
Exercise	Gave up movie	Supply of firewood	Missed a movie
Day with friend	Gave up time with wife	Day with friend	Sore and stiff next day
Approval from friend	Stiff and sore next day	Land cleared	Future obligation to John

We assume that both men bring the same "investments" to the situation. Therefore the "rewards minus costs" for John must equal the "rewards minus costs" for Joe in order that distributive justice be served. On first appearance, Joe gets more value in rewards than John, and John incurs more costs than Joe. However, a more important cost for Joe is implicit in the situation—Joe's future obligation to help John. That is a strong expense indeed, since it is open-ended. John may ask for a reciprocal favor at any time. Should Joe refuse a return favor, the present exchange would be inequitable, and it is possible that the friendship would be terminated.

Presumably the norm is internalized during the course of socialization. Gouldner noted that such a norm has a stabilizing effect in society. The norm motivates reciprocity in exchange relations and therefore tends to inhibit the emergence of exploitative relations. The internalized norm also serves as a brake on powerful people and hinders their exploitation of less powerful others. Finally, such a norm promotes positive acts of helping others, since the helper can confidently expect the act of helping to be repaid.

A series of statements on a JUSTICE MOTIVE and related topics has emerged out of general considerations in equity theory. People should get their just desserts, whether rewards or punishments. One form of this approach is the "just world" hypothesis (Lerner, 1970), which states that we want to believe that people deserve what they get and get what they deserve. Such a norm can lead to helping responses on occasion, but it can also lead to derogation and rejection of a victim of misfortune. More recently Lerner, Miller, and Holmes (1976) proposed that most people care deeply about justice for themselves and others and believe that justice and deserving are major organizing themes in our lives. At this point it is unclear how the general conception of the justice motive predicts precisely when and how people will behave altruistically. Nevertheless, the conception seems important and will be more fully developed in the future.

INDEBTEDNESS THEORY was proposed by Greenberg (1968) in an attempt to understand the process underlying reciprocity behavior. Basically, the norm of reciprocity is reformulated into a notion of psychological indebtedness that one person feels toward another. Indebtedness is viewed as an aversive motivational state, which one needs to reduce or get rid of. The primary way the feeling of indebtedness can be reduced is by reciprocating the help directly or reciprocating it indirectly to a third party.

The notion is interesting. Based on experience, it is clear that feeling obligated to another can sometimes be unpleasant. Receiving a Christmas card or gift can sometimes be irritating simply because one feels obligated to reciprocate in kind but really doesn't want to do so.

Social-norm theories. In general, this approach relies on a societal norm as the explanation for altruism. A NORM is a standard or expectation held by a group about how its members should behave. People often regard norms as rules that should be obeyed. We consider two normative theories of altruism.

Leeds (1963) proposed a NORM OF GIVING, which postulates that people should want to give for its own sake, not because of anticipated gains. People who have internalized the norm have a need or motive to give. This concept may be useful for explaining altruism in some areas of life, particularly the giving of one's service or ideas. Sometimes it is said of an individual that "so and so has so much to give." This may mean love and affection, ideas for a project, or overt behavior in the service of a cause.

According to Berkowitz (Berkowitz and Connor, 1966; Goranson and Berkowitz, 1966), the NORM OF SOCIAL RESPONSIBILITY prescribes that a person should help others who are dependent on his or her assistance. People follow this norm to gain self-approval and self-rewards for doing what is right. Such a norm would explain why parents take care of children, an often onerous, thankless task. More generally, the norm accounts for why people of high power and status often help less powerful others rather than exploit them. Berkowitz was able to support his theory to some extent in the laboratory. More recently he noted that both norms and the characteristics of the person and situation are involved in causing actual helping behavior in a specific situation (Berkowitz, 1972).

There have been criticisms of the normative approach. Darley and Latané (1970) note that an appeal to norms for explanations is not very sound, because any behavior can be called normative, norms are too vague to guide concrete action, norms are often contradictory, and people seem not to think about norms when they behave altruistically. The criticism has some merit, but it is true of almost any very general concept. Normative theories may continue to be useful, even though they are general statements.

Helping in emergency situations

Seldom does a single incident have a strong direct impact on social psychology. It is almost unheard of for such an incident to stimulate the creation of a whole area of research. Helping behavior in emergency situations is just such an area of research. It was stimulated by a single incident, the murder of a young woman. The effects of this incident also spilled over into other areas, such as nonemergency situations and theories of altruism.

In early 1964, a young woman named Catherine Genovese was attacked on the street late at night near her home and murdered. Her screams aroused many of her neighbors, but none of them went down to the street to help her. A detailed description of the incident appears in Box B.

At first the murder did not attract much attention from the news media. Then slowly, people became aware that there had been as many as 38 witnesses to the murder and that not a single one of them had helped. The story was documented in a book by Rosenthal (1964), a New York news editor. This book and other commentary on the case attracted much attention. The agonizing question of why nobody intervened to save Genovese's life haunted the public conscience. Two social psychologists, John Darley and Bibb Latané, became interested in the case and started a research program to investigate the antecedents of helping in emergency situations. Another major research program has been conducted by the Piliavins and others (Piliavin, Rodin, and Piliavin, 1969; Piliavin and Piliavin, 1972; Gaertner and Dovidio, 1977).

BYSTANDER INTERVENTION IN EMERGENCIES

The basic question to be answered is: Under what conditions will a bystander intervene to help in an emergency? In attempting to answer the question we first will consider the nature of an emergency. Then we will discuss the approach of Latané and Darley and that of the Piliavins.

The nature of an emergency. We have already discussed the general nature of helping. In particular, we examined the notion of perceived need in a situation that is out of the ordinary in one way or another. Most situations of need do not have the critical immediacy that we call emergency. A situation that may be called an EMERGENCY has several distinctive characteristics (Bar-Tal, 1976):

1. The situation involves harm or threat of harm. Because of the potential danger involved, intervention may be very costly to the helper.

2. An emergency is a rare and unusual event. Most people caught up in an emergency have no experience in handling such situations.

3. Each emergency is unique. The specific situation poses specific problems and specific needs for intervention. A fire is quite different from an imminent drowning, and both are different from a bank robbery.

4. Most emergency situations are unforeseen and unpredictable. It is not possible to plan for them in advance.

5. Analysis of the situation, a plan for intervention, and actual intervention must occur all at once. There is no time for careful deliberation.

Helping in an emergency may be either direct or indirect. Direct help is an actual stepping in to try to avert tragedy; indirect help is a notification or appeal to a third party to do something.

A decision-making model. Latané and Darley (1970) proposed a model (or theory) of the process by which a bystander comes either to intervene in an emergency or not to intervene. Their approach is a type of decision-making theory, because they view the bystander as having to make a series of five sequential decisions:

1. A person must *become aware that help is needed*. People are usually involved in their own thoughts and needs. In an environment full of stimulation (a crowd or other noisy setting), a call for help, the collapse of another person, or other unusual behavior may not be noticed. Thus the first basic choice or "decision" is whether an individual will become aware that something unusual has occurred.

2. An individual must *define the situation as an emergency*. Once one is aware that something unusual is happening, it is still necessary to decide whether the situation is an emergency. Emergencies happen quickly, and the situation is often ambiguous at first, so that events can be difficult to interpret. For example, a person lying in a doorway may have had a heart attack or may merely be sleeping off a hangover.

3. Once a bystander has defined an event as an emergency, he or she must *decide whether there is a personal responsibility to help*. Many variables are presumed to affect this decision, such as the bystander's sex, age, social role, general competence, and relationship to the victim, the victim's age, sex, and race, and so on.

B. The murder of Kitty Genovese

At 2:25 on Friday morning, March 13, 1964, a dark-eyed and attractive bar manager named Catherine Genovese said goodbye to the regulars at Ev's 11th Hour Bar on Jamaica Avenue in the Hollis section of Queens and walked out to her red Fiat parked at the curb. She had left it there at 6 o'clock while she went out on her night off for a first date with a young man named Louis Respo. At 2 o'clock, he had dropped her back at Ev's where, after chatting a bit with the regulars, she was ready to go home and sleep late.

She drove across Jamaica Avenue to the Grand Central Parkway, apparently not noticing a small white car making the same turns she did. She sped west on the parkway to the Queens Boulevard exit, turning into 82nd Road, a quiet, shaded street of two-family homes in the area called Kew Gardens. At Austin Street she turned left and drove for a block to the Kew Gardens station of the Long Island Railroad, where she usually parked in the lot in front of the station, deserted at this hour. The railroad management didn't like residents to do that, but Kitty's apartment was over an upholstery shop in a row of small stores right next to the parking lot, and it was close. Above each store were two apartments with entrances in the rear. Kitty simply had to walk behind the stores to 82-70 Austin Street, then up a narrow stairway to the small flat she shared with Marie Lozowsky—a mere 40 steps.

As she paused by her car in the absolute silence of the windless morning hour, Kitty sensed that something was wrong. Instead of walking those steps to the rear entrance, she ran from the lot along the sidewalk in front of the stores and, her heels clicking in the stillness, started up toward Lefferts Boulevard. She may have been heading for the police call box on the corner. She may have felt that the broader, well-lit boulevard was safer. Maybe she hoped that Anthony's Bar, in the middle of the row of stores, was still open. Whatever she had in mind, she got only as far as the card shop, the fourth store up.

On the seventh floor of the apartment building directly across from the card shop, Milton Hatch awoke when he heard the first scream. Bolting to the window, rubbing sleep from his eyes, he saw a woman kneeling on the sidewalk and a smallish man in an overcoat standing over her. "Help me! Help me! . . . Oh God, he's stabbed me!" she wailed.

Hatch leaned out the window, his wife beside him now. "Let that girl alone!" he shouted down.

The man looked up. For a few seconds nobody moved. Then the man suddenly turned and ran, pumping his knees high. He ran back on Austin Street to a car parked under the trees on the other side of the railroad station, jumped in, and backed into the next block, 82nd Road—one way, the wrong way. That put him out of sight of Hatch. But in a private house on 82nd Road, Isaac Hartz had also been awakened by the screams. Though a hedge blocked part of his view, he thought the car that had backed into a bus zone in front of his house was a gray or white compact car with a flat grill—maybe a 1960 Rambler.

In front of the card shop now, Kitty was being watched by others besides the Hatches. Some were in the same 7-story building, some in the 16 apartments over the stores, some in the apartment house on the far side of the railroad parking lot. So many eyes were on Kitty as she lay under the yellow street lamp that she might have been spotlighted on a stage. For some of her neighbors she really was. One woman went to the window to see what the screams were about, but could not quite make out the scene below. "Turn off the lights, dumbbell," her husband said, "then you can see." The woman did see better with the lights out. She and her husband pulled chairs up to the windows to watch.

Alone on the street now, though followed by eyes all around, Kitty got up. On the second floor of the Hatches' building, Molly Leffler glanced at her alarm clock. It was exactly 3:20 when Kitty walked slowly back past the card shop, the liquor store, the dry cleaner, and turned the corner toward the back of the stores.

In his apartment building with a side view of the parking lot, Emil Power picked up Kitty where the others had lost her. Power saw Kitty stagger as she rounded the corner. She made it past the first doorway, the entrance to the closed Interlude Coffee House. At the second entrance, a few doors from her own, she slipped inside. The door shut behind her. She may have thought that her friend Harold Kline, the strapping young man who lived upstairs, would come to help her. A woman leaning out her window a few doors down is sure she heard Kitty call Harold's name. She could not get up the stairs. She fell on her back in the narrow stairwell.

Ten minutes later, the neighbors saw the man in the overcoat return. Frances Hatch noticed that he was walking normally as if he didn't have a care in the world. Three floors below, Georgette Share was surprised to see that, while before he had had on a stocking cap, he was now wearing a Tyrolean hat with a feather in the band. Walking slowly, looking from side to side, he peeked into the doorway of the card shop. Nothing. He walked past the liquor store and the dry cleaner and turned the corner. Molly Leffler ran from one to another of her three windows facing Austin Street to keep him in view. He crossed the parking lot without even glancing into the locked Fiat. He gave a push at the door of the waiting room of the Kew Gardens railroad station and found it open. He spent only a minute inside. Emil Power picked up the phone to call the police but his wife Elaine said, "Don't. Thirty people must have called by now." Power saw the man wearing the Tyrolean hat come out of the side door of the Long Island Railroad waiting room and head for the rear walkway. He tried the first doorway, 82-60. Nothing. He went to the second, 86-62. Power held his breath. It had been 12 minutes since the last scream. As the man pushed open the door, only a few neighbors could hear a low cry, too weak for a scream, as the door closed behind him.

The neighbor closest to what was happening to Kitty now was Harold Kline, the young man who lived at the top of the stairs. A poodle-trimmer by profession, he often chatted over a drink with Kitty at her place or his. He had even sold her a poodle. The first attack had come almost right under his window. Now he didn't know what to do. He paced . . . went to the door . . . put his ear to it . . . unbelievable. He mustered his courage, opened the door, shut it quickly, went back to pacing. Should he call the police? Should he do nothing? He called a friend who lived in Nassau County, who advised him to call the police. But from his own phone? He called old Mrs. Lucchese, who lived three doors down. She called Evelyn Lozzi, who lived across the hall from Kitty. Often Ms. Lozzi would come in to answer the phone when Kitty was out. But now what should they all do? Rather than take the stairs and confront the horror in the vestibule, Harold Kline hoisted himself out of his window and scooted across the steep Tudor roof to Mrs. Lucchese's. From there, at 3:55, he called the 102nd Precinct to report that a girl had been attacked. From the time of Kitty's first scream, 35 minutes had elapsed.

The first patrol car from the 102nd swung into the parking lot beside Kitty's Fiat 2 minutes after Kline called. He and the three women now came down. A few minutes later at 4:05, Mitch Sang and Mike Pokstis, the duty detectives from the 102nd squad, pulled up in a black Ford. Kitty was lying where she had fallen—on her back at the bottom of the stairs in 82-62. Her suede jacket and blouse had been ripped open. So had her skirt and underclothing. Kitty was moaning very softly. It looked like a case of rape—until Evelyn Lozzi, who had reached her first, picked up Kitty's head and felt the blood underneath. Kitty was still alive when the ambulance came, but by the time it reached Queens General Hospital, a few minutes before 5 o'clock, she was dead.

Chief. New York: Avon Books, (Abridged from A. A. Seedman and P. Hellman, 1975, pp. 117–121).

4. Once personal responsibility to help has been assumed, the bystander must *decide how to intervene and help*. The basic options are direct and indirect help. It is possible to decide that one has personal responsibility to help and still not be able to decide how to intervene. In the Genovese murder, Harold Kline, the "strapping young man" who knew the victim well, apparently decided that he had some personal responsibility for helping, but was very uncertain about how to help. He opened the door, then shut it, called a distant friend for advice, called Mrs. Lucchese three doors down the hall, and finally crawled out the window and across the roof to Mrs. Lucchese's place where he called the police. Thus he gave indirect help in a very delayed and somewhat erratic fashion.

5. The last decision is how to implement the fourth decision and *carry out the intervention*. Kline's calling the police illustrates this step of the decision process.

Latané and Darley's decision model captures the complexities and confusion involved in an emergency. It also points out that it is not sheer callousness or hard-heartedness that keeps people from helping. Since uncertainty and ambiguity arise at several steps along the way, we might expect immediate situational variables to have a strong effect on helping. In some situations nearly everyone might try to help, but in other situations perhaps no one would help. Thus one should look to situational determinants to explain interventions in emergencies.

Suppose you are in a crowd of people watching some event, perhaps a clown in a shopping center. Suddenly someone just ahead of you moans and sinks slowly to the ground. You are startled and feel your heart begin to beat faster. You notice that several other people are also looking at the collapsed person. They look curious but not really upset. After a moment, they look away and begin watching the clown again. You are uncertain. Perhaps the person is kidding. Maybe it's part of the clown act. The other people did not seem concerned. Anyway, if the collapsed person really does need help, several other people are closer than you are. Even though you feel mildly upset, you also look away and resume watching the clown.

What you don't know is that each of the other people has inwardly gone through the same kind of turmoil that you experienced. They were uncertain about what was happening or what to do. There is a social norm that we should "keep our cool"; therefore all the people present masked their true feelings. But they were observing each other for cues as to how the others felt and how serious they judged the situation. Many people may also have angrily thought, "Why doesn't someone help?"

Everyone present was ignorant about the true reactions of the others in the crowd. Each person used the others as a source of information, but since everyone maintained a calm and collected front, everyone provided a false set of cues. Consequently some people may have defined the situation as a nonemergency; others may have defined it as an emergency but then decided that someone else should be responsible for helping. The situation was such that a DIFFUSION OF RESPONSIBILITY occurred, as each person decided that someone else should be responsible.

Now suppose that you and the person who collapsed were the only two people watching the clown. There are no other bystanders for you to observe to see how they react, and there is obviously no one else present to help except you. Responsibility cannot be diffused elsewhere. Will you help?

Via this reasoning, Latané and Darley arrived at the following dramatic prediction: In an emergency situation, the greater the number of people who are immediately present and could help, the less likely it is that any given one of them will help.

Research testing the model. Three different experimental situations were constructed to test the hypothesis of diffusion of responsibility (Latané and Darley, 1968; Latané and Rodin, 1969; Darley and Latané, 1968).

In the "smoke-filled room" experiment, male graduate and undergraduate students from Columbia University were invited to an interview to discuss problems of life in an urban university. When the students arrived for the experiment, they were seated in a room and started working on a questionnaire. Some of the students were working alone in a room; others were seated in groups of 3. After a few minutes, a cloud of whitish smoke began to pour into the room through a vent in the wall. The purpose of the experiment was to see if subjects would go to get help. The smoke continued to pour into the room for 6 minutes, after which the experiment was terminated if the subjects had not gone for help.

When subjects were alone in the room, most of

Why is it that the passersby do not consider the wino in need of emergency assistance? What factors must exist for someone to recognize a situation as an emergency? (Eugene Richards/ The Picture Cube)

them got up to check out the smoke as soon as they noticed it. During the 6-minute period, 18 of 24 subjects (75 percent) in the alone condition went for help. In the condition wherein there were 3 subjects in the room, the percent going for help was much lower. There were 8 different groups of 3 people, and someone went for help within 6 minutes in only 3 of the groups, a helping rate of only 38 percent. Thus the results confirmed the prediction: helping responses were fewer in groups faced with a potential emergency than among single individuals.

In the "injured lady" experiment, a total of 120 male undergraduate students were recruited for a survey of game and puzzle preferences by the "Consumer Testing Bureau" at Columbia University. Some of the students were asked to bring a friend to the interview. When subjects arrived they were met by a woman, ostensibly a market research representative, who escorted them to a room where they began working on a questionnaire. The woman said that she would work next door in her office while they filled out the forms. She then opened a room divider, went next door, closed the divider behind her but did not lock it, and began busily shuffling materials. The subjects then heard a series of sounds, which were actually on a tape recorder, indicating that a serious accident had occurred. There were sounds of a loud crash and screams as a chair collapsed. The woman said "Oh my God, my foot . . . I . . . I . . . can't move it. Oh . . . my ankle. I . . . can't get this . . . thing . . . off me." The recorded incident went on for 130 seconds. If subjects had not intervened to help by the end of this period, the lady "limped" next door, talked with the subjects, and explained the experiment to them.

The basic independent variable was the composition of the group working on the questionnaire. Some subjects worked alone, others with a friend, others with a stranger who was also a real subject, and others with a stranger who was really a confederate in the experiment and was trained to be nonresponsive to the screams. The percentages of subjects who helped under these conditions were as follows:

Alone	70 percent
Subject with confederate	7 percent
Two strangers	40 percent
Two friends	70 percent

These data clearly show that the composition of the two-person groups had a strong effect on how many people helped. When the other person was a programmed nonresponsive bystander, only 7 percent of the subjects helped, compared to 70 percent when subjects were alone. The percentage increased to 40 percent when both were strangers and to 70 percent when both were friends. Overall, these results indicate that the probability of helping was higher for a single bystander than when two bystanders were present.

In the "epileptic seizure" experiment, subjects were

According to Latané and Darley's theory of bystander intervention, the fewer the number of people at an emergency, the more likely the victim will be assisted. When only a few people are present, it is difficult to diffuse the responsibility for helping.

recruited to serve in a discussion experiment concerned with personal problems in college life. They were told that the discussion would be held over an intercom system with each person in a separate cubicle, in order to avoid personal embarrassment. The subject never saw anyone else, and in fact there were no other people. All the voices that the subject heard were prerecorded. Each subject in the group was supposed to take turns speaking to the others over the intercom microphone. The first voice was that of a person who would shortly become a victim of an epileptic seizure. This subject spoke for 2 minutes. Depending on the condition, either no other voice, 1 other voice, or 3 other voices spoke about their lives prior to the real subject's turn to speak. Thus, from the subject's point of view, he or she was serving in a group-discussion experiment consisting of either 2 persons (self and victim), 3 persons (self, victim, and 1 other), or 6 persons (self, victim and 4 others). During the second round of discussions, the first person had an apparent epileptic seizure while he or she was speaking. Gasping, choking, and requests for help went on for about 2 minutes. If the subject had not left the cubicle to seek help within 6 minutes, the experiment was terminated.

One important aspect of this experiment was that it varied perceived number of other people who could help, while keeping the physical characteristics of the experiment constant across the various conditions. Each subject was alone but thought that others were aware of the situation, except in the condition of two persons, which included only the subject and the seizure victim. This experiment also models, to some extent, the murder of Kitty Genovese. People were in their apartments, separated from other people, but they were probably aware that others were aware that Genovese was in trouble.

The percentages of subjects responding within 6 minutes were as follows:

Two persons (subject and victim)	85 percent
Three persons (subject, victim, and 1 other)	62 percent
Six persons (subject, victim, and 4 others)	31 percent

The larger the perceived size of the group of people who could help, the less likely a subject was to actually leave the cubicle and try to help.

The results across all three experiments represent an impressive bit of social science. Any given study might have had some flaw. Subjects in the smoke-filled room might have viewed themselves as engaged in a game of "chicken," the test being who would go first to report the fire (Latané and Darley, 1970). Such a factor, if it occurred, would give the predicted results for the wrong reasons. This specific artifact could not have occurred in the "injured lady" or "epileptic seizure" studies. The point is that, across the three very different experiments, the results consistently showed that helping was less likely the more people there were available to help. Since these were the predicted results, it seems unlikely that all three sets of data could have been caused by artifacts. Therefore the studies provide good support for Latané and Darley's hypothesis of diffusion of responsibility.

An arousal-reduction approach. Piliavin and Piliavin developed a second theory for bystander intervention. The basic propositions of the theory are as follows (Piliavin, Piliavin, and Rodin, 1975):

   1. Witnessing an emergency creates a state of physiological arousal in the bystander. The more severe the emergency, the stronger the arousal that is created. Also, the closer the bystander is to the emergency, the more similar the bystander is to the victim, and the longer the emergency lasts, the stronger the state of arousal.

   2. Arousal is unpleasant; and the stronger it is and the longer it lasts, the more unpleasant it is. Therefore the bystander will be motivated to reduce the arousal.

   3. The bystander will choose the response that most rapidly and completely reduces the arousal. There are four types of action that can be taken: direct intervention, indirect intervention, leaving the scene with no intervention, and staying at the scene without intervention.

   4. The choice of an action depends on the rewards and costs involved in helping and in not helping. Among the costs associated with helping are effort, embarrassment, and possible harm. Costs involved in not helping include self-blame and possible disapproval from others. Rewards of helping include self-praise and approval from the victim and others. Rewards of not helping include being able to continue with the activities one was engaged in before the emergency arose, avoidance of danger, and avoidance of possible embarrassment. The bystander computes rewards and costs by a kind of unconscious arithmetic, picks the least costly course of action that offers the most arousal reduction, and engages in the action.

This model is different from Latané and Darley's model. The latter is mostly a cognitive, decision-making model, while Piliavin and Piliavin's model is mostly a drive- or arousal-reduction approach. Piliavin and Piliavin conducted several field experiments to test their ideas. For example, Piliavin, Rodin, and Piliavin (1969) had teams of four experimenters travel on subway trains in New York City. Each team consisted of a model, a victim, and two observers who recorded such data as the number of people in the car, their sex, their race, and so forth. The "victim" was always male; one was black and the other three were white. The victim was standing near the front of the car. On some runs, the victim carried a cane; on other runs, he appeared drunk. At a prearranged time, the victim collapsed to the floor and stayed there until either a passenger or the model came to help. The model came to help only after a minimum of 70 seconds had passed.

The results were quite surprising when compared to Latané and Darley's studies. Usually people came to the victim's aid so fast that the model had no chance to intervene. Help was given on 100 percent of the trials, except when the victim was black and appeared drunk. In that case help was given on 73 percent of the trials. Another study (Piliavin and Piliavin, 1972), also conducted on the subway, varied whether or not blood came out of the victim's mouth, and a third study (Piliavin, Piliavin, and Rodin, 1975) varied whether the victim had a (fake) port wine stain birthmark on the face. The results of the second and third studies were comparable to the results of the first study. There was no diffusion of responsibility; people helped regardless of the number of people in the situation. It is an interesting apparent contradiction of results from two major research programs on bystander intervention. One resolution will be discussed in the next section.

WHEN WILL BYSTANDERS HELP?

One clear difference between the approach of Latané and Darley and that of the Piliavins is that in the former studies, the subjects clearly knew they were in an experiment. Subjects in the Piliavins' experiments did not know that an experiment was going on; it was real life. Evaluation apprehension, suspicion of deception, and the like (see Chapter 2) may prevent subjects from helping in a laboratory experiment. For example, in the alone condition of Latané and Darley's experiments, 70 to 85 percent of the subjects helped, which means that 15 to 30 percent of the alone subjects did nothing. If subjects had been in the same situation but did not know that it was an experiment, it is possible that helping would have approached 100 percent, as it did in the Piliavins' studies.

Another difference between the two approaches concerns the degree of ambiguity in the situation. Darley and Latané's studies were constructed to simulate the uncertainty and ambiguity experienced by the witnesses to the murder of Kitty Genovese. In contrast, there was almost no ambiguity in the situation the Piliavins used—a person obviously collapsed and was in need. It was not possible to define the situation as a nonemergency. Given that fact and the fact that it was a real-life situation, there was apparently very little diffusion of responsibility among the bystanders.

One interesting possibility is that bystanders' reactions in an emergency work to influence other bystanders in the direction of helping. We noted previously how norms for "keeping cool" might keep everyone ignorant of everyone else's feelings and prevent helping. However, in the dramatic situation created by a person collapsing in a subway car, witnesses might gasp, show startle responses, and so on. Each bystander would be aware of some of the others' startled responses, and this awareness should aid the process of quickly defining the situation as an emergency. Darley, Teger, and Lewis (1973) tested this possibility in an experiment in which subjects were working alone, in pairs facing each other, or in pairs facing away from each other. Subjects heard a crash and scream for help from next door. In the alone condition, 90 percent of the subjects went to help. In the condition of pairs facing away from each other, one of the subjects tried to help in only 20 percent of the cases. When subject pairs were directly facing each other, one or both subjects tried to help in 80 percent of the cases. Apparently the startle response from the crash and scream cued off the need for help when subjects faced each other. As the authors point out, the face-to-face condition was most similar to the seating arrangements on the subway in the Piliavins' studies showing a high rate of helping (Darley, Teger, and Lewis, 1973). Thus the reactions of a crowd can sometimes promote a helping response, but they can hinder helping at other times.

Helping in nonemergency situations

TO HELP OR NOT TO HELP

We have been looking at the way people help or do not help others in emergency situations, and much of the available literature focuses on this aspect of helping behavior. If someone faints, chokes, or goes into cardiac arrest, we expect certain kinds of behavior to occur. If we see someone being attacked or hear a woman screaming "rape," we may be a bit less sure about the appropriate response. But aside from dramatic, uncommon, emergency situations, how and why does altruistic behavior occur in everyday life? Bar-Tal (1976) views a nonemergency situation as (1) not involving threatened or real harm to person and property, (2) a common daily event, (3) a clear situation wherein appropriate action is obvious, and (4) a situation wherein planned and not immediate action is required. If we accept this definition, many situations that we encounter every day offer opportunities for altruism.

Awareness. In making a judgment about whether or not to help in a given situation, we must first be aware of the situation itself. For example, Bob is sitting at the kitchen table reading a magazine when his wife, Jean, gets home from the grocery store. He continues reading while Jean carries in several heavy grocery bags and reacts with surprise when Jean later criticizes him for not helping her. To meet a need we must first be aware of it, and like many of us, Bob is often quite unaware.

Assigning responsibility. If we become aware of a given need, we often look at the situation and try to assign responsibility for it. We try to determine what caused the situation before we decide whether or not to intervene. Is a person who is in need of help an innocent victim, or did he or she get himself or herself into this mess? Individuals are usually more willing to aid someone whose situation arose from factors beyond his or her control than someone whose problems are his or her own fault (Schopler and Matthews, 1965). People are also more willing to help others when they are not coerced to do so. Berkowitz (1972) proposed that an unwillingness to help due to coercion may be induced by reactance (Brehm, 1966) generated by the helper's perception of restrictions on his or her freedom.

Costs and benefits. Another factor in the initial decision to help or not to help is the cost–benefit analysis of the situation, which we discussed earlier in the context of equity theory. As Worchel and Cooper (1976) point out, the likelihood of helpful behavior increases as the need increases, until one reaches the point at which the physical or psychological cost to the helper becomes too great. The helpful behavior may decrease when this occurs, no matter what the perceived need.

We have discussed awareness of a need for help, determination of responsibility for the need, and analysis of the costs and benefits in meeting the need. However, these factors alone do not determine whether an individual will help in a given nonemergency situation. We must look further at both the personality and situational factors that affect this type of helping behavior.

WHAT MAKES A GOOD SAMARITAN?

What makes some people help and not others? Why do people help in some situations and not in others? Various researchers have studied the relationship between helping behavior and variables such as sex, race, age, and personality characteristics of the helper.

Sex, race, and personality variables. Although some studies (Gaertner and Bickman, 1971) found sex differences in helping, with males offering help more frequently and for a longer duration than females, other studies (Gruder and Cook, 1971) failed to find such differences. Bar-Tal (1976) notes that studies that do not involve sex-typed tasks reveal no sex differences in responses of helpers, while research involving traditionally "masculine" helping behavior elicits more responses from males. Since affective, interpersonal-relations tasks have traditionally been identified as "feminine," an interesting research question might look at whether females engage in more altruistic behaviors of an affective nature than do males.

Some researchers have found racial factors relevant to altruistic behavior, while other researchers have not. West, Whitney, and Schnedler (1975) found that black victims were helped faster in a black neighborhood, while white victims were helped faster in a white neighborhood. In another situation, whites showed more racial bias in their helping behavior than blacks. Wegner and Crano (1975) found the opposite, however, with black bystanders helping more black than white victims and white bystanders helping both races equally.

Numerous investigators have tried to establish relationships between specific personality factors and helping behavior. Although some studies (Berkowitz and Daniels, 1964) suggested a positive relationship between altruism and a general variable called social responsibility, Gergen, Gergen, and Meter (1972), in their attempt to relate ten trait dispositions to given altruistic acts, found no consistent relationship patterns and no good trait predictors of actions.

According to research by Carlsmith and Gross (1969), guilt may be a motivator toward altruistic action, since subjects who believed they had harmed someone else volunteered their time more readily than subjects who believed they had not harmed anyone. Guilt may motivate a person to help someone else, but it will probably be someone other than the individual whom the actor may have injured originally (Freedman, Wallington, and Bless, 1967).

A personality variable that has been looked at frequently in connection with helping behavior is empathy. We might consider empathy as the helper's attempt to put himself or herself into the victim's shoes to feel what the victim feels. Hornstein (1970) looked at empathic behavior on a more behavioral level, however, and found that empathy with a third person could actually facilitate altruistic behavior from the altruist to the victim. Finally, Krebs (1975) ascertained that experimental subjects who reacted most empathically behaved most altruistically.

Research on personality factors and helping behavior is disparate and often contradictory, but most researchers agree that a helper's moods and feelings do affect helping behavior.

Moods and feelings. Several efforts have been made to show that a person's good mood can increase his or her altruistic behavior, while a bad mood can decrease altruism. Berkowitz and Connor (1966) conducted an experiment in which subjects had an experience of either success or failure, presumably precipitating a good or a bad mood, respectively. They were then asked to work for someone who was either slightly or very dependent on them. It was found that the successful subjects worked harder in both high- and low-dependency conditions than did failure subjects or controls. In another experiment, Isen, Clark, and Schwartz (1976) found that for a brief time subjects who were put in a good mood by receiving a small gift were more helpful than control subjects. In another, widely cited mood experiment, Isen and Levin (1972) induced increased helping behavior in experimental subjects by giving them free cookies and arranging for them to find a free dime in the coin return of a public telephone during the experiment.

Perhaps the best evidence of the effect of mood on altruism can be gained from our own personal experience. If we've just gotten an A grade on an exam and are on our way to a party, we are presumably more likely to loan a friend $5 than if we have just gotten an F on the exam and need to study all evening for a make-up test. Many personality factors that influence helping are in turn affected by situational factors that originate in the external environment.

SITUATIONAL DETERMINANTS OF HELPING

Social norms. Social norms—the socially responsible, socially acceptable rules by which individuals operate—have been assumed to be quite powerful in influencing altruistic behavior, and several studies on them have been conducted. One early experiment (Berkowitz, 1957) indicated that a subject was more likely to work hard when both he and his partner could get a valuable prize than when only one of them could get the prize. Since one might propose that a desire for approval rather than a feeling of interdependency was the motivating factor, several experiments (Berkowitz and Daniels, 1963) varied both the experimenter's and the helpee's awareness of the helper's actions. Results confirmed that people worked harder to help other people who were greatly dependent on them and that these helpers were not influenced by the prospect of immediate or deferred social approval for their actions. In this situation, a person was more influenced by his or her internal norms or rules than by possible external influences. In discussing values and norms, it is useful to distinguish between wanting to do the *right* thing and wanting to help someone else (Staub, 1974), since different motivations may lead to different courses of action.

In most discussions of social norms and social responsibility, writers have looked at the powerful influence of dependency, or the degree to which a needful person is dependent on the altruist for help. The more dependent an individual is on someone else, the more likely he or she is to receive help. This formula for behavior works sometimes, though it is influenced by the rewards and costs of helping, as we pointed out earlier. Bar-Tal (1976) makes the point that we are often but not always more inclined to help when someone's dependency on us increases.

Modeling. Another situational factor influencing altruistic behavior is modeling, which we discussed earlier. Various experiments (Wheeler and Wagner, 1968) have demonstrated that a generous or helpful model increases generosity and helpfulness in a subject. Also, Wispe and Freshley (1971) found that an extremely unhelpful and even cynical model could inspire greater generosity and altruism in a subject. Perhaps the negative model violates so many social norms that an observer is motivated to do the opposite. Other studies have looked at the interesting inverse relationship between negative modeling and altruistic behavior. Explanations have included norm violation, sympathy for the helpee, guilt within the helper, and the cost–reward aspects of not helping, which a negative model can demonstrate.

Individuals can effectively model altruistic behavior for themselves. A number of studies (Freedman and Fraser, 1966) have indicated that when someone has complied with a small request, he or she is more likely to comply with a larger one. We called this the "foot-in-the-door" phenomenon in Chapter 9, and experiments on it have yielded fairly consistent results. When a person has been helpful in a small way, he or she is more likely to be helpful again.

An individual is more likely to help someone who has previously been helpful to him or her (Berkowitz, 1972). Whether we are more attracted to someone who has helped us, or whether we have a need for equity and want to balance the ledger with someone who has previously helped us, we are likely to help someone by whom we have already been helped.

Although personality characteristics and situational characteristics of helping are often intertwined, it is useful to consider the two influences separately. We shall now examine research on the helpee or recipient to see which factors are most influential in gaining help from someone else.

CHARACTERISTICS OF THE RECIPIENT OF HELP

Demographic characteristics. Sex, race, and similarity are three factors that have been studied in connection with the recipient of help. Females are more likely to be helped than males in most situations. The sex-role norms of our society are probably largely responsible for this result, because dependency is much more acceptable for females than for males. It will be interesting to see if this holds true in the future, as women become equal participants in both the rights and responsibilities of the society.

As we have seen, only a few studies have been concerned with race and helping, but these studies have shown that people are often more likely to help others of the same race. This appears to be less a function of racial attitudes, however, than a tendency for individuals to help others who are similar to themselves (Bar-Tal, 1976), for similarity has been shown to have a positive effect on helping.

Attractiveness. One of the most influential characteristics in human relationships is attractiveness, and many studies have examined this variable. It appears that physically attractive people are liked more, are more sought after socially, are credited with more intelligence and greater achievement potential, and are generally evaluated more positively under most circumstances than less attractive people. Some recent research on attractiveness as it affects helping was conducted by Benson, Karabenick, and Lerner

(1976), who looked at the specific task of helping to deliver a graduate school application ostensibly lost by a traveler in an airport. A picture attached to the application varied the attractiveness, sex, and race of the target or helpee. The researchers found that physical attractiveness did influence helping behavior. Attractive targets were helped more often than unattractive targets regardless of target sex or race.

We turn now to one of the most emotion-laden factors in the helping process—the feelings of the recipient of help. What is it like to be dependent and need help? What is it like to feel powerless?

SOMETIMES IT'S HARD TO BE GRATEFUL

More and more in recent years, writers have looked at the recipients of help as significant factors in any helping interaction. In fact, a review article by Gergen (1974) suggests that it might be profitable to develop a comprehensive psychology of receiving help. In reviewing the literature, he proposed several variables influencing the recipient. We will examine some of these variables.

The recipient's view of the helping process. The recipient's perceptions of the helper are extremely important. Gergen and Gergen (1974) found that positive attributions about a helper were associated with positive final evaluations of the helper and his or her actions, while negative attributions resulted in negative evaluations. In another instance, they found that negative attributions were made when the recipient saw the helper as having a specific purpose or an ulterior motive. It is easier to request help when it is offered voluntarily (Broll, Gross, and Piliavin, 1974), and it is easier to accept it from a friend than from an enemy. Fisher and Nadler (1974) found that receiving aid from a person who was very similar to the recipient had negative effects on a recipient's self-esteem and self-confidence in a given situation, while help from a dissimilar other actually increased esteem and confidence. Clark, Gotay, and Mills (1974) found that aid was more acceptable from a similar other when the opportunity existed to reciprocate the altruistic behavior, but when no opportunity for reciprocation was expected, dissimilar others became more acceptable helpers. Recipients find help less acceptable and more ego-threatening when it is offered by someone who is quite powerful (Fisher and Nadler, 1976). An interesting finding of Fisher and Nadler's study was that recipients who felt threatened by the help (high-resource helper) did more to help themselves than recipients who did not feel threatened. Perhaps some amount of ego threat is positively related to independence and achievement. One can see that many factors influence a recipient's attitude toward helping and the helper.

Recipient characteristics. Although little work has focused solely on recipient personality characteristics, Nadler, et al. (1974) found that individuals high in self-esteem reacted differently from low-esteem individuals when they were in the position of receiving help. High-esteem individuals found aid from a similar person more threatening than did low-esteem individuals and were also less likely to even ask for help in certain situations.

Context characteristics. Context characteristics include the helper, nature of the benefit, and recipient characteristics that we have just discussed. Individuals prefer to accept help from someone who volunteers it, from someone who is not too powerful, or from someone whom they can help in turn. People with high self-esteem receive help differently from people with low self-esteem, and people who believe that asking for help is an admission of failure are less likely to seek help than those for whom the help does not have such connotations (Morris and Rosen, 1973). When helping itself and the whole notion of reciprocating the helping become intertwined with a recipient's feelings of self-worth, of capability, and of control over his or her life and environment, the helping context can become a very threatening and hostile one. Witness the animosity of the welfare recipient to the social worker, the mistrust of the poor South American farmer toward the Peace Corps volunteer, and the resentment that can occur even in families when a successful family member gives financial help to someone in the family who hasn't "made it." It is clear that the complexity surrounding the helper and the helping process extends to the recipient as well.

Organized helping
By Susan Singer Hendrick

Americans have long been recognized as entrepreneurial wizards with a tendency to organize every aspect of their society. We have organized our businesses, industries, schools, government, and even our recreation, so it is no great surprise that we also have organized our ways of helping people. Our mode of organizing has basically channeled helping into two categories: volunteer helping (usually called VOLUNTARISM) and paid helping, which includes social service agencies, welfare departments, and private and governmental programs of all types. Both of these approaches have precedents which developed relatively early in Western history.

VOLUNTARISM

The history of voluntarism. Many writers, such as Manser and Cass (1976), view voluntarism as having two origins: the Greek and Roman tradition, wherein powerful social reform was brought about by the community as a whole, and the Judeo-Christian tradition, which emphasized the religious and moral necessity of one individual helping another individual. The secular tradition died out for a time, and during the Middle Ages, the Church was the only organized force for person-to-person helping. After the Reformation in Europe, the Church could no longer assume the awesome burden of helping the general populace, so Poor Laws were enacted in England. Eventually the Industrial Revolution stimulated the need for additional reforms and greater aid, and government was once again deeply involved in organized helping. The United States was particularly influenced by the Depression in the 1930s. From that time to the present, the two threads—social reform and individualized charity—have become even more intertwined and have greatly affected voluntarism in Western society.

How widespread is voluntarism? Voluntarism is big business. It involves the time and the money of a vast number of individuals in many countries throughout the world (Graham, 1974). And of course it occurs daily in every sector of our society. There are over 7 million volunteer groups in the United States, and writers have estimated that 1 out of every 4 Americans over the age of 13 does some kind of volunteer work (Manser and Cass, 1976). Manser and Cass estimate that about 50 percent of the time volunteered is spent in church-related work, another 30 percent in health and education, and the rest in civic and citizenship activities, recreational pursuits, and social welfare and political endeavors. The sheer quantity of volunteer time (for which society would otherwise have to pay a high price) is overwhelming. In addition to the savings incurred from all this freely donated time, actual contributions to volunteer organizations and related endeavors total approximately $25.15 billion annually, or about 1.8 percent of the United States' gross national product. Logical questions that follow any discussion of the massive impact of voluntarism on society concern the volunteer as an individual actor. Who volunteers? Why do people volunteer? What kinds of things do volunteers do?

The volunteer. Both voluntary associations and volunteers themselves vary. Many sociological studies of volunteer participation have been conducted, and the nearly unanimous opinion among researchers is that social class significantly affects participation, perhaps more than any other single factor (Smith and Freedman, 1972). Individuals in lower socioeconomic groups participate less. In fact, Stern and Nol (1973) found that upwardly mobile people participate more than nonmobile people. The individual influences of finances, status, education, and class norms all contribute to the differentiation between middle- and lower-class participation.

Women don't necessarily participate more than men, but they do participate differently. Women tend to be members more often than designated leaders in mixed-sex voluntary groups. They also tend to hold fewer board positions. Voluntarism usually declines with age; older people are harder to activate and thus are less active. Perhaps this trend will change as increasing numbers of older people make their presence felt in the society. Little work has been done on personality factors as they affect volunteers, though Smith and Freedman (1972) cite a study suggesting that volunteers have less need for autonomy than nonvolunteers.

Various studies have dealt with racial and ethnic factors that influence voluntarism, and several have found that blacks participate proportionately more than whites and that Hispanic Americans participate considerably less than either of these other groups (Smith and Freedman, 1972; Kutner, 1976). All these groups participate to some extent, however. Volunteers are heterogeneous.

ARE VOLUNTEERS ALTRUISTIC?

Bar-Tal (1976) states that altruism involves voluntary behavior and benefits another with no expectation of external reward for the altruist. The church school teacher, the Little League coach, and the person who collects door-to-door for a charity are all giving of themselves without thought of external profit, though there may be numerous internal rewards.

First of all, voluntarism can be viewed as an exchange process. Such things as skill training, status, working with professionals, and gratitude or recognition can all serve to balance the sacrifices inherent in volunteering. In addition, self-reward may be a powerful motivator for volunteers.

Voluntarism can also be thought of as a normative behavior. Volunteering always involves giving of one's time, money, or energy, so it may be an appropriate act for someone to whom giving is a rule of personal or social behavior. The norm of social responsibility is probably equally likely in this case of altruism, because volunteers are usually responsible citizens who feel a commitment to maintain or possibly improve their society. The very fact that so many people volunteer may be both a result and a cause of social norms supporting voluntarism.

Frequency of volunteering may also be related to the developmental approach to altruism, which emphasizes learning and modeling. Parents' altruistic behavior has been shown to be positively related to children's subsequent altruistic behavior (Middlebrook, 1974), so modeling apparently does operate in this area of life. Perhaps the prevalence of voluntarism offers frequent opportunities for people to learn that volunteer work is a valued and respected type of human behavior.

ALTRUISM BOUGHT AND PAID FOR

One cannot always discern a clear dividing line between voluntarism and paid helping, since financial factors are important to both and since volunteers and paid professionals are essential to the successful functions of both types of activity. In this section, we will refer to the aid given various types of needful clients by public and private social service agencies as paid helping.

Historical development in the United States.

Historically, it has been difficult for society to strike a balance between necessary social service that allows an individual to develop more fully and happily and the kind of dole or handout that fosters dependency and inertia.

Many examples of both kinds of "altruism" have been offered by our own government. Social Security legislation was developed to aid citizens in building a secure retirement, so that they could be self-sustaining when they were no longer employed. Franklin Roosevelt's domestic work programs, such as the W. P. A., were designed to get unemployed people working again and to allow people self-respect and a sense of accomplishment. Roosevelt's program was intended to be a help, not a handout, and it contrasts with the monolithic welfare system of our present day.

Other government programs that might be labeled altruistic include the Peace Corps and day-care centers. In the Peace Corps, an American is designated to work with a group of people in another country. By teaching and working, the volunteer transfers knowledge that promotes self-sufficiency and growth—values that do not necessarily accompany a straight gift of seed, fertilizer, or a plow. Similarly, day-care centers are designed to make it easier for parents to be self-supporting.

Paid altruism has proliferated throughout the twentieth century. From a pioneer society that prized independence and self-sufficiency has emerged a society that encourages one segment of the citizenry to take responsibility for another, less fortunate segment. One of the prime motives for this developing perspective seems to be a norm of social responsibility. Unfortunately, this norm sometimes seems to be mandated by income taxes rather than strictly voluntary. Although some motives for paid altruism are humanitarian ones, the social service agencies that offer paid altruism are also institutions that seek to perpetuate themselves.

Thus paid altruism presents us with some discrepancies. Does it promote individual welfare and growth, or does it foster dependency and inertia? Does it continue to develop because society wants greater egalitarianism and a better life for all, or does it grow because it is self-perpetuating and because no organization will willingly disband? We will explore these

Modern society has organized many professional helping services, such as hospitals, police, and firefighters. The work is often grim and poignant, as illustrated by the fireman attempting to revive a young victim of an early morning fire. (Wide World Photo)

questions as we briefly discuss the paid helping offered by community mental health centers.

The community mental health center. Although the concept of community psychiatry has been around for decades, responsibility for dealing with individuals experiencing mental disorders was haphazardly assumed by state and local agencies until World War II, when the large numbers of military recruits rejected for service because of psychiatric problems brought mental illness to public attention (Coleman, 1976).

The federal government then intervened and in 1946 created the National Institute of Mental Health (NIMH), which was supposed to emphasize both research and service, the latter primarily in the form of training and consultation for agencies to be set up in the field. In 1969, NIMH was instrumental in the passage of the Community Mental Health Centers Act, which provided for construction and staffing of comprehensive mental health centers all over the country (Coleman, 1976). Although the federal government has continued to provide massive funding for these centers, individual states and local areas provide additional funds, and the centers are urged to collect fees for services whenever possible.

Community mental health centers offer traditional one-to-one therapy, and new trends include marital and group therapy, supportive partial hospitalization programs, community education for adults, and consultation with other community institutions. General accountability to the community as well as to funding agencies is a current issue for mental health centers (Bloom, 1973).

As it has moved from an earlier, more isolated position to its present involvement in the community, the mental health center has changed its pattern of altruism. In the early years of this movement, service was given to only a few people, but services have been more widely offered in recent years, promoting greater helping as well as greater financial pressures. In order to survive, community mental health centers, like other social service agencies have become more concerned with costs and (sometimes out of necessity) less concerned with quality service. The emphasis on accountability can make agencies more responsive to public needs and less able to function in an "ivory tower"—hence the shift from individual to group therapy—but many agencies are not organized along efficient business lines. New services are added while outmoded ones are retained. Some centers have even gone bankrupt, both because the flow of federal dollars has been drastically stemmed in recent years and because sophisticated management is virtually unknown in such centers (Wray, 1978). Sometimes the strong altruistic, service orientation of the community mental health center seems diametrically opposed to the practical business techniques that could help make the best use of community funds.

Mental health centers present us with several dilemmas. Self-maintenance of the agency seems to be as important as service to the client. Valuable help is given, but often inefficiently and at high financial cost. Many individuals and families are probably helped by such centers, but still other individuals seem to use mental health services to avoid responsibility and maintain dependency. Paid altruism is a complex phenomenon that cannot automatically be labeled "good" but must rather be examined from many different perspectives.

Summary

Altruism or helping, as we have referred to it in this chapter, is a complex social response that is voluntary, intended to benefit another person, performed without expectation of reward, and performed with some degree of empathy for the other person. Helping incurs both costs and benefits, and various theories have been offered to explain altruistic behavior.

Altruism does not appear to be instinctive but is learned during the course of development. There are two general theoretical approaches to altruism. One approach tries to account for altruism as a type of reciprocity behavior. This approach includes exchange theory, equity theory, the reciprocity norm, the justice motive, and indebtedness theory. The other general theoretical approach includes social-norm theories such as the norm of giving and the norm of social responsibility. No one theory, however, provides a comprehensive explanation of altruism.

The study of helping in emergency situations and the study of helping in nonemergency situations have tended to develop as separate literatures with different research traditions. The study of helping in emergency situations was prompted by the murder of Kitty Genovese in 1964. Although 38 people witnessed the murder, none intervened to help. This startling fact stimulated several social psychologists to examine emergency helping. Latané and Darley (1970) proposed a "diffusion of responsibility" hypothesis predicting that the more people who potentially could help in a given situation, the less likely that any one person actually would help. Piliavin and Piliavin (1972) developed a different theory based on notions of drive reduction and reward–cost analysis.

Helping in nonemergency situations depends on many variables. We have looked at studies dealing with demographic and personality characteristics of the helper and have seen that similarity to the helpee, positive mood states, and perception of helpee dependence all increase helping. We have noted that such helpee characteristics as physical attractiveness also affect helping. The emotional impact of helping on the recipient of the help has recently been considered in the literature. Help can be aversive if it is given grudgingly or if it represents to the recipient a loss of control over his or her life.

Social psychology has studied altruism or helping primarily as an individual social behavior. However, helping has been organized at the level of social institutions in modern societies. We have discussed organized helping in the context of voluntarism, so important to our quality of life, and in the context of paid helping, which has both positive and negative impacts on our society.

11

Aggression

306
What is aggression?

The components of aggression
   Physical aspects of aggression
   Emotion
   Intention
   Personality disposition
   Social consensus
A definition of aggression

310
Conceptions of aggression: Instinct, drive, and social learning

Aggression as instinctive behavior
   Psychoanalytic theory
   Ethology and aggression
Aggression as drive: Does frustration cause aggression?
   Statement of the hypothesis
   Problems with the hypothesis
The revised frustration-aggression hypothesis
Aggression as a learned social behavior

317
Personality and individual differences in aggression

Are males more aggressive than females?
   Animals
   Humans
Genetic effects in aggression
Personality dispositions in aggression
   Personality dimensions in aggression
   What makes really violent people violent?

319 Situational and environmental factors in aggression

Experimental methods for studying aggression
   The Buss (1961) technique
   The Berkowitz (1962) technique
   The Taylor (1967) technique
Environmental factors in aggression
   Attack from another person
   The effects of noise
   The effect of heat
   The effect of crowding
   Alcohol and aggression
   Does presence of guns cause aggression?
Is television a cause of violence?
   Violence on television
   The effects of television on aggression
   The catharsis hypothesis

327 Forms of violence in society

Violence against individuals
   Crimes of violence
   Rape
Violence in the family
   Child abuse
   Wife battering
Violence as a social control mechanism: The Mafia
Large-scale violence

332 Control and prevention of aggression

Punishment
Nonaggressive models
Cognitive factors
Social change as prevention

333
Summary

The fact is that men are very dangerous to each other. They can at once want and not want to harm each other mortally. (Hallie, 1969)

On May 4, 1970, a group of Ohio National Guardsmen on the campus of Kent State University fired their rifles into a large crowd of milling students, killing four of them. This incident riveted the attention of the country. Many people were horrified, but equally as many were gratified and stated that even more students should have been killed (Johnson, 1972). The world seemed to have run amok, and civilized life as we knew it seemed temporarily suspended.

The violence at Kent State was unique in some respects, yet it is just one of literally millions of such episodes in human history. To actually experience such an episode is to know that the peaceful fabric of the social order is very fragile. Murder and other violent acts can apparently occur at almost any time in any setting. Since very few of us would claim to prefer violence—indeed, it is usually horrifying—why does it occur so frequently? Do human beings, as Hallie implies, have a dark side that really wants to maim and kill?

Aggression is a basic fact of social life. The purpose of this chapter is to explore this aspect of social behavior, to ponder why humans are aggressive and in what ways, and to ask whether aggression can be controlled.

What is aggression?

It would be satisfying to define aggression succinctly and proceed from that point to discuss it. Unfortunately, aggression cannot be simply defined. As a term used in everyday life, it has many, often contradictory meanings. Like beauty, aggression is sometimes in the eye of the beholder. Even social scientists who specialize in aggression do not agree on a definition. Some approach aggression from the point of view of society and vast disturbances such as war, while others view aggression as a behavioral process within the individual. Our concern in this chapter will be fairly broad, including both individual and collective approaches to aggression. In this section, we will first consider some examples of aggression and then discuss its more important components. Finally, we will adopt a tentative definition of aggression.

One way to approach aggression is to ponder whether given behaviors are aggresive. Consider the following examples:

1. Joe is an avid hunter with many shotguns and rifles. He hunts rabbits, quail, and deer, always in season, and he always obeys the hunting laws. Joe loves hunting, considers it a great sport, and agrees with an article title in the magazine *American Rifleman*, "Happiness is a warm gun" (Johnson, 1972). Is Joe basically an aggressive person?

2. Joan and George have been married for five years. They argue frequently and occasionally shout angrily at each other. On the last occasion, Joan became so enraged that she was almost beside herself. She lunged at George and slapped his face with all her strength. George looked stunned and was momentarily dazed. He snarled, clenched his fist, and smashed Joan in the face, breaking her nose. Were Joan and George aggressing against each other when they were merely quarreling? When they were shouting angrily at each other? Was the slap aggression? Was George's punch also aggression? Was George justified in retaliating?

3. Anna was finishing her Christmas shopping in a large mall and left the mall for her car in the parking lot about dusk. As she unlocked her car, a man grabbed her from behind and shoved her into the car. Anna began to scream but was stopped by a sharp slap and the threat "Be quiet or I'll kill you!" The intruder then roughly ripped off her clothes and forcibly raped her. Granted that the slap and perhaps the threat are

Prosocial and antisocial behavior

Groups in confrontation: May 4, 1970. The Ohio National Guard confronts student protesters at Kent State University. (Kent State University News Service)

examples of aggression, was the sexual activity involved in the rape also aggression?

4. Jake was the state's legal executioner for 19 years. In that role, he closed the switch on the electric chair for 38 condemned men and 4 women. Were Jake's actions aggressive?

5. Charlie borrowed his father's handgun, drove to a remote area, left a note absolving the world (and his father) for the miseries of his existence, and killed himself. Is suicide a type of self-aggression?

These examples suggest some of the problems involved in deciding when an action is aggressive. If the class were to vote on each of the five examples, there would undoubtedly be some disagreement on every one.

THE COMPONENTS OF AGGRESSION

The examples we have considered raise several questions about the components of aggression.

1. Is aggression an overt physical act?
2. Is strong emotion, such as anger, part of aggression?
3. Must aggression be intended, or can it sometimes be accidental?
4. Is aggression part of the personality of an individual?
5. Does labeling an act as aggression depend on a shared social consensus among a group of people?

Physical aspects of aggression. Some scholars define aggression primarily in physical terms. For example, Buss (1961) viewed aggression as the attempt of one individual to deliver noxious stimulation to another individual. But consider the following list of activities:

1. A dream about hurting someone
2. A fantasy about hurting someone
3. A cold, "overpolite" response to a person
4. A frown or cold stare directed toward someone
5. Gossiping with someone about a third person
6. A serious argument
7. Screams and yells at another
8. Attempts to physically hit or otherwise hurt another person (such as throwing rocks)
9. Attempts to maim another person (such as shooting or stabbing)
10. Physical injury to another resulting in death

This sequence of activities increases progressively in the amount of direct physical action. All of these activities may be considered aggression, though most people would consider the last three the most serious by far. All five examples that we presented earlier involved physical force or harm of one kind or another. Although it is reasonable, depending on one's purpose, to define any of the activities on our list as aggression, the most important forms of aggression do involve overt physical behavior.

Emotion. Given that a variety of behaviors may be considered aggressive, does a single type of emotion or several types of emotion accompany aggression? Does one have to be angry? Or must one experience any emotion at all to commit aggression? In the past, it was conventional to distinguish between angry or hostile aggression and instrumental aggression. ANGRY AGGRESSION is action pursued with the aim of harming or injuring another person. INSTRUMENTAL AGGRESSION has some goal or aim other than aggression, which is only a means to an end. For example, the "hit man" who carefully plans murders is committing instrumental aggression. The fight between Joan and George, on the other hand, is a clear instance of angry aggression.

Both instrumental and angry aggression are goal-directed, and in both the aggression is intended. We may conclude that anger or any other particular emotional state is not a necessary component of aggression. Angry arousal may sometimes lead to aggression, but a given act of aggression may or may not be accompanied by anger.

Intention. One can cause great harm without intending to do so. The concepts of negligence and recklessness recognize the possibility of unintended harm, which is not usually called aggression. When harm is intended, we usually do define the act as aggressive. We must be careful to emphasize that the object of the intention is *harm*. This is not the same as pain. A parent spanking a child intends to administer pain but does not usually intend to harm the child. Indeed, the parent usually feels that mild punishment will help the child mature properly.

The factor of intention was operating in each situation we described. Joe, the avid hunter, intended to kill animals; Joan intended to hurt George; the rapist intended to harm Anna; Jake intended to execute condemned prisoners; and Charlie intended self-destruction.

The focus and strength of the intent to cause harm may be disproportionate to the harm inflicted. For example, one may intend only to "rough up" an opponent and be quite surprised to learn that the opponent died. Conversely, murder may be intended but the bullet may miss. In some cases, the intent to harm may be carefully disguised—possibly even from oneself. In the latter case, it might make sense to speak of an unconscious intention to aggress. But regardless of the rough fit between intention and act, we would ordinarily say that a given act is aggression only if there is an intention to inflict harm. If no such intention exists, aggression cannot occur.

Personality disposition. Sometimes an individual is described as an aggressive person. Such a description implies that aggression is a personality trait that is part of the person to a greater or lesser degree. Joe the hunter is an instance of this conception. Hunting is a culturally conditioned activity. At one point in the history of the country, nearly everyone hunted to obtain food. But Joe hunts and kills purely for sport. It is legal, and Joe is joined by literally millions of other hunters on the first day of every new hunting season. For nonhunters, there is a vague feeling that Joe may be manifesting hidden aggression or an aggressive personality, that, if not given outlet in killing defenseless animals, might explode in the killing of humans. Most hunters would not, of course, accept this interpretation of their hunting behavior. We will consider aggression as a personality trait in a later section.

Social consensus. A given act may be considered aggressive in one society but not in another. Such variation across societies indicates that what is defined as aggression depends on a shared consensus among members of a society. The rape of Anna is an example of change in social conceptions. Fifty years ago, rape would not have been considered an act of aggression. Today it is increasingly viewed as an aggressive act, sex being the means for committing the aggression.

Charlie's suicide was clearly a violent act, and perhaps it could be called self-aggression. It is viewed as morally wrong in most Western societies, though there is a growing opinion that under some conditions (such as terminal illnesses), one should have the right to take one's own life. The act of legal execution is also clearly a violent act, but by social definition it is not wrong. For such acts, there is usually a great deal of ritual and an exactly prescribed method of procedure.

A DEFINITION OF AGGRESSION

The following definition was adopted by a distinguished scholar on aggression (Baron, 1977). AGGRESSION is any form of behavior directed toward the goal of harming or injuring another living being who is motivated to avoid such treatment. This definition has several interesting properties. Let us examine them separately.

1. *Any form of behavior.* This aspect of the definition allows a wide variety of acts, ranging from passive–imaginal to overt.
2. *Directed toward the goal.* Both goal direction and intention on the part of the aggressor are implied.
3. *Of harming or injuring.* The object of the goal is clearly specified as harm or injury, as opposed to pain. The slaughter of animals for food would be exempt, because there is no desire to harm as such, even though death occurs. Hunting for pleasure is an ambiguous case. It would probably be considered aggression.
4. *Another living being.* Although Baron is primarily concerned with human aggression, the phrasing allows for animal aggression and human–animal aggression.
5. *Who is motivated to avoid such treatment.* This is an interesting stipulation and an important one. It rules out sadomasochistic sexual relationships, suicide, and mercy killing which are excluded from the category of aggression because the victim is not motivated to avoid harm.

This definition is about as good as possible in our current state of knowledge. It implies that aggression is a social behavior and that a relationship is involved. In fact, a minimum of two social roles are involved: the role of AGGRESSOR and the role of VICTIM. Strong motive states are involved: the aggressor's motivation to cause harm or injury and the victim's motivation to avoid such harm. It is also implied that successful aggression involves a power difference in the relationship. Since the motive states of aggressor and victim are directly opposite, attempted aggression cannot succeed unless the aggressor has sufficient power to overcome the victim's resistance (Hallie, 1969). A type of "cooperation" is also involved. The victim must live in time and space in such a way that the aggressor has access to him or her. A potential victim who departs for Venus will not receive much (earthly) aggression. Thus aggressor and victim form a small, violent system in microcosm. The hope of many social scientists is that, if we can understand the dynamics of this miniature social system, we will be able to generalize that knowledge to larger collections of people.

In the remainder of the chapter, we will consider some of the important issues in the study of aggression. We first examine the controversy about the extent to which aggression is purely instinctive and the extent to which it is purely a learned behavior. In another section we consider situational factors in the instigation of aggression. Some attention is given to personality and sex differences in aggression. In another section, we discuss the nature and forms of violence at the societal level. Finally, we consider ways of controlling aggression.

Conceptions of aggression: instinct, drive, and social learning

One ancient controversy concerns the basic nature of human beings. Some writers have viewed human nature as basically evil, consisting of vile and hostile impulses which must be contained if civilization is to survive. Others have viewed human nature as basically good, or at least neutral. According to this view, evil is learned. It is something that innocent babes unfortunately acquire on their way to maturity. Actually, the question of whether human nature is basically good or evil cannot be answered. However, such primitive assumptions do influence the types of theories that are developed about human behavior, especially theories of aggression.

It is instructive to locate various theories of aggression on an instinct-learning dimension (see Figure 1), with pure instinct represented at one end of the dimension and pure learning represented at the other end. Let's look at three positions that represent different points on the dimension: instinct theories, drive

In recent years bombings have become frequent in many countries. Often terrorist groups give advance warning so that no one is killed, although property damage may be extensive. Does this kind of violence fit our social-psychological definition of aggression? Why or why not? (Wide World Photo)

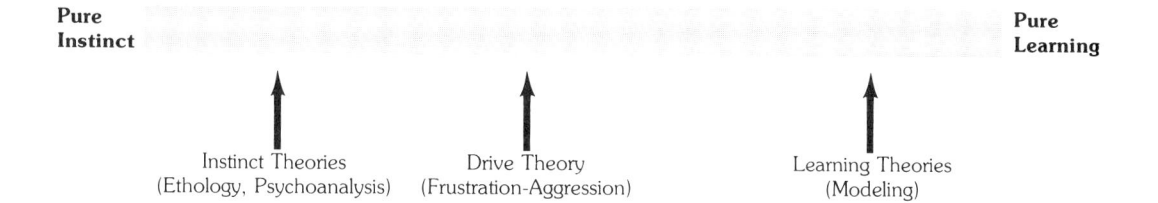

```
Pure                                                                              Pure
Instinct                                                                          Learning
   ↑                      ↑                              ↑
Instinct Theories      Drive Theory              Learning Theories
(Ethology, Psychoanalysis)  (Frustration-Aggression)    (Modeling)
```

theories, and learning theories. Ethology and psychoanalysis are the most popular instinct theories of aggression. The concept of aggression as a drive, represented by the classic frustration–aggression hypothesis, owes something to both positions, but it is probably somewhat closer to the instinct end than to the learning end of the dimension. Finally, there are several learning theories of aggression, but we will be concerned primarily with the theory that aggression can be imitated and learned through modeling.

AGGRESSION AS INSTINCTIVE BEHAVIOR

There are many definitions of instinct. Generally, an INSTINCTIVE BEHAVIOR is a complex behavior pattern that is fixed genetically, universal among members of a species, and only slightly (if at all) modified by experience. The nest-building behavior of various birds is a good example; they build nests in a fixed manner, even if they are raised in isolation from other members of their species (Berkowitz, 1962). Labeling more complicated behaviors, such as aggression, as instinctive is often questionable, because the actions involved in such behaviors are so intricate and varied. Nevertheless, two influential traditions have argued persuasively that aggression is instinctive: Freud and his followers in the psychoanalytic movement and the naturalistic zoologists known as ethologists.

Psychoanalytic theory. During the early part of his career, Freud believed that the life instinct, EROS, is the basic cause of all behavior. The energy of the life instinct, called libido, is directed toward pleasure seeking and avoidance of pain. According to Freud, aggression is a response to the blocking of the libido. Aggression is inevitable, because the libido is always oriented toward immediate pleasure, and some blocking of the pleasure urge is inevitable. Thus aggression is a result of the frustration of the libido, not a direct force in its own right.

1. The instinct-learning dimension in the study of aggression. Ethology and psychoanalysis represent relatively pure instinct theories. Drive theory assumes a mix of instinct and learning. Learning theories assume that aggression is acquired through experience.

World War I had a strong impact on Freud, to the extent that he changed his theory (Baron, 1977; Berkowitz, 1962). In addition to eros, Freud proposed a second major instinct—THANATOS, the death instinct. The energy of this instinct is directed toward self-destruction, based on the notion that the natural inclination of all life is to return to a nonliving form of matter. Since direct expression of thanatos would lead to the extinction of the species, Freud speculated that the death urge is directed outward (displaced) toward other people. In this way, thanatos becomes the basis for aggression toward others.

This dramatic turn in Freud's writing is an exceptionally pessimistic view of human nature. It suggests that aggression toward others is necessary to prevent self-destruction. However, some hope was restored in the idea that aggressive energy is also discharged through expressions of anger and hostility and that such expressions prevent more destructive acts.

Very few of Freud's followers accepted the concept of the death instinct. However, orthodox psychoanalysis still assumes that aggression stems from innate, instinctive urges and is therefore an intrinsic part of human nature.

Ethology and aggression. ETHOLOGY is the branch of biology concerned with the instincts and action patterns common to all members of a species operating in their natural habitat (Wrightsman, 1972). Ethologists patiently observe animals in their natural environment and try to extrapolate what they have observed to human behavior. The Nobel prize winner Konrad

Lorenz (1966) is perhaps the best-known representative of this tradition, but others have popularized the science as well (Ardrey 1970; Morris, 1967). The ethological approach draws on three key concepts in its explanation of aggression: evolution, territoriality, and dominance.

EVOLUTION has been characterized as the survival of the fittest, and aggression apparently plays a part in that process of natural selection. Aggression is common in the animal kingdom, though it is more precise to speak of fighting rather than aggression. Ethologists often emphasize that animals seldom fight to the death, because mechanisms have evolved to control the amount of fighting. Humans are presumed to be a failure in this regard (Lorenz, 1966) and consequently have become nature's most ferocious killers.

There is another side to the issue, however (Johnson, 1972; Marler, 1976). Few animals in the wild survive to a ripe old age. Observation of colonies of lions indicates frequent fighting, occasionally to the death (Johnson, 1972), with at least one recorded instance of adults killing cubs. Jane Goodall has reported aggressive behavior resulting in death among the chimps she has long observed at the Gombe Stream Reserve in Tanzania (*Science News,* April 29, 1978). In general, the statement that animals within a species seldom harm each other seems to be incorrect.

If destructive fighting is common in many species, why should it have been selectively favored in the course of evolution? There is no pat answer. One reasonable hypothesis was suggested by Johnson (1972):

> Evolution would seem to favor surplus aggression rather than surplus caution, for animals that failed to fight when it was essential probably fared worse than those who fought when it wasn't necessary. The net result might be a tendency to err on the high side and resort to aggressive behavior too often rather than not often enough (p. 17).

In any case, there are two basic reasons why animals fight. They fight to control territory and to achieve dominance, the other two key concepts in the ethological argument.

TERRITORIALITY has many meanings, but its most basic definition is any defended space. All animals require space in which to exist, and territoriality is very common, though not universal. Territories are often marked. An example is scent marking made by urinating along trails in the territory. The lovely songs of songbirds are often territorial in nature, warning potential intruders that the space is taken. Animals defend space to protect nesting, feeding, and mating areas and to protect their young. The types of defense vary enormously. Expressed willingness to fight, as in THREAT DISPLAYS, is much more common than actual fighting. In many respects, territoriality remains a puzzle because it is not universal. Closely related species may differ greatly, and the reason for such variation is not known. However, aggressive fighting in defense of territory is usually part of the behavior pattern of those species that are territorial.

DOMINANCE occurs in many animal groups that are small societies of unequals. The rigid dominance hierarchy, or "pecking order," among chickens is well known. Often the hierarchy is established by fighting, with the strongest and most threatening animal achieving preeminence. It has been argued that such dominance orders enhance sexual selection. In groups with dominance hierarchies, 10 percent of the males may control sexual access to 50 percent or more of the females. In this way, the species presumably perpetuates its most lively, assertive genes.

Ethology is an interesting science. Its specific theories are similar to psychoanalytic theory in many ways. For example, Lorenz (1966) viewed aggressive energy as accumulating within the organism in much the same way as Freud viewed it. A RELEASER STIMULUS is necessary to cue off the aggressive act. The longer the length of time since the last aggressive act, the easier it is to cue off a new one (Baron, 1977).

Ethology has been criticized for its extravagant generalizations about human behavior. It is not clear that observations of animals' social lives can be so readily extrapolated to the humans. In fact, some have seriously questioned whether the study of animal aggression has any relevance to the study of human aggression (Boice, 1976). It is true that humans struggle for dominance and stake out territory, but it is not clear that aggression is involved in the same ways as for animals. Humans have much greater behavior capabilities than other species because of their superior learning ability. Therefore, most social scientists doubt any theory that depends on instincts rather than learning. Nevertheless, the theory of aggression that has received the most attention assumes an instinctive causal mechanism and a learned disposition toward aggression in about equal proportions. That theory is the frustration–aggression hypothesis.

AGGRESSION AS DRIVE: DOES FRUSTRATION CAUSE AGGRESSION?

Suppose that a stereo receiver you want badly is advertised at half price. You rush madly to the store, only to be told that the last one was sold five minutes ago. How do you feel? Probably not happy. Most people would be upset, perhaps very angry. What do you do? Hit the clerk in the nose? Probably not, but you might swear at him or her. More likely you would express mild irritation and wait to tell a roommate or a friend what no-good so-and-so's they are, and possibly what a lousy state the world is in. Or you might even yell at your roommate for leaving the room messed up. If you are a rare type (usually considered undesirable), you might sneak back that night and smash a window in the store. Nearly everyone has experienced a similar angry disappointment. This everyday occurrence illustrates the FRUSTRATION—AGGRESSION HYPOTHESIS, which simply states that aggression is caused by various kinds of frustrations.

Statement of the hypothesis. The frustration–aggression hypothesis was formally proposed in a monograph by Dollard, Doob, Miller, Mowrer, and Sears (1939). Initially the hypothesis stated that frustration always causes some form of aggression and that the occurrence of aggression presupposes the prior existence of frustration. This is a very strong pair of assumptions. There are several concepts which feed into them.

1. Various drive states (such as hunger and thirst) within the organism instigate sequences of behavior, the purpose of which is to reduce the drive state.
2. An act that ends a self-directed sequence of behavior is a GOAL RESPONSE.
3. Anything that blocks or interferes with a goal response is a FRUSTRATION.
4. AGGRESSION is any sequence of behavior that has the goal response of injury of the person toward whom it is directed.
5. Aggression does not reduce the strength of the original drive state, only the SECONDARY STATE produced by frustration.

The magnitude of the aggression is presumed to depend on (1) the strength of the initial drive state, (2) the degree of blocking of the goal response, and (3) the frequency with which response sequences have been frustrated. Whether aggression is directly manifested also depends on factors that might inhibit it. The major such factor is anticipated punishment: the greater the anticipated punishment, the greater the inhibition of the expression of aggression. Inhibiting aggression does not mean that the instigation to aggression simply goes away. If a direct response cannot be made, aggression may be displaced into some other, indirect response.

The original statement of the frustration–aggression hypothesis at first seemed clear and elegant in its simplicity. It is worth noting that aggression was not discussed as an instinct, but was considered an automatic response to a blocked drive. The forms of aggression (that is, the types of overt responses and displacement activities) could be modified by experience. The fact that aggression of some type would occur as a result of frustration was, however, a biological given. In this sense, the theory implicitly assumed an instinct mechanism in aggression.

Problems with the hypothesis. The first half of the hypothesis—that frustration always causes some form of aggression—was objected to by many writers. Miller (1941) amended the hypothesis, saying that "frustration produces instigations to a number of different types of responses, one of which is an instigation to some form of aggression" (p. 338). This weakening of the hypothesis may be empirically laudable, but it leads to conceptual confusions. When will frustration lead to aggression and when to other types of responses? How can one tell whether a response (a fantasy, for instance) is a type of displaced aggression or a different kind of response altogether? These conceptual confusions are very difficult to resolve by experimental means.

The concept of frustration also proved problematic. Brown and Farber (1951) pointed out that frustrating conditions may consist of physical barriers, delays between the beginning and the completion of a response sequence, omission of a reward, or a tendency to a conflicting response that is incompatible with an ongoing response. Further, is frustration best defined as an external blocking (as in the original definition), or as the internal emotional response that occurs when behavior is blocked? These problems diverted much research to the nature and definition of frustration, largely without fruitful results.

A final issue concerns the nature of the frustration–aggression link. Actually the Yale group wished to make no assumption about whether the link was instinctive. It seems that some position has to be taken, however, and the original statement favored BIOLOGICAL DETERMINISM. Even with such an assumption, the nature of the link was not specified. In many ways, it remained mysterious. Because of such problems, this theory would probably have been abandoned except for the efforts of Leonard Berkowitz to revise and update it.

THE REVISED FRUSTRATION–AGGRESSION HYPOTHESIS

Berkowitz accepts the essential validity of the frustration–aggression hypothesis, but he has modified it in various ways (Berkowitz, 1962; 1965; 1969):

1. The emotional reaction arising from the blocking of a goal response is an important causal factor (Berkowitz, 1965). This emotional reaction is anger.
2. However, anger does not automatically instigate aggression. It only creates a *readiness* to aggress.
3. Given a state of readiness, aggression will only occur when suitable cues exist. These cues are stimuli associated with present or past instigators of anger (Berkowitz, 1965). It is implied that these cues are external to the organism. However, a later statement (Berkowitz, 1969) indicated that anger (particularly strong anger) may produce its own internal cues that are sufficient to elicit an aggressive response.
4. Aggression may, with practice, become a habit that can be activated without angry arousal. This notion assumes that aggression can occur habitually, without the necessity of prior frustration.

Berkowitz's revisions are summarized in Figure 2. Fortunately these revisions match the requirements of a good experimental design, as shown in the figure. Two basic factors are required. Anger either exists or it does not, as shown in the rows of Figure 2. An aggressive cue either exists or it does not, as shown in the columns. Aggression occurs only when both anger and the cue occur, as shown in the lower right-hand cell of the figure.

Berkowitz has conducted many experiments to test his ideas. The same basic approach was followed in several of the experiments. A subject was first introduced to another subject (actually an experimental confederate) who either behaved in a neutral manner or made the subject angry. The subject was then exposed either to one or more cues related to aggression or to neutral cues. Afterwards, the subject was given a chance to administer electric shocks to the confederate in a socially sanctioned atmosphere. The number and duration of the shocks were taken as dependent measures of aggression.

One example of this research is an experiment re-

2. Diagram of Berkowitz's revision of the frustration-aggression hypothesis. Both anger and an external cue must exist before aggression occurs.

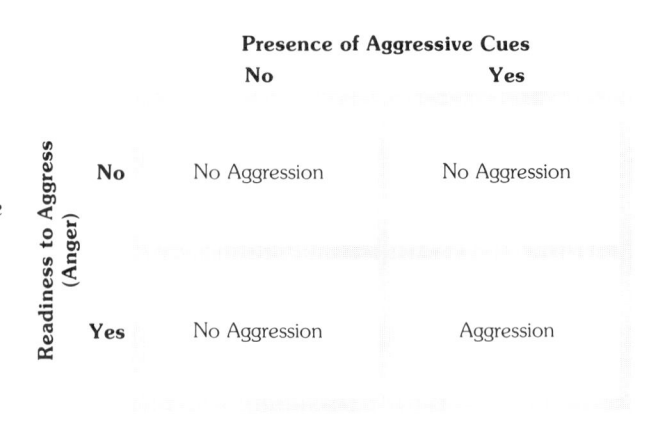

	Presence of Aggressive Cues	
Readiness to Aggress (Anger)	**No**	**Yes**
No	No Aggression	No Aggression
Yes	No Aggression	Aggression

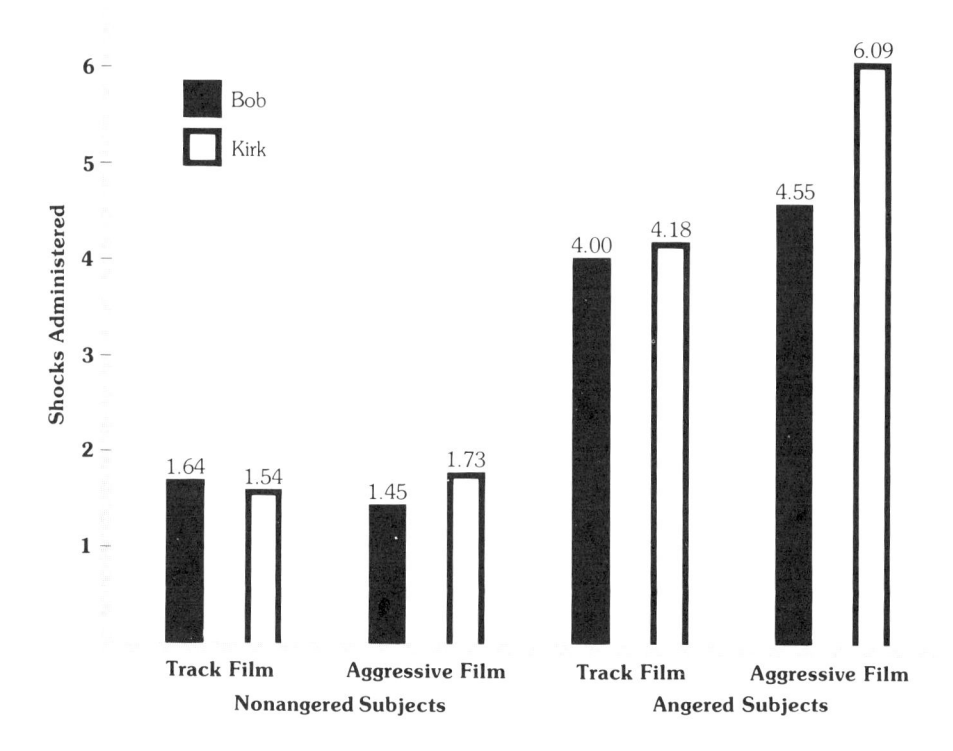

ported by Berkowitz and Geen (1966). After the initial interaction between confederate and subject, the subject watched either a brutal 7-minute clip from the movie *Champion*, in which the actor Kirk Douglas was badly beaten, or an active but neutral film about track racing. The film clip from *Champion* served as one type of aggressive cue. Another cue was the name of the confederate, who was introduced as either *Kirk* Anderson (similar to Kirk Douglas) or Bob Anderson (nonsimilar). The effects of the manipulation of anger or nonanger, and the two types of cues (type of film and name of confederate) on the number of shocks the subject later gave the confederate are shown in Figure 3. The figure shows that the manipulation of anger had the strongest effect. Angered subjects gave a minimum of 4.0 shocks, while nonangered subjects gave an average of less than 2.0 shocks. In the four Nonanger conditions, there should have been no differences due to presence or absence of cues, and indeed the four columns on the left of the figure indicate no significant differences in aggression. Results of the four Anger conditions were somewhat mixed. Subjects who were introduced to Kirk and saw the fight film were significantly more aggressive than those in any other condition (right-most column of the figure). Subjects who were introduced to Bob and saw the fight film should have delivered significantly more shocks than subjects who saw the track film, but this did not occur.

3. Number of shocks administered to confederate by the subject under several conditions. Data indicate that subjects who had been angered were most aggressive. Prior viewing of an aggressive film, plus interacting with Kirk (the similar-named confederate), also increased the amount of aggression to some extent. (Adapted from Berkowitz and Geen, 1966, p. 528.)

The data illustrated in Figure 3 suggest that anger had a general energizing effect on aggressive responding, and, while the external cues made some difference, their effects were minor compared to the impact of anger. It may be that the major effect of frustration (or anger) is to create a state of general arousal that energizes whatever response the subject happens to be engaged in. If so, then physiological arousal from other sources, such as vigorous exercise and stimulating drugs, might lead to increased aggression under some circumstances. There is some evidence in favor of these speculations (Baron, 1977). Thus it is unclear to what extent specific target-directed anger or a more diffuse general state of arousal is the necessary condition. The role of external cues and how they combine with the internal cues produced by anger are also unclear.

Berkowitz's research program continues to evolve over time, and the final word on his revision of the frustration–aggression hypothesis undoubtedly has not yet been written. At the very least, his research reminds us that frustration, and particularly anger-producing frustration, is one cause of aggression. At the same time, Berkowitz recognizes that aggression may be due to other causes as well. One such apparent cause is observational learning. Aggression may occur because people witness it, learn it, and later engage in similar behavior.

AGGRESSION AS A LEARNED SOCIAL BEHAVIOR

A child is led by an adult from nursery school class to a nearby room for a game. In one corner of the room, a small chair and table contain materials for making posters. The adult explains the task to the child and then escorts another adult to a far corner of the room. In that corner are also a chair, a table, and several toys, including a mallet, Tinker toys, and a large, inflated Bobo doll about 5 feet high. The second adult is left to play with these materials, and the first adult leaves the room. Very soon, the adult attacks the Bobo doll, pounding and kicking it vigorously and talking aggressively to the doll. The attack lasts 10 minutes. Afterwards the first adult returns and takes the child to another room that contains many toys, including a 3-foot Bobo doll. The adult soon leaves, and the child is free to play with the toys. How does the child play with the Bobo doll?

This is the scenario for a classic study relevant to aggression (Bandura, Ross, and Ross, 1961) and subsequently used for a long series of experiments (Bandura, 1973). The first adult was an experimenter. The second adult was a confederate who served as a model. For half of the children in the experiment, the model played quietly. For the other half, the model strenuously attacked the Bobo doll. Half of the children saw a model of their own sex, and half saw a model of the opposite sex. When the child was led to the second room, hidden observers watched carefully to see whether the child imitated the model's behavior. The results were clear. Children who observed an aggressive model were much more aggressive toward their Bobo doll than children who observed a model who played quietly.

This experiment illustrates social learning by observation. In particular, it demonstrates that aggression can be learned by observation of the behavior of another person.

During the past two decades, several social-learning theories have emerged that emphasize the importance of cognitive and perceptual processes, rather than the stimulus–response connections of earlier learning theories. Several labels have been applied to this type of learning, such as imitation, observational learning, and modeling. Modeling is the broader and most preferred term (Johnson, 1972). There are three important aspects of modeling as a type of learning:

1. *Response acquisition.* By watching a model, one may acquire a novel response not previously available. Often such responses may be reproduced with a high level of accuracy without much practice.
2. *Inhibition–disinhibition.* If a model is punished, similar behavior in the subject may be strongly inhibited. Likewise, a model's act may serve to disinhibit responses in another. For example, if one person in an angry, milling group of people throws a rock, that act may disinhibit everyone else. A barrage of stones may be thrown, and a full-fledged riot may result.
3. *Response facilitation.* Observing a model may facilitate a response already learned by the subject. For example, if a model looks up toward the sky, several other people soon do the same thing (Johnson, 1972).

These general learning principles have been applied

to the study of aggression, primarily by Bandura and his colleagues (Bandura and Walters, 1963; Bandura, 1973). In the example of the Bobo doll, the child acquired novel responses (ways of beating the doll), simply by observing the model. Later the child repeated the same responses in another situation. Other studies have shown that if the model is punished, the child will not aggress against the Bobo doll. Further, the child does not have to observe the model "in the flesh." One study (Bandura, Ross, and Ross, 1963) showed that children imitate the model whose behavior they watch on television. Bandura's work has received some criticism, in part because of the potential applicability of his findings to the mass media (Baron, 1977). Can beating an inflated rubber doll be considered aggression? Perhaps it is just raucous play. Furthermore, children almost never see adults behave as the model behaved toward the Bobo doll, so such findings are difficult to generalize to everyday life.

Such criticisms have a point. However, in the intervening years since the early 1960s, a great deal of research on observational learning has been conducted in a variety of formats. Clearly observational learning occurs for a variety of behaviors, including aggressive behavior. This approach shows that aggression stems from many causes. Frustration is one cause of aggression if other conditions are met. But it is *not* the case that for aggression to occur, frustration must precede it.

Personality and individual differences in aggression

People differ from each other in many ways. One of the more obvious differences, of course, is that of gender. Sex differences are currently the subject of much study and debate as a result of social trends toward economic and political equality between men and women. People also differ in their hereditary potential and personality attributes. This section, then, is concerned with how these differences in sex, hereditary background, and personality relate to aggressive behavior.

ARE MALES MORE AGGRESSIVE THAN FEMALES?

Animals. Throughout the animal kingdom, there is a strong tendency for males of a species to be more aggressive than females. This statement is true for invertebrates as well as vertebrates (Scott, 1958). Among mammals the tendency is quite pronounced. Animal breeders have long recognized the ferocity of stallions and bulls, and they often castrate the animals to make them docile. If castrated when young, the ferocious bull becomes a plodding ox, the stallion a tame draft horse. However, there are species exceptions to male aggressiveness. For example, female hamsters are more aggressive than males; indeed, a male placed in a cage with a female is likely to be killed unless the female is in heat.

Greater aggressiveness in males is related to two factors. In general, males of most species tend to be larger and physically stronger than females, conferring a competitive edge in fighting. The second factor is differences in sexual hormones—the sexes differ in relative balance of androgens and estrogens. There are several varieties of each type of hormone, but the most important one for aggression is testosterone, the male gonadal hormone involved in the onset of puberty (Johnson, 1972). Many experiments have shown that presence or absence of this hormone is related to fighting. For example, hens injected with testosterone tend to rise higher in the peck order and remain there as long as the injections are maintained. Castrated male mice are docile, but they become aggressive when injected with testosterone (Scott, 1958). Similar results have been found with male chimpanzees.

Apparently minute differences in hormone secretions during early stages of development cause permanent changes in neural organization related to sexual characteristics. Developmental changes include larger physical size of the male and growth of secondary sexual characteristics appropriate to the species. The neural patterning may also be responsible for sex differences in sensitivity to various kinds of stimulation. In general, males may require a lower level of stimulation to trigger fighting behavior, leading to more fighting by males.

Humans. We are much less confident that the physiological generalizations about other species are applicable to humans. Clearly, human males are often more aggressive than females, and the crime statistics indicate that males engage more often in illegal violence. However, such behavior may depend on cultural stereotypes that males should be "masculine" and "tough" while females should be "passive," rather than on innate biological differences (Deaux, 1976).

Careful scientific research yields mixed results. At low levels of provocation, males tend to initiate more aggression than females. When there is strong provocation, however, females respond just as aggressively as males (Baron, 1977). Men may have a lower "boiling point," or threshold for aggressive behavior, a conclusion consistent with the animal research.

It is very difficult to know how closely biological differences between the sexes may be related to differences in aggression. Humans seem to have outgrown their biology, because experience, cultural factors, and learning conditions are often more important than hormonal differences. Indeed, the difference between males and females in aggressiveness may be diminishing (Deaux, 1976; Baron, 1977) due to changes in cultural expectations about the role of women. Between 1960 and 1973, FBI data indicated that the arrest rate for serious crimes increased three times faster for women than for men—though in absolute terms, men were still arrested six times more often than women (Bruck, 1975). Other commentators (Adler, 1975) believe that women are becoming more violent in the types of crimes they commit.

A fair conclusion is that human males are more aggressive than females. This difference may be partially dictated by biological factors, but cultural and learning conditions are probably more important. The current sex differences in aggression may be reversed. Women of the year 2525 may be aggressive amazons, with males playing passive roles. In both cases, the difference will depend on cultural values more than innate biological differences.

GENETIC EFFECTS IN AGGRESSION

Animal research demonstrated many years ago that aggressiveness can be inherited to some extent. Animal breeders have been able to increase the aggressiveness of such species as chickens and dogs over several generations by interbreeding the most aggressive pairs of animals in a generation. In humans, the issue is whether aggressiveness is a personality trait that varies in amount in a population (Johnson, 1972; Berkowitz, 1962).

During the past decade, much interest has developed in the XYY syndrome. Human body cells have 46 chromosomes. Two of them, the X and Y chromosomes, are related to sex determination. Females have two X chromosomes, or an XX pattern. Males have an X and a Y chromosome, or an XY pattern. A small percent of males have an extra Y chromosome, or an XYY pattern. Early research revealed that the XYY pattern was more common among men in prison than in the population at large. Men with the XYY pattern tended to be quite tall and somewhat mentally retarded. They also exhibited occasional outbursts of extreme violence (Baron, 1977). Such reports led to great scientific controversy, and the issue is still not completely resolved. Extensive data indicate that XYY types are in fact overrepresented in prison populations. On the average, however, such individuals are no more aggressive than XY types. Rather, they are somewhat less intelligent—more likely, perhaps, to be caught when they commit a crime. Their crimes are more likely to be petty theft than violence. The image of the XYY as an aggressive supermale seems unwarranted, and the extra Y chromosome is not particularly related to aggressive behavior.

PERSONALITY DISPOSITIONS IN AGGRESSION

We touched on the issue of an aggressive personality in the previous section. A more profitable approach is to ask how specific personality dimensions are related to aggression. We will summarize research on this issue and then briefly consider the causes of extreme violence.

Personality dimensions in aggression. Much of the work on this topic has been done in controlled laboratory settings in which research subjects can administer some punishment (usually electric shock) to another person. Individuals are preselected as high or low on a selected personality dimension (such as need for approval or locus of control), which is usually measured by an objective test. Some of the more important findings to date are (Baron, 1977):

1. Subjects who strongly fear social disapproval are less aggressive than subjects who do not fear social disapproval. However, both types of individuals become much more aggressive as provocation from another person increases, to the point where both types show an equally high level of aggression (Dengerink, 1971).

2. In a similar vein, subjects high in the need for social approval are less aggressive than subjects low in this need (Taylor, 1970), though differences between the two types are minimal when provocation from another person is high.

3. Rotter (1966) developed a test called the Locus of Control Scale. People who score high on the scale have an EXTERNAL LOCUS OF CONTROL. Such people believe that the rewards they experience and the things that happen to them are largely in the hands of others. Their own efforts to control their world do not benefit them very much. In contrast, people with an INTERNAL LOCUS OF CONTROL believe that what happens to them and the rewards they receive depend on their own efforts and actions. Dengerink, O'Leary, and Kasner (1975) conducted an experiment in which subjects who were either external or internal in locus of control aggressed against a person who either increased or decreased his level of provocation over time. As expected, internal subjects matched the provocativeness of the other person very closely in degree of aggression expressed, but external subjects did not respond very strongly to the other person.

This area of research is still in its infancy. During the next several years, there will probably be an upsurge of research relating a wide variety of personality variables to aggressive behavior.

What makes really violent people violent? A small number of people lead extremely violent lives. They are immersed in violence as a way of life. Not surprisingly, they often end up in prison. Toch (1969) studied a sample of such people by arranging for other prisoners and parolees to serve as interviewers. The interviews were recorded on tape and later analyzed extensively. Toch did not find any single reason or cause for violent behavior. Instead he found several different types of people who had engaged in extensive violence. The three most common types accounted for over 50 percent of the cases.

1. *Self-image defenders* feel the world is out to belittle them. They respond with violence at the slightest imagined provocation.
2. *Self-image promoters* need to convince the world that they are formidable and fearless. They seek violent encounters as a way of proving their own worth.
3. *Reputation defenders* are often gang members and must maintain reputations as tough, formidable opponents. Aggressive encounters often seem the only way to maintain such reputations.

Extremely violent people are violent for many different reasons. Toch believes that they are basically children who use force as a way of compensating for inadequate social skills. With such people, aggression is an ingrained habit that could be considered a personality trait.

Newspaper headlines relate brutal murders so bizarre as to seem inhuman. Very often, however, such acts are committed by individuals who are passive and mild-mannered prior to the violent act and may be very well behaved after the act (Megargee, 1971). In fact, that single act of violence may be all the individual ever commits. Among samples of prisoners, Megargee (1966) found that such individuals are extremely overcontrolling of anger and hostility. Most of the time, their anger is rigidly repressed. On a rare occasion, the controls fail and gross violence occurs. The Overcontrolled Hostility Scale (Megargee, 1971) has been developed to identify such people. Although the scale is still in the developmental stages, it appears useful in identifying individuals prone to unexpected, isolated acts of violence. If valid, this instrument will be very useful, because such individuals could be encouraged to seek preventive therapy before they have committed an act of violence.

Situational and environmental factors in aggression

Situational and environmental factors in aggression are particularly amenable to experimental manipulations in the laboratory. Consequently, most of the relevant research consists of rigorous laboratory experiments. We present some of the major laboratory methods that have been devised to study aggression. Then we discuss some of the empirical research on such topics as the effects of noise, crowding, heat, and alcohol on aggression. We also consider the effects of violence in television and the mass media, and we examine the validity of a concept called the catharsis hypothesis.

EXPERIMENTAL METHODS FOR STUDYING AGGRESSION

Early research on aggression used verbal measures of aggression. However, there is always some question about whether a negative evaluation by the subject is really an act of aggression. Other approaches have used play measures of aggression, primarily with children. Bandura's research with the Bobo doll is the best-known example. Critics of this approach maintain that the subjects are engaging in play and not aggression and that it is hardly applicable to the study of adult aggression. In response to such problems, researchers devised techniques in which subjects could ostensibly engage in direct aggressive acts against another person. Deception is involved in these techniques in that subjects believe they can hurt another person, whereas in fact they cannot. The procedures are designed to measure a subject's intentions or desires to hurt another without allowing actual assaults. Three such techniques have been devised, and each is designated by the name of its inventor.

The Buss (1961) technique. Each subject is told that he or she will be participating with another subject (actually a confederate) in an experiment on the effects of punishment on learning. In a fake lottery, the real subject draws the role of teacher and the confederate the role of learner. The teacher's task is to present various materials to the learner (usually located in another room), who tries to master them. The teacher signals each correct response with a light and punishes each error with an electric shock. The teacher sits facing an electric box with a series of lights and 10 buttons on it. Pushing a button is supposed to administer a shock to the learner. The strength of the shock is graduated across the buttons, ranging from very weak to quite intense.

The range in amount of shock delivered to the learner is interpreted as variation in the degree of aggressiveness the teacher shows toward the learner. The duration for which a shock button is depressed is also sometimes considered a measure of aggression. In most experiments, there are between 20 and 35 different trials, so the teacher delivers that many shocks to the learner.

In actual fact, nobody receives shocks. The sequence of correct and incorrect responses from the learner is programmed in advance. The electric circuits measure the degree of shock intended by the teacher, but the confederate is usually not hooked up to the shock electrodes. Since this "aggression machine" registers precisely the level of intended punishment but no one actually gets shocked, the technique has been very popular. Hundreds of experiments have been conducted using the Buss technique (Baron, 1977).

One major question is whether the subjects' intent is actually aggressive in these experiments. Subjects may well believe that they are helping the learner and that the stronger the shocks, the better the learning. If so, the Buss technique would mix altruistic motives with aggressive motives. There is some evidence that such motive mixes do occur (Baron, 1977). Very recently, instead of using the teacher–learner deception, researchers have told subjects that the purpose of the experiment is to study the effect of shock on physiological responding. This change presumably reduces the altruistic motive, so that the shocks delivered are more purely a measure of aggression.

The Berkowitz (1962) technique. Each subject is told that he or she will be participating with another subject (a confederate) in a study of the effects of stress on problem solving. The experimenter poses some issue (such as improving labor–management relations) on which the subject and confederate will write essays. Stress is introduced by evaluation of each other's essay and resulting administration of electric shocks. After writing the essay, the confederate delivers 1 to 10 electric shocks to the subject; the more shocks, the poorer the essay is judged to be. In most studies, the confederate delivers either 1 or 7 shocks of fixed voltage. This aspect of the technique is supposed to vary the subject's anger toward the confederate.

After this phase of the experiment, various manipulations are introduced. Witnessing the fight sequence in *Champion* (see page 315) is a good example, though many other manipulations have been used. After this phase, the subject evaluates the confederate's work via electric shock. The number and duration of shocks is the measure of aggression.

One advantage of this approach is that a realistic but socially sanctioned basis is provided for a subject to aggress directly against the person who provokes anger. In addition, the effects of various environmental variables and the way they combine with anger arousal can be conveniently studied. The major disadvantage of the technique is that it is relatively complex, allowing errors and artifacts to intrude into the experiment.

4. Diagram of a Taylor aggression machine. When Ready Light comes on, the subject sets the shock desired for the opponent (a confederate), and then depresses the reaction-time key. The finger is removed from the key when the Off Light comes on. The subject loses the reaction-time contest and receives a shock from the opponent on half of the trials and wins the other half (thus avoiding a shock). The lights on top of the panel serve as signals indicating what shock intensity the opponent set for the subject on the previous trial.

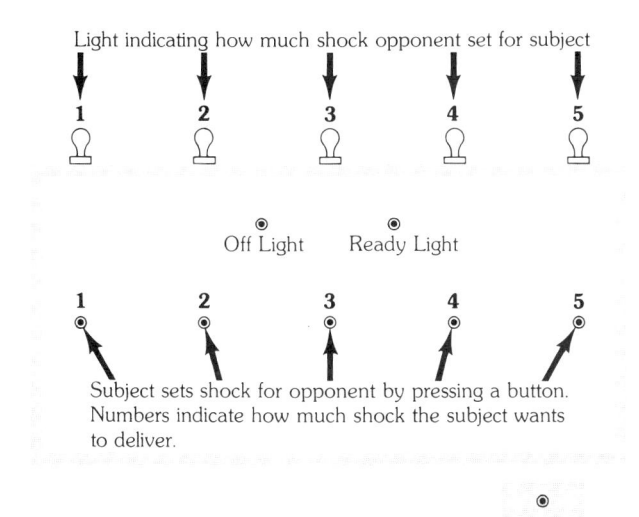

The Taylor (1967) technique. A subject arrives for the experiment and is told that he or she will engage in a competitive reaction-time test. The subject competes with another subject (a programmed confederate) on 20 to 30 trials. On a signal for each trial, the subject depresses a reaction-time key (see Figure 4). When an Off Light comes on, the subject removes his or her finger as quickly as possible. The incentive for speed is shock. Prior to each trial, the subject presses a shock button that indicates how much shock he or she wants the opponent to receive if the subject is faster on that trial. A set of signal lights indicates how much shock the opponent set for the subject to receive on that trial. The shocks are prescaled to the subject's threshold for pain. The most extreme button is mildly painful, and the least extreme button produces a light twinge. Usually 5, but occasionally 10, buttons are used.

This technique is quite versatile. Since the opponent is programmed, the aggressive intent of the opponent can be easily manipulated. Imagine sitting in front of an apparatus on which an unseen opponent constantly signals an intent to deliver maximum shock, compared to having a mild opponent who always signals minimum shock. Very different perceptions are created in the two cases. Taylor has usually conducted experiments in which both opponent and subject win about 50 percent of the time on a random basis, although the proportion of winning trials can be easily manipulated.

This approach contrasts with the Buss and Berkowitz techniques. In the latter two approaches, the confederate victim is helpless and cannot fight back. With Taylor's procedure, subject and confederate are in a mutual retaliatory situation. To an extent the procedure mimicks fighting, and so it is somewhat like many aggression situations in everyday life. The major problems with the technique are that subjects actually receive electric shock and that the competitive aspects of the situation may be partially confounded with aggressive motives.

All three techniques are ingenious methods for studying aggression in a controlled laboratory setting. Very few studies have compared the techniques, so we do not know whether the three approaches yield equivalent results. But these techniques are collectively a great advance in the study of environmental determinants of aggression.

ENVIRONMENTAL FACTORS IN AGGRESSION

Many environmental and situational factors have been studied as potential causes of aggression. In this section, we sample several of them and discuss examples of the relevant research.

Attack from another person. One of the primary instigators of aggression is attack from another person. This result has been found using all three techniques discussed in the previous section. Using the Taylor technique, Greenwell and Dengerink (1973) found that symbolic attack, rather than severity of actual attack, may be the more important variable. These investigators manipulated the severity of actual shocks that subjects received independently of the light signals for the amount of shock the opponent set for them to receive. Some opponents consistently flashed a moderate shock level; other opponents progressively increased the shock value that they signaled. Results showed that subjects responded more strongly to the symbolic values of the light signals than to variation in actual painfulness of the attacks. These data show that perceived aggressive intent is a powerful variable in eliciting an aggressive response.

The effect of noise. During the past few years, several commentators have warned of the harmful effects of "noise pollution." Aggression researchers have explored the effects of noise, and several experiments indicate that noise may cause increased aggressiveness under certain conditions. Donnerstein and Wilson (1976) conducted an experiment using the Buss technique. Subjects wrote an essay and were then evaluated harshly (9 shocks) or mildly (1 shock) by a confederate. This first phase manipulated the subject's anger. Afterwards the subject was given a chance to punish the confederate by administering shocks. During this teacher–learner phase of the experiment, the subject was exposed to uncontrollable bursts of white noise (a mixture of all sound frequencies) of moderate (55 decibels) or high (95 decibels) intensity.

Results showed that either moderate- or high-intensity noise made no difference in intensity of shocks when subjects had not been previously angered. When subjects had been previously angered, however, they showed significantly more aggression when exposed to the high-intensity noise than when exposed to noise of moderate intensity. In a second experiment, Donnerstein and Wilson (1976) gave the subjects apparent control over the noise by telling them that it would be stopped if they requested it. Under these conditions, the high-intensity white noise did *not* lead to increased aggression.

The laboratory research indicates that noise affects aggression under some conditions. Those conditions seem to be that the subject (1) is already in a state of angry arousal, and (2) has no control over the noise.

The effect of heat. There were many riots around the world in the late 1960s and early 1970s. The majority of the riots occurred during summer months. The news media and other commentators frequently blamed summer heat as a major cause. The idea was that exposure to heat increased irritability and lowered thresholds for outbursts of anger. Since inner-city houses are seldom air-conditioned, people go outdoors to find relief from the heat. Many people are thrown into close proximity, and the milling about can, with the proper spark, become an angry riot.

Led primarily by Baron (1977), several researchers attempted to explore in the laboratory the question of whether heat leads to increased aggression. The question proved surprisingly difficult to answer in a direct way. Several early experiments revealed that aggressiveness actually decreased when subjects participated in a hot room (92–95°F) compared to a cool room (72–75°F). After much effort, Baron concluded that the relationship between heat and aggression is actually quite complex and is mediated by an individual's mood state. Under cool conditions, mood is positive and there is little impact. As heat increases, irritability increases and so does aggressiveness. Beyond some point, however, the heat becomes debilitating. The subject's dominant response is to escape the situation, and his or her level of aggressiveness goes down. There is some evidence to support this complex hypothesis (Bell and Baron, 1976), but considerably more research is required. It already seems clear, however, that the social violence of riots in the summer is not caused in any simple way by the summer heat. Other effects of heat on social behavior are discussed in Chapter 15.

The effect of crowding. Much ethological research demonstrates that, in many species, individuals space themselves rather precisely from one another. When

Racial animosity sometimes triggers violence. Such violence has been attributed to overcrowding, heat, and scapegoating as a result of frustrations, among other possible causes. There does not seem to be one simple, direct cause of racial violence, and it remains an important social problem in need of a solution. (Eugene Richards/The Picture Cube)

one individual violates the space of another, fighting often breaks out. Aggression also seems to occur when animals are overcrowded. One famous series of experiments by Calhoun (reported in Hall, 1966) investigated the effects of gross overcrowding on rats. There was general social disorganization, including greatly increased aggressiveness.

There has been considerable speculation that overcrowding among humans also has detrimental effects, including increased aggression. In a book summarizing an extensive program of research, Freedman (1975) found that crowding had very little effect on various types of aggressive behavior. There was a slight trend for males to be more aggressive and females less aggressive under crowded conditions, but the trend was not very pronounced. Freedman proposed that crowding may act as an intensifier or energizer of ongoing behavior. If the behavior is typically pleasant (such as a restaurant meal), crowding will enhance the pleasure. If the behavior is negative (such as waiting in a shopping line after a tiring day), crowding will increase the unpleasantness of the behavior. Crowding seems to have no uniform effect on aggression. As with heat, the effects of crowding seem quite complex. The effects of crowding on other types of behavior are discussed in Chapter 16.

Alcohol and aggression. Common lore suggests that drinking makes people more prone to aggressive acts. Alcohol is often associated with acts of violence such as murder and rape. Only recently, however, has the association between alcohol and aggression been studied carefully. In one interesting study, Taylor and Gammon (1975) varied type and amount of liquor subjects drank before participating in a Taylor-technique aggression study. Subjects received either high or low doses of vodka or bourbon. Results showed that subjects receiving high doses of either drink were more aggressive than subjects receiving low doses.

In a later study, Taylor, Gammon, and Capasso (1976) had subjects first consume vodka or a placebo drink. While preparing for the experiment, they overheard the experimenter talking with the ostensible opponent. The nature of the discussion constituted a manipulation of threat. The experimenter asked the opponent and subjects if there were any questions after the procedures were presented. In the High Threat condition, the opponent said simply "no questions." In the No Threat condition, the opponent said that he had strong convictions about not hurting people and would feel more comfortable setting just the 1-button (the lowest setting) all the time. The experimenter assured him that was okay. Afterwards the experiment proceeded. In all conditions, the opponent set only the 1-button and was therefore not at all aggressive.

The results for the first trial setting are shown in Figure 5. Results for the remaining 18 trials showed a similar pattern. Of particular interest is the fact that an innocuous threat like "no questions" in conjunction with alcohol cued off a strong aggressive response. In fact, the subject's behavior could well be described as somewhat paranoid. The alcohol subjects were not simply disinhibited to aggress, because they were not at all aggressive in the No Threat condition. It is unclear exactly what cued off the aggressive response. At the very least, Taylor, et al. have shown that under some conditions, consumption of alcohol does cue off increased aggressiveness.

Does presence of guns cause aggression? Since 1900, guns have killed more than 800,000 Americans (Johnson, 1972). In fact, approximately 20,000 Americans are now killed each year by guns. Traditionally, people in the United States have been fond of guns. In contrast, Japan has never allowed the general population to own such weapons. The rate of homicide with guns in the United States is 214 times higher than in Japan (Johnson, 1972). Clearly possession and ownership of guns is associated with increased violence. But is the presence of guns a causal factor in violence?

This question was addressed by Berkowitz and LePage (1967) in an experiment that has received much publicity. The Berkowitz technique was used, and some subjects were first angered and others were not. Subjects were then given a chance to aggress against the confederate who had initially angered them. In some conditions, a .38-caliber revolver and a 12-gauge shotgun were lying on a table near the shock apparatus. In other conditions, there were either no objects or neutral objects such as badminton racquets on the table. Results showed that when weapons were

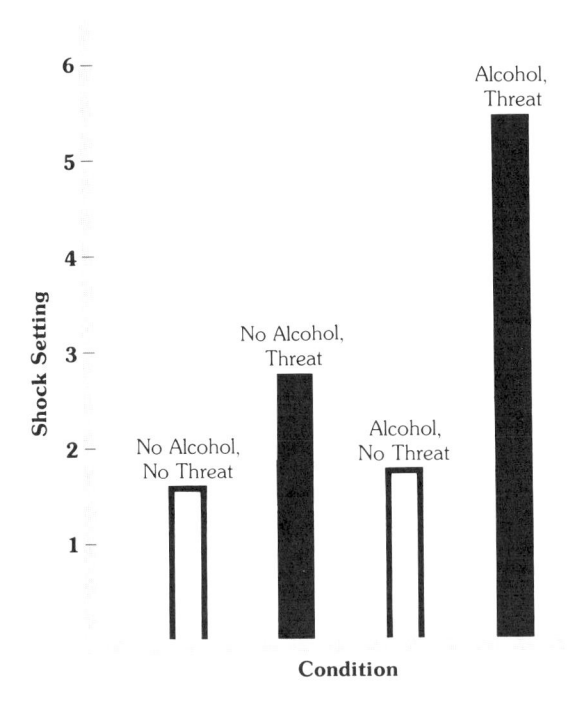

5. Subjects' first shock setting in the Taylor, et al., alcohol study. These data indicate that subjects who had been drinking and received a threat were very aggressive. Threat alone or alcohol alone did not cause an increase in aggression. (Adapted from Taylor, Gammon, and Capasso, 1976, p. 940.)

present and subjects were angry, they delivered significantly more shocks than when neutral objects or no objects were present.

This "weapons effect" implies that the suggestive presence of cues strongly associated with violence, such as guns, may increase an individual's level of aggressive behavior. Because of the importance of this experiment in terms of its implications for social life, several replications were conducted. Unfortunately, only some of the repeat experiments were successful (Baron, 1977), and the reasons for the failures are unclear. The failures suggest that the original results may have been artificial, and caution is required in making generalizations.

The various techniques for studying aggression have made possible the study of a whole host of environmental influences on aggression, but this does not necessarily mean that simple, clear-cut results will emerge readily. The causes of aggression are complex. Perception of intent to attack by another person seems to elicit aggressive behavior quite reliably. However, all the other variables examined reveal complications. There is no direct, simple effect of noise, heat, crowding, alcohol, or presence of guns on aggression. There undoubtedly are some effects due to each of these variables, but they occur in interaction with other variables and under special conditions. We are reminded once again that the world is not simple. The statement holds true for environmental determinants of aggression as well as for most other areas.

IS TELEVISION A CAUSE OF VIOLENCE?

During the last quarter-century, television has come to exert powerful effects on social life. By 1970, approximately 95 percent of the households in the United States owned at least one TV set (Liebert, Neale, and Davidson, 1973), and the impact in Europe and some other areas of the world is equally pervasive. The impact of TV on social life has been studied extensively (Howitt and Cumberbatch, 1975; Noble, 1975). Various commentators have noted that TV has resulted in a more factually knowledgeable public. Others have blamed TV for the decay in reading skills, reduced motivation for school work, and disruption of traditional patterns of neighborhood socializing.

It is easy to document the fact that people watch a great deal of television. It has been estimated that the average American TV set is turned on for slightly more than 6 hours per day (Liebert, Neale, and Davidson, 1973). Children watch extensively. In primary grades, viewing time ranges between 15 and 25 hours per week. It decreases to 12 to 14 hours during high school years. By the time children graduate from high school, they have spent more hours in front of the TV set than in the classroom. Therefore the potential influence of the medium is vast, rivaling that of parents and peers. It is not surprising that people have been concerned about violence on TV and the impact such violence has on society—particularly on children.

Violence on television. Common observation and numerous studies have shown that violent acts are very common in TV programs. Over the years, the amount of violence in prime-time television increased from about 17 percent in 1954 to 60 percent in 1961. Later studies showed that the percentage of dramatic programs containing violence during the years 1967–1971 was over 75 percent for each year. Other studies have shown that more than half of the major TV characters are violent, that nearly half of the killers depicted suffer no ill consequences from their acts, and that violence is often a successful means to an end (Johnson, 1972). It has been estimated that over 90 percent of children's cartoons contain violent episodes. Since children also watch many adult programs, they are truly exposed to a massive amount of violence on television. This degree of program violence has resulted in complaints, congressional inquiries, and research studies.

Brutal acts apparently inspired by television are common. For example, in October 1973, a young woman named Evelyn Wagler ran out of gas in Boston. She was returning to her car with a 2-gallon can of gasoline when she was accosted by several youths. They pushed her into a nearby yard, and, after beating her, forced her to pour gasoline over herself. One of the youths then struck a match and held it to her, and Evelyn Wagler became a screaming human torch. Police attributed this gruesome act to a TV film aired a few nights before that included a scene in which youths poured gasoline on sleeping tramps and set them on fire. Criminal acts attributable to television could be cited dozens and probably hundreds of times. They have provoked numerous public outcries about television as a cause of violence.

The effects of television on aggression. The best summary of the effects of television violence is expressed by Liebert, Neale, and Davidson (1973) in their excellent volume *The Early Window:*

> But the real issue is to weigh the evidence in light of the consequences of maintaining and teaching violence. While some quibble, violence continues to become a way of life. The quibbling is unwarranted. On the basis of evaluation of many lines of converging evidence, involving more than 50 studies which have included more than 10,000 normal children and adolescents from every conceivable background, the weight of the evidence is clear: The demonstrated teaching and instigating effects of aggressive television fare upon youth are of sufficient importance to warrant immediate remedial action (p. 197).

The statement is strong. It is based on the following types of evidence.

1. *Observational learning.* One line of evidence comes from social-learning experiments. New responses can be acquired by watching a filmed model. Such modeling can loosen inhibitions against aggression and actively facilitate it. Aggression does not have to be performed immediately after it is witnessed. Rather it is stored in the memory system and may be activated later. Along with modeling novel behaviors, pervasive TV violence also desensitizes people so that they become less emotionally responsive to later episodes of violence (Thomas, Horton, Lippincott, and Drabman, 1977). Stated differently, watching violence can blunt children's sensitivity to the suffering of others (Liebert, Neale, and Davidson, 1973).

2. *Laboratory studies.* Many of the observational-learning studies were criticized, because, it was claimed, striking a Bobo doll has nothing to do with human aggression. Several experiments were subsequently designed to overcome such criticisms. These experiments used more realistic measures of aggression with attacks against humans instead of toys, exposed subjects to more relevant portrayals of violence (such as actual TV episodes), and sought to vary the similarity between the exact nature of the observed violence and the type of situation in which subjects could express aggression (Baron, 1977). Most of these studies supported the conclusion that observing film violence leads to greater aggressiveness in the laboratory.

3. *Field research.* Even the laboratory studies received extensive criticism, particularly from spokespersons of the television industry, for not being sufficiently similar to real life. As a result, a wide variety of field experiments and correlational studies were conducted. In general, such studies measured how much violent television a person watched and obtained some measure of that person's aggressiveness. These studies rather consistently showed positive correlations between watching violence on TV and committing aggressive acts (see Baron, 1977, and Liebert, Neal, and Davidson, 1973, for reviews).

Data from all three types of studies consistently point to the conclusion that *aggression can be modeled by media, especially television.*

The catharsis hypothesis. Fairness requires that brief consideration be given to the notion that witnessing violence has a positive effect, the CATHARSIS HYPOTHESIS. The idea comes from Aristotle, who speculated that watching drama might purge an audience of feelings of grief, fear, and pity. Over the centuries, the idea has been extended to anger and expressions of aggression. The basic idea is that fantasy aggression can serve to drain off aggressive energy generated by frustration or other causes. Witnessing filmed violence may stimulate the fantasy process; and if it does, it should reduce the frequency of actual acts of aggression.

The major piece of evidence in favor of the catharsis hypothesis is a study reported by Feshbach and Singer (1971). Subjects were 400 adolescent boys living in several institutional settings. The boys were divided into two groups. One group watched aggressive TV programs for 6 weeks, and the other group watched only nonaggressive programs. Various measures of aggression showed that, in some institutions, the boys watching nonaggressive programs were more aggressive than boys watching aggressive programs.

There are several problems with this research. For one thing, the nonaggressive programs were relatively disliked. The frustration of being forced to watch only such programs for 6 weeks may have been responsible for the boys' increased aggressiveness. Furthermore, the boys in some of the institutions objected so strongly to not being allowed to watch *Batman* (an aggressive program) that the authorities relented and added it to the viewing list. Such a change makes any differences in the dependent variable difficult to interpret, to say the least.

Most authorities believe that Feshbach and Singer's work is not conclusive (Bandura, 1973; Baron, 1977; Goranson, 1970; Geen, 1976). Attempts to replicate the catharsis effect have not been successful. Indeed, more recent and better-designed research (Parke, Berkowitz, Leyens, West, and Sebastian, 1977) using cross-national samples indicates that watching TV violence is reliably associated with increased aggressiveness. The catharsis hypothesis is probably false, or it is valid only under extremely limited conditions that are presently unknown.

Forms of violence in society
By Susan Singer Hendrick

In the previous sections, we have been primarily concerned with aggression as an individual phenomenon. However, in asking about the effects of mass media on aggression, we shifted our emphasis from the individual to the society at large. We also began to use the word *violence* about as frequently as *aggression.*

Aggression is of interest to many sciences, and it can be studied at many levels. In this section, we will consider several types of social violence. We examine briefly the concept of violent crime in society. We give special consideration to rape, a type of aggression involving sex, and to violence within the family, a tragedy of increasing social concern. The instrumental use of violence to attain group goals is considered in an examination of organized crime. And finally, an example of large-scale social conflict is presented in a discussion of violence in Northern Ireland.

VIOLENCE AGAINST INDIVIDUALS

Crimes of violence. Every society defines some actions as violent and others as nonviolent. The definition of what is violent may vary from society to society and across historical periods. Also, each society considers some forms of violence legitimate and others illegitimate. Often the definition depends on which person in which social role performs the action. For example, if a police officer on duty shoots and kills an armed robber, the act is legitimate. If the robber happens instead to shoot and kill the police officer, the act is defined as murder. Any form of violence not considered socially legitimate may be defined as crime. Not all crime involves violence, of course, but there is a tendency to view the two as synonymous. Kahn (1972) interviewed a national sample and obtained opinions about what acts are violent. Among whites, only 32 percent of the sample defined the shooting of looters by the police as a violent act, but looting itself was considered violence by 87 percent of the sample. A related crime, burglary, was considered violence by 64 percent of the sample. In the public mind, crimes against property are perceived as violent acts about as strongly as crimes against persons.

One issue of concern to most people is whether violent crime is increasing. The FBI Uniform Crime Reports showed that during the decade of the 1960s, violent crimes increased in number by 130 percent. Murder increased by 44 percent, forcible rape by 93 percent, aggravated assault by 79 percent, and robbery by 146 percent (Johnson, 1972). There are some problems with these statistics. The definition of crimes and the methods of collecting and reporting data vary from time to time and place to place. Thus crime statistics contain large amounts of error. Some commentators (Wrightsman, 1977) speculate that rates for violent crimes may actually have been higher early in the century than now. It is not really clear that we are becoming a more violent society.

The National Commission on the Causes and Prevention of Violence (1969) summarized masses of data on crime, yielding a general profile for violent crime:

1. Violent crime occurs mostly in large cities. In 1969, the 26 largest cities contained 17 percent of the population, but produced 45 percent of the major violent crimes.
2. Violent crime is largely committed by males between the ages of 15 and 24.
3. Violent crime is committed primarily by individuals of lower socioeconomic status. Such crime is disproportionately frequent in ghetto areas.
4. Criminals and victims tend to be similar in socioeconomic and racial background. In fact, most homicides and assaults occur between relatives, friends, or acquaintances.
5. Violent crimes against persons are often provoked by the victim, often involve petty quarrels, and are often associated with alcohol.
6. The majority of crimes are committed by repeaters.

It appears that much crime against persons and property stems from adverse economic conditions and the social disorganization that goes with such conditions. Crimes against property are most often thefts for economic reasons. Economic frustrations, lack of jobs, prejudice, and discrimination may serve as perpetual frustrations, making individual acts of violence against persons more probable. On the societal level, as on the individual level, aggression in the form of crime seems largely determined by environmental (economic and social) variables.

Rape. During the 1970s, rape received much national attention. Rape crisis centers were established across the country, and a large and voluminous literature appeared. Books such as Susan Brownmiller's *Against Our Will* (1975) became best sellers. During this period, Congress passed a law establishing the National Center for the Control and Prevention of Rape, and many states revised their statutes on rape.

This strong social attack on rape seems to have developed out of the feminist movement. Rape is one of the few crimes that victims are reluctant to report because of the stigma attached and possibly because so few rapists are actually sent to prison. Consequently, estimates of the frequency of rape vary widely, with some estimates of up to half a million cases per year. Greer (1975) points out that

> a man has to be very unlucky to be convicted of the crime of rape. He has to be stupid enough, or drugged or drunk enough, to leave a mile-wide trail of blood, bruises, threats, semen, screaming and what have you. He has to have chosen the kind of woman about whom the neighbors have nothing but good to say, who has enough *chutzpah* to get down to the police station at once and file her complaint (p. 378).

It is small wonder that rape is so underreported.

There are many types of rape situations. One basic distinction is whether the victim and offender are acquainted. Estimates of the incidence of acquaintance rape vary from 48 percent (Amir, 1971) to 57 percent (Medea and Thompson, 1974). Neither Russell (1975) nor Kirkpatrick and Kanin (1957) found a single victim of acquaintance rape who had reported it to the police. Students are at high risk for rape; 61 percent of all victims are under age 25 (Amir, 1971).

Since so few rapists are imprisoned, studies of rapists have necessarily been conducted on very unrepresentative samples. A few attempts have been made to classify rapists diagnostically. For example, Cohen, Garofalo, Boucher, and Seghorn (1971) proposed three types. *Aggressive* rapists are angry men intent on humiliating the victim. *Sexual* rapists use minimal violence and are often defending against homosexual impulses. And *sex-aggression diffusion* rapists represent a combination of the other two types. Unfortunately, no work has been done to validate this classification.

Some men who rape may be suffering from emotional disorder. But for many more, rape is culturally conditioned by sex-role socialization. Manliness in Western society is often associated with strength and aggressiveness, including sexual aggression. Men are supposed to be dominant initiators of sexual activity, and when hostility is added to the mix, rape becomes a potential aggressive act (Weis and Borges, 1973). Thus rape may be viewed as an act of power and sex combined (Brownmiller, 1975; Griffin, 1971). Since females are often socialized to be passive and nonaggressive, they are in a sense trained to be victims of rape attacks (Weis and Borges, 1973).

These socialization tendencies are summarized and put in excellent perspective by Diana Russell in *The Politics of Rape* (1975). Russell presents a number of detailed case studies of rape victims. Her conclusions match closely the sociological perspective we have just outlined.

> Indeed, the view that emerges from this study is that rape is not so much a deviant act as an overconforming act. Rape may be understood as an extreme acting out of qualities that are regarded as supermasculine in this and many other societies: aggression, force, power, strength, toughness, dominance, competitiveness. To win, to be superior, to be successful, to conquer, all demonstrate masculinity to those who subscribe to common cultural notions of masculinity, i.e., the masculine mystique. And it would be surprising if these notions of masculinity did not find expression in men's sexual behavior. Indeed, sex may be the arena where these notions of masculinity are most intensely acted out, particularly by men who feel powerless in the rest of their lives, and men whose masculinity is threatened by their sense of powerlessness (p. 260).

Since men are expected to take the initiative sexually with women, "it is to be expected that they will often go beyond what the woman wants and 'offend' her in some way" (Russell, 1975). Thus, from the females' perspective, there will be a considerable amount of "ordinary" sexual aggressiveness directed against them during courtship. The evidence indicates that such is the case. Kanin (1965, 1967) conducted an interview study of college-age students to ascertain the frequency of aggressive attempts at coitus, usually among dating couples. An aggressive attempt was defined as behavior not so extreme as to be called rape, but something like forceful attempts to remove clothing in the dating situation. Of 341 college respondents, 25 percent reported some degree of sexual aggression in their previous relationships. Further, the number of aggressive sexual encounters by males was positively correlated with a generalized aggression scale (Kanin, 1965). The higher the male aggressiveness in general, the more likely that the male would attempt forceful seductions. Kanin (1965) suggested that actual sex offenders constitute a very biased sample of extremely sexually aggressive males.

There is yet a further facet of the socialization of the rapist to consider. What many females would view as rape may be viewed by the male as manly seduction. Most men would not want to be defined as rapists: "Men have a vested interest in maintaining the definition of the situation as primarily sexual and seductive rather than rapacious. If the man can call the act seduction, he may call himself a winner; if it is rape, he is a loser" (Weis and Borges, 1973, pp. 86–87). It would thus be expected that the average male would have a much higher threshold than the average female for viewing a given act as involving undue force. It is this sort of defensive maneuver that seems to leave many men genuinely confused and disbelieving that they have committed rape. The denial even exists in stranger-to-stranger rape situations. "Even convicted rapists who are serving long prison terms deny their culpability. They tenaciously insist women encourage and enjoy sexual assault. These men tell you that they are the greatest lovers in the world" (Selkin, 1975, p. 76).

It seems fair to conclude that the majority of rapes are acts of violent aggression. The act seems to be derivative of a supermasculine sex-role stereotype. Presumably, the long-term solution lies in changes in socialization, particularly in the belief that force is a suitable means of achieving goals while at the same time validating one's self-concept.

VIOLENCE IN THE FAMILY

Some of you reading these words will eventually abuse your children, some will beat your wives, and a few may kill a member of your family.

Aggressive behavior exists at all levels of modern society. This conclusion seems warranted by all the relevant research and social commentary. But what about the family? What about the haven from the storm, "the place where, when you have to go there, they have to take you in?" Family violence does occur, and it is best seen on a continuum ranging from mild verbal assaults, designed to deflate another's ego, to actual murder of a family member. Since few families are totally exempt from all violence, most families fall somewhere on this continuum. We will look at two examples of family violence:

Child abuse.

> And he [God] said, Take now thy son, thine only son Isaac, whom thou lovest, and get thee into the land of Moriah; and offer him there for a burnt offering upon one of the mountains which I will tell thee of. . . . And they came to the place which God had told him of; and Abraham built an altar there, and laid the wood in order, and bound Isaac his son, and laid him on the altar upon the wood. . . . And Abraham stretched forth his hand, and took the knife to slay his son." (*Genesis* 22:2, 9, 10)

Infanticide, one form of child abuse, is not new. In this particular story, infanticide did not actually occur, because God intervened to keep Abraham from killing Isaac. Yet the intent was there. Child sacrifice, infanticide with the purpose of pleasing or appeasing a God, was practiced by the Irish Celts, the Gauls, the Scandinavians, the Egyptians, the Phoenicians, and various other cultures (deMause, 1974). Killing infants and children was a means of population control, an attempt to ease socioeconomic stress, and a way to rid parents of the burden of child-rearing. Those reasons for infanticide among the ancients sound very similar to some of the reasons given for twentieth-century child abuse.

Children have also been mutilated throughout the centuries. Burns, lacerations, broken bones, and even amputations have always been perpetrated on children. It is only in the last couple of centuries that society has really begun to think of children as human beings deserving of humane treatment. But society has not changed enough, for child abuse continues. Al-

The battered child syndrome is a particularly ignominious form of aggression, and is much more prevalent than most people believe. Many states have introduced Child Abuse Hotlines which handle in excess of 10,000 calls per year. (Wide World Photo)

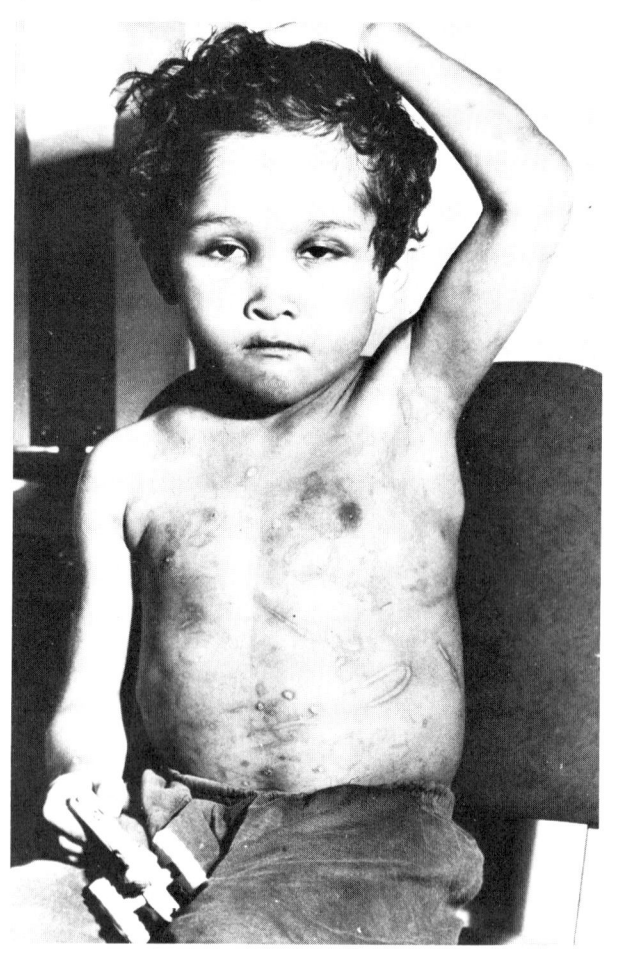

though the statistics are notoriously unreliable, some estimates of abuse run as high as 500,000 to 2.5 million cases per year (Sarles, 1976), and Fontana (1971) believes that abuse is probably the greatest cause of death in children, leading all childhood diseases.

As we mentioned before, various ethologists believe that aggression is largely instinctive (Lorenz, 1966; Morris, 1967). These writers might well agree with Bakan (1971) that child abuse may be a regression to an instinctive behavior natural to the human condition. Perhaps the decrease in aggression toward children through the centuries is due to the progressive social taming of instinctive drives.

Theories of modeling such as Bandura's (1973) would attribute some responsibility for child abuse to society at large, wherein violence is so ubiquitous (Gil, 1971). Various authors (Sage, 1975; Sarles, 1976) have pointed to corporal punishment within the schools as a significant model of aggression for both parents and children.

Environmental stresses related to child abuse include lower socioeconomic status, unemployment, youthful parents, high mobility, and unwanted pregnancies (Gil, 1971). The disproportionate amount of child abuse reported from families of lower socioeconomic class may reflect a tendency by such families to use violence to solve family problems (Sarles, 1976). Since a high level of frustration exists under such conditions, the frustration–aggression hypothesis would predict a high level of aggression also. In fact, this appears to be the case.

Wife battering. "There is no personal gratification from seeing someone close to you that's black and blue, with busted lips and a knocked-out front tooth trying to hide it with dark glasses" (Geracimos, 1976, p. 53). Thus speaks a self-described woman beater as he reviews his former relationships with women.

Wife beating or battering, like child abuse, is not new. It has always been part of the larger problem of inequality between the sexes. "The existence of civil and religious laws giving men superior rights over women nurtured the belief—born in the dim past in the smoke-filled caves of primitives—that men also had the right to beat their wives" (Langley and Levy, 1977, p. 32). Wives, along with children and property, have, throughout history, belonged to men to do with as they wished. Judge Blackstone, a noted English jurist, recorded the English "Rule of Thumb," which referred to a husband's right to "chastise his wife with a whip or rattan no bigger than his thumb, in order to enforce the salutory restraints of domestic discipline." Conditions slowly improved as women were allowed to own property, accorded voting rights, and in most instances treated as full citizens. Yet wife battering has continued to flourish.

Many of the causes of wife battering are the same as the causes of child abuse. Frustration resulting from environmental stress surely precipitates aggression, and wife battering does occur somewhat more frequently in lower socioeconomic groups. The norm of violence in Western society gives social support and modeling influence for violent action, and there is a historical precedent for wife battering. Personality disturbances of both husband and wife are also positively related to family violence of this type.

Yet wife-battering and, to a lesser extent, husband-battering take place in marital systems that often continue to function for years. This type of aggression is chronic, not acute, and it occurs between intimates. Although fear, economic dependency, and emotional attachment all serve to maintain abusive couples in their relationships, there often appears to be an aggressor-victim scenario that is acted and reenacted time after time in this type of marriage. Perhaps the proponents of aggression as instinct would offer the most convincing explanation for wife battering.

VIOLENCE AS A SOCIAL CONTROL MECHANISM: THE MAFIA

Although crime of all types contributes to violence in the world, organized crime is worth discussing because of its interesting use of both symbolic and actual violence. For example, the Mafia (also called the Cosa Nostra) uses only minimal violence in the public sector, because it wants to keep a low profile and avoid incurring public and possibly governmental wrath. Threats of violence appear perfectly sufficient to intimidate the small businessperson, politician, or law enforcement official who could potentially hurt the organization. However, actual violence is frequently used to (1) restrict the activities of criminal rivals or keep competing "families" in line, (2) depose a Mafia leader and gain power, and (3) keep fellow family members under control. In these cases, violence or the threat of violence is used primarily for *instrumental* purposes. *Angry* violence also occurs on occasion, usually in the form of retaliation against a rival family for injuries perpetrated.

LARGE SCALE VIOLENCE

The best example of large-scale aggression between groups is war. Northern Ireland offers an example. Berkowitz (1962) talks about the escalation of aggression when visibly different groups are thrust into proximity where they can create various kinds of frustrations for each other, and this is surely the case in Northern Ireland. Cultural, political, and economic issues all separate the Protestants and the Catholics.

Both rivalry and frustration influence aggression (Sherif and Sherif, 1953), and Catholics in Northern Ireland have been continually frustrated in their efforts to secure better jobs, better housing, voting parity, and equal treatment before the law (Schmitt, 1974; *London Sunday Times,* 1972). This frustration resulted first in mistrust and finally in disregard for the existing government and in sporadic violence used to aggress, defend, or retaliate against the Protestants (Schmitt, 1974).

Control and prevention of aggression

Most research and writing have concentrated on the causes of aggression, paying very little attention to variables that can control and prevent it. According to Baron (1977), there are two reasons for the lack of research on control and prevention. Until recently, many people (including psychologists) believed that punishment and catharsis were the most effective deterrents to aggression. However, we saw earlier that there is little evidence in favor of the catharsis hypothesis.

Second, many researchers apparently believed that if the cause of aggression could be found, simply removing the cause would eliminate aggression. This approach seemed reasonable when aggression was attributed to a single cause, such as frustration. However, as the number of factors implicated in aggression increased, this approach seemed less realistic. Instead, an active search for deterrents seemed more profitable, and in the last few years, aggression researchers have begun to explore the effectiveness of various deterrents.

PUNISHMENT

Punishment has been the most widely touted deterrent to aggression, as well as a means to modify other behaviors. Although it fell into disfavor as a technique of behavior change, largely because of the influence of Skinner (1971), it is now generally agreed that punishment can indeed affect aggression under certain specific conditions (Baron, 1977).

The mere threat of punishment can inhibit aggressive actions when both the magnitude and the probability of proposed punishment are very high—higher, in fact, than the person's motivation to commit aggression. When an individual is extremely angry and highly provoked, he or she will probably aggress no matter what the threatened punishment (Baron, 1977). Actual punishment also seems effective under specified conditions, such as when it follows aggression promptly and appropriately and can be seen by its recipients as the logical outcome of an aggressive act. The use of punishment can also be combined with reward as DIFFERENTIAL REINFORCEMENT, the providing of a reward for nonaggressive behavior and a punishment for aggressive behavior. Bandura (1973) felt that differential reinforcement should be particularly effective in controlling aggression.

NONAGGRESSIVE MODELS

Another possible control for aggression is the use of nonaggressive models (Baron, 1977; Aronson, 1976). If people who cope with life and its frustrations calmly and nonaggressively can be visible and respected models for others, aggressive models may become less powerful. Such nonaggressive models as Mahatma

Gandhi and Martin Luther King have had significant impact on individuals as well as social systems.

COGNITIVE FACTORS

When individuals understand their own frustration or another person's reason for behaving aggressively, they may well be able to monitor their own aggressive responses. If a wife realizes that her husband's irritability is caused by a flat tire on his way home from work, she may be less likely to lash out with biting comments of her own. Baron (1977) refers to this cognitive understanding as awareness of mitigating circumstances.

Another cognitive approach to aggression control is to create responses that are incompatible with aggressive behavior. Three such responses are empathy, amusement, and sexual arousal. Baron (1977) points out that studies in both laboratory and field settings have shown that these three responses all act to reduce aggression in a variety of situations. For example, an angry crowd can sometimes be induced to laugh at a joke, which of course greatly reduces the crowd's tendency toward violence.

SOCIAL CHANGE AS PREVENTION

Although no one has any guaranteed methods for prevention and control of aggression, nearly all writers in aggression research support the need for social change. Baron (1977) discussed the need to alter environmental conditions that provoke aggressive responses and to change the attitudes that allow violence as a viable behavioral alternative. In their classic study of groups, Sherif and Sherif (1953) found that integration of hostile groups reduced aggression. Increased contact between the groups, mutual group effort, and uniting against a common enemy all contributed to easing tensions. Johnson (1972) supported the learning of conflict-resolution techniques as a way of reducing violence. He also advocated early socialization of children in the control of aggression and stressed the need to model nonaggressive problem-solving techniques rather than violent confrontation. Following this notion, Bandura (1973) discussed the media's impact on society and proposed (1) a violence-rating of TV programs to be made available to the public, (2) news broadcasts that have greater in-depth coverage and less violent sensationalism, and (3) increased public broadcasting.

Summary

Aggression is a complex form of social behavior involving at least two roles, the role of aggressor and the role of victim. Aggression may be defined as any form of behavior directed toward the goal of harming or injuring another living being who is motivated to avoid such treatment. Theories of aggression may be located on a hereditary–environment dimension. Psychoanalytic and ethological theories view aggression as instinctive, though very few social scientists today believe that aggression is instinctually determined as strongly as these two theories imply. The most widely acclaimed theory, proposed by a group of psychologists at Yale in 1939, is that frustration causes aggression. The hypothesis first stated that aggression is always caused by frustration and that frustration always leads to aggression. There were many problems in substantiating the hypothesis, and it would probably have been abandoned were it not for the extensive efforts of Berkowitz (1962, 1965, 1969) to revise and update it. Berkowitz has shown that frustration may be considered one of several causes of aggression. The social-learning approach views aggression as largely a learned phenomenon. Bandura's (1973) observational-learning theory is most popular.

Several kinds of personality and individual differences affect aggression. The topic most frequently studied is that of sex differences; males of most species generally show more aggression than females. Several laboratory techniques have been devised to study situational and environmental causes of aggression. The techniques of Buss (1961), Berkowitz (1962), and Taylor (1967) are best known. Actual or intended attack from another person is one of the more reliable causes of aggression, and other causes include noise, heat, crowding, and alcohol. The effects of the mass media, particularly television, on aggression have been studied extensively. The evidence indicates that viewing violence on TV is associated with increased levels of aggressiveness.

There are many forms of violence in society. Violence is perpetrated against individuals, within the family, at the level of organized crime, and at the societal level in riots, rebellions, and civil wars. Economic and social frustrations seem causally implicated in much violent crime, as well as in various forms of violence in the family. Organized crime uses violence instrumentally. Political violence is somewhat different, because economic and social privations often contribute to it. Numerous ways to control and prevent aggression have been suggested. The more common ones are punishment, nonaggressive modeling, cognitive control, and social change.

VI

The nature of groups

12

The formation of groups: from "I" to "We"

338
Small groups

340
Sources of affiliation

Physical attractiveness
Similarity
Anxiety
Complementary
   The nature of roles
   The reciprocal character of roles
Forming the family: an integration of similarity and complementarity?
   The stimulus-value-role theory
   Evidence for the stimulus stage
   Evidence for the role stage
Which comes first, the membership or the motive?
   In groups of two
   In larger groups

355
Aberrations of affiliation

Groupthink
Risk and caution in groups
Commitment to the group
   The effects of initiation

362
Summary

*I*n preceding chapters, we have focused primarily on the behaviors, attitudes, and values of individuals. Even in the chapter on conformity, for example, a topic that clearly involves a relationship between an individual and a group, we focused on the individual's reaction to real or imagined group pressure and the individual's use of conformity as a strategy to manipulate others. In this chapter and the ones that follow, we shift to the study of groups.

GROUPS vary tremendously in size, purpose, composition, and the impact they have on the lives of the individuals involved. The most diffuse sorts of groups are often little more than categories. In *Cat's Cradle* (1963), novelist Kurt Vonnegut refers to such groups as *granfalloons,* pseudogroups that really exist only in the minds of some of the members. He gives the following example of an interaction between two people, one of whom is and one of whom is not impressed by their membership in such a granfalloon.

> . . . his wife Hazel recognized my name as an Indiana name. She was from Indiana, too.
> "My God," she said. "are you a *Hoosier?*"
> I admitted I was.
> "I'm a Hoosier, too," she crowed. "Nobody has to be ashamed of being a Hoosier."
> "I'm not," I said. "I never knew anybody who was."
> "Hoosiers do all right. Lowe and I've been around the world twice, and everywhere we went we found Hoosiers in charge of everything."
> "That's reassuring" (p. 80).

Vonnegut believes such granfalloons—Hoosiers, southerners, Catholics, Daughters of the American Revolution, communists, capitalists—are generally meaningless in terms of the day-to-day existence of most people.

Poets and novelists, of course, are licensed to overstate their case. Even if we ignore the wars that have been fought in the name of "Christianity" or for *Deutschland Über Alles* or to keep the world safe for "Democracy," there is good evidence that the groups people identify with do make a difference in their lives, even if these groups are only abstract entities, such as the "now generation," the New Left, or "Volvo owners." All of these entities could be reference groups for individuals, and we have seen (Chapter 9) that reference groups can serve as a basis for self-evaluation, attitude formation, and action. On the other hand, there is a great deal of insight in Vonnegut's cynicism about the everyday importance of large collectivities. Let us see why.

Small groups

The really important groups for most people appear to be family, friends, work groups, and other people with whom they interact on a daily or at least a frequent basis. The common feature of such groups is that they are generally very small. In 1973, for example, 82 percent of all households in the United States were inhabited by four or fewer people (U.S. Bureau of the Census, 1974). Further, in a series of field observations of people at play, working, shopping, conversing, and engaging in other spontaneous everyday activities, James (1951) found that 98 percent of all groupings consisted of four, three, or two people. As Shaw (1971) points out, one cannot infer from these data that small groups are necessarily more important than larger groups, but it does seem likely.

Apart from the simple fact that the vast majority of groups people experience in their daily lives are small, there are at least two additional reasons for believing that these small groups are the most important social aggregations. James points out that groups are limited in size by the information-processing capabilities of their individual members. Specifically, if we consider all that takes place between two individuals, two subgroups, or an individual and a subgroup as a single relationship, the number of potential relationships is related to group size as follows:

Most large aggregations of people are actually comprised of much smaller, more manageable groups. Apparently, to interact with all of the combinations of people and behaviors in the larger group puts too much of a strain on an individual's cognitive processing capabilities. (Eric Roth/The Picture Cube)

Group Size	Potential Relationships
2	1
3	6
4	25
5	90
6	301
7	966

Even if only a small percentage of the potential relationships in a group of, say, seven people were active at any given time, it would be confusing to try to comprehend the various coalitions and sentiments at work in the group. James (1951) argues that increases in group size above two or three result in unstable groups that tend to break up rather quickly into subgroups. This lack of stability of larger groups due to information overload on the individual supports the idea that smaller groups are indeed most important.

The third reason for concentrating on small groups is that even when the group in question is some large collectivity or organization, such as the Catholic church, the prescriptions and proscriptions of the larger body are mediated by a small group of associates, such as parents, priests, and peers. It is important to realize that the particular small group surrounding the individual may actually misinterpret the norms, beliefs, and doctrines of the larger collectivity and misrepresent them to the individual. Thus the immediate group of associates takes precedence even when its task is to represent the larger organization.

The way a small group selectively mediates the norms, values, and culture of a larger society is apparent in the family. The child is born into a social situation in which he or she usually encounters the two people who will be predominantly in charge of his or her socialization in the values, beliefs, and ways of perceiving the world that are shared by a group. But there is a catch here. The parents—the "significant others" in the child's environment—are imposed on the child. The way the parents define the world will be accepted by the child, at least for a few years, as the way the world really is. Parental prejudices are not likely to be seen as prejudices, for example, but as evidence of objective reality. If they say certain people are lazy and shiftless, it can only be because those people are lazy and shiftless. Reality is filtered by the parents; only certain parts of it get through to the child, and those parts that do get through may well be distorted.

Families differ in at least two ways from most other groups people encounter. First, people do not seek out and join a family; they are born into it. Second, the enormous power and status differences between parents and children are not usually present, or at least are not quite so extreme, in other groups. For both of these reasons, one could argue that the family is an atypical group and that the selectivity, filtering, and biased presentation of information that occurs in families would not occur in other groups. We shall see.

For now, then, we have three reasons for concentrating on small, face-to-face groups. First, such groups comprise the vast majority of groups encountered in daily life. Second, larger groups strain the information-processing capabilities of individuals and, as a result, tend to be unstable and break up into cliques and smaller groups. Third, small groups usually mediate between the individual and larger collectivities and organizations. Let us begin by asking about the formation of groups. Why do people seek out the company of others?

Sources of affiliation

Generally, people seek out the company of others when they anticipate being rewarded or reinforced for doing so. The rewards received do not have to be money and material goods, although these seem to hold many work groups together. Rather, the rewards can include such nebulous things as a heightened sense of self-esteem, a few moments of pleasure, or a reduction in uncertainty. We all know people who have never done anything for us in a material sense but whose company we seek at every opportunity, simply because they are pleasant to be around. They don't engage in petty gossip, they usually have something interesting to say, or they make us feel important by asking our opinions.

Thibaut and Kelley (1959) have devised a general framework for the analysis of social interaction in which the exchange of rewards is seen as the basic mechanism behind group formation and maintenance. In their view, each person has a set of possible behaviors, and the reward value associated with each behavior depends in part on the behavior performed in response by the other party to the interaction. Giving a stranger a friendly smile may be rewarding in itself (it allows you to think of yourself as a friendly person), but it is much more rewarding if it is met with a smile from the stranger than if he or she ignores you.

The major analytic tool employed by Thibaut and Kelley is a matrix displaying the behavioral repertoires of two people. As an example, consider two people who have just been introduced and whose behavioral repertoires are displayed in Figure 1. Each cell in the matrix represents one possible set of joint responses. The number above the diagonal in each cell is the reward value of that set for person A, and the number below the diagonal is the reward value of that set for person B. As Thibaut and Kelley point out, the initial interactions between two people are a process of exploring the matrix. The parties learn the values of the matrix by (1) experiencing samples of the outcomes in various parts of the matrix and (2) forecasting trends in the outcomes. Interaction between the parties will continue only if each believes his or her current and future rewards from the interaction will be greater than those obtainable in alternative relationships with other people. Person A will no doubt quickly tire of attempting to interact with person B if all B does is yawn and look bored. A receives no reward at all from such behavior on B's part.

The Thibaut and Kelley framework has a certain appeal, but, as Shaw (1971) points out, it is not sufficiently analytic about the way in which groups form. Specifically, one would expect that what constitutes a "reward" would vary as a function of the nature and purpose of the group being formed.

What, then, are some of the bases for anticipating that another will generally serve one's needs and desires and provide a rewarding sequence of interaction? Further, do these bases differ as a function of the type of group being formed? We discuss several bases for affiliation in the following sections, including physical attraction, similarity, anxiety, and complementarity. Then we use these bases for affiliation to discuss one type of group, the family, in more detail.

1. A portion of the Thibaut and Kelley interaction matrix for two people who have just been introduced.

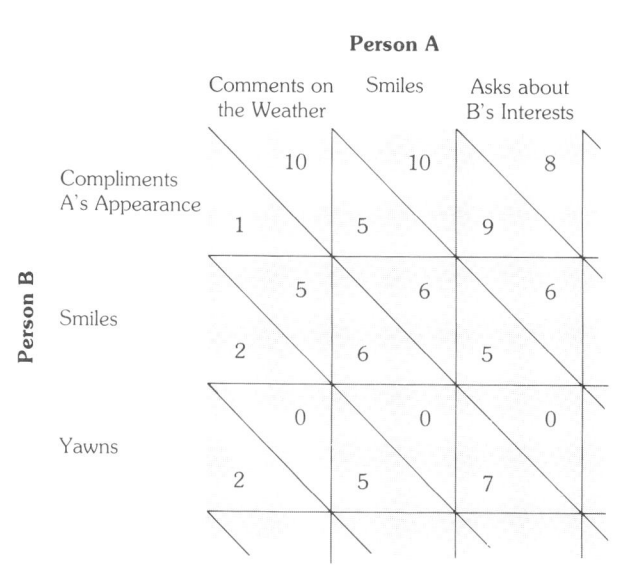

	Person A: Comments on the Weather	Person A: Smiles	Person A: Asks about B's Interests
Person B: Compliments A's Appearance	10 / 1	10 / 5	8 / 9
Person B: Smiles	5 / 2	6 / 6	6 / 5
Person B: Yawns	0 / 2	0 / 5	0 / 7

PHYSICAL ATTRACTIVENESS

There is nothing very mysterious about the fact that a well-formed face or a well-proportioned body of either sex is aesthetically appealing and therefore rewarding to others. We have already discussed this topic in Chapter 6 and shall not dwell on it here except to point out that what we *assume* about "beautiful people" may be as important to the development of interaction with them as their actual characteristics. Consider the following study.

Dion, Berscheid, and Walster (1972) hypothesized that people attribute desirable personality characteristics to physically attractive others and, in addition, that people expect physically attractive others to lead better lives than unattractive individuals. To check on their hypothesis, Dion, et al. asked male and female subjects to rate people shown in photographs on 27 different personality traits. The photos had previously been selected to represent three different levels of attractiveness, and each subject judged one attractive, one average, and one unattractive person. Subjects were also asked to assess which people would be most likely to have a number of different life experiences (such as divorce, professional success, or a happy marriage) and which would be most likely to engage in each of 30 different occupations. As anticipated, many more socially desirable personality traits were attributed to attractive individuals, who were also expected to have more prestigious jobs, to be more competent spouses, and to have happier marriages. These differences were not affected by the sex of the person making the judgments or by the sex of the person about whom the judgments were being made.

Thus we tend to assume that the physically attractive are more interesting people, hold higher-prestige jobs, and have more socially desirable characteristics than the unattractive. These assumptions are reinforced daily via advertisements in which beautiful people appear in elegant clothes, lounging in tastefully appointed rooms, or at their desks in private offices. However these assumptions are arrived at, they have at least two interesting consequences for the initial stages of group formation.

First, because we believe attractive others have certain additional characteristics, we may behave toward them in ways that lead *them* to behave as we expect. That is, if we believe certain people have a number of socially desirable characteristics, we may treat them with more than average esteem and respect. And when people are treated in such a manner, they are more likely to behave in socially desirable ways. If this cycle occurs repeatedly in the lives of attractive people, they may indeed develop an easy and graceful social manner, so of course people continue to treat them pleasantly and seek their company. Guthrie (1938) reports an example of this process, in which a group of male students

> agreed to cooperate in establishing a shy and inept girl as a social favorite. They saw to it . . . that she was invited to college affairs that were considered important and that she always had dancing partners. They treated her by agreement as though she were the reigning college favorite. Before the year was over she had developed an easy manner and a confident assumption that she was popular. These habits continued her social success after the experiment was completed and the men involved had ceased to make efforts in her behalf (p. 128).

By giving the physically attractive the benefit of the doubt about their additional characteristics during the initial stages of interaction and treating them as if they were "reigning favorites," we make it easier for them to be socially rewarding to us. Hence we confirm our initial assumption that the physically attractive are more pleasant to interact with than the unattractive. (For another example of this process at work, see Box A.)

The second consequence of our preexisting assumptions about the characteristics of the physically attractive is that such beliefs may lead us to infer mistakenly that the attitudes, beliefs, and values of physically attractive others are more similar to our own than are those of physically unattractive others. Most people believe that they themselves possess socially desirable characteristics. Rosenberg (1965) reports that the vast majority of a large sample of high school juniors and seniors described themselves as easy to get along with, respected, looked up to by others, pleasant, likable, popular, good-natured, and liked by many different people. It is possible that, in the initial stages of group formation, we seek out the physically attractive at least in part because we assume that their personality characteristics are more similar to our own. Let us see what evidence there is, then, about the effects of similarity on group formation.

SIMILARITY

In the early and middle 1950s, there was a great deal of research and speculation on the formation of small groups, especially friendship groups. In a well-known study, Festinger, Schachter, and Back (1950) investigated the patterns of friendship in two married-student housing projects at M.I.T. One of their major findings was that the closer together people lived in the projects, the more likely they were to become friends. Since then, a number of other studies (Byrne, 1961) have shown that propinquity is indeed an important factor in friendship and group formation. In fact, the effect of propinquity was so pronounced in some studies that it almost seemed that a decision to move into a certain neighborhood was also a decision about who one's friends would be (Caplow and Forman, 1950).

Recently, however, people have begun to take a closer look at propinquity as a determinant of group

A. Self-Fulfilling Stereotypes about the Physically Attractive

Mark Snyder, Elizabeth Tanke, and Ellen Berscheid use the phrase BEHAVIORAL CONFIRMATION to refer to how we may unknowingly induce others to treat us in such a way that our initial impressions of them are confirmed. For example, if we believe certain people are cold and hostile, we may be less friendly than if we believed they were warm and generous. They may be mildly offended by our cool and aloof approach and reciprocate in kind. Thus our initial impression of their lack of warmth is confirmed, though the confirmation is brought about by our own behavior.

To see whether this sort of self-fulfilling prophecy occurs with stereotypes about the physically attractive, Snyder, Tanke, and Berscheid (1977) designed an experiment in which male college students were to try to get acquainted with a female college student over the telephone. The male—female pairs of students who participated in the research were not allowed to see each other before the telephone conversation. However, each male student was given some information about the woman he would be talking with and shown a photograph that had supposedly just been taken with a Polaroid camera. The female phone partners were in another room. All of the information furnished the males was supplied by the actual person they were to get acquainted with over the phone. The photographs, however, were selected from one of two pools of photos: attractive or relatively unattractive females.

Each male—female pair engaged in a 10-minute phone conversation. The conversations were recorded, and raters were asked to listen to the tape tracks that contained the female voices and answer a number of questions about the females. For example, they rated each female participant on a number of bipolar scales and answered questions such as "How much is she enjoying herself?" and "How animated and enthusiastic is this person?" Remember that the raters heard only the females, who were just being themselves but who were believed to be either attractive or unattractive by the person to whom they were talking.

Before the phone conversations took place, the male students had indicated their initial impressions of their partners. Those who saw an attractive photo, for example, expected their partners to be poised, humorous, and sociable. These expectations, which initially existed only in their minds, became reality! The raters listening to the phone conversations rated the females whose partners thought they were attractive as sounding more poised, more humorous, more sociable, and generally more socially adept than the females whose partners thought they were unattractive. Those *believed* to be attractive actually came to *behave* in a more friendly, likable, and pleasant manner.

---

formation. It appears that propinquity, like physical attractiveness, has often been confounded with assumed similarity. Consider the Festinger, et al. (1950) study. The inhabitants of the housing project were a relatively homogeneous group to begin with. Festinger, et al. report that they all were married, all the men were veterans, and all were students at M.I.T. The subjects were older, more mature, and more serious than the average student. The great majority came from upper-middle class homes and majored in engineering or natural sciences. It should come as no surprise that propinquity was a determinant of group and clique formation. Since everyone was pretty much alike anyway, a simple least-effort principle predicts that one would make friends with the closest people. A number of other studies that identified propinquity as a factor in friendship formation can be similarly criticized.

Nahemow and Lawton (1975) examined spontaneous group development in a New York housing project. They see an individual's social activities as taking place in two concentric regions. The innermost region

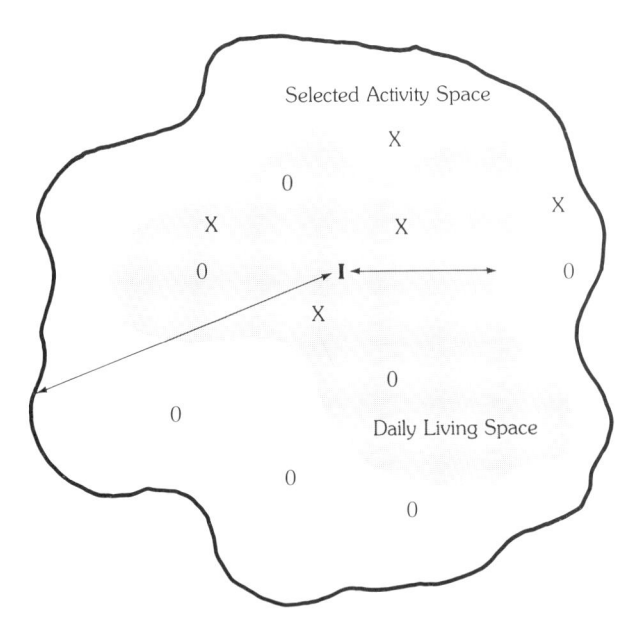

2. In this model of differentiated social space, similarity is not important in determining friendships within the individual's Daily Living Space. Within the Selected Activity Space, however, the individual (I) tends to interact more with similar others (O) than with dissimilar others (X). (From Nahemow and Lawton, 1975, Figure 2, p. 207.)

is termed the DAILY LIVING SPACE and consists of all those places where the individual is likely to be at some time during an average day. Surrounding this daily living space is a region they term the SELECTED ACTIVITY SPACE, consisting of those places where the person goes only occasionally when he or she has a specific reason for going. Nahemow and Lawton hypothesized that within the daily living space, similarity would not be a very important determinant of friendship formation. Within this region, the individual would become acquainted with both similar and dissimilar others. Outside of the daily living space, however, the individual would be more selective and would be more likely to interact with similar than with dissimilar others. These ideas are represented graphically in Figure 2.

To check on their ideas, Nahemow and Lawton interviewed 270 residents of a public housing project consisting of seven 14-story buildings in New York City. The interviewers asked respondents about their best friends in the project, where the friends lived, and how often they saw the friends. The interviewers also recorded whether the person being interviewed was white, black, or Puerto Rican; male or female; and young, middle-aged, or old. As anticipated, both proximity and similarity of age and race were significant predictors of friendship. Eighty-eight percent of the people mentioned as best friends lived in the same building as the person who mentioned them, and almost 50 percent lived on the same floor. Similarly, 60 percent of reported friends were in the same age category as the chooser, and approximately 70 percent were of the same race. However, when a person indicated a friend from a different age category, that person was more likely to live even closer than were friends in the same age category. Further, friends of the same race were found to live in different buildings 12 percent of the time, but there was not a single case of an interracial friendship in which the parties lived in different buildings. Sixty-nine percent of all interracial friendships were between people living on the same floors of the same buildings. People seem to go farther and put themselves out more to see similar others, but social contact with those who are different is likely to occur only if it is convenient.

As we saw in Chapter 6, interpersonal attraction is positively related to similarity on a number of dimensions. The more similar people are, the more attracted they are to each other and, as we just saw, the more likely they are to seek each other out. It makes sense that similarity would be an important determinant of group formation in friendship groups. After all, one way of validating our opinions, beliefs, and values is to surround ourselves with like-minded others. Having done so, we can firmly assert, with only a mild twinge of doubt, that we must be correct about the Republicans or the younger generation or the welfare system because everyone we know agrees with us. But what about situations in which we ourselves do not know what to think? What happens when our own opinions about some important topic or value are shaken or when we are confronted with some uninterpretable event?

ANXIETY

Although there are dozens of definitions of anxiety (Lazarus and Averill, 1972), investigators generally agree that both anticipation and uncertainty are components of anxiety. ANXIETY usually involves the belief that something is or is not going to happen, and it is something about which the person does not know quite what to do or even what to think.

Any event that unexpectedly disturbs the routine of one's life can produce anxiety. The anxiety may be fleeting, lasting only until one has gotten one's bearings and plotted a course of action, but during that temporary disorientation, it is real and unpleasant. Shibutani (1966) points out that, following any crisis or disaster, one of the first things people do is seek out information—news about what has happened and is happening. This need for information can be great:

> Amid the smoldering ruins of razed buildings survivors of the disastrous San Francisco earthquake and the fire huddled together in parks and squares, confronted with the possibility of starvation, thirst, and death. It was April 19, 1907 (sic), after two days of a holocaust that had charred four square miles of the city, demolished 28,000 buildings, and left 200,000 homeless. At various encampments the exhausted refugees, separated from friends and families and dragging along their few belongings, made inquiries about lost persons and the progress in fighting the fire. Staffs of the three San Francisco morning newspapers moved to Oakland and on borrowed presses put out a combined *Call-Chronicle-Examiner,* which they distributed free. Their cars were almost mobbed. In the end the distributors had to drive along at full speed, throwing out the sheets as they went along, or they could make no progress at all. No bread wagon, no supply of blankets aroused as much interest as the arrival of news. (Shibutani, 1966, p. 31; From Irwin, 1911.)

News, of course, is merely a form of information, and people must have information to adjust to changed or unusual circumstances. Further, most of our information (even a newspaper's information) is mediated by other people. If uncertainty is a component of anxiety and if people who are uncertain about what to do or think seek information, then anxious people will seek out the company of others.

Schachter (1959) arrived at this same prediction from a somewhat different starting point. In reviewing autobiographical reports of people who had undergone prolonged isolation experiences, Schachter found that they frequently tended to think about, dream of, obsess over, and even sometimes hallucinate about people. Isolation also seemed to produce severe anxiety. The co-occurrence of anxiety and preoccupation with people led Schachter to predict that anxiety would lead to an increase in the desire to be with other people.

To check on this hypothesis, Schachter set up a very simple, two-condition experiment. In the High Anxiety condition, female students at a university were led to believe that, as part of an experiment they had signed up for, they were going to have to experience some painful electric shocks. Each was told that she would have an electrode strapped to her hand and that the shocks she would experience would be quite intense, though there would be no permanent damage. A comparable group of subjects, assigned to the Low Anxiety condition, were told that the shocks would be very mild and, in fact, would "resemble more a tickle or a tingle than anything unpleasant."

After this induction of high or low anxiety, subjects were told there would be a short delay while some equipment was brought in and set up and that, since there were a number of small rooms close by, they could wait alone or in the company of others. The results (see Table I) show that a significantly greater proportion of the subjects experiencing high anxiety chose to wait together with others. An increase in anxiety apparently increases the desire to be with other people.

In a second experiment by Schachter, subjects participated in the experiment individually and high anxi-

Table I. **Relationship of anxiety to the need to affiliate**

	How subjects chose to wait	
	Together	Don't care or alone
High Anxiety	20	12
Low Anxiety	10	20

A greater proportion of subjects experiencing high anxiety chose to wait for the anxiety-arousing event in the company of others. (From Schachter, 1959, Table 2, p. 18.)

ety was induced in all of them; that is, all were told the shocks would be painful. However, when the experiment got to the part about a short delay for some equipment to be set up, two conditions were created by varying information about whom the subjects would wait with if they chose to wait with others. In the Same State condition, the subjects were given a choice between waiting alone and waiting with other women who were taking part in the same experiment. In the Different State condition, the subjects were given a choice between waiting alone and waiting with other women who happened to be in the building to see their advisors. The proportion of subjects choosing to wait with others was significantly higher in the Same State than in the Different State condition. As Schachter summarizes this result, "Misery doesn't love just any kind of company, it loves only miserable company" (p. 24).

Thus it does appear that anxiety heightens affiliative tendencies and, specifically, that anxious people prefer the company of others who they anticipate will understand what they themselves are experiencing. Schachter proposed the following five explanations for these phenomena:

1. Escape. Anxious people may seek the company of others as a preliminary to escaping the event or threat that produced the anxiety.
2. Cognitive clarity. Anxious prople may hope that others will be able to shed some light on the nature of the threat itself.
3. Direct anxiety reduction. The mere presence of others may be reassuring.
4. Indirect anxiety reduction. The presence of others may be diverting. Thus one can get one's mind off one's troubles.
5. Self-evaluation. By being with others, one can determine whether one is responding appropriately to the threat, overreacting, or underreacting.

All of these explanations sound plausible. Unfortunately, none of them has received clear support or refutation in the literature, although some additional research by Schachter and Gerard and Rabbie (1961) indicates that, in particular situations, these determinants and others may operate jointly in motivating anxious people to seek the company of others. Note, however, that similarity or assumed similarity again plays a role in the choice of the anxious. They want to be with others like themselves.

In work groups (groups with some purpose or some task to perform), similarity may not be so important. In fact, if the group's task is at all complex or involves a division of labor, similarity among group members may be counterproductive. It seems quite possible that in work groups, similarity may be inversely rather than directly related to attraction. Some complementarity of skills, roles, and personality characteristics may be essential to successful group performance and, hence, to member satisfaction.

COMPLEMENTARITY

To complement something is to add that which is lacking—to make something complete or whole. For example, a restaurant with a dozen excellent chefs, but with no one to wash dishes, wait on tables, or order supplies would not be in business long. The chef's role, while it might be the most important in a successful restaurant, simply could not be performed without the complementary roles of dishwasher and table server also being fulfilled. Within sociology and social psychology, the concepts of role and role-related behavior have a long history, reaching back to some distant time when they were pilfered from the theater. Roger Brown (1965) points out that, in spite of this lengthy past and numerous definitions and discussions of the concepts, little has been added to the terms that was not already present when they were slipped out through the stage door.

The nature of roles. If we define NORMS as relatively stable rules about behavior that are based on agreement or consensus and enforced by appeals to values or other suprapersonal agents (Thibaut and Kelley, 1959), it is easy to see that people apply various groups of norms to various categories of people. People who are similarly categorized by having the same subset of norms applied to them are said to occupy the same ROLE. Once a person has been categorized as occupying a certain role—father, mother, professor, student—certain definite behaviors are expected. The concept of role, then, calls attention to the *normative* nature of our *expectations* about the behavior of others. That is, not only do we expect others to behave in certain ways, but we often feel they *should* behave as we anticipate. When they fail to do so, we may get quite upset. The reason why we are surprised or even angry when others do not behave as we expect is that it is important to us to anticipate others' behaviors consistently. We cannot plot our own course of action unless we can make reasonable estimates of how others will respond.

Of interest for the initial stages of group formation is the possibility that, when others behave differently from what we anticipate or believe to be appropriate, we are less inclined to continue interacting with them. For example, Kiesler (1966) found that a favor results in increased attraction for the one who does the favor only when the favor (sharing rewards) was appropriate within the role relationship of the favor-doer and the recipient—that is, when the two were supposed to perform a task cooperatively. When the two were supposed to be competing, withholding the favor resulted in greater attraction than granting the favor. It appears that behavior in line with perceived role requirements elicits liking, whereas out-of-role behavior does not. Kiesler's demonstration is particularly interesting, because it counters the naive assumption that we like or are attracted to people who do nice things for us. Actually we are attracted to them only if it is appropriate for them to do nice things for us.

When people behave inappropriately (as defined by the expectations of those with whom they are interacting), the result depends on a number of factors, not the least of which is the relative power or status of those who are interacting. When the deviant is low in status, the reward and punishment options available to others are fairly obvious and may range from the strategic use of rewards in an attempt to shape the other's behavior (Thibaut and Kelley, 1959; Krasner, 1958) to more drastic measures involving assorted punishments. When the deviants are relatively high in status or power, the options available to those with whom they are interacting are more constrained and may be reduced to such tactics as breaking off the interaction. Overall and Aronson (1963) report some evidence that "leaving the field" (Lewin, 1935) may indeed result when the expectations of the low-power party in an interaction are violated. Psychiatric patients were interviewed by a social worker immediately before and immediately after their first sessions. The greater the discrepancy between what the patient expected to occur and what actually occurred in the first session, the less likely the patient would return for a second appointment.

The reciprocal character of roles. Thus roles have both a normative and an anticipatory character. Implicit in our discussion is a third and crucial component of roles. As we have seen, roles are defined in terms of norms that have to do with behavior toward other people. By definition, then, a given role implies a reciprocal or *complementary* role. For someone to be a wife, there must be a husband; for the physician, the patient; for the taxi driver, the passenger. Such standard role categories are important, but they are relatively uninteresting as far as the initial stages of group formation are concerned. Of greater interest are those ambiguous situations that occur frequently in interpersonal interaction and group formation when we are not quite sure how to relate to particular others or what we can anticipate and expect from them—when we are not quite sure of the role they intend to play.

Sarbin (1954), Berne (1961), and others have pointed out that in such undefined situations, individuals engage in a series of maneuvers designed to "locate the position of the other" or cast the other in an appropriate role vis-à-vis themselves. They do this by eliciting certain types of information and relying on what cues the other presents, even if these cues are minimal and themselves ambiguous. The results of these attempts at placing the other include both a definition of one's own role in the interaction and the development of what Goffman (1959) refers to as a WORKING CONSENSUS, which is defined as an interaction situation that the participants implicitly agree to sustain (temporarily, at least). A major component of the working consensus is agreement about the social identities of the participants. Since each role must have a reciprocal, when one of the participants attempts to assume a particular identity or play a particular role, he or she therefore creates an identity for the other—a process that Weinstein and Deutschberger (1963) refer to as ALTERCASTING.

It is important for the social identities that emerge as part of the working consensus to be mutually acceptable. Otherwise, the working consensus will dissolve— and with it the incipient group. Weinstein (1966) points out that one of the primary tasks facing an individual who wishes to assume a certain identity in a group (and thereby serve as casting director for the other group members) is to make certain that no one evaluates his or her assumed identity inappropriately. A series of communication tactics such as the icon (*identity con*firmation) can help prevent misunderstanding of the person's credentials. (Name dropping is an icon we are all familiar with.) There are vast individual differences in the extent to which people use such tactics. Everyone knows a few people who apparently need to be the center of attention at all times and dominate the conversation of every group they find themselves in. Hence, we would expect a relationship between an individual's personality characteristics and interpersonal needs and the roles he or she is willing (or tries) to assume in various groups. If the group's task is such that the individual's personality and needs mesh with the role he or she must perform, then attraction to the group should be relatively great. Note that this does not imply that the individual would necessarily like the other members of the group.

Some data on this reasoning are presented by Wagner (1975). Subjects were 70 male counselors employed in 3 summer camps. Observations and interviews at the camps led to selection of the following interpersonal needs, which were deemed especially relevant to the work requirements and role expectations of the camps: dominance, autonomy, succorance, nurturance, exhibitionism, deference, aggression, abasement, responsibility, and dissociation. The strength of each of these needs in each counselor was ascertained through intensive interviews; the counselors also rated each other on a number of items, including how much they liked working with each of the others. Then the interpersonal needs were grouped into complementary pairs (such as dominance–autonomy, succorance–nurturance, and exhibitionism–deference). The higher a counselor's own standing on the first member of a pair, the more likely he was to be attracted to working with counselors who were high on the second member of the pair. Exhibitionists were not interested in working with similar others. They wanted to work with others who were deferential and, presumably, yielded them the spotlight. Several counselors explicitly stated that they did not enjoy working with close friends. They apparently had little time for the niceties of friendship when they were working.

It appears that in informal friendship groups, similarity and assumed similarity are quite important in the initial stages of group formation. In work groups, these factors are less crucial. When some division of labor is necessary for the group to function, role differentiation takes place and complementarity becomes more important to one's attraction to the group and in the group's maintenance and continued development. Friendship groups and work groups, however, are only two of what Argyle (1969) refers to as the three most important types of groups. What about the family?

FORMING THE FAMILY: AN INTEGRATION OF SIMILARITY AND COMPLEMENTARITY?

Of the three basic types of groups, the family is by far the most complex, the most interesting, and, for many people, the most important. It is also the most difficult to obtain hard data on. There are many reasons for the family's resistance to research. For example, intimate questions about one's family life are usually considered an invasion of privacy, whereas the same questions about one's work group are likely to be answered readily. Similarly, investigators can form work groups at will and manipulate variables of interest. Not only is such experimental intervention impossible with families, but it is even difficult to do simple observational studies. Further, friendship groups and work groups were defined in essentially the same way in 1776 as in 1976, but we cannot say this about the family.

One way of looking at the modern family is that it is a friendship group at its inception (marriage) which must evolve into a work group later (with the birth of children). Accordingly, the factors that are important in the formation of friendship groups should be paramount during the early stages of family development, and the factors that are important in work groups should become increasingly important later on. Murstein (1971) has proposed a theory of marital choice that is very close to this conception.

The stimulus-value-role theory. Murstein's theory is termed the STIMULUS-VALUE-ROLE THEORY. Basically, it proposes that most couples pass through three stages in approaching marriage. In the first or stimulus stage, an individual may be attracted to another on the basis of obvious physical, social, or other qualities. This does not mean that people are attracted only to the most physically attractive others or only to others of high social standing. Rather, an implicit equity model is assumed to operate. In taking the first tentative steps toward forming a relationship with someone of the opposite sex, each person compares his or her total assets (qualities that would be rewarding to the other) with those of the other and attempts a rough balance. Thus an unattractive physician may assume that his or her professional standing more than compensates for unharmonious appearance and would not be hesitant about seeking the company of a more attractive companion of somewhat lower social standing.

The second or value stage is a period during which the couple compare values, attitudes, and philosophies. The range of topics covered may include politics, religion, sex, family life—anything and everything of importance to either or both of them. Murstein's prediction for the outcome of this stage is that the more similar the couple find themselves in basic values and attitudes, the more strongly attracted to each other they become.

As for the third or role stage, Murstein argues that

B. The American Ideal?

In the past few years, one of the more active areas of theory and research in social psychology has centered around the notion of psychological androgyny. As we pointed out in Chapter 3, in contrast to the "usual" conceptions of masculinity and femininity as opposites, the androgynous person is one who incorporates the best of what have traditionally been considered to be "feminine" qualities (concern for others, nurturance) as well as the best of what have traditionally been considered "masculine" qualities (such as independence and curiousity). It has been assumed that the truly androgynous person might be able to function better in a wider variety of situations than one who was bound by sex role stereotypes and who felt constrained to act in a masculine or feminine manner only. The androgynous person, then, has been put forward as something of an ideal we all should strive for, by becoming androgynous we could break out of the confines of our traditional sex roles.

Recently, Edward Sampson (1977), a social psychologist at Clark University, has suggested that by putting forward ideals such as the androgynous person we may be making too much of a demand on individuals and we may also be ignoring other, more viable, solutions for the problems created by forcing people into rigid sex roles. Sampson's point is simply that American society has always held up the rugged individual as an ideal, the person who needed no one else and who could handle everything himself or herself. Psychological androgyny may be nothing more than a straightforward extension of this respect for rugged individualism. Each person would have all the good "masculine" and all the good "feminine" qualities, hence there should be no need for a person with complementary qualities. Pushed to the limit, psychological health for the androgynous person would be total independence of others. As Sampson puts it, androgyny . . .

> as an ideal seems to contribute to further human isolation and alienation and to thwart necessary cooperative ventures that build upon and recognize the needs of interdependence for their solution (p. 774).

> It is important to note that Sampson is *not* suggesting that females should assume or continue to assume the traditional "feminine" roles and males the traditional "masculine" roles. His point is that we might be better off in the long run if we recognized our need for others and worked toward an interdependent harmony rather than pushing as an ideal an aggregation of self-contained, self-sufficient, and independent androgynous persons.

stimulus attraction and value similarity are necessary but not sufficient conditions for a lasting marriage and family development. The two individuals have to be able to function in compatible roles. This is where things get a little tricky. How they are going to function in the roles of husband and wife and what sorts of implicit and explicit expectations they hold about their reciprocal roles are not so easy to determine as their stimulus attributes (stage 1) or their values and attitudes (stage 2). The problem, of course, is that one would like to know these things before making a commitment, but one cannot really know them until some time after the commitment has been made. The best one can do is try to make educated guesses by obtaining as much information about the other in as wide a variety of situations as possible.

With this brief overview of the theory, let us examine the evidence. We have already seen ample evidence for the importance of value and attitude similarity in attraction, so we shall focus on stages 1 (stimulus) and 3 (role).

Evidence for the stimulus stage. The interesting aspect of stage 1 is the possibility that people tend to seek out as partners those who roughly match themselves in the "weighted pool of stimulus characteristics." Thus a person who thinks very highly of himself or herself should seek out more attractive others than one who thinks less well of himself or herself. Kiesler and Baral (1970) offer some data on this hypothesis.

Subjects in the Kiesler and Baral experiment were paid male volunteers recruited to take an intelligence test that was supposedly being validated for use with college students. The test was administered orally, and approximately half the subjects (those randomly assigned to the High Self-Esteem condition), were led to believe that they were really doing well. The remaining subjects were assigned to the Low Self-Esteem condition and were led to believe that they were doing rather poorly. After two parts of the test had been completed, the experimenter suggested that they take a break and escorted the subject to a small canteen in the same building for a cup of coffee. When they entered the canteen, the experimenter "recognized" a girl (actually an accomplice) who was either made up extremely well (the Attractive condition) or appeared rather sloppy and slovenly (the Unattractive condition). The girl sat down at the same table with the experimenter and subject, but after a minute the experimenter excused himself to make a telephone call, leaving the female confederate and the subject alone. The confederate continued talking with the subject in a very friendly and interested manner, while at the same time coding the subject's behavior into certain categories of "romantic behavior," such as asking for a date, offering to buy the confederate a snack, or coffee, or asking for information that could lead to a date. The results (see Figure 3) show that subjects high in self-esteem display more romantic behavior toward the attractive than the unattractive confederate. On the other hand, subjects low in self-esteem display more romantic behavior toward the unattractive confederate.

This study supports some "matching" of perceived net worth in the early stages of a relationship. Some

3. Romantic behavior toward attractive and unattractive others as a function of self-esteem. Subjects with a temporarily inflated view of themselves and their qualities attempt to establish relationships with more attractive others. (From Kiesler and Baral, 1970, Figure 1, p. 162.)

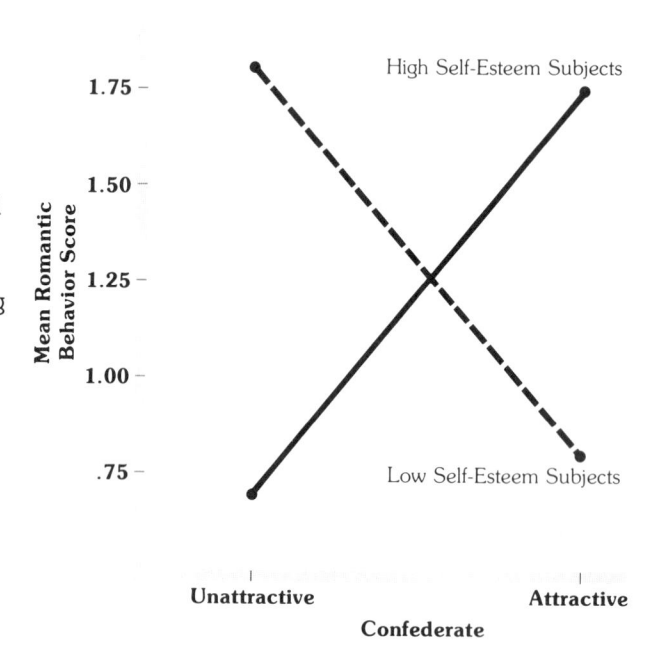

further evidence for matching comes from a study by Murstein (1971). Subjects were 99 college couples who were either engaged or going steady. Photos of each of the 198 people were judged for physical attractiveness. The mean discrepancy in physical attractiveness of actual couples was significantly smaller than the mean discrepancy in physical attractiveness when the photos of the 99 males were randomly matched with those of the 99 females.

Evidence for the role stage. The evidence for the role stage in Murstein's theory is less clear-cut than that for the other two stages. There are bits and pieces of evidence (Winch, 1963; Murstein, 1971), and the idea that some give and take (some degree of role and/or need complementarity) is essential to a long-term, stable relationship is certainly plausible. But Rubin (1973) cautions that

> The multiplicity of human needs and aspirations, the variety of ways in which they may be satisfied, and the problem of specifying which are more and which are less central to marriage have all presented obstacles that researchers have not yet succeeded in surmounting. . . . For one couple the dominance–submission dimension may be central to premarital and marital interaction; for another couple it may be rather unimportant. For the second couple a different sort of complementarity—in which the husband glories vicariously in his wife's artistic talent, while the wife is broadened by her husband's intellectual interests—may be the glue that keeps them strongly attracted to one another.
>
> As a result, it proves to be much easier to recognize need complementarity among established couples than it is to predict it ahead of time on the basis of the individual characteristics of the prospective partners. Need complementarity is best viewed as a pattern of interaction that emerges gradually in the course of a relationship (p. 200).

It does seem, however, that the initial stages of forming family groups are very similar to the initial stages of forming informal friendship groups. If there is any validity in our conception of the modern family as a friendship group that has to evolve into a work group, problems will arise if couples fail to anticipate this shift. Work groups generally run into difficulty when they are formed as if they were to be friendship groups.

We have been discussing group formation from a strictly cognitive point of view. Potential group members have been described as seeking each other out because of the rewards they anticipate from associating with similar others, for example, or because they anticipate that being with others will help alleviate anxiety. We have discussed complementarity in terms of norms and role expectations. We even gave physical attractiveness a cognitive slant by pointing out that its effects on the initial stages of group formation may be partially mediated by *assumed* similarity. Are people really as rational as we have depicted them? Perhaps we have overstated the case. Somehow the image of a person setting out to surround himself or herself with similar others so that his or her opinions, attitudes, and values will have social support does not quite ring true. Similarly, the image of a number of people sitting down and dividing up the task at hand into a set of complementary subtasks does not seem to be the way that informal work groups get started. There is, in fact, another way of looking at the phenomena we have been discussing, and it may be closer to the way spontaneous groups form in *everyday* life.

WHICH COMES FIRST, THE MEMBERSHIP OR THE MOTIVE?

There are several theoretical reasons for believing that the apparently rational motives behind group formation are more apparent than real. Perhaps people do not seek out a group and then interact with other members. Maybe it makes more sense to think of people interacting with others and groups emerging from the interaction. As Weick (1969) puts it, "It may be that cognition has little effect on behavior, because it follows rather than precedes behavior. Cognitions may be retrospective; they may make sense of what has happened rather than what will happen" (p. 30).

On a general level, the question is one of *meaning*. That is, how do we impose some sort of order and coherence on the numerous interpersonal stimuli that confront us daily? The difficulty is that the stimuli we confront are usually equivocal. If, for example, someone smiles at us, are we to take it as politeness, genuine liking for us, or condescension? Any given event may be completely ambiguous out of context. Using context and whatever other cues are available, we try to make sense of the event, interpret it, and give meaning to what occurred. Thus meaning is imposed retrospectively, after the event or events in question have occurred. Now let us take this general philosophical orientation and ask what it implies about group formation.

In Chapter 2, we made the point that science and daily life are basically similar. In both, events occur that we wish to understand and, in both, one of the best ways for gaining that understanding is to attempt to control the events in question. When we can control the events and make them occur at will, we feel we understand them better than when we cannot. Since people are daily immersed in streams of interpersonal events, one way in which they attempt to make sense of those events is by exercising some control over them. But it is very difficult to demonstrate control by individual acts. Weick (1969) believes individuals establish cycles of reciprocal behavior with others in order to produce "closure" or some ability to predict and control events. "The behaviors which are most likely to produce closure in a series of changing events are behaviors which A emits that are valuable to B and which in turn lead B to produce behaviors that benefit A" (p. 45). Once a set of such interlocking behaviors has been discovered, a simple reinforcement principle suggests that A and B will both try to preserve it and to make it recur.

In groups of two. If we consider the essential feature of a group to be sets of interlocked behaviors, we can think of groups as *emerging from interaction* rather than being formed in advance to allow people to interact with similar people. Further, a number of experiments involving what has been termed the MINIMAL SOCIAL SITUATION have demonstrated that a mutually rewarding relationship can develop between two people even when they are unaware of each other's presence and when each is pursuing purely egoistic goals. Consider the following example.

Sidowski, Wyckoff, and Tabory (1956) arranged an experimental setting in which two subjects—in separate rooms and unaware of each other's presence—were unknowingly able to reward (give points to) or punish (shock) the other subject. Both subjects had electrodes attached to their left hands and sat in front of a control board having two unmarked buttons and a digital counter. The object was to score as many points as possible by inducing the other subject to press the reward button rather than the punishment button, even though neither knew which button was which. For example, when A pressed the button that rewarded B, while B pressed the button that shocked A, B received a point. B would continue this pattern for as long as A continued to press the reward button. A, on the other hand, would soon tire of the exchange and would press the other button, thereby shocking B. This would result in a change of B's behavior, who, attempting to avoid the shocks, would press the other button, thus rewarding A. Sidowski, et al. found that after a few minutes in such situations, mutually rewarding sequences of behavior were learned and then maintained, even though the two people were acting independently and even though each was acting out of self-interest.

A series of subsequent experiments (Sidowski, 1957; Kelley, Thibaut, Radloff, and Mundy, 1962; Rabinowitz, Kelley and Rosenblatt, 1966) explored parameters of the minimal social situation. There is a fair amount of evidence for what Rabinowitz, et al. (1966) refer to as IMPLICIT ADJUSTMENT, "the development of mutually advantageous interaction *unconsciously* (without realization of the relationship), *unintentionally* (without deliberate planning to do so) and *tacitly* (without words or speech)" (p. 194). A number of authors have roundly criticized these findings. Argyle (1969), for example, argues that experiments employing the minimal social situation leave out most of what is important and interesting about interpersonal behavior: verbal communication, body movements, visual perception of the other, and inferences based on how the other looks, acts, smells, or talks. As a consequence, the results obtained may be exaggerated or even incorrect.

Other aspects of interaction are more important than the sorts of implicit adjustments that can be demonstrated in the minimal social situation. However, the interlocking, mutually rewarding sequences of behavior that emerge in the minimal social situation are a prototype of the way in which many groups get started. People interact with the people they happen to encounter. Aspects of some of these encounters turn out to be mutually rewarding, so the parties to the interaction try to make those aspects recur and we have an incipient group. Implicit here is the view that people are quite adaptable in their interpersonal choices—or fickle, to use a pejorative term for the phenomenon. Friendships, for example, may be largely a function of the person one is interacting with at the moment, not the result of an enduring relationship between people who were "made for each other."

In larger groups. Two field experiments by the Sherifs and their colleagues (Sherif, 1951; Sherif and Sherif, 1953; Sherif, Harvey, White, Hood, and Sherif, 1961) demonstrate the above point. Groups of boys aged 10 to 12 were recruited for a 3-week summer camp. When they arrived, all were housed in one large bunkhouse, and within a few days small cliques and groups of friends had begun to form. After this initial get-acquainted period, each boy was asked to name his best friends in the camp. The friendship choices at this point presumably reflected genuine friendships among like-minded boys. Once the data on initial choices had been obtained, however, the campers were split into two groups. Two cabins were now used, and the boys were assigned to the two cabins in such a way that about two-thirds of the "best friends" were in different cabins.

Although there was a good deal of grumbling about this among the campers, camp activities continued. Now, however, each cabin was a separate unit, and the two did not participate in most activities together. After several days of this new arrangement, the campers were again asked to name their best friends. It was emphasized that they could name anyone in the entire camp—not just those in their cabin. Table II shows that the majority of "best friend" choices shifted from the spontaneous choices of the first few days of camp to choices among cabinmates who had been arbitrarily assigned. These results were replicated in a second experiment.

As Sherif and Sherif (1969) point out, their findings cast doubt on the popular notion that we choose our friends strictly according to personal preferences. Members of exclusive clubs, segregated societies, and some fraternities and sororities may sincerely defend their restrictive practices by saying that the friendship choices of the members tend to be largely within their homogeneous group. The members may make friends with whomever they please, but look, they all choose each other. The Sherifs' results imply that if out-group members were let into the club, they would soon be preferred also.

The astute reader may have noticed that the theoretical position advanced by Bem (1965, 1967) and described in Chapter 9 seems pertinent here. Recall that the core of Bem's analysis of self-perception is that we often infer our attitudes and beliefs retrospectively

Table II. Reversal of friendship choices before and after group formation.

People chosen from:	People belonging to:					
	Group A			Group B		
	Before	After	Difference	Before	After	Difference
Group A	35.1	95.0	59.9	65.0	12.3	−52.7
Group B	64.9	5.0	−59.9	35.0	87.7	52.7

The majority of subjects changed their choice of best friends after the circle of people they interacted with regularly was restricted. For example, people in Group A chose 95.0 percent of their friends from Group A whereas prior to the formation of groups they chose only 35.1 percent of their friends from this group. People in Group B, however, chose only 12.3 percent of their friends from Group A, whereas prior to the formation of groups they chose as friends 65 percent of the people in Group A. (From Sherif and Sherif, 1969, Table 2, p. 232.)

from our behavior. We use the same evidence that an outside observer would use: how we have behaved. Seeing us interacting with the same two or three people repeatedly, an outside observer might well infer that those people are our best friends. Similarly, if we are asked who our best friends are, we may very well look back over the past few weeks or months and draw conclusions from the behavior we observe in ourselves.

Thus we may delude ourselves. We may convince ourselves that the people we regularly interact with are the people we would have chosen to interact with and that, consequently, those people are unique and irreplaceable. People are often hesitant, for example, to move to a new city or even across town because they would have to leave all their friends. But friendship groups and work groups are considerably more ephemeral and interchangeable in their membership than many people imagine.

Unfortunately, if people assume that their group is unique and irreplaceable, they may exaggerate its importance and overrate its ability to cope with the demands of the situation. The group atmosphere of congeniality and cohesiveness may become the thing to achieve and preserve at all costs. When this occurs, the group may be in danger of losing touch with reality. Like all powerful motives, the affiliative tendency can run amuck. Let us look at what can happen when it does.

C. Extremes of Commitment: The Cult That Killed Itself

A horrifying example of the ultimate in commitment to a group occurred in November of 1978, when over 900 members of the People's Temple, a California religious cult that had settled in the jungles of Guyana, committed suicide on the orders of their leader, Reverend Jim Jones. The only parallels in recorded history were mass suicides by Jews in Masada in 73 A.D. and by 1,000 Japanese on Saipan during World War II. In both these cases, however, capture and possible execution were imminent and made the suicides somewhat reasonable. In the case of the People's Temple no such immediate threat existed. Yet the ravings of the leader started a social mechanism that led 900 people to drink a potion laced with cyanide. How could it happen? How can 900 people be persuaded to kill themselves?

The answers seem to be a combination of three elements in the situation: (a) the nature of the leader, (b) the type of people recruited to the group, and (c) the specific living conditions in the isolated area where the group lived.

The leader. Jim Jones grew up in Indiana, the first son of a mother who believed that he was destined for greatness. At maturity he became a preacher who advocated peace and complete racial integration. Persecution led him to move to California and there he established the People's Temple. Over a decade his behavior changed. Increasingly he focused on himself as the object to be worshipped. He demanded total loyalty, heavy donation of property and money, and sexual favors from his followers. His style was charismatic and his ability to influence people seemed to contribute to his growing self-importance. He also became increasingly suspicious and hostile in a pattern classically described as paranoia. Jones left the United States and led his followers to Guyana in South America, where they established a settlement in a remote area. Over a period of 3 or 4 years, as his paranoia progressed, he became more coercive in the control of his members.

The followers. Idealism was one of the motives that led early followers to join Jim Jones. Belief in equality and good works was a powerful stimulant to follow a strong charismatic man. And many good works were done. In fact, Jones was developing a modest political power in California before he left the country. Many other people joined because they were "nobodies going nowhere," rootless, with no ties to the past and an unpromising future. The Temple gave meaning

Aberrations of affiliation

The feelings of solidarity and belongingness that often develop among group members is usually referred to as COHESIVENESS. Cohesiveness has been variously defined, but it always involves the attractiveness and importance of the group to the members. The more attractive the group is to its members and/or the more important the group is in satisfying its members' needs, the more cohesive the group.

Cohesiveness is generally assumed to be a good thing. When members are highly attracted to a group, they attend meetings more regularly, persist longer in goal-directed activities, are more accepting of others' opinions, change their minds to adopt the view of fellow members more often, are more likely to protect the group's standards by exerting pressure on those who disagree, adhere more closely to group standards, and are more likely to find relaxation and security in group activities. But *are* these good things? The behavior of highly attracted members is more likely to be beneficial to the group, but is it beneficial to the individual members? The group may take on a suprapersonal quality and that which was formed to benefit the members paradoxically takes precedence over them. One could argue that none of the behaviors we have listed, not even relaxation and a feeling of security (Harrington, 1959), are good for the individual members (see Box C for an extreme example of an aberration of affiliation).

---

to their lives, a purpose, an ordered existence, and, in the early years at least, comradeship with other group members. As with other cults, members of the Temple were made totally dependent on the leader and group. They gave all of their material possessions to the Temple and worked laboriously at assigned tasks. Commitment to a group is often increased by valiant labors for the group. Members joined freely because the group's values matched their own. By giving their assets to the group, they lost their power to resist; by giving their labor willingly they slowly developed a binding commitment to the group. Jones skillfully manipulated this commitment so that subconsciously at least, the commitment was to him, and he retained predominant power.

The situation. The move to Guyana left the cult almost totally isolated from the outside world. Living conditions were good at first, but deteriorated as Jones' mind deteriorated. Fear as well as commitment became a factor of life as the settlement slowly became an armed camp. People could not come and go freely. They were underfed and deprived of sleep during long indoctrination sessions. Fatigue, overwork, and malnourishment combined to keep people powerless and unable to think for themselves. One ominous element was periodic suicide drills. This kind of grim modeling was probably instrumental in inducing people to later perform the mass suicide.

What instigated the suicide was the assassination of Congressman Leo Ryan of California who visited the Temple because of complaints he had received from relatives of cult members. When he left, several members of the Temple left with him. The desertion of a few members apparently snapped Jones' mind, and he sent a death squad after Ryan. The congressman and several members of his party were killed as they tried to board a small plane.

When Jones heard of the deaths, he assembled his people at a central pavilion and told them the time had come; everyone had to die. Vats of a sweet fruit drink laced with deadly cyanide were set up. People gathered in an orderly way, to poison their children first, and then drink the potion themselves. Very few escaped. Many probably died willingly, even joyously; others went to their deaths meekly, simply because they no longer knew how to resist. The combination of charisma, indoctrination, and powerlessness had taken its toll, and people followed orders issued from the depths of their leader's insanity—truly an aberration of affiliation on a frightening scale.

Actually, it is not even clear that the behaviors produced by cohesiveness are beneficial to the group. We have already seen one potentially detrimental aspect of increased cohesiveness. In Chapter 9, we cited research (Schachter, 1951) revealing that, after a group discussion, members of highly cohesive groups were significantly more rejecting of a member who expressed deviant opinions during the discussion than were members of less cohesive groups. The catch is that one who expresses deviant opinions may have information that others in the group do not have or, at least, a different perspective that could later prove useful to the group. If all who express deviant opinions are forced out of groups, group performance suffers in the long run—particularly if new problems arise. Schachter's research was not designed to test the latter proposition, of course. His "deviates" were in fact confederates of the experimenter, so there could be no subsequent group sessions in which performances of groups that had rejected the deviate were compared with performances of groups that had not.

Consider another of the supposedly beneficial behaviors exhibited by members of highly cohesive groups: changing their minds to accept the views of fellow members. Deviates or potential deviates may acquiesce more readily to the majority opinion when they themselves are highly attracted to the group. The more highly attracted they are to the group, the less they want to risk rejection. Janis (1972) has argued that the greater pressure on deviates in cohesive groups to conform and their greater willingness to do so contribute to a pattern of concurrence-seeking behavior that may have disastrous consequences on the quality of the groups' decisions and actions. He has named this behavior syndrome "groupthink."

GROUPTHINK

According to Janis, GROUPTHINK is not the same as conformity to group pressures. Rather, the decisions that result from groupthink are a consensus of genuine judgments made by all members of a group. Being composed of mere individuals, decision-making and policy-formulating groups are subject to all the same errors of judgment as individuals: selective perception, wandering attention, wishful thinking, and other forms of information distortion. Groupthink, however, is a powerful source of error over and above these familiar individual limitations. Groupthink occurs when the members of a decision-making group become so concerned with maintaining a group atmosphere of congeniality and mutual acceptance that they fail to critically evaluate the information on which the decision is to be based. Hence, they fail to make the best possible decision given the information available.

Not all decisions that turn out poorly are necessarily instances of groupthink, and groupthink is more likely to occur under some conditions than others. Janis hypothesizes that three specific group features increase the probability of groupthink: (1) a highly cohesive group in which a strong "we-feeling" exists, (2) a group insulated from the opinions and judgments of outsiders, and (3) a leader who actively promotes his or her own preferred solution to the problem confronting the group. How well these conditions fit the popular image of a conspiracy: an insulated, highly cohesive group and a leader with a plan.

Under these conditions, a peculiar sort of psychological contagion is likely to occur. Its presence can be detected by various combinations of the following symptoms (Janis, 1972, pp. 197–198):

1. An illusion of invulnerability, shared by most or all the members, which creates excessive optimism and encourages taking extreme risks.

2. Collective efforts to rationalize in order to discount warnings which might lead members to reconsider their assumptions.

3. An unquestioned belief in the group's inherent morality, inclining the members to ignore the ethical or moral consequences of their decision.

4. Stereotyped views of enemy leaders as too evil to warrant genuine attempts to negotiate, or as too weak and stupid to counter whatever risky attempts are made to defeat their purposes.

5. Direct pressure on any member who expresses strong arguments against any of the group's stereotypes, illusions, or commitments.

6. Self-censorship of deviations from the apparent group consensus, reflecting each member's inclination to minimize to himself the importance of his doubts and counterarguments.

7. A shared illusion of unanimity concerning judgments conforming to the majority view.

8. The emergence of self-appointed mindguards—members who protect the group from adverse information that might shatter their shared complacency about the effectiveness and morality of their decisions.

According to Janis, when a group displays all or most of these symptoms, it is likely to do a poor job of decision making. Group morale and *esprit de corps* will be maintained, but the group is not likely to do a good job of gathering and evaluating the information on which to base its decisions.

In a series of intriguing historical analyses, Janis makes a case for groupthink as a contributing factor in four major United States foreign policy debacles: the Bay of Pigs invasion, crossing the 38th parallel in the Korean War, our failure to be prepared for the surprise attack on Pearl Harbor, and our escalation of the Vietnam War. In each of these four instances, he argues that the decision to act (or not to act, in the case of Pearl Harbor) was made by a small, highly cohesive group that was relatively insulated from outside advice and whose members, in a misguided attempt to maintain the group atmosphere of congeniality, were insufficiently aggressive in expressing their own doubts about the wisdom of the plan and insufficiently critical in evaluating the available information.

The Bay of Pigs invasion, for example, was planned by a small group of talented and experienced men who met repeatedly over a period of weeks immediately after President John F. Kennedy took office in 1961. The planning group consisted of Kennedy himself, Dean Rusk, Robert McNamara, Robert Kennedy, Arthur Schlesinger, McGeorge Bundy, and Douglas Dillon, together with representatives of the Central Intelligence Agency and the Pentagon. Schlesinger (1965) reports that the atmosphere at the White House in those first weeks of the New Frontier was one of unbounded optimism and unlimited hope for the future. This atmosphere of confidence and invulnerability permeated the planning group. Yet the decision of this group to invade Cuba with a small band of Cuban exiles (approximately 1400) was an unmitigated disaster. The exiles waded ashore on April 17, their supplies and reserve ammunition never arrived, they were promptly surrounded by thousands of Cuban soldiers, and within three days almost all were killed or captured. How could it happen? Janis' answer, of course, is that members of the planning group maintained their *esprit de corps* as daring young men of the New Frontier by unintentionally softening their criticism of the plan and assuming that if the others didn't object, the plan must be okay.

To see how the groupthink hypothesis works itself out in detail, consider one aspect of the invasion—the contingency plan for what the invaders were to do if they did not succeed in their prime military objective. If the invaders failed, they were to retreat into the Escambray Mountains and strengthen the anti-Castro guerrillas known to be operating there. This seems like a reasonable idea and the planning group approved, or at least no one objected. Someone should have objected. As Schlesinger later admitted, no one in the group seemed to realize that the Escambray Mountains were 80 miles from the Bay of Pigs—80 miles of almost impassable swamp and marshes. It seems difficult to believe that such a high-level advisory group would approve an invasion plan and contingency escape route without carefully plotting the physical details of the engagement on a map of the area. Apparently the members of the group felt that asking such obvious questions as whether the proposed escape route was really feasible would be construed as criticism of the plan. The obvious questions were not asked, and the plan failed. (Box D describes a group procedure in which members can ask *any* questions and make *any* suggestions, because criticism of all input, however outlandish, is specifically banned.)

Janis' ideas on groupthink and its consequences are intriguing, but the case studies he cites hardly constitute rigorous evidence for the reality of the phenomenon. In the Preface of his book, Janis describes his effort as "hypothesis construction," and the entire groupthink syndrome should be regarded as a set of interrelated hypotheses—intriguing possibilities, but not yet established facts. If Janis's ideas prove substantially correct, he will have identified a major way in which our affiliative tendencies can get us into trouble. According to Janis, the basic process underlying groupthink is "a mutual effort among the members of a group to maintain self-esteem, especially when they share responsibility for making vital decisions that pose threats of social disapproval and self-disapproval" (p. 203). Let us look at another line of research bear-

D. Brainstorming

In 1939, an advertising executive named Alex Osborn originated a group technique called BRAINSTORMING for producing creative ideas. When brainstorming to solve a problem, group members should make no criticisms of each others' ideas and each should simply try to produce as many solutions as possible, no matter how ridiculous some of them might sound. Not only would a large number of solutions be obtained, but there should be a better chance of obtaining a few unique solutions. The important thing was to get a lot of ideas. They could be evaluated later.

Donald Taylor, Paul Berry, and Clifford Block (1964) decided to see whether the claims made for brainstorming were really valid. They enlisted the help of Yale undergraduates enrolled in a course in the psychology of personnel administration. Some of the students were organized in groups of 4 and given a series of 3 problems to work on. One of the problems, for example, was to suggest ways of inducing more European tourists to come to America on their vacations. Other students were asked to work on these same problems alone. There was a time limit of 12 minutes for each problem.

The ideas produced by the groups and by the individuals working alone were recorded and the recordings transcribed so that the number of different ideas could be compared. For the tourist problem, 483 different possible solutions were produced by all the groups and all the individuals working alone. The question of interest was whether the brainstorming groups or the individuals working alone produced more and/or better ideas. It would be unfair, of course, to compare the production of four individuals working in a group to the production of one individual working alone, so the productions of those who actually worked alone were randomly assigned to nominal groups of four and compared to the productions of the real groups.

Somewhat surprisingly, especially for the advocates of brainstorming, the individuals working alone produced many more and better ideas. The solutions proposed by individuals working alone were rated as more feasible, more effective, and more general. It appears that brainstorming in a group may actually inhibit rather than facilitate the production of creative ideas. One possible reason for this is that the thoughts of group members may be constrained by listening to what others are saying. They may be induced to pursue a single, or at least a similar, line of thought.

---

ing on these mutual efforts to avoid self-disapproval and social disapproval—a line of research that again implicates our affiliative tendencies as a potential source of irrational behavior.

RISK AND CAUTION IN GROUPS

It is widely believed that groups are, in general, more cautious and conservative than individuals. The theme of one of the most popular social science commentaries of the 1950s, Whyte's *The Organization Man* (1956), was that American society was placing too much emphasis on "belongingness." The result, according to Whyte, was that groups were becoming increasingly important in everyone's lives and that the emphasis on belonging caused people to avoid doing anything that might antagonize other members of their groups. People had, in short, become "other-directed" and were too concerned with pleasing others and doing what they thought others wanted. Timid and conservative behavior was thought to be the rule in groups—from Congressional Committees to corporate board meetings to the P.T.A.

In the early 1960s, a line of research growing out of a master's thesis at M.I.T. (Stoner, 1961) came close to reversing the belief that groups are more conservative than individuals. It began to look as though groups in general made riskier decisions than individuals. Now it seems that the answer to the question of whether groups or individuals make riskier decisions is the same as the answer to most interesting questions: it depends. However, one of the main things it depends on is the extent to which the individual wants to maintain an image of himself or herself as an exemplar of the dominant values held by the group.

In the typical experiment in this line of research, small groups of subjects are asked to respond individually to a questionnaire, called the Choice Dilemmas Questionnaire (CDQ), containing 12 such items as the following:

> Mr. A, an electrical engineer, who is married and has one child, has been working for a large electronics corporation since graduating from college five years ago. He is assured of a lifetime job with a modest, though adequate, salary, and liberal pension benefits upon retirement. On the other hand, it is very unlikely that his salary will increase much before he retires. While attending a convention, Mr. A is offered a job with a small, newly founded company which has a highly uncertain future. The new job would pay more to start and would offer the possibility of a share in the ownership if the company survived the competition of the larger firms.
>
> Imagine that you are advising Mr. A. Listed below are several probabilities or odds of the new company's proving financially sound. Please check the lowest probability that you would consider acceptable to make it worthwhile for Mr. A. to take the new job.
>
> ____The chances are 1 in 10 that the company will prove financially sound.
>
> ____The chances are 3 in 10 that the company will prove financially sound.
>
> ____The chances are 5 in 10 that the company will prove financially sound.
>
> ____The chances are 7 in 10 that the company will prove financially sound
>
> ____The chances are 9 in 10 the the company will prove financially sound
>
> ____Place a check here if you think Mr. A should *not* take the new job no matter what the probabilities.

Each of the items is similar to this example in that alternative courses of action are described, some involving a degree of risk and the others somewhat more of a sure thing. After expressing their individual risk preferences, the individuals are asked to discuss each item and arrive at a group consensus of preferred risk. Following the discussions and group consensus, the individuals are again asked for their private opinion about each item. Brown (1965) summarizes the general results as follows:

> In experiments with several kinds of subjects and with payoffs both actual and hypothetical, both positive and negative, groups have arrived at unanimous decisions that were riskier than the average of the decisions made by the individuals prior to discussion. In addition the individual opinions taken after discussion have been riskier than they were before discussion (p. 660–661).

We should note several things about this brief summary. First, the dilemmas do not have objectively correct choices. There is no physical reality to use as a final arbiter. Second, the group consensus is not simply the mean of the initial individual preferences. It is generally somewhat riskier than the mean of the initial preferences. Third, while the majority of items in the original CDQ produced risky shifts, a few items consistently produced a group consensus more cautious than the mean of individual preferences. Subsequent research (Cartwright, 1971) has confirmed that additional caution-producing items can be designed, although they are somewhat more difficult to construct than risk-producing items. What do we make of all this?

A number of possible explanations have been proposed. Kogan and Wallach (1967) suggest that participation in group discussion of the dilemmas makes clear to each individual that the entire group, not he or she alone, will be responsible for any negative consequences or "wrong" answers. Hence, the members become more willing to endorse riskier alternatives. (It is not clear how this explanation can account for the shifts to caution found on some items.) Another explanation for increased risk-taking in groups is that the individuals who had originally taken risky positions were probably more influential during group discussions. The more daring individuals may have more of a flair for influencing others. Again, this explanation fails to account for the fact that certain items consistently produce shifts to caution, unless we assume that the latter items somehow bestow an ability to influence others on the more cautious members of the group.

There have been several additional proposals, but the one that appears best to account for the data was initially suggested by Brown (1965). Brown's basic idea is that choice situations engage one of two values, risk or caution, depending on the circumstances. A business decision, for example, would be likely to engage the value of risk. One must be bold and take chances in order to maximize profits. Nothing ventured, nothing gained. On the other hand, a medical decision about whether to operate on a patient would be more likely to engage the value of caution. Surgery can be dangerous, so it is the preferred course of action only when absolutely necessary. So far, no argument. But how does this account for risky and cautious *shifts* following group discussion?

The key to Brown's argument is that with values such as risk and caution, people like to believe they are appropriately risky or cautious, and "appropriately" is defined by how risky or cautious other people like themselves are. Consider what may happen when an item on the Choice Dilemmas Questionnaire describes a situation in which riskiness is generally valued. Brown reminds us that

> the individual who has not talked with anyone about the problems cannot know how to be truly risky because risk is relative to a group norm and the location of the norm on the scale of probabilities is not known. . . . When individuals talk together and disclose their decision the actual distribution is made known. Those who find themselves below the mean of the six members of the group discover that they are failing to realize the ideal of riskiness that they may have thought they were. . . . Consequently they feel impelled to move in a risky direction. . . . Subjects at or above the group mean feel no such impulsion, they are relatively risky just as they meant to be. The result would be, of course, a shift in the group decision toward greater risk than the mean of the individual decisions (p. 701).

Similar reasoning can be applied to those items that describe a situation in which caution is generally valued. In both cases, the apparent motive behind individual shifts is the desire to be an exemplar of what the group is assumed to value.

The evidence appears to be generally consistent with Brown's value theory of risky and cautious shifts. Ferguson and Vidmar (1971) found that on risk-evoking items, individuals estimated before group discussion that others were more cautious than themselves, whereas on caution-evoking items, they estimated that others were more risky than themselves. Further, on risk-evoking items, the more cautious an individual had been initially, the more he or she shifted toward a riskier alternative as a result of group discussion. Conversely, on caution-evoking items, the more risky an individual had been initially, the more he or she shifted toward caution after the discussion.

Our desire for social approval can make us do irrational things. Our desire to maintain an image of ourselves as appropriately risky or cautious, as defined by group norms, can induce us to take greater risks or to be more conservative than the circumstances of the problem alone seem to warrant. We are apparently greatly concerned about how we appear to others, especially others with whom we find ourselves interacting. But what about how those others appear to us? Do we remain clear-eyed evaluators of their virtues and vices? There is reason to believe that we do not.

COMMITMENT TO THE GROUP

A commitment is essentially a pledge or promise, and committing oneself to a certain group is binding oneself to the group for better or for worse. One can become committed to a group by (1) devoting a great deal of time and effort to qualifying for membership, (2) similarly exerting oneself in the group's activities and/or in defense of its interests, or (3) using legal and contractual means, as in taking marriage vows or pledging a fraternity or sorority. In each of these examples, the individual has done something that affects the subsequent course of events. And in each case, it would be difficult to deny or change what he or she had done.

Now suppose that an individual has in some way committed himself or herself to a group. Further, suppose that the group turns out to be a collection of duds. Their conversation is boring, they are lazy, they are petty and gossipy, or they just simply appear to genuinely dislike the individual in question. All the necessary and sufficient conditions of dissonance arousal are present. Recall that dissonance (Chapter 9) is a motivational state occurring when an individual simultaneously has cognitive elements that clash or disagree with each other. Knowledge that "I worked hard to get into this group" should be dissonant with "This group is boring." Similarly, knowledge that "I have done a great deal for this group" should be dissonant with "They don't seem to like me." Dissonance persists until some cognitive work is done to alter the dissonant cognitions. In the first of our examples, dissonance could be reduced by either denying that the group is boring or denying that one worked hard to get into the group.

This is where the notion of commitment becomes important. Commitments create cognitions about one's own behavior that are relatively resistant to change. In our example, the cognition that one has worked hard to become a member of the group results from a behavioral commitment and is relatively difficult to deny. On the other hand, the cognition that the group is boring is not tied to any behavioral commitment or objective evidence . . . and . . . maybe they're not so bad after all. Note that dissonance reduction helps us maintain an image of ourselves as rational. Rational people presumably do not work hard to become members of dull groups. Thus, if we commit ourselves to a group and the group turns out not to be rewarding, dissonance theory predicts that we will distort our perceptions of the group. Let us look at some pertinent research.

The effects of initiation. In an often cited and widely criticized experiment, Aronson and Mills (1959) examined the effects of severity of initiation on liking for a group. Subjects were college women who volunteered to participate in group discussions on the psychology of sex. Each subject was seen individually, and when she arrived for the "first" session, each was told that she would be joining a group that had already been meeting for several weeks. It was explained that since the topic of the discussion was sex, a topic many people are somewhat hesitant about discussing openly, the group members were assigned to separate rooms and the discussions were conducted via an intercom system. This, so the experimenter said, helped people relax and seemed to facilitate the discussions. However, since the subject had not read the group's assignment for the week, "Sexual Behavior in Animals," she would just be allowed to listen to the discussion via a headphone this week, and her microphone would be turned off. Thus all subjects believed they were listening to a live discussion carried on by three girls in separate rooms somewhere in the immediate vicinity. Actually, the discussion that all subjects heard had been pre-recorded and

> was deliberately designed to be as dull and banal as possible. The participants spoke dryly and haltingly on secondary sex behavior in the lower animals, "inadvertently" contradicted themselves and one another, mumbled several *non sequiturs,* started sentences that they never finished, hemmed, hawed, and in general conducted one of the most worthless and uninteresting discussions imaginable (p. 179).

The interesting feature of the experiment occurred just before the subjects heard this boring discussion. The subjects were randomly assigned to one of three treatment conditions. In the Control condition, each subject was simply asked whether she thought she could discuss sex freely. In the other two conditions, the experimenter explained that each subject had to take an "embarrassment test" so that the experimenter would be able to determine whether she would be able to contribute to the discussion without too much embarrassment. In the Mild Initiation condition, the subjects simply had to read aloud to the male experimenter five sex-related but not obscene words. In the Severe Initiation condition, the subject had to read aloud a number of obscene words and two vividly detailed descriptions of sexual activity from works of fiction. Then all subjects listened to the recorded discussion and rated both the discussion and the participants on a number of evaluative scales. The major results are shown in Table III.

Subjects who underwent the severe initiation rated both the discussion and the participants higher than did subjects in either of the other two conditions. The knowledge that one has undergone a painful experience to become part of a group is dissonant with the knowledge that the group has turned out to be dull

Table III. Evaluations of the group

Ratings of	Control	Experimental conditions Mild initiation	Severe initiation
Discussion	80.2	81.8	97.6
Participants	89.9	89.3	97.7

The higher the number, the more favorable the ratings. (From Aronson and Mills, 1959, Table 1, p. 179.)

and boring. One cannot easily deny that the initiation was severe, but one's perception of the group is much more malleable. Accordingly, one exaggerates the group's virtues, thus reducing dissonance.

The Aronson and Mills (1959) results have been the subject of a great deal of criticism, and a number of alternative hypotheses have been proposed to account for them. For example, it has been proposed that the severe initiation was sexually arousing and that subjects in this condition would evaluate anything remotely associated with sex more positively. Others have suggested that the severely initiated subjects were upset by the initiation. The banal discussion was a relief, so it was rated more highly. Gerard and Mathewson (1966) devised an experiment that cast doubt on these explanations. They used electric shocks instead of obscene material for the initiation rite. Other subjects were shocked before listening to the discussion, but the shock was not part of the initiation. The group discussion was rated more favorably only when shocks constituted an initiation into the group. These results, using shocks, support the validity of the original Aronson–Mills study.

The more committed we are to a group or the more we have endured to become part of the group, the more we exaggerate its virtues and soft-pedal its vices. These tendencies can help see us and the group through the occasional hard times that are bound to occur. It should be obvious, however, that these same tendencies may blind us to what the group is really like.

Summary

We began this chapter by calling attention to the importance of small groups in daily life. Families, work groups, and spontaneous informal groups are usually composed of four or fewer members, and the norms of larger groups are filtered to the individual through small groups of friends and associates.

Then we turned to the question of why people seek the company of others. In general, people associate with others whom they find rewarding and who they anticipate will provide favorable outcomes in the future. What constitutes a reward varies as a function of the nature and purpose of the group being formed.

With *informal friendship groups* and in the early stages of courtship and marriage, physical attractiveness appears to be a very important reward. And there is more to physical attractiveness than meets the eye. We tend to assume that physically attractive people have more desirable personality characteristics and life experiences than unattractive people. Furthermore, we behave differently toward attractive others, thereby making it easier for them to be rewarding to us. We also may assume that our own personality characteristics are more similar to those of physically attractive others.

Next we considered similarity itself. Propinquity is also an important determinant of friendship formation, partly because similar people tend to live in the same areas. One reason why similarity is so important is that we tend to validate our beliefs, opinions, and attitudes by surrounding ourselves with like-minded others. This point is reinforced by research linking anxiety to affiliation. When we are anxious and do not quite understand what is happening, we seek out the company of others—not just any others, but others in the same situation.

With *work groups*, complementarity of roles and personality characteristics appears to be much more important than in friendship groups. When there is some division of labor necessary in order for the group to function, role differentiation occurs and complementarity plays more of a part in attraction to the group, its maintenance, and its development.

The *family* is the most interesting and complex of small groups. It makes sense to consider the family as a friendship group that must evolve into a work group (and, perhaps, back into a friendship group). There is some evidence for a matching of perceived net worth in the early stages of romantic relationships, as Murstein's stimulus–value–role theory predicts. The evidence on complementarity of roles in the later stages is less clear-cut. Because complementarity emerges gradually in a relationship, the particular needs and roles that will be involved in the pattern are very difficult to predict.

Weick and others have argued that it often makes more sense to think of interaction as *preceding* group formation. From this perspective, the essential features of groups are sets of interlocked behaviors, and groups themselves emerge only when people retrospectively try to make sense of the streams of behavior in which they have been immersed.

In the last three sections of the chapter, we turned our attention to some aberrations of affiliation—things that can go wrong when we let our affiliative needs get the best of us. The groupthink syndrome identified by Janis seems to occur when members of a decision-making group become overly concerned with maintaining a group atmosphere of congeniality and mutual acceptance. As a result, they do not evaluate information critically and fail to make the best decision. Research on risky and cautious group decisions indicates that the individual's desire to be an exemplar of what the group values can induce the individual to take irrational stances—to be more risky or more cautious than circumstances alone warrant. Finally, we saw that when an individual makes a commitment to a group, he or she can no longer be relied on to evaluate the group objectively.

13

Interaction in groups

366
Incidental consequences of interaction

Social facilitation: When others matter
    Social facilitation and bystander inhibition
Deindividuation: When others don't matter
    Applying and testing Zimbardo's model
Nonverbal communication
    Nonverbal cues and interaction

375
Interaction processes

Attempts to analyze ongoing interaction
    Forming, storming, norming, performing
Stabilizing participation differences
    Why those who talk talk
    Why those who talk keep talking
    And talking
    And talking
Reacting to one's own behavior
    The prisoner's dilemma
    Research applications of the prisoner's dilemma
Individual versus group performance

386
Retrospective misinterpretations: What really happened here?

388
Summary

In Chapter 12, we examined some of the reasons why people seek out the company of others and how, in some instances, groups just seem to emerge from interaction. We also looked at two ways in which our desire to be accepted by groups can induce us to do irrational things and saw how the very effort expended to get into a group can blind us to its shortcomings. In this chapter, we shift our focus to ongoing interaction and its consequences.

A major consequence of group interaction is goal attainment. In fact, most discussions of ongoing social interaction focus on the goals that the participants, individually and collectively, are assumed to be pursuing. Jones and Thibaut (1958) even use different types of goals as a basis for classifying interactions. It seems clear that there are few totally purposeless interactions between people. People bring goals to interaction, and much of what is involved in the various interpersonal tactics and strategies—the attempts to define the situation in particular ways and/or to cast others in particular roles—can be seen as attempts by the individual participants to achieve their goals.

On the other hand, many of the most interesting aspects of social interaction appear to be independent of the particular goals a group or its members may be trying to attain. (We might call these things that happen simply because we are around other people the incidental consequences of interaction.) We behave in groups differently from the way we behave when alone—and we behave in these different ways regardless of why we are interacting with others. Let us begin our discussion by looking at some of these incidental consequences of interaction.

Incidental consequences of interaction

Recall that in Chapter 10 we described some research on the effect of different numbers of witnesses on the speed with which a victim in an emergency got help (Darley and Latané, 1968). Group inhibition of helping has been found in a number of studies, and one explanation offered for this phenomenon is that other people influence the potential helper's interpretation of the situation. The potential helper looks around and sees that no one else appears excited or is rushing forward to help, so he or she decides that the situation is not an emergency and, consequently, is less likely to help.

That is a very cognitive, rational approach to what happens in ambiguous, quickly unfolding, potentially serious emergency situations, and somehow it does not quite ring true. The intense arousal and instantaneous action (or inaction) often reported by people caught up in such situations does not mesh well with the image of someone coolly looking around to gather cues about how to interpret the situation and then deciding what to do. There is a body of literature that offers a more basic explanation for group inhibition of helping and also suggests when groups will have exactly the opposite effect on an individual—that is, when the individual will be disinhibited by the group.

SOCIAL FACILITATION: WHEN OTHERS MATTER

When researchers begin to investigate a problem, the initial results are often not only inconclusive but inconsistent. The problem turns out to be much more complex than it appeared at first, and the early, divergent results seem to drive some investigators on to easier pickings. Happily, those same inconsistent early returns often goad other investigators to reconsider the problem, restate the original question, and come up with a theory that can account for and integrate the initial results. The research on social facilitation is a case in point.

Actually, the term SOCIAL FACILITATION itself implies a half-truth, because the presence of others sometimes facilitates and sometimes inhibits what an individual is doing. For many years, the only generalization one could draw was that the presence of others had an effect, even when no competition was involved. Even in the same experiment, it was often found that the presence of others facilitated performance on some tasks and inhibited performance on others. In reviewing the pertinent research, Zajonc (1965) discovered a single thread of consistency in the results. The learning of new responses always seemed to be inhibited by the presence of others, while the performance of familiar responses seemed to be facilitated by the presence of others.

Reasoning inductively, Zajonc argued that there is a general class of psychological processes known to increase the likelihood of occurrence of DOMINANT (or well-learned) RESPONSES. This class consists of drive, arousal, and related processes. If it could be shown that the presence of others is physiologically arousing, this would account for the findings on social facilitation, because arousal is known to facilitate dominant responses. But what about social inhibition? Zajonc reasoned that in ambiguous situations or *learning* situations in which the individual has not yet mastered the task, the dominant responses are usually incorrect. If performance accuracy is used as the criterion, the presence of others will inhibit correct responding, because their presence facilitates dominant responses. Let us look at some studies designed to test this reasoning directly.

In the first phase of a two-part experiment, Zajonc and Sales (1966) trained subjects in the pronunciation of 10 seven-letter nonsense words. Two words were seen and pronounced by the subject 1 time each; another 2 words were seen and pronounced 2 times each; 2 words, 4 times; 2, 8 times; and 2, 16 times. Thus the latter words should have been much better learned than the former. During the second phase of the experiment, subjects were told that the words they had just learned to pronounce would be flashed on a screen and that their task would be to identify the words. On only about 25 percent of the trials in the second phase, however, were the flashes at a speed slow enough for subjects to recognize which of the 10 words had actually been presented. On the remaining trials, not only were the flashes too fast to interpret, but the material presented was simply irregular black lines and not words at all. The subjects were told that they should guess one of the 10 words on each trial, even when they could not clearly perceive which had been presented.

After the training phase and after the instructions for the second phase were given, subjects were assigned to one of two conditions. For control subjects, the second phase proceeded with each subject alone in a cubicle pronouncing aloud his or her best guess after each flash on the screen. Subjects in the experimental condition were told that "two students of the experimenter have asked if they can watch" and the two were brought in and seated a few feet away from the subject, who then proceeded to pronounce the "words" as they were flashed on the screen.

There were 124 pseudorecognition trials, trials on which none of the previously learned nonsense words were presented. The prediction was that, on these pseudorecognition trials, subjects responding in the presence of others would be more likely than those responding alone to guess by using well-learned (dominant) responses—words they had pronounced 16 times during the training session. Subjects responding in the presence of others should be less likely to use nondominant responses—words they had pronounced only once or twice during the training sessions. This is exactly what happened. It appears that the mere presence of others increases the likelihood of dominant, well-learned responses occurring at the expense of responses learned less thoroughly.

The "mere presence" of another may not be quite as simple as it sounds. Cottrell (1968; Cottrell, Wack, Sekerak, and Rittle, 1968) has argued that the mere proximity of a second person in the vicinity is not the crucial variable to enhance dominant responses. In an inital training period, Cottrell's subjects learned to pronounce 10 nonsense words. The 10 words were divided into 5 pairs, and the various pairs were pronounced 1, 2, 5, 10, and 25 times, respectively, during the training session. During the subsequent pseudorecognition trials, subjects performed Alone, in the presence of an Audience of two others who were interested in observing the experiment, or in the Mere Presence of two blindfolded confederates who were supposedly dark-adapting to take part in another experiment. The major results are shown in Figure 1.

The mere physical presence of others appears not to be the crucial variable. Rather, it is the presence of an audience capable of judging and evaluating one's performance that is arousing and that facilitates dominant responses at the expense of less well-learned responses. Subsequent research (Paulus and Murdoch, 1971; Cohen and Davis, 1973) is generally consistent with this idea. Recently Laughlin and Jaccard (1975) extended research on social facilitation by examining what effects being observed has on the performance of small groups. Using a relatively difficult concept-attainment task, they found that the performance of individuals suffered when they were being observed, compared to when they performed the task alone. However, the performance of pairs of cooperative subjects was unaffected by the presence of observers. The task used was easier for pairs than for individuals. One might expect the opposite effect to occur on tasks that are easier for individuals. The research on social facilitation continues and, though Zajonc's (1965) original formulation has been extended and refined in several respects, it remains the most robust theoretical statement about the effects of an audience on performance.

Social facilitation and bystander inhibition. The main value of a good theory, of course, is that it can assimilate diverse experimental findings. At the beginning of this section, we intimated that the social-facilitation framework might account for some of the research on bystander inhibition. Consider the Latané and Rodin (1969) experiment as an example. The basic findings were very simple. Compared to individuals waiting alone, both pairs of strangers and pairs of friends were less likely to help in an apparent emergency, and pairs of strangers were more inhibited about helping than pairs of friends. In order for Zajonc's (1965) formulation to account for these findings, we need only make one very plausible assumption: we need to assume that helping was not the dominant response in the situation. This seems a very reasonable assumption, because, as Latané and Rodin themselves point out, most people have very little ex-

perience with emergencies of any kind. Furthermore, the subjects were in a strange building and had been assigned a definite task by someone in authority. Hence the dominant responses were probably to sit in their seats and complete the questionnaires. Since the presence of others is arousing (Martens, 1969) and facilitates dominant responses, groups of friends and strangers were more likely to do just that—sit in their

1. Subjects working in the presence of an audience capable of judging their performance tend to give dominant, well-learned responses to ambiguous stimuli much more than subjects working alone or in the mere physical presence of others. (From Cottrell, 1968, Figure 2, p. 102.)

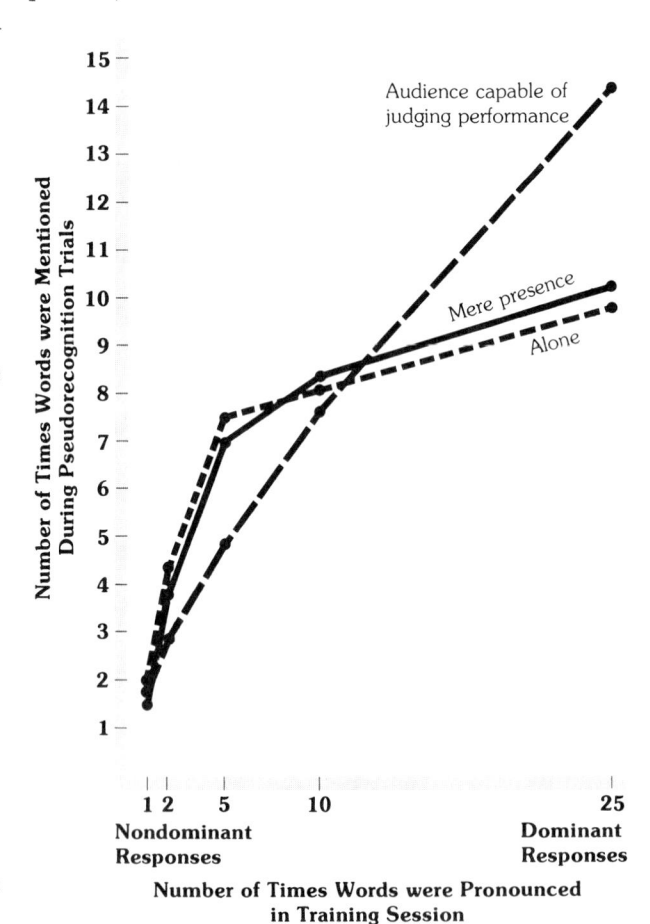

368
The nature of groups

seats and complete the questionnaires. Subjects waiting alone, on the other hand, were quite likely to perform the novel response: to try to help the lady in distress.

But how are we to account for the fact that friends were somewhat less inhibited about helping than strangers? There is some evidence that the presence of free fatty acids in the blood can be used as an indicator of stress and arousal (Bogdonoff, Klein, Back, Nichols, Troyer and Hood, 1964; Back and Bogdonoff, 1964). Back and Bogdonoff (1967) have found that levels of free fatty acids were higher among subjects participating in an experiment with a group of strangers than among subjects participating in the same experiment with a group of acquaintances. Back and Bogdonoff discuss this and similar findings in terms of the "buffering effect" of being surrounded by a group of friends and acquaintances. Perhaps the subject who comes into the experiment in a group feels shielded from the experimental situation. The individual with a friend nearby is less aroused and apprehensive than the individual surrounded by strangers. Hence the dominant responses (remaining seated and finishing the questionnaire) of the former would be facilitated less, and the groups of friends would be more likely to respond appropriately in the unusual helping situation they faced in the Latané and Rodin experiment. This, of course, is exactly what happened.

A little less apprehension about being evaluated and a little less concern about what other people will think may be a good thing. It can lead to better performance in ambiguous and unusual situations. Like most things, however, it can be carried too far. When one becomes totally unconcerned about the evaluative judgments of others, the effects may not be so beneficial. After all, the evaluative judgments of others are the major vehicle by which the ethical and moral values of society are sanctioned and transmitted. Let us look at some of the consequences when individuals lose all apprehension about being evaluated by the surrounding group.

DEINDIVIDUATION: WHEN OTHERS DON'T MATTER

A recurring figure in literature through the ages is the protagonist who is held in high esteem by his or her peers and who appears to exemplify all the characteristics valued by the surrounding society, but who is nevertheless subject to dark, forbidden impulses that must be forcefully suppressed. These socially undesirable urges are never quite successfully squelched, and that ingredient has thickened many a plot. Under certain social conditions, something happens to the individual, something that reduces the importance of adhering to socially accepted forms of behavior. The individual seems to see self and others in a different way temporarily, and behavior that is normally restrained is released. We shall soon look at some of the social conditions that trigger these events, but first, let us examine the notion of a conflict between appropriate and inappropriate behavior.

Slater (1970) points out that every culture finds some normal human responses unacceptable and attempts to socialize its members into foregoing those responses:

> . . . Yet there are always a few of these responses with which every society and every individual has trouble. They must be shouted down continually. . . . Thus although the Germans, for example, have always placed great stress on order, precision, and obedience to authority, they periodically explode into revolutionary chaos and are driven by romantic *Gotterdammerung* fantasies. In the same way there is a cooperative underside to competitive America, a rich spoofing tradition in ceremonious England, an elaborated pornography in all prudish societies. . . . Rather than saying Germans are obedient or Anglo-Saxon societies stuffy or puritanical, it is more correct to say that Germans are preoccupied with issues of authority, Anglo-Saxons with the control of emotional and sexual expression, and so forth. Those issues about which members of a given society seem to feel strongly all reveal a conflict one side of which is strongly emphasized, the other as strongly (but not quite successfully) suppressed. . . . These opposing forces are much more equally balanced than the society's participants like to recognize—were this not true there would be no need for suppression (p. 3-4).

The important question, of course, is, under what conditions are these normally restrained behaviors likely to be released. Casual observation seems to suggest (Festinger, Pepitone, and Newcomb, 1952) that the release of such behaviors may be facilitated by the presence of a group. In groups, individuals sometimes act as though they were no longer responsible for their actions, as though they were "submerged in the group." Festinger, et al. refer to this state of affairs as DEINDIVIDUATION. The deindividuated person does not seem to pay attention to group members and others as individuals. This is another way of saying that there is a lack of concern about social evaluation—about what other people will think of one's behavior.

2. **Zimbardo's representation of the causes (Input Variables), mechanisms (Inferred Subjective Changes), and results (Output Behaviors) of the deindividuation process. (From Zimbardo, 1969, Figure 1, p. 253.)**

This seems to be the key psychological process involved in deindividuation. If so, the presence of a group may be a sufficient condition, but not a necessary condition, for deindividuation to occur.

In a detailed descriptive analysis of the processes and products of deindividuation, Zimbardo (1969) argues that the phenomenon unfolds within the individual, though several things about being a part of a group increase the likelihood that one will lose all concern about social evaluation and thus become deindividuated. In groups, responsibility for antisocial behavior is diffused among many members, individual members may develop feelings of anonymity, the presence of others may increase levels of arousal, and the noise and activities of many nearby people may overload one's information-processing abilities. All of these effects could lead to a temporary lack of concern about self-observation and social evaluation. Such lack of concern is assumed to lower one's threshold for ex-

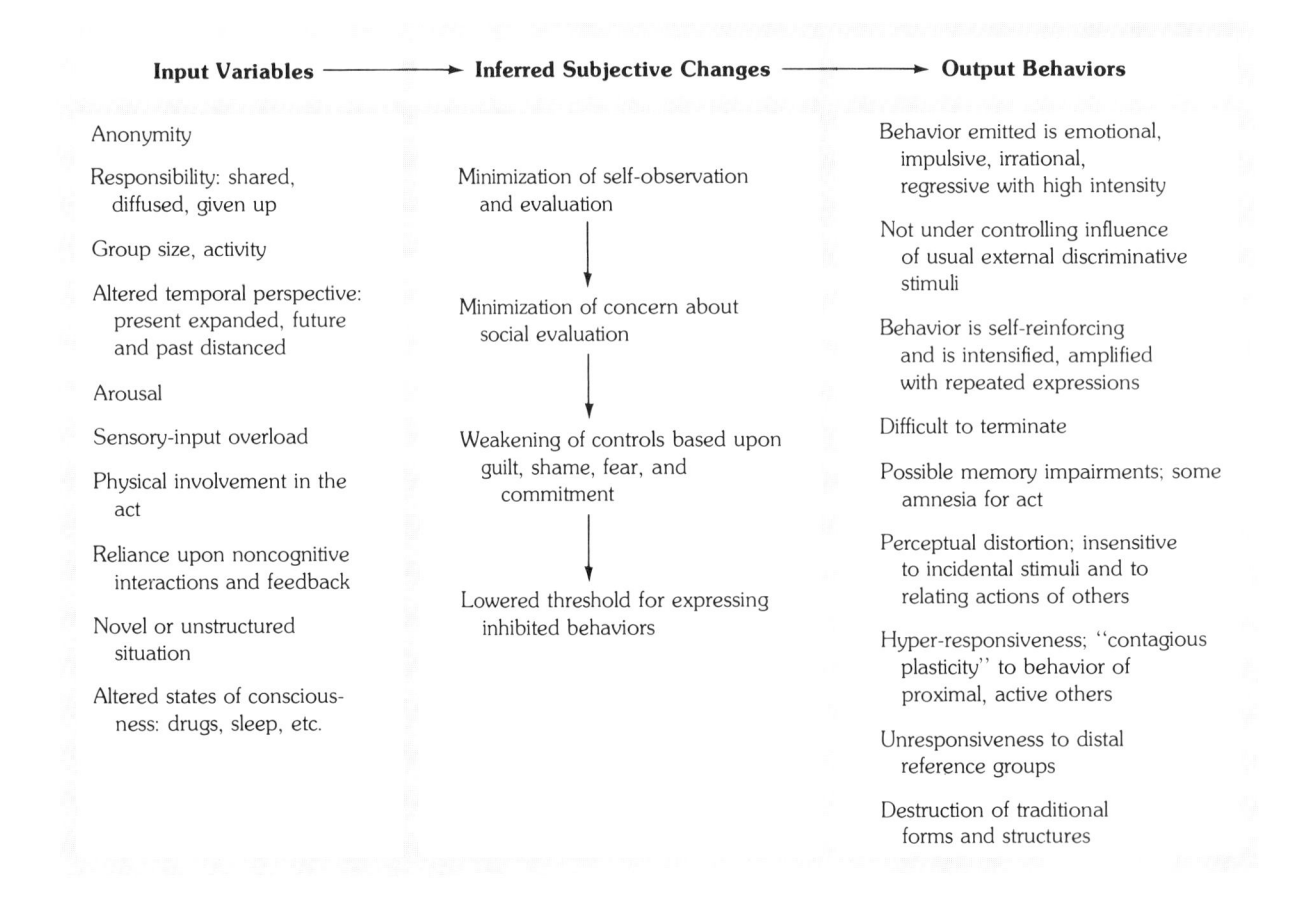

Input Variables	Inferred Subjective Changes	Output Behaviors
Anonymity	Minimization of self-observation and evaluation	Behavior emitted is emotional, impulsive, irrational, regressive with high intensity
Responsibility: shared, diffused, given up		Not under controlling influence of usual external discriminative stimuli
Group size, activity		
Altered temporal perspective: present expanded, future and past distanced	Minimization of concern about social evaluation	Behavior is self-reinforcing and is intensified, amplified with repeated expressions
Arousal		Difficult to terminate
Sensory-input overload	Weakening of controls based upon guilt, shame, fear, and commitment	Possible memory impairments; some amnesia for act
Physical involvement in the act		Perceptual distortion; insensitive to incidental stimuli and to relating actions of others
Reliance upon noncognitive interactions and feedback		
Novel or unstructured situation	Lowered threshold for expressing inhibited behaviors	Hyper-responsiveness; "contagious plasticity" to behavior of proximal, active others
Altered states of consciousness: drugs, sleep, etc.		Unresponsiveness to distal reference groups
		Destruction of traditional forms and structures

pressing normally inhibited behaviors, whether those behaviors involve such benign activities as shouting at a football game or such destructive acts as throwing rocks at buses taking children out of the ghetto to schools in the suburbs. A schematic representation of the deindividuation process as hypothesized by Zimbardo is shown in Figure 2.

It is clear from the figure that there are many facets to Zimbardo's deindividuation model. Many changes are hypothesized to occur in the behavior of a person experiencing deindividuation. The behavior of such a person should be difficult to terminate, unresponsive to the norms of the person's usual reference groups, self-reinforcing, and overresponsive to the behaviors of those in the immediate vicinity. Zimbardo's model of deindividuation is, in his own words, "complex and fuzzy," and most of the hypothesized relationships and implications have not yet been tested, though there has been an encouraging increase in research on deindividuation in the past few years (Diener, 1976; Diener, Dineen, Endresen, Beaman, and Fraser, 1975; Cannavale, Scarr, and Pepitone, 1970; Watson 1973). Let us look at some examples.

Applying and testing Zimbardo's model. When admonishing or reprimanding another, we are usually influenced by the characteristics of the other. If the other is a nice person who has simply made a mistake, we are inclined to be lenient. If the other is an obnoxious person, we may not be quite so even-handed. According to Zimbardo's hypothesis, the deindividuated person would be less likely to make such a distinction and would probably be equally harsh to both nice and obnoxious transgressors (this is the second "output behavior" listed in Figure 2).

To test this idea, Zimbardo (1969) arranged for subjects to administer shock to another who was supposedly undergoing a series of conditioning trials. The subjects had previously heard a taped interview in which the shock recipient came across as either a nice, altruistic person or a totally self-centered, conceited, obnoxious individual. Subjects took part in the experiment in small groups and observed the shock victim through a one-way mirror. On each of a series of trials, the victim could be shocked by the group members. Deindividuation was induced in some groups by preserving the anonymity of the individual members.

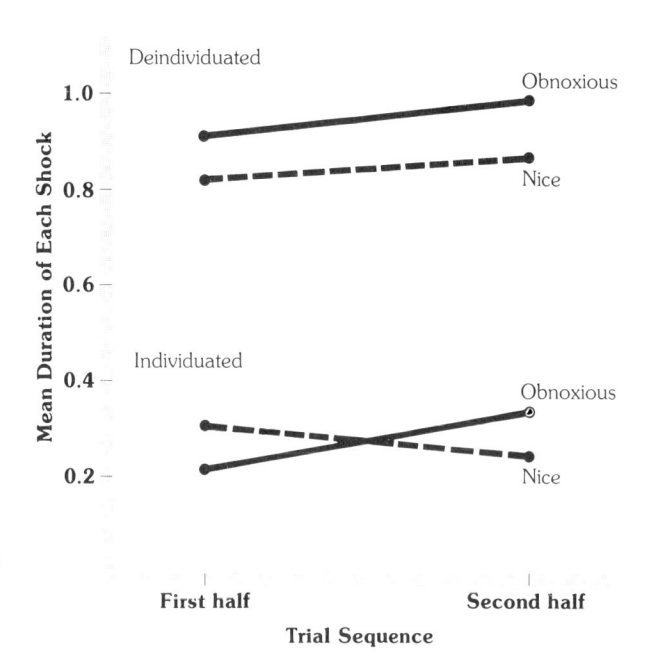

3. **Aggression measured by shock duration. Deindividuated subjects gave longer shocks to all victims and increased the shocks as time passed, whether the victim was nice or obnoxious. Individuated subjects shocked the nice victims less and the obnoxious victims more as the trials progressed, and, in both cases, administered less shock. (From Zimbardo, 1969, Figure 4, p. 269.)**

Their names were never used, they wore big hoods over their heads so they couldn't be identified, and the entire experiment was conducted in a darkened room. The victim was in a lighted room on the other side of a one-way mirror and could be easily seen. For other groups, the individuality and identifiability of the members was emphasized throughout. They wore name tags, the importance of their unique reactions was emphasized, they had no hoods over their heads, and the lights in the room were merely dimmed enough for subjects to see the victim in the next room through a one-way mirror.

The major results are shown in Figure 3, where it can be seen that the deindividuated subjects gave much longer shocks to the victim. Furthermore, the deindividuated subjects were relatively unresponsive to the characteristics of the victim. Individuated subjects shocked the nice victim less and the obnoxious victim more as the trials progressed. Deindividuated subjects increased the shock duration for both victims as the trials progressed. Thus feelings of deindividuation, apparently engendered by the anonymity treatment, led to greater aggression against the victim as well as a lack of attention to characteristics of the victim that normally would have reduced the aggression expressed.

In an intriguing cross-cultural use of Zimbardo's model, Watson (1973) obtained data from the Human Relations Area Files, a depository of descriptive information compiled by ethnographers about scores of cultures around the world. Watson reasoned that one aspect of deindividuation that could be examined using these data was the relationship between aggression in warfare and changes in appearance prior to battle. The files contained sufficient information on the extent of "killing, torturing, or mutilating the enemy" for Watson to categorize 23 independent cultures as aggressive or nonaggressive. These same cultures were also categorized in terms of whether there were specific changes in appearance of the individual before battle. A change of appearance might be accomplished, for example, by painting parts of the body or face, by wearing masks, or by wearing special war clothes. Watson's hypothesis, which was derived from Zimbardo's model, was that such changes in appearance would serve as a means of inducing deindividuation, so there should be a positive relationship between pre-warfare appearance changes and aggressiveness in battle. The data Watson obtained strongly supported this hypothesis.

Subsequent research has not been quite so kind to Zimbardo's model of the processes and products of deindividuation (Diener, 1976; Diener, et al., 1975), and the model will undoubtedly need to be refined as additional results accumulate. The presence of a group may not be necessary for deindividuation to occur, but it is clear that many of the conditions that encourage deindividuation seem to co-occur frequently with the formation of a group. It is equally clear, as Zimbardo (1969) notes, that

> we must insist on greater individuation in all aspects of our lives . . . we should not give up our names for more efficient numbers, and should resist urban planning which nurtures sterile, drab sameness and wipes out neighborhoods where people are recognized by others and are concerned about the social evaluation of those others (p. 344).

We have been discussing some rather dramatic phenomena that may occur when we are in the presence of others—inhibition of helping, social facilitation, and deindividuation. (For another example, see Box A.) While none of these phenomena always occur when we are with others, certain antecedent conditions increase the probability of their occurrence. There is, however, a more general class of phenomena that apparently does always occur when we are in the presence of others.

NONVERBAL COMMUNICATION AND INFORMATION MANAGEMENT

As we saw in Chapter 4, there is a growing interest in nonverbal communication. Many people appear to be rediscovering the importance of all the little signs and cues described by Freud in *The Psychopathology of Everyday Life*. Freud believed that most, if not all, of people's actions were of communicative significance. Body position, errors, slips of the tongue, manner of dress—everything was assumed to convey something. A growing experimental literature now supports these assumptions. It is almost impossible for two people not to communicate when they are in each other's presence. Trying not to communicate when in the presence of others is like trying to make your mind a complete blank. It cannot be done.

Knowing that others read significance into such cues as manner of dress, body position, gestures, and facial expressions, people often attempt to control the nonverbal aspects of their behavior in order to project a certain image. Goffman (1959) provides an interesting theoretical analysis of why people attempt to manage the nonverbal complements of their verbal communications. He distinguishes between an impression that one "gives," (one's conscious attempts to communicate particular information about oneself or the situation) and an impression that one "gives off," (the not-so-conscious nuances that may undercut the definition of the situation one wishes to maintain). For example,

A. How're we doing? Great!

When members of a group work together to achieve a goal, they often come to like each other a great deal. This effect seems to be heightened if the group in question is in competition with other groups. A genuine feeling that "it's us against them" may develop. Ludo Janssens and Joseph Nuttin (1976), two psychologists at the University of Leuven in Belgium, hypothesized that the positive feelings associated with this *esprit de corps* may cloud the group members' perceptions of how well the group is really doing.

To test this idea, they set up a task in which pictures of identical objects were flashed on a screen, each picture depicting somewhere between 25 and 95 of the objects. The task was for subjects in each of four conditions to estimate how many objects were presented on each of 22 trials. The four conditions were: (1) individual subjects making estimates and competing with another subject seated nearby, (2) individual subjects making estimates but not competing with another subject, (3) groups of four subjects making a group decision on each trial and competing with another group seated nearby, and (4) groups of four subjects making a group decision but not competing with another group. The individuals and groups in competition with other individuals and groups received feedback on each trial of either "Better" or "Worse," meaning that their answer had either been closer to the correct answer or further from the correct answer than that of their competitor. Individuals and groups in the No Competition conditions simply received feedback of "Right" or "Wrong" on each trial. In all four conditions, however, feedback was actually unrelated to performance and all subjects (individuals and groups) were led to believe they were "Right" (or "Better") on half of the trials and "Wrong" (or "Worse") on half of the trials. At the end of the series of trials, subjects were asked to estimate how many successes ("Right" or "Better") they had had during the series. The results, in terms of mean percentages of perceived successes, were as follows:

	Individuals	**Groups**
Competition	47.6%	57.3%
No competition	48.4%	52.6%

Compared to individuals, groups in competition with other groups significantly overestimate how well they have been doing. Competing groups are also more likely than noncompeting groups to overestimate their successes. It appears that positive interactions with one's co-workers may induce an overly optimistic assessment of the work the group is doing.

---

the projected definition of being dispassionate and objective and taking part in an intellectual discussion may fall apart when one's voice breaks or a particularly cutting remark escapes. The consequences of such inadvertently "given off" impressions are severe. As Goffman (1959) puts it,

> When these disruptive events occur, the interaction itself may come to a confused and embarrassed halt. Some of the assumptions upon which the responses of the participants had been predicated become untenable, and the participants find themselves lodged in an interaction for which the situation has been wrongly defined and is now no longer defined. . . . Society is organized on the principle that . . . an individual who implicitly or explicitly signifies that he has certain social characteristics ought in fact to be what he claims he is (p. 12).

The most important thread running through Goffman's work, then, is the concept of INFORMATION MANAGEMENT. The individual is seen as attempting to control the information about himself or herself to which others present have access.

Such control is especially important if what the individual is thinking would belie what the individual is doing. For example, the most chilling aspect of the totalitarian society depicted in Orwell's *1984* is that the Party attempted to enforce thought control. The Thoughtpolice were constantly alert to any nonverbal cue that might indicate the presence of thoughts contrary to Party doctrine:

> Your own worst enemy, he reflected, was your own nervous system. At any moment the tension inside you was liable to translate itself into some visible symptom . . . to wear an improper expression on your face (to look incredulous when a victory was announced, for example) was itself a punishable offense. There was even a word for it . . . *facecrime* it was called (Orwell, 1961, p. 54-56).

The extent to which impression management is conscious can vary from such overt, active attempts to keep a particular expression on one's face to those features of personal style and habit that are so routine that they have slipped from awareness. Gibbins (1969) presents evidence that the messages conveyed by particular types of women's clothing are clearly perceived and that, within a given social group, consensus exists about the characterstics of women who wear particular kinds of clothes.

The important point about nonverbal cues, as far as group interaction is concerned, is that such cues not only affect our perceptions of others but may also affect how we respond to others. The question is whether the nonverbal cues that occur during interaction affect the course of interaction—regardless of the verbal communication that is taking place.

Nonverbal cues and interaction. Consider the case of interaction between two or more people when one of them appears different in some way and has some clearly visible stigma, such as physical deformity or blindness. The problem such a stigmatized individual continually faces in interaction is a problem of acceptance. According to Goffman (1963), the stigmatized person is usually aware of the nature of his or her "differentness" and knows that "normal" others often construct what Goffman refers to as STIGMA THEORIES, systems of expectations about what such different people are really like. The major difficulty is that people usually incorporate into their expectations about the stigmatized a variety of imperfections in addition to the original one. As a result, there is likely to be a double uneasiness during contacts between those with visible or known differences and normals who can observe or know about the other's stigma. The normal individual may be uneasy because he or she does not know how to treat the stigmatized individual and may believe that people with such a stigma—whatever it may be—are not quite whole people. The stigmatized individual may be uneasy because he or she knows what the other is thinking and feels that he or she must be very careful to appear normal.

To see whether such uneasiness is really characteristic of interactions with the stigmatized, Kleck, Ono, and Hastorf (1966) recruited 40 male high school students for a study supposedly concerned with physiological reactions in face-to-face interaction. The subjects were run individually and, while having their galvanic skin response (GSR) monitored, were assigned the task of interviewing another subject (actually a confederate) who had either walked in or arrived in a wheelchair. The wheelchair employed had a false bottom where the confederate's left leg could be inserted in such a way as to make it appear that it had been amputated. There are several results of interest. As indicated by the GSR index, subjects showed a significantly greater decrease in skin resistance (presumed to be an indication of emotional arousal) when the confederate entered in a wheelchair than when he simply walked in. Subjects interviewing the confederate in the wheelchair also tended to terminate the interaction sooner. In a similar study, subjects committed considerably more errors in procedure when the confederate was in the wheelchair. It does appear that the subjects were somewhat less at ease when interviewing the apparent amputee.

A later study by Kleck (1969), using female subjects and two confederates who alternated playing a handicapped (in a wheelchair) and nonhandicapped fellow subject, afforded some evidence that normal subjects place themselves at a greater physical distance from the other when interacting with a handicapped as opposed to a normal other. It is interesting to note the discrepancy between this rather unobtrusive, nonverbal index of interpersonal distance and the finding that, in this same study, subjects rated the handicapped other more positively than the nonhandicapped. Kleck notes that the source of this rating may be a general norm in our society to be kind to disadvantaged persons. The nonverbal behavior of the subjects suggests that they may not feel what they say they feel.

It is important to note that nonverbal behaviors do not occur in isolation. In group interaction, such behaviors are usually embedded in a context of ongoing verbal communication, and the effects of any given nonverbal behavior may differ as a function of the context within which the behavior occurs. Bugental, Love, and Gianetto (1971) have found that, when interacting with their children, mothers are more likely to smile regardless of the content of what they are saying than are fathers. Similarly, increasing the frequency of mutual glances may lead to greater or less liking, depending on the nature of the verbal exchange involved (Ellsworth and Carlsmith, 1968). Any nonverbal behavior is likely to be ambiguous out of context and, like the other incidental consequences of interaction that we have discussed, may tell us more about what effects interaction is having on the individual participants than about the interaction itself. Let us look at that interaction.

Interaction processes

In this and the preceding chapter, we have already discussed a number of processes that may occur in group interaction. We have seen, for example, that the desire to maintain a group atmosphere of cohesiveness and congeniality may lead to inhibition of mutual criticism and result in poorer group decisions. Similarly, we have seen that the presence of others capable of judging one's performance affects that performance and, hence, may affect the social environment to which those others respond. There are literally hundreds of additional variables that can influence the processes of group interaction. Unfortunately, many of these variables are exceedingly complex, and the research that might delineate their individual and joint effects has simply not been done.

Take group size as an example. At first glance, size appears to be such a clear-cut, concrete variable that one might wonder why the effects of group size on the interaction processes in groups are not known. But size is actually a very complex variable. As Weick (1969) points out,

> Whenever there is a change in size, *several* things happen. This means that when groups of differing size are compared, one never knows how to interpret the comparison. For example, in a 12-man group, as compared to a three-man group, (1) it is more difficult to communicate to everyone, (2) there is not sufficient time for everyone to talk, (3) there is more need for a leader and greater likelihood that he will control what happens, (4) members are more likely to form into small clusters (p. 24).

Thus groups of different size do not consistently differ on any dependent measure—whether productivity or member satisfaction or whatever. Changes in group size result in simultaneous changes in several interaction processes.

Many investigators have attempted to get around such complexities by extracting one aspect of groups and studying that one aspect in isolation. As incredible as it may sound, they have often eliminated interaction itself. In many studies of small groups, interaction has been reduced to passing notes through a slot in a screen to "other group members" who can be neither seen nor heard. Such experiments are not necessarily worthless, and a great deal has been learned via such research about decision processes and individual satisfaction with different modes of decision making (Davis, 1969). However, such research tells us nothing at all about interaction in small, face-to-face groups. Fortunately, there are several lines of research that do tell us something about spontaneous, ongoing interaction in small groups. There is, in fact, a surprising degree of order and regularity in what occurs in such groups.

ATTEMPTS TO ANALYZE ONGOING INTERACTION

In the late 1940s, Robert Bales and his associates at Harvard began making detailed observations of the interactions that take place in groups, a task that many have attempted before and since. Bales, however, has pursued the task with more perseverance than anyone else. In a stream of research reports extending over three decades (Bales, 1945; 1970), he has provided the most commonly used system for observing and recording interaction, as well as a great deal of information about the nature of group interaction itself.

Interaction process analysis. The method developed by Bales (1950a) is called INTERACTION PROCESS ANALYSIS, and it consists of a set of 12 categories for coding what goes on in interaction. The set, shown in Figure 4, includes both verbal and nonverbal aspects of behavior. Observers classify each intelligible unit of behavior in a group into one of the 12 categories. In addition, the observers record who initiated each unit of behavior and to whom it was directed. The latter may, of course, be the group as a whole as well as any individual member. Thus Bales's method is basically a type of content analysis, which we discussed in Chapter 2. The content that it attempts to abstract from the raw material of observation is the relevance of each action that occurs in the group for the ongoing group process. A simple mechanical device constructed by Bales and Gerbrands (1948), the interaction recorder, allows observers to also keep track of the sequence of events in the group being observed. The interaction recorder consists of a metal case with a wide, slowly moving paper tape exposed on part of its surface. The tape has 12 rows (a row corresponding to each category), and as the observer makes entries on the various rows, the tape is gradually wound onto a roller within the case.

Using this relatively simple coding scheme, Bales and his associates have observed and recorded ongoing interaction in hundreds of groups. The groups observed have varied in size, composition of membership, nature of the problem(s) to be solved, and length of acquaintance of the members. In spite of this diversity, a number of distinct similarities characterize the interaction of all the groups. For example, there appears to be a number of phases through which groups consistently pass in their problem-solving attempts (Bales and Strodtbeck, 1951). During the early stages of interaction, a large proportion of behaviors of group members are coded into categories 6 and 7 of Figure 4, "Gives orientation" and "Asks for orientation." As interaction continues, such problem-defining and focusing behaviors decline sharply, while the proportion of behaviors coded into categories 4 and 9, "Gives suggestion" and "Asks for suggestion," show a rapid increase. Similarly, the proportions of behaviors in categories 1, 2, and 3 (Positive Reactions) and categories 10, 11, and 12 (Negative Reactions) both increase with the amount of time the group has been interacting, although positive reactions are consistently more frequent in all stages of interaction than negative ones. Bales and Strodtbeck (1951) claim that under the conditions characteristic of many different kinds of groups, especially those in which some problem is to be solved or a plan of action decided, the group process seems to begin with problems of orientation, to shift to problems of evaluation, and then to shift to problems of control. During this process, there is an increase in the relative frequencies of both positive and negative reactions.

Forming, storming, norming, performing. In a more recent and more comprehensive review of the literature on the developmental sequences found in therapy groups, naturally occurring groups, and laboratory groups, Tuckman (1965) proposes a model of the phases groups go through that is actually quite similar to the stages Bales and Strodtbeck found. Tuckman's model of the developmental course of group interaction consists of four stages, which he summarizes as forming, storming, norming and performing. During the first or FORMING stage, the primary concern of the members is orientation. What is the nature of the problem? What resources are available? How much time do we have? Do we have to do this? Has anybody here ever done this before? As the available resources and interpersonal characteristics of the other members become clearer, the group moves into the second stage, STORMING, which is characterized by conflict and polarization around interpersonal issues. During the storming phase, more emotions are expressed. The resistance to influence characterizing this stage gradually gives way to feelings of solidarity as the members begin to identify with the group. In the third or NORMING stage, members more freely express their opinions and suggestions about how to get on with the job at hand. In the last or PERFORMING stage, the members have settled the question of "how," resolved or submerged the interpersonal conflicts, and evaluated everyone's suggestions. They now focus their attention on getting the job done.

Given this sequential development of group con-

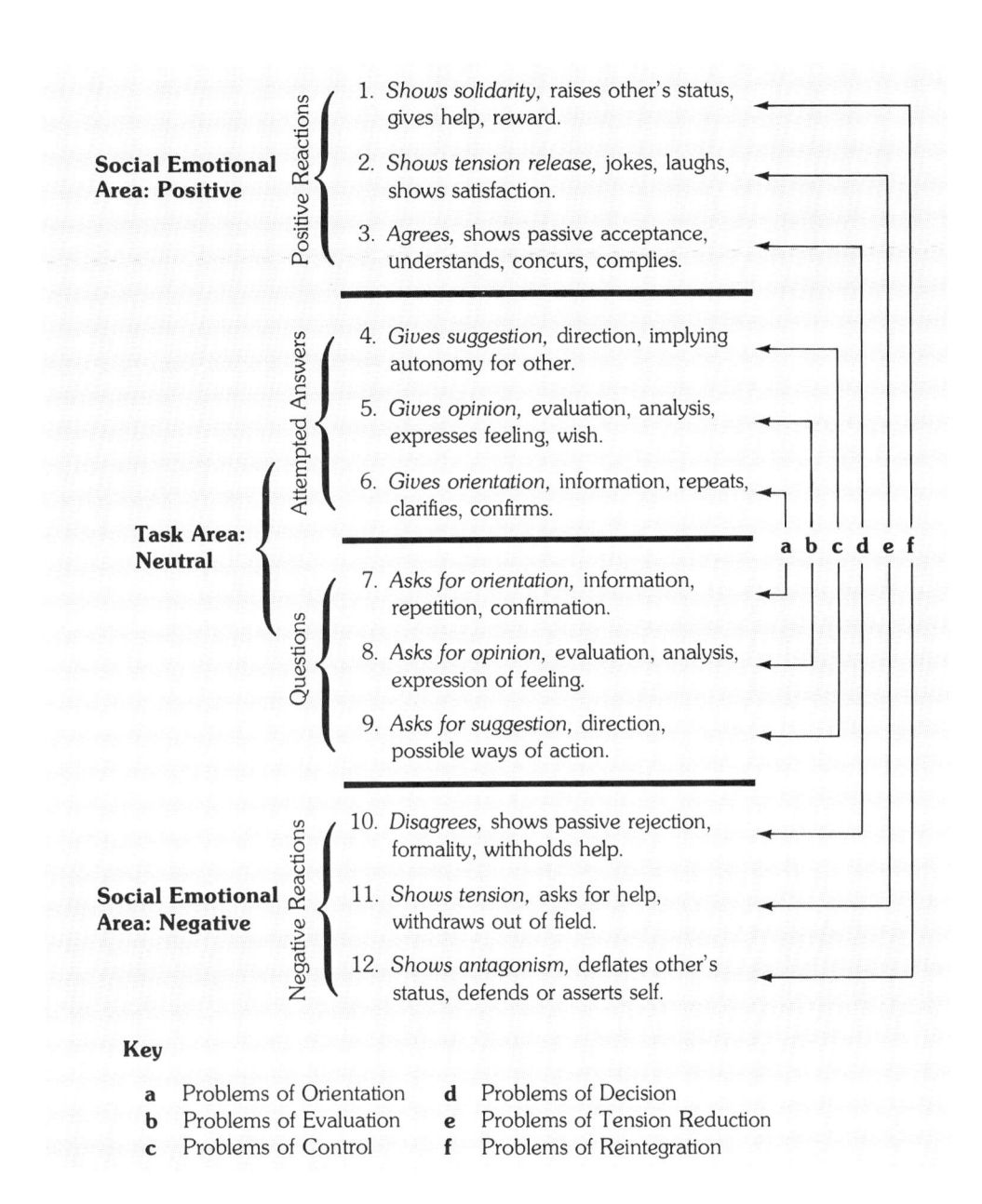

Social Emotional Area: Positive
- Positive Reactions
  1. *Shows solidarity,* raises other's status, gives help, reward.
  2. *Shows tension release,* jokes, laughs, shows satisfaction.
  3. *Agrees,* shows passive acceptance, understands, concurs, complies.

Task Area: Neutral
- Attempted Answers
  4. *Gives suggestion,* direction, implying autonomy for other.
  5. *Gives opinion,* evaluation, analysis, expresses feeling, wish.
  6. *Gives orientation,* information, repeats, clarifies, confirms.
- Questions
  7. *Asks for orientation,* information, repetition, confirmation.
  8. *Asks for opinion,* evaluation, analysis, expression of feeling.
  9. *Asks for suggestion,* direction, possible ways of action.

Social Emotional Area: Negative
- Negative Reactions
  10. *Disagrees,* shows passive rejection, formality, withholds help.
  11. *Shows tension,* asks for help, withdraws out of field.
  12. *Shows antagonism,* deflates other's status, defends or asserts self.

a b c d e f

Key

a	Problems of Orientation	d	Problems of Decision
b	Problems of Evaluation	e	Problems of Tension Reduction
c	Problems of Control	f	Problems of Reintegration

4. The system of categories used in Interaction Process Analysis. Brackets and arrows indicate categories that are related to each other. (From Bales, 1950b, Chart 1, p. 9.)

cern, one might expect that in a group of peers (a group in which everyone is equal in status), different group members would be maximally involved and/or talkative at various stages of group development. Surprisingly, this appears not to be the case. One of the most consistent findings to emerge from the analysis of ongoing group interaction in such homogeneous groups is that one person always seems to do most of the talking. As the size of the group is increased, the relative proportion of talking done by this one person increases rather than decreases. Consider the following report by Bales, Strodtbeck, Mills, and Roseborough (1951).

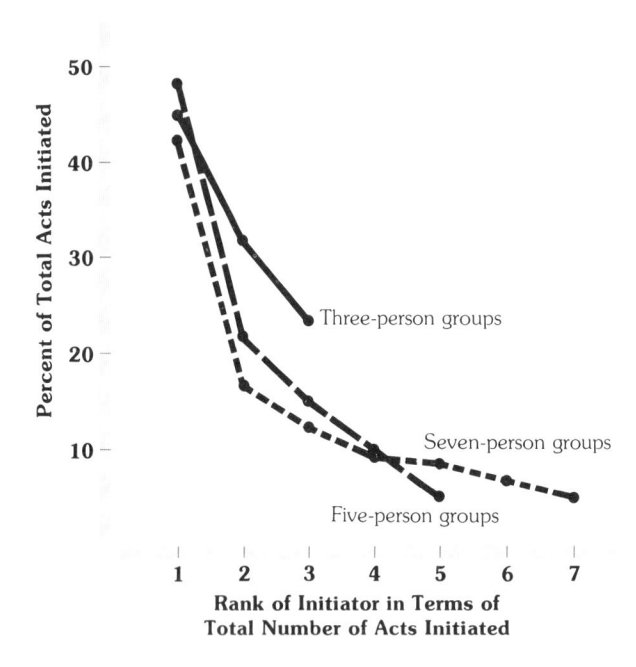

5. Relative contributions to total acts observed in groups of three, five, and seven. In each group, the person who initiated the most acts initiated *nearly half* of the acts. Acts for this study were the categories of interaction shown in Figure 4. (From Bales, et al., 1951, Chart 1, p. 467.)

A large number of groups ranging in size from three to ten people were observed and the interactions coded into Bales's categories. The groups observed consisted of nonstudent committees, work groups in natural settings, therapy groups, diagnostic councils and students brought into a laboratory for the purpose of forming problem-solving groups. Many of these groups met and were observed over a number of different sessions. At the conclusion of their observation of any given group, Bales, et al. tabulated the number of acts each participant had initiated, the number of acts that had been addressed to or directed to each participant, and the number of acts each participant had addressed to the group as a whole. These three classifications were highly related. That is, the more acts a person had initiated, the more acts he or she had addressed to the group as a whole, and the more acts others had addressed to him or her. Further, if the individual members were ranked on number of acts initiated and compared in terms of their relative contribution to the total acts observed in the group, distributions such as those shown in Figure 5 resulted. For groups of three, five and seven people, there was always one person who initiated between 40 and 50 percent of the observed behavior in the group. And as group size increased, the percentage of observed behavior initiated by the second most talkative person dropped from above 30 percent to below 20 percent.

What are we to make of this? First, if these phenomena occurred only in highly structured groups with a clearly defined leader, they would be of little interest. We would expect a leader to do most of the talking. However, the findings are not limited to such groups and occur regularly in unstructured groups composed of equal-status peers. Second, it is not just the amount of talking that differs, but the content of what is said. Bales (1953) reports that the people who talk the most have a higher percentage of their behaviors in categories 4, 5, and 6 of Figure 4. That is, they are more likely to be giving opinions, making suggestions, or contributing information. On the other hand, the people who talk less are more likely to be agreeing, disagreeing, or asking for information. The behaviors of the high participators look suspiciously like what leaders are supposed to do—directing, suggesting, and shaping the course of action. These findings may indeed point to the emergence of leadership in initially leaderless groups, and we shall return to them in the following chapter. For now, let us put aside the question of leadership and see whether we can understand something about the dynamics within a group that might contribute to and reinforce differential participation rates.

STABILIZING PARTICIPATION DIFFERENCES

Why those who talk talk. Even among individuals who are relatively homogeneous in whatever abilities are to be required for effective group performance, there are a variety of personality factors that might account for initial differences in talkativeness in an unstructured group setting. Some people, for example, do not tolerate ambiguity well (Budner, 1962). Being in an ambiguous situation is uncomfortable for such people, and they are quick to try to reduce their discomfort by either leaving the situation or structuring it themselves. Being part of an unstructured group fumbling through the first stages of interaction can be very unpleasant for such people. One way they can reduce this unpleasantness is to get the group moving, and to do this, of course, they have to start talking.

Other possibilities are that individual differences in impulsiveness (McCandless, 1969) or ability to delay gratification (Mischel, 1966) account for the initial differences in talkativeness. (Box B gives an example of another possible variable in participation differences.) Whatever the reasons, people differ consistently in the

B. Are Men or Women More Sociable? Yes.

Although many stereotypes exist about whether males or females are more "group-oriented," there are surprisingly few hard data on the issue. It is widely believed, for example, that males have more friends and associates and spend more time interacting with them. If this were true, however, it might be because more males than females work outside of the home and are likely to see and interact with more people in the course of a day. On the other hand, many people believe that females form closer, more intimate relationships with other females than men form with other men. But again, if this were true, it might simply be that females generally know fewer other people than males and therefore are more interested in and have more time for the people they do know.

In an attempt to determine whether males spend more time in social interaction with others than females do, or vice versa, Ladd Wheeler and John Nezlek (1977) of the University of Rochester conducted the following study. Male and female first-year residents in coed dormitories were asked to keep daily diaries of their social interactions. For 2 weeks in the fall semester and 2 weeks in the spring semester, the students were to keep records of every interaction they had with another person, or with other people, that lasted more than 10 minutes. They were given special forms to fill out for each interaction, recording such things as the date, time, and length of the interaction, who the interaction was with, and how pleasant or unpleasant the interaction was.

A number of interesting findings emerged. For example, for both males and females, most interactions occurred with one other person of the same sex. However, females initially spent much more time in interaction with others than did males, almost an hour a day more. By spring this had reversed, and females actually spent somewhat less time in interaction each day than males. Relative to males, females were also less satisfied with their social interactions in the spring than in the fall.

In speculating about this pattern of results, Wheeler and Nezlek suggest that one explanation may stem from

> the premise that the change from high school to college meant a greater increase in personal freedom for females than it did for males. Given our culture's prejudice regarding the submissive nature of females and the manner in which this belief is transmitted via the socialization process, such a notion is not farfetched. . . . it would follow that females would find the first semester to be very satisfying and would take full advantage of their newly found freedom . . . By the spring semester the novelty would have worn off.

Some additional evidence from a life-history questionnaire administered to subjects supports this interpretation. Those females who reported their parents as harsh and critical and as having restricted their activities as a form of punishment had longer interactions in the fall and reduced them more in the spring.

amount and timing of their spontaneous verbal output (Goldman-Eisler, 1951).

Why those who talk keep talking. Once a person has started talking, a number of interpersonal and intrapersonal processes come into play that tend to reinforce and perpetuate his or her control of the conversation. For example, politeness dictates that people are not to be interrupted, and, unless the discussion becomes heated, such rules of etiquette are likely to be obeyed. Ervin-Tripp (1969) points out that a number of more subtle linguistic rules and paralinguistic phenomena often produce the same effect as noninterruption. For example, when a person addresses a question to another, it is normally expected that the latter should answer and that his or her answer should be directed to the questioner, not to the group as a whole. It is also expected that the questioner is obligated to comment on, or at least acknowledge, the answer. Hence, if the questioner judiciously avoids pausing after acknowledging the answer and proceeds directly into another question or statement, he or she retains control of the conversation. If we use letters to represent the members of a group, the sequence of talking is likely to be closer to A, B, A, C, A, D than to A, B, C, D, E. . . . Ervin-Tripp also points out that a person who is talking does not have to ask direct questions in order to control who will talk next; eye contact can serve essentially the same purpose.

And talking. It is important to remember that we are discussing groups in which the members are all approximately equal in terms of task-related ability. In spite of this, linguistic rules about the sequencing of conversation tend to keep control of the discussion in the hands of some initially talkative group members. What is the likely result? As we have already mentioned, the evidence (Bales, 1953) indicates that the most talkative members of such unstructured, homogeneous groups are likely to be predominantly giving opinions and making suggestions. The evidence also indicates that the less talkative group members are more likely to agree with what others in the group say than they are to disagree. Hence, the agreement of the less talkative members may reinforce both the ideas and the verbal output of the initially talkative.

To see if this line of reasoning is correct, Bavelas, Hastorf, Gross, and Kite (1965) set up the following experiment. Subjects were recruited to participate in "group discussions of case problems." Eighteen four-man groups were assigned to either an experimental or a control condition. In the control condition, the groups simply discussed three case problems for ten minutes each. During their discussion, an observer recorded the total amount of time each person talked, as well as the number of times each talked. In the experimental condition, their first and third discussion periods were the same as in the control condition. That is, the groups were simply to discuss the pertinent facts that would affect a decision. Prior to their second discussion period, however, members of the experimental groups were told that they would each receive feedback during the discussion about whether what they were doing was contributing positively to the discussion. The feedback was to be given via two lights, one red and one green, in front of each subject. Any given subject's lights were arranged so that the other subjects could not see them. The red light was to come on whenever the subject behaved in a manner that would eventually detract from the group's performance. The green light was to appear whenever the subject behaved in a manner that was in the best interest of the group.

On the basis of results from the first discussion period, one person in each group (in both experimental and control groups) was selected who had not been very talkative during that first session. This person was designated the target person. Then, during the second session, the lights were used in the experimental groups only, and the experimental manipulation consisted of flashing the target person's green light whenever he expressed an opinion or made a statement. If the other subjects did either of these things, their red lights came on. On the other hand, if the target person was quiet for very long, his red light would come on. The remaining subjects received green lights every time they agreed with the target person. During the third session for the experimental groups, the lights were not used. Subjects were simply to discuss the problem given them.

The major results of interest here are presented in Table I. The target persons in the control groups talked about the same amount of time in each of the three discussion periods. However, the target persons in the experimental groups talked significantly more when others were being reinforced for agreeing with them (during the second discussion period), and although their talking time declined in the third discussion period, it remained at a considerably higher level than it had been during the first, or baseline, period. It does appear that the combination of giving opinions, making suggestions, and having others agree not only sustains but increases one's talkativeness. As we shall see in the next chapter, the other group members' perception of the target person also undergoes a significant change as he or she becomes more talkative.

Since there is only a finite amount of time that can be filled with talk during a group meeting, chances are that an increase in the talkativeness of one member will necessarily result in a decrease in the talkativeness of one or more other members. Banta and Nelson (1964) have demonstrated that in two-person groups, the more favorable feedback one member received for expressing her opinions, the less likely the other member was to express opinions subsequently. Hence, it may be that a cycle is set up in which the most talkative member of a group elicits greater agreement from others and, seeing this, the remaining group members inhibit their own expressions of opinion and "go along." Such a cycle might be involved in the groupthink phenomenon we discussed in Chapter 12. There are other processes that would reinforce this cycle. As a consensus forms around the opinions and suggestions of one member, there is a tendency to communicate less and less with deviates (Schachter, 1951). Hence deviates talk less and less themselves, further increasing the differences in participation rates.

Table I. Time talked by target persons

Discussion period	Control groups	Experimental groups
1	17.3	15.7
2	20.2	37.0
3	19.5	26.9

The numbers represent the percent of time talked by the target persons compared to the total group talking time. (From Bavelas, et al., 1965, Table 1, p. 60.)

And talking. Suppose an initially unstructured, homogeneous group is to meet repeatedly over a number of days or weeks. Does this whole process start over again? Does everybody come back to the second meeting and sit around and wait for whoever is most anxious on that particular day to start talking and get things moving? Probably not. People are creatures of habit, and it is amazing how quickly we adopt patterns of behavior. The pattern of interaction in a given group tends to be perpetuated. There is evidence, for example, that a completely arbitrary norm will be maintained within a group for some time, even after the initiator of the norm has left the group (Jacobs and Campbell, 1961). (For more on this finding, see Box C.) Bales and his associates have found that the relative rates of interaction of the various members are remarkably stable in repeated sessions of the same groups.

The whole process of structuring the group is not likely to be repeated at each group session unless there is a drastic change in the composition of the group or the nature of its task. Group members develop clearcut expectations about each other, expectations that include not only where the others are likely to sit, but how much the others are likely to talk and what sorts of things they are likely to say. This gives rise to an interesting possibility. If we expect others to behave in certain ways, our own behavior may be such as to make the expected response from others more likely. If everyone knows that Bob always sits at the head of the table and everyone gets to the meeting before he does, the only chair likely to be empty when he arrives is the one at the head of the table. Is it reasonable to suppose that, in ongoing social interaction, what we respond to in others has been largely shaped by our own behavior?

REACTING TO ONE'S OWN BEHAVIOR

The prisoner's dilemma. Earlier we were discussing the concept of impression management and remarked that the most important part of impression management is how one attempts to define the relationship(s) between oneself and the other person or persons in the situation. For example, if the others perceive that they are liked and respected, this may lead to con-

C. Authoritarianism of Group Members and Social Change

One of the characteristics of the authoritarian personality that we discussed in Chapters 2 and 7 is resistance to change. That is, those people who score high in authoritarianism seem to like the status quo better than those who score low on authoritarianism. Thus we might anticipate that a group whose members were predominantly high in authoritarianism would evolve more slowly or stick to old norms and values longer than a group whose members were less authoritarian.

To test this idea, Robert Montgomery, Stephen Hinkle, and Russell Enzie (1976) made use of the AUTOKINETIC PHENOMENON, the fact that a small point of light seen in a darkened room appears to move. When naive subjects observe this light, they usually estimate that it moves anywhere from 1 to 5 inches. Because of the ambiguity of the observation situation, it is very difficult to tell how much the light appears to move, so the autokinetic phenomenon has often been used to study conformity. Confederates present with a naive subject will say that the light appeared to move 12 inches (rather than 1 inch or so) and, sure enough, the naive subject is likely to say that the light seemed to move 10 or 11 inches.

But what happens if the confederate leaves and the naive subject continues to make estimates? Montgomery, Hinkle, and Enzie found that it depends on the authoritarianism of the subject. The arbitrary norm established by the estimates of the confederate continues to have an influence longer among authoritarian subjects than among nonauthoritarian subjects. Further, when new naive subjects were brought in, the original subject was more likely to pass on the arbitrary norm if he or she was high in authoritarianism. And the new subject was more likely to be influenced by the arbitrary norm if he or she was also high in authoritarianism. Apparently groups composed of authoritarian members are likely to change their beliefs more slowly than groups of nonauthoritarians, even when the beliefs have no basis in objective reality.

---

sequences quite different from those that will occur if the others perceive that they are disliked. The initial perception of being liked, say, may be quite groundless, but it may lead to behaviors such as cooperativeness and politeness that induce the very liking mistakenly thought to be present at the outset.

Since much of the research on this line of reasoning has used variations of an interpersonal situation termed the PRISONER'S DILEMMA, let us take a moment to describe the general structure of the situation. Suppose that two people are arrested on suspicion of committing a crime—say, armed robbery. They are taken to the police station and put in separate rooms for questioning. Suppose further that they are guilty and that each is sincerely interested in putting in as little time as possible behind bars. The dilemma stems from the fact that neither can be sure of what the other is going to do. If *neither* confesses, both are likely to be charged with a lesser offense, such as possession of illegal weapons, and both will get off with minimum sentences because the evidence on the armed robbery charge is only circumstantial. If *both* confess, both are likely to get a long jail term. However, if one confesses and the other does not, the one who confesses will get a light sentence in return for providing evidence against his or her (former) colleague, while the latter will be penalized much more severely. The prisoner's dilemma is whether to trust one's partner not to confess and not confess oneself (that is, to cooperate with one's partner) or to confess and save oneself before the partner confesses (that is, to compete with one's partner). The basic reward structure of this mixed-motive (cooperation versus competition) problem is illustrated in Figure 6.

Using the basic structure of the prisoner's dilemma as a model, a number of investigators have employed mixed-motive games as tools for studying various aspects of interaction. The rewards involved in labora-

	Prisoner A Can:	
	Refuse to confess	**Confess**
Prisoner B Can: Refuse to confess	A gets 6 months / B gets 6 months	A gets 90 days / B gets 10 years
Confess	A gets 10 years / B gets 90 days	A gets 5 years / B gets 5 years

6. The basic reward structure of the prisoner's dilemma. Each prisoner must decide whether to act competitively (confess) or cooperatively (refuse to confess), but the outcome is also affected by what the other prisoner decides to do.

tory analogies of the prisoner's dilemma are not jail terms, of course, but prizes of various sorts—usually points or money. In the laboratory versions, such games are usually played by two people for a series of trials. On each trial, each player is confronted with a choice between a cooperative and a competitive response and is also faced with the puzzle of what the other player will choose on that trial, since the outcome of a given trial is determined by what both players choose. A general pattern for the various possible combinations of responses and the rewards contingent in each combination is shown in Figure 7. If mutual cooperation occurs on a given trial, both players win a moderate amount (+5); if mutual competition occurs, both players lose (−5). The opportunity also exists for one to exploit a cooperative opponent by making a competitive choice when one's opponent makes a cooperative choice. In the latter case, the person making the competitive choice comes out way ahead (+10), while the person making the cooperative choice loses badly (−20).

Research applications of the prisoner's dilemma. Let us see how such laboratory games have been used in looking at the influence of expectations on interaction. As we mentioned, it seems reasonable to suppose that we will be more cooperative with people whom we think like us than with people we think dislike us. Using a version of the prisoner's dilemma game, Jones and Panitch (1971) found that, among male subjects, those who were falsely informed at the beginning of the game that their partner liked them made significantly more cooperative choices during the game. Further, they were actually rated by their partners as significantly more likable after the game than those who were initially led to believe that their partners disliked them. For male subjects at least, it appears that the belief that one is liked or disliked begins a sequence of events that results in the other person actually coming to like or dislike the subject. An important qualification of the Jones and Panitch result is that the same effects failed to occur with pairs of female subjects.

In another series of studies employing variations of the prisoner's dilemma game, Kelley and Stahelski (1970) identified groups of subjects who indicated, prior to the game, that they intended to be either cooperative or competitive in the game itself. Subjects were then paired off in one of three ways: two competitive players, two cooperative players, or one competitive and one cooperative player. After playing for a number of trials, the players were asked, individually, about what they believed their opponents' initial orientation had been. The most frequent error in the cooperative-competitive pairs was a judgment by the

7. Possible combinations of responses and the rewards in a typical prisoner's dilemma game. A's payoff is above the diagonal in each cell; B's payoff is below the diagonal.

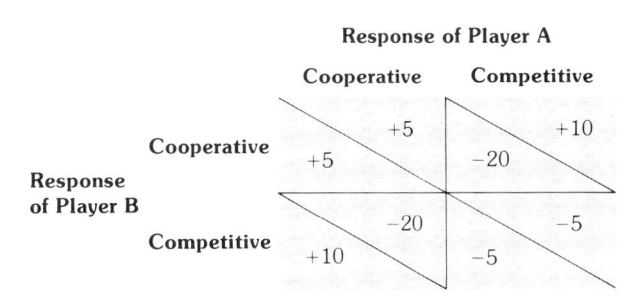

	Response of Player A	
Response of Player B	Cooperative	Competitive
Cooperative	+5 / +5	+10 / −20
Competitive	−20 / +10	−5 / −5

competitive member of such pairs that his or her cooperative opponent was also competitive. Analysis of trial-by-trial choices indicated that, when paired with a competitor, the initially cooperative players had indeed become competitive. Kelley and Stahelski term this a BEHAVIORAL ASSIMILATION EFFECT, and they review some evidence suggesting that overassimilation may occur. That is, when paired with a competitively oriented partner, the initially cooperative person behaves even more competitively than the competitor. On the other hand, when two cooperative players were paired, they maintained cooperation throughout the game. Competitively oriented people influence their social worlds in such a way that the behaviors they are reacting to in others are determined by their own behavior.

There is another implication of these findings. People who are generally cooperative in their interpersonal relations and people who are generally competitive may develop different views of what other people are like. Cooperators will be aware that there is variability in interpersonal style—that some are cooperative and some competitive. Competitors will not be aware of this variability, because they force all those with whom they interact to be competitive. Of course, the assumption here is that the goals and orientations people adopt for themselves in laboratory tasks such as the prisoner's dilemma reflect the goals and orientations they generally adopt in interaction with others.

Kelley and Stahelski (1970) cite data from studies employing the F-scale, a personality-assessment instrument designed to measure one's degree of authoritarianism (Adorno, Frenkel-Brunswik, Levinson, and Sanford, 1950), which lend some plausibility to this assumption. Several studies (Scodel and Mussen, 1953) have shown that people scoring low on the F-scale (non-authoritarians) tend to see others as being heterogeneous in their degree of authoritarianism. Those who score high on the F-scale (authoritarians) tend to believe that everyone is as authoritarian as they are themselves. Further, evidence indicates that people scoring low on the F-scale tend to be cooperative in the prisoner's dilemma game. When playing opposite a high F-scorer, however, they tend to be behaviorally assimilated to the high scorer, who tends to be competitive in play. The evidence is certainly not conclusive, but it is intriguing. As Kelley and Stahelski (1970) point out,

One wonders whether, in general, the belief that other people are very much alike may not be a clue that the person holding that belief plays a very influential causal role in his interpersonal relationships. . . . The interaction process described here would . . . constitute a mechanism by which the authoritarian interpersonal orientation is a self-fulfilling prophecy, maintaining and justifying itself by causing the person to experience a world in which the orientation is shared and, therefore, necessary and justified (p. 88–89).

It appears that the behavior of an individual engaged in social interaction cannot be interpreted except as part of a system composed of the individual's own behaviors as well as the behaviors of others. One's own behavior may induce responses in others that make the former behavior appropriate, but that would not have occurred had the original behavior been different.

One might well wonder whether there is anything to be said in favor of groups. If face-to-face groups tend to be dominated by the most talkative member(s), to be susceptible to the insidious effects of groupthink, to facilitate simple well-learned responses, and to inhibit more complex, novel responses, why would anyone ever give a group responsibility for an important decision or assign a group a complex or intricate task? The issue, of course, is the quality of group performance.

INDIVIDUAL VERSUS GROUP PERFORMANCE

It is easy to think of tasks on which groups readily and consistently outperform individuals. If the task is a strenuous physical one, such as unloading a moving van or clearing brush from a right-of-way, groups will get the task done more quickly, more safely, and with fewer mistakes. Further, if the task can be subdivided into a number of discrete elements, groups will probably do better (Kelley and Thibaut, 1969). To use our example from Chapter 12, one needs a group to run a good restaurant. We can also think of tasks on which an individual easily and consistently outperforms groups. Threading a needle is one such task. Instead of asking whether groups do better or worse than individuals, let us ask whether groups do better than individuals on what are loosely termed "intellectual tasks"—tasks requiring reasoning, considered judgments, decision making, and problem solving.

The question still needs a little work. Specifically, we are interested in whether group interaction has anything to do with the relative quality of group versus individual performance on such tasks. There is ample evidence in the literature for what have been termed PSEUDOGROUP EFFECTS (Argyle, 1969). For example, if the task to be performed involves solving a series of complex problems, a group is likely to do better simply because there may be at least one individual in the group who can work each problem. This, of course, has nothing to do with group processes or group interaction. To compare the performance of a group with that of an individual is inappropriate and unfair. Rather, one must compare the group's performance with the pooled performances of the same individuals working alone. And even this can be tricky. If we average the judgments of a number of subjects who have not interacted, this average is likely to be more accurate than the judgments of most individuals, simply because averaging removes random error.

With these few caveats in mind, let us seek an answer to our question. Hackman and Morris (1975) believe that the key to understanding group effectiveness lies in the interaction processes taking place among group members while they work on a task. They and a number of others (Wheeler, 1970; Kelley and Thibaut, 1969; Davis, 1969) argue that one reason why we know so little about group effectiveness is that most research on the question has attended primarily to group output (how many problems are solved, what final judgment is reached) with relatively little attention to the group dynamics by which the outcomes are attained. How would an understanding of interaction processes help clarify the group-effectiveness problem? Let us look at some examples.

Compared to the intrapersonal processes involved in thinking and problem solving, interpersonal processes are relatively awkward and cumbersome. When a group is presented a task, some implicit or explicit rules of procedure must be acknowledged before the group can address itself to the task. Are we going to just blurt out what we think is pertinent information? Are we going to be polite and not interrupt each other? In short, what strategy of attack is to be employed? Now, is that okay with everyone? An individual, of course, short circuits this initial planning stage and usually jumps right into the task. Hence, it seems reasonable

Table II. Mean words produced as a function of group size

	Group size		
	1	2	3
Real groups	17.1	23.4	27.4
Nominal groups		24.2	28.4

The similarity of results for real and nominal groups suggests a pseudogroup effect, but simple, overall mean scores fail to take into account variation over time. (From Anderson, 1961, Tables 1 and 2, pp. 70-71.)

to expect time to be an important variable in individual group comparisons. Initially an individual might take the lead, but a group might prove superior in the long run.

Anderson (1961) offers some evidence in support of this reasoning. Male and female subjects working either alone or in same-sex groups of two or three were given the task of making as many words as possible out of sets of letters. For the two- and three-person groups, it was emphasized that the group was a unit and would be so scored; it did not matter who contributed the words. For purposes of comparison, Anderson also composed nominal groups of two and three from the performance data of individuals who had actually worked alone. The overall results are shown in Table II. Groups of two produced more words than individuals working alone, and groups of three produced more words than groups of two. However, the results from the nominal groups of two and three were very similar to those for the real groups of two and three, respectively. The group effect appears to be a pseudogroup effect, but further examination indicates that such a conclusion is unwarranted. Looking at the rate of word production, Anderson found that, in the first two or three minutes of the task, nominal groups do better than real groups. Then the trend reverses, and real groups produce more words as time passes. The latter results emphasize that group output varies over time. A single measurement taken at some arbitrary time may not be very informative in the study of group efficiency.

As another example of the linkage between interaction processes and group performance, consider the issue of feedback and the relationship between the feedback one receives in a group and one's dominant motivations. French (1958) hypothesized that achievement-oriented people would improve in performance of a group task when given positive feedback about their apparent efficiency and mastery of the task. Conversely, she hypothesized that people who are less achievement-oriented but more concerned with affiliation and social relations would improve more in performance of the same task when given positive feedback about their apparent ability to work well together. As we saw in Chapter 7 (see page 186), the results of French's research were precisely in line with these expectations.

The nature of the interaction in a group and the extent to which group members feel that the interaction helps them achieve their own goals are crucial determinants of individual effort on the group's behalf and, hence, of group performance. A static comparison of individual performance versus group performance is not likely to be very meaningful in terms of the psychologically important factors in either performance. Unfortunately, the bulk of research on the group-effectiveness problem has made just such static comparisons, and, as we pointed out earlier, we still know relatively little about the conditions under which groups will or will not outperform individuals.

There are signs that the emphasis on outcome is shifting and that more and more investigators are looking at how group interaction processes relate to group performance. Anderson (1976), Hackman and Morris (1975), Kelley and Thibaut (1969), and others have recently proposed process-oriented theoretical frameworks for the study of group effectiveness that suggest relationships exist between what happens in group interaction and group performance or member satisfaction. Another reason why many have shied away from attempts to relate ongoing group interaction to group performance is that ongoing interaction is extremely complex and difficult to analyze. Let us take a brief look at another consequence of this complexity.

Retrospective misinterpretations: what really happened here?

It is important to keep in mind the sheer amount of behavior that occurs in a group. Bales, et al. (1951) report that, in observing groups of 5 people interact for 9 different sessions, a total of 10,700 behavioral acts were recorded. That is an average of 1,199 separate behavioral acts per group session, and since not all behavior can be coded into Bales's 12 categories it is a conservative estimate of what actually happened. Given that such a tremendous amount of behavior occurs in a typical group interaction, we would expect—and the evidence (D'Andrade, 1974) confirms—that group members will not recall precisely who said what to whom.

If group members are not able to keep track of who said what to whom, what are their retrospective reports of group interaction likely to reflect? As a partial answer to this question, let us recall some material discussed in Chapter 5. There we noted that we all have expectations about what other people are like and how they will behave. As Rosenberg and Jones (1972) point out, these expectations about others generally consist of: (1) the categories we employ to describe the range of abilities, attitudes, interests, physical features, traits, behaviors, and values that we perceive in others and (2) the beliefs we hold about which of these perceived characteristics tend to go together and which do not.

Given the tremendous amount of behavior that occurs in a typical group session and the impossibility of keeping track of it all, D'Andrade (1974) argues that, when asked what occurred in a group, members rely on their previously existing expectations about behaviors that are likely to go together. His hypothesis is that the judgments group members and group observers make from memory cannot be trustworthy, because there is a *systematic bias* in such judgments. Behaviors that one considers similar will be recalled as having been performed by the same person when, in fact, they were not. Thus, the relationships "found" between behaviors occurring in a group may be due to the observers' conceptions of similarities among behaviors rather than to actual covariation in the behaviors of the subjects.

In a reanalysis of some data originally reported by Newcomb in 1929, Shweder (1975) provides some evidence to support D'Andrade's hypothesis. The original study was conducted in a summer camp for boys. Two groups of campers attended a camp for about 3½ weeks each, and their day-to-day behaviors were recorded by 6 observers. The observers recorded every occurrence of 26 behaviors exhibited by the boys. Some examples of the behaviors recorded are as follows:

> Speaks with confidence of his own abilities,
> Spends more than an hour of the day alone,
> Painstaking in making up his bed,
> Works steadily, without stopping, at after-meal work,
> Talks more than his share of the time, and
> Gets into scraps with other boys (p. 460–461).

These day-to-day observations, recorded as soon as possible after they occurred, constitute the *actual behavior* of the boys. In addition, at the end of each 3½ week session, each of the 6 observers was asked to give an overall rating to each boy on each of the 26 behaviors. The latter constitutes what Shweder terms the *rated behavior* of the boys. These indices of actual and rated behavior were both obtained by Newcomb in the late 1920s.

In the early 1970s, Shweder asked 10 University of Chicago students to inspect the 26 behaviors from Newcomb's study and, for each possible pair of those behaviors, to rate the conceptual similarity of the behaviors. These ratings constitute what Shweder refers to as the *pre-existing conceptual scheme*—that is, the perceived similarities among the 26 behaviors. Shweder then correlated the actual behaviors performed by the boys, the rated behaviors as judged by the observers at the end of camp, and the pre-existing conceptual scheme of perceived similarities among the behaviors themselves.

The results are shown in Figure 8. The numbers in the figure are correlation coefficients, and a coefficient of 1.00 is the maximum possible, indicating a perfect correspondence. There are several points to note about the relationships in the figure, and these points hold true for both groups of campers. First, the actual behavior of a group does *not* correspond very closely to the rated behavior. Second, the pre-existing conceptual scheme corresponds much more closely to the

8. The relationship among subjects' actual behaviors, how those behaviors were rated by others, and how those behaviors were seen as being associated, conceptually. Note that rated behavior corresponds more closely to the pre-existing conceptual scheme than to actual behavior. (From Shweder, 1975, Figure 1, p. 463.)

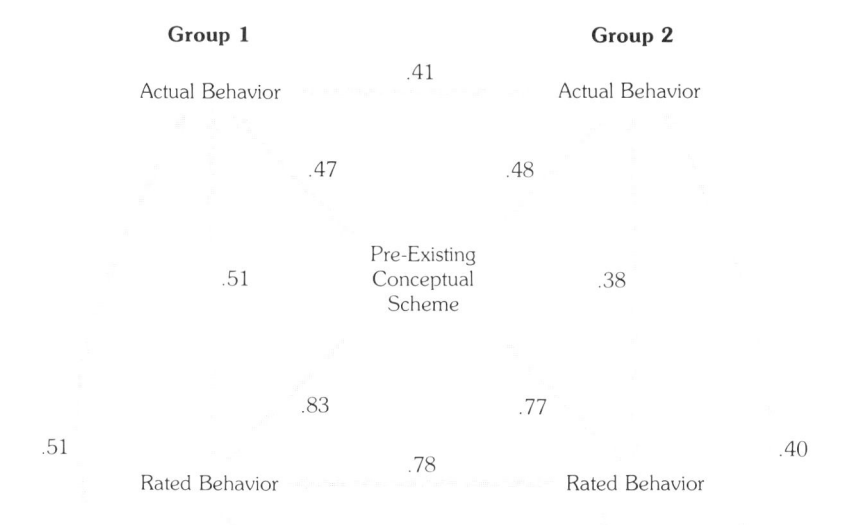

```
      Group 1                              Group 2
                         .41
   Actual Behavior ─────────────────── Actual Behavior

              .47                .48

                    Pre-Existing
              .51   Conceptual     .38
                      Scheme

              .83                .77
.51                                              .40
                         .78
   Rated Behavior ─────────────────── Rated Behavior
```

rated behavior than the actual behavior does. As Shweder puts it, "There seems to be a causal distorting relationship between conceptual factors and rating factors, i.e., conceptual factors control judgment and are not necessarily related to actual behavior" (p. 465). Note also that the actual behavior of each group corresponds as closely to the rated behavior of the other group as it does to its own rated behavior. The actual behaviors of the two groups do not, however, correspond very closely.

It appears that D'Andrade's (1974) argument is a valid one:

> The argument . . . is not just that there is memory drift when people make ratings or rankings of other people's behavior, but that this "drift" is systematic, nonrandom, biased in the direction of the rater's conception of "what is like what." (p. 175).

This is a particularly important point for the study of groups because, as we have seen, one of the major deficiencies in the group literature has been the failure to relate aspects of interaction to outcome. The existing techniques for interaction analysis, though they have yielded some useful knowledge, are cumbersome and crude. Taken together, these factors have tempted many investigators to forego a fine-grained analysis of interaction and rely on the postsession judgments of group members for evidence about what occurred in the group. Such evidence, as we have just seen, is of questionable value.

Summary

We began this chapter by examining several incidental consequences of social interaction: things that appear to happen simply because we are around other people.

The presence of many other people in ambiguous emergency situations apparently decreases the likelihood that the victims will be helped. The initial nonresponsiveness of other bystanders may lead one to define the situation as a nonemergency. The literature on social facilitation, however, suggests a somewhat different explanation for group inhibition of helping. Zajonc's reformulation of the social-facilitation literature postulates that the presence of others is physiologically arousing and consequently inhibits complex, novel responses—such as helping in an ambiguous situation—and facilitates dominant, well-learned responses. Subsequent research generally supports Zajonc's ideas, with one major exception. It is not the mere presence of others, but the presence of others who are capable of evaluating one's performance that produces social facilitation.

The literature on deindividuation shows that a complete lack of concern about the evaluations of others is socially destructive. The available data suggest that, when deindividuated, people are insensitive to the cues and norms that usually inhibit socially undesirable behavior. We also briefly examined some of the literature on nonverbal communication. The notion of information management was discussed to illustrate how people attempt to use nonverbal cues both to project a particular image of themselves and to "see through" the images that others attempt to project.

We then turned to interaction processes and pointed out that changes in one variable in a group, such as size, result in simultaneous changes in several interaction processes. In spite of this complexity, research on group interaction has yielded a number of well-established and intriguing findings. Researchers using Bales's interaction process analysis and other systems for recording ongoing interaction have found that many different kinds of problem-solving groups progress through definite stages.

Individual group members tend to differ tremendously in the extent to which they participate in group discussions and these differences in participation are remarkably stable, provided the group's composition and/or task does not change. In addition to linguistic rules and norms of etiquette that help to maintain these differences, group members quickly develop expectations about how the others in a group are going to behave. We cited some research employing the prisoner's dilemma game to show that our expectations about how others are going to behave can change our own behavior in ways that increase the probability that our expectations will prove correct.

We briefly examined the question of whether groups are more effective than individuals. The literature on groups versus individuals has been generally uninformative for three reasons: (1) too much emphasis on group outcomes or products, (2) too little emphasis on how and why group processes should relate to group production, and (3) too little attention to the methodological problems encountered in comparing group and individual performance.

Finally, we noted other factors that complicate the study of group interactions: the sheer amount of behavior that occurs in groups, the difficulty group members consequently experience in remembering who said what to whom, and the tendency of the members to "remember" by relying on their previously existing expectations about behaviors and what behaviors go together. For all these reasons, the recollections of group members are a questionable source of information about what really goes on in groups.

14

Leadership

392
The search for "leaders"

Dominance in nonhuman species
The Great Person theory of leadership

398
The situational approach to leadership

Presidential style and changing situations
All things to all people?
The contingency model of leader effectiveness

406
Leadership as a group process

Legitimacy and leadership
The influence of followers

409
Crises and change in leadership

412
Summary

During any election year, hardly a day passes that one does not hear people talk about leadership. Incumbents are accused of failing in it, and challengers promise to provide it. If one listens closely to the campaign rhetoric, however, it quickly becomes clear that *leadership* is an ambiguous word: it means whatever the speaker wants it to mean. Incumbents paint verbal images of leadership that are synonymous with portraits of themselves at the helm of the ship of state, steering a safe course through the night. Challengers, on the other hand, assert that all our problems—from crime in the streets to our high-fat diets—are somehow due to a failure of leadership. Scientifically, ambiguous words are usually considered useless. Instead of facilitating communication, such words retard it. Judging from the many apparent meanings it enjoys in political campaigns, the word *leadership* may well qualify as scientifically useless.

Nevertheless, most people seem to understand what is referred to when someone mentions leadership, and one can even discern a common core of meaning in the foregoing examples. That common core of meaning involves interpersonal influence within a group. Following Bass (1960), we shall define LEADERSHIP as the efforts of one group member to somehow change another group member in almost anything—attitudes, beliefs, values, behavior, and/or opinions. There are several things to note about this deceptively simple definition. First, leadership is not an all-or-none phenomenon. Each member of a group may exhibit leadership, with various group members differing only in the amount of leadership they exercise. Second, the definition allows us to distinguish attempted, successful, and effective leadership. ATTEMPTED LEADERSHIP is simply an effort by one person to influence or change another in some way. Such an attempt may or may not be SUCCESSFUL LEADERSHIP, which actually results in change. If the attempt is successful, it is considered EFFECTIVE LEADERSHIP if it results in satisfaction, reward, or goal attainment for the person influenced. Third, it is clear that several of the topics we have discussed in preceding chapters, such as conformity and attitude change, are directly relevant to the study of leadership.

With this definition in mind, let us examine some of the research, theory, and speculation about leaders, followers, and leadership. We shall begin by looking at the early research in which attempts were made to identify Leaders, with a capital L. In several nonhuman species, clear patterns of dominance and submission are established among members of groups, and we shall discuss examples of this type of behavior to see how it is similar to and different from leader–follower relations in humans.

We shall then examine the notion that leadership is a quality that some people exhibit by virtue of having certain dispositions or characteristics that others do not have. In its strong form, this notion has been called the Great Person theory of leadership. As we shall see, the evidence for leadership ability as an enduring attribute is mixed, and even the data cited as evidence for the Great Person theory suggest that the situation in which leadership is exhibited is often of crucial importance. Hence, we shall review some research on the situational approach to leadership, research which suggests that (1) groups often have more than one leader and (2) different types of leadership tactics are apparently called for under different circumstances. What works in the army does not necessarily work elsewhere. Along the way, we shall pay particular attention to the issues of exchange and reciprocal influence among leaders and followers. The fact that leaders have only as much power as followers give them makes for an intriguing paradox in leader–follower relations. The withholding of confidence and the refusal to be influenced can result in a *coup-d'état* and the emergence of new leaders. In the final section of this chapter, we shall examine some of the conditions under which such social changes occur.

The search for "leaders"

In 1859, Darwin presented a strong case for the existence of continuity in physical and mental characteristics between human and nonhuman species. It took only a small leap of imagination to extend this continuity to social characteristics as well. Casual observation had long suggested that many animal societies were not just random collections of individuals, but had definite social structure. In fact, it seemed that there were clearly defined "leaders" among many species of animals. At least, there were animals that were consistently deferred to by others in their group. Perhaps this was the archetype of leadership. If so, understanding this phenomenon, what functions it serves, how the hierarchy is established, and how it is maintained might tell us something about leader–follower relations in humans. On the other hand, preference and deference in nonhuman species might serve functions entirely unlike those they serve in humans. Let us see.

DOMINANCE IN NONHUMAN SPECIES

Observers of animal behavior report that all that you have to do to verify the existence of dominance hierarchies in many animal species is become familiar enough with the group you are observing so that you can reliably recognize individuals. As soon as you can distinguish one hen, one jackdaw, or one chimpanzee from another, you become aware of an asymmetry of behavior between any given pair of animals within the group. If food is repeatedly placed between the members of a pair, the same animal consistently gets a greater share (Leary and Slye, 1959). If the two animals meet on a narrow pathway, one consistently steps aside and lets the other pass (Van Lawick-Goodall, 1971). In short, between each pair of animals within a species group one is dominant and takes precedence with respect to the allocation of food, sex, freedom of movement, and other such amenities. The second animal is submissive and defers to the first whenever a potential conflict of interest arises.

The existence of apparent dominant–subordinate relationships among animals within species has been noted by many observers. Nearly 65 years ago, for example, Schjelderup-Ebbe (1913) reported what he, or some unknown translator, referred to as "despotism" among barnyard fowl. Further, since many of the early observations were done on various species of birds (mainly chickens), and since the major weapon with which such creatures keep subordinates in their places is a well-honed beak, the term PECKING ORDER was coined to refer to dominant–subordinate relationships. A number of serious questions have been raised about the validity of these early observations. As Maclay and Knipe (1974) note in commenting on Schjelderup-Ebbe's observations of chickens, the barnyard is a peculiar, unnatural environment. Nearly all of the inhabitants are female, they are often cooped up in a relatively small, fenced enclosure, and they are fed at predetermined times. Under more natural conditions, they would spend their days roaming freely over a wide area in search of food, and their behavior might or might not be similar to that seen in a chicken coop.

In the years since Schjelderup-Ebbe's study, a number of investigators have determined, under more natural conditions than those of a hen coop, that dominance hierarchies do exist within a number of animal species. For example, the famous Austrian naturalist Konrad Lorenz (1952) settled a colony of jackdaws in an aviary in the roof of his house, with access to the outdoors through a trap door. Lorenz's purpose was to raise an entire colony of tame, free-flying jackdaws and to study their social behavior. As in the more artificial environment of the barnyard, it soon became apparent that one of the main features of jackdaw society was a clear DOMINANCE HIERARCHY. Each bird appeared afraid of certain other birds, those above her in rank. The rank-ordering was determined by what Lorenz terms "disputes," but these disputes were not necessarily physical encounters. Further, once the rank-ordering had been determined, it was relatively resistant to change. Thus the existence of a pecking order among birds does not appear to be some aberration brought on by domestication and confinement.

What about the "higher" animals? After all, we want to see whether dominance in animals is in any way similar to leadership in humans. It is important to know whether dominance hierarchies exist within those species, such as the chimpanzee, that are closer to humans on the evolutionary scale than jackdaws and barnyard fowl. As with the studies of birds, early observations on the social behaviors of higher animals were almost always done on those in captivity. But there have now been a number of studies under more natural conditions.

One of the most significant of these has been in progress since the early 1960s in Africa, on the eastern shore of Lake Tanganyika at the Gombe Stream Chimpanzee Reserve (Van Lawick-Goodall, 1971). Participants in this study have tried to observe and record the behavior of chimpanzees under completely natural conditions, as the chimpanzee bands roam entirely free in the jungle. A number of significant findings have rewarded Van Lawick-Goodall and her associates for their years of tramping through jungle grass, peering through telescopes, climbing trees, taking pictures, perching on mountaintops, and observing chimpanzees endlessly. For example, it was discovered that chimpanzees eat meat, whereas they had previously been thought to subsist on fruit and insects only. Numerous examples of tool using have been observed and even instances of tool making. For our purposes, however, the most interesting observations involve the social behavior of the chimpanzees and, in particular, dominance and how it is established.

Early in her field work, Van Lawick-Goodall found clear evidence of a dominance hierarchy among the chimpanzees. After observing the chimpanzees long enough to distinguish individuals, Van Lawick-Goodall named each and soon

> began to suspect that Goliath might be the highest ranking chimpanzee in the area. . . . If William and Goliath started to move toward the same banana at the same time, it was William who gave way and Goliath took the fruit. If Goliath met another adult male along a narrow forest track, he continued—the other stepped aside. Goliath was nearly always the first to be greeted when a newcomer climbed into a fig tree to join a feeding group (p. 79).

Van Lawick-Goodall also noted something about dominance contests that Lorenz, Schjelderup-Ebbe, and numerous others had observed. That is, to the extent that the term *pecking order* implies that questions of dominance are always settled by physical aggression, the term is misleading. Dominance contests are usually settled by bluff—displaying, threatening, posturing, growling, hooting, and other behaviors designed to intimidate. Actual physical contact is usually avoided. And it is in this area of nonverbal behaviors, such as those employed in bluffing, that Van Lawick-Goodall believes the similarities between humans and chimps are particularly striking.

The similarities between dominance in nonhuman species and leadership in humans are indeed striking, and they do not stop with nonverbal display behaviors. Koford (1963), for example, reports that in free-ranging macaque monkeys, the sons of high-ranking females are more likely to rise to high rank in the band than the sons of low-ranking females. Tiger and Fox (1974) offer an interesting interpretation of this finding. The high-ranking mothers outrank even some of the males, and the youngster, accompanying his mother everywhere for the first year or so of life, becomes used to seeing other animals give way to him. Furthermore, the confident assurance of his dominant, high-ranking mother are his to share. Hence, if most dominance contests are settled by bluff anyway, an excess of confidence may make one king of the roost. Tiger and Fox (1974) see in this "inherited" ranking system of the macaque monkeys the archetype of aristocracies among humans.

Such analogies to human behavior are quite attractive, but we need to be sure we are really talking about leadershiplike phenomena. Russell and Russell (1957) argue that we are not. As they put it, dominance among most lower animals is primarily competitive. The dominant animal gets the food, the preferred roost, or the best mate, and the lower-ranking animal does without or gets second best. In humans, however, dominance can be, and often is, used to exploit others. This, of course, would not qualify as effective leadership by our earlier definition. Leadership in humans is used for the mutual benefit of leader and followers. If dominance in animals is to be considered similar to leadership in humans, the dominance hierarchy must serve the interests of both the dominant and the subordinate animals in the group.

What Russell and Russell refer to as constructive leadership is equivalent to what we defined earlier, following Bass (1960), as effective leadership. In terms of our definitions of attempted and successful leadership, dominance in animals qualifies as leadership, and it may even qualify in terms of the more stringent criterion of effective leadership. Several investigators have argued that dominance hierarchies are indeed beneficial for both dominant and subordinate animals within the hierarchy. For example, Price (1969) points out that, since animals often reach physical maturity sometime after sexual maturity, it is in the best interest of a species for young males to yield to older males in conflicts over sexually receptive females. Otherwise the young males might be destroyed. Similarly, a hierarchy is established in baboons prior to the age at which the lethal canine teeth develop. Once established, the hierarchy is maintained primarily by bluffs and threats, not by mortal combat, so even the smaller, weaker, subordinate animals can live to a ripe old age. Dominance hierarchies may also help ensure survival of the species as a whole. Wynne-Edwards (1962) points out that, since dominant animals take precedence in feeding, the hierarchy provides a social mechanism for ensuring that some animals will survive periods of prolonged food shortage.

Even if dominance in animals were nothing more than an attractive analogy to leadership in humans, there would be another reason for discussing it. The ease with which leaders can be identified among animals (dominance is usually correlated with age, sex, and physical size) suggested to many investigators in the first part of this century that leaders among humans might also be easy to identify. All one had to do was to find those personality characteristics and/or physical attributes associated with leadership, and one would be able to predict who in a group was most likely to lead. Leadership, in short, was assumed to be a phenomenon that stemmed from certain characteristics a person possessed. This notion came to be known as the Great Person theory of leadership or, among historians, as the "Bad King John" theory (Carr, 1961). Let us see how this approach has fared.

THE GREAT PERSON THEORY OF LEADERSHIP

When a particular problem-solving approach proves successful in one realm, it is difficult to resist the temptation to apply that same approach in other realms, even when the latter seem basically different. Take the two concepts of intelligence and leadership for instance. Intelligence is generally considered an attribute of an individual, something he or she has. Leadership, on the other hand, is an interpersonal phenomenon, a characteristic of the interaction between two people. In spite of this basic conceptual dissimilarity, the early research on leadership was heavily influenced by the successful development of tests to measure intelligence in the late 1800s and early 1900s.

Binet in France, Galton in England, Ebbinghaus in Germany, and Cattell in the United States were among the many who were actively investigating intelligence around the turn of the century. However, as Guilford (1967) points out, it was the advent of World War I and the development of the Army Alpha and Beta Examinations, two intelligence tests administered to more than 1.5 million recruits for selection, screening, and job assignment purposes, that really called attention to intelligence testing. One consequence was the almost immediate development of aptitude tests of various sorts. Thus, in the period immediately following World War I,

> psychologists gave a large part of their attention to problems of personality and the measurement of personality. What interest there was in the description of leader behavior during this period was caught up in this tide, and almost all the work reported took the form of a search for traits of personality which were supposed to characterize "the leader" (Gibb, 1969, p. 216).

For a while it seemed that this search was paying off. There were 10 or 12 personality characteristics that seemed to consistently differentiate leaders from nonleaders in the results of numerous investigations using diverse subject populations and group tasks. For example, in an extensive review of the literature on personality and leadership, Stogdill (1948) found 23 investigations that reported leaders to be brighter than their followers and only 5 that reported no differences in intelligence between leaders and followers. None reported leaders to be less intelligent than their fellow group members. Similarly, in a more recent review, Mann (1959) reported that in 28 studies, with a total of 196 results pertinent to the relationship between intelligence and leadership, 173 (88 percent) of the results indicated that leaders are likely to be more intelligent

The Camp David agreement, September 17, 1978. Egyptian President Anwar Sadat, United States President Jimmy Carter, and Israeli Prime Minister Menachem Begin reach agreement on a Middle East settlement after two weeks of negotiations. With the intense focus of the media on specific leaders and their accomplishments, it is easy to see why The Great Person theory of leadership has been so popular. (Wide World Photo)

than their followers. Mann also points out, however, that even though most of the results indicated a relation between intelligence and leadership, the median correlation in these studies was only .25, not a very impressive relation.

Several other personality characteristics seem to be consistently related to the probability of assuming leadership in a group. Stogdill reports uniformly positive evidence from 15 or more studies that the average person occupying a position of leadership is likely to be more intelligent, more dependable, more socially active, and higher in socioeconomic status than the average member of his or her group. Other traits that have been related to leadership, though somewhat less consistently, are persistence, self-confidence, adaptability, and extroversion.

In addition to this apparent consistency in the early correlational research on leadership, experimental studies seemed to yield results supporting the idea that leadership ability is a quality or attribute that some people have, an attribute that will shine forth regardless of the group in which those people find themselves. Borgatta, Couch, and Bales (1954) reasoned that a great man (The Great Man theory was an earlier version of The Great Person theory) would have to possess several qualities, including assertiveness, intelligence, task ability, and social acceptability, in order for there to be some transfer of his leadership ability from group to group. To identify some great men, Borgatta, et al. observed and recorded the interactions, using Bales's Interaction Process Analysis, of 42 three-man groups composed of Air Force enlisted men. Group members were always of the same rank. Then, on the basis of total activity rates, sociometric ratings of coparticipants, leadership ratings of coparticipants, and individual IQ's, Borgatta, et al. identified 11 great men—that is, 11 men who were high on all of these measures.

Now, if these 11 were truly great men, then in subsequent, different groups they should emerge as leaders, and the subsequent groups in which these men participated should be more productive and/or more satisfying for other members than comparable groups lacking a great man. To see if these predictions held, Borgatta et al. assigned all 126 men, sequentially, to 3 additional group sessions. Each person participated with 2 new participants in each session. The sessions were again observed and coded using Bales's Interaction Process Analysis, and, following each session, the participants again rated each other on leadership and social acceptability. Of the 11 men identified as high on all 4 criteria of "greatness" after the first session, 8 were at the top in the second and third sessions, and 7 still remained at the top in the fourth session. Further, analysis of the interaction process codings (see Table I) revealed that groups containing 1 of the 11 great men were more productive in terms of the number of suggestions generated *and* more satisfying for members in that less tension and more solidarity were exhibited during the interactions. Having a great man for a leader is likely to make the group a better group, both in terms of productivity and member satisfaction.

As we mentioned, the search for characteristics that differentiate leaders from followers was given impetus in the first few decades of this century by both studies of dominance among animals and the success of intelligence testing during World War I. Even more important, however, was the widespread belief that what really matters in history are the personalities and behaviors of individuals. This theory is one that we all learned as children. We are told of the exploits of Caesar, Columbus, and Robin Hood. We hear of

Table I. Mean rates of interaction for Great Man and non-Great Man groups

	Session 1	Sessions 2, 3, and 4
Rate of Giving Suggestions and Agreement		
Great Man Groups	867	530
Non-Great Man Groups	566	362
Rate of Showing Tension		
Great Man Groups	9.4	11.7
Non-Great Man Groups	14.1	16.4
Rate of Showing Solidarity and Tension Release		
Great Man Groups	39.6	28.6
Non-Great Man Groups	19.7	22.2

The higher the number, the greater the rate of giving suggestions, or showing agreement, tension, or solidarity. (From Borgatta, Couch, and Bales, 1954, Table 2, p. 758.)

Henry VIII, Hitler, Karl Marx, and George Patton. Seldom are we told of the complex social circumstances surrounding these figures. As Carr (1961) puts it,

> It is easier to call Communism "the brainchild of Karl Marx" . . . than to analyze its origin and character, to attribute the Bolshevik revolution to the stupidity of Nicholas II or to German gold than to study its profound social causes, and to see in the two world wars of this century the result of the individual wickedness of Wilhelm II and Hitler rather than of some deep-seated breakdown in the system of international relations (p. 57).

This does not mean, of course, that there are not great men and women who play crucial roles in a variety of settings. It means that, taken by itself, the Great Person approach is incomplete. It is not even a theory, because it specifies nothing about the antecedents or the attributes of greatness. It also seems reasonable to expect that these antecedents and attributes will be related. That is, the conditions conducive to a particular person emerging as a leader *determine* the attributes of leadership in that situation, the qualities or personal characteristics of the leader who will be effective in that context. One becomes a leader in a particular group because one has the qualities that will facilitate the attainment of the group's goals, whatever those goals may be. Thus the characteristics of the leader must mesh with the needs, goals, and activities of the group.

There is nothing contradictory between this statement and the finding cited earlier that leaders are generally more intelligent, persistent, dependable, and active than their followers. These are all qualities that would be expected to facilitate attainment of a wide variety of goals in a wide variety of situations. It is clear, however, that leadership is not just a quality that some people have. It is a relationship between individuals in a particular situation. The major reason why Borgatta, et al. (1954) found the great men identified in their first session to be leaders in the second, third, and fourth sessions with new coparticipants was probably that all four sessions were similar and called for the same type of leader. Let us look at this issue of how the situation influences leadership.

The situational approach to leadership

There are a number of lines of evidence bearing on the issue of how the situation affects leadership. Even the studies that identified apparently general characteristics of leaders provide data indicating the importance of situations. For example, Mann (1959) points out that intelligence appears to be more strongly related to leadership in small than in large groups, while good personal adjustment seems to be more characteristic of leaders of large groups. He hypothesizes that internal conflicts and squabbles become increasingly likely with increasing group size. Conflicts must be kept under control for the group to proceed smoothly toward its goals, and a well-adjusted, even-tempered leader is more likely to be able to minimize conflict. Relatively speaking, then, a small group, with fewer task-relevant resources, may have a greater need for an intelligent, task-oriented leader.

A number of other constraints on the generality of leadership qualities across groups emerged from the early correlational literature. Even within one group, however, the qualities and behaviors necessary for

Table II. Barber's classification of presidents

	Active	Passive
Positive	Franklin D. Roosevelt Harry S Truman John F. Kennedy	William H. Taft Warren G. Harding
Negative	Woodrow Wilson Herbert Hoover Lyndon Johnson Richard M. Nixon	Calvin Coolidge Dwight Eisenhower

The active-passive dimension refers to the amount of energy invested in work. The positive-negative dimension refers to whether the president seems to experience political life as happy or sad, enjoyable or discouraging, positive or negative. Classification as positive or negative is not an evaluation of the president or his conduct of the presidency. (Data from Barber, 1972.)

successful and effective leadership may change as the group's external and internal environments change. When such changes do occur, the very qualities of the leader's personality that were so important to the group earlier may prove to be his or her downfall.

PRESIDENTAL STYLE AND CHANGING SITUATIONS

One of the most perplexing and perennial political puzzles is that of predicting how an elected official, such as the president of the United States, is going to perform in office. The president elected in 1984 will be confronting the day-to-day problems of America and the world for several years, problems that to a large extent can neither be foreseen nor forestalled. If the problems cannot be foreseen, how is the voter of 1984 to make his or her choice?

In an intriguing analysis of U.S. presidents since Theodore Roosevelt, Barber (1972) argues that, while we may not be able to predict precisely how a future president will handle any particular problem, we may very well be able to predict the general "climate" and tone of his or her approach, the mode and manner of his or her attempts to solve problems. Barber's thesis is very straightforward and is based on the idea that a president's personality, which Barber sees as consisting of character, world view, and style, is an important determinant of presidential behavior. Presidents, of course, encounter changing national needs, and the resonance, or fit, between any given president's personality and the needs of the situation is what makes an apparently great president or one everybody would just as soon forget. Barber argues that presidents can be divided into four basic types, based on how actively and energetically they approach the office and whether or not they appear to enjoy political life. Culling his data from biographies, autobiographies, and political analyses, he offers the classification shown in Table II.

Of particular interest here is Barber's discussion of personal style. He claims that there are basically three aspects of a president's duties: (1) to speak to large audiences, (2) to deal in small private groups with individuals, usually other politicians, and (3) to "do his homework" and keep abreast of the mass of information necessary for him to do his job well. It is clear, of course, that presidents differ in the relative emphasis they place on these three duties, and a president's style is his habitual way of blending them, the balance that he strikes. Barber observes that a president's style is usually fixed at some point early in adult life by the manner in which he achieves his first independent political success.

The problem, of course, is that there is usually quite a difference between the situation in which the future president achieved his first independent success and the situations he must confront as president. According to Barber, rigid adherence to a style inappropriate to changed circumstances has been the downfall of several presidents. For example, Herbert Hoover's independent success was achieved as an engineering student at Stanford when he became treasurer of the student body and by hard work, attention to details, and efficient management wiped out a $2000 debt he had inherited as treasurer. As Barber puts it,

> Hoover was the man behind the scenes, the coordinator who transformed a bookkeeping function into the preeminent campus leadership function. The medium was the caucus—a small conference of the top men. The message was system, order, accountability . . . combined with a nearly complete absence of rhetoric (p. 128).

Years later, with the nation slipping into the worst depression in history, what was needed was a man who could inspire confidence—and that Hoover could not do.

In contrast, Barber depicts Woodrow Wilson as a man of high principle who appealed directly to the people: "The core of Woodrow Wilson's presidential style was rhetoric—especially 'oratory'—and he excelled in that" (p. 58). Yet Wilson too failed, because he could not or would not change his style to deal with the small group of senators and Congressmembers who could have insured ratification of the Covenant of the League of Nations. He refused to discuss any reservations or changes and went over the heads of the individual senators, appealing directly to the people. The Senate, of course, rejected the treaty. (Box A offers some additional evidence that the ability to change may be required for continued political success.)

Barber's intriguing analyses are the source of numerous hypotheses about presidents, politics, and

A. Revolutionary Leaders and Long-Term Success

The single-mindedness that seems to characterize revolutionary leaders, while often necessary to ensure the success of the revolution, can turn into a liability if the revolution is successful. As Suedfeld and Rank (1976) point out, the pretakeover revolutionist may often be characterized as a fanatic, a person with a one-track mind who sees everything in strict moralistic terms and who has the fixed idea that all that is evil and corrupt about society flows from "them"—his opponents, the current power structure, or the military–industrial complex. On the other hand, once the revolution has been accomplished, "generally, there is no longer a single overriding enemy, various factions must be reconciled and conciliated, policies must be based on diverse considerations in complex interactions, and both ideology and practice must be flexible and adaptable to dynamic events" (p. 172). In short, pretakeover revolutionaries may be characterized as low in cognitive complexity. Successful posttakeover revolutionaries, however, may need to be more flexible and to develop a more complex world view if they are to stay in power.

To check on this line of reasoning, Suedfeld and Rank obtained samples of the pre- and posttakeover writings of 19 leaders from 5 different revolutionary movements. Of the 19, 11 were judged successful on the basis of their having held important public office in the posttakeover government until their natural death or voluntary retirement. The 8 not meeting this criterion were judged unsuccessful. The pre- and posttakeover writings of these 19 leaders were then scored by a trained coder in terms of the complexity of the ideas expressed in the writings. Identifying material (names, dates, places) had been removed so that the coder would not know whose writings were being scored.

	Pretakeover	Posttakeover
Successful	1.67	3.65
Unsuccessful	2.37	2.22

The higher the mean, the greater the complexity of ideas.

The major results are shown in the table in terms of the mean complexity of ideas. It shows that "successful leaders were indeed those who exhibited a high degree of single-mindedness and complete dedication (i.e., conceptual simplicity) during the revolutionary struggle, with a change to more complex functioning after grasping power" (p. 173). Those who fell from power after their takeover exhibited less single-mindedness prior to the takeover and less complexity afterwards.

---

leadership. Of course, many of his conclusions are debatable, and, as with Janis's discussion of the groupthink syndrome, the historical case studies hardly constitute rigorous evidence for the reality of the phenomena. Even so, it is clear that individuals, including presidents, differ in their approaches to problems and in their relative strengths and weaknesses. Let us look at some rigorous evidence on how these stable individual differences among leaders and potential leaders interact with the internal and external environments of a group.

ALL THINGS TO ALL PEOPLE?

In Chapter 13, we described a study by Bavelas, et al. (1965) which revealed that in small, initially leaderless discussion groups, the participation rates of individuals can be dramatically increased by reinforcing them for stating opinions and by reinforcing others for agreeing with them. An additional finding in this study is of particular interest here. After each group session, subjects were asked to rank all group members on amount of participation, quality of ideas, effectiveness in guiding the discussion, and general leadership ability. Bavelas, et al. report that these rankings were highly correlated and that a sociometric index combining all four was closely related to the artificially induced talkativeness of the target subjects. That is, the subjects reinforced for stating opinions increased their overall verbal output, and other group members subsequently rated them more highly in quality of ideas, effectiveness, and leadership ability, as well as amount of participation.

Note, however, that even though Bavelas, et al. refer to their combined index as a sociometric index, they have left out any measure of the group members' likes and dislikes for each other. A number of people (Kahn and Katz, 1960) have pointed out that all work groups or task groups have two basically different yet closely intertwined problems. They must be competent to accomplish their assigned or chosen tasks, and they must be able to keep interpersonal tensions within the group under control so that conflict does not interfere with achievement of the group's goals. Given our earlier discussion of the stability of individual personality and style, one might well ask whether it is likely that, in general, a single person will be able to lead effectively in the solution of these different group problems.

Slater (1955), Bales (1958), and others observing initially leaderless discussion groups and recording their observations using interaction process analysis have reported some interesting findings that are pertinent here. If one plots total activity of the individual members (number of acts initiated) against how the other group members rate them on quality of ideas, likeableness, and dislike, the person rated highest on quality of ideas is usually not the most liked person. He or she is, in fact, the most disliked! Bales (1958) terms the person who is high on activity and ideas but low on likeableness a TASK SPECIALIST and the person high on likeableness but low on activity and ideas a SOCIAL SPECIALIST. The task specialist exercises leadership by his or her attempts to solve problems—by suggesting, guiding, giving opinions, and directing. The social specialist exercises a different kind of leadership by keeping tensions within bounds—by agreeing, showing solidarity, giving support, and providing for the release of tension. Bales argues that, except in those rare groups having a Great Person who is all things to all people, this differentiation of leadership roles is the norm in most problem-solving groups.

> The husband and wife in many families seem to play complementary roles of the sort described. Many administrators find cases from their experience where organizations in fact have two leaders, one who specializes on the task side, one on the social-emotional side. It is a kind of political maxim that it is almost impossible to elect the person who is technically best suited for an office—he is generally not popular enough (p. 443).

Small wonder that many politicians feel it is more important to smile and kiss babies than to get their facts straight.

There is another line of evidence bearing on this dilemma of social support versus task orientation in leadership. Consider the problems faced by a middle-level bureaucrat. Subordinates often expect consideration, sensitivity to their problems, and recognition for a job well done. On the other hand (Hemphill, 1950) superiors expect organizational ability and emphasis on output from the same person. During World War II, Stouffer, Suchman, DeVinney, Star, and Williams (1949) collected some data pertinent to this point by asking privates, noncommissioned officers, and officers about appropriate behavior for noncommissioned officers—the men in the middle. As Table III shows, the perceptions of privates and officers differed considerably. The privates believed the noncoms should be more willing to socialize and be "one of the boys," while the officers were more inclined to think noncoms should maintain their distance and discipline.

In commenting on these and related findings, Gibb (1969) points out that to be a "real" leader, an intermediate-level official in any hierarchy must play dual and conflicting roles. The values, rules, and procedures of the organization must be accepted and enforced if the person is to appear worthy to his or her superiors. Simultaneously, however, the person must be considerate and thoughtful of those lower in the

Table III. Comparison of privates, noncoms, and officers on attitudes toward noncom behavior

	Percent agreeing		
	Privates	Noncoms	Officers
A noncom will lose some of the respect of his men if he pals around with them off-duty.	13	16	39
A noncom should not let the men in his squad forget that he is a noncom even when off-duty.	39	54	81
A noncom has to be very strict with his men or else they will take advantage of him.	45	52	68
A noncom should teach his men to obey all rules and regulations without questioning them.	63	81	90
A noncom should always keep his men busy during duty hours, even if he has to make them do unnecessary work.	16	22	39
The harder a noncom works his men, the more respect they will have for him.	10	18	42

(From Stouffer, Suchman, DeVinney, Star, and Williams, 1949, Volume 1, Table 12, p. 408.)

hierarchy if he or she is to win and maintain their willing cooperation. The conflict between these two aspects of leadership can sometimes be quite sharp and painful. While the subordinates may be more concerned with effective leadership (that is, that they feel satisfied about what happens), superiors may only be concerned with successful leadership (that the man or woman in the middle gets the job done). Another curious phenomenon often associated with leadership in a hierarchy is described in Box B.

It seems clear that leaders are often called on to play conflicting roles. If the settings in which these conflicting roles are enacted can be kept segregated, then one person may be able to fill both roles well with relatively little stress. Similarly, if the group structure allows for the roles to be filled by two different people, all may proceed smoothly. Suppose, however, that the same individual must be both social leader and task leader in the same setting. What is likely to happen? Instead of following a maximizing principle in selecting a leader, the group is likely to follow a SATISFICING principle. That is, instead of the most technically competent *or* the most interpersonally rewarding member, the group will select someone who "suffices" in both roles. In a hierarchy, someone will be placed in the intermediate level who can fulfill the demands of both superiors and subordinates reasonably well, but who is not really first-rate in the eyes of either. Although casual observation attests to the truth of this idea, which we might call "the theory of mediocre management," it awaits definitive experimental verification.

Let us look more closely at how situations influence the leader's success in directing and coordinating task-relevant group activities. Fiedler (1964, 1971) has addressed this question directly and has developed a theory of leadership effectiveness.

THE CONTINGENCY MODEL OF LEADER EFFECTIVENESS

In Chapter 13, we described how the literature on social facilitation appeared inconsistent and uninterpretable for years, until Zajonc (1965) called attention to a very subtle but important consistency in that literature. By reorganizing the literature in terms of whether the task confronting the individual called for novel or well-learned responses, Zajonc demonstrated that the presence of others inhibits the former and facilitates the latter—a powerful generalization that has done much to clarify the apparent inconsistencies in the earlier literature. Similarly, Fiedler has attempted to systematize a number of apparently inconsistent results

B. The Peter Principle

Lawrence J. Peter, a professor at the University of Southern California, has formulated a possible explanation for occupational incompetence, which he and co-author Raymond Hull claim is all around us. This explanation, termed the PETER PRINCIPLE, can be stated very succinctly:

In a hierarchy, every employee tends to rise to his or her level of incompetence.

Like much satire, the Peter Principle contains a great deal of truth. The basic observation behind the principle is that, in most hierarchies, the criterion for promotion is competent performance at a lower level, and competent performance at the lower level usually requires different skills from those required at the level to which the person is promoted. Peter and Hull give the following example:

Military File, Case No. 8. Consider the case of the late renowned General A. Goodwin. His hearty, informal manner, his racy style of speech, his scorn for petty regulations and his undoubted personal bravery made him the idol of his men. He led them to many well-deserved victories.

When Goodwin was promoted to field marshal he had to deal, not with ordinary soldiers, but with politicians and allied generalissimos.

He would not conform to the necessary protocol. He could not turn his tongue to the conventional courtesies and flatteries. He quarreled with all the dignitaries and took to lying for days at a time, drunk and sulking, in his trailer. The conduct of the war slipped out of his hands into those of his subordinates. He had been promoted to a position that he was incompetent to fill (p. 6).

A number of interesting corollaries relevant to leadership follow from the Peter Principle:
1. Useful work is accomplished only by those who have not been promoted to their level of incompetence.
2. Those who are incompetent in their present positions will not, of course, be considered for promotion.
3. Contrary to the old belief that "Nothing succeeds like success," the Peter Principle clearly implies that *nothing fails like success.* A competent worker is bound to be promoted into a position calling for skills he or she does not have, and, hence, will sooner or later fail.

According to Peter and Hull, one of the few ways to fight the insidious operation of the Peter Principle is to find something that one can do well and *refuse* to be promoted. Unfortunately, even this commendable ploy entails certain risks.

---

about the circumstances under which particular types of leader attitudes and behaviors facilitate or hinder group performance. In doing so, Fiedler has constructed a contingency model of leader effectiveness and has indeed illuminated a very complex problem. Even so, this question of the relationships among leader characteristics, situational constraints, and group effectiveness has not yet yielded to the eloquent sort of simplification that Zajonc was able to impose on social facilitation.

Beginning with the very plausible hypothesis that the leader's attitudes toward other group members are important in group interaction and performance, Fiedler developed a measure of leaders' esteem for their least-preferred co-workers (LPC). The measure is simply a series of scales defined by adjective pairs, such as warm–cold, helpful–frustrating, and tense–relaxed. Group leaders in a variety of real-life and laboratory groups were asked to think of all the individuals with whom they have ever worked and then to use the rating scales to describe that person with whom they least preferred to work. The evidence seems to indicate that those who describe their least-preferred co-worker in relatively favorable terms (high–LPC subjects) tend to be more relaxed as leaders, more permissive and human-relations oriented—similar, in short, to Bales's social–emotional leaders. On the other hand, those who describe their least-preferred co-worker in relatively unfavorable terms (low–LPC subjects) tend to be more like Bales's task leaders. They are more directive and controlling, they give more suggestions, they are more serious and efficient, and they appear little concerned about whether their fellow group members like them.

Fiedler then correlated this measure with criteria of group effectiveness in a number of diverse groups. The correlations were usually highly significant, but inconsistent. For example, among a set of 14 high school basketball teams whose leaders had been identified by sociometric ratings, the LPC index correlated negatively with team performance. That is, the teams that won more games had leaders who were more controlling and psychologically distant. Other research (Fiedler, 1955) showed that whether the relationship between the LPC index and group performance was positive or negative depended on whether the leader had good or poor interpersonal relations with the other group members and also on the nature of the task: whether it was a highly structured or a relatively unstructured task.

In puzzling over these and related data, Fiedler reasoned that the relationship between a leader's attitude (managing and controlling versus relaxed and permissive) and group performance depends on the extent to which the group situation is favorable or unfavorable to the leader. For Fiedler, "group situation" refers to three variables: (1) whether the leader has good or poor interpersonal relations with key group members, (2) whether the task confronting the group is highly structured or not, and (3) whether the leader has much or little power and authority over the group members. His reasoning was that, in situations wherein all of these variables are favorable (a structured and clear task, good interpersonal relations with important group members, and a powerful leader), the group will be ready to get on with the task and a straightforward and directive leader is likely to be effective. When the conditions are very poor for the leader, a directive, controlling leader will *also* be most effective, because someone with the strength to step in and get the group organized and under way is needed. On the other hand, when conditions are only moderately favorable (or moderately unfavorable), a permissive, considerate leader might be most effective. Here the task is ambiguous or relations with group members are uneasy. The situation calls for someone who can coordinate conflicting views and smooth ruffled feathers.

To check on this line of reasoning, Fiedler gathered data from a large number of previous studies that had related leaders' LPC scores to group performance and organized the data in terms of whether the group situation was favorable or unfavorable to the leader. In doing so, he had to make some assumptions about the relative importance of the three situational factors—whether, for example, low power is more unfavorable to leadership than an unstructured task. Fiedler assumed that leader–member relations were most important, task structure was next, and leader power least important. Working under this assumption, Fiedler categorized previous research in terms of the three situational factors and plotted the median correlations between LPC scores and group performance. Although the relationships were not perfect, there was a surprising degree of consistency with the hypothesis that permissive, thoughtful (high–LPC) leaders would be more effective when the situation was moderately favorable or unfavorable to leadership and that controlling, directive (low–LPC) leaders would be more effective in situations very favorable or very unfavorable to leadership.

Research on leadership and group effectiveness was greatly stimulated by Fiedler's presentation of the contingency model, and a number of interesting derivations of the model have been tested recently. For example, Fiedler (1973) has pointed out that leadership training may not actually change leaders as much as it changes the situation. That is, training provides structure by clarifying what is expected and what the goals are or, at least, gives a set of rules, procedures, and hints about how to approach an ambiguous task. Thus, by helping to define and structure the situation, leadership training makes the situation more favorable to leadership. As we have seen, however, whether this will result in an increase or a decrease in group productivity should depend on (1) the leader's style, managing and controlling (low–LPC) or permissive and relaxed (high-LPC) and (2) whether the shift in favorableness of the situation is from very unfavorable to moderately unfavorable or moderately unfavorable to moderately favorable.

In other words, groups with untrained, task-oriented (low–LPC) leaders do quite well when the situation is very unfavorable for the leader. Hence, training low–LPC leaders should provide structure, make the situation slightly more favorable, but *decrease* group effectiveness because the situation would then be only moderately unfavorable—and in such situations, a relaxed, socially oriented (high-LPC) leader is called for. To test this line of reasoning, Chemers, Rice, Sundstrom, and Butler (1975) administered the LPC scale to a large group of ROTC cadets and selected leaders (low-LPC and high-LPC) on the basis of their responses. Three-person groups were then composed of two ROTC cadets and one non-ROTC undergraduate. Half of the groups were assigned a low-LPC leader and half a high-LPC leader. The task for all groups was to solve a series of cryptograms such as the following:

"GKKW GK MW WQK CWMWRFT WDKCOMZ
_ _ _ _ _ _ _ _ S _ _ _ _ _ _ _ S _ _ _ _ _ _ _

GFVTRTJ R BRSS NK OVKCCKO RT
_ R _ _ _ _ _ LL _ _ R SS _ _

M NSMLH FXKVLFMW"*
_ L _ _ _ _ _ R _ _ _ _ _ _ _.

Each cryptogram had a different code, but all followed a letter-substitution format in which letters of the alphabet are used to stand for other letters. Prior to the group sessions, half of the low–LPC leaders and half of the high–LPC leaders were given a 30-minute training session in cryptogram solution, which suggested a number of procedures for decoding and gave information about common word endings, letter frequencies, and one- and two-letter words. The result of the training session, according to Chemers, et al., was a drastic reduction in the ambiguity of the task.

Evidence from posttask questionnaires and anecdotal reports of the experimenters indicates that the group atmosphere was, generally, in the unfavorable region. Group-members ratings were significantly lower than similar ratings of groups in previous research. Further, as Chemers, et al. (1975) point out,

> The cadet leaders appeared agitated and expressed great concern with good performance. It was later learned that the ROTC cadre had admonished the cadets to perform at a high level. Tension may have been augmented by the presence in each group of a psychology student volunteer, who, it may be assumed, was considerably less motivated and involved in the task (p. 405).

Given these data about the group atmosphere, it was expected that groups with low–LPC leaders would perform best in the Untrained condition and that groups with high–LPC leaders would perform best in the Trained condition, the training having made the situation slightly more favorable and hence amenable to their brand of leadership. In terms of the number of cryptograms solved, the measure of group effectiveness, the results supported these expectations (see Figure 1).

Research on this model is proceeding, and the model has proved useful in furthering our understanding of a number of phenomena related to leadership. There are several ambiguities inherent in the model, however, some of which will be clarified by future research. For example, it is crucial to know what the dimension referred to as "favorableness to leadership of the group atmosphere" really is and how different groups can be rigorously compared on this dimension. In actual research, such as the study by Chemers, et al., placement along this dimension is often done on an *ad hoc* basis, and comparison across studies is very difficult.

---

*The solution is: "Meet me at the station Tuesday morning. I will be dressed in a black overcoat."

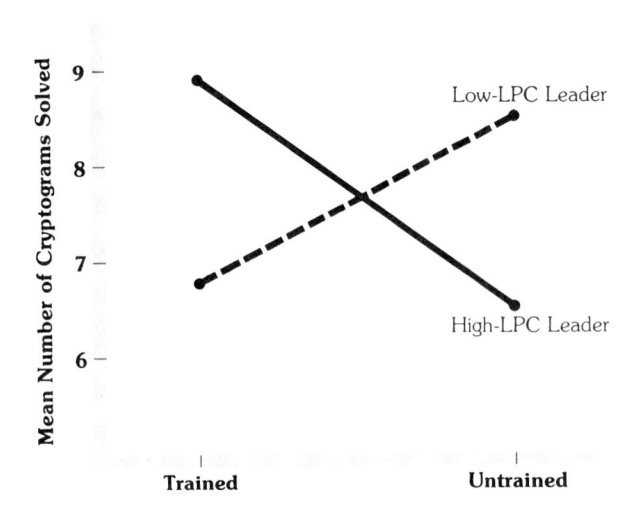

1. Interaction of training and leaders' LPC scores on group productivity. Training adversely affects the performance of groups headed by task-oriented (low-LPC) leaders because such leadership is more effective under relatively ambiguous circumstances. As training renders the situation less ambiguous, the relaxed, permissive (high-LPC) leader becomes more effective. (From Chemers, Rice, Sundstrom, and Butler, 1975, Figure 2, p. 406.)

Of course, a model does not have to account for everything. Although it does not detract from the model's usefulness, Fiedler's model addresses only indirectly some very important determinants of a leader's ability to influence his or her followers. These factors include the source of the leader's authority, the perceived competence of the leader, and the expectations of both leader and followers. Let us look at some of them.

Leadership as a group process

While both the personality trait approach and the strict situational approach to leadership are useful, they both tend to be overly static. The former views leadership as a property of the leader, and the latter argues that the type of leadership needed is a property of the situation. Neither approach tells us much about leadership as a *process*. Recently, Hollander and Julian (1969, 1970) suggested that it would be profitable and would shed some light on the process of leadership to view the relationship between leaders and followers as an exchange, or a transaction in which each party benefits and to which each party contributes.

LEGITIMACY AND LEADERSHIP

According to Hollander and Julian, the key to understanding the reciprocal influence between leaders and followers is the legitimacy of the leader. Legitimacy was a prominent concept in the study of leadership during the 1950s (French and Raven, 1959), but, with a few exceptions, it was not the subject of much research until its recent resurrection. Several variables contribute to legitimacy: (1) the leader's perceived ability or competence to deal with the tasks confronting the group, (2) the leader's apparent motivation to deal with those tasks and/or interest in the group's welfare, and (3) the perceived source of the leader's authority. There are a number of different sources of authority, such as election, appointment, and usurpation of power, and each source may have different implications for the leader's ability to influence his or her followers.

It is important to note that each of the variables affecting legitimacy is "in the eye of the follower." It is the followers' perception of the leader's motivation or interest in the group, for example, that is important for his or her ability to lead. It may be crucial, in fact, for leaders to conform rigidly to certain of their followers' expectations. The leader must appear interested in the group and competent to solve the group's problems, though he or she may deviate in other respects (Hollander, 1964). With respect to their competence and motivation, leaders may be overly concerned with their "image" and be quite practiced with the techniques of impression management discussed in Chapter 13.

As Hollander and Julian (1969) point out, there is a cycle in leader–follower relations that tends to perpetuate leadership in the absence of dramatic changes in the group's situation:

> The leader provides a *resource* in terms of adequate role behavior directed toward the

group's goal attainment, and in return receives greater influence associated with status, recognition and esteem. These contribute to his "legitimacy" in making influence assertions, and in having them accepted (p. 388).

The basic process of leadership, then, is one of exchange between leaders and followers. There are rewards for both leaders and followers, and the notions of equity and inequity apply to leader–follower relations as well as to other types of human behavior. For the leader to justify his or her greater rewards (esteem, power, financial benefits) and maintain harmony within the group, he or she must make apparent to other group members his or her greater inputs, such as competence to solve the group's problems and the interest and motivation to do so. One of the prime sources of revolutionary sentiment is the perception of inequity among followers (see Box C).

Hollander and Julian (1970) report a simple questionnaire study in which undergraduates were asked a series of questions about groups to which they belonged. For example, some were asked to think of a group to which they belonged and to imagine an elected leader of their own sex who could be described as a good performer and was interested in the group's activities and in its members. For other subjects, the description of the leader's performance and interest was omitted, and for still others, the leader was described as being interested in the members and group activities but a poor performer. All subjects were then asked to rate the leader they had thought of on a number of evaluation scales, such as how willing they would be to have that person continue as the leader. The major result of interest here is shown in Table IV. As expected, good performers are preferred to poor ones, but a poor performer may survive by convincing others that he or she has an abiding interest in the group.

There are problems in interpreting this sort of retrospective questionnaire data. However, Hollander and Julian (1970) report some additional evidence obtained in face-to-face interacting groups that supports their argument for the importance of perceived legitimacy in leadership. For example, in an experiment in which the perceived competence of the leader, the success or failure of the leader, and the source of the leader's authority (elected versus appointed) were all manipulated, they found that, in terms of the evaluations of followers, it makes little difference whether a highly competent appointed leader succeeds or fails. On the other hand, the evaluation of a highly competent *elected* leader is contingent on success or failure. This vulnerability can create a genuine problem for the elected leader. Subsequent research in the same series indicates that the very election process that makes the leader vulnerable to being ousted also makes him or her more confident, compared to an appointed leader and willing to deviate from group expectations. The research on legitimacy and exchange continues, but it already seems clear that the study of leadership cannot ignore the expectations, perceptions, and behaviors of followers.

Table IV. Competence of leader and interest in group as determined by followers' evaluations

	Competence of leader	
Leader's interest in group	Good	Poor
Mentioned	5.34	3.58
Not mentioned	5.22	2.80

The higher the number, the more favorable the reaction of the followers. Good performers were preferred, but if a poor leader's deep interest in the group was mentioned, evaluations became somewhat more favorable. (From Hollander and Julian, 1970, Table 2, p. 41.)

THE INFLUENCE OF FOLLOWERS

A recent study by Beckhouse, Tanur, Weiler, and Weinstein (1975) makes this point very clearly. Subjects were first selected, on the basis of their responses to a Leadership Self-Concept Scale, as being "natural leaders" or "natural nonleaders." Natural leaders were defined as those who indicated no hesitancy about speaking before a group, who enjoyed trying to get groups to solve problems, who said they were comfortable supervising others, and who answered a number of additional, similar questions in the affirmative. Each subject was then appointed the leader in two separate work sessions, each session involving two different students. Actually the additional "students"

C. Relative Deprivation and Revolutionary Sentiment

During World War II, the Information and Education Division of the Research Branch of the United States Army conducted an extensive series of studies investigating variables affecting the transition from civilian to military life and the mental and emotional adjustment of soldiers before and following combat. A concept used extensively in the multivolume report of the research (Stouffer, Suchman, DeVinney, Star and Williams, 1949) was RELATIVE DEPRIVATION, which includes "such well-known sociological concepts as 'social frame of reference,' 'patterns of expectation,' or 'definitions of the situation'" (p. 125). The concept of relative deprivation conveys the idea that while being a soldier is usually a sacrifice, the magnitude of the sacrifice and the personal anguish caused by having to make it depend to a large extent on with whom one compares one's lot. A clerk-typist serving behind the lines in France may have thought himself lucky compared to those G.I.'s ducking bullets and mortars behind snowbanks in the Argonne Forest. On the other hand, if he considered the hardships faced by similar clerk-typists serving in Honolulu, he may have been somewhat less satisfied.

Stouffer, et al. point out that, since most soldiers in World War II were not careerists and had been civilians in a relatively classless society (compared to the army) only a few weeks or months before,

> the privileges enjoyed by the officer class were so much out of line with democratic tradition and so unjustified in the eyes of the men that a smoldering resentment, which was to burst into flame with the end of the war, probably was inevitable.
>
> Why was the criticism of officers even more acute in inactive theaters and in rear areas of active theaters than in the United States? The most plausible hypothesis seems to turn on the concept of *scarcity*. If the supply of attractive women, liquor, or entertainment is severely limited, as was the case in many overseas areas, the problem of equitable distribution is much more acute than if there is plenty to go around. The charge which enlisted men repeated in theater after theater was that the officers used their rank to monopolize these desired objects. This was not expressed merely in indictments of particular officers . . . It was an indictment of a *system*—a system by which a privileged minority acquired, through their authoritarian position, a preponderant share of the scarce objects which were craved by others (p. 368-370).

The smoldering resentment and revolutionary sentiment created by such a system grew increasingly intense throughout the war and resulted in a series of sweeping recommendations for changes in officer/enlisted relations by General Doolittle's commission in 1946. One recommendation was that privileges accompanying rank be applied only to enable officers to better perform their duties and not for personal interest or gain.

---

were confederates of the experimenter. The behaviors of these confederates had been previously arranged. They had been trained to attempt to place the subject in a superordinate (leader) role or in a subordinate (follower) role. Each subject experienced *both* types of behavior on the part of his fellow students, one in the first session and one in the second.

The behavior employed by the confederates in the active situation (subordinate altercast) was designed to keep the subject in the leadership role in name only. This was accomplished in several ways. The confederates took over the division of labor, with one directing the subject to take notes while the other offered unrequested assistance. This had the effect of altercasting the subject into a support-seeking role, conveying to him that he was perhaps incapable of directing the activities.

In the passive situation (superordinate altercast) the confederates' behavior was designed to project the subject into a leadership role. Here they expressed bewilderment as to what should be done in the session and often acted passively. In this condition, the confederates made no attempt to define the situation . . . The job of the confederates here was not to force the subject to do all of the work, but rather to get him to make them do the work (p. 560-561).

It is important to note that, in both situations, the naive subject had "officially" been appointed the group leader and the confederates' actual contributions to task solution were held constant by having them make their *task-relevant* suggestions from a pool of uniformly poor items. Tape recordings of the interactions were made and the verbal exchanges coded using Bales's interaction process analysis. In addition, subjects were asked a number of questions about what had occurred during the interactions.

The results indicate that when subjects were altercast into a subordinate role by followers who "took over," they did indeed engage in significantly less task-relevant activity themselves and increased their activity in social-emotional areas (showing solidarity, agreeing, showing tension release). On the other hand, when confronted with followers who were willing to follow, the subjects significantly increased their task-relevant behaviors (giving suggestions, making opinion statements) and decreased their activity in social-emotional areas. Further, even though the quality and number of actual task-relevant suggestions made by the confederates was constant in the two situations, postexperimental questionnaires revealed that the subjects attributed a significantly greater amount and quality of suggestion to the confederates who had cast them (the naive subjects) into a subordinate role. It was as though the subjects were justifying to themselves their failure to lead. Two final results of interest are depicted in Table V. When the confederates assumed a passive role, the increase in task answers was much larger for natural leaders than for nonleaders. On the other hand, task questions (a measure of

Table V. Natural leaders versus natural nonleaders when followers assume an active versus a passive role

	TASK ANSWERS Confederates		TASK QUESTIONS Confederates	
	Active	Passive	Active	Passive
Natural leaders	54.23	70.41	12.24	13.80
Natural nonleaders	55.36	64.68	11.21	18.32

Mean numbers indicate answers offered or questions asked. When confederates are passive, leaders offer more answers while nonleaders solicit more answers from confederates. (From Beckhouse et al., 1975, Table 3, p. 564.)

direction being solicited *from* other members of the group) increased more among natural nonleaders when the confederates became passive.

The study by Beckhouse et al. underlines the dyadic character of leadership. It is a function of the expectations, perceptions, and behaviors of both leaders and followers. Leadership is a relationship between people in a social situation, and those who exercise leadership in one situation may not be able to do so when some aspect of the situation changes. The aspects of situations that may change include the needs of followers, the external environment of the group, the number and identity of group members, and many more. In the face of such changes, stability in a leader's personal style, level of expertise, and approach to problems can become a genuine liability.

Crises and change in leadership

A CRISIS is a situation in which something must be done quickly to prevent or at least delay negative consequences. A crisis calls for immediate, decisive action, and failure to act in a crisis has caused the downfall of many leaders. Bass (1960) points out that "In emergencies, it requires great ability and power for a leader to delay, to withhold decisive action without losing . . . control of the group under threat" (p. 438). One of the interesting things about this demand for fast action is that delay or inaction may be the most effective strategy, but ultimate effectiveness is not likely to be of great concern to a group under threat.

Simultaneously with the pressing need for action in a crisis, there arises in group members a need for cognitive clarity, a need to understand why the crisis has occurred. This, of course, has obvious adaptive advantages. If one understands why a crisis has occurred, one can fix the blame, take corrective measures, and avoid such crises in the future. Here group members have several options. They can (1) blame themselves, (2) find an external circumstance or scapegoat that supposedly caused their problem, (3) blame the group leader, or (4) use any combination of the foregoing. Consider these options. Blaming themselves is a psychologically uncomfortable and unsatisfying solution in most circumstances (Wicklund and Brehm, 1976) and will occur rarely. Finding an external circumstance or scapegoat is much more satisfying in terms of one's self-image. Hoffer (1951), in fact, argues that the ability to identify scapegoats and blame them, convincingly, for a group's problems has enabled many an ineffective leader to maintain his or her position of power:

> Like an ideal diety, the ideal devil is omnipotent and omnipresent. When Hitler was asked whether he was not attributing rather too much importance to the Jews, he exclaimed: "No, no, no! . . . It is impossible to exaggerate the formidable quality of the Jew as an enemy." Every difficulty and failure within the movement is the work of the devil, and every success is a triumph over his evil plotting (p. 87).

When no convenient scapegoat is available, the difficulty most people have in blaming themselves for failure often causes them to hold the group leader responsible for the crisis confronting the group. Marshall (1927) presents some intriguing data suggesting that a leader is even likely to be held responsible for things he or she cannot control. In the 100-year period between 1824 and 1924, there were 25 presidential elections. During this time, of course, the economy of the United States was primarily agricultural, and periods of drought constitute a severe crisis in any agricultural economy. Marshall reports that for 13 of the presidential elections, the rainfall in the preceding 4 years was below average and that the incumbent party was ousted from the presidency in 11 of these 13 elections. For the remaining 12 elections, the rainfall was above average in the preceding 4 years. In 11 of these 12 elections, the incumbent party maintained control of the presidency.

A number of other historical and biographical studies suggest that leaders are blamed for crises, even when they are not at fault, and will be ousted if they do not move quickly. We have already noted how Herbert Hoover was blamed for the Great Depression (Barber, 1972) and was defeated by Franklin Roosevelt in 1932 because he failed to initiate any dramatic steps to convince people that something was being done to invigorate the economy. Roosevelt, on the other hand, won a great deal of popularity by making many rapid decisions in his attempts to cope with the Depression. And his popularity seemed to be independent of the effectiveness of those decisions (Bass, 1960). As plausible as many of these historical analyses may be, they are ambiguous. We simply cannot know what the crucial factor was in Herbert Hoover's fall from grace or what factors influenced the presidential elections between 1824 and 1924. Fortunately, experimental studies have addressed the issue of what happens to leaders in times of crisis.

Hamblin (1958), for example, set up 24 three-person groups and assigned them the task of discovering the rules in a modified shuffleboard game. They were to do this essentially by guessing and trying various things. A red light was to flash when they violated a rule, and a green light was to come on each time they scored. The experimental session was divided into two periods. During the first period, all groups were treated alike. Their interactions were observed and coded in terms of who made suggestions, how frequently suggestions were made, and whether or not suggestions were accepted. By the end of the first period, most groups had discovered the rules of the game and were doing quite well, making successful shots, and surpassing the scores of some high school groups they had been given for comparison. In the second period, half of the groups (the control groups) continued as in the first period. For the remaining groups (the crisis groups), a crisis was introduced at the beginning of the second period by changing the rules of the game—unannounced to the group members, of course.

Procedures that were permissible before the change were now against the rules; procedures that were against the rules now became permissible. Lights had been used in teaching the participants the original rules and they could be used in indicating the changes. As the participants saw it, they were receiving red lights for doing the very things for which they had been receiving green lights. But this was not all. As soon as the participants learned a new rule and received a green light, the rule was changed again . . . As they saw it, their leads vanished, and then their scores fell farther and farther behind those of their rivals (p. 326–327).

Hamblin reports that this situation was genuinely involving for the subjects and that there was much running about, shouting, and a real perception of threat in the crisis groups when the rules were changed.

On the basis of observers' recordings, group members within each group were ranked on the amount of influence they exerted in period I. Similar observations made during period II revealed whether the person who had emerged as the leader in period I continued to lead in period II. The results appear in Figure 2. As the figure shows, for the control groups, the person who was most influential in period I was also most influential in period II. The crisis groups on the other hand, turned to another leader when the original leader's suggestions failed in period II. The person who was second in amount of influence exerted in period I usurped the leadership position in period II. It is important to note, however, that this was not because the latter's suggestions were more effective. The groups continued to do poorly even with new leaders.

2. Relative amounts of influence of group leaders in Periods I and II. Period I proceeded normally, but a crisis was precipitated in the crisis groups during Period II. In this condition, the second-ranking members emerged as the new leaders of the crisis groups. In the control groups, no change in leadership occurred. (From Hamblin, 1958, Figure 3, p. 332.)

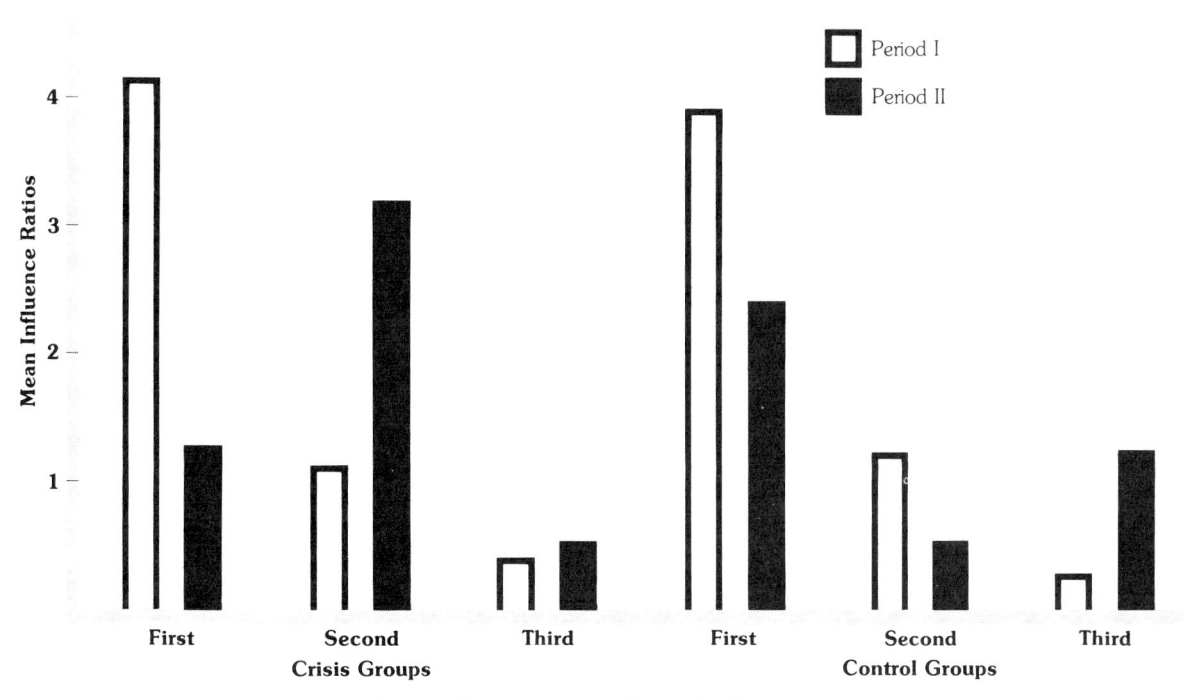

The second-ranking persons in the control groups did not, of course, emerge as new leaders in period II. Even though they were as qualified as their counterparts in the crisis groups, there was no need for them. Hoffer (1951) makes this point on a more grandiose scale with respect to mass movements:

> there is no doubt that the leader cannot create the conditions which make the rise of a movement possible. He cannot conjure a movement out of the void. There has to be an eagerness to follow and obey, and an intense dissatisfaction with things as they are, before movement and leader can make their appearance. When conditions are not ripe, the potential leader, no matter how gifted, and his holy cause, no matter how potent, remain without a following (p. 103).

Recently Firestone, Lichtman, and Colamosca (1975) provided some additional experimental evidence extending and confirming Hamblin's results. Five-person discussion groups were confronted with a medical emergency—an incipient diabetic coma—by an experimental confederate posing as one of the group members. Prior to this emergency, a leader had been either elected for the group by an apparent consensus of the members or appointed by the experimenter. Further, on the basis of observational data, the elected and appointed leaders were either high or low in discussion group leadership ability (LGD). That is, they either had or did not have a relatively high rate of making suggestions and attempting to control the discussion in an earlier group session.

Of interest here is what happened to these various types of leaders when the medical emergency occurred. Firestone, et al. defined leadership overthrow as occurring whenever someone other than the designated leader directed the help offered or served as the intermediary with the victim. The results are shown in Table VI. Whether the leader had been appointed or elected was relatively unimportant in his or her being maintained or overthrown during the emergency. However, leaders who were high in discussion group leadership ability (those who tended to make suggestions at a high rate) were more likely to be maintained during the emergency than those low in that ability.

In times of crisis, a leader who does not act quickly will be deposed. The manner in which a leader is deposed is seldom dramatic; there are usually no armed revolutionaries fighting in the streets. When a crisis occurs and the leader fails to act, group members simply allow themselves to be influenced by someone else. They begin to take someone else's suggestions and accord that someone greater esteem and status than before. The old leader simply "fades away."

Summary

We began this chapter by defining leadership in terms of interpersonal influence and pointing out that, within most groups, leadership is distributed quantitatively among various group members. We then examined some of the early research, which attempted to identify leaders under the assumption that leadership was not simply a matter of greater or lesser influence, but was a capacity that some people had and others did not. Observations of both captive and free-roaming animals revealed the existence of clearly defined dominance hierarchies in many species. Further, dominance in animal societies was usually correlated with certain characteristics such as age, sex, weight, and height. This fact, coupled with successful and widespread testing of human intelligence, encouraged many people to believe that the characteristic(s) associated with leadership ability in humans could be similarly identified and measured. We also discussed the "Great Person" approach to leadership. Since it is difficult to remember the complex social circumstances

Table VI. Effect of conferral process and perceived ability on leadership continuity during a crisis

Leader type and conferral process	Maintained	Overthrown
Low LGD, Elected	4	9
Low LGD, Appointed	1	6
High LGD, Elected	13	0
High LGD, Appointed	5	1

LGD means discussion group leadership ability. (From Firestone, et al., 1975, Table 3, p. 347.)

surrounding historical events, we tend to focus on some prominent actors associated with the events and forget the rest.

The search for characteristics of leaders revealed several personality traits that seemed to differentiate leaders and followers. In a wide variety of groups, leaders were generally found to be more intelligent, persistent, and dependable than their average followers. However, the strongest finding to come out of the search for leader attributes was that the personal characteristics of leaders must be relevant to their followers' needs, activities, and goals. Even within one group, the qualities necessary for successful and effective leadership may change as the group's external and internal environments change. We then looked at some experimental evidence bearing on the situational approach to leadership and found that many groups have two leaders—one who is primarily concerned with task-relevant activities and one who is primarily concerned with social–emotional relationships within the group. Similarly, the middleperson in a hierarchy is often subjected to conflicting expectations and demands by those above and below.

Fiedler's contingency model of leader effectiveness represents one of the few attempts to systematize the vast literature on the relationship between a leader's style and the situation in which he or she must lead. Although the relationship is not perfect, controlling leaders fare somewhat better in situations either very favorable or very unfavorable to leadership, and easy-going leaders do better in moderately favorable or unfavorable situations.

We then turned to the process of leadership and, in particular, to the view of leadership as a transaction between leaders and followers in which each party benefits and to which each contributes. The perceived legitimacy of the leader is important in the reciprocal influence between leaders and followers. Several variables contribute to legitimacy: (1) the leaders' perceived ability to deal with the tasks confronting the group, (2) the leader's apparent motivation to deal with those tasks and/or interest in the group's welfare, and (3) the perceived source of the leader's authority.

Finally, we discussed leadership and crises. When a crisis occurs and the leader of a group fails to act, a new leader is likely to emerge.

VII

Social psychology and the environment

15

Environmental psychology

418 *The urban environment*

The suburban way of life
City life
Cognitive representation of cities
   "Images"
   Beneath the surface
Neighborhoods
   Roots and uprooting
The cognitive mediation of stress
Environmental load
   Adapting to overload
   Attention and altruism
Effects of noise
   In the laboratory
   In the street

433 *The natural environment*

Weather and behavior
Effects of heat
Suicides and mental hospital admissions
The value of wilderness
Energy conservation

440 *Summary*

The "Green Revolution" is upon us. In the past decade, increasing concern has been voiced about smog and pollution, the exploitation of our natural environment, and the need for energy conservation. Other voices cry out about the dangers of our overpopulated world and our crowded cities. Social psychologists have explored some of these issues, and now the emerging discipline of environmental psychology investigates the psychological aspects of environmentally related issues. In this chapter and the one to follow, we will discuss what environmental psychology is, focus on some of the questions it has raised, and describe some of the answers that research in environmental psychology suggests.

Irwin Altman, a leading figure in the field, has defined environmental psychology in a way that the majority of environmental psychologists would probably agree with. According to Altman (1976), the subject matter of ENVIRONMENTAL PSYCHOLOGY includes how people perceive, represent, and come to terms with their environment (see Figure 1).

Environmental psychology deals with the effects of places. These places may be those that people have built, such as offices, homes, neighborhoods, cities, or submarines. Alternatively, the places may be part of the natural environment, such as national parks, deserts, tornado-prone areas, or arctic regions. Salient features of both the natural and the built environment have been studied. These include pollution, crowding, weather, territoriality, privacy, land use, and transportation.

Figure 1 lists certain important processes and behaviors in which various types of actors engage. These processes and behaviors (such as cognitive mapping, spatial behavior, territorial behavior, and efforts to attain privacy) are used by individuals, small groups, and larger social units in a variety of places or settings. Although (or perhaps because) the field is young, it is consumed with fiery visions, boundless energy, and youthful enthusiasm. A field that ranges from the physiological effects of crowding to the effects of air pollution, and from land-use legislation to architectural interventions to improve hospital and prison facilities, is so broad that only a sampling of it can be conveyed in two brief chapters. However, our goal is to describe some representative areas of study in the field and use the Altman framework to look at important issues involved in several settings.

In this chapter, our major focus will be on the built environment, especially on urban settings. We will describe the urban setting and contrast it with the suburban way of life. Among the processes and behaviors we will note in this chapter are the way we cognitively "map," or represent to ourselves, the urban environment, the way in which high levels of stimulation overload and even stress us, and how we react to high noise levels—a major urban problem. While much of our discussion will focus on the reactions of individuals, we will also consider families, and an entire section will be devoted to a discussion of the neighborhood. Some other important issues (such as privacy, territoriality, personal space, and crowding) will be discussed in Chapter 16.

The last portion of this chapter will be devoted to the natural environment—especially to climate and the conservation of energy. Although we have treated the natural environment in less detail than the built environment, environmental psychologists are equally concerned with both of these issues. In a recent chapter in the *Annual Review of Psychology,* Stokols (1978) has summarized a large body of research on attitudes toward the natural environment.

The urban environment

The social ills of the 1960s and 1970s seemed to center on our cities. Crime in the streets, poverty, inadequate housing—all are a part of modern city life. Yet the city is an exciting and diverse place to live. While environmental psychologists have only recently begun to study the effects of city life, sociologists have long been interested in the city. Let us first look at what the sociologists have found and then return to research by psychologists.

With the coming of the industrial revolution and the rapid growth of cities, sociologists began to ask how the urban way of life affected behavior and social organization. They tried to relate the urban lifestyle to social pathologies. In particular, they wanted to know whether high-density living and the hustle and bustle of city life contributed to increases in crime, mental illness, and family disorganization.

Early in the twentieth century, George Simmel pointed out that, in contrast to the relative peace and quiet of the country, people in cities are constantly bombarded with an overabundance of complex stimuli. Milgram (1970) cites some sobering statistics in support of Simmel's contention. He writes that the Regional Planning Association has calculated that if you work in Nassau County, which is a suburb of New York City, you could meet 11,000 other people within a 10-minute driving radius of your office. You could certainly find a date without venturing far from the office! But consider this. If you worked in Newark, New Jersey, a city with a population of several hundred thousand, that same 10-minute drive would give you the opportunity to meet more than twice the number of people you could meet in Nassau County. But we're still in minor league standards. If you worked in New York City, with an excess of 8 million people, you could meet about 220,000 in your 10-minute spree. Staggering, isn't it? In New York City, you could meet about as many people in a 10-minute foray as there are in all of Newark.

1. Irwin Altman's view of the subject matter of environmental psychology is used as an organizing framework in this chapter and in the section on crowding in Chapter 16. (From Altman, 1976, p. 103.)

Actors	Processes/Behaviors	Places
Individuals (young, old, personality, etc.)	Environmental Perceptions and Behaviors (cognitive mapping, environmental preferences and attitudes, aesthetics, etc.)	Built Environment (homes, neighborhoods, cities, extreme environments)
Small Groups (families, teams, small work units, etc.)	Social Processes (privacy, territory, personal space, crowding, spatial behaviors)	Natural Environment (land, vegetation, resources)
Larger Social Units (neighborhoods, communities, cities, etc.)		Associated Issues (energy, pollution, land use, transportation)

Louis Wirth, an urban sociologist, notes that large numbers of people increase the likelihood that a city dweller will encounter a very heterogeneous population. Compare the types of people you are likely to meet on the streets of Manhattan with the types you will meet in the suburbs. A walk down Broadway in Manhattan is likely to take you past a man hobbling along on a cane, a group of Hare Krishna members, someone prophesying the apocalypse, several Columbia University students eating ice cream at the Baskin Robbins ice cream parlor, a drunk huddled against the wall, a handicapped person in a motorized wheel chair, two mothers pushing baby carriages, two men picketing a barber shop, and you still haven't gotten to the end of the block. A walk down Oakey Drive in suburban Kendall Park is likely to take you past two children riding tricycles, three children riding bikes, a teenager on a moped, three mothers pushing baby carriages, and two men mowing their lawns. The suburban population is also much more homogeneous ethnically and economically.

Another sociological tradition is the analysis of the neighborhood. Interest in this topic began with the work of Robert Park, who was identified with the Chicago school of sociology. Park was concerned with such issues as the types of interaction that take place in housing units, playgrounds, and neighborhoods. His ideas stimulated pioneering studies in PSYCHIATRIC EPIDEMIOLOGY, which relates emotional disorders to local social conditions.

In a well-known study entitled *Mental Disorders in Urban Areas,* Faris and Dunham (1939) looked at the distribution of such disorders as paranoid schizophrenia and manic depressive psychosis in the various neighborhoods of Chicago. Their findings are intriguing. If you look at where patients lived prior to their hospitalization, you find that the greatest number come from the center of the city, and the number decreases steadily as you move from the center to the outer edges of the city. This same pattern has been observed for the distribution of unemployment, juvenile delinquency, infant mortality, and other social ills. Faris and Dunham also found that different psychiatric disorders are concentrated in different types of areas. Most of the paranoid schizophrenics are found in the rooming-house districts in the central core of the city. Manic depressives, however, live closer to the suburbs in the higher rental areas.

Faris and Dunham related psychiatric and social problems to community characteristics. Residents in the rooming-house districts lived a life of isolation. According to Faris and Dunham, the lack of communication with neighbors was an important contributor to their schizophrenic disorder. Since the research was correlational, however, it is impossible to determine whether schizophrenics choose to live an isolated life and therefore gravitate to rooming houses, or whether marginally schizophrenic individuals develop a full-blown psychosis because of their isolation. Moreover, a great deal of recent research suggests that schizophrenic and manic depressive psychosis have an organic basis. Nevertheless, a life of isolation is likely to encourage bizarre behaviors.

In order to understand the city environment, let's examine how different it is from life in the suburbs.

THE SUBURBAN WAY OF LIFE

Sociological concern with the neighborhood led to studies of the effects of suburban as well as city living. One well-known study, *the Levittowners,* (1967) was published by Herbert Gans, a defender of the suburban way of life. (See Box A for a dissenting view.) He finds that people's lives are not drastically changed by the move from city to suburb. In general, the time it takes to commute from home to work is not significantly greater than it was before. Most of the commuters in Gans's sample report spending more time with their family after the move than before. The typical suburbanite is also less bored than when he or she lived in the city, probably because of the many tasks that must be done to maintain the home. Lawns must be mowed, fences erected and painted, gardens weeded, windows puttied, and other jobs completed, even though there is never enough time. Moreover, when a new community is first developed, residents must cope with numerous difficulties (such as how to replace mudflats with lawns, rectify problems created

The urban environment, in many cases bleak, crowded and containing an abundance of complex visual stimuli, has long afforded behavioral scientists with both a "laboratory" to study behavior and a setting in which to effect change. (Bobbi Carrey/The Picture Cube)

420
Social psychology
and the environment

421
Environmental
psychology

A. The Poet's Image of Suburbia

Gans's view of life in the suburbs is a positive one, and we have described some of the positive features he sees in suburban living. Yet to others, suburban living is intolerable. Particularly offensive is the plastic sameness of dwellings in housing developments. More recently, developers have tried to relieve the monotony by using several variations on the front elevations of a house. One of a pair of three-bedroom colonials will sport a Tudor front and the other a more rustic facade to disguise the fact that they are the same house. Some developers have instituted a policy of offering six or seven different models (ranches, colonials, split levels, bilevels, and so on) and forbidding purchasers to select the same style house within a certain distance of a similar one. But these efforts are rather superficial. The trained eye can still detect the "little boxes" (and the other kinds of sameness) that Malvina Reynolds sang about in the early 1960s:

> Little boxes on the hillside
> Little boxes made of ticky tacky
> Little boxes on the hillside
> Little boxes all the same.
> There's a green one and a pink one
>   and a blue one and a yellow one.
> And they're all made out of ticky tacky
>   and they all look just the same.
> And the boys go into business
>   and they marry and raise a family
> Boxes made of ticky tacky
>   and they all look just the same.

by a builder trying to cut corners, and develop adequate recreational facilities). Because these needs are common to the newly arrived residents, they band together and form homeowners' associations and other social groups. Since the population is largely homogeneous in its values, these social groupings develop easily. Almost overnight, a community and a lifestyle evolve that are highly desirable to the majority of the residents. According to Gans, most of the stress that the suburbanite experiences stems from the financial crunch created by home ownership. Many people have overextended themselves financially in an effort to purchase their "piece of the rock" and find that they are now "house poor." However, since all the neighbors are in the same boat, they find ways to socialize without spending a great deal of money.

There are, however, certain groups of deviants who are adversely affected by suburban living. Two such deviant groups are the cosmopolites and the working-class. The COSMOPOLITES are people who used to live in the city, were much involved with its culture and were excited by its hectic pace and diversity. They reluctantly decided to move because of the high cost of living, rampant crime, their need for more space, and a desire for better schools. These people are generally unhappy, because they lack like-minded individuals to share their interests. They can't get involved in the hyperfertilized lawn syndrome that is a major occupation for most of their neighbors. They would rather talk of their voyage to Pisa than their trip for Pizza, and discuss the politics of European neighbors rather than the problems of their next-door neighbors. They yearn for the city and feel out of place among their neighbors. They often cope with the situation by becoming active in local civic and educational organizations and trying to persuade their neighbors to adopt their standards for education, government, and appropriate community activities. While they appear to carry more weight

The houses, the song implies, are merely outer shells reflecting similar lifestyles among people all cut from the same mold:

> And the people in the houses
>   all went to the university
> Where they were put in boxes
>   and they came out all the same.
> And there's doctors and there's lawyers
>   and there's business executives
> And they're all made out of ticky tacky
>   and they all look just the same.
> And they all play on the golf course
>   and drink their martini dry
> And they all have pretty children
>   and the children go to school
> And the children go to summer camp
>   and then to the University
> Where they are all put in boxes
>   and they come out all the same.
> Little boxes on the hillside
> Little boxes made of ticky tacky
> Little boxes on the hillside
> Little boxes all the same.

(Words and music by Malvina Reynolds, © 1962 by Schroder Music Co. [ASCAP]. Used by permission.)

than their numbers suggest, they usually lack the votes necessary to implement their policies.

A second group of deviants are the working-class people who are most financially burdened by the cost of their home. Often they are less educated than their neighbors, have different standards of child rearing, and feel socially awkward. They may have moved to the suburb directly from a neighborhood where they spent their entire lives; lacking adequate public transportation, they are cut off from family members and former friends. For them, life in suburbia is lonely and isolated.

There is a third group that has difficulty thriving in a suburban environment: the adolescent population. Recreational facilities are generally sparse, and the handful that exist are seldom within walking or biking distance. Since public transportation is usually inadequate, teenagers must either depend on their parents to transport them or find ways to amuse themselves in the absence of recreational facilities. Gans notes that some turn to delinquency, but because of family values the majority do not. Perhaps things have changed somewhat since Gans' 1967 study. The majority of suburban teenagers do not turn to crime, yet petty theft, malicious mischief, and vandalism in suburbia are increasing. Town councils have begun to seriously consider the need for providing recreational facilities and means of transportation to relieve teenager boredom. Unfortunately, these needs are recognized only after parents notice increases in teenage alcohol consumption, drug use, and sexual activity.

CITY LIFE

Every year, hordes of people flee the ravages of the city to the relative tranquility of the suburbs. What are they running from?

Ask a new arrival in suburbia why he or she left the

city and you are likely to be told, "It was the noise. I lived in a neighborhood where trucks kept rolling down the street. Horns were constantly honking. The elevated train kept rumbling by. And jackhammers banging away. Early in the morning the garbage cans would clang, and there was my neighbor's TV, and the guy across the courtyard never stopped blasting his acid rock music. I had to get out."

Ask a second person, and you get another horror story. "Crime and pollution. Every day another robbery or mugging. And the vandalism. You buy a brand new car, and you expect the radio antenna to be broken off. But they break the windows, scratch the sides with penknives and bang nails into the tires. And the dirt. The sidewalks, they're full of litter. You clean your floors and dust your windowsills and in no time they're full of soot again. There's nothing you can do about it. You look up in the sky and it's always overcast. The weather report says the sun is shining, but you'd never know it looking outside. You get accustomed to hearing the weather report that 'today's air quality is unacceptable,' and you think nothing of it. Is that any way to live?" Yet another person talks about the crowds. Crowds on the busses and on the subway. Crowds when you wait in line to cash a check at the bank. Crowds and lines at the movies. These are the views of the refugees from the cities.

Nevertheless, people are constantly migrating to the cities. Many of these people have returned from the suburbs to partake again of urban delights. Where else but in a large metropolitan area can they find such a wide variety of restaurants to satisfy their palates? Can anything compare with the cultural opportunities of the city? And there are so many different types of people with so many different interests, values, and beliefs that you are bound to find your niche. If you are into primal scream therapy, there's a group of devotees meeting downtown. If you are gay, there are several nightspots to choose from.

The city is different things to different people. Because perception is selectively different, people choose to emphasize differing aspects of the city. Moreover, the same features of city life mean different things to different people. Earlier in this book, we described work on person perception that demonstrated how our impression of a person differs depending on certain central traits that we believe he or she possesses.

An industrious, intelligent, witty, warm person and an industrious, intelligent, witty, cold person would appear to have very different personalities. Cities too have personalities, so perhaps our impressions of them depend on which critical traits they seem to possess. For example, some people may view the city as vibrant and thrilling. Others, looking at the same features of the city, may see it as a hassle. To the former, the crowds, noise, and traffic jams all testify to the excitement of city life. Pandhandlers are quaint, sidewalk hawkers interesting rather than annoying. How different this is from the way it appears to the person who sees the city as a nerve-wracking anthill.

Several studies have examined the way in which people cognitively represent cities. Let us look at what they have shown.

COGNITIVE REPRESENTATION OF CITIES

In order to survive in a city, we need a cognitive "map" of the area. (Even rats form mental maps of their environment. They develop a cognitive representation of the mazes in which they are trained, and this enables them to locate food when they are hungry.) Your cognitive map of a city can likewise have survival value. If you are in New York, for example, it is important to know which areas to avoid after dark, where to go for medical help, and where to find a pizzaria that is open all night. In addition to the survival value of maps, our cognitive representation of the city helps to explain our emotional reaction to it. Some cities excite us, while others are places we could just as well do without. And not everyone has the same reaction to a given city. If we understand how people represent the city, we can begin to understand how they respond to it.

"Images." An early attempt to understand the way people cognitively represent cities was made by Kevin Lynch (1960), a planner at M.I.T. Consider yourself a participant in his study. You are asked to take a walk through a city, either Boston, Los Angeles, or Jersey City. As you walk along, you look around and note things that stand out. On returning from your walk, you are asked to sketch a map of what the city looks like to you. You might try to do this now (on the basis of prior acquaintance with a city of your choice) before reading about what Lynch found. After collecting categories with reference to New York City (Figure 2).

In the first category were things that Lynch called PATHS. A path might be an expressway or a freeway—a mechanism for moving from one part of the city to another. The second feature that regularly appeared on the subjects' maps was EDGES. These are boundaries such as riverfronts that set the city off from its surroundings. A third prominent feature of the map is LANDMARKS. In New York, the Empire State Building, the World Trade Center, Central Park, St. Patrick's Cathedral, and Radio City Music Hall are well-known landmarks. A fourth category is what Lynch termed NODES. These are important transition points—places that allow you to gain access to other parts of the city. Airports, railroad stations, and bus depots are nodes. In New York, nodes include Kennedy Airport, the Port Authority Bus Terminal, and Grand Central Station. Finally, DISTRICTS figured in the maps subjects drew. Districts are prominent geographical areas such as neighborhoods. Districts in New York would include Greenwich Village, the Upper West Side, Brooklyn Heights, Harlem, and so on. Lynch suggested that people use these features to form an IMAGE of the city. Because some of these features are more prominent in some cities than in others, some cities are easier to form an image of and evoke a stronger emotional reaction than others. New York and Boston are both highly "imageable" cities.

While Lynch's work concerned people's images of cities, his ideas might be extended to the images that we have of our homes, our communities, our schools, and our houses of worship. Think for a minute about the high school you attended and see if you can draw a map of it. While Lynch's analysis never covered a school environment, let's see whether we can use his ideas to map it. Clearly the corridors and the "up" and "down" staircases function as paths along which people move from one area to another. There are sometimes restricted paths as well, such as elevators available to teachers and administrators but usually off limits to students. Edges, too, appear in schools in the form of fences and schoolyards, and signs to motorists saying "School Zone" or "Watch for Children" make it clear to all that this is a special environment differentiated from its immediate surroundings. Schools also have landmarks: statues, plaques, and trophy cases. Lynch's other two categories, districts and nodes,

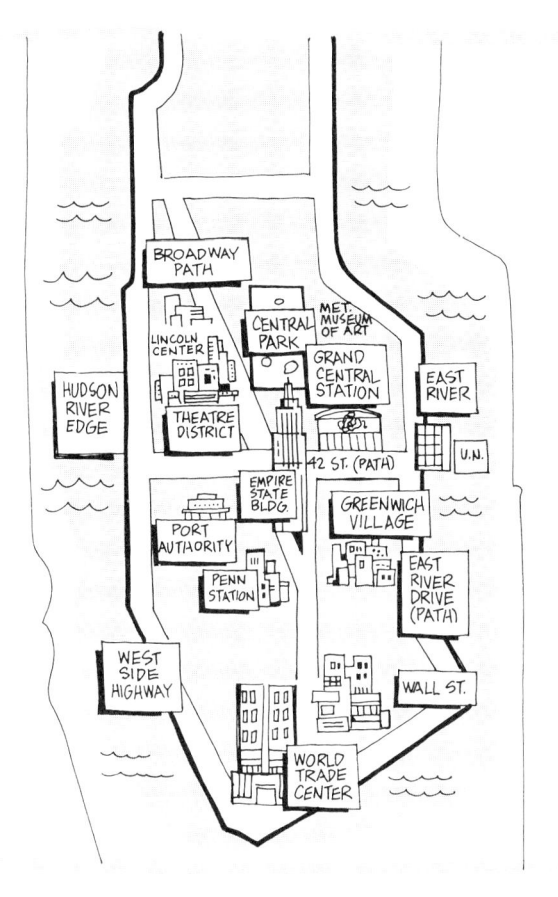

2. This cognitive map of New York City illustrates Lynch's ideas about features of cities which people most frequently visualize. *Paths* **that stand out are the East River Drive and the West Side Highway.** *Districts* **such as the theatre district and Greenwich Village, and** *Edges,* **including the East and Hudson Rivers, contribute to the image of a city. People converge on cities at central transportation hubs, for example, the Port Authority and Grand Central Station, which Lynch calls** *nodes.* **And what city does not have its** *landmarks?* **Ask anyone for a New York City landmark and the odds are that they will mention the Empire State Building.**

these maps from his subjects and interviewing them, Lynch organized the material into five categories. For the sake of our example, we will illustrate these seem less applicable to schools. On the other hand, other important categories are probably highly imageable in schools. Perhaps we could label one such category as *breaks*—places where students break out of their role as information consumers and assume other roles. In the gymnasium or on the football field, for example, students become athletes or spectators. In the auditorium, they become actors.

Beneath the surface. Lynch's work on the imageability of cities focused only on the visual surface of the environment. Wood (1971), a geographer, has extended Lynch's work by including political, economic, and social considerations as well. He was interested in learning how inhabitants pictured San Cristobal las Casas, in Mexico. In doing so, he took into account the physical features of the environment and the social institutions at the same time.

San Cristobal las Casas was selected because it has a high degree of "replicability;" there are features in the home that are replicated at the neighborhood level and at the larger level of the city itself. For example, the home has a patio, which is an open space available to the individual. At the neighborhood level, there is a common open space (the barrio plaza) that is available to residents of the neighborhood. On the citywide level, there is a central "zocalo," a square in which community activities occur. Here is a physical space replicated on the three levels of home, neighborhood, and city. There is also replication in religious and recreational activities. With respect to religion, each home has its own shrine, each neighborhood its own local church, and the city its cathedral. Fiestas are celebrated at each level of social organization, as are marriages and deaths. Thus, the functional as well as spatial aspects are important to the individual in forming an image of this city.

NEIGHBORHOODS

Terrence Lee (1970), a British psychologist has suggested that residents tend to organize information about their neighborhoods into SCHEMATA—mental pictures of the environment that represent physical space and its social significance. Lee gave people a map of their city with an X marked at the spot where their house was located. He asked them to "please draw a line around that part which you consider acts as your neighborhood or district." When he had collected a sufficient number of such maps from people located in various parts of the city, he superimposed them on a single, larger map. The picture that emerged showed that regardless of the portion of the city in which people lived, the average size of the area they considered their neighborhood was about the same—roughly 75 acres. In some high-density parts of the city, of course, these 75 acres would contain considerably more people than 75 acres in lower-density areas. But residents do not think of their neighborhood in terms of population; they think of it in terms of area. Lee finds that the number of friends an individual has is related to the *size* of the neighborhood map he or she draws rather than to density of the population found in this area. Size of area is also related to the number of clubs to which a person belongs and the person's tendency to use local shops rather than nonlocal ones.

A closer look at Lee's data revealed that community involvement was related not only to the size of the perceived neighborhood but also to the kind of neighborhood that each person perceived. A neighborhood really consists of the places you go to and consider "just around the corner" or "down the block." People who are actively involved in their community tend to know the barbershop operator several blocks east and the drugstore owner three blocks west. The involved resident uses these stores and thinks of them as part of his or her neighborhood. The uninvolved resident, on the other hand, is unaware that a better pizzaria can be found three blocks south or that a cheaper cleaning store is not far away. His perceived neighborhood is not extended by the presence of these shops. Lee believed that the neighborhood extended through the area within a ½-mile radius of the individual's home. He drew a circle representing a ½-mile radius extending from the person's home on a map of the city and counted how many shops, dwelling units, and amenity buildings (such as churches and schools) were located wtihin that area. He then looked at how many of these buildings the subject included on the neighborhood map that he or she drew (see Figure 3). Lee found that those people who were more involved in their communities drew maps with a greater number of shops and amenity buildings than people who were less involved and active in their neighborhood.

Roots and uprooting. To Lee, the neighborhood is an important institution. It can provide the individual with a sense of belonging and security. Lee conducted a study of bussing in England based on that assumption. He compared teachers' ratings of the degree of adjustment of children who walked to school and children who were bussed. He found that, given equal time to make the trip to school by foot or by bus, the children who were bussed were rated less well adjusted. Through a series of other comparisons, Lee was able to demonstrate that this difference could not be accounted for on the basis of child-rearing practices or ethnicity. He prefers to explain this finding on the basis of the neighborhood concept. He believes that children who are bussed are unfamiliar with the neighborhood of the school. All they really know is the path they observe through the bus window on the way to school. Once the bus drops them off, they feel cut off from their home neighborhood. Since urban bussing in the United States is undertaken to relieve social ills, the possibility that it may create one warrants further study.

There is some other evidence that Lee is correct about the importance of neighborhoods for the psychological well-being of many individuals. In recent years, the federal government in this country has constructed many housing projects for the poor. These houses provided adequate space, plumbing, heating, and electricity for poor families who formerly lived in run-down slum dwellings. Yet many people became more unhappy after they moved from their old slum neighborhoods to the new houses in other neighborhoods.

There seems to be a number of reasons for this dissatisfaction. Marc Fried studied the largely Italian

3. Schema A and Schema B represent maps made by two housewives living next door to each other. Their hypothetical neighborhood is represented by the circle with the half-mile radius drawn around their homes, but person A has a very different picture of the neighborhood than person B. Although both women think of their neighborhood as covering approximately the same amount of area, person B's neighborhood includes more shops and amenity buildings. On the basis of these maps Lee would predict that housewife B would be more highly involved in her neighborhood than housewife A.

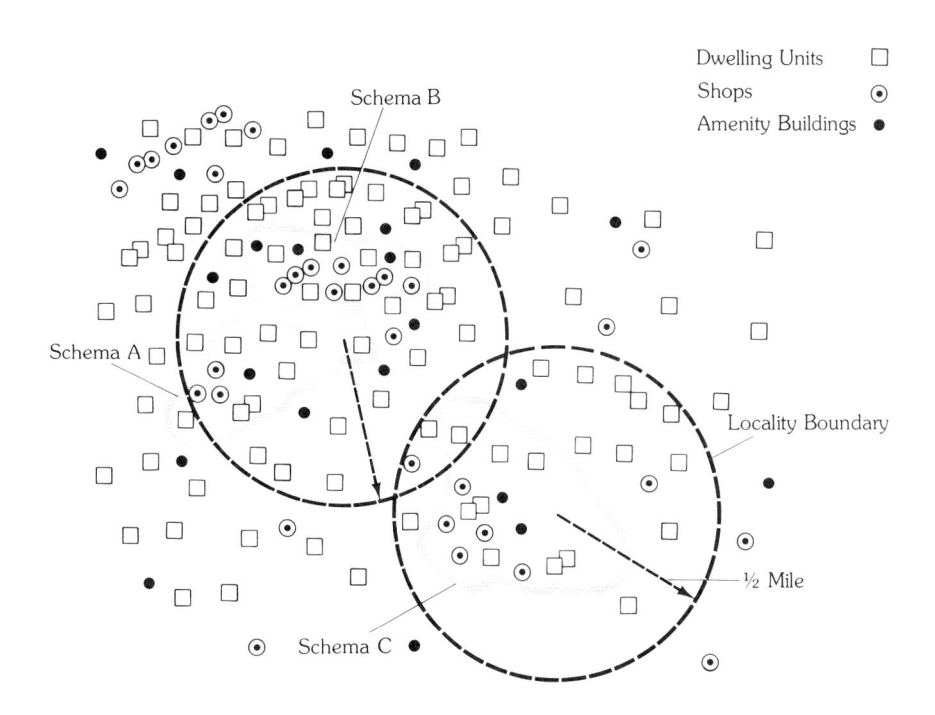

population of Boston's West End, who were forced to relocate as part of an urban redevelopment project. Prior to redevelopment, the West End of Boston was a cohesive and warm environment. The largely working-class inhabitants shared a common set of experiences, social activities, and values. For West Enders, home was not just an apartment but a whole area, full of familiar shops, churches, schools, friends, and acquaintances. When forced to relocate, many people suffered severe grief reactions and were upset and depressed for months and years afterward. They felt alienated in their new environment. When their run-down houses were destroyed, they felt that an important part of them had died. Further, patterns of living to which they were accustomed ceased to exist. In the old neighborhood, men spent most of their time with men, and women with women. The new surroundings discouraged the traditional pattern of same-sex groupings, and couples were isolated in their own homes. While many would applaud this increase in intimacy, it had adverse effects on some of the marriages studied.

Patterns of interaction differ in lower- and middle-class neighborhoods. About 60 percent of lower-class residents find their neighborhoods very satisfactory (Foote, et al., 1960; Fried, 1963). The same percentage of middle-class residents find their neighborhoods satisfactory, but the reasons for the satisfaction of these two groups differ. In lower-class neighborhoods, people are part of important social networks. Their close friends live nearby. It is a small and often warm world. People cooperatively adapt to the limitations of poverty, provide child care for each other, and in countless ways help to make each other's lives more livable (see Box B).

Herberle (1960) found that the intensity of social interaction decreases as one moves from working-class areas to upper-income residential suburbs. For lower-class residents, neighborhood satisfaction is related to the presence of close friends in the nearby vicinity. If close friends are neighbors, people are satisfied. For the middle class, the physical proximity of friends is not so important. They tend to form friendships based on common interests. Neighbors tend to be casual acquaintances (Blum, 1964; Herberle, 1960; Gans, 1961). Certainly there are serious problems in poverty-stricken neighborhoods, but it is generally possible for people to work out some sort of satisfactory lifestyle.

Ittelson, et al. (1974) suggest that a person's cognitive representation of his or her city is related to factors such as age, sex, and race. They note that the students of U.C.L.A. had an image of Los Angeles which was quite different from the one that black residents in Watts had. While the students at U.C.L.A. saw various features of the whole city, the view from Watts focused mainly on the county hospital and the jail.

We have begun our discussion of the urban environment by looking at the cognitive representation of the city, because we believe that an important determinant of people's reactions to their environment is how they think about it. The popular press frequently depicts the city as a stressful environment. Yet research has failed to find any clear pattern indicating that people are negatively affected by the stresses they encounter. One of the reasons for this may be the role of cognitive processes in mediating reactions to stress.

THE COGNITIVE MEDIATION OF STRESS

Richard Lazarus has conducted extensive research on psychological stress. He believes that, in order to understand how a person is affected by a stressful event, we must first ask what he or she thinks of that event—or, in Lazarus's terms, appraises it. Consider the following experiment. Subjects viewed a film depicting gruesome industrial accidents, such as a board flying off a table saw and impaling a worker. In the control condition, subjects' heart rate and skin conductance were recorded as they watched. These physiological measures were used to measure the subjects' stress. Lazarus found a noticeably accelerated heart rate and level of skin conductance and reactivity in subjects who had just seen the filmed accidents. He used these data as his baseline condition—an indication of the standard response to these gruesome events.

The point of Lazarus' experiment was to demonstrate that the stressfulness of these scenes could be modified depending on how the subject appraised the information. He used a clever technique to do this. He superimposed a sound track on the film. In one condition, the sound track gave a highly intellectualized account of what the subject was viewing on the screen.

B. A Superstar's Boyhood Neighborhood

When outsiders hear the term *ghetto,* they conjure up images of rubble, crime, and depressing living conditions. To the youngster growing up there, however, the neighborhood often has a vibrant quality and a certain warmth despite its problems. A good example is provided by O. J. Simpson's description of what life was like in his neighborhood when he was growing up. Here is how he described life in the Potrero Hill district of San Francisco, as it appeared in an interview in *Playboy* magazine:

> . . . PLAYBOY: How much trouble did you get into when you were young?
>
> SIMPSON: Oh, I wasn't bad, just mischievous. Some of that had to do with growing up in the Potrero Hill district of San Francisco, which to me was the greatest place in the world. My mother worked—my father didn't live with us—and me, my brothers and my two sisters always had a terrific time. Blacks talk about other blacks' bein' your brothers and sisters, and that applies even more in the projects, where everybody's momma is your momma and three or four nights a week you'll be eatin' over at somebody else's house. It's like living in a Federally funded commune. On a real level, Potrero Hill was an area where 70 percent of the people were on welfare, and it's bullshit to think they sat on their asses waiting for Government checks, because the fathers were always out looking for jobs, but there wasn't any work for them. I wasn't aware of all that, of course. To me, Potrero Hill was America the Beautiful, and I think most of the people who lived there felt the same way. I remember that at world-series time, everybody would crowd around a radio to listen to the games, and when the national anthem was played, the whole room would stand up. Everybody—mothers, fathers, kids—would be on their feet, and this was in the projects. Mostly, I remember all the adventures we had. There was a polliwog pond, railroad tracks, a lumberyard and lots of factories nearby, and in the summer, when there wasn't anything to do, somebody would say, "Hey, let's go hit the pie factory." So we'd go down there, sneak around the fence and set up what looked like a little bucket brigade, and we'd steal maybe 30 pies. My favorite was blackberry; man that was good. Or we'd hit the Hostess Bakery or the milk factory. We had a good group of dudes and my best friends then are still just about my best friends now. We also had the toughest gang on Potrero Hill; couldn't nobody whup us on the Hill. . . .

O. J. Simpson and his friends adapted to the problems of their neighborhood. They were able to find ways to make it home, a refuge and haven from the outside world.

(Originally appeared in *Playboy* Magazine, © 1976 by Playboy)

By intellectualizing what they saw, subjects reinterpreted the meaning of the event, and it became less stressful. This reduction in stress was obvious in the physiological recordings obtained. In contrast, heightened stress reactions were observed when a different sound track, pointing out and emphasizing all the gory details, was superimposed. The study nicely illustrates that the severity of stress reactions depends on how we appraise the situation. In a city, we can become stressed by the sight of a panhandler if we appraise him as dangerous. On the other hand, if we consider him a quaint diversion, we are unlikely to be stressed. More generally, appraising the environment as uncontrollable increases our stress reactions.

No doubt some people consider even the most benign environments threatening. But this is the exception. The threats that many city dwellers attach to various aspects of the urban environment are genuine. The threats may sometimes be to their safety, but there are also threats to their psychological well-being. What is it about the urban environment that can threaten a person's sense of psychological and emotional well being? One useful answer lies in the concept of environmental load.

ENVIRONMENTAL LOAD

People have limited capacities to attend to environmental stimuli. Imagine that you have a final exam in social psychology next week and have returned home to visit your family for the weekend. The only place available for study is the kitchen table. While you are trying to read this text, your mother is talking on the telephone, your teenage sister is listening to rock music, your little brother is watching TV, your father is using the power saw in the basement, and the dog is barking. It would not be surprising if, under these conditions, you had a difficult time concentrating on your reading. You would probably have even greater difficulty if the lighting in the kitchen were inadequate and you could smell food cooking. Each of these distractions competes for your attention and depletes your limited supply of it. Given the pressure of having to study for the exam, you would probably feel stressed under these conditions. Sheldon Cohen has proposed the concept of ENVIRONMENTAL LOAD to explain how environments stress people. The load an environment imposes is the degree to which it taxes the amount of attention available to you. Attention is needed not only to perform work, but also to engage in social behavior. What happens when we are placed in an environment that overloads our attentional capacities?

Adapting to overload. We humans are highly adaptive creatures. Perhaps this ability to adapt to difficult environmental circumstances has enabled us to survive for as long as we have. One way in which we adapt to an overloaded environment is to develop a set of priorities to handle incoming information. We are like successful busy executives, telling our internal secretaries which calls to put through and which to hold, which letters to respond to immediately and which to throw out, which appointments to schedule immediately and which to delay. We make decisions, sometimes conscious and sometimes not, about which information we will attend to. Usually, we attend to the inputs most relevant to the task most important to us and sacrifice attention to less relevant inputs. Sitting in the kitchen trying to study for your exam, you would probably consider your mother's remarks about your brother's problems at school less relevant and pay less attention to them than to the material in the text.

In addition to developing priority systems, we activate a monitoring process that evaluates inputs in order to decide how important they are and how we will respond to them. Some inputs indicate the existence of a problem that demands an immediate response. If we can predict when such inputs will occur, we need not constantly maintain a vigil waiting for them. Other inputs are unpredictable, however, and we have to expend a considerable amount of attention waiting for them to happen. Some stimuli are clear, while others are ambiguous. Ambiguous stimuli make us stop to interpret them and, in so doing, detract from our attentional capacity. If our environment is filled with ambiguous, unpredictable, or intense stimuli demanding immediate action, our ability to work productively and engage in satisfying social relationships will be diminished.

Finally, we can become cognitively fatigued. If you have just expended a great deal of your attentional capacity being vigilant or working in an overloaded environment, your ability to function effectively will be decreased for a while. Keeping these ideas in mind, we can examine how the urban environment is likely to affect people negatively.

Attention and altruism. Saegert, MacIntosh, and West (1975) invited people to participate in an experiment in the shoe department of Macy's in New York City. Participants were asked to look at 12 different pairs of shoes and to write descriptions of them. Half of the subjects looked at the shoes when the department was crowded and half when it was uncrowded. Later, subjects were taken to an uncrowded isolated part of the store. There, they again described the details of the shoes they had seen and also drew a map of the shoe department, including as many details as they could remember. For all subjects, paying attention to the details of the shoes had been the primary task, and picking up information about the surroundings of the department was secondary. If there were many people present while they worked on this primary task, the high density taxed their attentional capacity so that less attention could be devoted to the peripheral task of noticing their surroundings. The results of the study revealed that subjects who had originally described the shoes under crowded conditions gave less detailed information about the environment of the shoe department than subjects who had responded when the population density was lower. In both cases, however, recall for the characteristics of the shoes was equally good. This study demonstrates that attentional priorities are developed such that attention is focused on the primary task. When the environment taxes attentional capacity, low-priority tasks suffer.

Admittedly, it is no great tragedy not to remember the details of the shoe department of Macy's. But the mechanism of withdrawing attention from peripheral tasks in order to devote yourself to central tasks has high costs for social behavior. Milgram (1970) suggested that this mechanism may account for "bystander apathy" in crisis situations. Imagine that you have just emerged from a crowded bus and are walking down a densely packed street in the city. A woman is lying on the sidewalk, her face contorted in pain. Do you stop to help her? Laboratory studies by Latané and Darley have shown that as the number of other bystanders increases, the likelihood of helping decreases. They explain their results on the basis of "diffusion of responsibility" (see Chapter 10), but other factors must also be considered.

First, in the hustle and bustle of the crowded street, your attention may be focused on other things and you may not even notice the woman lying on the sidewalk. Second, you may notice the woman but, since you have less attention available, you may incorrectly evaluate the significance of cues indicating her distress. You may think she is drunk rather than hurt. Moreover, considering the number of incoming stimuli you need to process, any given stimulus may be less able to attract your attention away from the focus you have given to your own pressing needs. City life may not have hardened your heart, but it may have taxed your brain too severely.

Additional support for the idea that overload lessens our ability to respond helpfully to distress cues appears in a study by Sherrod and Downs (1974). In the laboratory, they simulated either overloaded or adequate environmental conditions. All subjects had to proofread some text material and detect errors that were interspersed throughout, while at the same time listening to a tape recording of a voice reading random numbers. Overloaded subjects heard the recording of random numbers together with Dixieland jazz music and the sound of a man reading prose that had nothing to do with the other information. Their attentional capacity was severely taxed and they underwent a mildly unpleasant experience. In the No Overload condition, subjects heard the random numbers together with the sound of waves lapping against the seashore—a rather soothing sound.

Sherrod and Downs also employed a condition identical to the Overload condition except that subjects were given the opportunity to turn off the distracting sounds if necessary. While equally overloaded, these subjects felt that they had some measure of control over their environment. After participating in this phase of the experiment, subjects were debriefed and told they could leave. As they left the laboratory, they encountered a second experimenter who asked if they would volunteer to help in pre-testing some experimental materials. The most help was given by subjects who had not been overloaded. The least help was given by previously overloaded subjects who had no control, while an intermediate amount of help was given by subjects who had been overloaded, but who had control. Whether overloaded subjects helped less because they were in a bad mood or because they were less able to attend to the request for help is not clear. But in either case, overload is costly to helping behavior. The results also suggest that giving people a means to control the overloaded environment will make them more likely to engage in prosocial behavior.

EFFECTS OF NOISE

Urban environments are often noisy. Truck and car horns blare, construction crews tear down buildings with explosive crashes, and airplanes land and take off with a deafening roar. What effect does all this noise have on the urban dweller?

In the laboratory. Glass and Singer (1972) conducted a program of laboratory studies investigating the effects of noise. In the typical study, subjects listened to short bursts of tape-recorded office machines, conversations, and a variety of other sounds all occurring simultaneously. These noises were either loud (comparable to a machine shop) or soft (comparable to quiet conversation), were either predictable or unpredictable, and could either be turned off or could not be controlled. Some subjects worked on such tasks as performing arithmetic computations, while others worked on more complex tasks that required them to do two different things simultaneously. For example, a subject would be required to turn a steering wheel to make sure that an arrow stayed on a line while at the same time listening to a voice reading numbers out loud in order to repeat the last number he or she heard.

In general, Glass and Singer found that loud, unpredictable, and uncontrollable sounds had the worst effects. Performance on complex tasks deteriorated markedly under these conditions. Effects were found not only while subjects were listening to the noise but also after the noise had ended. Compared to a situation in which subjects had not been exposed to noise previously, exposure to unpredictable noise, whether loud or soft, resulted in a lessened ability to detect errors on a proofreading task and a lowered toleration for frustration. Note that the type of noise that led to the worst effects in these studies is very much like the type of noise to which city dwellers are usually exposed. Most city noises, such as the passing of a garbage truck, the use of a jackhammer, or the landing of an airplane, only occur from time to time and are not usually predictable. Thus the results of the Glass and Singer research do not bode well for city dwellers.

In the street. Interestingly, some people can tolerate noise much better than others, and people seem able to exert some control over the amount of noise that bothers them. Noise at work is tolerated to a much greater extent than noise at home (Moos, 1976). Although many people complain to friends about noise, few see it as enough of a threat to do anything about it. Burrows and Zamarin (1972) studied people living near the Los Angeles International Airport. While many people considered the noise a problem because it disturbed their sleep and domestic life, only 4 percent had ever complained to the authorities. Over 40 percent stated that they were aware of the aircraft noise before they moved into the neighborhood. People who owned their own homes reported that their property had increased in value as much as property in other areas of Los Angeles. And 60 percent were unwilling to make any kind of money payment to alleviate the noise problem.

Appleyard and Lintell (1972) studied the effect of noise on neighborhood life. They looked at three San Francisco streets. One had heavy truck traffic and was very noisy; the second had moderate traffic and noise levels; the third had light traffic and low noise levels. On the noisy street, one elderly couple reported sleeping during the day to make up for the sleep they lost at night. People scurried to and from their apartments, virtually never interacting with one another on the street. In fact, they reported that their street was a lonely place to live. It may be important to note that this was a working-class Italian neighborhood similar to the West End of Boston, which we described previously. Thus the disruption of social interaction was a great loss. On the low-noise street, people engaged in a great deal of interaction. They sat together on their doorsteps and gathered in front of the corner drugstore. This street was perceived as a very friendly, sociable place.

Cohen, Glass, and Singer (1973) studied children who lived in a high-rise apartment house situated atop a busy interstate highway near its approach to the George Washington Bridge in New York City. Residents of the "Bridge apartments" live in a building in which cars and trucks pass right under them. Thus the lower the floor, the closer occupants are to the highway. Cohen believed that an important precondition for learning to read is learning to understand speech adequately. Children who live in a noisy environment may not hear words as distinctly as children living in a quieter environment. Perhaps they pay more attention to nonverbal cues and the context of what they are hearing. They do not learn to discriminate speech sounds as carefully and accurately as children raised in quieter environments. When they try to learn to read, they face a difficult task. "Sounding out a word" may not help them as much, because the exact sound of a word is not as important to them as it is to other children. Cohen found that children living on lower floors of the bridge apartments both suffered from deficits in auditory discrimination and read less well than children living on a higher floor. Reading impairment is a high price to pay for living in a noisy environment.

The federal government has become concerned with environmental problems such as noise levels and requires environmental impact statements before approving new projects that are likely to disrupt the existing environment. Sometimes interesting research studies are conducted in preparing environmental impact statements. One such study was conducted on a controversial road project scheduled to be built in New Brunswick, New Jersey, the home of Rutgers University. A bridge across the Raritan River was under construction, but construction was halted in midstream by vociferous community opposition. The road was to pass right next to several structures that served as both dormitories and classroom buildings. Two Rutgers psychologists, Larry Ward and Peter Suedfeld, conducted a field simulation to forecast the effects of this road. They tape-recorded traffic noises generated during the morning and evening rush hours on an existing section of this highway. Then they played back these sounds over loudspeakers situated outside the building so that the sound level approximated the actual sound level on the highway. They found less participation and less attentiveness in class when the noise was present than when there was no noise. Classes tended to be conducted as lectures, because discussion was difficult to carry on. Students became so annoyed that they cut the power cable to the sound equipment twice during the 3-day experimental period. Dormitory life was disrupted along with classroom activities. Students became tense and disagreeable and were generally in a bad mood during the noisy portion of the study. Accordingly, the effect of this road is expected to be rather negative.

We have examined the effect of some of the important environmental variables in urban life. In the next chapter, we will consider the effects of overpopulation, another very important aspect of urban life. Before concluding this chapter, however, let us look at some environmental research that is not concerned with the city but with the effects of weather and climate on behavior.

The natural environment

How are you affected by variations in weather and climate? Do long periods of rain depress you? When a professor we know was once considering moving to Vancouver, British Columbia, he was very concerned about the effects of the weather on his mood. Vancouver is a charming city surrounded by the spectacular Canadian Rockies and beautiful vistas. Of all Canadian cities, it probably has the most moderate climate because of the warming effects of the Japanese current. However it has a great deal of rain. Vancouverites tell visitors that if you cannot see the mountains it means that it's raining. If you can see the mountains, it means that it's going to rain. Our friend felt that a rainy climate would encourage his tendency toward mild depression. He felt the same way about extremely cold weather. The thought of bundling up in layers of clothing, donning boots, and plodding through the snow was repugnant to him. Could he adapt to these climatic changes? Given what we know about the limits of human adaptability, the answer is probably yes. But the effect of his negative attitude and unfavorable expectations are difficult to predict.

Imagine the task of a researcher trying to conduct experiments to answer this question. Laboratory studies are probably of little use. To try to understand the effects of the weather on our friend's moods, we would have to take into consideration such things as his physical health (damp weather would cause him physical pain if he had arthritis), his preferences in leisure activities, his wife's reactions, and on and on. But moods are a relatively minor issue compared with the effects of climate on such outcomes as suicides, mental illness, accident rates, work efficiency, and crime and aggression. In this section, we will discuss several studies that have examined the influence of climate on human behavior.

WEATHER AND BEHAVIOR

There is some experimental evidence that weather directly affects physiological responses and subjective reactions. People suffering from arthritis often say that they experience pain when it is damp. To test this experimentally is difficult, but not impossible. It requires the use of a sophisticated laboratory environment. Such a laboratory, called a CLIMATRON, has been created at the University of Pennsylvania. In it, 225 square feet of area are comfortably furnished so that two people can live there for long periods of time. Special devices allow the researchers to precisely vary temperature, humidity, rate of air flow, and more esoteric factors such as ion charge and ion concentration. Hollander and Yeostros (1963) asked arthritis sufferers to spend time in the climatron. They observed their behavior and obtained subjective reports of pain in response to changes in air pressure only, humidity only, and combinations of simultaneous changes in pressure and humidity. By manipulating these variables, the researchers were able to simulate the effects of stable, fair, or foul weather and of unstable (stormy) weather. Arthritis sufferers seemed to suffer less in stable weather conditions, even if the weather was foul, than they did in simulated unstable weather.

Other experiments have probed the effects of heat in somewhat less elaborate laboratory environments. One general finding is that there are no significant differences in preferred warmth. Contrary to popular opinion, old people have the same optimal comfort temperature as young people. Since they are often less active, however, they generate less body heat. So if a room is slightly chilly, they feel less comfortable than young people who are more active. Much of the research on the effects of heat has been conducted by "human factors" psychologists—researchers concerned with performance measures. In one study, Mackworth (1950) tested military personnel on such tasks as Morse code reception and visual tracking using a pursuit rotor. Subjects worked for a period of several hours in an environment in which humidity was kept constant at 67 percent but temperature varied. The results indicated that performance worsened as the temperature increased.

Colquohoun and Goldman (1968) required subjects to exercise and thus made them hotter. After sufficient exercise and exposure to temperature of about 100°F, they measured performance on a signal-detection task. The increased temperature led to more correct detections of the signal when it was present but also to more false alarms—that is, reports of hearing the signal when it was not sounded. There are many other such performance studies in the literature. In a review of this literature, Pepler (1965) concludes that psychomotor performance is negatively affected by temperature variations of between 37 and 41°F either above or below optimum. While significant, the effects are small, and whatever decrements are observed can be offset by appropriate use of incentives.

So far, we have touched on the effects of unpleasant and uncomfortable weather conditions. Rainfall, humidity, and heat may be a nuisance, but they are not dangerous conditions. Some people live in environments where the weather is actually hazardous. One example of such hazardous weather is a tornado. People living in the midwest and south know that they inhabit a dangerous environment. How do they cope with it? How do they prepare to face potential disasters?

Research on people living in tornado-prone areas reveals that psychological factors mediate reactions to these natural hazards. Sims and Baumann (1972) noticed that deaths from tornados were higher in the south than they were anywhere else in the country. Further investigation revealed that tornados in the south were not more fierce, nor was the tornado warning system in the south less effective, nor was southern housing less able to withstand the winds. Why, then, was the death rate higher in the south? The authors hypothesized that the steps that southerners took to cope with tornados must be different from those of other people and that behind their strategy were strongly held beliefs. They questioned samples of Illinois and Alabama residents about their behavior in preparation for, and in response to, tornados. They also measured the degree to which these people were internally oriented—(felt in control of their destiny) or externally oriented (felt that they were at the mercy of luck or chance). They found that the southerners were much more externally oriented than the midwesterners.

Sims and Baumann argue that this difference in orientation is responsible for the actions that these populations take in response to the threat and occurrence of a tornado. For example, the two populations differ greatly in their usage of weather bureau information in preparing for tornados. Midwesterners feel that the best way to identify tornado weather is to listen to the radio or use barometers or other weather devices. Southerners, on the other hand, would rather rely on the shape of the clouds or some other personal observations. During the tornado, midwesterners take more active steps than southerners. Southerners have a fatalistic outlook, ascribing survival to God's plan. Midwesterners, on the other hand, think of survival as luck rather than part of a master plan. Hence southerners rely less on the weather forecasts and take less action in the face of the disaster. Sims and Baumann explain the differences in terms of personality characteristics. An alternative explanation might emphasize the role of group norms about reaction to and preparation for natural hazards. Understanding the effects of the environment in this case requires a multilevel analysis, including personality, geography, and social pressures.

EFFECTS OF HEAT

There have also been a few studies of the effects of heat on social behavior. Griffitt (1970) used Byrne's attraction paradigm to investigate the effects of heat on interpersonal attraction. Recall that Byrne's research generally indicates that we like people whose opinions are similar to ours. In his study, Griffitt led half the subjects to believe that they would become acquainted with a stranger whose beliefs were similar to those of the subjects, while the other subjects expected to meet a stranger with a very different set of beliefs. Further, half the subjects in each condition were situated in an uncomfortable hot room (90°F), while the remainder worked in a comfortable room (68°F). The results indicated that attraction to the stranger was more strongly influenced by the temperature in the room than by similarity of opinions. Regardless of opinion similarity, negative evaluations were given when the room was hot.

Based on Griffitt's work, Baron (1972) expected that subjects who had been instigated to aggress would be more likely to do so if they were uncomfortably hot than if they were comfortable. Using a "Rube Goldberg" setup involving turning on the air conditioner or leaving it off and augmenting temperature with portable heaters, he paired subjects with a confederate who gave written evaluations of their work. The evaluation also consisted of the number of times the confederate delivered a 67-volt shock to the subject. Subjects given appropriate instigation to aggression received negative written evaluations and were shocked 9 out of 10 possible times. Those given little instigation to aggress received favorable evaluations and only 1 shock in 10 trials.

In the next phase of the study, the experimenter told subjects that they would participate in a learning task. The subject was led to believe that he or she would teach the confederate a list of nonsense syllable pairs. To enhance learning, the teacher delivered an electric shock when the learner made an incorrect response. The experimenter provided the teacher with an efficient incentive machine—a device in which a number of switches supposedly delivers increasingly high levels of electric shock. The teacher can choose the level that he or she wishes to deliver when the learner makes a mistake. The intensity of the shock and its duration are used as the measures of aggression. Baron found that angered subjects delivered longer and more intense shocks than less angered subjects. However, the hotter the room, the *less* intense the shock and the shorter its duration.

Baron's data contradict popular opinion (and the conclusions of the U.S. Riot Commission) that heat contributes to aggression. He offers several explanations for his finding, the most plausible of which seems to be that subjects who were hot and uncomfortable wanted to finish the experiment as quickly as possible. Here we see an example of how the constraints of the laboratory environment can lead to very different conclusions from what might be observed outside the laboratory.

In a subsequent experiment, Baron and Lawton (1972) investigated the effect of an aggressive model in the same situation. Half of the subjects in each condition saw a teacher administer frequent high-intensity shocks and were then asked to serve as teachers. The remaining subjects first served as teachers themselves and subsequently witnessed the aggressive actions of another teacher. The pattern of results for subjects who served as teachers prior to observing the aggressive model was the same as in the previous experiment. For hot subjects, however, the presence of the aggressive model led to more frequent shocks of higher intensity. One interpretation of these data is that people who take part in riots are modeling the antisocial behavior of others under conditions of hot weather and sufficient anger. An alternative explanation is that the results are artifacts of the demand characteristics of the setting. Placing subjects in hot rooms together with a model who aggresses may cue the subject that the experimenter expects this behavior. It may also create conformity pressures to behave in the same aggressive way as the model. It should be noted that there was no significant difference between the amounts of aggression the model elicited in the hot room and in the comfortable room. The only significant difference was between the Model condition and the No Model condition in the hot room. Beyond the few experimental studies we have cited, most research on the effects of heat has been correlational. The general approach involves the use of archival data such as accident rates, suicide rates, and the like.

SUICIDES AND MENTAL HOSPITAL ADMISSIONS

Several studies have attempted to relate suicides and psychiatric hospitalization to seasons of the year (see Box C for a related phenomenon). The majority of these studies have found a consistent pattern of increasing admissions to mental hospitals beginning in the spring and reaching their peak during the summer months. Admissions begin to decrease after the summer and are lowest in the winter. In a review of the evidence collected in many countries on various continents, Abe (1964) finds the same strong, consistent relationship. The fact that the same pattern occurs in cultures as different as Japan, Australia, and several South American countries suggests that the explanation is probably not culture specific. Moreover, the same seasonal pattern has been reported for suicide rates. Durkheim (1951), investigating suicides committed in the nineteenth century, found that the greatest number of suicides occurred during the summer months.

Why should this relationship between season, suicide, and hospitalization exist? The answer is not clear, but we can consider several possibilities. Some writers have suggested that mood and stress should be considered as intervening variables. Seasonal variations may affect mood, which is in turn reflected in the state of mental health. Perhaps the summer months are more stressful than the other months and lead to more negative moods. Dealing with children who are home from school, depression resulting from greater unemployment during the summer, and the discomfort of excessive summer heat may all contribute to more negative moods. The long hours of daylight provide increasing opportunities for interaction between people in public, and this, too, might increase the probability of stressful and unpleasant interactions. Children stay up later and parents have less privacy. Similarly, in the absence of air conditioning, people are likely to spend time outside in front of their homes to escape the oppressive indoor heat. There they are more likely to be forced to interact with neighbors, further limiting their privacy.

Clearly, all these suggestions are speculations. And although we have speculated about mediating social conditions that may contribute to the relationship, it is not possible to rule out the idea that the weather may contribute directly to these pathologies. Perhaps changes in air pressure, temperature, humidity, or ionization contribute to physiological stress. We have no direct evidence on these questions. The only suggestive finding is by Sanborn, et al. (1970), who, found that in New Hampshire, suicide rate increases when barometric pressure is low.

Thus far, our discussion may have inadvertently painted a one-sided picture of individual–environment transactions. As we have described noisy cities and hazardous weather conditions, people have appeared to be passive victims of the environment. Environmental psychologists, however, are more likely to subscribe to an interactional view of person and environment. People influence the environment, and the environment influences them. We will discuss two areas in which the individual actively engages the environment. The first involves the choice of recreational activities in wilderness environments. The second concerns ways in which people actively engage in conserving natural supplies of energy.

THE VALUE OF WILDERNESS

Moos (1973) emphasizes the reinforcement value of environments. By this he means that we can choose to spend time in environments that help us fulfill desired goals. Wilderness environments serve this purpose. Think about a trip to the Rocky Mountains. As you climb a moderately difficult mountain trail, you observe majestic scenery, you breathe clean air, it's quiet,

C. Madness and the Moon

Remember those midnight movies or Saturday matinee monster flicks showing werewolves or other demented creatures baying at the moon or murdering innocent victims when the moon was full? Several researchers also remembered them and conducted research to see if there was any connection between the phases of the moon and psychotic behavior.

Two researchers at the University of Miami Medical School, Arnold Lieber and Carolyn Sherin, believe that the human body can be thought of as a microcosm—a miniature world—consisting of the same chemical elements in roughly the same proportions as are found on the earth's surface. Lieber and Sherin speculate that, because the earth and the human body share this chemical similarity, they may also share other similarities. Of particular interest is the possibility that, just as the moon exerts a gravitational pull on the earth's tides, it may also exert a gravitational pull on our internal body fluids. They speculate that these internal biological tides are associated with electrolytic and hormonal shifts. These shifts change our thresholds for neural firing and subject predisposed individuals to emotional stress. With these theories in mind, Leiber and Sherin (1972) developed a model that predicted higher rates of emotional disturbances during the new moon and full moon than at other times of the month.

To test their ideas, they collected statistics on the homicide rate for a 15-year period in Dade County, Florida, and for a 13-year period in Cuyahoga County, Ohio. They developed a complex system for scoring the data and looked at the association between homicides and lunar phases. In Ohio, there was a trend showing a relationship between lunar phase and homicides, but the relationship was not statistically significant. In Dade County, however, a significant relationship was found. Homicides increased significantly at times close to the new moon and full moon phases. There are, of course, several possible explanations for the association. Our cultural myths of weird things happening when the moon is full may create expectancies for deviant behavior. Antisocial individuals may excuse their behavior to themselves by thinking that the moon made them lose control. This explanation is problematic, however, because our cultural myths deal only with the effects of a full moon, while the data also indicate an increase in homicides for the new moon phase.

Several hundred years ago, many people believed that the insane behavior of inmates in mental hospitals was caused by exposure to the moon. Staff members in mental hospitals at that time noticed that patients were more restless and active than usual when the moon was full. Benjamin Rush, a physician practicing at that time, proposed a simple explanation for the change in the patients' behavior. According to Rush, the light of the full moon illuminated the ward and disturbed the patients' sleep, because the wards had no window shades. Patients who could not sleep would wake the other patients, and a disturbance would result. So a "field experiment" of sorts was performed. Someone hung a curtain over the windows in the hospital when the moon was full. Lo and behold, the "lunar effect" diminished greatly. Perhaps someone will find a similar explanation for the Lieber and Sherin results.

---

and few people are around. Several researchers have investigated people's feelings about the value of such environments. Cicchetti and Smith (1973) gave campers in the Spanish Peaks Wilderness area in Montana an interesting choice. To see how much these campers valued their wilderness experiences, they asked them how much they would be willing to pay for a variety of wilderness experiences. The main difference between the situations they described was in the number of other people the campers would be likely to encounter. As you might expect, campers were willing to pay more for experiences that minimized the number of people they would expect to meet. Avoidance of congestion seems to be one of the values of wilderness experiences.

Before considering in greater detail the responses of students to a survey assessing the value of wilderness experiences, we might consider how the choice of recreational activity in general fits with the individual's personality. For example, what kinds of people would be most likely to benefit from experiences such as camping out alone, climbing mountains, or fishing in secluded mountain streams? Ask some gregarious people how they would feel about such a vacation, and you might well hear that they would be bored. Research on this topic seems to indicate that people who prefer this sort of isolated recreational activity are rather low in their need for affiliation.

One recent study on the value of wilderness activities was conducted by Rossman and Ulehla (1977). They gave students a Reward Value questionnaire that allowed the students to indicate the importance to them of each of 30 possible rewards they could obtain in the wilderness. The results of the questionnaire were factor analyzed, and several different factors were described. One important aspect of the wilderness was found to be the religious or spiritual experience encountered there. Respondents felt that the experience enlarged their spirits, contributed to personal growth, uplifted them, and gave them a chance to feel a part of the life cycle. A second important value of the wilderness experience was the opportunity to challenge one's survival skills—to pit self against nature. It was seen as a healthy antidote to the "soft way of life fostered by our overgrown technology." Another value of the wilderness experience is aesthetic. Communing with nature gives one the opportunity to appreciate beauty, provides a different perspective on life, and inspires a sense of tranquility. Finally, the wilderness experience provides a respite from the problems of the urban environment. Time spent in a natural environment breaks up the hectic city pace, offers a welcome change of scenery, and relieves the tensions of life.

The choice of outdoor recreational activity is one way in which a person can demonstrate ability to use the environment profitably. Another way we benefit from our natural environment is through the transformation of its resources into energy. But we have been wasteful in our use of energy. We are now painfully aware of our dependence on energy and the price we have paid for its indiscriminate use. Recent efforts by environmental psychologists have focused on applying principles of social psychology, such as attitude change techniques, and principles of behavior modification to instill attitudes favorable to energy conservation. We conclude this chapter with a description of several studies on conservation attitudes and practices.

ENERGY CONSERVATION

The winter of 1973 suddenly shocked most Americans into awareness that we face an energy crisis. Automobile fuel prices suddenly skyrocketed. Normally a routine job, filling the family car, suddenly became a chore and a source of anxiety. Long lines formed outside filling stations. Flags of different colors were used in certain states to inform motorists whether the station was rationing gas or was completely out of fuel. Many homeowners were afraid that local oil companies would run out of fuel and their houses would freeze during the cold season. The president of the United States appeared on television, urging homeowners to turn down their thermostats and to wear sweaters instead of increasing their home heating. He also announced that highway speed limits would be reduced to 55 mph nationwide, a law that is still being enforced.

Social scientists became interested in this issue. They wanted to learn why Americans failed to conserve energy and what could be done to change this behavior. The federal government attempted to change energy consumption by mounting an information campaign urging apartment dwellers to use less energy. Similar campaigns were launched by local energy conservation groups. What determines whether people try to conserve energy?

Clive Seligman and his colleagues (Seligman, Kriss, Darley, Fazio, Becker, and Pryor, 1979) provided some important answers to this question. They designed a questionnaire investigating a variety of attitudes toward the energy crisis and beliefs about energy conservation. They distributed the questionnaire during the summer to a sample of married couples living in a planned development. They also obtained records of each couple's electricity consumption during the summer months. With this information, they were able to determine how attitudes about energy predicted actual energy consumption.

Responses (given in terms of extent of agreement with various statements) could be grouped into several different types of attitudes. One group dealt with feelings about how energy conservation would affect the resident's comfort. A sample item tapping feelings about comfort was: "I find I can't relax or work well unless the house is air conditioned." A second group, typified by the statement, "American technology in the past has come to grips with all major crises and it will no doubt soon discover a solution to the energy crisis," indicated attitudes about technology's ability to solve the energy crisis. A third group of attitudes revealed the subject's opinion about whether the individual can play an important role in energy conservation. A person believing that his or her actions do matter would agree with the statement, "If everyone in the country tried to conserve energy at home, there would probably be a real impact on the nation's overall energy consumption." In addition to these three attitude clusters, the investigators found three others. One cluster consisted of beliefs that conserving energy at home requires a great deal of effort for too little dollar savings. A second cluster consisted of beliefs that conserving energy by methods such as not using air conditioners might be detrimental to the health of family members. A final attitude cluster measured the belief that the energy crisis is a hoax fabricated by oil companies so that they could raise fuel prices.

The research team investigated how well husbands' and wives' scores on each of these attitude clusters predicted their energy consumption during the summer months. They found that the most important predictor was the set of beliefs about comfort and health. The more husbands and wives perceived that energy conservation would lead to discomfort and ill health, the more energy the household consumed. Of somewhat lesser importance, but still predictive of energy consumption, were beliefs about the relationship between effort and dollar savings. The more people believed that it takes a great deal of effort to conserve energy and that the savings are only minimal, the more energy they consumed.

Knowing how these attitudes predict behavior suggests ways to try to change consumer patterns of energy consumption. For example, educating people about the health consequences of less air conditioning should help reduce the use of these devices. While no study has tried to do this, several studies have used the financial angle to change conservation behavior. According to Seligman et al., an important reason for not conserving energy is the belief that you just don't save enough money to warrant the discomfort and inconvenience of conservation measures. If ways can be found to show people that they can save a substantial amount by conserving energy, they ought to do so.

In one study using this technique, Slavin and Wodarski (1977) used energy rebates for a group of apartment residents whose energy consumption was metered on a group basis rather than individually. These conditions make it difficult to change behavior, because individuals are unaware of how much energy they are using and probably feel less responsible than they would if their apartment were individually metered. The investigators set up three conditions. In the control condition, 48 apartments whose energy conservation was monitored on 4 common meters received an appeal to conserve energy and tips on how to do it. In a Small Group condition, another group of 48 apartments was divided into 4 groups of 12 apartments each having a common meter. In addition to receiving the appeal and the tips on how to save energy, these persons were also offered a 75-percent rebate on the dollar savings corresponding to their reduced energy usage. The Large Group condition was the same as the Small Group condition, except that 2 groups of 24 apartments rather than 4 groups of 12 were used. The program was only slightly effective. Only people in the Large Group condition saved energy, and then only for the first month of the study. It appears that they found that all their energy conservation efforts resulted in only a 95-cent rebate. This was hardly worth the trouble and inconvenience that conservation necessitated.

A more successful approach to changing conservation behavior is outlined in a study by Seaver and Patterson (1976), who used operant conditioning principles to change behavior. Three groups of energy users, whose rates of consumption the previous year were equivalent, were studied during the winter and early spring of 1974. The control group received only the usual monthly delivery ticket from the oil company indicating how many gallons of oil they used and how much they paid. One experimental group also received information about the *rate* of their fuel consumption during the current delivery period compared to the same period in the previous year. The information slip also noted the dollars saved or lost compared to what the customers would have paid had they used fuel at the rate at which they used it the previous winter. The third condition gave the same information as the second condition but also provided a sticker commending the consumer for saving oil. The results of the study clearly show that people need to be commended in addition to learning about their consumption and savings in order to conserve more energy. While all three groups used less fuel than the previous year, the biggest reduction was found when the consumer was commended. There was no difference in amount of energy conservation between the feedback and the control conditions. A little praise coupled with knowledge of money saved may be one way to encourage energy conservation.

Summary

In this chapter, we discussed environmental psychology. We used Altman's framework of places, processes, and actors to look at responses to urban and natural environments. We gave considerable attention to the urban environment. Throughout our discussion, we were concerned with the ways in which city dwellers may be stressed and the possible psychological costs of living in the city. We noted some of the potentially stressful features of city life, including the large numbers and high density of people, the heterogeneity of the population, the noise, and the pollution of the urban environment. We contrasted these features with the suburban environment, looked at the suburban way of life, and sketched Gans's argument in favor of suburban living.

Next, we discussed the factors that influence how stressful city life may be. We emphasized the role of cognitive factors in mediating urban stress and illustrated this notion with Richard Lazarus's work on the mediation of psychophysiological stress. We also highlighted the importance of the neighborhood as a means for reducing the stress of city life.

We then discussed Sheldon Cohen's model of environmental load. We showed how city life may tax the attentional capacity of the urban dweller and how behaviors such as bystander apathy may result. We then turned to research on the effects of noise, which showed how the unpredictability of noise and the belief that one has little control over it can adversely affect behavior and physiological functioning. We also examined research on the effects of noise on reading impairment, classroom instruction and social behavior, and life in close proximity to airports.

The final section dealt with the natural environment. We first considered the effects of humidity and heat on performance and social behavior. Our discussion included the relationship of weather to suicides and admissions to mental hospitals. We then turned to a more pleasant topic, the value of wilderness experiences. The chapter ended with a consideration of attitudes predicting energy conservation and studies on attempts to change energy conservation practices.

16

Environmental Influences on Social Behavior

443 The use of space to regulate social behavior

Interaction distance
Spatial intrusion
   Being intruded on
   Intruding on others
The equilibrium model
Privacy
   Maintaining privacy
   Kinds of privacy needs
Territoriality
   The "home court advantage"
   Within the home
Cultural differences in human interaction

455 Crowding

The what and why of crowding
Crowded transportation settings
Sex differences in reaction to crowding
Residential crowding
   Ecological correlations
   Interview studies
Prisons
Architectural effects in reactions to crowding
"Tripling" students in two-person rooms

465 Effects of institutional environments

Total institutions
   Responses to life in total institutions
The physical environment of mental hospitals

470 Summary

We are rapidly approaching the end of this textbook. You have learned about numerous factors that influence our social behavior, perhaps more than you care to remember. Before concluding, however, we would like to discuss how environmental variables also affect social behavior.

We begin with an examination of the "hidden dimension" of social behavior (Hall, 1966), which involves how far away we stand from people with whom we are conversing, how closely we allow others to approach us, whether we look directly at them, or whether we turn our bodies toward or away from them. These behaviors are observable, but we consider them hidden because we are usually unaware of the full extent of their influence on our behavior. We will show how we use these spatial behaviors to obtain privacy. Territoriality is another aspect of spatial behavior, and we will show how it is used to structure and reflect the quality of our interpersonal relationships. This section will conclude with a look at how our use of space and the attainment of privacy differ from one culture to another.

The second section of this chapter examines the effects of crowding, a problem that frequently results from inappropriately close spacing or a lack of privacy due to an overabundance of people. We will review studies with animals and with humans in an attempt to learn whether crowding is stressful.

In the final section, we consider institutional environments, concentrating especially on mental hospitals. We demonstrate how these environments limit the privacy of their occupants and examine the types of social adjustments inmates attempt in order to cope with restricted privacy. Finally, we discuss the effects of certain architectural changes on the behavior of people living in institutions.

The use of space to regulate social behavior

INTERACTION DISTANCE

One important aspect of spatial behavior is how far we stand from others with whom we interact. Edward Hall (1966), an anthropologist, coined the term proxemics to designate the scientific study of interaction distance. As a student of human spatial behavior, Hall noted that we are often unaware of our use of space. According to Hall, we treat spatial behavior as we treat sexual behavior: it's there, but we don't talk about it. Things change in a decade; we now talk about both sex and space in great detail.

Hall identified four spatial zones of human interaction: the intimate, personal, social, and public zones. The INTIMATE ZONE extends from physical contact to an 18-inch separation between two people. Both lovemaking and fighting can occur within this zone. In public, people usually try to stay out of each other's intimate zones.

Social existence being what it is, strangers must occasionally inhabit each other's intimate space—for example, when riding in crowded elevators or subways. When we are crowded, the unwritten rule is to ignore our neighbor, so, almost involuntarily, we stand erect with slightly tensed muscles. Thus, even though we are physically close to others, our tense posture removes us from them psychologically.

The PERSONAL ZONE extends from about 18 inches to 4 feet. This zone is used by people primarily involved in conversation. The personal zone is the zone of friendship and convivial social interaction.

The SOCIAL ZONE extends from about 4 feet to 12 feet. Within this zone, people tend to relate to each other formally, as in business transactions, negotiations, or state ceremonies. When two people are linked by an official role relationship without the benefit of friendship, they usually prefer to maintain the customary social distance.

The PUBLIC ZONE extends from about 12 feet to 25 feet. Communication within this zone tends to be formal and one-way, as in public lectures, plays, and musical performances. One person (or group) presents a performance of some kind to a passive audience. Beyond 25 feet, contact with another person *as a person* is rapidly lost. Watching people on the sidewalk from the observation deck of a tall building is a strange sensation. We know that the army of orderly moving ants below are people, but to experience another individual fully seems to require spatial proximity.

These different interaction distances limit the types of comunication possible. Space acts as a channel of communication, a medium through which meaningful information is conveyed. Intimate distances, for example, accentuate visual cues, heighten the impact of sounds and smells, and make touch possible. Distances in the personal zone maintain some of the communication features of distances in the intimate zone, but at a reduced level of intensity. Smells are less prevalent, but eye contact remains an important channel of communication. The use or avoidance of eye contact in this zone functions to regulate the level of intimacy in the interaction. At a social distance, gestures needed for heightened intimacy are not possible, whispers used to convey intimate feelings cannot easily be heard, touches used to convey feelings of emotional closeness are not possible, and fine details of facial expression are less easily discernible. Yet the formality of the interaction is not nearly so great as when people interact at public distances. At these greater public distances, speech and gestures must be exaggerated in order to be comprehensible. The techniques actors and actresses learn which enable them to project their voices illustrate how clarity of communication is achieved without intimacy. Actually, interaction distance, while the most easily identifiable aspect of an interaction, is not the most important regulating factor. Rather, the verbal and nonverbal communicational gestures that result from distance are the key to regulating the intimacy of interactions.

Altman and Vinsel (1977) reviewed 106 studies of human spatial behavior in an effort to determine whether Hall's distance zones were, in fact, applicable to people interacting in different social situations. In . reviewing Hall's studies, they found that whether the subjects were seated or standing made a difference. When seated, people maintained either social or personal distance and rarely maintained intimate or public distance. In contrast, if interactions occurred while people were standing, the personal zone was most commonly used but the intimate zone was also used frequently. The social and public zones, however, were rarely used when standing. These findings support Hall's theory of the way people use space in interactions.

We have discussed how space is used to define and regulate types of social relationships. Space is also used as a mechanism for defining the boundary between the self and others. We behave as though the boundary surrounding our body extends beyond our skin out into the space adjacent to us. By maintaining control over this boundary, we attempt to regulate our privacy. When we wish to increase our sense of privacy, we try to extend these boundaries and keep others farther away. Conversely, when we want to be more intimate, we allow others to come closer, even to penetrate this personal space surrounding us. But we don't always have control over these boundaries. Sometimes others intrude on them, and sometimes we intrude into the personal space of others. Invasion of personal space has been studied extensively. The results of these studies paint a consistent picture of the effects of spatial intrusion: people react negatively to intrusions, try not to intrude on others, and feel uncomfortable when they do so. Let's look at some of the studies that have examined the effects of spatial intrusion.

SPATIAL INTRUSION

The effects of intrusion on personal space have interested Robert Sommer for many years. Sommer (1969) uses the concept of PERSONAL SPACE to refer to "the emotionally charged zone around each person, sometimes described as a soap bubble or aura, which helps to regulate the spacing of individuals." He and his students have studied the effect of violating that "emotionally charged soap bubble."

Being intruded on. Sommer studied personal space in a mental institution. He conducted the study outdoors, where patients spend much of their time sitting alone. Some patients served as controls and were observed unobtrusively in order to identify the baseline time for sitting alone. Other patients sitting alone were approached by an experimenter who, without a word, sat about 6 inches from the patient. Fully half of the experimental subjects had left by the end of 9 minutes, but within the same period, only 8 percent of the control subjects had moved to another location.

Sommer conducted another experiment at a university library. Some subjects sitting alone at a table were considered the control condition and observed at a distance. Others sitting alone were approached by the experimenter, who took a seat immediately next to them. By the end of the 30-minute observation period, only 10 percent of the control subjects had left their seats, while 70 percent of the experimental subjects had moved away.

Sommer's research captured the imagination of many researchers, and studies of spatial intrusion proliferated. These studies were conducted in a variety of settings, including mental hospitals, college hallways, libraries, and restrooms. Patterson, Mullens, and Romano (1971) investigated nonverbal responses to invasion of personal space by others. They also arranged a situation in which a confederate invaded the personal space of a student studying in a college library. One factor they were interested in was the degree of discomfort resulting from the closeness of the intruder to the subject. In one condition, the intruder sat next to the subject; in a second condition, three seats away; and in a final condition, across the table. It was clear that the intrusion made students feel uncomfortable. The closer the invasion, the less time it took students to get up and change their seats, and before changing seats, the students engaged in nonverbal behaviors indicating discomfort. They fidgeted, turned away from the intruder, leaned in the opposite direction, or placed their elbows on the table to create a boundary between themselves and the unwanted intruder. Clearly they did not appreciate the invasion.

You may never have had this sort of experience when studying in your college library. Anyone who wanted to sit next to you probably asked whether the seat was occupied and, if not, whether he or she might take it. There is evidence that people avoid such intrusions. Two studies show this clearly. Knowles (1973) arranged a situation wherein people walking down the corridor in a university building had to choose whether to walk through or around a group of people engaged in conversation. The group contained either 2 or 4 people. In a control condition, 2 wastebaskets, rather than interacting individuals, were used to determine whether people would walk between or around two inanimate objects.

Knowles also varied the status of the interactants. In a High Status condition, interactants were about 30 years old and dressed formally. In a Low Status condition, they were about 20 years old and dressed casually. An observer stationed down the hall unobtrusively recorded the reactions of passersby. Knowles hypothesized that groups set up boundaries around their interaction and that these boundaries deter would-be invaders. The higher the status of the interactants, the less permeable the boundaries and the more passersby should walk around rather than between the interacting members of the group. Knowles found that 75 percent of the passersby walked down the center of the corridor between the two wastebaskets in the control condition. Fewer people (only 25 percent) walked between interacting people. As the size of the group increased, the boundaries deterring interaction increased. While 30 percent of the passersby walked between interacting members of the 2-person group, only 20 percent invaded the boundaries of the 4-person group. Additionally, high-status groups formed less penetrable boundaries than low-status groups. While 30 percent of the passersby walked through the low-status groups, only about 18 percent walked through the high-status groups.

The results of this study indicate that people avoid intruding on the space of others and that the forces preventing intrusion increase as the importance of the people to be intruded upon increases. It is interesting to note that most people did not hesitate to invade the space between the wastebaskets. Later in the chapter we will discuss the nature of social relationships between staff and inmates of mental institutions. We will show that staff members who disregard the human value of inmates and begin to think of them as objects rather than humans engage in these same violations of personal space.

Intruding on others. Now let us consider a study

that examined the nonverbal reactions of people who invaded the space of others. Efran and Cheyne (1974) unobtrusively filmed the nonverbal behaviors of subjects who walked from one room to another in a psychology laboratory. In the Invasion condition, they were forced to pass between a male in a lab coat and a female who were conversing. In the No Invasion condition, they had to walk past a camera mounted on a tripod. In the Minimal Invasion condition, they had to walk past but not between two conversing individuals. Efran and Cheyne found strong nonverbal indications of discomfort when invasions occurred. Invaders walked with head down, avoided looking at the conversing individuals whose space they invaded, closed their eyes partially or completely when invading, and made many long negative mouth gestures. People who did not have to invade showed the fewest signs of discomfort, while people in the Minimal Invasion condition were intermediate in their display of discomfort.

When our personal space is invaded, we feel psychologically distant from others even though we are physically close to them. Frequently, we may experience a disequilibrium between the spatial and psychological aspects of an encounter with another person. Under these conditions, an equilibrium process designed to restore the proper balance to the interaction takes place. (See Box A.)

THE EQUILIBRIUM MODEL

Argyle and Dean (1965) proposed a model to account for the way people control and regulate the degree of intimacy in their interactions. They suggest that the level of intimacy in any interaction is affected by factors such as amount of eye contact, interaction distance, smiling, and other nonverbal and verbal behaviors. Their EQUILIBRIUM MODEL OF INTIMACY postulates that in any interaction approach forces move the interaction toward greater intimacy and avoidance forces move it toward lesser intimacy. Interactants engage in a subtle negotiation process to attain a comfortable equilibrium point where the approach forces balance the avoidance forces. If this equilibrium point is somehow disturbed, such that intimacy rises above the desired level, a process of compensatory behaviors is set into motion to restore the intimacy to the comfortable level. Conversely, if the interaction starts to become too formal, compensatory behaviors raise the level back to the comfortable equilibrium point. We can illustrate these ideas with the case of George and Harry.

George wants to be very friendly with Harry, but Harry prefers to have little to do with George. It's not that he dislikes George—he just doesn't want him for a close friend. One evening, George and Harry meet at a party. Geroge wants to share his anguish about his divorce and is equally eager to learn about Harry's personal problems. Harry would just as soon talk about the cold snap in Florida. When George begins to discuss his divorce, Harry tries to shift the topic back to the weather, thereby lowering the intimacy to the superficial level he prefers. Finding that George persists, Harry backs away, gradually increasing the physical distance between them. By moving away, Harry is nonverbally communicating that he is uncomfortable with George's topic of conversation. If George is at all sensitive, he will pick up the signal and change the subject.

Harry has other strategies. He can change his body's AXIS OF ORIENTATION, the angle at which he faces George. When two people face each other directly, they are being most intimate. As they turn away from one another, they decrease their level of intimacy. Harry can also avoid looking at George. Since eye contact is associated with intimacy, avoidance of eye contact signals a desire to maintain psychological distance.

Smiling is another mechanism available to Harry. Just as Harry's smile would signal that he wanted to be invited further into George's world, his refusal to return a smile indicates that he wishes to go no further. With all these techniques at his disposal, Harry should succeed in keeping George at bay.

In an experiment testing their equilibrium model, Argyle and Dean (1965) had a confederate converse with a subject at 2-foot, 6-foot, and 10-foot distances. The confederate gazed at the subject throughout the conversation. Based on their model, Argyle and Dean hypothesized that subjects would compensate for the decreasing intimacy experienced at the greater distances by returning the confederate's gaze more frequently. This was indeed the case. The greater the distance between subject and confederate, the greater the frequency of eye contact.

Argyle and Dean's equilibrium model stresses the compensatory aspects of the regulation of intimacy. In a review of the literature testing the model, Patterson (1976) finds a good deal of support for this compensation. Studies by Goldberg, Kiesler, and Collins (1969), by Schulz and Barefoot (1974), and by Stephenson, Rutter, and Dore (1972) all showed that subjects compensated for the heightened level of intimacy resulting from close proximity to others by decreasing their use of eye contact, thus reducing intimacy to a more acceptable level. Other studies revealed that heightened intimacy due to close proximity can be reduced by facing the other person less directly (Mehrabian and Diamond, 1971; Pellegrini and Empey, 1970; Watson and Graves, 1966).

However, Patterson also finds that subjects often reciprocate intimate behaviors. Patterson proposes a model that attempts to explain when the intimacy of person A leads to compensatory behaviors by person B and when person B reciprocates person A's display of intimacy. Patterson hypothesizes that great increases in the intimacy of person A's behavior arouse person B and cites a number of studies supporting this assumption. Patterson then draws on Schachter's work on emotions to explain what happens once the intimacy of person A arouses person B. According to Schachter, people experience emotions when they attach a label, or an explanation, to the arousal they experience. Thus it is possible for people who are aroused as a result of another person's intimacy to attach a positive label, such as attraction or liking, to the arousal or to attach a negative label, such as fear or embarrassment. Patterson suggests that people are likely to attach a negative label to arousal when they feel they lack control over the interaction. If the label attached to the arousal is negative, the individual will engage in compensatory behaviors, such as reduced eye contact or increased interpersonal distance in order to reduce intimacy to a more comfortable level. On the other hand, if the individual positively labels the arousal, he or she will reciprocate by engaging in similar intimacy-maintaining gestures, such as increased eye contact.

Another way to think about the intimacy level of interactions is in terms of privacy. There are times when we want to discuss intimate matters with others and times when we want to keep them to ourselves. We use spatial and nonverbal behaviors to regulate the amount of privacy available to us. Let's consider the concept of privacy in greater detail.

PRIVACY

After reviewing many definitions of PRIVACY, Irwin Altman (1975) defines it as "selective control of access to the self or to one's group." In other words, Altman suggests that each person or group uses boundaries to separate the self from others.

Maintaining privacy. There are many ways to control the degree of access others have to us. In our own families, for example, we maintain privacy from others with private jokes or sayings, the meaning and humor of which are known to us but not to others. Various ethnic groups have a slang of their own that separates them from members of the out-group. During the Korean War, prisoners of war who were made to confess to crimes they had allegedly committed mouthed the words required of them but communicated to members of the in-group, through nonverbal behaviors known only to the in-group, that they didn't mean what they were saying. In this way, they maintained their separation from the out-group and achieved some privacy.

Altman refers to privacy as a DIALECTIC PROCESS. By this he means two things. First, he assumes that within the same individual there are oppositional forces: a force that impels the person to let others into his or her world (reducing privacy) and a force that motivates the person to tighten up the boundary and keep others out (increasing privacy). These oppositional forces are much the same as the approach and avoidance forces that Argyle and Dean described as central to the regulation of intimacy in interactions. The second aspect of the dialectic process reflects the individual's constantly changing position about how much privacy he or she desires. There are times when, like Greta Garbo, we all "vant to be alone." Yet there are other times when we feel starved for human companionship—so starved that almost anyone will do. Likewise, there are times when we don't have enough privacy and times when we have too much. We try to maintain a balance, says Altman, between desired levels of privacy and achieved levels of privacy. To regulate this balance, we

447
Environmental influences on social behavior

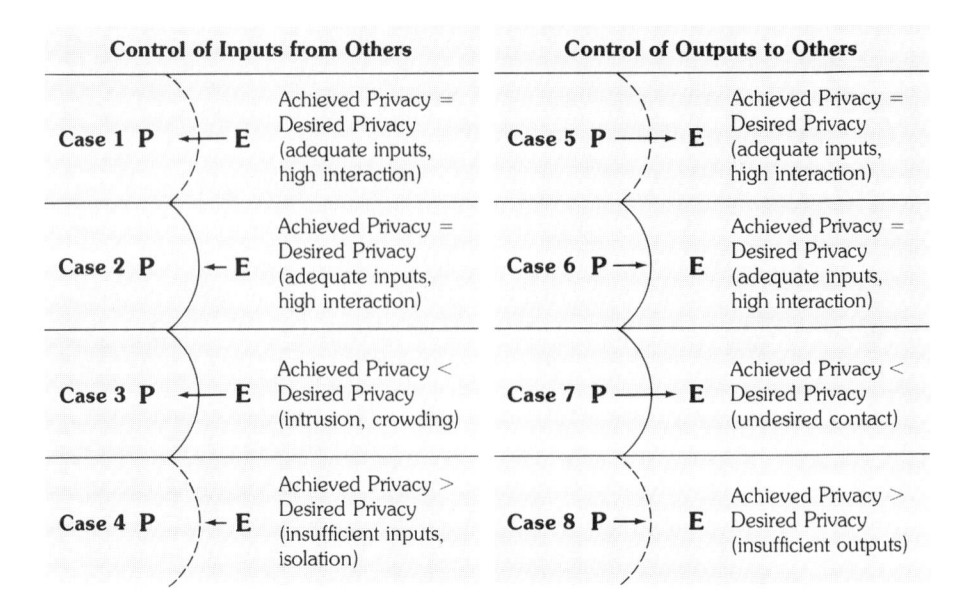

	Control of Inputs from Others	Control of Outputs to Others
Case 1	P ←⫫— E Achieved Privacy = Desired Privacy (adequate inputs, high interaction)	Case 5 P —⫫→ E Achieved Privacy = Desired Privacy (adequate inputs, high interaction)
Case 2	P ←— E Achieved Privacy = Desired Privacy (adequate inputs, high interaction)	Case 6 P → E Achieved Privacy = Desired Privacy (adequate inputs, high interaction)
Case 3	P ←— E Achieved Privacy < Desired Privacy (intrusion, crowding)	Case 7 P —→ E Achieved Privacy < Desired Privacy (undesired contact)
Case 4	P ← E Achieved Privacy > Desired Privacy (insufficient inputs, isolation)	Case 8 P → E Achieved Privacy > Desired Privacy (insufficient outputs)

1. Boundaries control the degree of access of the person (P) to the environment (E), and vice versa. There are times when the boundaries are permeable and interaction can occur. At other times, the boundaries close, preventing interchange between the person and the environment. (From Altman, 1975, p. 29.)

control our inputs to others and their outputs to us. Altman illustrates ways of doing this in Figure 1.

As Figure 1 illustrates, sometimes we succeed in maintaining the proper balance between desired and achieved privacy (Cases 1, 2, 5, and 6), and sometimes we fail (Cases 3, 4, 7, and 8). Of critical importance in the process of regulating privacy is the use of boundaries. These boundaries can take many forms. They can be verbal mechanisms, for instance, such as the choice of a topic of conversation. When we want to increase privacy, we discuss nonintimate topics. When we want to decrease privacy, we engage in intimate self-disclosure. The boundaries can also consist of nonverbal behaviors, such as the ones used by Harry to keep George at bay. They can also consist of environmental factors, such as our choice of clothing. Sunglasses, for example, are often worn by individuals who wish to maintain privacy.

Another environmental means for regulating privacy is the use of personal space. Harry moved farther away from George to try to increase his level of privacy. Other types of environmental mechanisms, differing from one culture to another, can be used to regulate privacy:

> In Java people live in small, bamboo-walled houses, each of which almost always contains a single nuclear family—i.e., mother, father, and unmarried children. . . . The houses face the street with a cleared front yard in front of them. There are no walls or fences around them, the house walls are thinly and loosely woven, and there are commonly not even doors. Within the house people wander freely just about any place any time, and even outsiders wander in fairly freely almost any time during the day and early evening. In brief, privacy in our terms is about as close to nonexistent as it can get. You may walk freely into a room where a man or woman is stretched out (clothed, of course) sleeping. You may enter from the rear of the house as well as from the front, with hardly more warning than a greeting announcing your presence. . . .

> The result is that their defenses are mostly psychological. Relationships even within the household are very restrained; people speak

softly, hide their feelings, and even in the bosom of a Javanese family you have the feeling that you are in the public square and must behave with appropriate decorum. Javanese shut people out with a wall of etiquette (patterns of politeness are very highly developed), with emotional restraint, and with a general lack of candor in both speech and behavior. It is not, in short, that the

A. "Don't Break My Bubble"

Robert Sommer (1969) has suggested that each person has a space surrounding him or her that can be thought of as an emotionally charged "soap bubble." The person tries to keep others out of this region. Mardi Horowitz, Donald Duff, and Lois Stratten (1964) devised a technique to measure the size of this area, which they referred to as body buffer zone. The technique is simple; you can try it yourself to determine your own body buffer zone and those of your friends.

The technique involves having a person approach a second person who is standing still. When the person stops, measures are taken of the distance between them. There are some subtleties and many variations on this basic technique. First, efforts are usually made to measure the distance between people unobtrusively. One way to do this is to use a room having floor tiles of a certain size—say one foot square. Distance is then measured by counting the number of tiles between people. Second, approaches to the other person can be obtained from several directions—from the front, the rear, and either side.

Asking the subjects to approach another provides data about the size of their zone when they are in control of the interaction. But we often want to know how people feel about having others approach them. One way to find out is to have the subject stand still and ask someone else to approach. The subject is told to tell the other person to stop when the subject begins to feel uncomfortable with the closeness. Variations on this technique involve using different people to approach the subject. No doubt our "bubble" expands and contracts, depending on how we feel about the person approaching us. We allow friends to approach closer than strangers, and we keep people who seem hostile at greater distances than people who seem friendly.

Once the individual has approached another from several directions, or has been approached by others from several directions, and distances are measured, maps of his or her body buffer zones are drawn, as shown in the diagram.

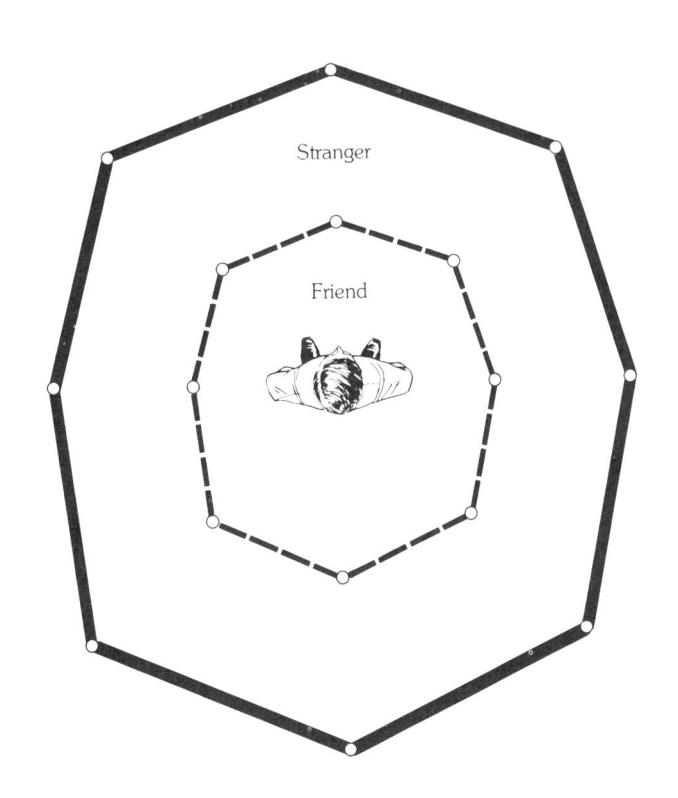

Javanese do not wish or value privacy; but merely that because they put up no physical or social barriers against the physical ingress of outdoors into their household life they must put up psychological ones and surround themselves with social barriers of a different sort. . . .

Now, in Bali people live in house yards surrounded by high stone walls into which you enter by a narrow, half-blocked-off doorway. Inside such a yard lives some form of what anthropologists call a patrilineal extended family. Such a family may consist of from one to a dozen or so nuclear families of the Javanese sort whose heads are related patrilineally: i.e., father, his two married sons, his two married brothers, *his* father. . . .

In contrast to Java, nonkinsmen almost never enter one's houseyard . . . Within the yard one is in one's castle and other people know better than to push their way in . . . Other patrilineal relatives of yours may do so, but except for these, when you are in your houseyard you are free of the public. Only your immediate family is around.

However, the Balinese home is characterized by . . . a tremendous warmth, humor, (and) openness . . . As soon as the Balinese steps through the doorway to the street and the public square, market and temples beyond, however, he becomes more or less like the Javanese (Geertz, 1970, cited in Altman, 1975, p. 15).

Kinds of privacy needs. Nancy Marshall (1972) has suggested several types of privacy needs. Her analysis is nondialectic: she focuses only on the "keep out" aspects of privacy. In public, the need for privacy is expressed as a desire for ANONYMITY. In contrast to small towns in which all the townspeople know intimate details of each other's lives, large cities afford anonymity.

With a circle of friends or in one's family, privacy may be expressed as a need for INTIMACY. Here intimate privacy is evidenced by the ability to reveal personal facts with the assurance that such revelations will remain confidential. Two other privacy needs focus on the home. The first, SECLUSION, reflects the need to have a home out of sight and sound of neighbors and traffic. The second, NOT NEIGHBORING, is closely related to the Indonesian example we cited. It reflects a need to limit the unannounced "dropping in" of friends and neighbors. People often fulfill this need by choosing personal friends who do not live nearby and seeking little social involvement with their nearest neighbors. Yet another need is the need for SOLITUDE, a desire to be completely alone. Cutting across all these needs except solitude is the need for RESERVE, which expresses a reluctance to disclose intimate information about oneself to others.

Marshall developed a privacy preference scale to measure the extent of these six privacy needs (see Box B). She found substantial individual differences. In general, however, she found that older people have more need for avoidance of involvement with neighbors and for reserve, while college students have more need for solitude and for intimacy with close friends. Women tended to have higher needs for reserve, solitude, intimacy, and anonymity than did men.

Our discussion of privacy has shown that people have a variety of privacy needs. When these needs are unfulfilled, people act to restore the balance and regain a comfortable privacy. Territorial behavior is one mechanism used to regulate the amount of available privacy.

TERRITORIALITY

Irwin Altman (1975) has written at length about territorial behavior. He defines territorial behavior as follows:

Territorial behavior is a self/other boundary-regulation mechanism that involves personalization of or marking of a place or object and communication that it is "owned" by a person or group. Personalization and ownership are designed to regulate social interaction and to help satisfy various social and physical motives. Defense responses may sometimes occur when territorial boundaries are violated (p. 107).

Altman (1975) distinguishes among primary territories, secondary territories, and public territories. PRIMARY TERRITORIES are nonpublic areas over which we exercise absolute territorial control. In a primary terri-

B. How Private Are You?

To measure the extent to which people differed in the strength of their needs for privacy, Nancy Marshall (1972) developed a questionnaire that measured preferences for six aspects of privacy. The following is an abbreviated version of the items on her questionnaire. You may test yourself to find out how strong your needs are for reserve, one of Marshall's six aspects of privacy. Questions are answered on a five-point scale as follows:

        0   Strongly Agree (SA)
        1   Agree (A)
        2   Uncertain (U)
        3   Disagree (D)
        4   Strongly Disagree (SD)

Simply write the number that best represents your response next to the question. After you have taken the test, add up the total of your responses to assess the strength of your need for reserve. Scores can range from 0 to 28. The *lower* your score, the *greater* your need for reserve.

1. I dislike talking about personal matters to a friend in a crowded place where other people can overhear us.
2. Acquaintances often ask questions which I consider rude and personal.
3. I usually don't tell personal things about myself to people I don't know very well.
4. I don't like to talk about personal things with friends until I have known them for a long time.
5. I would dislike having a patio or balcony that neighbors or passersby could see into.
6. "Good fences make good neighbors."
7. I would be very upset if a friend read something I had written or my personal correspondence without my permission.

Marshall found that women have higher needs for reserve than men. Compare the scores of the men and women in your class to see if the results are consistent with her findings.

Reprinted by permission of Plenum Publishing Corporation.

---

tory, the occupants are the only ones who have the right to determine who enters, who remains, and what activities take place. Our home is a good example of a primary territory. Primary territories usually play a central role in our lives; they are places to which we usually have unrestricted access at any time, day or night.

SECONDARY TERRITORIES contain a mixture of public and semiprivate access. The neighborhood bar is a secondary territory. It is a public environment and anyone may patronize it. But within the bar, distinctions are made between the regulars and strangers. Regulars have their corner of the bar or their special table. A stranger who unwittingly sits in a regular's seat will get an icy stare to match his icy brew.

PUBLIC TERRITORIES, as their name suggests, are available to everyone. Playgrounds, libraries, museums, and beaches are several examples. A distinction must be made, however, between freedom of access and freedom of activities in public territories. Anyone may bathe in the ocean or soak up the sun on a public beach. However, littering is prohibited to all. Furthermore, there are usually specific times when access is denied in public territories. Libraries are often closed to the public between 9:00 P.M. and 9:00 A.M. Beaches are usually not available as overnight sleeping grounds. Violation of these regulations leads to the kind of conflict we witnessed in 1968, when many college students camped out in Grant Park in Chicago during the Democratic National Convention.

The "home court advantage." Many studies of territorial behavior have focused on primary territories. Patterson (1978) compared people who clearly signaled that their home was their territory with others who did not. Older people tended to mark their homes with such signs as "No Trespassing" or "Keep Out" and to use barriers such as fences and surveillance devices such as peepholes. When old people live alone, territorial marking reduces apprehension. Those who mark their property feel less afraid of property loss or personal assault than those who do not mark their property. Perhaps people feel greater control over their territory when they personalize it with special markers. When they feel in control, people feel less threatened by such potential dangers as crimes (see Box C).

Several other investigators also studied how effec-

C. Territorial Control and Crime

The belief of Patterson's subjects that personalizing the environment increases safety is consistent with research findings on crime in housing projects.

Oscar Newman (1973) compared crime rates in high-rise and low-rise housing projects in New York City. There are, of course, many differences between these two types of buildings. One outstanding difference, for example, is the number of people inhabiting each type of building. High-rise projects have many more residents than low-rise buildings. Yet both high-rise and low-rise buildings in this study had similar population densities. Newman was able to demonstrate dramatic differences in numbers of crimes committed in these different forms of housing. Robberies, for example, were much more frequent in the high-rise than in the low-rise buildings. Why?

The answer appears to involve differences in the architecture of these two types of buildings. As it turned out, the low-rise buildings contained architectural features leading to the perception that their space was more "defensible" than the space of the high-rise buildings. It should be emphasized, however, that it is possible to construct high-rise buildings that give the sense of defensible space and low-rise buildings that do not. Let's consider what made the space in the high-rise buildings studied by Newman less defensible than the space in the low-rise buildings.

In the high-rise buildings, eight families share a floor. The floor is reached by an elevator that stops in the center of the floor. After getting off the elevator, one walks left or right down a corridor containing two apartments on either side of the corridor. Newman believes that this arrangement of apartments minimizes the feeling that the hallway is part of the apartment dweller's territory. This belief is consistent with the observation that children never play in these hallways. Discussions with residents of these hallways reveal that they feel little responsibility for what goes on there.

Six families share a floor in the low-rise buildings. There is an unlocked swinging door in the middle of the floor and, on either side of it, two vestibules that are shared by three families each. The individuals living in these types of corridors consider the hallways an extension of their territory. They allow their children to play in the hallways and maintain surveillance over their activities. Because they consider this space their territory, they protect it and take care of it. They watch to see whether strangers are roaming around, and if they see any, they alert their children. They feel a sense of control over their hallways and, as a result of their belief that they have a stake in this area, deter would-be criminals. The dramatic difference in amount of crime in these two types of housing suggests that architecture that increases feelings of territorial control can play an important part in crime prevention.

tive markers were in preventing territorial encroachment. Earlier in the chapter, we mentioned that people usually will not sit down in a seat next to you in the library without first asking if the seat is taken. This tendency to ask and to hesitate to sit down is noticeably increased if you leave some form of marker—books, clothing, or papers—to indicate that you have claimed that territory. For example, in one study investigating the effectiveness of different types of markers, Sommer and Becker (1969) found that, compared to times when no markers were present, fewer people sat at empty tables that had books, jackets, or sandwich wrappers left on them. This was true regardless of whether the setting was a college sweet shop, a library, or a dormitory study room. And the more personal the marker, the more effective it was in protecting the territory from encroachment.

We have shown that people are able to defend their territory by using markers. Indeed, people go to great lengths to stake out their own territories and to defend them from encroachment. They place fences around their homes, mark out their little domain on public beaches, and even stake out their chair at the dinner table. It would seem that there is something advantageous about having a territory of one's own. Indeed, sports teams frequently talk about the advantages of playing at home on their own territory. Does any empirical evidence support the idea that there is an advantage to playing or working in one's own territory? Martindale (1971) studied pairs of male college students. Each pair role-played prosecuting and defense attorneys in a criminal case and negotiated a sentence for the criminal. The role playing took place in the room—that is, the territory—of one of the members of the pair. Residents exerted more influence in the negotiations and talked longer than visitors in this study. Thus Martindale's study illustrates the importance of the "home court advantage."

In a similar study, Edney (1975) asked pairs of college students to perform a task in the college dormitory room of one member of the pair. Half the time, the resident was asked to act as an assistant while the visitor was in charge of the task. The reverse was true for the remainder of the pairs. Regardless of who was supposed to be in charge, residents resisted their partners' attempts to control their behavior more than visitors.

In both the Martindale and Edney studies, there was an element of competition, just as one might expect in a sporting event. But do we invite people into our homes merely to dominate them? Visiting is a uniquely human institution. No other species invites same-sex members into its home territory. What happens when noncompetitive visitors arrive?

Conroy and Sundstrom (1977) studied residents and visitors who had differing opinions on a particular subject. In a room belonging to one member of the pair, the students discussed whether the university should recognize the campus Gay Liberation group. When the students disagreed, residents spoke longer than visitors and generally dominated the conversation. It was as though they were communicating: "On my turf you'll listen to what *I* have to say." However, when the students agreed on the issue, a "hospitality" effect emerged. The visitor spoke more and seemed to control the conversation. In other words, residents appeared willing to give their guest the floor.

Within the home. Inside the home, territoriality functions in several ways. We have seen how it enables people to dominate others. But within the family, territoriality reflects a stable structuring of social relationships among family members. For example, Rosenblatt and Budd compared the territorial behavior of married couples and unmarried couples who were living together. There are many indications of territoriality in the home. For example, the man has his dresser and the woman hers, and each has a particular chair at the dinner table, side of the bed, and area of the bathroom. Rosenblatt and Budd found that married couples were far more territorial than unmarried couples living together. Because married couples were committed to an enduring relationship, they needed a way to delineate distinct roles. By clearly marking what was the man's territory and what was the woman's, they were attempting to create a stable role structure. On the other hand, unmarried couples more often had places to be alone. Commenting on this, Altman (1975) concluded that "unmarried couples were less committed to the relationship, wanted to maintain their separateness by having places to be alone, but did not commit themselves to the detailed organization of space and living habits necessary for long-term group stability" (p. 142).

Several other studies have demonstrated the way in which territorial behavior expresses and structures social interaction. Esser (1965) and his colleagues studied patients on psychiatric wards. They found that the more dominant patients claimed an entire ward as their personal territory and roamed about freely. Patients in the middle of the dominance hierarchy claimed territory in the most interesting part of the ward—near the main areas of traffic flow, for example. Patients lowest in the dominance hierarchy had territories in secluded corners and other less desirable locations.

Sundstrom and Altman (1974) found a similar pattern in the territorial behavior of delinquent boys at a rehabilitation center. The most dominant boys claimed territories in the most desirable areas. For example, they had rights to the first and second row of seats in the TV area. The territories of less dominant boys were dispersed throughout the cottage and were correspondingly less desirable. The least dominant boys were forced to congregate near the supervisor's desk—a highly undesirable area for delinquent boys. Once this hierarchy was established, disruptive behavior was minimal. Disobeying, fighting, stealing, and other antisocial behaviors rarely occurred. After five weeks, the administration removed two dominant boys and replaced them with two new boys. Now each boy went where he pleased and no clearcut territories existed. The absence of established individual territories disrupted group stability and resulted in a marked increase in disruptive behavior.

Territorial behavior is only one means by which humans stabilize relationships with one another. We also use verbal, nonverbal, and spatial behaviors to structure our relationships. Even if we are forced to share a dresser with a roommate or use a communal dormitory bathroom, we can develop a cooperative social structure that enables us to interact in relative harmony. Different societies and cultures call for various strategies for managing human interactions. Let us briefly look at how some other cultures handle these issues.

CULTURAL DIFFERENCES IN HUMAN INTERACTION

When people of two cultures interact, some amusing things can happen. The story is told of an Arab and an Englishman who were trying to carry on a conversation in a hallway. The Englishman was trying to maintain a "proper" distance of 5 feet; the Arab preferred 2 feet. Whenever the Arab approached 3 feet, the Englishman politely retreated 3 feet. The Arab would then move closer. At the end of a largely unsatisfactory 15-minute conversation, the Arab had backed the helpless Englishman down the long corridor. From the Englishman's point of view, the Arab persisted in penetrating his private space, so he exhibited a mild flight reaction. From the Arab's point of view, the Englishman was persistently unfriendly. Those who expect to deal with people from other cultures must learn the other cultures' norms governing nonverbal behavior in different situations and at different levels of intimacy.

Such learning can be observed in the spatial behaviors of children of different ages. A study by Aiello and Aiello (1974) demonstrated that as children grow older, their spatial behavior more closely approximates the behavior of adults. In the first grade, conversing children stand very close together. In the third grade, they stand farther apart; in the fifth grade, farther yet; and by the time they reach the seventh grade, they converse standing as far apart as adults. Aiello and Aiello also observed that, prior to the fifth grade, interactions between two males resemble those between two females. The distance between children and the angle at which they face each other are roughly equivalent. However, differences begin to emerge by the seventh grade. Males stand farther apart and face each other less directly than females.

Aiello and Aiello demonstrated that as they grow older, children learn to adjust their spatial behavior to fit the requirements of the situation. But who are the role models for teaching children about appropriate spatial behavior? The answer is not clear. Some evidence suggests that children imitate the spatial behavior of their ethnic group. Other evidence, however, suggests that similarity in spatial behaviors follows social class lines rather than displaying an ethnic pattern. Two studies can be cited to illustrate each of these views. Aiello and Jones (1971) compared the spatial behavior in black, white and Puerto Rican children among elementary school populations in the New York City vicinity. Unfortunately, the investigators chose different locations and populations differing in socioeconomic status as well as ethnicity. Lower-class

Puerto Rican children and lower-class black children were found to stand closer together during conversations than middle-class white children. However, it is possible that the observed differences reflected social class rather than racial differences.

To examine this possibility, Scherer (1974) conducted two studies of interacting pairs of school children in Toronto playgrounds. In the first study, pairs of black chidlren and pairs of white children interacting in the same school playground in a lower socioeconomic area were studied. Scherer found no differences in the spatial behavior of these two groups. In the second study, Scherer compared the behavior of four groups of interacting pairs: lower-class black children, lower-class white children, middle-class black children, and middle-class white children. Results of this study indicated that middle-class white children stood farther apart than lower-class white children. Middle-class black children also stood farther apart than lower-class black chidlren, although the difference was not statistically significant. Taken together, the studies by Aiello and Jones and by Scherer indicate that members of different groups differ in their spatial behavior. Whether these differences are due primarily to ethnicity or to social class, however, is still in doubt.

Body contact and touching also vary between cultures. Because English-speaking societies tend to be nontouching societies, body contact in public places may be stressful. A simple observational study conducted by Sidney Jourard (1966) dramatically illustrates the resistance to physical contact in English speaking societies. He observed people in cafés in San Juan, Paris, London, and Gainesville, Florida, and recorded the number of times per hour that people touched each other in any way at all. In San Juan, Jourard counted 180 touches per hour. In Paris, the rate was about 110 per hour. In Gainesville, it plummeted to about 2 touches per hour. And though he lingered over tea and crumpets in a London café for quite some time, Jourard was unable to record a single instance of touching.

The infrequency with which people in English speaking societies touch is surprising in view of the fact that members of these societies report finding touch pleasant. So great is the touch taboo that there is scarcely any literature on the effects of bodily contact. The few studies on touch which have been conducted suggest that Americans generally refrain from touching in public. When they do touch someone, they usually know that person well, and people usually touch by mutual choice.

Each culture, then, teaches its members how to react to differing levels of intimacy. Usually, we "keep our distance" from others with whom we are not intimate. When it is not possible to do so, we resort to a variety of other behaviors such as reduced eye contact and less direct angle of body orientation to reduce the intimacy level. These behaviors tacitly signal the level of intimacy desired. However, we are seldom conscious of either the desires themselves or the overt behaviors; conscious awareness varies between cultures, just as the behaviors themselves do.

Having briefly considered some of the relevant theories and research concerned with humans and the way they inhabit physical space and interact within it, we now turn quite logically to the phenomenon of crowding.

Crowding

In the early 1960s, John Calhoun, working in the laboratory of Brain Evolution and Behavior of the National Institute of Mental Health, shocked scientists and the public alike with a report published in *Scientific American* (Calhoun, 1962).

Calhoun built a special rat colony. The colony was designed to accommodate 48 rats, but Calhoun allowed the population to grow until there were 80 adult rats present. After this point, any newborn rat that survived birth and weaning was removed from the colony. A diagram of this colony appears in Figure 2. As you can see, the colony was divided into four pens each containing a food hopper, a water supply, and an elevated burrow with five nest boxes. Ramps connected pen 4 with pen 3, pen 2 with pen 3, and pen 1 with pen 2. The arrangement of this colony soon created problems. Since rats usually roam around, and since pens 2 and 3 had more ramps leading to them than pens 1 and 4, a large number of rats tended to congregate in pens 2 and 3. Most rats also avoided pens 1 and 4 because, in each of these pens, one dominant rat claimed the pen as his territory and chased all would-be intruders away. The middle pens became a

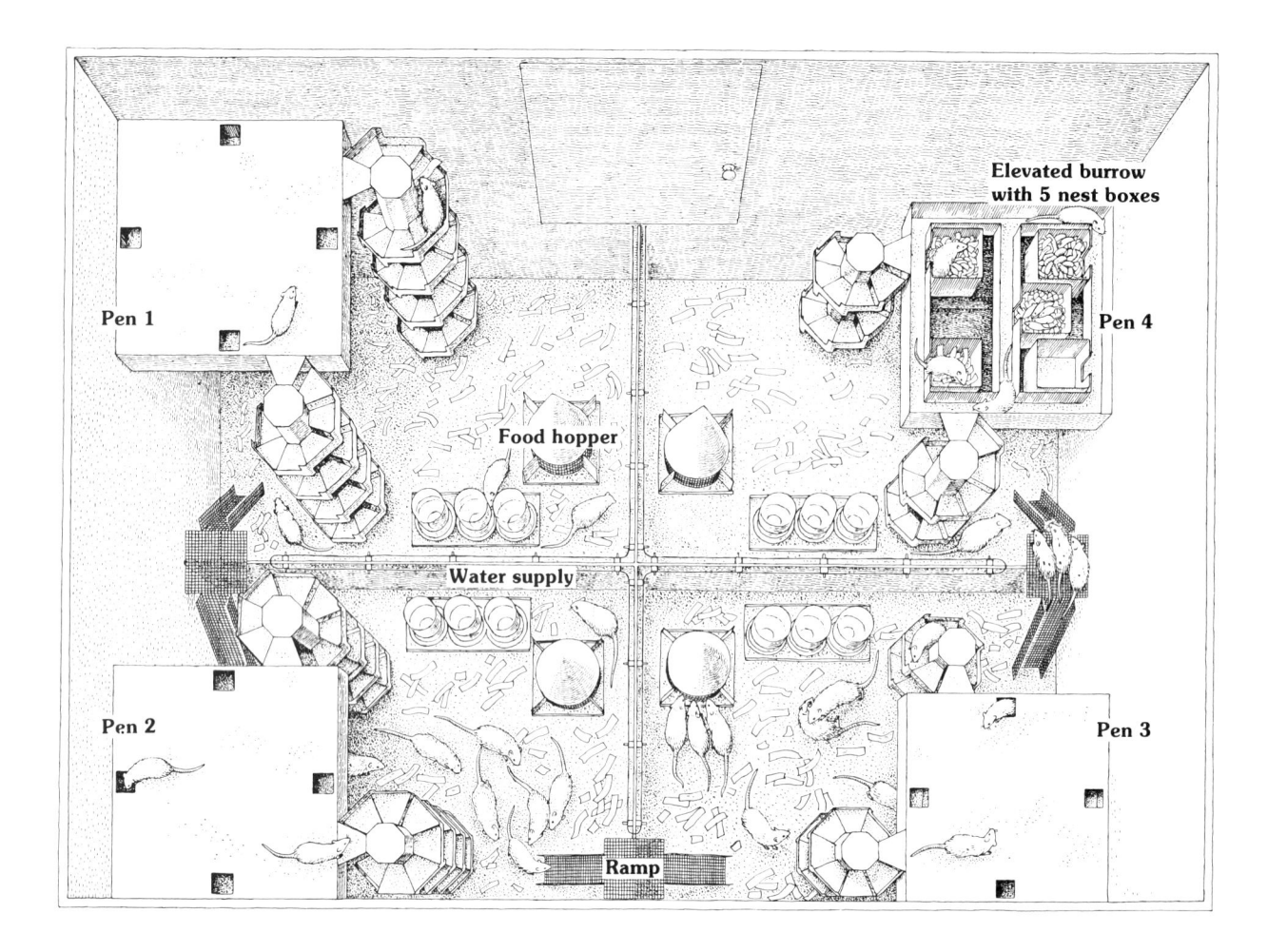

2. In this specially constructed environment, a group of rats was allowed to multiply. Each had nest boxes, a food hopper, and a water supply. Because of traffic patterns, however, pens 2 and 3 became a crowded "behavioral sink." (From Calhoun, 1962, p. 137.)

"behavioral sink." The greatest number of animals occupied these pens and remained there, crowded together. The rats soon began to eat and drink together, roaming back and forth between the middle pens several times daily. Instead of avoiding the crowding, they actually seemed to seek it out.

The effects soon became apparent. Females in the middle pens showed a complete breakdown of maternal behavior. They failed to build nests for their offspring, abandoning them instead in the middle of the pen where they would starve and then be eaten by adult rats. Adult male rats in the middle pen were of two types: fighters and probers. No really stable dominance hierarchy ever emerged in these middle pens, but the fighters had more status than the probers. The probers took no part at all in the status struggle; instead they became hyperactive, hypersexual, homosexual, and cannibalistic. After 16 months, the colony was beginning to die off. Calhoun moved the four healthiest males and the four healthiest females to another pen. These animals were six months old and in the prime of their lives. Although they no longer lived in a crowded environment, not one of their offspring survived to maturity.

A similar study was conducted with deer that inhabited an island in Chesapeake Bay. In this study, conducted by Christian, Flyger, and Davis (1961), a group of deer had expanded the size of their population due to favorable environmental conditions. However, since they were restricted to a small island, they could not expand their territory beyond a certain limit. The following summer, deer with plenty of food and water and in otherwise perfect health began to die. Post-mortem examinations revealed increases in the size of the adrenal gland, signifying that these deer were subjected to high levels of stress. Overpopulation was killing them.

These two animal studies and other similar studies were carried out before the research on the effects of crowding on humans. Based on the animal studies, people began to speculate about the possible grim consequences for humans living in crowded conditions. Soon studies with humans were under way.

THE WHAT AND WHY OF CROWDING

Calhoun's research stimulated a great deal of interest and numerous studies on the way humans are affected by crowding. To the student first approaching this literature, conclusions about the effects of crowding seem difficult to draw. Some studies find that crowding negatively affects people, some find that it affects them positively, and some find that it makes no difference. We believe, however, that it is possible to describe the effects of crowding in a meaningful way. To do so, we must return to the Altman framework of settings, processes and actors, which we described in Chapter 15. We assume that crowding always involves several people who are facing an environmental problem that they describe and label as crowding. The nature of the problem they face depends on the setting and the characteristics of the actors in that setting. Crowding can occur in such varied settings as residences, mass transit facilities, stores, and classrooms.

All these settings pose different problems. In crowded homes, for example, the major problem is lack of privacy and scarcity of resources. People living in an apartment in which the only place to study is a room where others watch TV are likely to complain that the apartment is crowded. They also would be likely to complain if they all had to share one bathroom in the morning and found that they were late to school or work because of the early morning wait to use this facility. Their problems differ from those of the rush-hour subway rider, who feels crowded because he or she is packed into the car like a sardine and has to touch strangers in a public place.

The characteristics of the actors and their relationships to each other also differ in these settings. In homes, the actors are part of a group in which members share common norms and have obligations to each other. They have a history of interaction and a stake in their interrelationship. They are able to exert influence on each other. In mass transit settings, riders are a collectivity rather than a group. They are, for the most part, strangers. They have no relationship and minimal obligations to each other. Thus, while both trains and homes may be described by their occupants as crowded, the problems are different and the resources available to solve them differ as well.

An individual feeling crowded in each of these two different settings will try to solve the problem posed by the environment. In residences the attempt is likely to be a group effort, while on subways the attempt is more likely to be individual. If the attempt to solve the problem fails, the individual is likely to be upset because he or she feels unable to control the situation. Lack of control contributes to a sense of helplessness and depression (Seligman, 1975) and has been singled out as an important contributor to the problems of crowding (Baron and Rodin, 1978).

With these distinctions in mind, we can expect that the effects of crowding in residences are likely to differ from the effects of crowding in mass transit facilities. The subway or bus rider probably has little ability to solve the problems he or she faces and is likely to feel a loss of control and experience stress. The resident of a crowded dwelling, on the other hand, may be able to influence the people he or she lives with, especially if the occupants are cooperatively linked to one another. Cooperation and competition seem to be critical processes influencing the effects of crowding in various settings. Thus we might expect that in middle-class homes where cooperative bonds exist, the problems of crowding will be solved and few ill effects should be observed. In crowded college dormitories, however, where occupants have a shorter history of relating to one another, problems should be more noticeable and outcomes should depend to a greater extent on other factors that create either cooperative or competitive re-

458
Social psychology
and the environment

lationships. We will examine research on the effects of crowded mass transit settings and crowded residences, noting how the results are a function of the setting, the actors, and the processes they engage in. We begin with research on crowded transportation settings.

CROWDED TRANSPORTATION SETTINGS

In the main, research has shown that crowded transportation facilities usually are stressful, whereas crowded residences usually are not. Most of the research done on transportation crowding has been conducted by a group of researchers at Rutgers University headed by Yakov Epstein. Their research is conducted in a laboratory setting wherein they attempt to recreate the high degree of crowding and body contact strangers usually experience on crowded buses and subways.

Subjects in the Rutgers experiments, whether male or female, always find the crowded environment uncomfortable and unpleasant. Both physiological and task performance measures showed that these subjects are stressed. For example, a study by Aiello, Epstein, and Karlin (1976) showed that crowded people had higher skin conductance levels than noncrowded people and that these levels continued to increase over the course of a session. Epstein, Lehrer, and Woolfolk (1978) found that even over the course of a three-week period, the systolic blood pressure of crowded subjects was higher than that of noncrowded subjects, and in each session it continued to rise. Crowded subjects also reported that they felt a lack of control over the problems posed by the crowded environment. Performance on tasks also suggested that these subjects were stressed. According to the YERKES-DODSON LAW (Kahneman, 1973), under moderately high levels of arousal or stress, performance on simple cognitive tasks should improve, but performance on complex cognitive tasks should deteriorate. A study by Epstein and Karlin (1975) found greater improvement in performance of simple tasks for crowded people than for noncrowded people. In a different study, Aiello, DeRisi, Epstein, and Karlin (1977) found that crowded subjects did worse on a complex creativity task than noncrowded subjects. The researchers believed that the stress in this situation stemmed from the unwanted body contact. In one experiment, the research teams (Nicosia, Hyman, Aiello, Epstein, and Karlin, in press) used Plexiglas barriers that eliminated body contact and found a reduction in physiological stress and an increased tolerance for frustration.

SEX DIFFERENCES IN REACTION TO CROWDING

One important actor characteristic that appears to influence reactions to crowding in a variety of settings is gender. A number of studies have found that men and women react differently in crowded environments. These laboratory studies have simulated both classroom and mass transit settings.

Freedman, Levy, Buchanan, and Price (1971) measured the degree of cooperation of men and women in crowded and noncrowded classroom environments. Compared to subjects who were not crowded, crowded women were more cooperative and crowded men less so. Men and women were also asked to listen to court cases describing violent crimes, to decide the guilt of the accused, and (if guilty) the severity of the sentence. Crowded men meted out harsher sentences than noncrowded men, while crowded women handed down more lenient sentences than noncrowded women.

Epstein and Karlin (1975) obtained similar results in a mass transit setting. They found that crowded women were more cooperative than noncrowded women, while the reverse was true for men. Crowded men competed more than noncrowded men. Epstein and Karlin also found that, unlike noncrowded women, crowded women formed closer bonds with their group members and liked them better, while once again the reverse was true for men. Though both crowded men and crowded women were upset, they handled distress differently. Crowded women shared their distress with other group members, while crowded men tried to hide theirs.

Why should men and women who are experiencing equal stress respond so differently? Epstein and Karlin

Crowding in mass transit facilities frequently contributes to a sense of helplessness and depression because the individual does not feel able to control the situation. (New York Daily News Photo)

believe the answer lies in the way men and women in our society are socialized to handle distress. Women are taught to share their distress with other women who reciprocate. Sharing their feelings is comforting and "binding." It enables women to form a cohesive and cooperative group. Men, on the other hand, are conditioned to hide their distress from others, because it is considered unmanly. In the crowded environment, men felt closely scrutinized by others. They were upset, and hiding this feeling in such close quarters is difficult. Furthermore, the presence of other men contributed more tension and augmented the men's tendency to cope with the situation in isolation. They became the "lonely crowd."

The differences between male and female social behavior in crowded environments are not the result of inherited sex differences. With special training, the sex-specific pattern of social behavior can be reversed. Karlin, McFarland, Aiello, and Epstein (1976) modified the level of interaction among women in a crowded room to more closely resemble the male pattern. Crowded women were informed that successful and intelligent people cope with crowded environments by keeping to themselves. Two confederates who were part of the four-person group modeled noninvolvement. Under these circumstances, the social behavior of crowded women was similar to that of the crowded men in the Epstein and Karlin experiment.

Crowded classrooms, crowded subways and crowded stores are certainly an unpleasant part of our daily lives, but they are not so central to our existence as the crowded home we may have to occupy. In the next section, we will look at the effects of crowded residences.

RESIDENTIAL CROWDING

We will consider several kinds of studies used to investigate the effects of residential crowding: archival studies using the technique of ecological correlation; interview studies; and the field experiments outlined in later sections.

Ecological correlations. At first glance, determining whether crowding in residences has negative effects appears simple. We need only follow the behavior of people who live in crowded houses and that of people who live in noncrowded ones. If crowding has negative effects, residents of crowded houses should show a greater degree of impairment than noncrowded residents on measures of crime, suicide, disease, death, and mental hospital admissions.

Several early investigators used a technique known as ECOLOGICAL CORRELATION and found moderate support for the expectation that crowded homes exert negative effects. The technique involved correlating measures of population density with measures of social pathology. For example, a city may be divided into a number of neighborhoods. In each neighborhood, the investigator determined the total population, the total number of dwelling units, the number of rooms in each dwelling, and the number of people living in each dwelling unit. From this data base, it was possible to calculate the average number of people per room, the average number of people per dwelling unit, and a variety of similar statistics. Along with the information about population density, we can obtain information about the number of robberies, murders, and admissions to mental hospitals, all of which are indices of social pathology.

The cautious investigator can also obtain information about the so-called DEMOGRAPHIC CHARACTERISTICS of the population. In this category are such variables as race, level of education, income, and occupation of the neighborhood residents. (The U.S. Bureau of the Census has collected much of this information and published it for various "census tracts.") With this information at hand, we can correlate measures of population density with measures of social pathology. The results of such correlations usually reveal a positive association between population density and social pathology. The more crowded an area, the more crime, health problems, and other pathologies there are. But can we conclude that crowding causes these problems?

People may commit crimes or have health problems because of poverty rather than overcrowding. But poverty and crowding usually go hand in hand. Combined with poverty, frustration, and social factors, living in a crowded slum has a generally detrimental effect on a person's behavior. Thus the cautious investigator attempts to statistically control the influence of these so-called extraneous demographic factors. Unfortunately, criteria for choosing control variables are usually arbitrary and therefore inadequate. To illustrate the problem, let us look at two related studies.

Galle, Gove, and MacPherson (1972) studied the effects of residential crowding on the health and social behavior of Chicago residents. They divided the city of Chicago into 75 neighborhood areas and obtained information on the average number of people per room and per acre. They also obtained information on death rates, birth rates, number of families receiving public assistance, instances of juvenile delinquency, and number of mental hospital admissions. They found that the more crowded the neighborhood, the higher the level of public assistance, amount of juvenile delinquency, and birth and death rates. No relationship, however, was found between degree of crowding and number of admissions to mental hospitals. When Galle, et al. statistically controlled for factors such as ethnicity and social class, the results remained stable. They concluded that crowding rather than poverty was responsible for these results.

Shortly thereafter, Sally Kent Ward (1975) voiced doubts about the findings of the Galle, et al. study. She believed that Galle, Gove, and MacPherson had used an inappropriate criterion for determining economic poverty. They had essentially defined poverty in terms of median family income for people living in Chicago. Ward, on the other hand, classified poverty in terms of a family income of $3,000 a year or less. Using this new criterion of poverty and adjusting the criteria for education and occupation, she reanalyzed Galle, Gove, and MacPherson's data, concluding that negative social pathology is attributable to poverty rather than to crowding.

One recent investigation has managed to avoid the pitfalls of arbitrary definition in its study of crowding. Freedman, Heshka, and Levy (1975) examined how the number of people per acre and per room affected incidence of juvenile delinquency, infant mortality, out-of-wedlock births, and venereal disease in the population. They compared crowded and non-crowded neighborhoods in which income level and ethnic composition were equivalent. They found no relationship between number of people per room and degree of social pathology. The most reasonable conclusion to be drawn from the many correlational studies of density and pathology is probably that crowding itself does not lead to pathology. However, crowding in urban areas is frequently associated with many social problems.

Interview studies. Mitchell (1971) investigated living conditions among Hong Kong residents. An extremely densely populated city, an average-sized dwelling unit in Hong Kong measured only about 400 square feet. Ten or more people often lived in such an apartment, 39 percent of Hong Kong families shared a dwelling unit with another unrelated family, and 28 percent of the population slept three or more to a bed. Many apartments had only one room and no tap water, flush toilets, or cross-ventilation. Clearly, people who live under these conditions lack privacy, cannot control their territory, and have very scarce resources. Mitchell interviewed over 500 married couples. He also interviewed over 2,600 other people who were married and living in a family unit but whose spouse was unavailable for an interview.

In assessing the effects of crowding, Mitchell used three types of measures—superficial strain, severe strain, and behavioral impairment. Superficial measures included general happiness and amount of worry, while severe strain was indicated in an index of emotional illness and in an index of hostility. Behavioral impairment was measured by withdrawal from work and family roles. While crowding affected the superficial measures to some degree, only the families suffering from the most severe conditions showed deficits on measures of severe strain. These families lived in dwelling units shared by at least one other family. They also lived on the second or higher floor of their apartment house. (Families in Hong Kong who live on the ground floor use the street as an extension of their living space, while families who live on upper floors cannot easily escape into the street.)

Ability to work or function effectively within the family unit was not affected by crowding. Only two aspects of family life showed any deficits. Since crowded families preferred to have their children spend a good deal of time out of the house, there was some loss of parental control over children. However, as we saw in Chapter 15, supervision is often provided by other adults in poor communities. Second, those with crowded homes did not have others visit them as often. Mitchell felt this might lessen their involvement in neighborhood life.

The Mitchell study is a testament to the human ability to adapt to difficult environmental conditions. We can speculate that the residents of Hong Kong have learned to use the available space in cooperative ways that enable them to live in and cope with this environment. But Hong Kong is a culture very different from our own. Let us turn to a study of a Canadian city and a culture more similar to ours.

Booth (1975) studied residents of two sections of Toronto, the downtown area and an area several miles away but still within the city. About 80 percent of the sample lived in private dwellings, row houses, or townhouses like large apartments. The remainder lived in ordinary apartments or apartments above stores. Most of the dwellings were typical of older urban residential areas and included some public housing. The sample contained 560 families from which 522 wives and 344 husbands were willing to be interviewed. About 500 adults and 900 children in these families also underwent a physical examination at a local clinic. The investigators studied the effects of crowding on health, as determined by physical examinations and blood and urine analyses. They also studied psychiatric impairment, family relations, aggression within and outside the family, social perception, political activity, reproduction, and child development. Crowded families tended to have more arguments and use more physical punishment to discipline their children, but crowding had little or no effect on any of the other measures. Booth and his colleagues concluded that socioeconomic status and general health had a much greater impact than crowded living conditions on the quality of life. The interview studies, like the correlational studies, seem to indicate that crowded housing conditions do not negatively affect residents.

PRISONS

Field studies of crowding have been conducted in two major settings: prisons and college dormitories. In a study of the effects of crowding in prisons, D'Atri (1975) compared the blood pressure of prisoners living in dormitory-type rooms that housed several prisoners with the blood pressure of prisoners housed alone or two to a cell. In the dormitories, prisoners had less ability to control and regulate the frequency and nature of their interaction with others. D'Atri found that prisoners living in dormitory rooms had higher blood pressure than the other prisoners. This heightened blood pressure was interpreted as indicating greater stress.

McCain, Cox, and Paulus (1976) compared the rates of illness among prisoners who lived in dormitory cells with the rates among prisoners who lived alone or with one other inmate in their cell. As in the D'Atri study, prisoners who lived with several others in dormitory rooms complained more of illness than those who lived alone or with one other person. McCain and his colleagues interpret these results as indicating that heightened stress is associated with lack of ability to control and regulate interactions in crowded prison environments.

We turn now to a problem that has recently become

3. Although the number of people living on a floor having suites is approximately the same as the number in a corridor dormitory, these different architectural styles have markedly different effects on social behavior. People living in suites can regulate their contacts with others and become a cohesive group. People living on corridors frequently find themselves running into others when they would rather avoid them. They do not become cohesive and engage in more competitive behaviors than suite residents. (Baum and Valins, 1977, p. 21–22.)

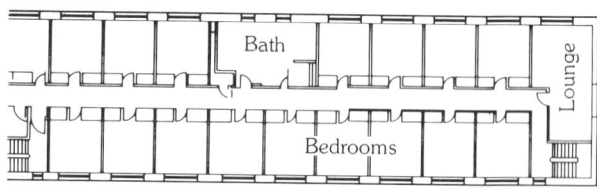

Floorplan of a Corridor-Design Dormitory

Floorplan of a Suite

widespread across our nation's campuses. Due to shortages in existing facilities and the high cost of construction, college dormitories have become increasingly crowded. Gone are the days when a student could choose to live in a single room. It is much more common for students to live in double rooms or suites housing four to six people. Some colleges are even finding it necessary to house three students in rooms intended for two. In the next two sections, we will consider the effects of the architecture of suites versus more traditional dormitory designs and then look at the effects of housing three students in rooms intended for two.

ARCHITECTURAL EFFECTS IN REACTIONS TO CROWDING

In an extensive program of reserach on the effects of dormitory architecture on the social behavior of college students, Baum and Valins (1977) compared the reactions of students who lived in ordinary 2-person double rooms with those of students living in groups of 6 in 3-room suites. The amount of space per person was approximately the same in these forms of housing. In the corridor dormitories, students lived 2 to a room. Each floor in the dormitory was inhabited by 36 students who occupied 18 rooms. As in most college dormitories, residents of each floor shared a communal bathroom and a large lounge. Thus students who wished to do anything other than sit in their room had to interact with all of the other residents of their floor who happened to be around at the time. On the other hand, students who lived in suites shared essentially 2- or 3-bedroom apartments. Although, like the corridor residents, students in suites lived 2 to a bedroom, they shared their bathroom and living room space only with the other members of their suite. Thus a corridor resident shared nonbedroom space with 35 others, while a suite resident shared nonbedroom space with 3 or 5 other people (see Figure 3).

Baum and Valins found that these different architectural arrangements had major effects on the social interaction of residents. Suite residents tended to form cooperative, cohesive groups, while corridor residents tended to remain alone or compete with each other. For example, suite residents reported that they resolved their problems more as a group, felt more accepted as individuals, disclosed more, and shared similar attitudes with others in their suite far more often than did corridor residents. When presented with a group decision-making task, suite residents reached a greater degree of consensus than corridor residents. Corridor residents felt that they often met people on their floor when they didn't want to. Suite residents rarely felt this way.

Baum and Valins conducted several experiments to investigate the social consequences of these different living spaces. In one experiment, suite and corridor residents were asked to wait in a room with a confederate before an experiment began. The investigators expected corridor residents to nonverbally demonstrate their wish to avoid being involved with others. The data confirmed this expectation. Corridor residents sat farther from the confederates, looked less often at them, and reported feeling less comfortable in this situation than suite residents, thereby signifying their greater desire to avoid interaction with others.

In a second experiment, Baum and Valins told subjects ahead of time that they would be involved in either a cooperative or a competitive game with another person. In the Cooperative condition, results were similar to those in the first experiment. Corridor residents sat farther away and felt more uncomfortable than suite residents. When the situation was reversed, however, and subjects were told to expect to play a competitive game, corridor residents sat much closer to the confederate than they had before, while suite residents sat slightly farther away. When the situation was defined as competitive, the corridor residents were more comfortable. Baum and Valins noted that a competitive situation by its very nature imposes greater psychological distance from others. Thus, in the Competitive condition, corridor residents could sit closer without getting involved in unwanted interactions with others.

In a third experiment, corridor and suite residents were asked to solve anagrams in competitive and noncompetitive circumstances. Suite residents performed better in noncompetitive situations than in competitive ones, while the reverse was true for those who lived on corridors. In an experiment conducted by Reichner (1979), corridor and suite residents were placed in a discussion group with several confederates. In one condition, the confederates included the subject in a discussion; in the second condition, the confederates ignored the subject and excluded him or her from the conversation. Being ignored in social situations is unpleasant, and people so ignored are generally angry. Reichner reasoned that, since corridor residents wished to avoid social interaction, they would be less bothered by being ignored than suite residents. The results supported this expectation.

These studies paint a picture of markedly different social behavior resulting from architectural arrangements that vary available privacy and the opportunity to control and avoid unwanted interactions. The suite architecture maximizes privacy and control over unwanted interactions, while the traditional corridor architecture fails to do so. As a result, suites promote the development of cohesive and cooperative groups, while corridor arrangements alienate residents and lead them to engage in less productive social behavior. Furthermore, not only did corridor residents state that they felt more crowded, but they also demonstrated their heightened sensitivity to crowding in a projective test.

Living in a typical corridor-style college dormitory is not the best of all possible worlds. But surely things could be worse. What would happen if a housing shortage necessitated the addition of a third person to a room that was designed to accommodate two people? This is not a hypothetical question, for universities all across the country are adopting this solution to a shortage of campus housing. Judging by the reactions of many students, it is a very unpopular solution.

"TRIPLING" STUDENTS IN TWO-PERSON ROOMS

Baron, Mandel, Adams, and Griffen (1976) compared tripled and doubled students living in corridor dormitories at the University of Connecticut. Triples felt less satisfied with their living conditions and said they had less control over them. Although there was a tendency for their grades to be poorer than the grades of students housed two to a room, the difference was not statistically significant.

In a second study of the effects of tripling, Karlin, Epstein, and Aiello (1978) studied the behavior and reactions of tripled and doubled male and female students living in a corridor dormitory at Rutgers University. Results indicated that tripled women fared worst. They reported the greatest number of physical and psychological symptoms, were most frustrated in their desire to make their room homey, disclosed less intimate information to their roommates than noncrowded women, and were more likely than were males to break up their threesome at the first possible opportunity. Since these results may have been due to the formation of coalitions rather than the crowding that resulted from placing three students in a room, subsequent analyses compared the reactions of isolates with those of coalition members. Coalitions formed among the females but not among the males. However, isolates fared no worse than members of coalitions.

In the second semester of their first year, most of the tripled men continued to live as threesomes, while most of the women managed to move into two-person groups. None of the students were tripled after the end of the first year. At the end of the first semester of their junior year, Rosen (1976) contacted most of these students, who agreed to participate in a follow-up study. She administered a questionnaire on the students' adjustment to college life and obtained transcripts of their grades.

Beginning with the sophomore year, the reactions of all students were very similar. Grade-point averages and indices of adjustment to college life seemed unrelated to whether students had been tripled or doubled during the first year. However, when reactions to college during the first year were compared to reactions later when students were no longer crowded, clear effects of tripling emerged. While all students were less well adjusted to college during the first semester of their first year, the effect was significantly stronger for tripled students. During the first semester, male and female tripled students were more disappointed about various aspects of college life and had more negative emotional reactions than doubled students. They also had a greater desire to change roommates, felt more strongly that their roommates and their living conditions contributed to the unpleasantness of college life, and reported that they spent less time studying. Finally, an examination of grade-point averages revealed that both doubled and tripled students earned poorer grades in the first semester of their first year than later. However, the degree to which grade-point averages had been depressed during the first semester of the first year was significantly greater for triples than for doubles.

Effects of institutional environments

We have discussed several environmental processes that have important consequences for social behavior. We have looked at spatial behavior, territoriality, and privacy and discussed their importance in regulating behavior in crowded environments. The final section of this chapter extends these ideas to behavior in institutional environments, particularly mental hospitals. In addition to considering the importance of privacy and spatial behavior, we must also understand the norms and patterns of adaptation that characterize life in what Goffman (1961) calls total institutions. Finally, we will look at the ways in which the architecture of total institutions conveys the institutional philosophy and influences behavior.

TOTAL INSTITUTIONS

Erving Goffman, an astute sociologist, has written extensively about total institutions (Goffman, 1961). Examples of TOTAL INSTITUTIONS include prisons, mental hospitals, and homes for the elderly. The institutions are considered "total," because the three major aspects of the inmates' existence—work, recreation, and sleep—all occur within the confines of the institution. In these total institutions, all the individuals' daily activities are conducted with a group of others and follow a rigid time schedule.

The total institution is populated by two groups: a large group called inmates and a small supervisory staff. Each group conceives of the other in terms of narrow and hostile stereotypes. When an inmate enters the total institution, a process of MORTIFICATION begins, designed to make inmates see themselves as the degraded individuals that the staff consider them to be. One important way of degrading patients is to deprive them of privacy. The environment is designed to minimize available privacy. Inmates in prisons or mental hospitals usually sleep in dormitory rooms together with many others and often use toilets that have no doors. Inmates are frequently searched and their bodies touched or pawed by staff members. This violation of one's body is highly degrading. Privacy is also violated by having one's mail read and censored by the staff.

Goffman also shows how staff members capitalize on the lack of privacy to tyrannize and humiliate inmates. Because the environment is total, the staff knows about the inmates' behavior in a variety of different settings. If a mental patient, for example, is trying to portray his or her positive assets in a group therapy session, a staff member may well embarrass him or her by pointing out some negative behavior, such as nonparticipation in a recreational setting. Nowhere can the patient escape this ever-present surveillance. And though staff members watch inmates, they interact with them infrequently.

In Chapter 2 we described the study of Rosenhan (1973) who, along with a group of associates, got admitted to a mental hospital by saying that they were hearing voices. Other than this one dramatic falsehood, they gave the admitting staff accurate information about their backgrounds but were diagnosed as schizophrenics. On the wards, they kept notes of interaction patterns and the way inmates were treated. Rosenhan reports that there was very little contact between staff and patients. Staff members isolated themselves in a glassed-in enclosure and spent most of their time socializing with other staff members. They emerged only to give medication, conduct therapy sessions, and instruct or reprimand patients. Attendants spent only 11.3 percent of their time outside the glassed enclosure, and that time included such activities as folding laundry, supervising patient clean-up and overseeing shaving. Nurses spent even less time than attendants with patients, emerging from their glass enclosures only about 11 times per 8-hour shift. And physicians spent even less time than nurses making contact with patients.

The staff stereotyped the patients as "crazy" and treated them as less than human. Rosenhan and the other pseudopatients approached staff members to ask questions and recorded the responses they received. For example, patients approached staff members and politely asked, "Pardon me, could you tell me when I will be eligible for grounds privileges?" The usual response to this question was to move on with head averted and give no answer. This response occurred 71 percent of the time among psychiatrists and 88 percent of the time among nurses. Only 23 percent of the time did psychiatrists make eye contact with the patient, and nurses made eye contact only 10 percent of the time. Through their nonverbal behavior, these

Social psychology and the environment

physicians and nurses conveyed that they considered the patient was a worthless individual not even deserving the common courtesy of a look, far less a reply to his question.

Many other aspects of total institutions make the inmate feel worthless. For example, things we take for granted in our daily lives, such as watching TV, eating a snack, or reading a newspaper, become special privileges that the inmate has to earn. The staff constantly use the threat of punishment or denial of these privileges to keep the inmates in line. Clothing cannot be used to express individuality in institutions. Because institutions are designed to run efficiently, it is cheaper to have a standard uniform for all inmates, and these uniforms rarely fit well.

In addition, the architecture of the institution may graphically convey the attitude of staff toward the inmates. Many prisons and mental institutions are conceived of as "warehouses" where undesirable or malfunctioning individuals are stored away from society to protect other members of society from their contaminating effects. How do inmates cope with these dehumanizing environments and how are they affected by them? We consider these issues in the next section.

Responses to life in total institutions. Some inmate responses to the dehumanizing aspects of institutional life can be considered positive adaptations. There is a considerable amount of reactance against the negative ways in which the staff portray the patients. Typically, many patients become "intransigent," challenging the institution by refusing to cooperate with the staff. In the Rosenhan study, one typical mode of rebellion was the refusal to take medication. Patients would not swallow pills given to them. Instead they would hide them and later flush them down the toilet. Another response an inmate frequently makes is to develop a story or a tale of woe to explain how and why he or she has come to be incarcerated. The norms of the inmate culture ensure that others will refrain from challenging the inmate's story.

Other responses, however, represent capitulation to the views of the staff. Some inmates become model patients, imitating the posture and gestures of staff members. These patients are often given special privileges and are used to help take care of other inmates. But the price they pay for these privileges is admitting that they are failures in need of help.

Regardless of whether the inmates resist or acquiesce, life in the institution creates anxiety about leaving. Much of the inmate's time is spent yearning for freedom from the confines of the institution, but when the time to leave approaches, the inmate becomes fearful that he or she can't "make it" in the outside world. To some extent, the staff's view has rubbed off. Inmates are concerned about whether people in the outside world will stigmatize them because of the time they spent in the institution. They are also unaccustomed to taking care of themselves. Inside the institution, all their decisions about what to eat, what to wear, when to partake in what form of recreation, and who to associate with were made by the staff. Inmates are frightened when they think about having to make all these decisions for themselves. In response to this anxiety, many inmates do something wrong that prevents their release from the institution. Others who manage to avoid this pitfall are released, but they may become overwhelmed with the problems of making it in the outside world after many years away from normal life. Relapse may result, and they find themselves back in the institutions they so desperately yearned to leave.

So far, we have considered the social nature of institutional life and its generally negative effect on inmates. There has also been some work on the effects of the physical environment on inmates.

THE PHYSICAL ENVIRONMENT OF MENTAL HOSPITALS

Apart from the exterior of the mental hospital, which frequently conveys the feeling that inmates are being stored in a warehouse, many interior features have

An institutionalized mental patient faces loss of individuality and total dependence on the system. Feeling worthless, the patient is frequently treated as such by the institution's staff, thereby creating an even greater degree of alienation. As a result, the effectiveness of total institutions for the mentally ill is largely coming into question. (Wide World Photo)

negative effects on patient behavior. Humphrey Osmond (1966) pointed out, for example, that long corridors in mental hospitals provoke anxiety in normal people, let alone schizophrenics whose perception of space and time is already distorted. Wards are usually designed to minimize privacy. Since schizophrenics are generally withdrawn and have higher needs than others for being by themselves, the traditional ward fails to meet their needs. They respond by withdrawing to corners of the dayroom, where they sit by themselves. Staff members observing this behavior find their stereotypes of these "crazy people" reinforced.

The physical environment of mental hospitals probably has an even greater effect on the behavior of institutionalized children than on that of institutionalized adults. Ittelson, Proshansky, Rivlin, and Winkel (1974) cite a study by Tars and Appelby (1973) showing that a 10-year-old boy who was hospitalized because he was withdrawn actually became *more* withdrawn in the hospital than he was at home. The increased withdrawal in the face of added opportunities to socialize appears to have been due, in large part, to the architecture and regimenting rules of the hospital, which minimized opportunities for privacy. At home, what little contact did occur was the result of a limited amount of creativity and exploration. The hospital environment snuffed this out.

Ostensibly, mental hospitals are supposed to heal patients and make them better able to function when they are released. Yet architecture so different from what they will find on the outside is not suited to this purpose. Living, sleeping, and eating in a group with many large rooms devoid of privacy are poor preparation for life in a home or apartment. Ittelson, Proshansky, and Rivlin (1970) redesigned a dayroom with more comfortable seating and found that there was a decrease in isolated and withdrawn behavior in this area. If patients wanted to behave in an unsociable way, they went elsewhere. Holahan and Saegert (1973) compared behaviors of psychiatric patients in two wards that had at one time been identical but one of which had been repainted and fitted with partitions in dayrooms and bedrooms to increase privacy. This innovation reduced the incidence of isolated and withdrawn behavior.

The final study we will describe was conducted by Knight, Zimring, Weitzer, and Wheeler (1976) at a state school for the mentally retarded. The research team investigated how architectural modifications of an existing facility affected personal space and social behavior. The renovation was an attempt to create a NORMALIZED ENVIRONMENT (Wolfensberger, 1973), one that so far as possible permitted the types of behaviors and norms that occur in noninstitutional environments. The researchers believed that they could normalize the patients' environment and help teach them to behave in a more social manner.

The inmates in this study were male and female adults who were considered severely retarded. Prior to the renovations, they slept 15 or 20 to a room that measured 30 feet x 40 feet. They had a dayhall, a dining room, and a multipurpose room, all of which were drab and sparsely furnished. Two different types of architectural renovations were used. One created facilities much like college dormitories. Rather than sleeping in large halls, inmates now slept in single or double rooms that had doors they could lock. The renovated space also had two large activity rooms, TV rooms, and two small conversation areas. The second type of renovation maintained the concept of a common large sleeping room but erected 4½-foot partitions around the beds to provide a sense of personal space and privacy.

The original sleeping hall and the two different bedroom designs are shown in Figure 4. The researchers believed that, in order for inmates to learn to recognize and use personal space, they needed a physical environment that clearly defined personal space and a staff who would model appropriate behaviors, such as respecting the inmate's right to privacy. If these condi-

4. Architectural modifications of an institution for the retarded. (a) Open sleeping ward before renovations. (b) One- or two-person bedroom after renovations. (c) Module design after renovations. These changes sometimes led to changes in the behavior of both staff and inmates, but at other times they did not. The incomplete partitions were not as successful as the total partitions in changing behavior. The effect of incomplete partitions on patient behavior seems to depend largely on the attitude of staff members. (Alyce Kaprow Photo)

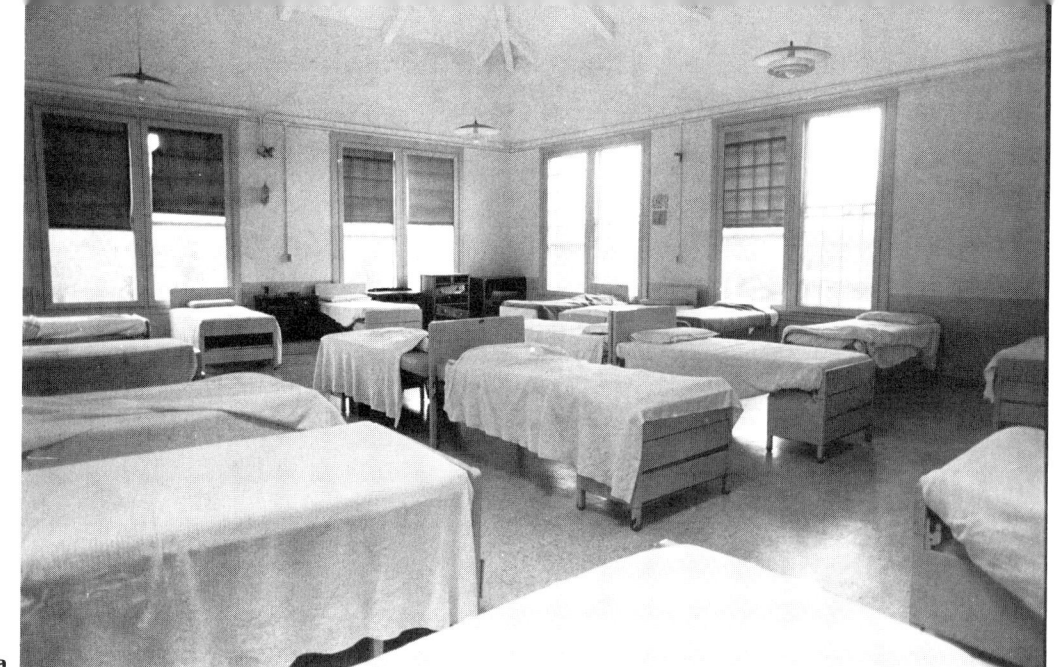

469
Environmental
influences
on social behavior

tions were met, patients were expected to engage in more appropriate social behaviors.

Observers stationed on the wards coded various types of personal space and social behaviors of the inmates before and after the renovations took place. When lockable bedrooms were provided, staff members began to respect the privacy of the inmates and taught them appropriate behaviors. The result was a dramatic increase in inmates' appropriate use of space and respect for the privacy of other inmates. Where the renovation introduced partitions in the common sleeping area, the degree of inmate learning depended on the attitudes and behaviors of the staff. When staff members respected the privacy of inmates, they imitated this behavior in their responses to fellow inmates. When staff failed to do so, inmates likewise failed to learn. Note that an important consequence of the different architectural modifications was their effect on staff behavior. Private bedrooms clearly signaled the staff to respect the privacy of inmates, while partitions had this effect only some of the time. Rather than merely providing privacy, it appears necessary to make the environment more homelike if we want to socialize mentally retarded patients.

Summary

In this chapter, we have described a variety of environmental influences on human social behavior. The use of space was seen as a vehicle for regulating the quality and intimacy of interpersonal encounters. Nonverbal mechanisms, such as how far we stand from someone, the angle at which we face someone, and the frequency with which we engage in eye contact, regulate the intimacy of our interactions. We discussed the equilibrium model of Argyle and Dean, which describes the process of regulating the intimacy level of interactions, and we discussed Patterson's extension of the model. We also described Hall's work on interaction distances, emphasizing the constraint that distances place on communication and paying particular attention to the effects of interactions that violate expectations about appropriate distances.

Our discussion of these spatial and nonverbal behaviors led to a consideration of mechanisms for attaining privacy. Then we noted Altman's suggestion that privacy is a dialectical process: privacy needs vary from individual to individual and situation to situation, sometimes indicating that the individual desires more privacy and sometimes less. Marshall's nondialectical approach emphasized different types of privacy needs, including anonymity, intimacy, solitude, seclusion, not neighboring, and reserve. We also considered territorial behavior and showed that interactions occurring on one's own territory differ from interactions taking place on someone else's territory. Finally, we concluded our discussion of spatial behavior with a look at cultural differences in appropriate spatial behavior.

Human spatial behavior served as our background for understanding an important environmental problem—crowding. We noted that crowding occurs in a variety of settings and that the problems faced by people crowded in each of these settings differ. We used Altman's setting, process, and actor framework to account for the effects of crowding and explain why the results of studies conducted in different settings are often contradictory. We reviewed the research on transportation crowding, noting that people usually find it stressful, and we discussed literature on sex differences in reactions to mass transit crowding and crowding in classrooms. While women frequently react more positively to these crowded environments than men, the difference is a culturally conditioned one, not genetic.

The remainder of our discussion of crowding focused on crowded residences. Life in crowded apartments has only minor negative effects on social behavior and few negative effects on health and stress. On the other hand, a few studies conducted in prisons showed that prisoners living in dormitory quarters had more health problems than prisoners living in individual or two-person cells. We also considered architectural variations in college dormitory design that influenced feelings of crowding and patterns of social behavior. These studies showed that residents of suites were more sociable and felt less crowded than residents of corridor dormitories. Finally, we reported on two studies of the effects of placing three students in college dormitory rooms built to accommodate only two people. These studies showed that "tripled" students were less satisfied and tended to have poorer grade-point averages than students who were not tripled.

The final section of this chapter dealt with institutional environments. Goffman's work on the characteristics of total institutions was discussed. We focused in particular on the environment of the mental hospital and examined how this environment influenced the treatment of inmates and their responses to it. We concluded with a discussion of a recent study that varied some architectural features of an institution for mentally retarded adults. A new design that increased the inmate's privacy led to changes in staff behavior and promoted positive behaviors on the part of the inmates.

GLOSSARY

accessibility The degree to which information requested by an interviewer is readily available in the memory of the person being interviewed.

accommodation One aspect of adaptation in Piaget's theory. An organism's attempts to meet the demands of the environment by modifying its schemata to deal with discrepant information about objects.

achievement motivation A desire to excel or attain success in one's endeavors; a tendency to evaluate one's performance with respect to personal standards of excellence.

acquiescent response style The tendency to agree with statements on a questionnaire regardless of the content of the statements.

adaptation A Piagetian process by which the organism "fits into" its environment. Adaptation occurs through the twin processes of assimilation and accommodation.

adaptation level theory Helson's theory that we notice and react to changes in stimuli or deviations from the level of stimulation to which we have become accustomed.

affiliation The tendency to associate with other people or seek them out.

aggression Any behavior with the goal or intent of harming or injuring another living being (human or animal) who is motivated to avoid such treatment.

aggressor An individual who commits an act of aggression. The role of aggressor may be viewed as a social role which requires the complementary role of victim.

altercasting The processes by which we try to induce those with whom we are interacting to play roles that complement the roles we ourselves play in the interaction.

altruistic behavior A type of prosocial behavior. In a pure case the behavior is performed voluntarily, with empathy, and without expectation of reward.

anal stage The second Freudian psychosexual stage, which occurs during the second year of life. The anal area is very sensitive to stimulation during this period.

androgynous Possessing the sex-stereotyped qualities of both males and females.

angry aggression Aggression which has the aim of harm or injury. The emotion of anger is a driving force in this type of aggression, which is usually contrasted with instrumental aggression.

anonymity The degree to which a person wants to maintain privacy in a public environment.

anxiety A feeling of intense subjective discomfort characterized by the belief that something bad is going to happen.

archival data Information that is available in public records. For example, information gathered by the U. S. Census is public information and can be used archivally. Similarly, the local telephone book is an archive of other types of information which can be used for research purposes.

archival research Investigation that makes use of existing public records such as police reports, library withdrawals, or book sales to obtain information pertinent to the hypotheses of interest.

assimilation One aspect of adaptation in Piaget's theory. An organism's ability through perception to "take in" (assimilate) its environment and fit new experiences and objects into existing schemata.

assisting One type of helping behavior which involves devoting one's effort, time, or material goods to another who has a specific need. Often there is no expectation of reciprocation or reward.

attachment A term coined by Bowlby to describe the infant's attempts to maintain physical closeness to the mother. The concept also signifies the baby's affection and love for people around him or her.

attempted leadership An effort made by someone to influence another.

attitude In the classical view, an attitude is assumed to have three components: beliefs about some object, positive or negative feelings toward the object, and a tendency to behave toward the object in particular ways. We infer that people have attitudes toward an object on the basis of how they behave toward the object and what they say about the object.

attraction A type of attitude directed toward other people. A positive affective state toward others is liking; a negative affective state toward others is disliking.

attribution Inferring that someone has a particular characteristic or trait on the basis of observing something about the person's behavior. For example, motivation may be inferred by observing how hard a person tries to perform a task.

audience The person or people to whom a persuasive communication is addressed.

authoritarianism A personality syndrome characterized by excessive obedience to and respect for authority, fear of being different, condemnation of others who differ from the norm, and a tendency to adopt mystical, superstitious beliefs in certain areas.

autokinetic effect Perceptual phenomenon in which a small, stationary light in an otherwise dark area appears to move.

availability When we judge the frequency of various events from memory, examples of some of the events may be more easily brought to mind than others. Availability refers to the ease with which an example can be brought to mind.

axis of orientation The angle at which a person's body faces the body of a person with whom he or she is interacting. The more directly the two people face each other, the greater the intimacy of the interaction.

behavioral assimilation effect When two people are interacting and one of them behaves in a very competitive manner, the second person may be led to behave in a similarly competitive manner. The behavior of the second person thus becomes quite similar to the behavior of the first person.

behavioral confirmation The processes whereby we induce others to behave as we expect them to behave and thereby confirm our initial impression of them.

bias A distortion or error. Research results may be biased if the investigator does not control for certain influences, such as his or her own desire to obtain particular results.

biological determinism A general viewpoint that assumes that much behavior is genetically determined and that complex social behavior may be preprogrammed biologically. This viewpoint is usually opposed by learning theorists, who view social behavior as almost entirely a product of learning and cultural conditioning.

body buffer zone Area surrounding an individual's body, which, if intruded on by another individual, leads to feelings of anxiety.

bonds Ties governing a relationship. People who like each other and share with each other might be described as being cooperatively bonded to each other.

boomerang effect A result of social influence in which change is produced in a direction opposite to that desired by the person attempting to influence the other.

brainstorming A technique in which group members generate as many solutions to a problem as they can dream up in a setting in which criticism is forbidden. The idea is that criticism inhibits novel thinking, so new and better solutions should be forthcoming in the absence of criticism.

break point In observing another's behavior, people tend to organize the behavioral sequence into segments. Break points are the points in ongoing behavior sequences where one segment is seen as ending and another beginning.

catharsis hypothesis The concept that "blowing off steam" or engaging in fantasy aggression will drain aggressive energy so that actual aggression will be less likely.

central traits In forming impressions of other people, we see some of their characteristics as more informative than other characteristics about what kind of people they are. Such characteristics or traits are considered central traits in that they exert an organizing influence on the impression.

classical conditioning A type of learning theory

often associated with the name Pavlov. If a dog salivates when meat is presented, the meat is an unconditioned stimulus, and the salivation is the unconditioned response. If a bell is sounded when the meat is presented, it eventually elicits salivation when sounded alone. The bell is called a conditioned stimulus, and salivation to the bell is a conditioned response.

climatron A laboratory environment designed for research on the effects of climate on behavior. It is specifically constructed to allow individuals to live in it for long periods of time. The researchers are able to vary such factors as temperature, humidity, rate of air flow, ion change, and ion concentration.

cognition The processes involved in thinking or knowing or being aware of the events and people around us.

cognitive complexity The extent to which one's knowledge of the world is organized into simple or complicated categories. Some people, for example, see the world in terms of black or white, either-or categories, whereas other people are less absolute in their perceptions.

cognitive conceit A common source of bias in person perception, whereby we overestimate our ability to take in and utilize data about others when making judgments.

cognitive-developmental theory A theory of social development proposed by Piaget. The emphasis is on the ways in which cognitive development and natural processes of maturation affect children's social behavior at different ages.

cognitive element A single item of knowledge, such as "the sun is shining," "the car is red," or "Sam is unpleasant."

cognitive structure In Piaget's theory, a cognitive structure is a mental organizational framework. Reflexes are the basis of structures, but complex behavior patterns become part of structures as the child matures. For example, thumbsucking is a structure which develops early in life.

cohesiveness A central property of groups relating to the degree to which members of the group are attracted to it and wish to remain part of it. A cohesive group is one whose members want to be a part of the group.

commitment A nonrevocable behavior or set of behaviors by which one binds oneself to a particular course of action.

common effects A concept from Jones and Davis' attribution theory. Any act is usually only one of several a person might have performed, and each possible act has one or more effects. Some effects would result from all the possible acts and are therefore common to them all. Because it belongs to all the possible choices, a common effect cannot explain why an individual performed the chosen act.

communication The processes by which we convey information to each other.

comparative function of reference groups An individual may use a reference group as a basis for judging the adequacy of his or her own behavior.

competition Two or more people or groups are said to be in competition when they are each trying to obtain the same nondivisible outcome or resources.

complementarity To complement something is to provide that which is missing. Under some conditions people are attracted to others who are different from themselves, but who complement them in tastes or the roles they assume in life and, in particular, in marriage. Complementarity refers to the idea that long-term relationships may often require a certain matching of different, rather than similar, characteristics.

compliance An observable change in behavior, usually resulting from the request of another person or a group.

concrete operations Third development stage in Piaget's theory of cognitive development. During this stage, the child learns to think logically about concrete objects and events.

conditioned response Any response, similar in form to an unconditioned response, which is elicited by a conditioned stimulus.

conditioned stimulus Any stimulus paired with an unconditioned stimulus which comes to elicit a response similar in form to the unconditioned response.

confederate A person who poses as a naive subject in research, particularly in an experiment, but who is really an accomplice of the experimenter and who behaves in certain predetermined ways. The point is usually to see how the programmed behavior of the confederate affects the behavior of real subjects in the research.

conflict A situation in which a person would like to perform two or more mutually exclusive behaviors, but in which only one can be performed.

conformity Involves a conflict between the desires or beliefs of an individual and the desires or beliefs of another individual or group. If the individual resolves the conflict by doing something he or she does not believe in and would not have done were it not for the real or imagined pressure from others, then the behavior is an example of conformity.

connotative meaning The ideas that we associate with a particular word beyond those that constitute the primary, or denotative, meaning of the word.

conscience One aspect of the superego. The child internalizes parental prohibitions; any transgressions cause feelings of guilt. The set of internalized prohibitions is called the conscience.

content analysis A research method in which characteristics of verbal material are systematically and objectively identified, usually to facilitate comparison with other verbal material. (For example, the number of aggression themes in newspaper editorials might be identified and counted.)

contingency model A theoretical scheme proposed by Fiedler in which the necessary qualities of a good leader are seen as being contingent on certain characteristics of the situation, such as the ambiguity of the task facing the group.

control In any research, only a certain number of variables can be investigated at any one time. In order to keep other, extraneous variables from influencing the results, these other variables must be held constant or controlled. In an experiment there is often a control condition in which no independent variables are manipulated and which serves as a basis of comparison for the effects of the independent variables manipulated in the other conditions.

cooperation A reciprocity behavior between at least two people. One person helps a second person in some way, and the second person helps the first in return. Usually the term applies to a situation in which the reciprocity maximizes the outcomes for both people.

correspondence A term used by Jones and Davis in their analysis of the attribution process to refer to the match between an act we observe and the characteristic or personality trait we attribute to the actor on the basis of observing that act.

cosmopolites A group of people living in the suburbs who identify with the city, would rather live there, but have moved reluctantly to the suburbs because they can afford to live there more economically.

credibility The perceived expertise and trustworthiness of a communicator. The more expert and trustworthy the communicator, the greater his or her credibility.

cultural relativism The conception that each society has a distinct or unique set of beliefs, habits, customs, and values.

cultural truism Any belief that is so widely accepted within one's culture that it is unlikely that one would have ever heard it contradicted. An example used by McGuire is the belief that brushing your teeth helps prevent tooth decay.

customs Patterns of behavior that are widespread and recurring within a culture; the usual ways of behaving in that setting.

daily living space A phrase used by Nahemow and Lawton to refer to the areas that one occupies or frequents in the course of a normal day. It is distinguished from selected activity space, the areas that one frequents only on special occasions or for specific purposes.

deindividuation A complex psychological process in which an individual becomes relatively unconcerned about the evaluations of others and performs behaviors that are usually inhibited. Deindividuation sometimes occurs when the individual is engaging in group activities.

demand characteristics In research, the unintentional cues given off by the investigator may induce a subject to behave in particular ways, usually ways that will confirm the investigator's hypotheses. It is as if the investigator and the setting in which the research takes place implicitly "demand" a particular type of response from the subject.

demographic characteristics Such characteristics of a population as age, sex, ethnicity, religion, and socioeconomic status.

denial hypothesis The idea that if a persuasive communication arouses a great deal of fear in the audience and does not give sufficient reassuring recommendations, the audience members will be motivated to ignore or minimize the importance of the threat.

denotative meaning The object or idea that a word stands for; that which the word designates.

dependent variable The index that is used in research to see whether changes in the independent variable have any effect. It is called dependent because our interest is in seeing how changes in it are affected by, or depend on, changes in the independent variable.

deprivation dwarfism A term coined by Gardner, who discovered that some children not given adequate attention as infants develop glandular disturbances which lead to a stunted, dwarflike appearance.

deviance Any behavior that is different from the norms that govern behavior in a particular situation.

dialectic process A process consisting of opposing forces that change in relative strength over time. One's need for privacy, for example, is often the result of a dialectic process.

differential reinforcement A mixture of both reward and nonreward for different acts. For example, a child might be rewarded for behaving nonaggressively and not rewarded, or even punished, for behaving aggressively.

diffusion of responsibility Concept used by Latané and Darley to explain why people often do not help in an emergency. Each person expects others to help, and in this way each person's responsibility diffuses to the other people present.

dissonance The psychological state produced when a person does something that is inconsistent with one of his or her beliefs or attitudes.

dissonance theory Festinger's theory that behavior inconsistent with one's beliefs produces an aversive motivational state that people will seek to reduce. A state of cognitive dissonance may be reduced, for example, by changing one's beliefs to be consistent with one's behavior.

distributive justice A concept proposed by Homans which states that interaction between two people is equitable when the ratio of one person's profits (rewards minus costs) to investments is the same as the second person's ratio.

district A prominent feature in the individual's image of a region. A district is a geographical area such as a neighborhood. For example, Greenwich Village is a well-known district in New York City.

dominance hierarchy An ordering of individuals in terms of the amount of influence they are capable of exerting. Individuals low in the dominance hierarchy are least influential, while those highest are most influential.

dominant response In a situation in which new responses are to be learned, it is often the case that old, inappropriate responses have to be inhibited before the new responses can be performed. At the outset of learning, these old, inappropriate responses are said to be dominant, because they are what the person has usually done in that situation.

donating A type of prosocial behavior which involves giving one's goods or services to another person, organization, or cause, usually without expecting to receive any reward in return.

drive A strong need or motive state. The term derives from learning theories which propose that behavior is energized and directed by various drive states.

drive state A strong stimulus state within the organism which impels activity to try to reduce the stimulation. Hunger and thirst are examples of drive states.

dyadic system Any two elements in some kind of interaction. Two people in conversation compose a dyadic system.

ecological correlation A measure of the relationship between composite rather than individual items. For example, ecological correlations of the relationship between number of people per residential room and amount of juvenile delinquency in Chicago have been computed. To arrive at the ecological correlation, the *average* number of people per room in a neighborhood is correlated with the *average* rate of juvenile delinquency in that neighborhood. Then the neighborhood statistics become the units of analysis in the ecological correlational technique.

edge A prominent feature in an individual's image of an area. An edge is a boundary, such as a riverfront, that sets off one region from another.

effectance A need or motive state to understand,

cope with, and master one's environment; hence, a need to be effective in dealing with one's environment.

effect interdependence Two people are said to be effect interdependent when they are dependent on each other for rewards and reinforcements.

effective leadership When someone attempts to influence another, when he or she is successful in the attempt, and when the resulting state of affairs is beneficial to both, the first person is said to have exercised effective leadership.

ego A system of personality in psychoanalytic theory which comes into existence to channel the desires of the id into appropriate outlets. The ego follows the reality principle and eventually becomes the "executive" or master of the personality.

egocentricity The state of being in which a person believes his or her interpretation of a situation is the only possible interpretation. Egocentric people assume that everyone sees things as they do.

ego ideal An aspect of the superego. The ego ideal is the set of internalized values and standards of society as represented to the child by his or her parents.

emergency A situation which involves threat of harm, occurs rapidly, and is unforeseen and unpredictable.

environmental load The degree to which a given environment taxes the attention capacity of the individual.

environmental psychology A newly emerging area of psychology concerned with the relationship between the individual and the physical environment. Research within this area centers on different natural settings, on populations within these settings, and on the important processes involved in the behavior of the particular population in the given setting.

eponym A person's name that has been taken as a label for a set of ideas or a period of history, such as the McCarthyism of the early 1950s or Victorian England.

equilibrium model of intimacy A model proposed by Argyle and Dean describing the process by which humans regulate the intimacy level of their interaction with others. The main idea is that when intimacy is greater or less than the desired level, a process of compensation takes place which restores intimacy to the equilibrium level. Compensation takes the form of nonverbal behaviors such as eye contact, physical distance from the other person, and smiling.

equity A state that occurs in the interaction between two or more people when the ratio of inputs to outputs or costs to rewards is about the same for everyone. Equity is contrasted with inequity, which occurs when one person is doing more than his or her share of the work and getting less than his or her share of the rewards.

equity theory A general theory which uses the concept of distributive justice as an explanatory mechanism to account for a wide variety of human interaction.

eros A psychoanalytic term for the life instinct.

ethnomethodology A branch of social science that is concerned with the way in which individuals construct meaning out of their experiences. The task of an ethnomethodologist is to uncover the assumptions and premises that seem to underlie social interaction.

evaluation apprehension A phrase coined by Rosenberg to label a potential source of bias in psychological research. The idea is that subjects in such research are typically concerned about the self-image they present to the investigator and do not want to appear foolish, inconsistent, or immature. Hence, their behavior may not be typical of the way they would behave if they were not worried about what the investigator will think of them.

evolution The theory proposed by Darwin that all life forms evolve from previous forms due to genetic selectivity.

exchange theory A general theory of human interaction which views people as exchanging goods and services, or more generally rewards and punishments. Homans, Thibaut, and Kelley helped develop exchange theory.

experimental realism The amount that an experimental setting is involving and holds the subjects' attention. It is contrasted with mundane realism in which an experimental setting is representative of a "real-world" setting.

experimentation A form of research in which the investigator actively manipulates or changes something (the independent variable) in order to see what effects the change has on something else (the dependent variable).

expiatory punishment Punishment for its own sake because a rule has been broken, with no conception of making the punishment fit the transgression. Young children usually advocate this kind of punishment.

external locus of control A concept developed by Rotter. People who have this external orientation believe that the events they experience are not in their own control; the control exists in the external environment.

external validity A term used by Campbell and Stanley to refer to the generalizability of research results. Results are said to have external validity when they hold in different settings, with different subjects, and/or under altered conditions.

factor analysis A technique for analyzing large bodies of data in order to reduce many variables to a few underlying, essential components.

feedback Information about how one is doing on a particular task. Feedback allows one to make the changes necessary to improve one's performance.

foot-in-the-door technique Getting someone to yield to a small request in order to increase the probability that he or she will grant a larger, subsequent request.

formal operations The last developmental stage in Piaget's theory, which occurs at about age 12. Abstract conceptual ability and other adult modes of thinking develop in this stage.

forming stage The first of four stages of group interaction processes identified by Tuckman. In this stage, the primary concern of the group members is that of orientation or defining the problem confronting the group. The four stages, in the order in which they seem to occur in most groups, are forming, storming, norming, and performing.

free association A research technique in which the subject is required to give the first word that comes to mind in response to each of a series of cue words. Free association is often used in psychoanalysis to explore the relationships that a subject sees among various ideas.

frustration-aggression hypothesis A theory proposed in 1939 that frustration always causes aggression, but since modified to the point where there are now many recognized causes of aggression.

galvanic skin response (GSR) An electrical property of the skin used to measure physiological arousal.

genital stage The last Freudian stage of psychosexual development. It occurs at onset of puberty and involves the direction of libido toward the opposite sex with the aim of reproduction.

goal response The last response of some sequence of activity directed toward achieving a goal.

great person theory The idea that leadership ability is a quality a person has, a quality that will emerge no matter what situation the person finds himself or herself in. According to the great person theory, circumstances and the match of an individual's characteristics to circumstances are relatively unimportant.

group Two or more people, at least one of whom perceives them all as forming a unit.

group dynamics A sub-area of social psychology concerned with the interaction processes that occur in groups.

group pressure The implicit and explicit forces acting on an individual group member to encourage conformity to group norms.

groupthink A psychological phenomenon investigated by Janis, in which a feeling of cohesiveness among group members inhibits mutual criticism. As a result of the lack of critical evaluation of group procedures and products, the group may produce inferior products or make poor decisions.

halo effect The effect produced when one's overall evaluation of another person is allowed to color one's evaluation of that person's specific attributes.

hedonic relevance A phrase used by Jones and Davis in their analysis of attribution processes. Observed actions of another person that have consequences that are pertinent to the life of the observer are said to be hedonically relevant to the observer.

hedonism The idea that the goal of all human behavior is to obtain pleasure and avoid pain.

helping A prosocial act directed toward another person which helps the person solve a problem or reduces a need state of the person in some way.

horizontal structure of an attitude Jones and

Gerard suggest that if we regard an attitude as the conclusion of a syllogism in which the minor premise is a belief statement and the major premise is an evaluative statement, then the same attitudinal conclusion can often be arrived at by other combinations of beliefs and evaluations. Horizontal structure refers to the fact that the same attitude may be the conclusion of several different syllogisms.

hospitalism A term coined by Spitz that refers to a pattern of behavior in which children raised in an institutional setting gradually become more retarded and withdrawn from the world.

hypersexual Unusually or excessively concerned with sexual activity.

identification In psychoanalytic theory, the process by which the person learns to match an image in the mind with the actual physical object. Because parents satisfy so many of the child's needs, the child may seek to become like them. Thus, the child identifies with the parents.

idiosyncracy credits Group members who have proven their loyalty and support of the group in the past can be thought of as having built up "credits" with the group. As a result, they are allowed occasional deviations from group norms and procedures without incurring sanctions.

illusory correlation Belief in a relationship between two variables when there is no relationship, the relationship is weaker than believed, or the relationship is the inverse of that believed.

image A term used by Lynch to describe the individual's cognitive representation of a particular physical location, such as a city or neighborhood.

immanent justice The notion held by young children that transgressions are invariably punished by God or nature. A young child might, for example, interpret a bicycle accident as retribution for some previous bad behavior.

immediacy An aspect of verbal communication that can be used to identify how the speaker feels about the person or object being referred to. Nonimmediate verbalizations are those which put some psychological distance between the speaker and the object and are used as a basis for inferring that the speaker dislikes the object.

imprinting Some species, especially birds, become attached to and follow any moving object shortly after birth. The animal is said to imprint on the object, because the attachment occurs so rapidly and is resistant to later change.

id According to psychoanalytic theory, the original primitive system of personality. The id is pleasure-oriented and strives for instinctual satisfaction without concern for the demands of reality.

indebtedness theory A theory proposed by Greenberg which assumes that if a person is helped by another, the person holds a psychological state of indebtedness toward the other. This state is aversive, and it may be reduced by reciprocating the help, either directly or to a third party.

independent variable The variable that the experimenter actively manipulates or changes in order to see what effect these changes will have on the dependent variable.

inequity A state that occurs in social interaction when the ratios of investments or costs to outcomes or rewards of all the participants are not equal. Inequity might exist, for example, if a husband and wife both work, but the husband refuses to help around the house.

information interdependence The state in which two or more people are dependent on each other for information about the validity of their perceptions and interpretations of reality.

information management A concept used by Goffman to refer to the task facing those who want to make a particular impression on others. In order to maintain the impression, or front, the individual must be able to control or manage the information to which the other person has access.

ingratiation Attempts on the part of one person to win the approval of another by such tactics as agreement with the other or flattery.

inhibition-disinhibition The notion that certain stimuli, such as punishment, may inhibit or prevent a response from occurring. Other stimuli, such as observing an act, may disinhibit or unblock a response so that it may occur.

innate purity A view of human nature (proposed by philosophers such as Rousseau and Kant) which assumes that people are born into a state of natural innocence.

instinctive behavior A complex behavior pattern

which is inherited, universal among a species, and only slightly modified by experience.

instrumental aggression Aggression which is a means to some other end; usually contrasted with angry aggression.

instrumental conditioning A type of learning, also called operant conditioning, often associated with the name of B. F. Skinner. Some reward or reinforcement which follows a response may increase the frequency of the response. For example, a rat will repeatedly press a small bar if pressing is rewarded by food pellets.

intention One's purpose in performing a particular behavior; the reason behind the action.

interaction Reciprocal social exchange between two or more people. Usually interaction is face-to-face, but it may also take place via such devices as telephones or letters.

interaction matrix The symbolic depiction of the behavioral repertoires of two people engaged in social exchange. For each behavior that one performs, the other has a choice of several behaviors. The matrix usually depicts the rewards that accrue to each person when a given pair of behaviors is carried out.

interaction process analysis A type of content analysis invented by Bales for analyzing what goes on in groups. The verbal material produced by members of the group is coded into twelve categories.

interaction processes The social exchanges, including verbal and nonverbal interchanges, that occur between two or more people.

internalize To incorporate the rules or values held by society. The child who has internalized the rules will follow them. When fully incorporated, the rules become a part of the self.

internal locus of control A concept developed by Rotter. People who have this orientation believe that the events they experience are within their control. Such people view themselves as causes of their own fate.

internal validity A phrase used by Campbell and Stanley to refer to whether a piece of research actually measures the variables of interest. In an experiment, for example, the question of internal validity might focus on whether the experimenter actually manipulated the independent variable he or she claimed to be manipulating.

interview The process of asking another person a series of questions on a certain topic. Interviews can range from a rigid format in which a number of people are all asked precisely the same questions, to relatively unstructured formats in which the person asking the questions has some freedom to decide the next question to be asked.

intimacy A privacy need identified by Marshall, reflecting the degree to which a person wishes to reveal personal facts about himself or herself to others.

intimate zone Interaction distances of 18 inches or less; usually used for intimate interactions such as lovemaking and fighting.

justice motive A concept proposed by Lerner and others, which states that people are preoccupied with the notion of justice in human affairs and need to believe that people receive what they deserve in life.

landmark A prominent feature in the individual's image of an area. A landmark is a well-known structure that comes readily to mind when the individual thinks about the area. The Empire State Building is an example of a landmark in New York City.

language An arbitrary system of symbols by which we convey information to each other. Those who wish to communicate by means of a language must, of course, agree on what each symbol is to represent.

latency stage A quiescent stage in Freudian theory which occurs after the Oedipus or Electra complex and lasts for several years prior to the onset of the genital stage.

latitude of acceptance A phrase used by the Sherifs, originators of social-judgment theory, to refer to those positions along an attitude continuum that a person would find acceptable or would agree with to some extent.

latitude of noncommitment A phrase from social-judgment theory that refers to those positions along an attitude continuum about which a person feels relatively neutral, positions with which the person neither clearly agrees nor disagrees.

latitude of rejection Those positions along an attitude continuum that a person disagrees with or finds objectionable for one reason or another.

leadership The process or state of exerting influence over other people.

learned helplessness The perception that one's outcomes are independent of one's responses, a perception that tends to inhibit or suppress future attempts to solve problems and achieve goals.

least preferred co-worker From Fiedler's contingency model of leadership effectiveness. To identify different types of leaders, Fiedler asked people to think of all those people they had worked with in the past and to describe the one with whom they had least enjoyed working. Those people who describe this least preferred co-worker in relatively warm, accepting terms tend to exert a different type of leadership from those who describe their least preferred co-worker in more negative terms. The latter tend to be much more directive and controlling as leaders.

libido In psychoanalytic theory, a general form of energy which drives the life instincts. Since the sex instincts are most prominent in the theory, libido is primarily a general sexual energy.

logical error An inferential bias that occurs in person perception. When we know one item of information about another person, we may assume that other, logically related things (such as a correlated trait) are also characteristic of the person when, in fact, they are not.

Machiavellianism An interpersonal style that is characterized by the cool, detached manipulation of other people to achieve one's own purposes.

Mach Scale A questionnaire designed by Christie and his associates to measure the extent to which one takes a manipulative attitude toward other people. The name derives from Niccolò Machiavelli, author of *The Prince*.

mandate phenomenon The label given the finding that elected leaders often act as if having won by a large margin gives them the right to do whatever they like while in office.

manipulation In the context of an experiment, the active changes in the independent variable introduced by the experimenter. The purpose is to see what effect these changes have on the dependent variable.

matching hypothesis In attraction research, the concept that people will become attracted to others approximately equal to them in physical attractiveness.

minimal social situation An artificial setting in which two people, each unaware of the other's presence, interact by making choices such as pushing one of two buttons and being rewarded or punished for the choices. Each person's reward or punishment is contingent on the choices made by the other person. Surprisingly, after some initial fumbling, a pattern of reciprocally rewarding choices often develops.

modeling Observational learning. A child may observe someone (a model) perform an act, and then engage in the act.

models Other people whose behaviors we imitate.

mortification Process by which an inmate in a total institution comes to see himself or herself as degraded and worthless, thus making his or her self-conception consistent with the staff's view.

motivation The desire to perform a particular set of behaviors or to achieve a particular goal.

multiple operationism The use of more than one method for investigating the relationships among variables. To see if frustration leads to aggression, for example, one might conduct an experiment, use participant observation, and conduct a survey.

mundane realism The phrase used by Aronson and Carlsmith to refer to how much an experimental setting simulates some aspect of the world outside the laboratory. Usually contrasted with experimental realism, how much the experimental setting is involving and holds the subject's interest.

node A prominent feature in the individual's image of a region. A node is an important transportation link that allows the individual to gain access to other areas in the region. Airports, railroad stations, and bus depots are examples of nodes.

nonconformity When a conflict exists between the desires or beliefs of an individual and the desires or beliefs of another individual or group, nonconformity occurs when the individual resolves the conflict by doing what he or she believes in spite of the pressure from others.

noncommon effects A concept from Jones and Davis' attribution theory. When a specific act is chosen over several alternatives and the effects of the act are not ones that could result from the other alternatives, these effects are called noncommon effects.

nonmonotonic A curve or graph that rises and then falls one or more times; a relationship between two variables that neither steadily increases nor decreases.

nonverbal communication The face-to-face conveying of information to others in ways that do not use words: facial expressions, posture, mode of dress, or interaction distance.

norm An implicitly or explicitly agreed upon standard of behavior; an expectation shared by members of a group about how one should behave.

normalized environment An environment which supports the norms and behaviors that typically prevail in normal noninstitutionalized environments.

normative function of reference groups Groups both set and enforce standards of behavior for those who belong, or would belong, to the group. The enforcing of standards of behavior among members or aspirants is the normative function of reference groups. (The setting of standards of behavior allows the individual to compare his or her own behavior to that of others and is thus the comparative function of such groups.)

norming stage The third of four stages of group interaction processes identified by Tuckman. In this stage, the group members predominantly express their opinions and suggestions about how to get on with the job at hand. The four stages, in the order in which they seem to occur in most groups are forming, storming, norming, and performing.

norm of giving A general norm postulated by Leeds that giving is intrinsically good. People want to give because of the norm, not because of anticipated gains in return.

norm of reciprocity A general norm of reciprocal behavior proposed by Gouldner. The norm states that people should help others who have helped them and should not hurt others who have helped them.

norm of social responsibility Proposed by Berkowitz as a general social rule which states that people should help others who are dependent on them. People follow this norm because of resulting self-rewards.

not neighboring A privacy need identified by Marshall reflecting the degree to which a person is concerned about having friends or neighbors dropping in to visit without previous warning.

obedience Doing as one is told; submission to another's real or imagined authority.

object-cathexis See *object-choice*.

object-choice An investment of energy by the id in forming a wish-fulfilling image of a need-satisfying object. The id is said to make an object-choice by investing energy to form such images.

object permanence A Piagetian concept which means that the child comes to realize that an object still exists even though it is out of sight. Object permanence develops during the stage of preoperational thought.

observational learning From social-learning theory, "learning by watching." Much of the child's knowledge of the social world is acquired simply by observation.

Oedipus complex A process in psychoanalytic theory which occurs in the phallic state (age 3–5 years). The male child becomes sexually attracted to his mother and jealous of his father. The complex is resolved by the child's identification with the father and transformation of desire for the mother into gentle affection. (The *Electra complex* is the equivalent for females, with minor variations.)

operant conditioning A process of learning whereby the subject is instrumental in producing an action that is then reinforced. In typical operant conditioning experiments conducted by B. F. Skinner and his students, a rat presses a bar which then activates a mechanism that drops a pellet of food into a food hopper.

operationalize To decide on a technique or method for defining or measuring a particular concept. One might, for example, define thirst as the length of time since one's last drink: the longer the time interval, the greater the thirst.

oral stage The first Freudian psychosexual stage, which occurs during the first year of life. The mouth and oral zone are very sensitive to stimulation during this period.

organization A term from Piaget's theory which indicates that mental structures tend to be organized in wholes as systems.

original sin A religious doctrine which views humans as born into an impure or evil state. The task of socialization is to tame and control the natural evil impulses of the child.

paradigm A type or characteristic research strategy. For example, one paradigm for studying cognitive dissonance involves "forced compliance," wherein a person engages in an act that he or she would not normally engage in. The experimenter then studies the resulting cognitive processes.

participant observation A research method in which the investigator enters into the routine of the people or setting to be examined, informally or formally interviews other participants in the setting, and gathers all available information about the setting.

path A prominent feature in an individual's mental image of a geographical area. A path includes both the route and the means for moving from one part of the area to another.

pecking order A slang expression used to refer to a dominance hierarchy among people or nonhuman animals. Originated from early studies of dominance that were conducted with groups of chickens.

perceptual defense The notion that people are slow to perceive those objects and events that they dislike or in some way find upsetting or threatening.

perceptual vigilance A heightened alertness and readiness to perceive certain classes of stimuli, especially those that the person feels positively toward or those that may serve as a signal for some avoidable danger.

performing stage The fourth of four stages of group interaction processes identified by Tuckman. During this stage, the group gets down to work. The four stages, in the order in which they seem to occur in most groups, are forming, storming, norming, and performing.

peripheral traits Characteristics that do not seem to make much of a difference when we are forming an impression of another person. These peripheral traits are seen as contributing little new or differentiating information about the person.

person To be a person means that one has decision-making powers, a distinct sense of self, a definite sex-role identity and organized and distinctive behavior patterns.

personalism A word used by Jones and Davis to describe the effect on an observer's attributions when the observer believes that the actor's behavior was intended to help or harm the observer. Personalism is hypothesized to decrease the correspondence of the inferences made by the observer.

personal space The emotionally charged zone surrounding an individual's body, which helps regulate the spacing between individuals. The term sometimes refers to the processes by which people mark out and personalize the space they inhabit.

personal zone Interaction distance extending from 18 inches to 4 feet. Used typically for friendly conversations.

person cognition The processes involved in thinking about, making inferences about, and making attributions to other people.

person perception The processes involved in perceiving other people. Often used interchangeably with impression formation, social perception, and person cognition.

persuasive communication paradigm The setting in which a source or communicator conveys a message to an audience with the intention of changing the attitudes of members of the audience.

Peter principle In any hierarchy, people will rise or be promoted until they occupy a job at which they are incompetent. Being incompetent in that role, they will not be promoted further but will remain at their level of incompetence.

phallic stage The third Freudian psychosexual stage, which occurs at ages 3–5 years. The genital area is sensitive to stimulation, and during this period the crucial Oedipus complex occurs.

physical reality The real world as it exists all around us. In social comparison theory, physical reality is contrasted with social reality, the agreed upon interpretations of the world or "proper" attitudes, beliefs, and values.

pleasure principle In psychoanalytic theory, the id is viewed as constantly striving for tension reduction, which is achieved by reflex actions and wish fulfillment. The concept of tension reduction is called the pleasure principle.

pluralistic ignorance A situation in which everyone privately deviates from the norms of a reference group, but believes that everyone else conforms to these norms.

power motivation The desire to exert influence over other people.

power semantic Nonreciprocal forms of speech in which one person is recognized as being in a superior position and one in a subordinate position.

precision One of the requirements of a good measuring instrument. The more precisely something is measured, the closer the result is to its true value.

prejudice An overall negative attitude toward another person or group. The term is usually used in discussing attitudes toward groups, and prejudice is assumed to be accompanied by beliefs that associate predominantly negative characteristics with the group and by behavioral tendencies to avoid or aggress against members of the group.

preoperational thought Second developmental stage in Piaget's theory. Children gain the power of language, learn to symbolize at an elementary level, and develop object permanence during this period.

prestige suggestion The idea that telling someone that a persuasive communication came from a respected and admired person would make the communication more effective in changing the person's attitude.

primary process In service of tension reduction, the id forms images of objects which satisfy its needs. The mechanism of forming wish-fulfilling images is called the primary process.

primary territory Nonpublic areas, such as homes, over which we exercise absolute territorial control.

prisoner's dilemma An experimental game derived by analogy with the situation in which two prisoners have been arrested for a crime, separated, and each exhorted to confess. The dilemma is posed by the fact that if neither confesses, there is limited evidence against them and they are likely to get moderate punishment. If one confesses and the other does not, the former gets off easy and the latter gets a heavy sentence. If both confess, they both get long sentences. The question is whether each can trust the other not to confess.

privacy Selective control of access to the self or to one's group.

private acceptance When the conformity conflict is resolved by an individual doing something he or she did not initially believe to be the right course of action, the person may later come to believe that what he or she was pressured into doing was indeed correct. If so, private acceptance is then said to have occurred.

propinquity Nearness or proximity to each other. The term is usually used in research on attraction and friendship formation, where it has often been found that mere propinquity, such as living close together, is a major factor in the probability of friendship formation.

prosocial behavior General term indicating positive acts or sentiments directed toward other people; includes behaviors such as altruism, donating, helping, assisting, sharing, and cooperation.

proxemics The scientific study of interaction distances and the way in which these distances constrain the various types of communication between individuals.

pseudogroup effect When we compare group performance with individual performance on certain tasks, groups sometimes appear to do better simply because a group has a greater number of individuals working and there is a better chance that at least one member of the group will be able to solve the problem. This effect has nothing to do with group processes or interaction.

pseudopatients In the Rosenhan study, researchers were admitted to a mental hospital by falsely informing admitting interviewers that they were hearing voices. After being admitted, these people took notes on life in a mental hospital.

psychiatric epidemiology A field of research in which investigators attempt to find the antecedent conditions or causes that lead to emotional disorders.

psychoanalytic theory A theory of social development proposed by Freud. The theory emphasizes the instinctual, emotional determinants of human nature and views socialization as the process of teaching the child to control these instincts.

psychosexual In psychoanalytic theory, a number of bodily zones are sensitive to pleasurable stimulation. At maturity, these various zones fuse to create a generalized sensitivity to pleasurable stimulation. Freud viewed adult psychology as primarily a sexual psychology; hence the emphasis on the psychosexual nature of humanity.

psychosocial A term applied to Erikson's theory, in contrast to Freud's psychosexual theory. Erikson was more concerned with ego development and the social—cultural determinants of personality development. Thus his emphasis was social rather than sexual.

public territory Places available to everyone, such as a public beach or public library.

public zone Interaction distances ranging from 12 feet to 25 feet. Used for public gatherings such as lectures or speeches.

punctuation In ongoing interaction, the meaning you assign to what occurs may depend on where you perceive a given sequence as beginning and ending, or where you punctuate the sequence.

random assignment A procedure employed by experimenters in assigning subjects to the conditions of an experiment. When subjects are randomly assigned, each has an equal probability of being assigned to a given condition. Thus, differences in the results of the experiment should not be due to any pre-existing differences among subjects assigned to the different conditions.

reactance A motivational state aroused by threat to or loss of one's freedom of behavior and directed toward safeguarding or restoring the free behaviors in question.

reactance theory Brehm's theory that threats to or elimination of one's freedom of behavior results in a motivational state directed toward safeguarding or restoring freedom of behavior.

reception tuning When forming an impression of another person, reception tuning is a state in which one anticipates learning more about the other. A final, decisive impression is postponed, and the person remains receptive to new information.

reciprocal punishment Punishment contingent on the nature of the misdeed. Children of age 10 and 11 years begin to reject expiatory punishment and advocate reciprocal punishment.

reciprocity behavior From "reciprocate," meaning to trade off. If one person helps a second person and the second returns help, he or she is reciprocating, or engaging in reciprocity behavior. Reciprocity behavior is often related to attraction.

reference group Any group to which we belong or aspire to belong and which we use as a basis for judging the adequacy of our behavior.

referential communication The attempt to convey information to another in such a way that the other can distinguish the object or objects being referred to from an array of similar or dissimilar objects.

reinforcement Consequences of an act or behavior. Behavior followed by positive consequences, or positive reinforcement, is likely to occur more frequently in the future. Behavior followed by negative consequences, or negative reinforcement, is likely to occur less frequently in the future.

relationship An imagined or real connection between two people in which at least one of the two is influenced by the other or by what he or she thinks the other might say or do, or in which at least one of the two thinks of the other from time to time.

relative deprivation The perception that one is less well off in some respect than others.

releaser stimulus In ethology, some definite stimulus pattern in another organism that is required to cue off an aggressive response.

reliability Repeatability of measurement. An instrument is said to be reliable if it gives the same results on repeated occasions when used under the same circumstances.

reserve A privacy need identified by Marshall, reflecting the degree to which a person is reluctant to disclose intimate information about himself or herself to others.

response acquisition The process of learning a new response or a new response pattern. According to social-learning theory, much response acquisition occurs by observation.

response competition In novel or ambiguous situations, a person may not know exactly how to behave. A state similar to conflict, wherein the person is torn between performing any of several different behaviors, or responses.

response facilitation Any stimulus which increases the probability of a response is said to facilitate the response. For example, observing someone else perform an act may facilitate another's performance of the act.

restitution Some behavior by which one tries to make amends or compensate for harm done to another person.

retrospective rationality Interpreting behavior

after it has occurred so that the behavior seems to have been a more logical response to the situation than it really was at the time.

risky shift The finding that group decisions following discussion of a problem are often riskier than the average of the decisions the individual members made prior to the discussion.

role A category of people, such as taxi drivers, and the expectations about how people in that category should behave.

role-taking Symbolically putting oneself in another person's position and trying to see the world, or a particular situation from that person's perspective.

sampling A statistical procedure whereby one selects a small number of people for participation in research. The small number of people, or sample, is selected in such a way that it is representative of the larger group, or population, from which it is drawn.

satisficing principle The idea that since one cannot always obtain the "best" outcome, one tries to obtain an outcome that is at least satisfactory or one that suffices.

scapegoat A person or object bearing blame that should fall on others. In ancient Jewish religious ceremonies, a scapegoat was a goat to which the chief priest symbolically transferred the sins of the people. The goat was then allowed to escape into the wilderness, thus cleansing the community of sin.

scapegoat theory of prejudice Based on the frustration—aggression hypothesis, the idea that aggression against the people or circumstances that produce frustration is often impossible. Hence, the frustrated may seek a less powerful object, person, or group as a target for aggression.

schema Some aspect of an individual's cognitive structure or organization of knowledge. Used by Terrence Lee, for example, to refer to a mental picture of the environment and the social significance of various places in the environment. In its more general sense, cognitive structure is an important aspect of Piaget's theory of development.

schizophrenic A person diagnosed as having a severe psychological disorder characterized by the presence of certain "thought disorders," among other symptoms.

seclusion A privacy need identified by Marshall, reflecting the degree to which a person is concerned with having a home out of sight of neighbors.

secondary drive state A second-order drive caused by frustration. In the frustration—aggression hypothesis, aggression was supposed to reduce the secondary drive state of frustration.

secondary territory Territory, such as a neighborhood bar, containing a mixture of public and semi-private access.

selected activity space A phrase used to refer to those areas that we frequent only occasionally and only for specific purposes. It is contrasted with daily living space, those areas that we frequent in the course of a normal day.

self-concept The complex perceptions that we have of ourselves, our abilities, beliefs, attitudes, skills, goals, aspirations, and niche in the social world, as well as our feelings about and evaluations of each of these aspects.

self-perception theory Bem's theory that the evidence we use in making judgments about ourselves is often the same as that used by an outside observer. We look at how we have behaved in the past to judge how we feel about a particular object or person.

self-reward Positive feelings about oneself, or an increase in self-esteem, that occurs because of some valued behavior one performs.

semantic differential A measuring technique devised by Osgood and his associates in which concepts are rated on a series of bipolar scales in order to obtain a measure of the connotative meaning of the concepts.

sensorimotor stage First developmental stage in Piaget's theory. During this period, many physical habits and action patterns develop.

sex-role identity An individual's basic concept of self as a sexual creature. Sex-role identity consists of a complex of values and expectancies about what is appropriate and desirable for one's sex.

sharing The prosocial behavior of dividing one's goods with another person so that he or she may partake in the use of the goods.

significant others A phrase usually used with reference to the socialization process in which the developing child is dependent on the ministrations of a few people, usually the parents, who are quite important to the child's well-being and development.

simple and sovereign theories Explanations of human behavior that make use of a single, all-encompassing principle, such as hedonism.

sleeper effect Increased agreement over time with a persuasive communication from a negative source, the communication at first having produced little or no agreement.

social-comparison theory Festinger's theory that, in the absence of physical evidence on which to base our beliefs, we rely on social reality or the degree to which our beliefs coincide with those of the people around us in evaluating our attitudes and beliefs. Further, in order to evaluate a particular belief, we usually seek out those who are similar to us in relevant respects.

social facilitation When one is in the presence of other people, well-learned responses seem to be facilitated and to occur with more vigor than when one is alone. However, the learning of novel responses seems to be inhibited by the presence of others.

social-judgment theory Sherif's theory that attitude change is a function of the discrepancy between one's initial position on the issue and the position advocated by a persuasive communication. Communications advocating positions that fall in one's latitudes of acceptance and noncommitment produce greater change the more discrepant they are from one's initial position. Communications advocating positions that fall in one's latitude of rejection produce less change the more discrepant they are from one's initial position.

social-learning theory A theory of social development in which such development is viewed primarily as a process of learning. Observational learning, modeling, and imitation are important concepts in the theory.

social psychology The study of social relationships and the behavioral, cognitive, and emotional processes accompanying such relationships. What this book is all about!

social reality The attitudes, beliefs, abilities, values, and perceptions of those other people all around us. Often used as a basis for evaluating our own attitudes, beliefs, values, abilities, and perceptions.

social specialist In many groups, two types of leaders may emerge: one who focuses on the task at hand and getting it done and one who focuses on the emotional dynamics of the group. The latter is considered to be a social specialist, the one who takes a meliorative role and keeps tensions among the members at a minimum.

social zone Interaction distances ranging from 4 feet to 12 feet. Used for formal interactions such as negotiations.

socialization All the aspects of learning and training that transform a biological infant into the social being we call a human.

socratic effect Delayed attitude change that occurs some time after the receipt of a persuasive communication and which is due to the gradual thinking through of the implications of the communication.

solidarity semantic Forms of speech that emphasize or point up the equality of the speaker and the person addressed.

solitude A privacy need identified by Marshall, reflecting the degree to which a person desires to be completely alone.

stereotype A preconceived belief about the characteristic associated with some object, person, or group. Usually the term is used to refer to the beliefs that we have about members of various national, religious, or racial groups.

stigma theories A term Goffman used to refer to the beliefs we have about stigmatized people. We often appear to assume that they have imperfections in addition to the stigma. These assumptions constitute an implicit theory about what people so stigmatized are like.

stimulus-value-role theory Murstein's theory that during the initial stages of heterosexual contact, the stimulus attributes of the other person, such as physical attractiveness, assume greatest importance. Later, shared values and agreement on basic issues are crucial to the continued development of the relationship, and finally, long-term adjustment requires some complementarity of roles.

storming stage The second of four stages of group interaction processes identified by Tuckman. During this stage, there is a great deal of emotional expressiveness and the group has yet to settle down to work. The four stages, in the order in which they seem to occur in most groups, are forming, storming, norming, and performing.

subjective norm A term from the theoretical position of Fishbein. Whether or not one actually carries out a given intention to behave depends in part on how one thinks other people would perceive and evaluate one's behavior. One's perception of what others would think is the subjective norm that applies to the behavior.

successful leadership When one person attempts to influence another and actually does so, successful leadership is said to have occurred.

superego According to psychoanalytic theory, the final system of personality to emerge. It is the internalized representative of society and consists of the conscience and the ego ideal.

surrogate Anything that serves as a substitute for something else. In some of Harlow's experiments, for example, young monkeys were given a "surrogate mother" built out of terry cloth.

survey research A method of research in which all the members of a selected group of people, the sample, are interviewed. The interview usually consists of a standard set of questions pertinent to some topic. All interviewees are asked the same questions in the same order, and their answers are tabulated.

tabula rasa "Blank slate." The philosopher John Locke's concept of the infant's basic nature as initially neutral, waiting to be shaped in many different directions.

task specialist In many groups, two types of leaders may emerge: one who focuses on the group's assignment or job and the best way to get it done and one who focuses on the emotional dynamics of the group. The former is the task specialist.

TAT (Thematic Apperception Test) A projective technique developed by Henry Murray consisting of a series of ambiguous pictures designed to measure individual needs and environmental presses. Subjects are asked to construct a story about each picture which is then scored to assess needs and presses.

territoriality A boundary-regulation mechanism that involves personalization or marking of a place or object and communication that it is owned by a person or group.

territorial marker An object or sign, such as a coat or books, indicating to others that a particular territory belongs to you.

thanatos A psychoanalytic term for the death instinct.

threat display Various gestures or movements indicating willingness to fight. Such displays are usually an attempt to defend territory.

total institutions Institutions, such as prisons and mental hospitals, in which all of the major facets of a person's life, such as eating, sleeping, work, and recreation, occur within the institution and are conducted together with other inmates of the institution.

transmission tuning A state said to exist when someone forming an impression of another person thinks he or she is going to have to describe that person to a third party. The necessity of having to communicate the impression tends to lead to a greater consistency in the impression formed than is otherwise the case.

triangulation of measurement Use of more than one method of measurment in the investigation of a particular phenomenon. The idea is that every method is imperfect, but different methods have different imperfections. Hence, if the same result is obtained by different methods, it is unlikely to be an artifact of the methods employed.

validity A measuring instrument is said to be valid when it measures just what it purports to measure—nothing more, nothing less.

value system The interrelated sets of beliefs that we all have about desireable states of affairs, goals worth striving for, and appropriate modes of behavior.

vertical structure of an attitude If we regard an attitude as the conclusion of a syllogism in which the minor premise is a belief statement and the major premise is an evaluative statement, then the major and minor premises may themselves be the conclusions of other syllogisms. Vertical structure refers to the fact that the syllogistic components of an attitude may themselves have been derived from other syllogisms.

victim An individual who is aggressed against. The role of victim may be viewed as a social role which requires the complementary role of aggressor.

voluntarism General term which designates a wide variety of volunteer helping and the complex of motive states which cause such helping.

weighted average In combining evaluations of specific attributes into an overall evaluation, we often seem to average the individual evaluations. However, some of the individual attributes may be more salient or important than others, so we give them greater weight in the final evaluation.

working consensus When we begin interaction with others, we make certain assumptions about the nature of the interaction that is going to take place and give cues to the others by our posture, mode of speech, and so on about what we have assumed. If they accept and share our assumptions or have made similar assumptions on their own, a working consensus is said to have developed and the interaction is likely to run smoothly.

Yerkes-Dodson Law Performance on simple cognitive tasks improves under moderately high levels of arousal, whereas performance on complex tasks deteriorates under moderately high levels of arousal.

yoking A control procedure used in experimental research whereby subjects in different conditions are matched in terms of exposure to an independent variable.

BIBLIOGRAPHY

Abe, K. Seasonal fluctuations of psychiatric admissions based on the data for seven prefectures of Japan for seven-year period 1955-61 with a review of the literature. In *Proceedings of the Joint Meeting of the Japanese Society of Psychiatry and Neurology and the American Psychiatric Association.* The Japanese Society of Psychiatry and Neurology, 1964, 173-176. Cited in R. Moos, *The human context,* New York: Wiley, 1976.

Abelson, R. P. Simulation of social behavior. In G. Lindzey and E. Aronson (Eds.), *The handbook of social psychology* (Vol. 2), 2nd ed. Reading, Mass.: Addison-Wesley, 1968.

Adams, J. S. Inequity in social exchange. In L. Berkowitz (Ed.), *Advances in experimental social psychology* (Vol. 2). New York: Academic Press, 1965.

Adler, A. *Social interest: A challenge to mankind.* London: Faber and Faber, 1945. (Translated by J. Linton and R. Vaughn. Capricorn Books, 1964.)

Adler, F. *Sisters in crime: The rise of the new female criminal.* New York: McGraw-Hill, 1975.

Adorno, T. W., Frenkel-Brunswik, E., Levinson, D. J., and Sanford, R. N. *The authoritarian personality.* New York: Harper & Row, 1950.

Aiello, J. R., and Aiello, T. The development of personal space: Proxemic behavior of children 6 through 16. *Human Ecology,* 1974, *2,* 177-189.

Aiello, J. R., DeRisi, D. T., Epstein, Y. M., and Karlin, R. A. Crowding and the role of interpersonal distance preferences. *Sociometry,* 1977, *40,* 271-282.

Aiello, J. R., Epstein, Y. M., and Karlin, R. A. Effects of crowding on electrodermal activity. *Sociological Symposium,* 1975, *14,* 43-57.

Aiello, J. R., and Jones, S. E. Field study of the proxemic behavior of young school children in three subcultural groups. *Journal of Personality and Social Psychology,* 1971, *19,* 351-356.

Ainsworth, M. D. S. The development of infant–mother attachment. In B. M. Caldwell and H. N. Ricciuti (Eds.), *Review of child development research* (Vol. 3). Chicago: University of Chicago Press, 1973.

Allport, F. H. *Social psychology.* Boston: Houghton Mifflin, 1924.

Allport, G. W. Attitudes. In C. Murchison (Ed.), *Handbook of social psychology.* Worcester, Mass.: Clark University Press, 1935.

Allport, G. W. The historical background of modern social psychology. In G. Lindzey and E. Aronson (Eds.), *The handbook of social psychology* (Vol. 1), 2nd ed. Reading, Mass.: Addison-Wesley, 1968.

Altman, I. *The environment and social behavior: Privacy · personal space · territory · crowding.* Monterey, Calif.: Brooks/Cole, 1975.

Altman, I. Environmental psychology and social psychology. *Personality and Social Psychology Bulletin,* 1976, *2,* 96-113.

Altman I., and Taylor, D. A. *Social penetration: The development of interpersonal relationships.* London: Holt, Rinehart and Winston, 1973.

Altman, I., and Vinsel, A. M. Personal space: An analysis of E. T. Hall's proxemics framework. In I. Altman and J. F. Wohlwill (Eds.), *Human behavior and environment: Advances in theory and research* (Vol. 2). New York: Plenum, 1977.

Amir, M. *Patterns of forcible rape.* Chicago: University of Chicago Press, 1971.

Anderson, N. H. Group performance in an anagram task. *Journal of Social Psychology,* 1961, *55,* 67-75.

Anderson, N. H. Cognitive algebra: Integration theory applied to social attribution. In L. Berkowitz (Ed.),

Advances in experimental social psychology (Vol. 7). New York: Academic Press, 1974.

Anderson, N. H. *Social perception and cognition* (Technical Report No. 62). Center for Human Information Processing, University of California, San Diego, 1976.

Anglin, J. M. (Ed.). *Beyond the information given.* New York: Norton, 1973.

Appleyard, D., and Lintell, M. The environmental quality of city streets. The residents' viewpoint. In W. J. Mitchell (Ed.). *Environmental Design: Research and Practice. Proceedings of the Third Environmental Design Research Association Conference.* University of California, Los Angeles, January, 1972.

Apsler, P., and Sears, D. O. Warning, personal involvement, and attitude change. *Journal of Personality and Social Psychology,* 1968, *9,* 162-166.

Ardrey, R. *The social contract.* New York: Atheneum, 1970.

Argyle, M. *Social interaction.* Chicago: Aldine, 1969.

Argyle, M., and Dean, J. Eye contact, distance and affiliation. *Sociometry,* 1965, *28,* 289-304.

Aronfreed, J. *Conduct and conscience: The socialization of internalized control over behavior.* New York: Academic Press, 1968.

Aronfreed, J. The socialization of altruistic and sympathetic behavior: Some theoretical and experimental analyses. In J. Macaulay and L. Berkowitz (Eds.), *Altruism and helping behavior,* New York: Academic Press, 1970.

Aronfreed, J. Moral development from the standpoint of a general psychological theory. In T. Lickona (Ed.), *Moral development and behavior: Theory, research, and social issues.* New York: Holt, Rinehart, and Winston, 1976.

Aronson, E. Some antecedents of interpersonal attraction. In W. J. Arnold and D. Levine (Eds.), *Nebraska symposium on motivation* (Vol. 17). Lincoln, Neb.: University of Nebraska Press, 1969.

Aronson, E. *The social animal.* San Francisco: W. H. Freeman, 1976.

Aronson, E., and Carlsmith, J. M. Experimentation in social psychology. In G. Lindzey and E. Aronson (Eds.), *The handbook of social psychology* (Vol. 2), 2nd ed. Reading, Mass.: Addison-Wesley, 1968.

Aronson, E., and Cope, V. My enemy's enemy is my friend. *Journal of Personality and Social Psychology,* 1968, *8,* 8-12.

Aronson, E., and Golden, B. The effect of relevant and irrelevant aspects of communicator credibility on opinion change. *Journal of Personality,* 1962, *30,* 135-146.

Aronson, E., and Linder, D. Gain and loss of esteem as determinants of interpersonal attractiveness. *Journal of Experimental Social Psychology,* 1965, *1,* 156-171.

Aronson, E., and Mills, J. The effect of severity of initiation on liking for a group. *Journal of Abnormal and Social Psychology,* 1959, *59,* 177-181.

Aronson, E., Turner, J. A., and Carlsmith, J. M. Communicator credibility and communication discrepancy as determinants of opinion change. *Journal of Abnormal and Social Psychology,* 1963, *67,* 31-36.

Aronson, E., Willerman, B., and Floyd, J. The effect of a pratfall on increasing interpersonal attractiveness. *Psychonomic Science,* 1966, *4,* 227-228.

Asch, S. E. The doctrine of suggestion, prestige and imitation in social psychology. *Psychological Review,* 1948, *55,* 250-276.

Asch, S. E. Forming impressions of personality. *Journal of Abnormal and Social Psychology,* 1946, *41,* 258-290.

Asch, S. *Social psychology.* New York: Prentice-Hall, 1952.

Ashmore, R. D. Prejudice: Causes and cures. In B. Collins, *Social psychology,* Reading, Mass.: Addison-Wesley, 1970.

Ashmore, R. D., Ramchandra, V., and Jones, R. A. Censorship changes attitudes. *New Jersey Education Association Review,* 1971, *45,* 17-47.

Back, K. W., and Bogdonoff, M. D. Plasma lipid response to leadership, conformity, and deviation. In P. H. Leiderman and D. Shapiro (Eds.), *Psychobiological approaches to social behavior.* Stanford, Calif.: Stanford University Press, 1964.

Back, K. W., and Bogdonoff, M. D. Buffer conditions in experimental stress. *Behavioral Science,* 1967, *12,* 384-390.

Backman, C. W., and Secord, P. F. The effect of perceived liking on interpersonal attraction. *Human Relations,* 1959, *12,* 379-384.

Bakan, D. *Slaughter of the innocents: A study of the battered child phenomenon.* San Francisco: Jossey-Bass, 1975.

Bales, R. F. Social therapy for a social disorder: Compulsive drinking. *Journal of Social Issues,* 1945, *1,* 14-22.

Bales, R. F. A set of categories for the analysis of small group interaction. *American Sociological Review,* 1950, *15,* 257-263. (a)

Bales, R. F. *Interaction process analysis.* Cambridge, Mass.: Addison-Wesley, 1950. (b)

Bales, R. F. The equilibrium problem in small groups. In T. Parsons, R. F. Bales, and E. A. Shils (Eds.), *Working papers in the theory of action.* New York: The Free Press, 1953.

Bales, R. F. Task roles and social roles in problem-solving groups. In E. E. Maccoby, T. M. Newcomb, and E. L. Hartley (Eds.), *Readings in social psychology,* New York: Henry Holt and Co., 1958.

Bales R. F. *Personality and interpersonal behavior.* New York: Holt, Rinehart, and Winston, 1970.

Bales, R. F., and Gerbrands, H. The interaction recorder: An apparatus and check list for sequential content analysis of social interaction. *Human Relations,* 1948, *1,* 456-463.

Bales, R. F., and Strodtbeck, F. L. Phases in group problem-solving. *Journal of Abnormal and Social Psychology,* 1951, *46,* 485-495.

Bales, R. F., Strodtbeck, F. L., Mills, T. M., and Roseborough, M. E. Channels of communication in small groups. *American Sociological Review,* 1951, *16,* 461-468.

Bandler, R. J., Madaras, G. P., and Bem, D. J. Self-observation as a source of pain perception. *Journal of Personality and Social Psychology,* 1968, *9,* 205-209.

Bandura, A. *Principles of behavior modification.* New York: Holt, Rinehart and Winston, 1969.

Bandura, A. *Aggression: A social learning analysis.* Englewood Cliffs, N.J.: Prentice-Hall, 1973.

Bandura, A. *Social learning theory.* Englewood Cliffs, N.J.: Prentice-Hall, 1977.

Bandura, A., Ross, D., and Ross, S. A. Transmission of aggression through imitation of aggressive models. *Journal of Abnormal and Social Psychology,* 1961, *63,* 575-582.

Bandura, A., Ross, D., and Ross, S. A. Imitation of film-mediated aggressive models. *Journal of Abnormal and Social Psychology,* 1963, *66,* 3-11.

Bandura, A., and Walters, R. H. *Social learning and personality development.* New York: Holt, Rinehart and Winston, 1963.

Banta, T. J., and Nelson, C. Experimental analysis of resource location in problem solving groups. *Sociometry,* 1964, *27,* 488-501.

Barber, J. D. *The presidential character.* Englewood Cliffs, N.J.: Prentice-Hall, 1972.

Barker, R. G. *Ecological psychology.* Stanford, Calif.: Stanford University Press, 1968.

Baron, R. A. Aggression as a function of ambient temperature and prior anger arousal. *Journal of Personality and Social Psychology,* 1972, *21,* 183-189.

Baron, R. A. *Human aggression.* New York: Plenum, 1977.

Baron, R. A., and Lawton, S. Environmental influences on aggression: The facilitation of modeling effects by high ambient temperatures. *Psychonomic Science,* 1972, *26,* 80-82.

Baron, R. M., Mandel, D. R., Adams, C., A., and Griffen, L. M. Effects of social density in university residential environments. *Journal of Personality and Social Psychology,* 1976, *34,* 434-446.

Bass, B. M. *Leadership, psychology, and organizational behavior.* New York: Harper & Brothers, 1960.

Bar-Tal, D. *Prosocial behavior: Theory and research.* New York: Halstead, 1976.

Baum, A., and Valins, S. *Architecture and social behavior: Psychological studies of social density.* Hillsdale, N.J.: Erlbaum, 1977.

Bavelas, A., Hastorf, A. H., Gross, A. E., and Kite, W. R. Experiments on the alteration of group structure. *Journal of Experimental Social Psychology,* 1965, *1,* 55-70.

Becker, H. S. *Outsiders: Studies in the sociology of deviance.* New York: The Free Press, 1963.

Becker, H. S., and Geer, B. Participant observation and interviewing: A comparison. In W. J. Filstead (Ed.), *Qualitative Methodology: Firsthand Involvement with the Social World.* Chicago: Markham, 1970.

Beckhouse, L., Tanur, J., Weiler, J., and Weinstein, E. . . . And some men have leadership thrust upon them. *Journal of Personality and Social Psychology,* 1975, *31,* 557-566.

Bell, P. A., and Baron, R. A. Aggression and heat: The mediating role of negative affect. *Journal of Applied Social Psychology,* 1976, *6,* 18-30.

Bem, D. J. An experimental analysis of self-persuasion. *Journal of Experimental Social Psychology,* 1965, *1,* 199-218.

Bem, D. J. Self-perception: An alternative interpretation of cognitive dissonance phenomena. *Psychological Review,* 1967, *74,* 183-200.

Bem. S. L. The measurement of psychological androgyny. *Journal of Consulting and Clinical Psychology,* 1974, *42,* 155-162.

Bem, S. L., and Bem, D. J. Case study of a nonconscious ideology: Training the woman to know her place. In D. J. Bem, *Beliefs, attitudes, and human affairs.* Belmont, Calif.: Brooks/Cole, 1970.

Benedetti, D. T., and Hill, J. G. A determiner of the centrality of a trait in impression formation. *Journal of Abnormal and Social Psychology,* 1960, *60,* 278-280.

Benson, P. L., Karabenick, S. A., and Lerner, R. M. Pretty pleases: The effects of physical attractiveness, race, and sex on receiving help. *Journal of Experimental Social Psychology,* 1976, *12,* 409-415.

Bergin, A. The effect of dissonant persuasive communications upon change in a self-referring attitude. *Journal of Personality,* 1962, *30,* 423-438.

Berkowitz, L. Effects of perceived dependency relationships upon conformity to group expectations. *Journal of Abnormal and Social Psychology,* 1957, *55,* 350-354.

Berkowitz, L. *Aggression: A social psychological analysis.* New York: McGraw-Hill, 1962.

Berkowitz, L. (Ed.). *Advances in experimental social psychology* (Vol. 2). New York: Academic Press, 1965.

Berkowitz, L. *Roots of aggression: A re-examination of the frustration-aggression hypothesis.* New York: Atherton, 1969.

Berkowitz, L. Social norms, feelings, and other factors affecting helping and altruism. In L. Berkowitz (Ed.), *Advances in experimental social psychology* (Vol. 6). New York: Academic Press, 1972.

Berkowitz, L., and Walster, E. (Eds.). *Advances in experimental social psychology* (Vol. 9). New York: Academic Press, 1976.

Berkowitz, L., and Connor, W. H. Success, failure, and social responsibility. *Journal of Personality and Social Psychology,* 1966, *4,* 664-669.

Berkowitz, L., and Daniels, L. R. Responsibility and dependency. *Journal of Abnormal and Social Psychology,* 1963, *66,* 429-436.

Berkowitz, L., and Daniels, L. R. Affecting the salience of the social responsibility norm: Effects of past help on the response to dependency relationships. *Journal of Abnormal and Social Psychology,* 1964, *68,* 275-281.

Berkowitz, L., and Geen, R. G. Film violence and cue properties of available targets, *Journal of Personality and Social Psychology,* 1966, *3,* 525-530.

Berkowitz, L., and LePage, A. Weapons as aggression-eliciting stimuli. *Journal of Personality and Social Psychology,* 1967, *7,* 202-207.

Berne, E. *Transactional analysis in psychotherapy.* New York: Grove Press, 1961.

Berscheid, E., Brothen, T., and Graziano, W. Gain-loss theory and the "law of infidelity": Mr. doting versus the admiring stranger. *Journal of Personality and Social Psychology,* 1976, *33,* 709-718.

Berscheid, E., and Walster, E. *Interpersonal attraction.* Reading, Mass.: Addison-Wesley, 1969.

Berscheid, E., and Walster, E. A little bit about love. In T. L. Huston (Ed.), *Foundations of interpersonal attraction.* New York: Academic Press, 1974. (a)

Berscheid, E., and Walster, E. Physical attractiveness. In L. Berkowitz (Ed.), *Advances in experimental social psychology* (Vol. 7). New York: Academic Press, 1974. (b)

Berzins, J. I. Sex roles and psychotherapy: New directions for theory and research. Paper presented at the 6th annual meeting of the Society for Psychotherapy Research. Boston, Mass.: June 13, 1975.

Betz, M., and Judkins, B. The impact of voluntary association characteristics on selective attraction and socialization. *The Sociological Quarterly,* 1975, *16,* 228-240.

Beveridge, W. I. B. *The art of scientific investigation.* New York: Vintage, 1957.

Birdwhistell, R. L. *Kinesics and context: Essays on body motion communication.* Philadelphia: University of Pennsylvania Press, 1970.

Blake, R. R., Mouton, J. S., and Hain, J. D. Social

forces in petition signing. *Southwestern Social Science Quarterly,* 1956, *36,* 385-390.

Blake, R. R., Rosenbaum, M., and Duryea, R. Gift-giving as a function of group standards. *Human Relations,* 1955, *8,* 61-73.

Blanchard, W. A. Relevance of information and accuracy of interpersonal prediction: A methodological note. *Psychological Reports,* 1966, *18,* 379-382.

Blau, P. M. *Exchange and power in social life.* New York: Wiley, 1964.

Block, J. H. Conceptions of sex role: Some cross-cultural and longitudinal perspectives. *American Psychologist,* 1973, *28,* 512-526.

Bloom, B. L. *Community mental health: a historical and critical analysis.* Morristown, N.J.: General Learning Press, 1973.

Blum, A. Social structure, social class, and participation in primary relationships. In A. Shostak and W. Gomberg (Eds.), *Blue collar world.* Englewood Cliffs, N.J.: Prentice-Hall, 1964.

Bogardus, E. S. *The development of social thought,* 4th ed. New York: David McKay, 1960.

Bogdonoff, M. D., Klein, R. F., Back, K. W., Nichols, C. R., Troyer, W. G., and Hood, T. C. Effect of group relationship and of the role of leadership upon lipid mobilization. *Psychosomatic Medicine,* 1964, *26,* 710-719.

Boice, R. In the shadow of Darwin. In R. G. Geen and E. C. O'Neal (Eds.), *Perspectives on aggression.* New York: Academic Press, 1976.

Booth, A. *Final report: Urban crowding project.* Unpublished manuscript, Ministry of State for Urban Affairs, Canada, August, 1975.

Borgatta, E. F., Bales, R. F., and Couch, A. S. Some findings relevant to the great-man theory of leadership. *American Sociological Review,* 1954, *19,* 755-759.

Bowlby, J. The nature of the child's tie to his mother. *International Journal of Psychoanalysis,* 1958, *39,* 350-373.

Bowlby, J. *Attachment and loss.* New York: Basic Books, 1969.

Bram, J. *Language and society.* Garden City, N.Y.: Doubleday, 1955.

Brehm, J. W. *A theory of psychological reactance.* New York: Academic Press, 1966.

Brehm, J. W., and Cohen, A. R. *Explorations in cognitive dissonance.* New York: Wiley, 1962.

Brehm, J. W., and Sensenig, J. Social influence as a function of attempted and implied usurpation of choice. *Journal of Personality and Social Psychology,* 1966, *4,* 703-707.

Brock, T. C. Communicator-recipient similarity and decision change. *Journal of Personality and Social Psychology,* 1965, *1,* 650-654.

Broll, L., Gross, A. E., and Piliavin, I. Effects of offered and requested help on help seeking and reactions to being helped. *Journal of Applied Social Psychology,* 1974, *4,* 244-258.

Brown, J. S., and Farber, I. E. Emotions conceptualized as intervening variables—with suggestions toward a theory of frustration. *Psychological Bulletin,* 1951, *48,* 465-495.

Brown, R. *Words and things: An Introduction to language.* New York: The Free Press, 1958.

Brown, R. *Social psychology.* New York: The Free Press, 1965.

Brown, R., and Gilman, A. The pronouns of power and solidarity. In T. A. Sebeok (Ed.), *Style in language.* Cambridge, Mass.: MIT Press, 1960.

Brownmiller, S. *Against our will: Men, women, and rape.* New York: Simon and Schuster, 1975.

Bruck, C. Women against the law. *Human Behavior,* 1975, *4,* 24-33.

Bruner, J. S. IV. Perceptual theory and the Rorschach test. *Journal of Personality,* 1948, *17,* 157-168.

Bruner, J. S. Personality dynamics and the process of perceiving. In R. R. Blake and G. V. Ramsey (Eds.), *Perception—An approach to personality.* New York: Ronald Press, 1951.

Bruner, J. S., and Tagiuri, R. The perception of people. In G. Lindzey (Ed.), *Handbook of Social Psychology* (Vol. 2). Reading, Mass.: Addison-Wesley, 1954.

Bryan, J. H., and Walbek, N. H. Preaching and practicing generosity: Children's actions and reactions. *Child Development,* 1970, *41,* 329-353.

Budner, S. Intolerance of ambiguity as a personality variable. *Journal of Personality,* 1962, *30,* 29-50.

Bugental, D., Love, L. R., and Gianetto, R. M. Perfidious feminine faces. *Journal of Personality and Social Psychology.* 1971, *17,* 314-318.

Burke, W. W. Social perception as a function of dogmatism. *Perceptual and Motor Skills,* 1966, *23,* 863-868.

Burrows, A., and Zamarin, D. Aircraft noise and the

community: Some recent survey findings. *Aerospace Medicine,* 1972, *43,* 27-33.

Burton, R. V. The generality of honesty reconsidered. *Psychological Review,* 1963, *70,* 481-499.

Buss, A. *The psychology of aggression.* New York: Wiley, 1961.

Byrne, D. The influence of propinquity and opportunities for interaction on classroom relationships. *Human Relations,* 1961, *14,* 63-69.

Byrne, D. Attitudes and attraction. In L. Berkowitz (Ed.), *Advances in experimental social psychology* (Vol. 4). New York: Academic Press, 1969.

Byrne, D. The *attraction paradigm.* New York: Academic Press, 1971.

Byrne, D., and Clore, G. L., Jr. Effectance arousal and attraction. *Journal of Personality and Social Psychology Monograph,* 1967, *6,* (4, Part 2, Whole No. 638).

Byrne, D., Clore, G. L., Jr., and Worchel, P. Effect of economic similarity-dissimilarity on interpersonal attraction. *Journal of Personality and Social Psychology, 1966, 4,* 220-224.

Byrne, D., Griffitt, W., and Stefaniak, D. Attraction and similarity of personality characteristics. *Journal of Personality and Social Psychology,* 1967, *5,* 82-90.

Byrne, D., and Nelson, D. Attraction as a linear function of proportion of positive reinforcements. *Journal of Personality and Social Psychology,* 1965, *1,* 659-663.

Caldwell, B. M. The effects of infant care. In M. L. Hoffman and L. W. Hoffman (Eds.), *Review of child development research* (Vol. 1). New York: Russell Sage, 1964.

Calhoun, J. B. Population density and social pathology. *Scientific American,* 1962, *206,* 139-148.

Campbell, D. T. Ethnocentric and other altruistic motives. In D. Levine (Ed.), *Nebraska symposium on motivation* (Vol. 13). Lincoln, Neb.: University of Nebraska Press, 1965.

Campbell, D. T. Reforms as experiments. *American Psychologist,* 1969, *24,* 409-429.

Campbell, D. T. On the genetics of altruism and the counterhedonic components in human culture. *Journal of Social Issues,* 1972, *28*(2), 21-37.

Campbell, D. T., and Stanley, J. C. *Experimental and quasiexperimental designs for research.* Chicago: Rand McNally, 1966.

Cannavale, F. J., Scarr, H. A., and Pepitone, A. Deindividuation in the small group: Further evidence. *Journal of Personality and Social Psychology,* 1970, *16,* 141-147.

Cannell, C. F., and Kahn, R. L. Interviewing. In G. Lindzey and E. Aronson (Eds.), *The handbook of social psychology* (Vol. 2), 2nd ed. Reading, Mass.: Addison-Wesley, 1968.

Caplow, T., and Forman, R. Neighborhood interaction in a homogeneous community. *American Sociological Review,* 1950, *15,* 357-366.

Carlsmith, J. M., and Gross, A. E. Some effects of guilt on compliance. *Journal of Personality and Social Psychology,* 1969, *11,* 232-239.

Carr, E. H. *What is history?* New York: Vintage, 1961.

Cartwright, D. Risk taking by individuals and groups: An assessment of research employing choice dilemmas. *Journal of Personality and Social Psychology,* 1971, *20,* 361-378.

Cartwright, D., and Zander, A. (Eds.). *Group dynamics: Research and theory,* 2nd ed. New York: Harper & Row, 1960.

Chapman, L. J. Illusory correlation in observational report. *Journal of Verbal Learning and Verbal Behavior,* 1967, *6,* 151-155.

Chapman, L. J., and Chapman, J. P. Genesis of popular but erroneous psychodiagnostic observations. *Journal of Abnormal Psychology,* 1967, *72,* 193-204.

Chemers, M. M., Rice, R. W., Sundstrom, E., and Butler, W. M. Leader esteem for the least preferred co-worker score, training, and effectiveness: An experimental examination. *Journal of Personality and Social Psychology,* 1975, *31,* 401-409.

Christian, J. J., Flyger, V., and Davis, D. E. Phenomena associated with population density. *Proceedings of the National Academy of Science,* 1961, *47,* 428-449.

Christie, R., and Geis, F. L. *Studies in Machiavellianism.* New York: Academic Press, 1970.

Chu, G. C. Prior familiarity, perceived bias, and one-sided versus two-sided communications. *Journal of Experimental Social Psychology,* 1967, *3,* 243-254.

Cialdini, R. B., Levy, A., Herman, C. P., Kozlowski, L.

T., and Petty, R. E. Elastic shifts of opinion: Determinants of direction and durability. *Journal of Personality and Social Psychology*, 1976, *34*, 663-672.

Cicchetti, C. and Smith, V. Congestion, quality deterioration, and optimal use: Wilderness recreation in the Spanish Peaks primitive area. *Social Science Research*, 1973, *2*, 15-30.

Cicourel, A. V. *Cognitive sociology: Language and meaning in social interaction.* New York: The Free Press, 1974.

Clark, M. S., Gotay, C. C., and Mills, J. Acceptance of help as a function of similarity of the potential helper and opportunity to repay. *Journal of Applied Social Psychology*, 1974, *4*, 224-229.

Clark, R. D., and Sechrest, L. The mandate phenomenon. *Journal of Personality and Social Psychology*, 1976, *34*, 1057-1061.

Clore, G. L., and Byrne, D. A reinforcement-affect model of attraction. In T. L. Huston (Ed.), *Foundations of interpersonal attraction.* New York: Academic Press, 1974.

Clore, G. L., Wiggins, N. H., and Itkin, S. Gain and loss in attraction: Attributions from nonverbal behavior. *Journal of Personality and Social Psychology*, 1975, *31*, 706-712.

Coale, A. The history of human population. *Scientific American*, 1974, *231*(3), 40-51.

Cohen, A. R. Cognitive tuning as a factor affecting impression formation. *Journal of Personality*, 1961, *29*, 235-245.

Cohen, J. L., and Davis, J. H. Effects of audience status, evaluation, and time of action on performance with hidden-word problems. *Journal of Personality and Social Psychology*, 1973, *27*, 74-85.

Cohen, M. L., Garofalo, R., Boucher, R., and Seghorn, T. The psychology of rapists. *Seminars in Psychiatry*, 1971, *3*, 307-327.

Cohen, R. Altruism: Human, cultural, or what? *Journal of Social Issues*, 1972, *28*(3), 39-57.

Cohen, S. *Social and personality development in childhood.* New York: Macmillan, 1976.

Cohen, S. Environmental load and the allocation of attention. In A. Baum (Ed.), *Advances in environmental psychology.* Hillsdale, N.J.: Erlbaum, 1977.

Cohen, S., Glass, D., and Singer, J. Apartment noise, auditory discrimination, and reading ability in children. *Journal of Experimental Social Psychology*, 1973, *9*, 407-422.

Cole, M., and Scribner, S. *Culture and thought: A psychological introduction.* New York: Wiley, 1974.

Coleman, J. C. *Abnormal psychology and modern life*, 3rd ed. Glenview, Ill.: Scott, Foresman, 1976.

Collins, B. *Social psychology.* Reading, Mass.: Addison-Wesley, 1970.

Colquhoun, W., and Goldman, F. The effects of raised body temperature on vigilance performance. *Ergonomics*, 1968, *11*, 48.

Conroy, J., and Sundstrom, E. Territorial dominance in a dyadic conversation as a function of similarity of opinion. *Journal of Personality and Social Psychology*, 1977, *35*, 570-576.

Cook, T. D., and Insko, C. A. Persistence of attitude change as a function of conclusion reexposure: A laboratory-field experiment. *Journal of Personality and Social Psychology*. 1968, *9*, 322-328.

Cooley, C. H. *Human nature and the social order.* New York: Scribner, 1902.

Cooper, J., Darley, J. M., and Henderson, J. E. On the effectiveness of deviant- and conventional-appearing communicators. *Journal of Personality and Social Psychology*. 1974, *29*, 752-757.

Coser, L. A. *Masters of sociological thought: Ideas in historical and social context.* New York: Harcourt, Brace, Jovanovich, 1971.

Cottrell, N. B. Performance in the presence of other human beings: Mere presence, audience, and affiliation effects. In E. C. Simmel, R. A. Hoppe, and G. A. Milton (Eds.), *Social facilitation and imitative behavior.* Boston: Allyn and Bacon, 1968.

Cottrell, N. B., Wack, D. L., Sekerak, G. J., and Rittle, R. H. Social facilitation of dominant responses by the presence of an audience and the mere presence of others. *Journal of Personality and Social Psychology*, 1968, *9*, 245-250.

Cronbach, L. J. Processes affecting scores on "understanding of others" and "assumed similarity." *Psychological Bulletin*, 1955, *52*, 177-193.

Cronbach, L. J. Proposals leading to analytic treatment of social perception scores. In R. Tagiuri and L. Petrullo (Eds.), *Person perception and interpersonal behavior.* Stanford, Calif.: Stanford University Press, 1958.

Cronbach, L. J. *Essentials of psychological testing,*

2nd ed. New York: Harper & Row, 1960.

Dabbs, J. M., and Janis, I. L. Why does eating while reading facilitate opinion change? An experimental inquiry. *Journal of Experimental Social Psychology*, 1965, *1*, 133-144.

Dabbs, J. M., and Leventhal, H. Effects of varying the recommendations in a fear-arousing communication. *Journal of Personality and Social Psychology*, 1966, *4*, 525-531.

Daher, D. M., and Banikiotes, P. G. Interpersonal attraction and rewarding aspects of disclosure content and level. *Journal of Personality and Social Psychology*, 1976, *33*, 492-496.

Dailey, C. A. The effects of premature conclusions upon the acquisition of understanding of a person. *Journal of Psychology*, 1952, *33*, 133-152.

D'Andrade, R. G. Memory and the assessment of behavior. In H. M. Blalock, Jr. (Ed.), *Measurement in the social sciences: Theories and strategies.* Chicago: Aldine, 1973.

Daniels, R. *The politics of prejudice.* New York: Atheneum, 1968.

Darley, J. M., and Latané, B. Bystander intervention in emergencies: Diffusion of responsibility. *Journal of Personality and Social Psychology*, 1968, *8*, 377-383.

Darley, J. M., and Latané, B. Norms and normative behavior: Field studies of social interdependence. In J. Macaulay and L. Berkowitz (Eds.), *Altruism and helping behavior.* New York: Academic Press, 1970.

Darley, J. M., Teger, A. I., and Lewis, L. D. Do groups always inhibit individuals' responses to potential emergencies? *Journal of Personality and Social Psychology*, 1973, *26*, 395-399.

Darlington, R. B., and Macker, C. E. Displacement of guilt-produced altruistic behavior. *Journal of Personality and Social Psychology*, 1966, *4*, 442-443.

Darwin, C. *The origin of species by means of natural selection.* New York: New American Library, 1958 (originally published in 1859).

D'Atri, D. A. Psychophysiological responses to crowding. *Environment and Behavior*, 1975, *7*, 237-252.

Davidson, A. R., and Jaccard, J. J. Population psychology: A new look at an old problem. *Journal of Personality and Social Psychology*, 1975, *31*, 1073-1082.

Davis, J. H. *Group performance.* Reading, Mass.: Addison-Wesley, 1969.

Dawes, R. M. Shallow psychology. In J. S. Carroll and J. W. Payne (Eds.), *Cognition and social behavior.* Hillsdale, N.J.: Erlbaum, 1976.

Deaux, K. *The behavior of women and men.* Belmont, Calif.: Wadsworth, 1976.

Deaux, K. Looking at behavior. *Personality and Social Psychology Bulletin*, 1978, *4*, 207-211.

deMause, L. The evolution of childhood. In L. deMause (Ed.), *The history of childhood.* New York: Psychohistory Press, 1974.

Dengerink, H. A. Anxiety, aggression, and physiological arousal. *Journal of Experimental Research in Personality*, 1971, *5*, 223-232.

Dengerink, H. A., O'Leary, M. R., and Kasner, K. H. Individual differences in aggressive responses to attack: Internal-external locus of control and field dependence-independence. *Journal of Research in Personality*, 1975, *9*, 191-199.

Derlega, V. J., Wilson, M., and Chaikin, A. L. Friendship and disclosure reciprocity. *Journal of Personality and Social Psychology*, 1976, *34*, 578-582.

Diener, E. Effects of prior destructive behavior, anonymity and group presence on de individuation and aggression. *Journal of Personality and Social Psychology*, 1976, *33*, 497-507.

Diener, E., Dineen, J., Endresen, K., Beaman, A. L., and Fraser, S. C. Effects of altered responsibility, cognitive set, and modeling on physical aggression and de-individuation. *Journal of Personality and Social Psychology*, 1975, *31*, 328-337.

Dillehay, R. C. On the irrelevance of the classical negative evidence concerning the effect of attitudes on behavior. *American Psychologist*, 1973, *28*, 887-891.

Dion, K., Berscheid, E., and Walster, E. What is beautiful is good. *Journal of Personality and Social Psychology*, 1972, *24*, 285-290.

Dollard, J., Doob, L. W., Miller, N. E., Mowrer, O. H., and Sears, R. *Frustration and aggression*, New Haven, Conn.: Yale University Press, 1939.

Dollard, J., and Miller, N. E. *Personality and psychotherapy: An analysis in terms of learning, thinking, and culture.* New York: McGraw-Hill, 1950.

Donnerstein, E., and Wilson, D. W. Effects of noise and perceived control on ongoing and subsequent aggressive behavior. *Journal of Personality and Social Psychology,* 1976, *34,* 774–781.

Dooley, B. B. *Crowding stress: The effects of social density on men with close or far personal space.* Doctoral Dissertation, University of California, Los Angeles, 1974.

Dornbusch, S. M., Hastorf, A. H., Richardson, S. A., Muzzy, R. E., and Vreeland, R. S. The perceiver and the perceived: Their relative influences on the categories of interpersonal perception. *Journal of Personality and Social Psychology,* 1965, *1,* 434–440.

Draguns, J. G., and Phillips, L. *Psychiatric classification and diagnosis: An overview and critique.* New York: General Learning Press, 1971.

Dubin, R., and Dubin, E. R. Children's social perception: A review of research. *Child Development.* 1965, *36,* 809–838.

Durkheim, E. *Suicide: A study in sociology* (J. Spaulding and G. Simpson, trans.). New York: The Free Press, 1951.

Eagly, A. H., and Himmelfarb, S. Attitudes and opinions. In M. R. Rosenzweig and L. W. Porter (Eds.), *Annual review of psychology* (Vol. 29). Palo Alto, Calif.: Annual Reviews, 1978.

Eckman, P. (Ed.). *Darwin and facial expression: A century of research in review.* New York: Academic Press, 1973.

Edney, J. Territoriality and control: a field experiment. *Journal of Personality and Social Psychology,* 1975, *31,* 1108–1115.

Efran, M. G., and Cheyne, J. A. Affective concomitants of the invasion of shared space: Behavioral, physiological and verbal indicators. *Journal of Personality and Social Psychology,* 1974, *29,* 219–226.

Ellsworth, P. C., and Carlsmith, J. M. Effects of eye contact and verbal content on affective response to a dyadic interaction. *Journal of Personality and Social Psychology,* 1968, *10,* 15–20.

Ellsworth, P. C., Carlsmith, J. M., and Henson, A. The stare as a stimulus to flight in human subjects. *Journal of Personality and Social Psychology,* 1972, *21,* 302–311.

Elworthy, F. T. *The evil eye: The origins and practices of superstition.* London: John Murray, 1895.

Endleman, R. *Personality and social life.* New York: Random House, 1967.

Epstein, S. The self-concept revisited: Or a theory of a theory. *American Psychologist,* 1973, *28,* 404–416.

Epstein, Y. M., and Karlin, R. A. Effects of acute experimental crowding. *Journal of Applied Social Psychology,* 1975, *5,* 34–53.

Epstein, Y., Lehrer, P., and Woolfolk, R. *Physiological, cognitive, and behavioral effects of repeated exposure to crowding.* Unpublished manuscript, Rutgers University, 1978.

Epstein, Y., Suedfeld, P., and Silverstein, S. The experimental contract: Subject's expectations of and reactions to some behaviors of experimenters. *American Psychologist,* 1973, *28,* 212–221.

Erikson, E. H. *Childhood and society,* Revised ed. New York: Norton, 1963.

Erikson, E. H. *Identity, youth, and crisis.* New York: Norton, 1968.

Ervin-Tripp, S. M. Sociolinguistics. In L. Berkowitz, (Ed.), *Advances in experimental social psychology* (Vol. 4). New York: Academic Press, 1969.

Esser, A., Chamberlain, A., Chapple, E., and Kline, N. Territoriality of patients on a research ward. In J. Wortis (Ed.), *Recent advances in biological psychiatry.* New York: Plenum, 1965.

Exline, R. V., Thibaut, J., Hickey, C. B., and Gumpert, P. Visual interaction in relation to Machiavellianism and an unethical act. In R. Christie and F. Geis, *Studies in Machiavellianism.* New York: Academic Press, 1970.

Eysenck, H. J. *Sense and nonsense in psychology.* Baltimore: Penguin, 1957.

Farina, A., Chapnick, B., Chapnick, J., and Misiti, R. Political views and interpersonal behavior. *Journal of Personality and Social Psychology,* 1972, *22,* 273–278.

Faris, R., and Dunham, H. *Mental disorders in urban areas.* Chicago: University of Chicago Press, 1939.

Ferguson, D. A., and Vidmar, N. Effects of group discussion on estimates of culturally appropriate risk levels. *Journal of Personality and Social Psychology,* 1971, *20,* 436–445.

Ferré, F. (Ed.). *Introduction to positive philosophy: Auguste Comte.* New York: Bobbs-Merrill, 1970.

Ferris, C. B., and Wicklund, R. A. An experiment on importance of freedom and prior demonstration. In

Wicklund, R. A. *Freedom and reactance.* Hillsdale, N.J.: Erlbaum, 1974.

Feshbach, S., and Singer, R. D. *Television and aggression: An experimental field study.* San Francisco: Jossey-Bass, 1971.

Festinger, L. Informal social communication, *Psychological Review,* 1950, *57,* 271–282.

Festinger, L. A theory of social comparison processes. *Human Relations,* 1954, *7,* 117–140.

Festinger, L. *A theory of cognitive dissonance.* Stanford, Calif.: Stanford University Press, 1957.

Festinger, L., and Aronson, E. The arousal and reduction of dissonance in social contexts. In D. Cartwright and A. Zander (Eds.), *Group dynamics: Research and theory,* 2nd ed. New York: Harper & Row, 1960.

Festinger, L., and Carlsmith, J. M. Cognitive consequences of forced compliance. *Journal of Abnormal and Social Psychology,* 1959, *58,* 203–210.

Festinger, L., Pepitone, A., and Newcomb, T. Some consequences of de-individuation in a group. *Journal of Abnormal and Social Psychology,* 1952, *47,* 382–389.

Festinger, L., Riecken, H. W., and Schachter, S. *When prophecy fails.* Minneapolis: University of Minnesota Press, 1956.

Festinger, L., Schachter, S., and Back, K. *Social pressures in informal groups.* Stanford, Calif.: Stanford University Press, 1963 (Originally published by Harper and Brothers, 1950).

Fiedler, F. E. The influence of leader–keyman relations on combat crew effectiveness. *Journal of Abnormal and Social Psychology,* 1955, *51,* 227–235.

Fiedler, F. E. A contingency model of leadership effectiveness. In L. Berkowitz (Ed.), *Advances in experimental social psychology* (Vol. 1). New York: Academic Press, 1964.

Fiedler, F. E. Validation and extension of the contingency model of leadership effectiveness: A review of empirical findings. *Psychological Bulletin,* 1971, *76,* 128–148.

Fiedler, F. E. Predicting the effects of leadership training and experience from the contingency model: A clarification. *Journal of Applied Psychology,* 1973, *57,* 110–113.

Firestone, I. J., Lichtman, C. M., and Colomosca, J. V. Leader effectiveness and leadership conferral as determinants of helping in a medical emergency. *Journal of Personality and Social Psychology,* 1975, *31,* 343–348.

Fishbein, M. (Ed.). *Readings in attitude theory and measurement.* New York: Wiley, 1967.

Fishbein, M., and Ajzen, I. Attitudes towards objects as predictors of single and multiple behavioral criteria. *Psychological Review,* 1974, *81,* 59–74.

Fishbein, M., and Ajzen, I. *Belief, attitude, intention and behavior: An introduction to theory and research.* Reading, Mass.: Addison-Wesley, 1975.

Fisher, J. D., and Nadler, A. The effect of similarity between donor and recipient on recipient's reactions to aid. *Journal of Applied Social Psychology,* 1974, *4,* 230–243.

Fisher, J. D., and Nadler, A. Effect of donor resources on recipient self-esteem and self-help. *Journal of Experimental Social Psychology,* 1976, *12,* 139–150.

Flavell, J. H. *The development of role-taking and communication skills in children.* New York: Wiley, 1968.

Fontana, V. *The maltreated child: The maltreatment syndrome in children.* Springfield, Ill.: Charles C. Thomas, 1971.

Foote, N., Abu-Lughod, J., Foley, M., and Winnick, L. *Housing choices and housing constraints.* New York: McGraw-Hill, 1960.

Ford A., Casualties of our time. *Science,* 1970, *167,* 23–30.

Freedman, J. L. Long-term behavioral effects of cognitive dissonance. *Journal of Experimental Social Psychology,* 1965, *1,* 145–155.

Freedman, J. L. *Crowding and behavior.* San Francisco: Freeman, 1975.

Freedman, J. L., and Fraser, S. C. Compliance without pressure: The foot-in-the-door technique. *Journal of Personality and Social Psychology,* 1966, *4,* 195–202.

Freedman, J. L., Heshka, S., and Levy, A. Population density and pathology: Is there a relationship? *Journal of Experimental Social Psychology,* 1975, *11,* 539–552.

Freedman, J. L., Levy, A., Buchanan, R., and Price, J. Crowding and human aggressiveness. *Journal of Experimental Social Psychology,* 1971, *8,* 528–545.

Freedman, J. L., Wallington, S. A., and Bless, E. Compliance without pressure: The effect of guilt. *Journal of Personality and Social Psychology*, 1967, 7, 117–124.

Freedman, R., and Berelson, B. The human population. *Scientific American*, 1974, 231(3), 30–39.

French, E. G. Effects of the interaction of motivation and feedback on task performance. In J. W. Atkinson (Ed.), *Motives in fantasy, action, and society*. Princeton, N.J.: Van Nostrand, 1958.

French, J. R. P., Jr., and Raven, B. The bases of social power. In D. Cartwright (Ed.), *Studies in social power*. Ann Arbor, Mich.: Institute for Social Research, 1959.

Freud, S. *Beyond the pleasure principle*. London: International Psychoanalytical Press, 1922.

Freud, S. *A general introduction to psychoanalysis*. New York: Boni and Liveright, 1924.

Freud, S. *The basic writings of Sigmund Freud*. Edited by A. A. Brill. New York: Random House, 1938.

Freud, S. *The interpretation of dreams*. In J. Strachey (Ed.), *The standard edition of the complete psychological works of Sigmund Freud* (Vols. 4 and 5). London: Hogarth Press, 1953. (First German Edition, 1900.)

Fried, M. Grieving for a lost home. In L. Duhl (Ed.), *The urban condition*. New York: Basic Books, 1963.

Friendly, M. L., and Glucksberg, S. On the description of subcultural lexicons: A multidimensional approach. *Journal of Personality and Social Psychology*, 1970, 14, 55–65.

Fromm, E. *The art of loving*. New York: Harper and Row, 1956. (Perennial Library Edition, 1974.)

Gaertner, S., and Bickman, L. Effects of race on elicitation of helping behavior: The wrong number technique. *Journal of Personality and Social Psychology*, 1971, 20, 218–222.

Gaertner, S. L., and Dovidio, J. F. The subtlety of white racism, arousal, and helping behavior. *Journal of Personality and Social Psychology*, 1977, 35, 691–707.

Galle, O., Gove, W., and McPherson, J. Population density and pathology: What are the relations for man? *Science*, 1972, 176, 23–30.

Gallimore, R., Weiss, L. B., and Finney, R. Cultural differences in delay of gratification: A problem of behavior classification. *Journal of Personality and Social Psychology*, 1974, 30, 72–80.

Gans, H. Planning and social life: Friendship and neighbor relations in suburban communities. *Journal of the American Institute of Planners*, 1961, 27, 135–139.

Gans, H. *The Levittowners: Ways of life and politics in a new suburban community*. New York: Pantheon, 1967.

Gardner, L. I. Deprivation dwarfism. *Scientific American*, 1972, 227(1), 76–82.

Gardner, R. A., and Gardner, B. T. Teaching sign language to a chimpanzee. *Science*, 1969, 165, 664–672.

Gardner, R. A., and Gardner, B. T. Comparative psychology and language acquisition. In K. Salzinger and F. Denmark (Eds.), *Psychology: The State of the Art*. Annals of the New York Academy of Science, 1978, 309, 33–76.

Garfinkel, H. *Studies in ethnomethodology*. Englewood Cliffs, N.J.: Prentice-Hall, 1967.

Geen, R. G. The study of aggression. In R. G. Geen and E. C. O'Neal (Eds.), *Perspectives on aggression*. New York: Academic Press, 1976.

Geis, F., and Christie, R. Overview of experimental research. In R. Christie and F. Geis *Studies in Machiavellianism*. New York: Academic Press, 1970.

Geracimos, A. How I stopped beating my wife. *Ms.*, 1976, 5(2), 53.

Gerard, H. B. Disagreement with others, their credibility, and experienced stress. *Journal of Abnormal and Social Psychology*, 1961, 62, 559–564.

Gerard, H. B., and Mathewson, G. C. The effects of severity of initiation on liking for a group: A replication. *Journal of Experimental Social Psychology*, 1966, 2, 278–287.

Gerard, H. B., and Rabbie, J. M. Fear and social comparison. *Journal of Abnormal and Social Psychology*, 1961, 62, 586–592.

Gerbasi, K. C., Zuckerman, M., and Reis, H. T. Justice needs a new blindfold: A review of mock jury research. *Psychological Bulletin*, 1977, 84, 323–345.

Gergen, K. J. Toward a psychology of receiving help. *Journal of Applied Social Psychology*, 1974, 4, 187–193.

Gergen, K. J., and Gergen, M. M. International assistance in psychological perspective. *1971 Yearbook of world affairs* (Vol. 25). London: Institute of World Affairs, 1971.

Gergen, K. J., Gergen, M. M., and Meter, K. Individual orientations to prosocial behavior. *Journal of Social Issues,* 1972, *28*(3), 105-130.

Gergen, K. J., and Marlowe, D. (Eds.). *Personality and social behavior.* Reading, Mass.: Addison-Wesley, 1970.

Gewirtz, J. L. (Ed.). *Attachment and dependency.* Washington, D.C.: V. H. Winston and Sons, 1972.

Gibb, C. A., Leadership. In G. Lindzey and E. Aronson (Eds.). *The handbook of social psychology* (Vol. 4), 2nd ed. Reading, Mass.: Addison-Wesley, 1969.

Gibbins, K. Communication aspects of women's clothes and their relation to fashionability. *British Journal of Social and Clinical Psychology,* 1969, *8*, 301-312.

Giesen, J. M. Effects of eye contact, attitude agreement, and presentation mode on impressions and persuasion. Unpublished doctoral dissertation, Kent State University, 1973.

Giglioli, P. P. (Ed.). *Language and social context.* Baltimore: Penguin, 1972.

Gil, D. G. Violence against children. *Journal of Marriage and the Family,* 1971, *33*, 637-648.

Gilbert, G. M. Stereotype persistence and change among college students. *Journal of Abnormal and Social Psychology,* 1951, *46*, 245-254.

Gillig, P. M., and Greenwald, A. G. Is it time to lay the sleeper effect to rest? *Journal of Personality and Social Psychology,* 1974, *29*, 132-139.

Gingold, J. "One of these days—pow! Right in the kisser." *Ms.,* 1976, *5*(2), 51-52; 54; 94.

Glass, D., and Singer, J. *Urban stress: Experiments on noise and social stressors.* New York: Academic Press, 1972.

Glucksberg, S., Krauss, R. M., and Higgins, E. T. The development of referential communication skills. In F. D. Horowitz (Ed.), *Review of child development research.* Chicago: University of Chicago Press, 1975.

Glucksberg, S., Krauss, R. M., and Weisberg, R. Referential communication in nursery school children: Method and some preliminary findings. *Journal of Experimental Child Psychology,* 1966, *3*, 333-342.

Goethals, G. R., and Nelson, R. E. Similarity in the influence process: The belief–value distinction. *Journal of Personality and Social Psychology,* 1973, *25*, 117-122.

Goffman, E. On cooling the mark out: Some aspects of adaptation to failure. *Psychiatry,* 1952, *15*, 451-463.

Goffman, E. *The presentation of self in everyday life.* Garden City, N.Y.: Doubleday-Anchor, 1959.

Goffman, E. *Asylums.* Garden City, N.Y.: Doubleday-Anchor, 1961.

Goffman, E. *Stigma: Notes on the management of spoiled identity.* Englewood Cliffs, N.J.: Prentice-Hall, 1963.

Goldberg, G. N., Kiesler, C. A., and Collins, B. E. Visual behavior and face-to-face distance during interaction. *Sociometry,* 1969, *32*, 43-53.

Goldberg, P. A., Gottesdiener, M., and Abramson, P. R., Another put-down of women?: Perceived attractiveness as a function of support for the feminist movement. *Journal of Personality and Social Psychology,* 1975, *32*, 113-115.

Goldman-Eisler, F. The measurement of time sequences in conversational behavior. *British Journal of Psychology,* 1951, *42*, 355-362.

Gollin, E. S. Organizational characteristics of social judgment: A developmental investigation. *Journal of Personality,* 1958, *26*, 139-154.

Goranson, R. E. Media violence and aggressive behavior: A review of experimental research. In L. Berkowitz (Ed.), *Advances in experimental social psychology* (Vol. 5), New York: Academic Press, 1970.

Goranson, R. E., and Berkowitz, L. Reciprocity and responsibility reactions to prior help. *Journal of Personality and Social Psychology,* 1966, *3*, 227-232.

Gouldner, A. W. The norm of reciprocity: A preliminary statement. *American Sociological Review.* 1960, *25*, 161-178.

Graham, J. D. Who participates? *Australian Journal of Social Issues,* 1974, *9*, 133-141.

Granberg, D., and Brent, E. E. Dove–hawk placements in the 1968 election: Application of social judgment and balance theories. *Journal of Personality and Social Psychology,* 1974, *29*, 687-695.

Gray, J. G. *The warriors: Reflections on men in battle.*

New York: Harper & Row, 1959. (Perennial Library Edition, 1973.)

Green, F. P., and Schneider, F. W. Age differences in the behavior of boys on three measures of altruism. *Child Development,* 1974, *45,* 248-251.

Greenberg, M. S. A preliminary statement on a theory of indebtedness. Paper presented at the meeting of the Western Psychological Association, San Diego, 1968.

Greenwell, J., and Dengerink, H. A. The role of perceived versus actual attack in human physical aggression. *Journal of Personality and Social Psychology,* 1973, *26,* 66-71.

Greer, G. Seduction is a four-letter word. In L. G. Schultz (Ed.), *Rape victimology.* Springfield, Ill.: Charles C. Thomas, 1975.

Griffin, S. Rape: The all-American crime. *Ramparts,* 1971, *10*(3), 26-35.

Griffitt, W. Environmental effects on interpersonal affective behavior. Ambient effective temperature and attraction. *Journal of Personality and Social Psychology,* 1970, *15,* 240-244.

Gruder, C. L., and Cook, T. D. Sex, dependency, and helping. *Journal of Personality and Social Psychology,* 1971, *19,* 290-294.

Guilford, J. P. *Psychometric methods,* 2nd ed. New York: McGraw-Hill, 1954 (originally published in 1936).

Guilford, J. P. *The nature of human intelligence.* New York: McGraw-Hill, 1967.

Gurin, G., Veroff, J., and Feld, S. *Americans view their mental health: A nationwide interview survey.* New York: Basic Books, 1960.

Guthrie, E. R. *The psychology of human conflict.* New York: Harper & Brothers, 1938.

Hackman, J. R., and Morris, C. G. Group tasks, group interaction process, and group performance effectiveness: A review and proposed integration. In L. Berkowitz (Ed.), *Advances in experimental social psychology* (Vol. 8). New York: Academic Press, 1975.

Hall, C. S., and Lindzey, G. *Theories of personality.* N.Y.: Wiley, 1957.

Hall, E. T. *The hidden dimension.* Garden City, New York: Doubleday, 1966.

Hallie, P. P. *The paradox of cruelty.* Middletown, Conn.: Wesleyan University Press, 1969.

Hamblin, R. L. Leadership and crises. *Sociometry,* 1958, *21,* 322-335.

Hamilton, D. L., and Gifford, R. K. Influence of implicit personality theories on cue utilization in interpersonal judgment. *Proceedings of the 78th Annual Convention of the American Psychological Association,* 1970, *5,* 415-416.

Haney, C. A., and Michielutte, R. Selective factors operating in the adjudication of incompetency. *Journal of Health and Social Behavior,* 1968, *9,* 233-242.

Hardin, G. The tragedy of the commons. *Science,* 1968, *162,* 1243-1248.

Harlow, H. F. The nature of love. *American Psychologist,* 1958, *13,* 673-685.

Harlow, H. F., and Harlow, M. K. Learning to love. *Scientific American* 1966, *54,* 244-272.

Harlow, H. F., and Harlow, M. K. The young monkeys. In P. Cramer (Ed.), *Readings in developmental psychology today.* Del Mar, Calif.: CRM Books, 1970.

Harrington, A. *Life in the crystal palace.* New York: Knopf, 1959.

Harris, M. *The rise of anthropological theory.* New York: Thomas Y. Crowell, 1968.

Harris, M. *Cows, pigs, wars, and witches: The riddles of culture.* New York: Random House, 1974.

Hartley, E. L., Rosenbaum, M., and Schwartz, S. Children's use of ethnic frames of reference: An exploratory study of children's conceptualizations of multiple ethnic group memberships. *Journal of Psychology,* 1948, *26,* 367-386.

Hartshorne, H., and May, M. A. *Studies in the nature of character; Studies in deceit* (Vol. 1). New York: Macmillan, 1928.

Hartup, W. W., and Lempers, J. A problem in life-span development: The interactional analysis of family attachments. In P. B. Baltes and K. W. Schaie (Eds.), *Life-span developmental psychology: Personality and socialization.* New York: Academic Press, 1973.

Hass, R. G., and Linder, D. E. Counterargument availability and the effects of message structure on persuasion. *Journal of Personality and Social Psychology,* 1972, *23,* 219-233.

Heberlein, T. A., and Black, J. S. Attitudinal specificity

and the prediction of behavior in a field setting. *Journal of Personality and Social Psychology,* 1976, *33,* 474-479.

Hediger, H. *Wild animals in captivity.* London: Butterworth, 1950.

Heider, F. Attitudes and cognitive organization. *Journal of Psychology,* 1946, *21,* 107-112.

Heider, F. *The psychology of interpersonal relations.* New York: Wiley, 1958.

Helfer, R. E., and Kempe, C. H. (Eds.). *The battered child.* Chicago: University of Chicago Press, 1968.

Helms, D. B., and Turner, J. S. *Exploring child behavior.* Philadelphia: Saunders, 1976.

Helson, H. Adaptation-level as a basis for quantitative theory of frames of reference. *Psychological Review,* 1948, *55,* 297-313.

Helson, H., Blake, R. R., and Mouton, J. S. Petition signing as adjustment to situational and personality factors. *Journal of Social Psychology,* 1958, *48,* 3-10.

Hemphill, J. K. *Leader behavior description.* Columbus, Ohio: Ohio State University Personnel Research Board, 1950.

Hendrick, C., and Brown, S. R. Introversion, extroversion, and interpersonal attraction. *Journal of Personality and Social Psychology,* 1971, *20,* 31-36.

Hendrick, C., and Page, H. Self-esteem, attitude similarity, and attraction. *Journal of Personality,* 1970, *38,* 588-601.

Henninger, M., and Wyer, R. S., Jr. The recognition and elimination of inconsistencies among syllogistically related beliefs: Some new light on the "Socratic Effect." *Journal of Personality and Social Psychology,* 1976, *34,* 680-693.

Herberle, R. The normative element in neighborhood relations. *Pacific Sociological Review,* 1960, *3,* 3-11.

Hersey, J. *My petition for more space.* New York: Knopf, 1974.

Hess, E. H. Imprinting in birds. *Science,* 1964, *146,* 1128-1139.

Hess, E. H. Attitude and pupil size. *Scientific American,* 1965, *212*(4), 46-54.

Hofer, M. A. (Ed.), *Parent-infant interaction.* Ciba Foundation Symposium 33. New York: American Elsevier, 1975.

Hoffer, E. *The true believer: Thoughts on the nature of mass movements.* New York: Harper & Row, 1951.

Hoffman, L., and Hoffman, M. The value of children to parents. In J. Fawcett (Ed.), *Psychological perspectives on population.* New York: Basic Books, 1973.

Hoffman, M. L. Moral development. In P. H. Mussen (Ed.), *Carmichael's manual of child psychology* (Vol. 2). New York: Wiley, 1970.

Hoffman, M. L., and Saltzstein, H. D. Parent discipline and the child's moral development. *Journal of Personality and Social Psychology,* 1967, *5,* 45-57.

Holahan, C., and Saegert, S. Behavioral and attitudinal effects of large-scale variation in the physical environment of psychiatric wards. *Journal of Abnormal Psychology,* 1973, *82,* 454-462.

Hollander, E. P. Conformity, status, and idiosyncrasy credit. *Psychological Review,* 1958, *65,* 117-127.

Hollander, E. P. *Leaders, groups, and influence.* New York: Oxford University Press, 1964.

Hollander, E. P., and Julian, J. W. Contemporary trends in the analysis of leadership processes. *Psychological Bulletin,* 1969, *71,* 387-397.

Hollander, E. P., and Julian, J. W. Studies in leader legitimacy, influence, and innovation. In L. Berkowitz (Ed.), *Advances in experimental social psychology* (Vol. 5). New York: Academic Press, 1970.

Hollander, J., and Yeostros, S. The effect of simultaneous variations of humidity and barometric pressure on arthritis. *Bulletin of the American Meteorological Society,* 1963, *44,* 489-494.

Holsti, O. R. *Content analysis for the social sciences and humanities.* Reading, Mass.: Addison-Wesley, 1969.

Homans, G. C. *Social behavior: Its elementary forms.* New York: Harcourt, Brace & World, 1961.

Hornstein, H. A. The influence of social models on helping. In J. Macaulay and L. Berkowitz (Eds.), *Altruism and helping behavior.* New York: Academic Press, 1970.

Horowitz, M., Duff, D., and Stratton, L. Body-buffer zone. *Archives of General Psychiatry,* 1964, *11,* 651-656.

Hostetler, J. A. *Amish society.* Baltimore: Johns Hopkins Press, 1963.

Hovland, C. I. Reconciling conflicting results derived

from experimental and survey studies of attitude change. *American Psychologist,* 1959, *14*, 8–17.

Hovland, C. I., Lumsdaine, A. A., and Sheffield, F. D. *Experiments on mass communication.* Princeton: Princeton University Press, 1949.

Hovland, C. I., and Mandell, W. An experimental comparison of conclusion-drawing by the communicator and by the audience. *Journal of Abnormal and Social Psychology,* 1952, *47*, 581–588.

Hovland, C. I., and Sears, R. R. Minor studies of aggression. VI. Correlation of lynchings with economic indices. *Journal of Psychology,* 1940, *9*, 301–310.

Hovland, C. I., and Sherif, M. Judgmental phenomena and scales of attitude measurement: Item displacement in Thurstone scales. *Journal of Abnormal and Social Psychology,* 1952, *47*, 822–832.

Hovland, C. I., and Weiss, W. The influence of source credibility on communication effectiveness. *Public Opinion Quarterly,* 1951, *15*, 635–650.

Howitt, D., and Cumberbatch, G. *Mass media, violence and society.* New York: Wiley, 1975.

Hunter, J. E. Images of woman. *Journal of Social Issues,* 1976, *32*(3), 7–17.

Husek, T. R. Persuasive impacts of early, late, or no mention of a negative source. *Journal of Personality and Social Psychology,* 1965, *2*, 125–128.

Hyman, H. H., and Sheatsley, P. B. Some reasons why information campaigns fail. *Public Opinion Quarterly,* 1947, *11*, 412–423.

Insko, C. A., and Schopler, J. *Experimental social psychology.* New York: Academic Press, 1972.

Irwin, W. What is news? *Collier's,* 1911, *46*(March 18), 16–18.

Isen, A. M., Clark, M., and Schwartz, M. F. Duration of the effect of good mood on helping: "Footprints on the sands of time." *Journal of Personality and Social Psychology,* 1976, *34*, 385–393.

Isen, A. M., and Levin, P. F. Effect of feeling good on helping: Cookies and kindness. *Journal of Personality and Social Psychology,* 1972, *21*, 384–388.

Ittelson, W. H., Proshansky, H. M., and Rivlin, L. G. The environmental psychology of the psychiatric ward. In H. Proshansky, W. Ittelson, & L. Rivlin (Eds.), *Environmental psychology: Man and his physical setting.* New York: Holt, Rinehart, and Winston, 1970.

Ittelson, W. H., Proshansky, H. M., Rivlin, L. G., and Winkel, G. H. *An introduction to environmental psychology.* New York: Holt, Rinehart, and Winston, 1974.

Jacobs, R. C., and Campbell, D. T. The perpetuation of an arbitrary tradition through several generations of a laboratory microculture. *Journal of Abnormal and Social Psychology,* 1961, *62*, 649–658.

James, J. A preliminary study of the size determinant in small group interaction *American Sociological Review,* 1951, *16*, 474–477.

James, W. *The principles of psychology.* New York: Henry Holt & Co., 1890.

Janis, I. L. *Air war and emotional stress.* New York: McGraw-Hill, 1951.

Janis, I. L. *Victims of groupthink.* Boston: Houghton Mifflin, 1972.

Janis, I. L., and Feshbach, S. Effects of fear-arousing communications. *Journal of Abnormal and Social Psychology,* 1953, *48*, 78–92.

Janis, I. L., and Field, P. B. Sex differences and personality factors related to persuasibility. In C. I. Hovland and I. L. Janis (Eds.), *Personality and persuasibility,* New Haven, Conn.: Yale University Press, 1959.

Janssens, L., and Nuttin, J. R. Frequency perception of individual and group successes as a function of competition, coaction, and isolation. *Journal of Personality and Social Psychology,* 1976, *34*, 830–836.

Johnson, R. N. *Aggression in man and animals.* Philadelphia: Saunders, 1972.

Jones, E. E. *Ingratiation.* New York: Appleton-Century-Crofts, 1964.

Jones, E. E., and Davis, K. E. From acts to dispositions: The attribution process in person perception. In L. Berkowitz (Ed.), *Advances in experimental social psychology* (Vol. 2). New York: Academic Press, 1965.

Jones, E. E., and Gerard, H. B. *Foundations of social psychology.* New York: Wiley, 1967.

Jones, E. E., and Nisbett, R. E. *The actor and the observer: Divergent perceptions of the causes of be-

havior. New York: General Learning Press, 1971.
Jones, E. E., and Sigall, H. The bogus pipeline: A new paradigm for measuring affect and attitude. *Psychological Bulletin,* 1971, *76,* 349–364.
Jones E. E., and Thibaut, J. W. Interaction goals as bases of inference in interpersonal perception. In R. Tagiuri and L. Petrullo (Eds.), *Person perception and interpersonal behavior.* Stanford, Calif.: Stanford University Press, 1958.
Jones, R. A. *Self-fulfilling prophecies: Social, psychological, and physiological effects of expectancies.* Hillsdale, N.J.: Erlbaum, 1977.
Jones, R. A., and Brehm, J. W. Persuasiveness of one- and two-sided communications as a function of awareness there are two sides. *Journal of Experimental Social Psychology,* 1970, *6,* 47–56.
Jones, S. C., and Panitch, D. The self-fulfilling prophecy and interpersonal attraction. *Journal of Experimental Social Psychology,* 1971, *7,* 356–366.
Jorgenson, D. O., and Dukes, F. O. Deindividuation as a function of density and group membership. *Journal of Personality and Social Psychology,* 1976, *34,* 24–29.
Jourard, S. M. *The transparent self.* Princeton, N.J.: Van Nostrand Reinhold, 1964.
Jourard, S. M. An exploratory study of body-accessibility. *British Journal of Social and Clinical Psychology,* 1966, *5,* 221–231.

Kagan, J., and Klein, R. E. Cross-cultural perspectives on early development. *American Psychologist,* 1973, *28,* 947–961.
Kahn, R. Who buys bloodshed and why. *Psychology Today,* 1972, *6*(1), 47–48, 82–84.
Kahn, R. L., and Katz, D. Leadership practices in relation to productivity and morale. In D. Cartwright and A. Zander (Eds.), *Group dynamics: Research and theory,* 2nd ed. New York: Harper & Row, 1960.
Kahneman, D. *Attention and effort.* Englewood Cliffs, N.J.: Prentice-Hall, 1973.
Kanin, E. J. Male sex aggression and three psychiatric hypotheses. *Journal of Sex Research,* 1965, *1,* 221–231.
Kanin, E. J. An examination of sexual aggression as a response to sexual frustration. *Journal of Marriage and the Family,* 1967, *29,* 428–433.
Kaplan, A. *The conduct of inquiry.* San Francisco: Chandler, 1964.
Karlin, R., Epstein, Y., and Aiello, J. R. Strategies for the investigation of crowding. In A. Esser and B. Greenbie (Eds.), *Design for communality and privacy.* New York: Plenum Press, 1978.
Karlin, R., McFarland, D., Epstein, Y., and Aiello, J. R. Normative mediation of reactions to crowding. *Environmental Psychology and Nonverbal Behavior,* 1976, *1,* 30–40.
Karlins, M., Coffman, T. L., and Walters, G. On the fading of social stereotypes: Studies in three generations of college students. *Journal of Personality and Social Psychology,* 1969, *13,* 1–16.
Katz, D. The functional approach to the study of attitude. *Public Opinion Quarterly,* 1960, *24,* 163–204.
Katz, D., and Braly, K. Racial stereotypes of one hundred college students. *Journal of Abnormal and Social Psychology,* 1933, *28,* 280–290.
Katz, D., and Stotland, E. A preliminary statement to a theory of attitude structure and change. In S. Koch (Ed.), *Psychology: A study of a science* (Vol. 3). New York: McGraw-Hill, 1959.
Kelly, G. A. The autobiography of a theory. In B. Maher (Ed.), *Clinical psychology and personality.* New York: Wiley, 1969.
Kelley, H. H. The warm–cold variable in first impressions of persons. *Journal of Personality,* 1950, *18,* 431–439.
Kelley, H. H. The two functions of reference groups. In G. E. Swanson, T. M. Newcomb, and E. L. Hartley (Eds.), *Readings in social psychology,* 2nd ed. New York: Holt, Rinehart and Winston, 1952.
Kelley, H. H. Attribution theory in social psychology. In D. Levine (Ed.), *Nebraska symposium on motivation* (Vol. 15). Lincoln, Neb.: University of Nebraska Press, 1967.
Kelley, H. H. The processes of causal attribution. *American Psychologist,* 1973, *28,* 107–128.
Kelley, H. H., and Stahelski, A. J. Social interaction basis of cooperators' and competitors' beliefs about others. *Journal of Personality and Social Psychology,* 1970, *16,* 66–91.
Kelley, H. H., and Thibaut, J. W. Group problem solving. In G. Lindzey and E. Aronson (Eds.), *The*

Kelley, H. H., Thibaut, J. W., Radloff, R., and Mundy, D. The development of cooperation in the "minimal social situation." *Psychological Monographs*, 1962, *76*, No. 19 (Whole No. 538).

Kelman, H. C., and Hovland, C. I. "Reinstatement" of the communicator in delayed measurement of opinion change. *Journal of Abnormal and Social Psychology*, 1953, *48*, 327–335.

Kerckhoff, A. C., and Davis, K. E. Value consensus and need complementarity in mate selection. *American Sociological Review*, 1962, *27*, 295–303.

Kiesler, C. A. *The psychology of commitment: Experiments linking behavior to belief.* New York: Academic Press, 1971.

Kiesler, C. A., and Kiesler, S. B. *Conformity*. Reading, Mass.: Addison-Wesley, 1969.

Kiesler, C. A., Nisbett, R. E., and Zanna, M. P. On inferring one's beliefs from one's behavior. *Journal of Personality and Social Psychology*, 1969, *11*, 321–327.

Kiesler, S. B. The effect of perceived role requirements on reactions to favor doing. *Journal of Experimental Social Psychology*, 1966, *2*, 198–210.

Kiesler, S. B., and Baral, R. L. The search for a romantic partner: The effects of self-esteem and physical attractiveness on romantic behavior. In K. J. Gergen and D. Marlowe (Eds.), *Personality and social behavior*, Reading, Mass.: Addison-Wesley, 1970.

Kinsey, A., Pomeroy, W., and Martin, C. *Sexual behavior in the human male.* Philadelphia: Saunders, 1948.

Kinsey, A., Pomeroy, W., Martin, C., and Gebhard, P. *Sexual behavior in the human female.* Philadelphia: Saunders, 1953.

Kinzel, A. Body-buffer zone in violent prisoners. *American Journal of Psychiatry*, 1970, *127*, 59–64.

Kirkpatrick, C., and Kanin, E. Male sex aggression on a university campus. *American Sociological Review*, 1957, *22*, 52–58.

Kirscht, J. P., and Dillehay, R. C. *Dimensions of authoritarianism: A review of research and theory.* Lexington, Ky.: University of Kentucky Press, 1967.

Klapper, J. T. *The effects of mass communication,* Glencoe, Ill.: The Free Press, 1960.

Klaus, M. H., and Kennell, J. H. (Eds.) *Maternal-infant bonding.* St. Louis: Mosby, 1976.

Kleck, R. Physical stigma and task oriented interactions. *Human Relations*, 1969, *22*, 53–60.

Kleck, R., Ono, H., and Hastorf, A. The effects of physical deviance upon face-to-face interaction. *Human Relations*, 1966, *19*, 425–436.

Kleinke, C. L., and Pohlen, P. D. Affective and emotional responses as a function of other person's gaze and cooperativeness in a two-person game. *Journal of Personality and Social Psychology*, 1971, *17*, 308–313.

Knight, R., Zimring, C., Weitzer, W., and Wheeler, H. *Social development and normalized institutional settings: A preliminary research report.* Amherst, Mass.: Environment and Behavior Research Center, University of Massachusetts, 1976.

Knowles, E. S. Boundaries around group interaction: The effect of group size and member status on boundary permeability. *Journal of Personality and Social Psychology*, 1973, *26*, 327–331.

Koford, C. B. Rank of mothers and sons in bands of Rhesus monkeys. *Science*, 1963, *141*, 356–357.

Kogan, N., and Wallach, M. A. Group risk taking as a function of the situation, the person, and the group. In G. Mandler, P. Mussen, N. Kogan, and M. A. Wallach (Eds.), *New directions in psychology III.* New York: Holt, Rinehart and Winston, 1967.

Kohlberg, L. Stage and sequence: The cognitive-developmental approach to socialization. In D. A. Goslin (Ed.), *Handbook of socialization theory and research.* Chicago: Rand McNally, 1969.

Kohlberg, L. Continuities in childhood and adult moral development revisited. In P. M. Baltes and K. W. Schaie (Eds.), *Life-span developmental psychology: Personality and socialization.* New York: Academic Press, 1973.

Kohlberg, L. Moral stages and moralization: The cognitive-developmental approach. In T. Lickona (Ed.), *Moral development and behavior: Theory, research, and social issues,* New York: Holt, Rinehart and Winston, 1976.

Krasner, L. Studies of the conditioning of verbal behavior. *Psychological Bulletin*, 1958, *55*, 148–170.

Krauss, R. M., and Glucksberg, S. The development of communication: Competence as a function of age. *Child Development*, 1969, *40*, 255–266.

Krauss, R. M., and Weinheimer, S. Concurrent feedback, confirmation, and the encoding of referents in verbal communication. *Journal of Personality and Social Psychology,* 1966, *4,* 343-346.

Krebs, D. L. Altruism—An examination of the concept and a review of the literature. *Psychological Bulletin,* 1970, *73,* 258-302.

Krebs, D. Empathy and altruism. *Journal of Personality and Social Psychology,* 1975, *32,* 1134-1146.

Krebs, D., and Adinolfi, A. A. Physical attractiveness, social relations, and personality style. *Journal of Personality and Social Psychology,* 1975, *31,* 245-253.

Krech, D., and Crutchfield, R. S. *Theory and problems of social psychology.* New York: McGraw-Hill, 1948.

Krech, D., Crutchfield, R. S., and Ballachey, E. L. *Individual in society.* New York: McGraw-Hill, 1962.

Kutner, N. G. Low income, ethnicity, and voluntary association involvement. *Journal of Sociology and Social Welfare,* 1976, *3,* 311-321.

Labov, W. The study of language in its social context. *Studium Generale,* 1970, *23,* 66-84.

Lamale, H. H. *Methodology of the survey of consumer expenditures in 1950.* Philadelphia: University of Pennsylvania Press, 1959.

Lambert, W. E., Hodgson, R. C., Gardner, R. C., and Fillenbaum, S. Evaluational reactions to spoken languages. *Journal of Abnormal and Social Psychology,* 1960, *60,* 44-51.

Landy, D., and Sigall, H. Beauty is talent: Task evaluation as a function of the performer's physical attractiveness. *Journal of Personality and Social Psychology,* 1974, *29,* 299-304.

Langer, E. J. The illusion of control. *Journal of Personality and Social Psychology,* 1975, *32,* 311-328.

Langer, E. J., and Saegert, S. Crowding and cognitive control. *Journal of Personality and Social Psychology,* 1977, *35,* 175-182.

Langley, R., and Levy, R. C. *Wife beating: The silent crisis.* New York: Dutton, 1977.

LaPiere, R. T. Attitudes vs. actions. *Social Forces,* 1934, *13,* 230-237.

Laughlin, P. R., and Jaccard, J. J. Social facilitation and observational learning of individuals and cooperative pairs. *Journal of Personality and Social Psychology,* 1975, *32,* 873-879.

Latané, B. (Ed.). Studies in social comparison. *Journal of Experimental Social Psychology, Supplement 1,* 1966.

Latané, B., and Darley, J. M. Group inhibition of bystander intervention in emergencies. *Journal of Personality and Social Psychology,* 1968, *10,* 215-221.

Latané, B., and Darley, J. M. Social determinants of bystander intervention in emergencies. In J. Macaulay and L. Berkowitz (Eds.), *Altruism and helping behavior.* New York: Academic Press, 1970.

Latané, B., and Rodin, J. A lady in distress: Inhibiting effects of friends and strangers on bystander intervention. *Journal of Experimental Social Psychology,* 1969, *5,* 189-202.

Lazarus, R. S., and Averill, J. R. Emotion and cognition: With special reference to anxiety. In C. D. Spielberger (Ed.), *Anxiety: Current trends in theory and research* (Vol. 2). New York: Academic Press, 1972.

Leary, R. W., and Slye, D. Dominance reversal in drugged monkeys. *Journal of Psychology,* 1959, *48,* 227-235.

Le Dantec, F. *L'égoisme: Seul base de toute société.* Paris: Flammarion, 1918. (Cited in Allport, 1968.)

Lee, J. A. *The colors of love: An exploration of the ways of loving,* Don Mills, Ontario: New Press, 1976.

Lee, T. Urban neighborhood as a socio-spatial schema. *Human Relations,* 1968, *21,* 241-267. Reprinted in Proshansky, H., Ittelson, W., and Rivlin, L. (Eds.), *Environmental psychology: Man and his physical setting.* New York: Holt, Rinehart and Winston, 1970, 349-370.

Leeds, R. Altruism and the norm of giving. *Merrill-Palmer Quarterly,* 1963, *9,* 229-240.

Lerner, M. J. The desire for justice and reactions to victims. In J. Macaulay and L. Berkowitz (Eds.), *Altruism and helping behavior.* New York: Academic Press, 1970.

Lerner, M. J., Miller, D. T. and Holmes, J. G. Deserving and the emergence of forms of justice. In L. Berkowitz (Ed.), *Advances in experimental social psychology* (Vol. 9). New York: Academic Press, 1976.

Lerner, M. J., and Simmons, C. H. Observer's reaction to the "Innocent victim": Compassion or rejection? *Journal of Personality and Social Psychology,* 1966, *4,* 203-210.

Leventhal, H. Findings and theory in the study of fear communications. In L. Berkowitz (Ed.), *Advances in experimental social psychology* (Vol. 5). New York: Academic Press, 1970.

Levinger, G. A three-level approach to attraction: Toward an understanding of pair relatedness. In T. L. Huston (Ed.), *Foundations of interpersonal attraction.* New York: Academic Press, 1974.

Levinger, G., Senn, D. J., and Jorgensen, B. W. Progress toward permanence in courtship: A test of the Kerckhoff-Davis hypotheses. *Sociometry,* 1970, *33,* 427-443.

Lewin, K. *A dynamic theory of personality: Selected papers,* New York: McGraw-Hill, 1935.

Lewin, K., Lippitt, R., and White, R. Patterns of aggressive behavior in experimentally created "social climates." *Journal of Social Psychology,* 1939, *10,* 271-299.

Lewis, M., and Rosenblum, L. A. (Eds.). *The effect of the infant on its caregiver.* New York: Wiley, 1974.

Lickona, T. A cognitive-developmental approach to interpersonal attraction. In T. L. Huston (Ed.), *Foundations of interpersonal attraction.* New York: Academic Press, 1974.

Lieber, A., and Sherin, C. Homicides and the lunar cycle: Toward a theory of lunar influence on human emotional disturbance. *American Journal of Psychiatry,* 1972, *129,* 69-74.

Liebert, R. M., Neale, J. M., and Davidson, E. S. *The early window: Effects of television on children and youth.* New York: Pergamon, 1973.

Linder, D. E., and Jones, R. A. Discriminative stimuli as determinants of consonance and dissonance. *Journal of Experimental Social Psychology.* 1969, *5,* 467-482.

Linton, H., and Graham, E. Personality correlates of persuasibility. In C. I. Hovland and I. L. Janis (Eds.), *Personality and persuasibility.* New Haven, Conn.: Yale University Press, 1959.

Linton, R. *The study of man.* New York: Appleton, 1936.

London, P. The rescuers: Motivational hypotheses about Christians who saved Jews from the Nazis. In J. Macaulay and L. Berkowitz (Eds.), *Altruism and helping behavior.* New York: Academic Press, 1970.

London Sunday Times Insight Team. *Northern Ireland: A report on the conflict.* New York: Random House, 1972.

Lorenz, K. *King Solomon's ring.* New York: Thomas Y. Crowell, 1952.

Lorenz, K. *On aggression.* New York: Harcourt, Brace & World, 1966.

Lorge, I. Prestige, suggestion, and attitude. *Journal of Social Psychology,* 1936, *7,* 386-402.

Lott, A. J., and Lott, B. E. The role of reward in the formation of positive interpersonal attitudes. In T. L. Huston (Ed.), *Foundations of interpersonal attraction.* New York: Academic Press, 1974.

Lott, D. F., and Sommer, R. Seating arrangements and status. *Journal of Personality and Social Psychology,* 1967, *7,* 90-95.

Lynch, K. *The image of the city.* Cambridge: M.I.T. Press, 1960.

Machiavelli, N. *The prince.* New York: Mentor, 1952 (Originally published in 1513).

Mackworth, N. *Researches on the measurement of human performance.* Medical Research Council Special Report Series No. 268, London: HMSO, 1950.

Maclay, G., and Knipe, H. *The dominant man: The pecking order in human society,* New York: Dell, 1972.

Malpass, R. S., and Kravitz, J. Recognition for faces of own and other race. *Journal of Personality and Social Psychology,* 1969, *13,* 330-334.

Mann R. D. A review of the relationships between personality and performance in small groups. *Psychological Bulletin,* 1959, *56,* 241-270.

Manser, G., and Cass, R. H. *Voluntarism at the crossroads.* New York: Family Service Association of America, 1976.

Marler, P. On animal aggression: The roles of strangeness and familiarity. *American Psychologist,* 1976, *31,* 239-246.

Marshall, N. J. Privacy and environment. *Human Ecology,* 1972, *1,* 93-110.

Marshall, R. Precipitation and presidents. *The Nation,* 1927, *124,* 315-316.

Martens, R. Effect of an audience on learning and performance of a complex motor skill. *Journal of Personality and Social Psychology,* 1969, *12,* 252-260.

Martindale, D. Territorial dominance behavior in dyadic verbal interactions. *Proceedings of the 79th Annual Convention of the American Psychological Association,* 1971, *6,* 305–306.

Maslow, A. H. *The psychology of science: A reconnaissance.* New York: Harper & Row, 1966.

Matlin, M. W. Response competition as a mediating factor in the frequency-affect relationship. *Journal of Personality and Social Psychology.* 1970, *16,* 536–552.

Mauldin, W. P., and Marks, E. S. Problems of response in enumerative surveys. *American Sociological Review,* 1950, *15,* 649–657.

McArthur, L. Z., and Eisen, S. V. Achievements of male and female storybook characters as determinants of achievement behavior by boys and girls. *Journal of Personality and Social Psychology,* 1976, *33,* 467–473.

McBride, G., King, M. G., and James, J. W. Social proximity effects of galvanic skin responses in adult humans. *Journal of Psychology,* 1965, *61,* 153–157.

McCain, G., Cox, V., and Paulus, P. The relationship between illness complaints and degree of crowding in a prison environment. *Environment and Behavior,* 1976, *8,* 283–290.

McCandless, B. R. *Childhood socialization.* In D. A. Goslin (Ed.), *Handbook of socialization theory and research.* Chicago: Rand McNally, 1969.

McClelland, D. C. *The achieving society.* Princeton, N.J.: Van Nostrand, 1961.

McClelland, D. C., Atkinson, J. W., Clark, R. A., and Lowell, E. L. *The achievement motive.* New York: Appleton-Century-Crofts, 1953.

McDavid, J. W. Approval-seeking motivation and the volunteer subject. *Journal of Personality and Social Psychology,* 1965, *2,* 115–117.

McDougall, W. *An introduction to social psychology.* London: Methuen, 1908.

McGuire, W. J. Inducing resistance to persuasion: Some contemporary approaches. In L. Berkowitz (Ed.), *Advances in experimental social psychology* (Vol. 1). New York: Academic Press, 1964.

McGuire, W. J. Personality and susceptibility to social influence. In E. F. Borgatta and W. W. Lambert (Eds.), *Handbook of personality theory and research.* Chicago: Rand McNally, 1968.

McGuire, W. J. The nature of attitudes and attitude change. In G. Lindzey and E. Aronson (Eds.), *The handbook of social psychology* (Vol. 3), 2nd ed. Reading, Mass.: Addison Wesley, 1969.

McGuire, W. J., and Millman, S. Anticipatory belief lowering following forewarning of a persuasive attack. *Journal of Personality and Social Psychology,* 1965, *2,* 471–479.

Mead, G. H. *Mind, self, and society.* Chicago: University of Chicago Press, 1934.

Medea, A., and Thompson, K. *Against rape.* New York: Farrar, Straus & Giroux, 1974.

Megargee, E. I. Undercontrolled and overcontrolled personality types in extreme antisocial aggression. *Psychological Monographs,* 1966, *80* (Whole No. 611).

Megargee, E. I. The role of inhibition in the assessment and understanding of violence. In J. L. Singer (Ed.), *The control of aggression and violence: Cognitive and physiological factors.* New York: Academic Press, 1971.

Mehrabian, A., and Diamond, S. G. Seating arrangement and conversation. *Sociometry,* 1971, *34,* 281–289.

Mensh, I. N., and Wishner, J. Asch on "forming impressions of personality": Further evidence. *Journal of Personality,* 1947, *16,* 188–191.

Mettee, D. R., and Aronson, E. Affective reactions to appraisal from others. In T. L. Huston (Ed.), *Foundations of interpersonal attraction.* New York: Academic Press, 1974.

Middlebrook, P. N., *Social psychology and modern life.* New York: Knopf, 1974.

Midlarsky, E., Bryan, J. H., and Brickman, P. Aversive approval: Interactive effects of modeling and reinforcement on altruistic behavior. *Child Development,* 1973, *44,* 321–328.

Milgram, S. Behavioral study of obedience. *Journal of Abnormal and Social Psychology.* 1963, *67,* 371–378.

Milgram, S. Group pressure and action against a person. *Journal of Abnormal and Social Psychology.* 1964, *69,* 137–143.

Milgram, S. The experience of living in cities. *Science,* 1970, *167,* 1461–1468.

Milgram, S. *Obedience to authority.* New York: Harper & Row, 1974.

Miller, C. E., and Norman, R. M. G. Balance, agreement, and attraction in hypothetical social situations. *Journal of Experimental Social Psychology,* 1976, *12,* 109-119.

Miller, N. E. The frustration–aggression hypothesis. *Psychological Review,* 1941, *48,* 337-342.

Miller, N. E., and Dollard, J. *Social learning and imitation.* New Haven, Conn.: Yale University Press, 1941.

Mills, J. Opinion change as a function of the communicator's desire to influence and liking for the audience. *Journal of Experimental Social Psychology,* 1966, *2,* 152-159.

Mischel, W. Theory and research on the antecedents of self-imposed delay of reward. In B. A. Maher (Ed.), *Progress in experimental personality research* (Vol. 3). New York: Academic Press, 1966.

Mischel, W. Processes in delay of gratification. In L. Berkowitz (Ed.), *Advances in experimental social psychology* (Vol. 7). New York: Academic Press, 1974.

Mitchell, R. E. Some social implications of high-density housing. *American Sociological Review,* 1971, *36,* 18-29.

Montgomery, R. L., Hinkle, S. W., and Enzie, R. F. Arbitrary norms and social change in high- and low-authoritarian societies. *Journal of Personality and Social Psychology,* 1976, *33,* 698-708.

Moore, H. T. The comparative influence of majority and expert opinion. *American Journal of Psychology,* 1921, *32,* 16-20.

Moos, R. *The human context: Environmental determinants of behavior.* New York: John Wiley, 1976.

Morris, D. *The naked ape.* New York: McGraw-Hill, 1967.

Morris, S. C., III, and Rosen, S. Effects of felt adequacy and opportunity to reciprocate on help seeking. *Journal of Experimental Social Psychology,* 1973, *9,* 265-276.

Murphy, G. *Personality: A biosocial approach to origins and structure.* New York: Harper & Brothers, 1947.

Murstein, B. I. A theory of marital choice and its applicability to marriage adjustment. In B. I. Murstein (Ed.), *Theories of attraction and love.* New York: Springer, 1971.

Murstein, B. I. Physical attractiveness and marital choice. *Journal of Personality and Social Psychology,* 1972, *22,* 8-12.

Murstein, B. I., and Christy, P. Physical attractiveness and marriage adjustment in middle-aged couples. *Journal of Personality and Social Psychology,* 1976, *34,* 537-542.

Nadler, A., Fisher, J. D., and Streufert, S. The donor's dilemma: Recipient's reactions to aid from friend or foe. *Journal of Applied Social Psychology.* 1974, *4,* 275-285.

Nahemow, L., and Lawton, M. P. Similarity and propinquity in friendship formation. *Journal of Personality and Social Psychology,* 1975, *32,* 205-213.

National Commission on the Causes and Prevention of Violence. *To establish justice, to insure domestic tranquility.* New York: Award Books, 1969.

Neisser, U. *Cognition and reality: Principles and implications of cognitive psychology.* San Francisco: Freeman, 1976.

Nemeth, C., and Endicott, J. The midpoint as an anchor: Another look at discrepancy of position and attitude change. *Sociometry,* 1976, *39,* 11-18.

Newcomb, T. M. The consistency of certain extrovert–introvert behavior patterns in 51 problem boys. *Teachers College Contributions to Education* (No. 382). New York: Teachers College, 1929.

Newcomb, T. M. An experiment designed to test the validity of a rating technique. *Journal of Educational Psychology.* 1931, *22,* 279-289.

Newcomb, T. M. *The acquaintance process.* New York: Holt, Rinehart and Winston, 1961.

Newman, O. *Defensible space.* New York: Collier, 1973.

Newtson, D. Attribution and the unit of perception of ongoing behavior. *Journal of Personality and Social Psychology,* 1973, *28,* 28-38.

Newtson, D. Foundations of attribution: The perception of ongoing behavior. In J. H. Harvey, W. J. Ickes, and R. F. Kidd (Eds.), *New directions in attribution research* (Vol. 1). Hillsdale, N.J.: Erlbaum, 1976.

Newtson, D., Engquist, G., and Bois, J. The objective basis of behavior units. *Journal of Personality and Social Psychology,* 1977, *35,* 847-862.

Nicosia, G., Hyman, D., Karlin, R., Epstein, Y., and

Aiello, J. Effects of bodily contact on reactions to crowding. *Journal of Applied Social Psychology*, (in press).

Nisbett, R. E., Caputo, C., Legant, P., and Marecek, J. Behavior as seen by the actor and as seen by the observer. *Journal of Personality and Social Psychology.* 1973, *27*, 154-164.

Nisbett, R. E., and Schachter, S. Cognitive manipulation of pain. *Journal of Experimental Social Psychology*, 1966, *2*, 227-236.

Nisbett, R. E., and Wilson, T. D. The halo effect: Evidence for unconscious alteration of judgments. *Journal of Personality and Social Psychology*, 1977, *35*, 250-256.

Noble, G. *Children in front of the small screen.* Beverly Hills, Calif.: Sage, 1975.

Olshan, K. The multidimensional structure of person perception in children. Unpublished doctoral dissertation, Rutgers, The State University, 1970.

Orne, M. T. On the social psychology of the psychological experiment: With particular reference to demand characteristics and their implications. *American Psychologist*, 1962, *17*, 776-783.

Orwell, G. *1984.* New York: New American Library, 1961. (Originally published by Harcourt, Brace in 1949.)

Osgood, C. E., Suci, G. J., and Tannenbaum, P. H. *The measurement of meaning.* Urbana, Ill.: University of Illinois Press, 1957.

Oskamp, S. *Attitudes and opinions.* Englewood Cliffs, N.J.: Prentice-Hall, 1977.

Osmond, H. Design must meet patient's needs. *Modern Hospital*, 1966, *106*(3), 98-100.

Overall, B., and Aronson, H. Expectations of psychotherapy in patients of lower socioeconomic class. *American Journal of Orthopsychiatry*, 1963, *33*, 421-430.

Overmier, J. B., and Seligman, M. E. P. Effects of inescapable shock upon subsequent escape and avoidance responding. *Journal of Comparative and Physiological Psychology*, 1967, *63*, 28-33.

Papageorgis, D., and McGuire, W. J. The generality of immunity to persuasion produced by preexposure to weakened counterarguments. *Journal of Abnormal and Social Psychology*, 1961, *62*, 475-481.

Parke, R. D., Berkowitz, L., Leyens, J. P., West, S. G., and Sebastian, R. J. Some effects of violent and nonviolent movies on the behavior of juvenile delinquents. In L. Berkowitz (Ed.), *Advances in experimental social psychology* (Vol. 10). New York: Academic Press, 1977.

Patterson, A. Territorial behavior and fear of crime in the elderly. *Environmental Psychology and Nonverbal Behavior*, 1978, *2*, 131-144.

Patterson, M. L. An arousal model of interpersonal intimacy. *Psychological Review*, 1976, *83*, 235-245.

Patterson, M. L., Mullens, S. and Romano, J. Compensatory reactions to spatial intrusion. *Sociometry*, 1971, *34*, 114-126.

Paulus, P. B., and Murdoch, P. Anticipated evaluation and audience presence in the enhancement of dominant responses. *Journal of Experimental Social Psychology*, 1971, *7*, 280-291.

Peevers, B. H., and Secord, P. F. Developmental changes in attribution of descriptive concepts to persons. *Journal of Personality and Social Psychology*, 1973, *27*, 120-128.

Pellegrini, R. J., and Empey, J. Interpersonal spatial orientation in dyads. *Journal of Psychology*, 1970, *76*, 67-70.

Pepler, R. Performance and well-being in heat. In *Temperature: Its measurement and control in science and industry*, *3*, Part 3. New York: Reinhold, 1963. Cited in D. Canter and P. Stringer (Eds.), *Environmental interaction.* New York: International Universities Press, 1975.

Peter, L. J., and Hull, R. *The Peter principle.* New York: Morrow, 1969.

Pettigrew, T. Regional differences in anti-Negro prejudice. *Journal of Abnormal and Social Psychology*, 1959, *59*, 28-36.

Petty, R. E., Wells, G. L., and Brock, T. C. Distraction can enhance or reduce yielding to propaganda: Thought disruption versus effort justification. *Journal of Personality and Social Psychology*, 1976, *34*, 874-884.

Pheterson, G. I., Kiesler, S. B., and Goldberg, P. A. Evaluation of the performance of women as a function of their sex, achievment, and personal history. *Journal of Personality and Social Psychology*, 1971, *19*, 114-118.

Piaget, J. *The child's conception of the world.* New York: Harcourt, Brace, 1929.

Piaget, J. *The child's conception of physical causality.* London: Kegan Paul, Trench, Trubner & Co., 1930.

Piaget, J. *The moral judgment of the child.* New York: Harcourt, Brace, 1932.

Piaget, J. *The psychology of intelligence.* London: Routledge and Kegan Paul, 1950.

Piaget, J. *The origins of intelligence in children.* New York: International Universities Press, 1952.

Piaget, J. *The construction of reality in the child.* New York: Basic Books, 1954.

Piliavin, I. M., Piliavin, J. A., and Rodin, J. Costs, diffusion, and the stigmatized victim. *Journal of Personality and Social Psychology,* 1975, *32,* 429–438.

Piliavin, I. M., Rodin, J., and Piliavin, J. A. Good samaritanism: An underground phenomenon? *Journal of Personality and Social Psychology,* 1969, *13,* 289–299.

Piliavin, J. A., and Piliavin, I. M. Effect of blood on reactions to a victim. *Journal of Personality and Social Psychology,* 1972, *23,* 353–361.

Plath, S. *The bell jar.* New York: Harper & Row, 1971.

Pohlman, E. H. *Psychology of birth planning.* Cambridge, Mass.: Schenkman, 1969.

Poussaint, A. F. A Negro psychiatrist explains the Negro psyche. *New York Times Magazine,* 1967, August 20, 52–53; 55–57; 73; 75–76; 78; 80.

Price, J. S. Ethology and behavior. *Proceedings of the Royal Society of Medicine,* 1969, *62,* 1107–1110.

Price, R. H., and Blashfield, R. K. Explorations in the taxonomy of behavior settings. Analysis of dimensions and classification of settings. *American Journal of Community Psychology,* 1975, *3,* 335–351.

Proshansky, H. M., and Newton, P. The nature and meaning of Negro self-identity. In M. Deutsch, I. Katz, and A. R. Jensen (Eds.), *Social class, race, psychological development.* New York: Holt, Rinehart, and Winston, 1968.

Provence, S., and Lipton, R. C. *Infants in institutions: A comparison of their development with family-reared infants during the first year of life.* New York: International Universities Press, 1962.

Rabinowitz, L., Kelley, H. H., and Rosenblatt, R. M. Effects of different types of interdependence and response conditions in the minimal social situation. *Journal of Experimental Social Psychology.* 1966, *2,* 169–197.

Rainwater, L. *Family design: Marital sexuality, family size, and contraception.* Chicago: Aldine, 1965.

Rappoport, L., and Fritzler, D. Developmental responses to quantity changes in artificial social objects. *Child Development,* 1969, *40,* 1145–1154.

Redd, W. H., Morris, E. K., and Martin, J. A. Effects of positive and negative adult–child interactions on children's social preferences. *Journal of Experimental Child Psychology,* 1975, *19,* 153–164.

Reichner, R. Differential response to being ignored: The effects of architectural design and social density on interpersonal behavior. *Journal of Applied Social Psychology,* (in press).

Ribble, M. *The rights of infants.* New York: Columbia University Press, 1943.

Rice, S. A. Contagious bias in the interview: A methodological note. *American Journal of Sociology,* 1929, *35,* 420–423.

Riecken, H. A program for research on experiments in social psychology. In N. F. Washburne (Ed.), *Decisions, values, and groups* (Vol. 2). New York: Pergamon Press, 1962.

Rockway, A. Cognitive factors in adolescent person perception development. Unpublished manuscript, University of Miami, 1969.

Rodin, M. J. The informativeness of trait descriptions. *Journal of Personality and Social Psychology,* 1972, *21,* 341–344.

Rogers, R. W., and Mewborn, C. R. Fear appeals and attitude change: Effects of a threat's noxiousness, probability of occurrence, and the efficacy of coping responses. *Journal of Personality and Social Psychology,* 1976, *34,* 54–61.

Rokeach, M. *Beliefs, attitudes, and values.* San Francisco: Jossey-Bass, 1968.

Rokeach, M., and Kliejunas, P. Behavior as a function of attitude-toward-object and attitude-toward-situation. *Journal of Personality and Social Psychology,* 1972, *22,* 194–201.

Rosen, L. *The effects of residential social density on human behavior: A follow-up study.* Undergraduate honors thesis, Rugers University, 1976.

Rosenbaum, M. E. The effect of stimulus and background factors on the volunteering response.

Rosenbaum, M. E., and Blake, R. R. Volunteering as a function of field structure. *Journal of Abnormal and Social Psychology,* 1955, *50,* 193-196.

Rosenberg, M. J. When dissonance fails: On eliminating evaluation apprehension from attitude measurement. *Journal of Personality and Social Psychology,* 1965, *1,* 28-42.

Rosenberg, S., and Cohen, B. D. Toward a psychological analysis of verbal communication skills. In R. L. Schiefelbusch, R. H. Copeland, and J. O. Smith (Eds.), *Language and mental retardation.* New York: Holt, Rinehart and Winston, 1967.

Rosenberg, S., and Jones, R. A. A method for investigating and representing a person's implicit theory of personality: Theodore Dreiser's view of people. *Journal of Personality and Social Psychology,* 1972, *22,* 372-386.

Rosenberg, S., Nelson, C., and Vivekananthan, P. S. A multidimensional approach to the structure of personality impressions. *Journal of Personality and Social Psychology,* 1968, *9,* 283-294.

Rosenblatt, P., and Budd, L. Territoriality and privacy in married and unmarried cohabiting couples. *Journal of Social Psychology,* 1975, *97,* 67-76.

Rosenhan, D. L. Learning theory and prosocial behavior. *Journal of Social Issues,* 1972, *28*(3), 151-163.

Rosenhan, D. L. On being sane in insane places. *Science,* 1973, *179,* 250-258.

Rosenthal, A. M. *Thirty-eight witnesses.* New York: McGraw-Hill, 1964.

Rosenthal, R. *Experimenter effects in behavioral research.* New York: Appleton-Century-Crofts, 1966.

Ross, E. A. *Social psychology.* New York: MacMillan, 1908.

Ross, L. D., Amabile, T. M., and Steinmetz, J. L. Social roles, social control, and biases in social-perception processes. *Journal of Personality and Social Psychology,* 1977, *35,* 485-494.

Rossman, B. and Ulehla, Z. Psychological reward values associated with wilderness use. *Environment and Behavior,* 1977, *9,* 41-66.

Rotter, J. B. Generalized expectancies for internal versus external control of reinforcement. *Psychological Monographs,* 1966, *80,* (Whole No. 609).

Rubin, K. H., and Schneider, F. W. The relationship between moral judgment, egocentrism, and altruistic behavior. *Child Development,* 1973, *44,* 661-665.

Rubin, Z. Measurement of romantic love. *Journal of Personality and Social Psychology,* 1970, *16,* 265-273.

Rubin, Z. *Liking and loving: An invitation to social psychology.* New York: Holt, Rinehart and Winston, 1973.

Rubin, Z. From liking to loving: Patterns of attraction in dating relationships. In T. L. Huston (Ed.), *Foundations of interpersonal attraction.* New York: Academic Press, 1974.

Rubovits, P. C., and Maehr, M. L. Pygmalion black and white. *Journal of Personality and Social Psychology,* 1973, *25,* 210-218.

Rushton, J. P. Generosity in children: Immediate and long-term effects of modeling, preaching, and moral judgment. *Journal of Personality and Social Psychology,* 1975, *31,* 459-466.

Russell, C., and Russell, W. M. S. An approach to human ethology: Behavioral sciences. *Behavioral Science,* 1957, *2,* 169-200.

Russell, D. E. H. *The politics of rape: The victim's perspective.* New York: Stein and Day, 1975.

Saegert, S., Mackintosh, E., and West, S. Two studies of crowding in urban public spaces. *Environment and Behavior,* 1975, *7,* 159-184.

Sage, W. Violence in the children's room *Human Behavior,* 1975, *4,* 40-47.

Sales, S. M. Threat as a factor in authoritarianism: An analysis of archival data. *Journal of Personality and Social Psychology,* 1973, *28,* 44-57.

Sampson, E. E. Psychology and the American ideal. *Journal of Personality and Social Psychology,* 1977, *35,* 767-782.

Sanborn, D., Casey, T., and Niswander, G. Suicide: Seasonal patterns and related variables. *Diseases of the Nervous System,* 1970, *31,* 702-704.

Sarbin, T. R. Role theory. In G. Lindzey (Ed.), *Handbook of social psychology,* (Vol. 1). Reading, Mass.: Addison-Wesley, 1954.

Sarbin, T. R., and Allen, V. L. Role theory. In G. Lindzey and E. Aronson (Eds.), *The handbook of*

Sarles, R. M. Child abuse. In D. J. Madden and J. R. Lion (Eds.), *Rage-hate-assault and other forms of violence.* New York: Spectrum, 1976.

Schachter, S. Deviation, rejection, and communication. *Journal of Abnormal and Social Psychology,* 1951, *46,* 190-207.

Schachter, S. *The psychology of affiliation.* Stanford, Calif.: Stanford University Press, 1959.

Schachter, S. The interaction of cognitive and physiological determinants of emotional state. In L. Berkowitz (Ed.), *Advances in experimental social psychology* (Vol. 1). New York: Academic Press, 1964.

Schachter, S. *Emotion, obesity, and crime.* New York: Academic Press, 1971.

Schachter, S., and Gross, L. P. Manipulated time and eating behavior. *Journal of Personality and Social Psychology,* 1968, *10,* 98-106.

Schachter, S., and Singer, J. E. Cognitive, social, and physiological determinants of emotional state. *Psychological Review,* 1962, *69,* 379-399.

Schank, R. L. A study of a community and its groups and institutions conceived of as behaviours of individuals. *Psychological Monographs,* 1932, *43,* No. 2.

Schaffer, H. R. *The growth of sociability.* Baltimore: Penguin, 1971.

Schaffer, H. R., and Emerson, P. E. The development of social attachments in infancy. *Monographs of the Society for Research in Child Development,* 1964, *29*(3).

Schaffer, R. *Mothering.* Cambridge, Mass.: Harvard University Press, 1977.

Scheff, T. J. The societal reaction to deviance: Ascriptive elements in the psychiatric screening of mental patients in a midwestern state. *Social Problems,* 1964, *11,* 401-413.

Scheff, T. J. *Being mentally ill: A sociological theory.* Chicago: Aldine, 1966.

Scheff, T. J. The labeling theory of a mental illness. *American Sociological Review,* 1974, *39,* 444-452.

Scheflen, A. E. *Stream and structure of communicational behavior.* Philadelphia: Eastern Pennsylvania Psychiatric Institute, 1965.

Schegloff, E. A. Notes on a conversational practice: Formulating place. In D. Sudnow (Ed.), *Studies in social interaction.* New York: The Free Press, 1972.

Schein, E. H. Reaction patterns to severe, chronic stress in American army prisoners of war of the Chinese. *Journal of Social Issues,* 1957, *13*(3), 21-30.

Schjelderup-Ebbe, T., *Revue naturen,* Bergen, Norway (1913). Cited in T. Schjelderup-Ebbe, Social behavior of birds, in C. Murchison (Ed.), *A handbook of social psychology.* Worcester, Mass.: Clark University Press, 1935.

Schleifer, M., and Douglas, V. I. Effects of training on the moral judgment of young children. *Journal of Personality and Social Psychology,* 1973, *28,* 62-68.

Schlesinger, A. M., Jr. *A thousand days.* Boston: Houghton-Mifflin, 1965.

Schmitt, D. E. *Violence in Northern Ireland: Ethnic conflict and radicalization in an international setting.* Morristown, N.J.: General Learning Press, 1974.

Schopler, J., and Matthews, M. W. The influence of the perceived causal locus of partner's dependence on the use of interpersonal power. *Journal of Personality and Social Psychology,* 1965, *2,* 609-612.

Schulman, J., Shaver, P., Colman, R., Emrich, B., and Christie, R. Recipe for a jury. *Psychology Today,* 1973, *6*(12), 37-44, 77-84.

Schulz, R., and Barefoot, J. Non-verbal responses and affiliative conflict theory. *British Journal of Social and Clinical Psychology,* 1974, *13,* 237-243.

Schur, E. M. *Labeling deviant behavior: Its sociological implications.* New York: Harper & Row, 1971.

Scodel, A., and Mussen, P. Social perceptions of authoritarians and nonauthoritarians. *Journal of Abnormal and Social Psychology,* 1953, *48,* 181-184.

Scott, J. P. *Aggression.* Chicago: University of Chicago Press, 1958.

Scott, W. A. Attitude measurement. In G. Lindzey and E. Aronson (Eds.), *The handbook of social psychology* (Vol. 2), 2nd ed. Reading, Mass.: Addison-Wesley, 1968.

Sears, R. R. Social behavior and personality development. In T. Parsons and A. Shils (Eds.), *Toward a general theory of action.* Cambridge, Mass.: Harvard University Press, 1951.

Sears, R. R., Maccoby, E. E., and Levin, H. *Patterns of child rearing.* Evanston, Ill.: Row, Peterson, 1957.

Seaver, W. B. and Patterson, A. H. Decreasing fuel oil consumption through feedback and social commendation. *Journal of Applied Behavior Analysis,* 1976, *9,* 147-152.

Seedman, A. A., and Hellman, P. *Chief.* New York: Avon Books, 1975.

Segal, M. W. Alphabet and attraction: An unobtrusive measure of the effect of propinquity in a field setting. *Journal of Personality and Social Psychology,* 1974, *30,* 654-657.

Seligman, C., Kriss, M., Darley, J. M., Fazio, R. H., Becker, L. J., and Pryor, J. B. Predicting residential energy consumption from homeowners' attitudes. *Journal of Applied Social Psychology* (in press).

Seligman, M. E. P. *Helplessness: On depression, development, and death.* San Francisco: Freeman, 1975.

Selkin, J. Rape. *Psychology Today,* 1975, *8*(8), 70-76.

Sensenig, J., Jones, R. A., and Varney, L. Inspection of faces of own and other race as a function of subjects' prejudice. *Representative Research in Social Psychology,* 1973, *4,* 85-92.

Seyfried, B. A. Complementarity in interpersonal attraction. In S. Duck (Ed.), *Theory and practice in interpersonal attraction.* London: Academic Press, 1977.

Shaffer, D. R. Social psychology from a social-developmental perspective. In C. Hendrick (Ed.), *Perspectives on social psychology.* Hillsdale, N.J.: Erlbaum, 1977.

Shaffer, D. R. *Personality and social development.* Monterey, Calif.: Brooks/Cole, 1979.

Shaw, M. E., *Group dynamics: The psychology of small group behavior.* New York: McGraw-Hill, 1971.

Sheehy, G. *Passages: Predictable crises of adult life.* New York: Dutton, 1974.

Sherif, M. A study of some social factors in perception. *Archives of Psychology,* 1935, *27,* 1-60.

Sherif, M. *The psychology of social norms.* New York: Harper & Brothers, 1936.

Sherif, M. A preliminary experimental study of intergroup relations. In J. H. Rohrer and M. Sherif (Eds.), *Social psychology at the crossroads.* New York: Harper & Brothers, 1951.

Sherif, M., Harvey, O. J., White, B. J., Hood, W. R., and Sherif, C. W. *Intergroup conflict and cooperation: The robbers' cave experiment.* Norman, Okla.: Institute of Group Relations, The University of Oklahoma, 1961.

Sherif, M., and Hovland, C. I. *Social judgment: Assimilation and contrast effects in communication and attitude change.* New Haven, Conn.: Yale University Press, 1961.

Sherif, M., and Sherif, C. W. *Groups in harmony and tension.* New York: Harper & Row, 1953.

Sherif, M., and Sherif, C. W. *Social psychology.* New York: Harper & Row, 1969.

Sherif, C. W., Sherif, M., and Nebergall, R. E. *Attitude and attitude change: The social judgment-involvement approach.* Philadelphia: Saunders, 1965.

Sherman, R. C., and Ross, L. B. Liberalism-conservatism and dimensional salience in the perception of political figures. *Journal of Personality and Social Psychology,* 1972, *23,* 120-127.

Sherrod, D. R., and Downs, R. Environmental determinants of altruism: The effects of stimulus overload and perceived control on helping. *Journal of Experimental Social Psychology,* 1974, *10,* 468-479.

Shibutani, T. *Improvised news: A sociological study of rumor.* Indianapolis, Ind.: Bobbs-Merrill, 1966.

Shweder, R. A. How relevant is an individual difference theory of personality? *Journal of Personality,* 1975, *43,* 455-484.

Sidowski, J. B. Reward and punishment in a minimal social situation. *Journal of Experimental Psychology,* 1957, *54,* 318-326.

Sidowski, J. B., Wycoff, L. B., and Tabory, L. The influence of reinforcement and punishment in a minimal social situation. *Journal of Abnormal and Social Psychology,* 1956, *52,*115-119.

Siegel, A. E., and Siegel, S. Reference groups, membership groups, and attitude change. *Journal of Abnormal and Social Psychology,* 1957, *55,* 360-364.

Sigall, H., and Aronson, E. Liking for an evaluator as a function of her physical attractiveness and nature of the evaluations. *Journal of Experimental Social Psychology,* 1969, *5,* 93-100.

Sigall, H., and Helmreich, R. Opinion change as a function of stress and communicator credibility. *Journal of Experimental Social Psychology,* 1969, *5,* 70-78.

Sigall, H., and Landy, D. Radiating beauty: Effects of having a physically attractive partner on person perception. *Journal of Personality and Social Psychology,* 1973, *28,* 218-224.

Sigall, H., and Page, R. Current stereotypes: A little fading, a little faking. *Journal of Personality and Social Psychology,* 1971, *18,* 247-255.

Signell, K. Cognitive complexity in person perception and nation perception: A developmental approach. *Journal of Personality,* 1966, *34,* 517-537.

Sills, D. L. *The volunteers.* Glencoe, Ill.: The Free Press, 1957.

Simmel, G. Sociology of the senses: Visual interaction, In R. E. Park and E. W. Burgess (Eds.), *Introduction to the science of sociology.* Chicago: University of Chicago Press, 1924.

Simons, H. W., Berkowitz, N. N., and Moyer, R. J. Similarity, credibility, and attitude change: A review and a theory. *Psychological Bulletin,* 1970, *73,* 1-16.

Sims, J., and Baumann, D. The tornado threat: Coping styles of the North and South. *Science,* 1972, *176,* 1386-1392.

Singer, I. B. *The Spinoza of Market Street.* New York: Farrar, Straus, and Cudahy, 1961.

Sistrunk, F., and McDavid, J. W. Sex variable in conforming behavior. *Journal of Personality and Social Psychology,* 1971, *17,* 200-207.

Skinner, B. F. *Walden two.* New York: Macmillan, 1948.

Skinner, B. F. *Science and human behavior.* New York: Macmillan, 1953.

Skinner, B. F. *Beyond freedom and dignity.* New York: Knopf, 1971.

Slater, P. E. Role differentiation in small groups. *American Sociological Review,* 1955, *20,* 300-310.

Slater, P. E. *The pursuit of loneliness.* Boston: Beacon Press, 1970.

Slavin, R. and Wodarski, J. Using group contingencies to reduce natural gas consumption in master-metered apartments. Technical Report Number 232. Baltimore, MD: The Johns Hopkins University Center for Social Organization of Schools, August, 1977.

Smith, C., and Freedman, A. *Voluntary associations: Perspectives on the literature.* Cambridge, Mass.: Harvard University Press, 1972.

Smith, M. B. Is experimental social psychology advancing? *Journal of Experimental Social Psychology,* 1972, *8,* 86-96.

Snyder, M., Tanke, E. D., and Berscheid, E. Social perception and interpersonal behavior: On the self-fulfilling nature of social stereotypes. *Journal of Personality and Social Psychology,* 1977, *35,* 656-666.

Sommer, R. *Personal space.* Englewood Cliffs, N.J.: Prentice-Hall, 1969.

Sommer, R., and Becker, F. D. Territorial defense and the good neighbor. *Journal of Personality and Social Psychology,* 1969, *11,* 85-92.

Spitz, R. A. Hospitalism: An inquiry into the genesis of psychiatric conditions in early childhood. *Psychoanalytic Study of the Child,* 1945, *1,* 53-74.

Spitz, R. A. *The first year of life.* New York: International Universities Press, 1965.

Staats, A. W., and Staats, C. K. Attitudes established by classical conditioning. *Journal of Abnormal and Social Psychology,* 1958, *57,* 37-40.

Staub, E. A child in distress: The effect of focusing responsibility on children on their attempts to help. *Developmental Psychology,* 1970, *2,* 152-153.

Staub, E. The use of role playing and induction in children's learning of helping and sharing behavior. *Child Development,* 1971, *42,* 805-816.

Staub, E. Helping a distressed person: Social personality, and stimulus determinants. In L. Berkowitz (Ed.), *Advances in experimental social psychology* (Vol. 7). New York: Academic Press, 1974.

Staub, E. *The development of prosocial behavior in children.* Morristown, N.J.: General Learning Press, 1975.

Steiner, I. D. Self-perception and goal-setting behavior. *Journal of Personality,* 1957, *25,* 344-355.

Stephenson, G. M., Rutter, D. R., and Dore, S. R. Visual interaction and distance. *British Journal of Psychology,* 1972, *64,* 251-257.

Stern, S. E., and Noe, F. P. Affiliation-participation in voluntary associations: A factor in organized leisure activity. *Sociology and Social Research,* 1973, *57,* 473-481.

Stewart, A. J., and Rubin, Z. The power motive in the dating couple. *Journal of Personality and Social Psychology,* 1976, *34,* 305-309.

Stockwell, R. P. Generative grammar. In A. A. Hill (Ed.), *Linguistics today.* New York: Basic Books, 1969.

Stogdill, R. M. Personal factors associated with leadership: A survey of the literature. *Journal of Psychology,* 1948, *25,* 35-71.

Stokols, D. Environmental Psychology. *Annual Review of Psychology,* 1978, *29,* 253-295.

Stone, L. J., Smith, H. T., and Murphy, L. B. (Eds.). *The competent infant: Research and commentary.* New York: Basic Books, 1973.

Stone, P. J., Dunphy, D. C., Smith, M. S., and Ogilvie, D. M. *The general inquirer: A computer approach to content analysis.* Cambridge, Mass.: The M.I.T. Press, 1966.

Stoner, J. A. F. A comparison of individual and group decisions involving risk. Unpublished master's thesis, School of Industrial Management, M.I.T., 1961.

Stouffer, S. A., Suchman, E. A., DeVinney, L. C., Star, S. A., and Williams, R. M., Jr. *The American soldier: Adjustment during army life.* Princeton, N.J.: Princeton University Press, 1949.

Suedfeld, P., and Rank, A. D. Revolutionary leaders: Long-term success as a function of changes in conceptual complexity. *Journal of Personality and Social Psychology,* 1976, *34,* 169-178.

Sundstrom, E., and Altman, A. Field study of territorial behavior and dominance. *Journal of Personality and Social Psychology,* 1974, *30,* 115-124.

Suomi, S. J., and Harlow, H. F. Social rehabilitation of isolate-reared monkeys. *Developmental Psychology.* 1972, *6,* 487-496.

Survey Research Center, *Interviewer's manual.* Ann Arbor, Mich.: Institute for Social Research, 1969.

Swain, M., and Kiser, C. Social and psychological factors affecting fertility. *Millbank Memorial Fund Quarterly,* 1953, *31,* 51-84.

Swingle, P. G. *The management of power.* Hillsdale, N.J.: Erlbaum, 1976.

Szasz, T. S. *The myth of mental illness.* New York: Harper & Row, 1961.

Tars, S. E., and Appleby, L. The same child in home and institution: An observational study. *Environment and Behavior,* 1973, *5,* 3-28.

Taylor, D. W., Berry, P. C., and Block, C. H. Does group participation when using brainstorming facilitate or inhibit creative thinking? In W. E. Vinacke, W. R. Wilson, and G. M. Meredith (Eds.), *Dimensions of social psychology.* Chicago: Scott, Foresman, 1964.

Taylor, S. P. Aggressive behavior and physiological arousal as a function of provocation and the tendency to exhibit aggression. *A Journal of Personality.* 1967, *35,* 297-310.

Taylor, S. P., and Gammon, C. B. Effects of type and dose of alcohol on human physical aggression. *Journal of Personality and Social Psychology,* 1975, *32,* 169-175.

Taylor, S. P., Gammon, C. B., and Capasso, D. R. Aggression as a function of the interaction of alcohol and threat. *Journal of Personality and Social Psychology,* 1976, *34,* 938-941.

Terkel, S. *Working.* New York: Avon Books, 1975.

Thibaut, J. W., and Kelley, H. H. *The social psychology of groups.* New York: Wiley, 1959.

Thistlethwaite, D. L., de Haan, H., and Kamenetsky, J. The effects of "directive" and "nondirective" communication procedures on attitudes. *Journal of Abnormal and Social Psychology,* 1955, *51,* 107-113.

Thomas, M. H., Horton, R. W., Lippincott, E. C., and Drabman, R. S. Desensitization to portrayals of real-life aggression as a function of exposure to television violence. *Journal of Personality and Social Psychology,* 1977, *35,* 450-458.

Thorndike, E. L. Animal intelligence: An experimental study of the associative process in animals. *Psychological Review Monograph Supplement* (No. 8), 1898.

Thorndike, E. L. A constant error in psychological ratings. *Journal of Applied Psychology,* 1920, *4,* 25-29.

Tiger, L., and Fox, R. *The imperial animal.* New York: Dell, 1974.

Toch, H. *Violent men.* Chicago: Aldine, 1969.

Toffler, A. *Future shock.* New York: Bantam, 1971.

Triandis, H. C. Some universals of social behavior. *Personality and Social Psychology Bulletin,* 1978, *4,* 1-16.

Triplett, N. The dynamogenic factors in pacemaking and competition. *American Journal of Psychology,* 1897, *9,* 507-533.

Trow, M. Comment on "Participant observation and interviewing: A comparison." In W. J. Filstead (Ed.), *Qualitative methodology: Firsthand involvement with the social world.* Chicago: Markham, 1970.

Tuckman, B. W. Developmental sequence in small groups. *Psychological Bulletin,* 1965, *63,* 384–399.

Turk, A. T. *Criminality and legal order.* Chicago: Rand McNally, 1969.

Tversky, A., and Kahneman, D. Availability: A heuristic for judging frequency and probability. *Cognitive Psychology,* 1973, *5,* 207–232.

Ullmann, L. P., and Krasner, L. *A psychological approach to abnormal behavior.* Englewood Cliffs, N.J.: Prentice-Hall, 1975.

Uris, L. *Trinity.* New York: Bantam, 1976.

U. S. Bureau of the Census. *Statistical abstract of the United States: 1974,* 95th ed. Washington, D.C.: Government Printing Office, 1974.

Van Lawick-Goodall, J. *In the shadow of man.* Boston: Houghton Mifflin, 1971.

Vidmar, N., and Rokeach, M. Archie Bunker's bigotry: A study in selective perception and exposure. *Journal of Communication,* 1974, *24,* 36–47.

Vonnegut, K. *Cat's cradle.* New York: Dell, 1963.

Wagner, R. V. Complementary needs, role expectations, interpersonal attraction, and the stability of working relationships. *Journal of Personality and Social Psychology,* 1975, *32,* 116–124.

Wallechinsky, D., Wallace, I., and Wallace, A. *The book of lists.* New York: Bantam, 1977.

Walster, B., and Aronson, E. Effect of expectancy of task duration on the experience of fatigue. *Journal of Experimental Social Psychology,* 1967, *3,* 41–46.

Walster, E. Passionate love. In B. I. Murstein (Ed.), *Theories of attraction and love.* New York: Springer, 1971.

Walster, E., Aronson, E., and Abrahams, D. On increasing the persuasiveness of a low prestige communicator. *Journal of Experimental Social Psychology,* 1966, *2,* 325–342.

Walster, E., Aronson, V., Abrahams, D., and Rottmann, L. Importance of physical attractiveness in dating behavior. *Journal of Personality and Social Psychology,* 1966, *4,* 508–516.

Walster, E., and Piliavin, J. A. Equity and the innocent bystander. *Journal of Social Issues,* 1972, *28*(3), 165–189.

Ward, L., and Suedfeld, P. Human responses to highway noise. *Environmental Research,* 1973, *6,* 306–326.

Ward, S. K. Methodological considerations in the study of population density and social pathology. *Human Ecology,* 1975, *3,* 275–286.

Watson, J. B. *Psychology from the standpoint of a behaviorist.* Philadelphia: Lippincott, 1919.

Watson, O. M., and Graves, T. D. Quantitative research in proxemic behavior. *American Anthropologist,* 1966, *68,* 971–985.

Watson, R. I., Jr. Investigation into de-individuation using a cross-cultural survey technique. *Journal of Personality and Social Psychology,* 1973, *25,* 342–345.

Watzlawick, P., Beavin, J. H., and Jackson, D. D., *Pragmatics of human communication: A study of interactional patterns, pathologies, and paradoxes.* New York: Norton, 1967.

Webb, E. J., Campbell, D. T., Schwartz, R. D., and Sechrest, L. *Unobtrusive measures: Nonreactive research in the social sciences.* Chicago: Rand McNally, 1966.

Wegner, D. M., and Crano, W. D. Racial factors in helping behavior: An unobtrusive field experiment. *Journal of Personality and Social Psychology,* 1975, *32,* 901–905.

Weick, K. E. *The social psychology of organizing.* Reading, Mass.: Addison-Wesley, 1969.

Weiner, B., Heckhausen, H., Meyer, W. U., and Cook, R. E. Causal ascriptions and achievement behavior: A conceptual analysis of effort and reanalysis of locus of control. *Journal of Personality and Social Psychology,* 1972, *21,* 239–248.

Weinstein, E. A. Toward a theory of interpersonal tactics. In C. W. Backman and P. F. Secord (Eds.), *Problems in social psychology.* New York: McGraw-Hill, 1966.

Weinstein, E. A. The development of interpersonal competence. In D. A. Goslin (Ed.), *Handbook of socialization theory and research.* Chicago: Rand McNally, 1969.

Weinstein, E. A., and Deutschberger, P. Some dimensions of altercasting. *Sociometry,* 1963, *26,* 454–466.

Weis, K., and Borges, S. S. Victimology and rape: The case of the legitimate victim. *Issues in Criminology,* 1973, *8*(2), 71–115.

Weitzman, L. J., Eifler, D., Hokada, E., and Ross, C. Sex-role socialization in picture books for preschool children. *American Journal of Sociology,* 1972, *77,* 1125–1150.

Weller, J. E. *Yesterday's people: Life in contemporary Appalachia.* Lexington, Ky.: University of Kentucky Press, 1965.

Welsh, R. S. Severe parental punishment and delinquency: A developmental approach. In M. Wertheimer and L. Rappoport (Eds.), *Psychology and the problems of today.* Glenview, Ill.: Scott, Foresman, 1978.

Werner, H. *Comparative psychology of mental development.* Chicago: Follett Press, 1948.

Werner, H., and Kaplan, B. *Symbol formation.* New York: Wiley, 1963.

West, S. G., Whitney, G., and Schnedler, R. Helping a motorist in distress: The effects of sex, race, and neighborhood. *Journal of Personality and Social Psychology,* 1975, *31,* 691–698.

Wheeler, L. *Interpersonal influence.* Boston: Allyn and Bacon, 1970.

Wheeler, L., and Nezlek, J. Sex differences in social participation. *Journal of Personality and Social Psychology,* 1977, *35,* 742–754.

Wheeler, L., and Wagner, C. M. The contagion of generosity. Paper presented at the meeting of the Eastern Psychological Association, Washington, D.C., 1968.

White, R. W. Motivation reconsidered: The concept of competence. *Psychological Review,* 1959, *66,* 297–333.

White, T. H. *Breach of faith: The fall of Richard Nixon.* New York: Atheneum, 1975.

Whiting, J. W. M., and Child, I. L. *Child training and personality: A cross-cultural study.* New Haven, Conn.: Yale University Press, 1953.

Whorf, B. L. Science and linguistics. In J. B. Carroll (Ed.), *Language, thought, and reality: Selected writings of Benjamin Lee Whorf.* New York: Wiley, 1956.

Whyte, W. H., Jr. *The organization man.* New York: Simon and Schuster, 1956.

Wicker, A. W. Undermanning, performances, and students' subjective experiences in behavior settings of large and small high schools. *Journal of Personality and Social Psychology,* 1968, *10,* 255–261.

Wicker, A. W., and Kauma, C. E. Effects of a merger of a small and a large organization on members' behavior and experiences. *Journal of Applied Psychology,* 1974, *59,* 24–30.

Wicker, A. W., and Kirmeyer, S. *From church to laboratory to National Park: A program of research on excess and insufficient populations in behavior settings.* Paper presented at conferences on "Experiencing the Environment" Clark University, Worcester, Mass., January 1975.

Wicklund, R. A., and Brehm, J. W. *Perspectives on cognitive dissonance.* Hillsdale, N.J.: Erlbaum, 1976.

Wiener, M., and Mehrabian, A. *Language within language: Immediacy, a channel in verbal communication.* New York: Appleton-Century, 1968.

Wiggins, N., Hoffman, P. J., and Taber, T. Types of judges and cue utilization in judgments of intelligence. *Journal of Personality and Social Psychology,* 1969, *12,* 52–59.

Williams, J. A., Jr. Interviewer–respondent interaction: A study of bias in the information interview. *Sociometry,* 1964, *27,* 338–352.

Winch, R. F. *Mate selection: A study of complementary needs.* New York: Harper & Brothers, 1958.

Winch, R. F. *The modern family,* rev. ed. New York: Holt, Rinehart and Winston, 1963.

Wispé, L. G., and Freshley, H. B. Race, sex, and sympathetic helping behavior: The broken bag caper. *Journal of Personality and Social Psychology,* 1971, *17,* 59–65.

Wolfensburger, W. *The principle of normalization in human services.* Toronto: National Institute on Mental Retardation, 1973.

Wolff, P. H. The natural history of crying and other vocalizations in early infancy. In B. M. Foss (Ed.), *Determinants of infant behavior.* London: Methuen, 1969.

Wood, D. Fleeting glimpses: Adolescent and other images of the entity called San Cristobal Las Cases, Chiapas, Mexico. Unpublished master's thesis, Clark University, 1971. Cited in D. Canter and P. Stringer (Eds.), *Environmental interactions.* New York: International Universities Press, 1975.

Worchel, S., and Arnold, S. E. The effects of censorship and attractiveness of the censor on attitude change. *Journal of Experimental Social Psychology,* 1973, *9,* 365-377.

Worchel, S., and Cooper, J. *Understanding social psychology.* Homewood, Ill.: Dorsey Press, 1976.

Wortman, C. B. Causal attributions and personal control. In J. H. Harvey, W. J. Ickes, and R. F. Kidd (Eds.), *New Directions in Attribution Research* (Vol. 1). Hillsdale, N.J.: Erlbaum, 1976.

Wray, H. Kentucky CMHC bankruptcy draws federal attention. *APA Monitor,* June 1978, 1 & 9.

Wrightsman, L. S. *Social psychology in the seventies.* Monterey, Calif.: Brooks/Cole, 1972.

Wrightsman, L. S. *Social psychology,* Monterey, Calif.: Brooks/Cole, 1977. (Second edition)

Wylie, R. C. *The self concept: A critical survey of pertinent research literature.* Lincoln, Neb.: University of Nebraska Press, 1961.

Wynne-Edwards, V. C. *Animal dispersion in relation to social behaviour.* Edinburgh and London: Oliver and Boyd, 1962.

Yarrow, M., and Campbell, J. Person perception in children. *Merrill-Palmer Quarterly of Behavior and Development,* 1963, *9,* 57-72.

Zadny, J., and Gerard, H. B. Attributed intentions and informational selectivity. *Journal of Experimental Social Psychology,* 1974, *10,* 34-52.

Zajonc, R. B. The process of cognitive tuning in communication. *Journal of Abnormal and Social Psychology,* 1960, *61,* 159-167.

Zajonc, R. B. Social facilitation. *Science,* 1965, *149,* 269-274.

Zajonc, R. B. Attitudinal effects of mere exposure. *Journal of Personality and Social Psychology Monograph Supplement,* 1968, *9,* No. 2, Part 2, 1-27.

Zajonc, R. B., and Brickman, P. Expectancy and feedback as independent factors in task performance. *Journal of Personality and Social Psychology,* 1969, *11,* 148-156.

Zajonc, R. B., and Sales, S. M. Social facilitation of dominant and subordinate responses. *Journal of Experimental Social Psychology,* 1966, *2,* 160-168.

Zanna, M. P., and Hamilton, D. L. Attribute dimensions and patterns of trait inferences. *Psychonomic Science,* 1972, *27,* 353-354.

Zanna, M. P., Kiesler, C. A., and Pilkonis, P. A. Positive and negative attitudinal affect established by classical conditioning. *Journal of Personality and Social Psychology,* 1970, *14,* 321-328.

Zanna, M. P., and Pack, S. J. On the self-fulfilling nature of apparent sex differences in behavior. *Journal of Experimental Social Psychology,* 1975, *11,* 583-591.

Zigler, E., and Child, I. L. Socialization. In G. Lindzey and E. Aronson (Eds.), *The handbook of social psychology* (Vol. 3), 2nd ed. Reading, Mass.: Addison-Wesley, 1969.

Zimbardo, P. G. The human choice: Individuation, reason, and order versus de-individuation, impulse, and chaos. In W. J. Arnold and D. Levine (Eds.), *Nebraska Symposium on Motivation* (Vol. 17). Lincoln, Neb.: University of Nebraska Press, 1969.

CREDITS

The following figures have been redrawn from material copyrighted by the American Psychological Association and used by permission:
Figure 1, p. 23 copyright 1969
Figure 2, p. 30 copyright 1974
Table 1, p. 95 copyright 1965
Figure 4, p. 107 copyright 1966
Figure 1, p. 124 copyright 1968
Table, Box A, p. 125 copyright 1972
Figure 2, p. 128 copyright 1977
Table 1, p. 129 copyright 1977
Table 2, p. 131 copyright 1960
Table 5, p. 140 copyright 1973
Table 2, p. 166 copyright 1968
Figure 3, p. 173 copyright 1970
Table 4, p. 174 copyright 1970
Table 1, p. 185 copyright 1969
Figure 2, p. 190 copyright 1968
Table 3, p. 199 copyright 1968
Figure 3, p. 200 copyright 1952
Table 1, p. 219 copyright 1965
Table 2, p. 219 copyright 1973
Table 4, p. 221 copyright 1968
Table 5, p. 230 copyright 1963
Table 6, p. 234 copyright 1953
Figure 6, p. 234 copyright 1976
Figure 8, p. 240 copyright 1976
Figure 9, p. 243 copyright 1953
Table 1, p. 256 copyright 1967
Figure 2, p. 262 copyright 1959
Table 2, p. 268 copyright 1966
Table 3, p. 270 copyright 1972
Figure 5, p. 325 copyright 1976
Figure 2, p. 344 copyright 1975
Table 3, p. 362 copyright 1959
Table, Box A, p. 373 copyright 1976
Table, Box A, p. 400 copyright 1976
Figure 1, p. 406 copyright 1975
Table 5, p. 409 copyright 1975
Table 6, p. 412 copyright 1975

Figure 2, p. 15 from G. W. Allport, "The historical background of modern social psychology." In G. Lindszey and E. Aronson (Eds.), *Handbook of social psychology.* Copyright 1969, Addison-Wesley Publishing Company. Reprinted by permission.

Quotes, p. 34, 37, 38 from E. J. Webb et al., *Unobtrusive measures: Nonreactive research in the social sciences.* Copyright 1966, Rand McNally and Company. Reprinted by permission.

Figure 2, p. 73 from L. I. Gardner, "Deprivation dwarfism." Copyright 1972 by Scientific American, Inc. All rights reserved.

Material in Boxes B and C, pp. 81–82 from D. R. Shaffer, *Social and personality development.* Copyright 1979 by Wadsworth Publishing Company. Reprinted by permission of Brooks-Cole Publishing Company.

Quotes from *1984* by George Orwell on pp. 104 and 374 reprinted courtesy of Mrs. Sonia Brownwell Orwell, Martin, Secker & Warburg, and Harcourt Brace Jovanovich, Inc.

Quote, p. 184 from S. Terkel, *Working.* Copyright 1975. Used by permission of Pantheon Books, a division of Random House.

Material in Box C, p. 201 from E. H. Hess, "Attitude and pupil size." Copyright 1965 by Scientific American, Inc. All rights reserved.

Figure 2, p. 214 from A. E. Bergin, "The effect of dissonant persuasive communications upon changes in a self-referring attitude." *Journal of Personality* 30:423–438. Copyright 1962 by Duke University Press.

Quotes, pp. 220 and 243 from W. J. McGuire, "The nature of attitudes and attitude changes." In G. Lindszey and E. Aronson (Eds.), *Handbook of social psychology.* Copyright 1969 by Addison-Wesley Publishing Company. Reprinted by permission.

Figure 7, p. 236 from W. J. McGuire, "Personality and susceptibility to social influence." In E. F. Borgatta and W. W. Lambert (Eds.), *Handbook of personality theory and research.* Copyright 1968 by Rand McNally and Company. Reprinted by permission.

Figure 1, p. 252 from S. Asch, *Social psychology.*

Copyright 1952. Reprinted by permission of Prentice-Hall, Inc.

Quote, p. 328 copyright 1972 by Germaine Greer. Originally appeared in *Playboy* Magazine. Reprinted by permission of the author and her agent, James Brown Associates Inc.

Quote, p. 329 from D. E. H. Russell, *The politics of rape.* Copyright 1975. Reprinted by permission of Stein and Day Publishers.

Quote, p. 338 from K. Vonnegut, *Cat's Cradle.* Copyright 1963. Reprinted courtesy of Delacorte Press/Seymour Lawrence.

Figure 3, p. 350 from S. B. Kiesler and R. L. Baral, "The search for a romantic partner." In K. G. Gergen and D. Marlow (Eds.), *Personality and social behavior.* Copyright 1970 by Addison-Wesley Publishing Company. Reprinted by permission.

Figures 2 and 3, pp. 370–371 from P. G. Zimbardo, "The human choice." In W. J. Arnold and D. Levine (Eds.), *Nebraska Symposium on Motivation 1969.* Copyright 1969 by the University of Nebraska Press.

Figure 8, p. 387 from R. A. Shweder, "How relevant is an individual difference theory of personality?" *Journal of Personality* 43:455–484. Copyright 1975 by Duke University Press.

Quote, p. 374 from J. van Lawick-Goodall, *In the shadow of man.* Copyright 1971 by Hugo and Jane van Lawick-Goodall.

Table 3, p. 402, and Box C, p. 408 from S. A. Stouffer et al. (Eds.), *Adjustment during Army life.* Copyright 1949 and 1977 by Princeton University Press. Reprinted by permission of Princeton University Press.

Material in Box B, p. 403 from L. J. Peter and R. Hull, *The Peter Principle.* Copyright 1969 by William Morrow and Company, Inc. Reprinted by permission of the publishers.

Material in Box A, p. 449 from M. J. Horowitz et al., "Personal space and the body-buffer zone." *Archives of General Psychiatry* 11:651–656. Copyright 1964 by the American Medical Association.

Figure 2, p. 456 from J. B. Calhoun, "Population density and social pathology." Copyright 1962 by Scientific American, Inc. All rights reserved.

Figure 4, p. 469 from R. C. Knight, W. H. Weitzer, and C. M. Zimring, *Opportunity for control and the built environment: the ELEMR project.* Photos copyright 1978 Alyce Kaprow. Reprinted by permission of Alyce Kaprow and The Environmental Institute, University of Massachusetts at Amherst.

AUTHOR INDEX

Abe, K., 436
Abelson, R.P., 45
Abrahams, D., 158, 215
Abramson, P.R., 186
Adams, C.A., 464
Adams, J.S., 196, 255, 283
Adinolfi, A.A., 161
Adler, A., 12, 57
Adler, F., 318
Adorno, T.W., 36, 129, 197, 384
Aiello, J.R., 454, 455, 459, 464
Aiello, T., 454
Ainsworth, M.D.S., 70
Ajzen, I., 187, 202, 203–204
Allport, F.H., 14
Allport, G.W., 10, 12, 184
Altman, I., 156, 418, 419, 444, 447–448, 450, 453, 454, 457
Amabile, T.M., 128
Amir, M., 328
Anderson, N.H., 188, 385, 386
Anglin, J.M., 93
Appelyard, D., 432
Appleby, L., 468
Apsler, P., 221
Ardrey, R., 312
Argyle, M., 348, 352, 385, 446–447
Aristotle, 10, 327
Arnold, S.E., 239
Aronfreed, J., 77, 279, 281
Aronson, E., 40, 44, 144, 157, 158, 161, 163–164, 165–166, 167, 215, 219, 228–230, 231, 332, 361–362
Aronson, H., 347
Asch, S.E., 123, 125–126, 212–213, 251–252, 255
Ashmore, E.R.D., 195, 204, 207, 239
Atkinson, J.W., 12
Averill, J.R., 344

Back, K.W., 342, 369
Backman, C.W., 155
Bakan, D., 331
Bales, R.F., 375–376, 377–378, 380, 381, 386, 397, 401, 404, 409
Ballachey, E.L., 255
Bandler, R.J., 147
Bandura, A., 67, 77, 248, 316, 317, 327, 331, 333
Banikiotes, P.G., 157
Banta, T.J., 381
Baral, R.L., 350
Barber, J.D., 398, 399–400, 410
Barefoot, J., 447
Barker, R.G., 133
Baron, R.A., 309, 311, 312, 316, 317, 318, 320, 322, 325, 326, 327, 332, 333, 435
Baron, R.M., 457, 464
Barrett, Elizabeth, 170
Bar-Tal, D., 278, 279, 281, 282, 285, 293, 295, 297, 298
Bass, B.M., 392, 394, 409, 410
Baum, A., 462, 463
Baumann, D., 434–435
Bavelas, A., 380, 400–401
Beaman, A.L., 371
Beavin, J.H., 111
Becker, F.D., 453
Becker, H.S., 26
Becker, L.J., 438
Beckhouse, L., 407–409
Begin, Menachem, 396
Bell, P.A., 322
Bem, D.J., 86, 98, 147, 148, 262–264, 353
Bem, S.L., 86, 87
Benedetti, D.T., 131
Benson, P.L., 295
Bentham, Jeremy, 11

Bergin, A., 214
Berkowitz, L., 279, 283, 284, 293, 294, 295, 311, 314–316, 318, 320–321, 324, 327, 332
Berkowitz, N.N., 218
Berne, E., 110, 347
Berry, P.C., 358
Berscheid, E., 126, 155, 158, 159, 167, 174, 175, 341, 343
Berzins, J.I., 87
Bickman, L., 293
Binet, 395
Birdwhistell, R.L., 114
Black, J.S., 202, 203
Blackstone, Judge, 331
Blake, R.R., 257
Blanchard, W.A., 135
Blau, P.M., 171, 280
Bless, E., 256, 294
Block, C.H., 358
Block, J.H., 86
Bloom, B.L., 300
Blum, A., 428
Bogardus, E.S., 10
Bogdonoff, M.D., 369
Boice, R., 312
Bois, J., 134
Booth, A., 462
Borgatta, E.F., 397, 398
Borges, S.S., 329
Boucher, R., 329
Bowlby, J., 69
Braly, K., 184
Bram, J., 92
Brehm, J.W., 225, 260, 266–268, 293, 410
Brent, E.E., 29–30
Breuer, J., 57
Brickman, P., 142, 281
Brock, T.C., 218, 238–240

Broll, L., 296
Brothen, T., 167
Brown, J.S., 314
Brown, R., 93, 108–109, 346, 359, 360
Brown, S.R., 157
Brownmiller, S., 328, 329
Bruck, C., 318
Bruner, J.S., 93, 122, 129, 135, 195
Bryan, J.H., 281, 282
Buchanan, R., 459
Budd, L., 453
Budner, S., 378
Bugenthal, D., 375
Bundy, McGeorge, 357
Burke, W.W., 131
Burrows, A., 432
Burton, R.V., 76
Buss, A., 308, 320, 321, 322
Butler, W.M., 405, 406
Byrne, D., 40, 152, 164–165, 342, 435

Caldwell, B.M., 74
Calhoun, J.B., 324, 455–456, 457
Campbell, D.T., 20–22, 23, 33, 39, 41, 94, 204, 281, 381
Cannavale, F.J., 371
Cannell, C.F., 27, 28, 29
Capasso, D.R., 324, 325
Caplow, T., 342
Caputo, C., 139
Carlsmith, J.M., 40, 44, 116, 228, 261–262, 294, 375
Carr, E.H., 395, 398
Carter, Jimmy, 396
Cartwright, D., 359
Cass, R.H., 297
Cattell, 395
Chaikin, A.L., 156
Chapman, J.P., 25
Chapman, L.J., 25, 138
Chapnick, B., 270
Chapnick, J., 270
Charcot, J.M., 56
Chemers, M.M., 405, 406
Cheyne, J.A., 446
Child, I.L., 55

Christian, J.J., 457
Christie, R., 12, 236, 254
Christy, P., 159
Chu, G.C., 225
Cialdini, R.B., 222
Cicchetti, C., 437
Clark, M.S., 294, 296
Clark, R.A., 12
Clark, R.D., 4, 7
Clore, G.L., Jr., 152, 164, 165, 166
Coffman, T.L., 184
Cohen, A.R., 135, 260
Cohen, B.D., 106
Cohen, J.L., 368
Cohen, M.L., 329
Cohen, R., 279
Cohen, S., 430, 432–433
Cole, M., 101
Coleman, J.C., 300
Collins, B.E., 447
Colman, R., 236
Colomosca, J.V., 412
Colquhoun, W., 434
Comte, Auguste, 13, 14, 15
Connor, W.H., 284, 294
Conroy, J., 453
Cook, R.E., 139
Cook, T.D., 243–244, 293
Cooley, C.H., 98
Cooper, J., 216, 293
Cope, V., 163–164
Coser, L.A., 14
Cottrell, N.B., 367, 368
Couch, A.S., 397
Cox, V., 462
Crano, 294
Cronbach, L.J., 100, 199
Crutchfield, R.S., 255
Cumberbatch, G., 325

Dabbs, J.M., 233, 234, 235, 236
Daher, D.M., 157
Dailey, C.A., 126–127
D'Andrade, R.G., 386, 388
Daniels, L.R., 294
Daniels, R., 204
Darley, J.M., 216, 284, 285–291, 292–293, 366, 431, 438
Darlington, R.B., 256
Darwin, Charles, 20, 69, 392
D'Atri, D.A., 462
Davidson, A.R., 188–189
Davidson, E.S., 325, 326, 327
Davis, D.E., 457
Davis, J.H., 368, 375, 385
Davis, K.E., 135, 136–137, 154
Dean, J., 446–447
Deaux, K., 133, 318
de Haan, H., 227
deMause, L., 330
Dengerink, H.A., 319, 322
DeRisi, D., 459
Derlega, V.J., 156
Deutschberger, P., 347
DeVinney, L.C., 401, 408
Diamond, S.G., 447
Diener, E., 371, 372
Dillehay, R.C., 197
Dillon, Douglas, 357
Dineen, J., 371
Dion, K., 126, 127, 159, 341
Dollard, J., 67, 313
Donnerstein, E., 322
Doob, L.W., 313
Doolittle, General, 408
Dore, S.R., 447
Dornbush, S.M., 94, 95
Douglas, V.I., 80
Douglass, F., 206
Dovidio, J.F., 285
Downs, R., 431
Drabman, R.S., 326
Draguns, J.G., 269
Dubin, E.R., 94
Dubin, R., 94
Duff, D., 449
Dukes, F.O., 6
Dunham, H., 420
Durkheim, E., 436
Duryea, R., 257

Eagly, A.H., 182
Ebbinghaus, H., 395
Eberhard, Wolfram, 215

Edney, J., 453
Edward, Duke of Windsor, 170
Efran, M.G., 446
Eifler, D., 86
Eisen, S.V., 88
Ekman, P., 113
Ellsworth, P.C., 116, 375
Elworthy, F.T., 116
Emerson, P.E., 70
Empey, J., 447
Emrich, B., 236
Endicott, J., 230–232
Endleman, R., 55
Endresen, K., 371
Engquist, G., 134
Enzie, R.F., 382
Epicurus, 11
Epstein, S., 98, 141
Epstein, Y.M., 459, 464
Erikson, E.H., 59–60, 63, 69, 76
Ervin-Tripp, S.M., 111, 112, 380
Esser, A., 453
Exline, R.V., 113, 116, 254
Eysenck, H.J., 109

Farber, I.E., 314
Farina, A., 270
Faris, R., 420
Fast, Julius, 113
Fazio, R.H., 438
Ferguson, D.A., 360
Ferre, F., 14
Ferris, C.B., 228
Feshbach, S., 232–234, 235–236, 327
Festinger, L., 23, 97, 165, 228, 249, 259, 261–262, 342, 343, 370
Fiedler, F.E., 402–406
Field, P.B., 238
Fillenbaum, S., 110
Finney, R., 33
Firestone, I.J., 412
Fishbein, M., 187, 188, 202, 203–204
Fisher, J.D., 296
Flavell, J.H., 100
Floyd, J., 157

Flyger, V., 457
Fontana, V., 331
Foote, N., 428
Forman, R., 342
Fox, R., 394
Franklin, Benjamin, 222
Fraser, S.C., 257, 295, 371
Freedman, A., 297
Freedman, J.L., 256, 257, 265, 294, 295, 324, 459, 461
French, E.G., 185, 386
French, J.R.P., Jr., 406
Frenkel-Brunswik, F., 36, 384
Freshley, H.B., 295
Freud, S., II, 56–58, 69, 75, 76, 101, 116, 311, 372
Fried, Marc, 427
Friendly, M.L., 94
Fritzler, D., 96
Fromm, Erich, 175

Gaertner, S.L., 285, 293
Galle, O., 461
Gallimore, R., 33
Galton, F., 395
Gammon, C.B., 324, 325
Gandhi, Mahatma, 332–333
Gans, H., 420–423, 428
Gardner, B.T., 105
Gardner, L.I., 72, 73
Gardner, R.A., 105
Gardner, R.C., 110
Garofalo, R., 329
Garfinkel, H., 113
Geen, R.G., 315, 327
Geer, B., 26
Geertz, C., 450
Geis, F.L., 12, 254
Genovese, Catherine ("Kitty"), 285, 286–287
Geracimos, A., 331
Gerard, H.B., 134, 189, 194, 252, 253, 255, 346, 362
Gerbasi, K.C., 236
Gerbrands, H., 376
Gergen, K.J., 238, 294, 296,
Gergen, M.M., 294, 296

Gewirtz, J.L., 69
Gianetto, R.M., 375
Gibb, C.A., 395, 401
Gibbins, K., 112, 374
Giesen, J.M., 116
Gifford, R.K., 132
Giglioli, P.P., 110
Gil, D.G., 331
Gilbert, G.M., 184
Gillig, P.M., 243
Gilman, A., 108–109
Glass, D., 431–432
Glucksberg, S., 94, 99, 100, 104
Goethals, G.R., 218–219
Goffman, E., 97–98, 112, 158, 268, 347, 372–374, 465
Goldberg, G.N., 447
Goldberg, P.A., 87, 126, 186
Golden, B., 219
Goldman, F., 434
Goldman-Eisler, F., 380
Gollin, E.S., 93
Goodall, J., 312
Goranson, R.E., 284, 327
Gotay, C.C., 296
Gottesdiener, M., 186
Gouldner, A.W., 155, 283–284
Gove, W., 461
Graham, J.D., 238, 297
Granberg, D., 29–30
Graves, T.D., 447
Gray, J.G., 174–175
Graziano, W., 167
Green, F.P., 281
Greenberg, M.S., 284
Greenwald, A.G., 243
Greenwell, J., 322
Greer, G., 328
Griffen, L.M., 464
Griffin, S., 329
Griffitt, W., 152, 435
Gross, A.E., 294, 296, 380
Gross, L.P., 146
Gruder, C.L., 293
Guilford, J.P., 122, 395
Gumpert, P., 254
Guthrie, E.R., 342

Hackman, J.R., 385, 386
Hain, J.D., 257

527
Author index

Hall, C.S., 56
Hall, E.T., 324, 443, 444
Hallie, P.P., 306, 310
Hamblin, R.L., 410–411
Hamilton, D.L., 126, 132
Haney, C.A., 269
Harlow, H.F., 70, 71–72
Harlow, M.K., 71
Harrington, A., 355
Harris, M., 14, 24
Hartley, E.L., 93
Hartshorne, H., 76
Hartup, W.W., 68, 69
Harvey, O.J., 206, 353
Hass, R.G., 226
Hastorf, A.H., 94, 374, 380
Heberlein, T.A., 202, 203
Heckhausen, H., 139
Heider, F., 29, 135, 136, 139, 162
Helmreich, R., 215
Helson, H., 257
Hemphill, J.K., 401
Henderson, J.E., 216
Hendrick, C., 153, 157
Henninger, M., 243
Henson, A., 116
Herberle, R., 428
Herman, C.P., 222
Heshka, S., 461
Hess, E.H., 52, 201
Hickey, C.B., 254
Higgins, E.T., 104
Hill, J.G., 131
Himmelfarb, S., 182
Hinkle, S.W., 382
Hitler, Adolph, 410
Hobbes, Thomas, 12, 56
Hodgson, R.C., 110
Hofer, M.A., 68
Hoffer, E., 410, 412
Hoffman, M.L., 76
Hoffman, P.J., 132
Hokada, E., 86
Holahan, C., 468
Hollander, E.P., 268, 406–407
Hollander, J., 434
Holmes, J.G., 284
Holsti, O.R., 31, 32, 33
Homans, G.C., 171, 255, 280, 282
Hood, W.R., 206, 353
Hood, T.C., 369
Hoover, Herbert, 399, 410
Hornstein, H.A., 294

Horowitz, M., 449
Horton, R.W., 326
Hostetler, J.A., 190–191
Hovland, C.I., 135, 199, 200, 207, 213, 214, 220, 225, 227, 299, 230, 242–243
Howitt, D., 325
Hull, C., 67
Hull, R., 403
Humphrey, Hubert, 29–30
Hunt, M., 169
Hunter, J.E., 86
Husek, T.R., 214, 215
Hyman, D., 459
Hyman, H.H., 226

Insko, C.A., 243–244, 262
Irwin, W., 345
Isen, A.M., 294
Itkin, S., 166
Ittelson, W., 428, 468

Jaccard, J.J., 188–189, 368
Jackson, D.D., 111
Jacobs, R.C., 381
James, J., 338, 339
James, William, 92, 98
Janis, I.L., 232–234, 235–236, 238, 249, 356
Janssens, L., 373
Johnson, Lyndon, 4, 5
Johnson, R.N., 306, 312, 316, 317, 318, 324, 326, 328, 333
Jones, E.E., 135, 136–137, 139, 141, 189, 194, 199, 253, 254, 255, 366
Jones, Jim, 354
Jones, R.A., 100, 122, 195, 225, 239, 264, 386
Jones, S.C., 383
Jones, S.E., 454, 455
Jorgensen, B.W., 154
Jorgenson, D.O., 6
Jourard, S.M., 155, 455
Julian, J.W., 406–407
Jung, C., 57

Kagan, J., 72
Kahn, R.L., 27, 28, 29, 327, 401
Kahneman, D., 138, 459
Kamenetsky, J., 227
Kanin, E.J., 328, 329
Kant, Immanuel, 56

Kaplan, A., 38
Kaplan, B., 98
Karabenick, S.A., 295
Karlin, R.A., 459, 460, 464
Karlins, M., 184
Kasner, K.H., 319
Katz, D., 184, 194, 196, 401
Keech, M., 23
Kelley, H.H., 123, 135, 137–138, 171, 218, 251, 255, 280, 340–341, 346, 347, 352, 383–384, 385, 386
Kelly, G.A., 20, 21
Kelman, H.C., 242–243
Kennedy, John F., 157, 357
Kennedy, Robert, 357
Kennell, J.H., 68
Kerckhoff, A.C., 154
Kiesler, C.A., 147–148, 190, 202, 248, 447
Kiesler, S.B., 87, 126, 248, 347, 350
King, Martin Luther, 333
Kirkpatrick, C., 328
Kirscht, J.P., 197
Kite, W.R., 380
Klapper, J.T., 228
Klaus, M.H., 68
Kleck, R., 374–375
Klein, R.E., 72
Klein, R.F., 369
Kliejunas, P., 203
Knight, R., 468
Knipe, H., 393
Knowles, E.S., 445
Koford, C.B., 394
Kogan, N., 359
Kohlberg, L., 60, 64, 79, 80–84
Kozlowski, L.T., 222
Krasner, L., 347
Krauss, R.M., 99, 104, 106–107
Kravitz, J., 195
Krebs, D.L., 161, 279, 294
Krech, D., 255
Kriss, M., 438
Kutner, N.G., 297

Labov, W., 109–110
Lamale, H.H., 31
Lambert, W.E., 110
Landy, D., 159–161
Langer, E.J., 143
Langley, R., 331
LaPiere, R.T., 197

Latané, B., 270, 284, 285–291, 292, 366, 368, 369, 431
Laughlin, P.R., 368
Lawton, M.P., 343–344
Lawton, S., 435
Lazarus, R.S., 344, 428
Leary, R.W., 393
Le Dantec, F., 12
Lee, J.A., 176–179
Lee, T., 426–427
Leeds, R., 280, 284
Legant, P., 139
Lehrer, P., 459
Lempers, J., 68, 69
LePage, A., 324
Lerner, M.J., 141, 284
Lerner, R.M., 295
Leventhal, H., 234, 235, 236
Levin, H., 76, 294
Levinger, G., 154, 156
Levinson, D.J., 36, 384
Levy, A., 222, 459, 461
Levy, R., 331
Lewin, K., 14–16, 347
Lewis, L.D., 292–293
Lewis, M., 68
Leyens, J.P., 327
Lichtman, C.M., 412
Lickona, T., 155
Lieber, A., 437
Liebert, R.M., 325, 326, 327
Linder, D.E., 165, 167, 226, 264
Lindzey G., 56
Lintell, M., 432
Linton, R., 169, 238
Lippincott, E.C., 326
Lippitt, R., 15
Lipton, R.C., 72
Locke, John, 56
London, P., 269
Lorenz, K., 311–312, 331, 393
Lorge, I., 212
Lott, A.J., 164
Lott, B.E., 164
Love, L.R., 375
Lowell, E.L., 12
Lumsdaine, A.A., 225
Lynch, K., 424–426

Maccoby, E.E., 76
Machiavelli, Niccoló, 12
MacIntosh, E., 430
Macker, C.E., 256

Mackworth, N., 434
Maclay, G., 393
MacPherson, J., 461
Madaras, G.P., 147
Maehr, M.L., 206
Malpass, R.S., 195
Mandel, D.R., 464
Mandell, W., 227
Mann, R.D., 395–397, 398
Manser, G., 297
Marecek, J., 139
Marks, E.S., 31
Marler, P., 312
Marlowe, D., 238
Marshall, N., 450, 451
Marshall, R., 410
Martens, R., 368
Martin, J.A., 78
Martindale, D., 453
Maslow, A.H., 20
Mathewson, G.C., 362
Matlin, M.W., 190
Matthews, M.W., 293
Mauldin, W.P., 31
May, M.A., 76
McArthur, L.Z., 88
McCain, G., 462
McCandless, B.R., 379
McCarthy, Eugene, 216
McClelland, D.C., 12, 31, 89, 129, 195
McDavid, J.W., 253, 257
McDougall, W., 14
McFarland, D., 460
McGuire, W.J., 184, 185, 215, 220–221, 222, 228, 236, 237, 240–241, 243
McNamara, Robert, 357
Mead, G.H., 98
Medea, A., 328
Megargee, E.I., 319
Mehrabian, A., 108, 447
Mensch, I.N., 123
Meter, K., 294
Mettee, D.R., 166
Mewborn, C.R., 234–236
Meyer, W.U., 139
Michielutte, R., 269
Middlebrook, P.N., 298
Midlarsky, E., 281
Milgram, S., 258–259, 269, 419, 431
Miller, C.E., 163

Miller, D.T., 284
Miller, N.E., 67, 313
Millman, S., 220–221
Mills, J., 220, 296, 361–362
Mills, T.M., 377
Mischel, W., 77, 379
Misiti, R., 270
Mitchell, R.E., 461
Montgomery, R.L., 382
Moore, H.T., 218
Moos, R., 432, 436
Morris, C.G., 385, 386
Morris, D., 312, 331
Morris, E.K., 78
Morris, S.C., 296
Mouton, J.S., 257
Mowrer, O.H., 313
Moyer, R.J., 218
Mullens, S., 445
Mundy, D., 352
Murdoch, P., 368
Murphy, G., 93
Murphy, L.B., 52
Murstein, B.I., 154, 159, 348–351
Mussen, P., 130–131, 384
Muzzy, R.E., 94

Nadler, A., 296
Nahemow, L., 343–344
Neale, J.M., 325, 326, 327
Nebergall, R.E., 198
Nelson, C., 123, 381
Nelson, D., 152
Nelson, R.E., 218–219
Nemeth, C., 230–232
Newcomb, T.M., 122, 162–163, 370, 386, 387
Newman, O., 452
Newton, P., 206
Newtson, D., 133–134
Nezlek, J., 379
Nichols, C.R., 369
Nicosia, G., 459
Nisbett, R.E., 127–128, 139–140, 141, 145, 147
Nixon, Richard, 7, 29–30
Noble, G., 325
Nol, F.P., 297
Norman, R.M.G., 163
Nuttin, J., 373

O'Leary, M.R., 319
Olshan, K., 97

Ono, H., 374
Orne, M.T., 44
Orwell, George, 104, 374
Osborn, Alex, 358
Osgood, C.E., 101–102
Oskamp, S., 186, 202
Osmond, Humphrey, 468
Overall, B., 347
Overmier, J.B., 142

Pack, S.J., 42–44
Page, H., 153
Page, R., 198–199
Panitch, D., 383
Papageorgis, D., 241
Park, R., 420
Parke, R.D., 327
Patterson, M.L., 439, 447, 452
Paul, Saint, 178
Paulus, P.B., 368, 462
Peevers, B.H., 96
Pellegrini, R.J., 447
Pepitone, A., 370, 371
Pepler, R., 434
Peter, L.J., 403
Pettigrew, T., 204, 207
Petty, R.E., 222, 238–240
Pheterson, G.I., 87, 126
Phillips, L., 269
Piaget, J., 56, 60–64, 70, 75, 79–80, 93
Piliavin, I.M., 40, 285, 291–292, 296
Piliavin, J.A., 40, 279, 285, 291–292
Pilkonis, P.A., 190
Plath, Sylvia, 112
Plato, 10
Postman, L., 129, 195
Poussaint, A.F., 112
Price, J.S., 395, 459
Proshansky, H., 206, 468
Provence, S., 72
Pryor, J.B., 438

Rabbie, J.M., 346
Rabinowitz, L., 352
Radloff, R., 352
Ramchandra, V., 239
Rank, A.D., 400
Rank, O., 57
Rappoport, L., 96
Raven, B., 406
Redd, W.H., 78

Reichner, R., 463–464
Reis, H.T., 236
Reynolds, M., 422–423
Ribble, M., 72
Ribicoff, Abraham, 20
Rice, R.W., 405, 406
Rice, S.A., 31
Richardson, S.A., 94
Riecken, H.W., 23
Rittle, R.H., 367
Rivlin, L., 468
Rockway, A., 96, 97
Rodin, J., 40, 285, 288, 291–292, 368, 369, 457
Rodin, M., 125
Rogers, R. W., 234–236
Rokeach, M., 130, 196, 203
Romano, J., 445
Roosevelt, Franklin, 297, 298
Roseborough, M.E., 377
Rosen, L., 464
Rosen, S., 296
Rosenbaum, M.E., 93, 257
Rosenberg, M.J., 342
Rosenberg, S., 106, 122, 123–125, 386
Rosenblatt, P., 453
Rosenblatt, R.M., 352
Rosenblum, L.A., 68
Rosenhan, D.L., 25–26, 279, 281, 465, 467
Rosenthal, A.M., 285
Rosenthal, R., 37, 42
Ross, C., 86
Ross, D., 316, 317
Ross, E.A., 14
Ross, L.B., 132
Ross, L.D., 128–129
Ross, S.A., 316, 317
Rossman, B., 438
Rotter, J.B., 319
Rottman, L., 158
Rousseau, Jean Jacques, 56
Rubin, K.H., 281
Rubin, Z., 13, 156, 168, 172–173, 175, 351
Rubovits, P.C., 206
Rush, B., 437
Rushton, J.P., 281
Rusk, Dean, 357
Russell, C., 394
Russell, E.H., 328, 329

Russell, W.M.S., 394
Rutter, D.R., 447
Ryan, Leo, 355

Sadat, Anwar, 396
Saegert, S., 430, 468
Sage, W., 331
Sales, S.M., 36–37, 367
Saltzstein, H.D., 76
Sampson, E., 349
Sanborn, D., 436
Sanford, R.N., 36, 384
Sarbin, T.R., 347
Sarles, R., 331
Sartre, Jean Paul, 116
Scarr, H.A., 371
Schachter, S., 23, 144–147, 174, 270, 342, 345–346, 356, 381, 447
Schaffer, H.R., 68, 69, 70, 74
Schaffer, R., 54, 68, 71
Schank, R.L., 255
Scheff, T.J., 25, 269–270
Scheflen, 114–116
Schein, E.H., 258, 261
Scherer, S., 455
Schjelderup-Ebbe, T., 393
Schlegloff, E.A., 112–113
Schleifer, M., 80
Schmitt, D.E., 332
Schnedler, R., 294
Schneider, F.W., 281
Schopler, J., 262, 293
Schulman, J., 236
Schulz, R., 447
Schur, E.M., 268
Schwartz, M.F., 294
Schwartz, R.D., 20, 33
Schwartz, S., 93
Scodel, A., 130–131, 384
Scott, J.P., 198, 317
Scribner, S., 101
Sears, D.O., 221
Sears, R.R., 67, 76, 207, 313
Seaver, W.B., 439
Sebastian, R.J., 327
Sechrest, L., 4, 7, 20, 33
Secord, P.F., 96, 155
Segal, M.W., 151–152
Seghorn, T., 329
Sekerack, G.J., 367
Seligman, C., 438–439
Seligman, M.E.P., 142–143, 457

Selkin, J., 329
Senn, D.J., 154
Sensenig, J., 195, 266–268
Shaffer, D.R., 63, 64, 73, 75, 76, 77, 78, 79, 89
Shaver, P., 236
Shaw, M., 338, 341
Sheatsley, P.B., 226
Sheehy, G., 60
Sheffield, F.D., 225
Sherif, C.W., 198, 206, 230, 231, 332, 333, 353
Sherif, M., 8, 9, 135, 198, 199, 200, 206, 230, 231, 249, 332, 333, 353
Sherin, C., 437
Sherman, R.C., 132
Sherrod, D.R., 431
Shibutani, T., 345
Shweder, R.A., 386–388
Sidowski, J.B., 352
Siegal, A.E., 191–194
Siegal, S., 191–194
Sigall, H., 159–161, 198–199, 215
Signell, K., 96
Simmel, G., 116, 419
Simmons, C.H., 141
Simons, H.W., 218
Simpson, O.J., 429
Sims, J., 434–435
Singer, J., 431–432
Singer, R.D., 144–145, 327
Sistrunk, F., 253
Skinner, B.F., 11, 64–67, 75, 332
Slater, P.E., 369, 401
Slavin, R., 439
Slye, D., 393
Smith, C., 297
Smith, H.T., 52
Smith, V., 437
Snyder, M., 343
Sommer, R., 444–445, 449, 453
Spencer, Herbert, II,
Spitz, R.A., 69, 71, 72
Staats, A.W., 189
Staats, C.K., 189
Stakelski, A.J., 383–384
Stanley, J.C., 39, 41
Star, S.A., 401, 408
Staub, E., 281, 282, 295
Stefaniak, D., 152
Steiner, I.D., 142
Steinmetz, J.L., 128

Stephenson, G.M., 447
Stern, S.E., 297
Stewart, A.J., 13
Stockwell, R.P., 93
Stogdill, R.M., 395, 397
Stokols, D., 418
Stone, L.J., 52
Stone, P.J., 31, 33
Stoner, J.A.F., 358
Stotland, E., 194
Stouffer, S.A., 401, 408
Stratten, L., 449
Strodtbeck, F.L., 376, 377
Suchman, E.A., 401, 408
Suci, G.J., 102
Suedfeld, P., 400, 433
Sundstrom, E., 405, 406, 453, 454
Suomi, S.J., 72
Szasz, T.S., 25, 268

Taber, T., 132
Tabory, L., 352
Tagiuri, R., 122
Tanur, J., 407
Tanke, E., 343
Tannenbaum, P.H., 102
Tars, S., 468
Taylor, D.A., 156
Taylor, D.W., 358
Taylor, S.P., 319, 321, 322, 324, 325
Teger, A.I., 292–293
Terkel, S., 184
Thibaut, J.W., 171, 254, 255, 280, 340–341, 346, 347, 352, 366, 384, 385, 386
Thistlethwaite, D.L., 227–228
Thomas, M.H., 326
Thompson, K., 328
Thorndike, E.L., 11, 127
Tiger, L., 394
Toch, H., 319
Toffler, A., 249
Triandis, H.C., 54
Triplett, N., 13, 14
Trow, M., 26
Troyer, W.G., 369
Tuckman, B.W., 376
Turk, A.T., 268
Turner, J.A., 228
Tversky, A., 138

Ulehla, Z., 438

Ulrich von Lichtenstein, 168–169

Valins, S., 462, 463
Van Lawick-Goodall, J., 394
Varney, L., 195
Vidmar, N., 196, 360
Vinsel, A.M., 444
Vivekananthan, P.S., 123
Vonnegut, Kurt, 338
Vreeland, R.S., 94

Wack, D.L., 367
Wagler, Evelyn, 326
Wagner, C.M., 295
Wagner, R.V., 294, 348
Walbek, N.H., 282
Wallach, M.A., 359
Wallington, S.A., 256, 294
Walster, E., 126, 144, 155, 158–159, 174, 175, 215, 279, 341
Walters, G., 184, 248, 317
Ward, L., 433
Ward, S.K., 461
Watson, J.B., 11
Watson, O.M., 447
Watson, R.I., 371, 372
Watzlawick, P., 111, 112
Webb, E.J., 20, 33, 34, 35, 37, 38, 45
Weick, K.E., 351, 352, 375
Weiler, J., 407
Weiner, B., 108, 139, 142
Weinheimer, S., 106–107
Weinstein, E.A., 99–100, 347, 407
Weis, K., 329
Weisberg, R., 99
Weiss, L.B., 33, 242
Weiss, W., 213, 214, 220, 242
Weitzer, W., 468
Weitzman, L.J., 86
Welch, R., 96
Weller, J.E., 101
Wells, G.L., 238–240
Werner, H., 93, 98
West, S.G., 294, 327
Wheeler, H., 468
Wheeler, L., 295, 379, 385
White, B.J., 206, 353
White, R.W., 15, 89
White, T.H., 7
Whiting, J.W.M., 55
Whitney, G., 294
Whorf, B.L., 101

531
Author index

Whyte, W.H., Jr., 358
Wicklund, R.A., 228, 410
Wiggins, N.H., 132, 166
Willerman, B., 157
Williams, J.A., Jr., 31
Williams, R.M., Jr., 401, 408
Wilson, D.W., 322
Wilson, M., 156
Wilson, T.D., 127–128
Wilson, Woodrow, 399
Winch, R.F., 154, 351
Winkel, G.H., 468
Wirth, L., 420
Wishner, J., 123

Wispé, L.G., 295
Wodarski, J., 439
Wolfensburger, W., 468
Wolff, P.H., 69
Wood, D., 426
Woolfolk, R., 459
Worchel, P., 152
Worchel, S., 239, 293
Wortman, C.B., 140
Wray, H., 300
Wrightsman, L.S., 311, 328
Wyckoff, L.B., 352
Wyer, R.S., Jr., 243
Wylie, R.C., 86

Wynne-Edwards, V.C., 395

Yarrow, M., 94
Yeostros, S., 434

Zadny, J., 134
Zajonc, R.B., 135, 142, 190, 191, 367, 368, 402, 403
Zamarin, D., 432
Zanna, M.P., 42–44, 126, 147, 190
Zigler, E., 55
Zimbardo, P.G., 370–372
Ziming, C., 468
Zuckerman, M., 236

Subject Index

A-B-X model of attraction, 162–163
Accessibility, and survey research, 28
Accommodation, and cognitive development, 63
Accountability of social service agencies, 300
Accretion of evidence in archival research, 35
Achievement motivation, 12, 55, 88, 89
Acquiescent response style, 199
Activity, scales of, 101
Adaptation, and cognitive development, 63
Adaptation-level theory, 257
Adolescents, 423
Affective components of attitudes, 182–189
Affective state(s), 108
Affects, attitudinal, and behavior, 197–204
Affiliation, aberrations of, 355–362
  commitment to the group, 360–362
  groupthink, 356–358
  risk and caution, 358–360
Affiliation, sources of, 340–354
  anxiety, 344–346
  complementarity, 346–348
  family formation, 348–351
  membership and motive, 351–354
  physical attractiveness, 341–342
  similarity, 342–344
Against Our Will (Brownmiller), 328
Agape, agapic love, 175, 177, 178–179
Age differences
  and friendship, 344
  and voluntarism, 297
Aggregation vs. group, 6
Aggression, 55, 306–333

angry/instrumental, 308, 332
and bluffing, 394
control, 322–333
defined, 306–310
environmental factors, 322–325, 435–436
experiments, 319–321
and frustration, 207, 311, 313–316, 331
and individual differences, 317–319
inhibited/displaced, 313
and prejudice, 195
sexual, 329–330
and social violence, 327–332
and television, 325–327
theories, 310–317
threshold, 317, 318
"Aggression machine," 320
Aggressive cues, internal/external, 314–316
Aggressive intent, 308–309, 322
Aggressive rapists, 329
Aggressor, role of, 309–310
Alcohol, and aggression, 324, 325
All in the Family, 196
Altercasting, 347, 408–409
Altruism, 277–301
  and agapic love, 178
  definition, 278–279
  demographic/personal characteristics, 293–296
  in emergencies, 284–293
  and environmental overload, 430–431
  nature of, 277–284
  in nonemergencies, 293–296
  paid, 298–300
  and voluntarism, 298
Ambivalent feelings, 174, 178
Americans, beliefs about, 198–199

Amish, 190–191
Anal stage, 58
Androgens, 317
Androgyny, 87, 349
Anger
  and aggression, 308, 314–316, 322
  and sexual arousal, 174–175
Animals
  aggressive behavior, 311–313, 317, 322–324, 331
  crowding of, 455–457
  dominance in, 312, 393–395
Anxiety
  and affiliation, 344–346
  and attraction, 166
  and comformity, 249
  and moral development, 77–78
Aptitude test, 395
Archie Bunker, 196
Architecture, 452, 463–464, 467, 468, 469
Archival research, 34–38
Arousal, labeling of, 447
Arthritis, 433–434
Assimilation, and cognitive development, 63
Attachment, 55, 64, 69–71. *See also* Love
Attitudes
  and attraction, 151, 162
  and behavior consistency, 197–204
  change of, 211–245
  components of, 182–189
  functions of, 194–197
  interrelatedness of, 194
  measurement of, 198–200
  origins and maintenance of, 189–197
  specificity of, 202–203

533
Subject index

Attraction, 151–168
  determinants of, 151–162
  effect of heat on, 435
  law of, 165
  theory of, 162–168
Attractiveness. *See* Physical attractiveness
Attribution processes, 135–139
  internal/external, 136, 139, 141
  and self-perception, 141–148
  and success/failure, 139–141
Audience
  effect on performance, 366–368
  and persuasive communication, 236–244
Authoritarian personality
  and ego defense, 196–197
  and environmental threat, 36–37
  and group formation, 382
  and prejudice, 204
  and prisoner's dilemma, 384
  and social perception, 129–131
Authoritarian Personality, The (Adorno et al.), 197
Autokinetic phenomenon, 7–9, 249, 382
Autonomy vs. shame and doubt stage, 59
Availability, and attribution, 138
Avoidance behavior, and prejudice, 195
Avoidance learning, 77–78

Balance theory, 28–30, 162–164
Balinese, 450
Bay of Pigs invasion, 357
Behavior
  actual/rated, 387–388
  and attitudes, 182–189, 197–204
  and conformity, 248–249
  consistency of, 194, 197, 200–204
  and heat, 322, 435–436
  and moon, 437
  prediction of, 202–203
  systems, 54–56
  and weather, 433–435
Behavioral assimilation effect, 384
Behavioral confirmation, 343
Beliefs, 182–189
  and conformity, 259–265
Bias
  and attitude measurement, 199–200

and person perception, 126–129, 386–388
  systematic, 386–388
Bible, 170, 178, 277, 330
Biological determinism, 314
Blacks, beliefs about, 198–199. *See also* Prejudice
Blood pressure, 459, 462
Bluffing, 394, 395
Bobo doll, 316–317, 320, 326
Bodily states, self-labeling of, 144–147
Body buffer zone, 449
Body contact, 455, 465
Body language, 113–116
Body orientation, 446, 455
Body position, sitting/standing, 444
Boomerang effect, 230, 265
Boston's West End redevelopment, 428
Brainstorming, 358
Break points, in perceived behavior, 134
"Bubbapsychology," 220
Buffer zone, personal, 449
"Buffering effect" of friends, 369
Bussing, 427
Bystander intervention/inhibition, 285–292, 366, 368–369, 431

Camp David agreement, 396
Capital punishment, 309, 331
Castration, 76, 317
Category construction, 32
Catharsis hypothesis, 327, 332
Cat's Cradle (Vonnegut), 338
Censorship, 239
Child abuse, 330–331
Child Training and Personality (Whiting and Child), 55
Children
  aggression, 316–317, 333
  altruism, 281, 282
  institutionalized, 468
  rearing practices, 74
  social development, 68–74
  spatial behavior, 454–455
  and television violence, 325, 326
Choice Dilemmas Questionnaire, 359
Cities, cognitive maps of, 424–426
City life, 423–424
Climatron, 434
"Closure" of events, 352

Coalitions, 464
Cognition, 28
  retrospective, 351
Cognitive components of attitudes, 182–189
Cognitive conceit, 129
Cognitive-development theory, 56
  and altruism, 281
  and moral development, 75, 79–84
  person concepts, 93
  Piaget and Kohlberg, 60–64
Cognitive factors of aggression control, 333
Cohesiveness of groups, 355–356
Colours of Love (Lee), 176
Commitments to groups, 361–362
Communication, 103–116
  context and imbeddedness, 110–113
  forms of, 107–110
  nonverbal, 113–116
  one-sided vs. two-sided, 222–226
  social nature of, 103–107
  and spatial behavior, 444
  See also Persuasive communication paradigm
Communicator characteristics, 212–222
Community Mental Health Centers Act (1969), 300
Competence, sense of, 89, 165, 166
Competition
  and cooperation, 55
  and crowding, 457, 463
  and dominance, 394
  and prejudice, 204–206
  and prisoner's dilemma, 382–384
Complementarity
  and attraction, 153–154
  and family group, 351
  and group formation, 346–348
  and roles, 346–348
Compliance
  and conformity, 255–259
  and dissonance, 259–262
Conclusion drawing, 226–228
Concurrence-seeking behavior, 356
Conditioning
  affective, 189
  instrumental, 164
  operant, 439
Confirmation in communication,

106–107
Conflict-resolution, 333
Conformity, 248–271
  and compliance, 255–259
  and nonconformity, 265–270
  and private beliefs, 259–265
Conscience, 57, 59–60, 76
Conservation of volume cognition, 64
Content analysis, 31–34, 94, 95. *See also* Interaction process analysis
Context and embeddedness in communication, 110–113
Contrast, positive/negative, in attraction, 166
Control, experimental, 38–40
Cooperation
  and competition, 55
  and prisoner's dilemma, 382–384
Correspondence of inference, 137
Cosa Nosta, 331–332
Cosmopolites, 422–423
Cost–benefit analysis, and altruism, 293
Courtship-like behavior, 114–116
Credibility of communicator, 213–215
Crime
  and architecture, 452
  family, 330–331
  organized, 331–332
  rape, 328–330
  sex differences, 318
  socioeconomic factors, 328
  statistics, 328
  violent, 318, 327–332, 437
Crisis
  and altruism, 280
  and leadership, 409–412
Crowding, 455–464
  and aggression, 322–324
  and architecture, 463–464
  in college dormitories, 463, 464
  in prisons, 462–463
  residential, 460–462
  sex differences, 459–460
  transportation, 459
  and wilderness, 438
Crying, 69
Cuba, 357
Cue utilization, 135
Cultural differences in spatial behavior, 448–450, 454–455
Cultural relativism, 51, 54

Cultural truisms, 240

Day-care centers, 298
Death instinct, 57, 311
Decision-making
  and bystander intervention, 285–288
  and groupthink, 356–357
Defense mobilization, 238–242
Deindividuation, 369–372
Demand characteristics, of the experimental situation, 44–45
Demographic characteristics, 460
  and altruism, 295–296
  and violent crime, 328, 331
  and voluntarism, 297
Denial hypothesis of persuasion, 234
Dependency, 55, 69
  and altruism, 295, 296, 300
  independence/interdependence balance, 89
Dependent variables, 8, 40
Depression, 143
Deprivation dwarfism, 72, 73
Despair vs. ego integrity, 60, 63
Deviant behavior, 268–270
  and crowing of rats, 455–456
  and group affiliation, 347, 356
  and lunar phases, 437
  in suburbs, 422–423
  and talkativeness, 381
Dialectic process, privacy as a, 447
Differential reinforcement, 332
Differentiation and cognitive development, 93
Diffusion of responsibility, 288–291, 431
Discipline
  and aggression, 308
  and morality, 76–77
Discrepancy, audience, 228–232
Dissonance theory, 216, 228–230
  and forced compliance, 259–262
  and group commitment, 360–362
Distributive justice, 282–283
Dominance, in animals, 312, 393–395
Dominant responses, facilitation of, 367–368
"Doomsday cults," 23
Dormitories, crowing in, 462–464
Drives, 67
  and theories of aggression,

313–316
Dyadic system, mother–infant, 69

Early Window (Liebert et al.), 336
Eating behavior, 55
  of obese people, 145–147
Ecological correlation, 460
Effect commonality, 136–137
Effect interdependence, 255
Effectance motive, 165
Ego, 57, 76
Ego ideal, 57
Ego integrity vs. despair stage, 60, 63
Ego threat, and altruism, 296
Egocentrism, 64, 80, 96
Emergency situations, helping in, 284–293, 366
Emotion, and aggression, 308
Emotional development, 55, 64. *See also* Attachment; Love
Empathy, 278, 279, 294
Energy conservation, 438–440
Environment, normalized, 468
Environmental load, 430–431
Environmental psychology, 417–471
  cowding, 455–464
  natural environment, 433–440
  spatial behavior, 443–455
  total institutions, 465–470
  urban environment, 418–433
Environmental variables, 443
  and aggression, 322–325, 331
  and social behavior, 443
Equilibrium model of intimacy, 446–447
Equity theory, of reciprocal behavior, 283–284
Eros, erotic love, 175, 177
  and aggression, 311
Erosion measures of archival evidence, 34–35
Estrogens, 317
Ethnic factors, and spatial behavior, 454–455
Ethnomethodology, 113
Ethology, and aggression, 311–313, 322–224, 331
Evaluation scales, 101
Evaluations of attraction, sequencing of, 165–168
"Evil eye," and visual interaction, 116
Evolution, and aggression, , 312

535
Subject index

Exchange theory
    of altruism, 280, 282–283, 298
    of love, 171–172
Existential problems, universal, 56
Expectations
    experimental, 42
    and person perception, 122, 386
    and prejudice, 206–207
    and sex roles, 84–88, 126
Experience, prior, and attitudes, 189–190
Experimentation, 38–45
    and aggression studies, 319–321, 326, 327
    on effects of temperature, humidity, etc., 434
Exploitation, in love, 171–172
External validity, 37, 39
Eye contact, 116, 380, 444, 446, 447, 455, 465

F-scale, 384
FBI Uniform Crime Reports, 328
Family
    group formation, 340, 348–351
    territoriality, 453
    violence, 330–331
Fatigue, 144
Fatty acids level in blood, 369
Fear and anger, and sexual arousal, 174–175
Fear-arousing messages, 232–236
Feedback and performance, 106–107, 185–186, 380–381, 385–386
Feminist movement, 186, 328
Fighting, 312. *See also* Aggression
Filter hypothesis of attraction, 154
Frustration–aggression hypothesis, 207, 311, 313–316, 331
Free association, 101
Frauendienst, 168
Flirting, 171
Foot-in-the-door technique, 257–258, 295

Gain–loss theory of attraction, 165–168
Galvanic skin response, 374, 459
Genetic factors, in aggression, 318
Genital stage, 58
Generativity vs. stagnation stage, 60
Ghettos, 429

Giving, norm of, 284
"Global evaluation," and person perception, 127
Goal attainment, 366
Goal response, 313
"Good boy"/"good girl" orientation, 81, 82–83
Good Samaritian, 277, 293–294
"Granfalloons," 338
Gratification, delay of, 32–33, 76
Great Depression, 399, 410
Great Person theory, 392, 395–398
Group, 6
    conflict, 204–206, 333
    cohesiveness, 355–356
    commitment, 360–362
    dynamics, 14
    "forming, storming, morning, performing," 376–378
    inlibition of helping, 366
    leadership, 378, 404–406
    performance vs. individual performance, 384–386
    power, 251–254
    risk/caution, 358–360
    "situation," 404
    size, 375
    status, and spatial intrusion, 445
    talkativeness, 377–381
Group formation, 337–363
    affiliation aberrations, 355–362
    affiliation sources, 340–354
    small groups, 338–340
Group interaction, 365–389
    deindividuation, 369–372
    interaction processes, 375–386
    nonverbal communication and information management, 372–375
    retrospective misinterpretations, 386–388
    social faciliation, 366–369
Groups
    and aggression, 333
    and authoritarianism, 382
    in competition, 373
    and prejudice, 204–206
    and social change, 382
"Groupthink", 356–358, 381
Guatemalan Indian children, 72
Guilt
    and altruism, 294
    and compliance, 256–257

vs. initiative, 59–60
Guns, and aggression, 324

Halo effect, 127, 128
Handicapped people, interaction with, 374–375
Hare Krisha, 193
Harrisburg Conspiracy, 236
"Hawks" and "doves," 29–30
Heat, effect on behavior, 322, 435–436
Hedonic relevance, 137
Hedonism, 10–11
    and liking/disliking, 168
    naive, 81, 82
Helping acts, direct/preventive, 280
Helping behavior. *See* Altruism
Helping costs, 280, 293
Heterosexual relationships, 158, 168, 176
Homicide rate, and lunar phases, 437
Homosexual impulses, and rape, 329
Homosexual love, 176
Hong Kong, 461–462
Hormones, 317
Hospitalism, 71, 72
Human nature, 168
    and aggression, 310
Hunting as aggression, 309
Hypnotism, 56

Id, 57
Identification, psychoanalytic, 57–58, 76
Identity confirmation ("Icon"), 348
Identity crisis, 60, 61
Idiosyncrasy credit, 268
Ik tribe of Uganda, 54
Illusion of control, and attribution theory, 143
Illusory correlation of variables, 138
Imitation, 69
    and aggression, 316–317
    role in moral development, 78–79
    See also Modeling
Immediacy/non-immediacy, in verbal communication, 108
Implicit adjustment, 352
Impression formation, 123–126, 129, 132
Impression management, 42–44, 112, 374, 381–382
Imprinting, 52–54

Incompetence, occupational, 403
Incongruent postures, 114–116
Indebtedness theory of reciprocity, 284
Independence–interdependence balance, 89, 349
Independent variables, 8
  levels and treatments, 40
Index construction, archival, 35–36
India, 24
Individual performance vs. group performance, 384–386
Indoctrination, 190–194
Industry vs. inferiority stage, 60
Indonesia, 448–450
Inequity and guilt, 255–257
Infant, social development of, 68–74
Infant sensory and response capabilities, 68–69
Infanticide, 330
Inference, correspondence of, 137
Infidelity, 167
Information management, 255, 345
  and groupthink, 356, 357
  and nonverbal communication, 372–375
Ingratiation strategy, 254
Inhibition–disinhibition, and aggression, 316
Initiative vs. guilt stage, 59–60
Innate purity doctrine, 56
Insanity. See Mental illness
Instinctive behavior
  and aggression, 311–313, 331
  and altruism, 281
Instincts, 57
  life/death, 57, 311
Institute for Righteous Acts, 269
Institutional environments, 465–470
Institutionalized infants, 71, 72
Instrumental aggression, 308, 332
Instrumental orientation, 81, 82
Integration, and cognitive development, 93
Intelligence, 63
  and leadership ability, 395–397
  tests, 63, 395
Intentions, 187
  to harm, 308–309
  to persuade, 220–222
Interaction distance, 374–375, 443–444

Interaction in groups, 365–389
Interaction matrix, 341
Interaction processes, 375–386
  analysis, 375–378
  individual vs. group performance, 384–386
  participation difference, 378–381
  prisoner's dilemma, 381–384
  retrospective misinterpretations, 386–388
Interaction recorder, 376
Internal validity, 39, 41
Interpretation of Dreams, The (Freud), 57
Intimacy
  cultural differences, 455
  equilibrium model of, 446–447
  intimate zone of interaction, 443
  vs. isolation stage, 60
  and reciprocity, 155, 156, 157
Intrinsic/extrinsic relationships 171
Introversion/extroversion, 157
Isolation, urban, and mental illness, 420
Israeli kibbutz children, 73

Japanese
  homicide rate, 324
  mass suicides on Saipan, 354
Javanese, 448–450
Jealousy effect in same-sexed peers, 159, 161
Jews in Masada, mass suicides of, 354
Justice, 79–80, 284

Kent State killings, 306, 307
Kinemes, kinesics, 114
Korean War, 258, 357, 447

Labeling process, 174, 175, 447
LPC (least-preferred co-workers) scores, 403–406
Laboratory studies. See Experimentation
Language, 52, 92, 100–103, 108–109, 447
Latency stage, 58
Latitude of acceptance/rejection/noncommitment, 230
Law-and-order orientation, 81, 83
"Law of infidelity," 167

Leadership, 378, 391–413
  change in crisis, 409–412
  and dominance in animals, 393–395
  Great Person theory, 395–398
  influence of followers, 407–409
  and intelligence, 395–397
  leader effectiveness model, 402–406
  and legitimacy, 406–407
  mandate phenomenon, 4, 5
  middle-level officials, 401–402
  presidential style, 399–400
  task vs. social specialists, 400–402
  training, 404–406
Learned helplessness, 142–143
Legalistic orientation, 81–82, 83
Levittowners, The (Gans), 420
Libido, 57
  and aggression, 311
Life instincts, 57, 311
Likes/dislikes, 151, 162, 168, 182–189
  being liked/disliked, and prisoner's dilemma, 383
  likeableness and leadership, 401
  liking/love scales, 172–174
  reciprocity of liking, 155
Linguistic rules, and sequencing of conversation, 380
Locus of Control Scale, 319
Logical error, 122
London Sunday Times, 332
Los Angeles Water district, 428
Love, 55, 64
  colors of, 175–179
  historical examples, 170
  liking/love scales, 172–174
  nature of, 168–179
  passionate, 174–175
  and psychoanalytic theory, 76, 77
Love-Story Card-Sort (Lee), 176
Loyalty oaths, 36
Ludus, ludic love, 177
Lunar phases, and mental illness, 437
Lying and cheating, 254–255, 261

Mach Scale, 12, 254–255
Machiavellianism, 254
Mafia, 331–332
Mandate phenomenon, 4, 5
Mania, manic love, 177, 178

Manipulation
   and conformity, 254–255
   experimental, 38
Marriage, attraction and love in, 154, 167, 168, 169–171, 348–351
Mass suicide, 354–355
Matching hypothesis of physical attractiveness, 158–159, 350–351
Maternal separation and deprivation, 71–74
Meaning
   denotative/connotative, 100, 101–103
   referential, 103–107
Measurement, 27–28
   of attitudes and behavior, 198–200
   triangulation of, 20–34
Membership groups and attitude stability, 191–193
   motives, 351–354
Mental Disorders in Urban Areas (Faris and Dunham), 420
Mental health centers, 300
Mental hospitals, 467–470
Mental illness, 25–26, 268–270
   in cities, 420
   effect of moon on, 437
   effect of seasons on, 436
Message, nature of, 222–236
Minimal social situation, 352
Mixed-motive games, 382–383
Modeling, 67
   and aggression, 316–317, 326, 331, 332–333
   and altruism, 282, 295, 298
   and attraction, 156
   and moral development, 78–79
Moon, effect of, on behavior, 437
Moral conduct, consistency in, 75–76
Moral development, stages of, 57, 74–84
   Kohlberg, 80–84
   Piaget, 79–80
Morality
   autonomous/heteronomous, 79–80
   pre-/post-conventional, 81–82
Mortification of institutional inmates, 465

Mother–infant interaction, 68–69
Motivation, 28, 29
Multiple operationism, 20
Mundane realism, 44
Mutuality. *See* Reciprocal behavior

National Center for the Control and Prevention of Rape, 328
National Commission on the Causes and Prevention of Violence, 328
National Institute of Mental Health, 300
Natural environment, 433–440
   energy conservation, 438–440
   heat effects, 435–436
   suicides and mental hospital admissions, 436
   weather, 433–435
   wilderness, 436–438
Natural hazards, regional reaction to, 434–435
Nazis, resistance to, 269
Need complementarity, 351
Negative orientation, 195. *See also* Prejudice
Neighborhoods, 426–428, 429
   effect of noise on, 432
Neoanalytic theory, 76–77
Neo-Hullian theory, 67
New Brunswick, N.J., 433
New York City
   "Bridge apartments" noise, 432–433
   cognitive map of, 425
Newspeak, 104
1984 (Orwell), 104, 374
"Noble savage," 56
Noise, effects of, 322, 431–433
Nonconformity, 265–270
Nonemergency situations, helping in, 293–296
Nonmonotonic relationship, 237
Nonverbal behavior
   and bluffing, 394
   and communication, 113–116
   in-group/out-group, 447
   and information management, 372–375
   of institutional staff, 465–466
   and spatial intrusion, 446
Normative beliefs, perceived, 188–189

Normative theories of altruism, 284
Norms, 284
   development of, 249–251
   of giving, 284
   of reciprocity, 283–284
   and roles, 346–347
   social, 207, 284, 294–295, 298
   subjective, 188–189
Northern Ireland, 332
Nurturance, 153

Obedience, 258–259
Object-choice (cathexis), 57
Object permanence, 64, 70
Observational learning, 66, 67
   and aggression, 316–317, 326
   See also Modeling
Observing behavior, 133–135
Oedipus complex, 58, 60, 76
Operant conditioning, and energy conservation, 439–440
Operational thought, 64–65
Operationalizing, 32
Oral behavior, 55
Oral stage, 58
Organization, and cognitive development, 63
Organization Man, The (Whyte), 358
Organized crime, 331–332
Orientation
   instrumental/legalistic, 81–82, 83
   internal/external, 434–435
Original sin, 56
Orphan homes, 71, 72
Overassimilation, 384
Overcontrolled Hostility Scale, 319

Parents,
   as "significant others," 340
Participant observation, 22–27
Participation
   differentials, 378–381
   reinforcement, 380–381, 400–401
Peace Corps, 296, 298
Pearl Harbor, 357
"Pecking order," 312, 317, 393, 394
Peer groups
   same-sex jealousy, 159, 161
   talking/leadership, 377–378
People's Temple, 354–355
Perceived need, 279–280

Perception. *See* Social perception
Perceptual defense/vigilance, 195–196
Perceptual errors, 194–195
Person concepts, differentiation and integration, 93–94
Person perception. *See* Social perception
Personal characteristics. *See* Personality variables; Physical attractiveness
Personal pronouns, familiar/polite, 108–109
Personal space, 444–446, 448
Personal zone of interaction, 443–444
Personalism, 137
Personality, psychoanalytic theory of, 57
Personality assessment and prediction. *See* Social perception
Personality variables, 123–126
  and aggression, 309, 317–319
  and altruism, 293–296
  and attraction, 157–158
  central/peripheral traits, 123–124
  and persuasibility, 237–238
  and recreational activity choice, 438
  regional, 434–435
  and social perception, 129–133
Personhood, 51, 88–89
Persuasive communication paradigm, 212–245
  audience, 236–244
  message, 222–236
  source, 212–222
Peter principle, 403
Phallic stage, 58, 76
Phonemes, 114
Physical attractiveness
  and altruism, 295–296
  and attraction, 158–160
  and group formation, 341–342
  and person perception, 126
  self-fulfilling stereotypes, 343
Physical evidence in archival research, 34–35
Physiological stress
  of crowding, 459
  of weather, 436

Pleasure motive, 10–11
Pleasure principle, 57
Pluralistic ignorance, 255
Political terrorism, 310
Politics of Rape (Russell), 329
Polycentrism, 98
Population, experimental, 27
Population density, and social pathology, 460–462
Potency scales, 101
Poverty, 461
Power difference, in aggression, 309–310
Power motive, 11–13
Power semantic, 108–109
Pragma, pragmatic love, 177, 178
Precision criterion, 27, 28
Pre-existing conceptual scheme, 387–388
Prejudice, 195, 196–197, 204–208
Preoperational thought stage, 63–64
Prestige suggestion, 212–213
Primary process, in psychoanalytic theory, 57
Prisoner's dilemma, 382–384
Prisons, crowding in, 462–463
Privacy, 447–450
  institutional lack of, 465, 468
Private beliefs, effects of conforming and compliance on, 259–265
Pronunciation differences, 109–110
Propinquity, and attraction, 151–152, 169
  and group formation, 342–343
Prosocial behavior, 278. *See also* Altruism
Proxemics, 443
Pseudogroup effects, 385
Psychiatric epidemiology, 420
Psychoanalytic theory, 56–58
  of aggression, 311
  and free association, 101
  of morality, 76–77
Psychological indebtedness, 284
Psychological reactance, 265–268
Psychological stress
  and crowding, 457
  urban, 428–430
Psychological tension and dissonance, 260
Psychopathology of Everyday Life (Freud), 372

Psychomotor performance, and temperature and humidity, 434
Psychosexual theory, 57–59
Psychosocial theory, 59–60
Psychotherapy, 20, 21, 116
Public zone of interaction, 444
"Punctuation" of sequence of events, 111
Punishment
  and aggression, 313, 332
  and attraction, 164–165
  and moral development, 77–82
Pupil dilation, 201

"Quasi-courtship behavior," 114–116

Racial factors and
  altruism, 294–295
  communication, 112
  friendship 344
  marriage, 169
  recognition and memory of faces, 195
  social choice, 130
  spatial behavior, 454–455
  voluntarism, 297
  See also Prejudice; Demographic characteristics
Racial violence, 323
"Radical behaviorism," 67
Random assignment, 41
Rank ordering. *See* dominance in animals
Rape, and aggression, 309, 328–330
Reactance theory, 225, 265–268
Reaction, internal/external, 77
Reading impairment, and noisy environment, 431–432
Reception tuning, 135
Reciprocal behavior, 69
  and altruism, 278, 282–284, 296
  and attraction, 154–157
  and roles, 347–348
Recognition and memory of faces, 195
Recreational choice, and personality, 438
Reference groups, 338
  and attitude stability, 191–193
  and conformity, 251, 269
  and indoctrination, 190–194

Referent
    communal/idiomatic, 98
    and nonreferents in communication, 103–107, 108
Refutational defense, prior, 240–241
Regional personality charactericties, 434–435
Reinforcement, 11, 67
    and altruism, 281
    and attraction theory, 164–168
    differential, 332
    extraneous, and persuasive communications, 233
    in moral development, 77
Rejection, 268–270
Relative deprivation, 408
Releaser stimulus for aggression 312
Reliability criterion, 27, 28
Religion
    Amish, 190–191
    Christian, 56, 175, 178–179, 297
    Hare Krishna, 193
    Hinduism, 24
    Jewish, 56, 297
    and marriage, 169
    People's Temple, 354–355
    Protestants vs. Catholics, 332
    and wilderness, 438
Research methods, 18–45
    archival research, 34–38
    content analysis, 31–34
    experimentation, 38–45
    interview, 27, 31
    participant observation, 22–27
    strategy, 20–22
    survey research, 27–31
Research tradition, 14–16
Residential crowding, 457, 460–462
Response acquisition/facilitation, and aggression, 316
Response competition, 190
Responsibility. *See* Social responsibility
Retardation, 71, 72
Revolutionary leaders, 400
Reward-cost theory, 164–165. *See also* Exchange theory
Riots, civil, 322, 435
Risk/caution in groups, 358–360
Role confusion, 60, 61
Role-playing, and altruism, 282
Role-taking, 98–100

Roles
    aggressor/victim, 309–310
    and complementarity, 346–348
    nature of, 346–347
    reciprocal character of, 347–348
    See also Social roles
Rutgers University; noise experiment, 433

Sadomasochistic sexual relationships, 309
Sampling in research, 27, 31
San Cristobal las Casas, Mexico, 426
San Francisco earthquake victims, 345
Satisficing principle of leader selection, 402
Scapegoating, 197, 207, 410
Selective deposit/survival in archival research, 38
Selective exposure, *de facto*/motivated, and reference groups, 194
Self-concept, 55–56, 60, 64, 88, 94–98, 141
Self-control, 77–79
Self-criticism, 78
Self-definition, and compliance, 257–258
Self-destruction, 311
Self-determining, 75
Self-development, 92–100
Self-disclosure, reciprocal, 155–157
Self-esteem
    and altruism, 296
    of authoritarian personality, 197
    and prejudice, 206
    and romantic behavior, 350
Self-fulfilling prophecy, 195, 384
Self-image, 112 and violent behavior, 319
Self-labeling of bodily states, 144–147
Self-perception, 141–148 and conformity, 262–265
Self-reinforcement, and altruism, 281–282
Self-rewards, 279, 298
Self-theories, 141
Semantic components of language, 93

Semantic differential scales, 101–102, 103
Sensorimotor stage, 63
Sex differences
    aggression, 317–318, 324
    altruism, 293–294, 295
    conformity, 238, 253
    crime, 318
    crowding reaction, 459–460, 464
    liking/love scales, 173
    persuasibility, 238, 253
    privacy need, 451
    self-disclosure, 155
    social interactions, 379
    voluntarism, 297
Sex hormones, 317
Sex-roles, 51
    and rape, 329–330
    and stereotypes, 84–88, 126, 349
Sexual aggression, 329–330
Sexual arousal, and fear and anger, 174–175
Sexual deviation, 36, 37
Sexuality, 54, 55
    diffusion of, 116
    in love, 177, 178, 179
Shakespeare, 170
Sign language, 105
"Significant others," parents as, 340
Similarity/dissimilarity
    and altruism, 295, 296
    and attraction/love, 40, 152–153, 165, 169–171
    and communication, 215–220
    and group formation, 342–344, 346, 348
Sitting/standing, and spatial interaction, 144
Situational constraints and self-disclosure, 155
Situational definitions, 112
Skin conductance levels, 374, 459
Slang, and privacy, 447
Sleeper effect, 242–244
Smiling, 69, 446
Social approval, need for, and aggresssion, 319
Social behavior
    and environmental variables, 443
    and heat effects, 435–436
    and spatial behavior, 443–455
Social change, 333, 382

Social choice, 130
Social class. *See* Socioeconomic factors
Social-comparison theory, 97
Social consensus, and aggressive behavior, 309, 327
Social contract, 81–82, 83
Social development, 49–89
   and altruism, 281–282
   and children, 68–74
   and morality, 74–84
   and sex roles, 84–88
   theories, 56–68
   universal issues, 51–56
Social facilitation, 13, 366–368, 402, 403
   and bystander intervention, 368–369
Social inhibition, 367
Social interaction, 6
   class differences, 428
   sex differences, 379
Social-judgment theory, 230–232
Social-learning theories, 56, 64–67
   and aggression, 316–317
   and altruism, 281–282
   and moral development, 77–79
Social norms, 207, 284
   and altruism, 294–295, 298
Social pathology, and population density, 460–462
Social penetration, theory of, 156
Social perception, 121–148
   and personality variables, biases, illusions, conceits, 126–129
   of others, 122–141
   of self, 141–148
Social psychology, 3–16
   definition, 4–7
   history, 9–14
   relation to psychology and sociology, 7–9
   research, 14–16, 18–45
Social reality, 165, 249
Social relationship, 6
Social responsibility
   and altruism, 282, 293
   diffusion of, 288–291, 431
   norm of, 284, 294–295, 298
Social roles
   and altruism, 280
   and legitimate/illegitimate violence, 309, 327
   and person perception, 128
Social Security, 298
Social service agencies, 296, 297, 298–300
Social specialist, 401
Social violence, 310, 322, 327–332
Social zone of interaction, 444
Socialization, universal issues of, 51–56
Socially desirable responses, 198–199
Socioeconomic factors and
   crime, 328
   family violence, 331
   neighborhoods, 428
   spatial behavior, 454–455
   voluntarism, 297
Sociolinguistic variable, 109
Socratic effect, 243–244
Solidarity semantic, 109
Source characteristics, in communication, 212–222
Spatial behavior, 312, 322–324, 344, 443–455
   of children, 454–455
   cultural differences, 448–450, 454–455
   equilibrium model of intimacy, 446–447
   interaction distance, 443–444
   privacy, 447–450
   spatial intrusion, 444–446
   territoriality, 450–454
   See also Crowding
Spatial intrusion, 444–446
Spatial zones of interaction, 443–444
Speech, internal/external, 98
Stage theories. *See*
   Cognitive-development theory
   Psychosexual theory
   Psychosocial theory
Stagnation vs. generativity, 60
Staring, 116
Status, and spatial intrusion, 445
Stereotyping
   and aggression, 318, 329–330
   "beautiful is good," 159–162, 341–342, 343
   and beliefs, 184–185, 186
   and passionate love, 175
   and prejudice, 204
   and psychological androgeny, 87, 349
   and rape 329–330
   and sex roles, 84–88, 126, 318
Stigma theories, 374
Stimulus deprivation, 71–74
Stimulus–value–role theory of marital choice, 348–351
Storge, storgic love, 177–178
Stress
   physiological, 436, 459
   psychological, 428–430, 457
Subjective norms, 188–189
Suburban life, 420–423
Success and failure, 139–142
Succorance, 153
Suffering, derogation of, 141
Suicide
   individual, 309, 436
   mass, 354–355
Superego, 57, 76
Surrogate mothers, 70
Survey research, 27–31
Survival
   and the interaction system, 69
   in dominance hierarchies, 395
   and wilderness experience, 438
Syllogisms, and attitudes, 194

Tabula rasa, 56
Talkativeness, 377–381
"Talking cure," 56–57
Task groups, 346, 348, 351, 401
Task specialist, 401
Television violence, 325–327, 333
Temptation resistance to, 78
Territoriality, 312, 450–454
Terrorism, political, 310
Testosterone, 317
Thanatos, 311
Threat displays, 312
Time factor
   in group performance, 385
   in love, 172, 174
Time–series analysis, 20–22, 23
Toilet training, 55, 58
Tornados, 434–435
Total institutions, 465–467
Touching, 455, 465
Transmission tuning, 135

Transportation crowing, 457, 458, 459
Triangulation of measurement, 20, 34
Trust
   vs. mistrust stage, 59
   and reciprocal self-disclosure, 156

Ugandan Ik tribe, 54
United States
   Army, 395, 401, 402, 408
   presidency, 4, 398, 399–400, 410
   Riot commission, 435
Universal ethical principles orientation, 82, 83. *See also* Behavior, systems
"Universal parenting machine," 51–54
Urban environment, 418–433
   city life, 423–424
   cognitive maps, 424–425
   environmental load, 430–431
   neighborhoods, 426–428
   noise effects, 431–433
   stress reduction, 428–430
   suburban life, 420–423
   vs. wilderness, 438

Validation by consensus, 249
Validity
   criterion, 27, 28
   external, 37, 39
   internal, 39, 41
Value systems, 194
Variables, 39. *See also* Dependent variables; Independent variables
Verbalizations, immediate/non-immediate, 108
Victim, role of, 309–310
Vietnam War, 357
Violence, 319
   and crime, 327–332
   legitimate/illegitimate, 309, 327
   and television, 325–327
Visual interaction, 116
Voluntarism, 297–298

War, and behavior, 174–175, 332, 372, 408
"Weapons effect," 324
Weather, effect on behavior, 433–435, 436
Weighted average, 188
Wife battering, 331
Wilderness, value of, 436–438
Women. *See* Rape; Sex differences; Wife battering
Women's liberation, 186, 328
Work, connotative meaning of, 101
Work groups, 346, 348, 351, 401
Working consensus, 347

XYY syndrome, 318

Yerkes–Dodson Law, 459
Yoking of experimental subjects, 157

Zones of interaction, spatial, 443–444